TOPICS IN MANAGERIAL ACCOUNTING

TOPICS IN MANAGERIAL ACCOUNTING

Third Edition

Edited by
L.S. Rosen
York University

McGraw-Hill Ryerson Limited

Toronto Montreal New York Auckland Bogotá Cairo Guatemala
Hamburg Johannesburg Lisbon London Madrid Mexico New Delhi
Panama Paris San Juan São Paulo Singapore Sydney Tokyo

TOPICS IN MANAGERIAL ACCOUNTING, Third Edition

2 3 4 5 6 7 8 9 0   W   3 2 1 0 9 8 7 6 5

Printed and bound in Canada

Care has been taken to trace ownership of copyright material contained in this text. The publishers will gladly take any information that will enable them to rectify any reference or credit in subsequent editions.

Because most of the material in this book has been previously published and, therefore, cannot be altered in any way, it has not been possible for the publisher to apply the standard guidelines for representing the sexes in a fair and equitable manner.

Canadian Cataloguing in Publication Data

Main entry under title:
Topics in managerial accounting

Includes bibliographical references.
ISBN   0-07-548709-8

1. Managerial accounting - Addresses, essays, lectures.
2. Cost accounting - Addresses, essays, lectures.
I. Rosen, L.S. (Lawrence Sydney), date

HF5629.T66   1983   658.1'5   C83-099083-6

TABLE
OF
CONTENTS

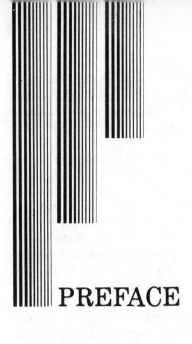

PREFACE

Many instructors seem to agree that students are able to grasp the techniques or basic concepts of management accounting fairly well after a little practice. However, these instructors also seem to agree that students have great difficulty being able to apply their knowledge in broader (less directive) situations, especially simulations of real life. Too often students lock into a favourite technique, perhaps variance analysis, and try to use it where it does not fit. Why does this tend to happen, and how serious an educational deficiency is it? These questions are not easily answered. As to the former question, we can speculate that too much time is being spent on learning many techniques at the expense of acquiring diagnostic, judgmental, evaluative, and application skills. A better balance between techniques and skills is needed in courses. As to the latter question about educational deficiencies, no doubt a range of opinions would be expressed.

Accounting is a very practical subject. If a student cannot apply what she/he has learned in management accounting courses, what then was the point of the course(s)? A strong argument can be made that accounting instructors have not spent sufficient time evaluating their classroom effectiveness. What do the students recall months later?

A main objective of this collection of articles is to try to help accounting instructors and students find a sensible balance between learning management accounting techniques and acquiring vital application skills. The largest number of the readings were selected because they describe how a textbook technique, or variation thereof, has been used in real life. This is to assist students, especially undergraduates, who may have little practical experience against which to evaluate a technique they are being asked to learn. It is hoped that these examples will ease the transition to learning how to apply techniques in different situations. Learning can then be reinforced by using less directive cases, for example.

The next largest group of articles was chosen because they provide linkages among two or more techniques, or provide an overview — sometimes from a practitioner's point of view. Some other articles were chosen because they illustrate a technique that is not in most textbooks and then give some applications.

Preceding the articles is an introduction that attempts to encourage students to link up the techniques that they will be learning with some common management evaluations or decisions. Obviously, such a link up will have imperfections. But without such deliberate attempts to force a decision orientation it is too easy for students to reach false conclusions about the universality of techniques they are being asked to learn. Ideally, students should try to devise their own charts, analytical frameworks, and taxonomies. When they make their own decision linkages, less attention need be given to memorization, a skill that probably absorbs too much attention in accounting education.

Section IX of the book provides questions for each article. Some of these questions are useful for class discussion purposes, whereas others are helpful for homework assignments. Several of the articles can be used to compare and contrast authors' viewpoints, using many of the questions.

The combination of a textbook, articles, and cases seems to provide a rich environment for learning management accounting techniques and their uses.

Suggestions are welcome.

L.S. Rosen

Toronto
Canada

ACKNOWLEDGEMENTS

Many instructors have given me helpful suggestions about portions of the previous editions of this book. They include T.H. Beechy, J.W. Bolla, J.E. Boritz, L.J. Brooks, R.J. Chambers, D.T. DeCoster, J. Dewhirst, B.M. Harnden, B. Irvine, H.A. Kennedy, W. King, D.L. McDonald, C.L. Mitchell, J.R.E. Parker, C.A. Prentice, C. Schandl, M.J. Vertigan, and J. Waterhouse. Prime thanks for this third edition must be extended to the authors who wrote articles especially for the book: A.A. Atkinson, T. Jick, and C. McMillan. Others who have helped make the third edition possible are: K. Dye and G.D. Richardson.

Gratitude must be expressed to permission editors and editors/publishers of journals who granted me rights to reprint articles from their journals. My secretary, Nancy Johnstone, merits praise for efficiently handling several tasks associated with the third edition. Finally, I would like to thank instructors who have the courage to work with students in conveying the importance of a decision orientation as well as judgmental, diagnostic, and analytical skills.

L.S. Rosen

TOPICS IN MANAGERIAL ACCOUNTING

I.

THE DISCIPLINE
OF MANAGEMENT
ACCOUNTING

A Decision Orientation

A discipline may be learned or studied from many different points of view. The readings in this book stress a *decision orientation*. The reasons are simple. The subject of management accounting encompasses a considerable amount of terminology that is new to most people. In addition, many new procedures, tools, and techniques have to be explained. A decision orientation helps to convey how each procedure, tool, and technique may fruitfully be used, and where its application would be useless or dangerous. Accounting is a practical subject; we have to know how to apply it.

A decision orientation helps to prevent undue worship of a particular tool or technique and helps us to cultivate needed business skills such as judgment, diagnostic, assessment, application, and evaluative ability. It is too easy, in an introductory course, to reach the *invalid conclusion* that each new tool or technique that you have just learned has universal application. Nothing could be further from reality! Each has its place of importance. Each can be misapplied.

For example, what does the word *"cost"* mean to you? If you have recently completed a financial accounting course that stressed "generally accepted accounting principles" (GAAP) your initial response may be: "cost is what we *paid*." On reflection you might add: "but there can be *more than one* cost; for example, for inventory, FIFO cost, LIFO cost, or weighted average cost."

The message, in financial accounting, that there is more than one cost figure becomes of even greater importance in management accounting. This is because (1) there are many types of decisions that might be made using management accounting data and, potentially, *each could employ a different figure for "cost"*; and (2) there are fewer legal constraints (such as GAAP) that confine or limit the preparation of different cost figures. With all this potential diversity we obviously have to focus our attention on "what fits where?"

Cost data might be used by management for the following potentially different types of judgments. (At an early date in your course the listing that follows is unlikely to be fully grasped. You are advised to refer to it frequently as the course progresses. Each reading will improve your understanding of the subject of management accounting.)

1. Performance Appraisal or Evaluation.

This category includes the various possible attempts to evaluate the performance of people, as individual managers or employees, or as a group. How well — or efficiently — did they perform compared to what was expected of them? Are we evaluating the people fairly given their environmental situation and how they are motivated? (There are several purposes of this evaluation. One is to determine what action might result in improved performance: more training needed? would an incentive plan help? should the work be split up so that some portion ought to be performed by machines?)

If the organization can be more *economic* in purchasing its raw material inputs — such as material and labour — and more *efficient* in transforming its inputs into finished products, or outputs, profitability is enhanced. Various performance appraisal tools exist.

2. Pricing or Setting Selling Prices for the Company's Products or Services.

Price setting is a function of several factors; often the most important would be the policies of the company's competitors. Prices may be set in the short term or long term. They may be based on cost, or on what the market will bear. When they are "cost-based," management accounting has an important role to play in ascertaining the cost of the product or service. (When prices are primarily "market-based," management accounting has a different role, one of computing profit. This is discussed shortly under the Inventory Valuation category.)

3. Output of Products or Services.

What quantity and quality of each product ought to be manufactured to enhance the profitability of the company? (Or improve the quality of service, if the organization is not-for-profit, such as a hospital.) Can the mix of products or services be altered so as to improve profitability?

Output decisions can be viewed in another dimension. Was the organization *effective* in accomplishing what it intended to accomplish? This is especially important in governments, where various social programs are voted into law to attain a particular effect (e.g., rehabilitate persons convicted of a crime). Do the programs work? What percentage of the participants in the program become rehabilitated? How can we measure effectiveness?

4. Financing. Where will the money needed to operate the organization come from? Possible sources are from internal funds flow (from operations), or from selling debt or bank borrowing, or from selling equity/shares. Which source ought to be used at the present time? How much money is needed? When is it needed? Management accounting can combine with finance and economics to answer these questions.

As is the case with other items on our list of management evaluations that have to be made, a variety of tools and techniques exist for helping management. Some tools are sensitive, complex, and expensive to use; others are cruder, less sensitive measures but are less expensive to implement. Learning has to include a sense of which tool and technique is the most appropriate under the circumstances.

5. Investing and Disinvesting. What should be acquired with available funds? — temporary investment in marketable securities? buy inventory? make a longer term investment in plant and equipment that will generate cash inflows over many years? The financing and investment evaluations are closely interlinked; both involve the flow of *cash*. Hence, the sophisticated tools and techniques to aid in financing and investment evaluations would attempt to track cash receipts (inflows) and cash disbursements (outflows). The cruder management accounting techniques may employ *accrual* accounting methods. This accrual effect makes the tool less sensitive to short term cash flows, and therefore a less effective measure in some circumstances.

6. Inventory Valuation. What cost ought to be attached to work in process and finished goods inventory for a manufacturing company? *One* unit cost figure is needed for each product so that an income statement and balance sheet may be prepared by companies that manufacture goods. A large number of alternative methods of computing unit costs exist. The most appropriate cost would be chosen after examining such factors as the other decisions (e.g., pricing) that management has to make, how expensive each of the alternative bookkeeping procedures would be, how the product is being manufactured (using people or machines?), and so forth.

A cost figure assembled for an inventory valuation that is needed to permit the preparation of financial accounting statements could be *highly misleading* for pricing or output evaluations. But under some circumstances one figure may be acceptable for both inventory valuation and pricing/output needs. The cost figure must always be tailored to the specific decision needs of management.

7. Income Taxation. An organization that is seeking a profit that will be subject to income tax has to consider whether one "cost" valuation method has advantages over the other in reducing or postponing income taxes. For many small manufacturers their *only* reason for accounting may be to prepare financial statements that accompany their annual income tax forms. Accordingly, the managers of these small businesses will want to choose accounting policies and techniques that keep their tax payments as low as is permitted by tax laws and regulations.

The financial statements of these small businesses could therefore report relatively low net income figures. A bank loan officer who has not fully comprehended the small business manager's objective of minimizing tax may reach an invalid conclusion about the valuation of inventory and success (profitability) of the business.

An important theme of this book is that financial statements and management accounting *reports have to be interpreted in light of the objectives of the preparer.* As readers or users of the reports we must ascertain what the preparer had in mind when a particular cost figure was chosen. Quite possibly the figure is not the one we need for our evaluation and decision. Communication with the preparer is needed to get the cost data you require.

A few management evaluation/decisions exist in addition to the seven just briefly described. Two examples are: strategic planning, and ascertaining the geographical area in which the company's products or services ought to be distributed. Some accountants would regard these two as subdivisions of one or more of the seven. On balance, the number of categories that we set up is not important at any early stage in a course. What is important is that a positive attitude or viewpoint be established for *linking* management accounting tools and techniques. When a strong orientation is missing, a course can easily become a confusion of techniques lacking a purpose. Memorization can too easily take the place of understanding and application.

One Broader Framework

How do the various management decisions/evaluations fit the broader objective of managing an organization? This question is given attention in many business courses. Unfortunately, we can comment on it in only general terms at this early stage in your study of management accounting. Nevertheless, we must address the point as forcefully as we can and as soon as we can because it is so vital to understanding our subject.

In hard practical terms we can say that most organizations have a few factors that are *critical to the success or failure of the organization.* A hospital, for example, may have continuing goals-objectives-purposes of "providing the best available health care at a reasonable cost." To do this, however, it may have to specialize in treating just a few illnesses (unless it happens to be the sole hospital in the region, and is forced to handle everything). Only the very large hospitals can afford the equipment and trained specialists to offer a high quality service for a broad range of illnesses.

What is critical to the success or failure of a medium-sized hospital (and therefore is of *prime importance* in choosing an appropriate management accounting system)? We previously hinted at two factors: (1) highly trained doctors and nurses; and (2) keeping costs reasonable by giving due regard to economy and efficiency. Other crucial success and failure factors may exist, but let us focus on the two above. The need for qualified staff should be obvious. If patients do not recover in a reasonable time, the reputation of the hospital is affected. Management accounting can play only a minor role in this regard — that of collecting data on the length of a patient's stay in this hospital, illnesses treated, and so forth. This data may help in giving an assessment of professional quality as long as comparative data for other similar hospitals exists.

In contrast, management accounting has a *major* role to play in cost and cash control of a hospital. Without strong cost and cash controls the hospital could approach financial collapse. If the hospital is government-supported it may be forced to cut back in certain areas until its financial health returns. Maybe patients may suddenly be required to pay for services that were previously paid for by the government. A variety of drastic steps could become necessary, most or all of which would likely affect the reputation of the hospital. The loss of reputation, in turn, could affect long run pursuit of the hospital's prime goals-objectives-purposes. Circular cause and effect interrelationships likely would occur.

A worse fate (i.e. bankruptcy) could await a profit-seeking organization that does not give adequate attention to those factors that are critical to its success or failure. Every organization has factors that will bring forth success or cause failure, and it is the responsibility of the person trained in management accounting to identify those factors. Sometimes management accounting can help; sometimes it cannot. The key skill to acquire is having the judgment to know when management accounting *can* prove useful. This skill can be acquired — through practice with cases and various illustrations from daily life. You have to ask yourself "what brings success or failure" to each of the organizations that you encounter: a law firm, a manufacturing plant, a corner grocery, a fastfood enterprise, an automobile dealership, and so forth. Different businesses will have different success/failure factors.

Let us follow through the example of a law firm. In some senses it is similar to the hospital, where quality of service is important. But lawyers have one additional factor, which can lead to failure — that is, clients' funds held in trust. A lawyer can easily be disbarred from his profession for using clients' funds for personal use. Auditors visit each lawyer's office from time to time to see that adequate records are maintained and that clients' funds are being used according to what is specified in contracts. A system of cash control must therefore be set up by lawyers. (This system may be part of financial accounting or of management accounting.) Without it the risk of being disbarred, or failure, is high. (Hence, adequate monitoring of trust funds would be a critical "success" factor for a law firm.)

A manufacturing plant could be automated or have many skilled craftsmen. If it is automated, with few employees, a performance appraisal system to evaluate *people* obviously would be of little benefit. A cost control system for measuring the efficiency of the machines (investment decision) could prove quite useful. A thorough knowledge of factors critical to the success or failure of the manufacturing plant must therefore *precede* any prescription or recommendation of management accounting tools and techniques.

In summary, comprehending the subject of management accounting involves more than just doing course assignment material. A tie-in to an organization's objectives and critical success/failure factors has to be grasped, and this can be done by asking instructors and fellow students about the internal workings of businesses that you encounter in everyday life. See Illustration I. The readings in this book attempt to give practical settings and sensible applications, and are therefore a beginning upon which you might build. But, learning a decision orientation requires us to become inquisitive about more than just the businesses described in textbooks.

Illustration I   Tailoring Management Accounting Systems To
An Organization's Objectives

---

1. Ascertain the organization's immediate, intermediate, and long term objectives or goals.
2. Identify the factors that are important in achieving the organization's objectives. (Critical success/failure factors.)
3. Identify those evaluations (from the seven listed) that frequently have to be made to monitor the critical success/failure factors.
4. Build into your management accounting system those accounting tools and techniques that help management make the evaluations noted in 3. (The tools and techniques are briefly outlined in Illustrations II and III.)

The process of designing an accounting system that is consistent with the steps in Illustration I requires us to ascertain which evaluations and decisions are made frequently and which are made only occasionally. The critical success/failure factors have to be monitored frequently.

Designing Analytical Frameworks

The linking of each management accounting tool or technique (explained in most cost accounting textbooks) with one or more of the foregoing management evaluations or decisions is not easy. Illustrations II and III show one possible linkage. Any attempt (such as these two illustrations) will have some shortcomings and exceptions to the generalizations that are noted. Nevertheless, we have to devise some sort of tailoring chart, or we risk being unable to apply what we have learned in the course to a real corporation or organization (or to a case simulation thereof).

The starting point for grasping Illustration II is column A. After a real situation has been analyzed in terms of the goals-objectives-purposes of the participants and the factors that are critical to success/failure, we must ask "which management evaluations are needed to aid success and minimize failure"? Is one or more of them listed in column A? If the answer is "yes" we then have to decide whether management accounting can play a large, or only minor, role in aiding management. For instance, maybe the evaluation

Illustration II Tailoring Accounting Techniques to Management Evaluations

A. Management Evaluation or Decision	Management Accounting Technique or Tool		D. Reading References in this book	
	B. Broad, Crude or Overall Technique	C. Specific or Refined Technique	Article Number	Author(s)
1. Performance Appraisal (primarily of individual managers, or of cost/revenue/ profit centres)	• Return on investment using historic costs • Fixed budgets and some variances from actual • Perhaps cost and revenue accumulation by profit centre or cost/revenue centre compared to previous periods (and not to flexible budgets/ standard) • Long run standards that are not currently attainable	• Responsibility accounting • Flexible budgets and variances from actual • Standard costs and some variances from actual cost (e.g., a price/cost variance may be the responsibility of a particular purchasing manager) • Some economy, efficiency, and effectiveness evaluations	6 23 9 8 1 7 10 2	Anthony *Control Systems* Parker Ridgway Simon Villers Wells Zmud
2. Pricing; setting selling prices for products or services	• Direct or variable costing • Master budgets; profit (accrual) budgets using fixed and variable costs • Break-even analysis and cost-volume-profit analysis (in multi-product companies) • Full inventory cost plus profit (See Illustration III)	• Contribution margin analysis • Sometimes differential or incremental cost and revenue analysis • Break-even analysis and cost-volume-profit analysis (in a single product division or company) • Program flexible costs/budgets • Some variance analysis may prove useful in the intermediate term for revising prices	13 16 12 11 15 14	*Accounting Logic* Eiler *et al* Greer Harder Kallimanis Pérusse
3. Output or production (Deciding upon quantities and qualities of products and services; e.g., make or buy decisions)	• Return on investment using historic costs • Master budgets; profit (accrual) budgets using fixed and variable costs • Break-even analysis and cost-volume-profit analysis (in multi-product companies)	• Contribution margin analysis • Sometimes differential or incremental cost and revenue analysis • Break-even analysis and cost-volume-profit analysis (in a single product division or company) • Learning curves and cost effects	5 3 35 36 21 23 16 18 19 4 24 22 14 1 20 17 2	Ackoff Anthony Atkinson Atkinson Chesley Control Systems Eiler *et al* *Fable* Greer Hanold Jick McMillan Pérusse Simon Treacy Vatter Zmud

Illustration II (cont'd)

A. Management Evaluation or Decision	Management Accounting Technique or Tool		D. Reading References in this book	
	B. Broad, Crude or Overall Technique	C. Specific or Refined Technique	Article Number	Author(s)
3. (cont'd)	• Direct or variable costing	• Some variances between actual and standard costs (e.g., some quantity, price, and volume variances) • Program flexible costs/budgets • Perhaps linear and nonlinear programming • Perhaps network and similar analysis		
4. Financing Requirements (Number of dollars required for which period of time from which sources?)	• Accrual profit budgets • Accrual basis statement of changes in financial position	• Cash budgeting • Cost of capital computations • Perhaps cash basis statement of changes in financial position (including cash effects of taxation, not accrual or deferral)	25 26	Gale & Branch Johnson et al
5. Investment and Disinvestment (e.g., of companies, divisions, segments, machines, or person/machine trade-offs)	• Accounting (accrual) return on investment • Profit budgets • Pay back methods of return on investment • Break-even or cost-volume-profit analysis conducted on a broad basis in a multi-product company	• Discounted cash flow capital budgeting techniques • Sensitivity analysis • Risk analysis and the use of objective or subjective probabilities • Contribution margin analysis used with one or more of the above • Break-even and cost-volume-profit analysis conducted in a single product firm or on a micro basis • Differential or incremental cost/revenue analysis • Post audit of previous capital expenditures	13 27 31 30 28 29	Accounting Logic Bierman Ijiri Main Seed Van Breda

Illustration II (cont'd)

A. Management Evaluation or Decision	Management Accounting Technique or Tool		D. Reading References in this book	
	B. Broad, Crude or Overall Technique	C. Specific or Refined Technique	Article Number	Author(s)
6. External Reporting (to stockholders, general creditors, and the public)	• Consolidated GAAP (historic cost) financial statements • See Illustration III • Some cash basis financial statements	• Profit forecasts prepared with the aid of various management accounting-budgeting tools) • Product, division, or segment profits (when divisible) • See Illustration III • Perhaps supplementary current cost or "changing price" income measures	33 34 32	Ferrara Itami & Kaplan Todd
7. Income Taxation (or financial reports required by governments)	• Similar to external reporting (but, in Canada, consolidated financial statements are not used for income tax purposes)	• Various tax planning tools might be used. (For example, although direct costing may not be used in the U.S., LIFO can be. The exact opposite applies in Canada.)		
8. Other Evaluations (E.g., determining the market area in which a product may be sold)	• Perhaps accrual profit budgets	• Perhaps contribution margin, or incremental cost/revenue analysis		

Illustration III　Inventory Cost Systems

A. Basic Accounting Procedure	B. Actual vs. Predetermined vs. Standard Costs (Which cost should be used for each cost element?)	C. Include vs. Exclude Fixed Manufacturing Overhead Cost?
1. Process Costing Approach	1. Actual Direct Material Actual Direct Labour Actual Manufacturing Overhead	1. Full or Absorption Costing (Includes the Fixed Portion of Manufacturing Overhead in Inventory Cost)
2. Other than Pure Process or Job Order	2. Actual Direct Material Actual Direct Labour Predetermined Manufacturing Overhead	2. Direct or Variable Costing (Does *Not* Include the Fixed Portion of Manufacturing Overhead in Inventory Cost)
3. Job Order Costing Approach	3. Actual Direct Material Predetermined Direct Labour and Manufacturing Overhead	
	4. Standard Direct Material, Direct Labour, and Manufacturing Overhead	

requires much more marketing than accounting input. Hence, if the answer is "minor" we look to column B. However, if the answer is "large" accounting input, we would tend to look to column C, because this lists the specific, refined, or sophisticated techniques that might aid management.

Ideally, the thinking as to whether a column B or column C technique ought to be selected occurs when the overall management accounting system is designed. That is, the overall system is designed only after accountants and management have anticipated the types of evaluations that will have to be made over the next several years. Some of the evaluations may be recurring (e.g., costing inventory); others may be infrequent (e.g., contribution margin). For the latter evaluation, the system must be flexible enough to permit the accounting technique (e.g., contribution margin) to be completed quickly at a reasonable cost.

The cost-benefit theme has to be prominent throughout the design of management accounting systems. Generally speaking, the accounting techniques in column C are not only more complex or sophisticated, they are also more expensive than those in column B. Consequently, we do not want to use a column C technique when one from column B would suffice. Extensive planning is needed to design an efficient and effective management accounting system.

Illustrations II and III appear overwhelming at first. They obviously have to be used on a weekly basis throughout any course in managerial or cost accounting. Some textbooks are better than others in conveying a decision orientation. In general, though, most students find the linkage of decisions and management accounting techniques challenging.

Linking Decisions and Techniques

This section is not designed to be read in *one sitting*; but it might be used as an overview or summary for someone who has completed a management accounting course. Its purpose is to help a little in explaining some of the differences between a technique that is listed in column B and one listed in column C of Illustration II. The words and thoughts provided here have to be used alongside a good managerial or cost textbook which explains the prime features of each technique.

1. Performance Appraisal or Evaluation. The techniques listed under column B of Illustration II tend to give an aggregate or overall picture of a company, division, or operating segment. The aggregate view does not tell you whether specific portions of the entity did better than others. Thus, it may not be possible to pinpoint the corrective action that is needed to improve those portions that are functioning below par.

Sometimes *both* column B and C techniques are needed to ensure that improvement at the individual portion or departmental level is not detrimental to the overall or aggregate picture. An example would be a foreman who improves productivity for assembly of multi-part products by having extra work in progress at each of the assembly "stations," in order to reduce waiting or idle time. The excess work in process inventory might prove costly to finance, store, and insure, and therefore exceed any savings that might be generated by not having idle workers. (The idle workers would be waiting for the assembly station ahead of them to finish their job and send along the work in process that is being assembled.)

There may be times when you have no alternative but to use a crude column B technique even though the decision is critical to an organization's success, and you would prefer to use a refined column C tool or technique. One example would be when an organization's lines of authority and responsibility are not adequate, or the accounting personnel are not sufficiently trained for responsibility accounting. Another example may be when older standards, which do not represent currently-attainable levels of cost or revenue, have to be used to assess efficiency because no other figures are available. Fixed budgets may have been set well in advance of the current year, and have not been revised (to flexible budgets) as a result of changes in actual production quantities, or due to strikes, or due to many internal and external factors. Under such less-than-desired conditions it becomes necessary to be extra careful how one uses any variances derived from comparisons of fixed budget versus actual costs. The longer term solution is to improve the organization's management accounting system. Meanwhile, users may have to search for other techniques to assess current performance and plan improvements.

2. Price Setting. Before discussing the differences between column B and column C it is necessary to establish the circumstances where management accounting figures might prove useful in setting selling prices of products or services. The initial questions to ask are:

A. Is the company a price leader or price follower? (What competitive conditions exist? Are prices set in a worldwide market — e.g., oil — and similar situation, or by the one organization we are studying?) If the organization has to accept an industry-set selling price, and therefore is a price follower — it does *not* have a pricing decision to make, but does have an *output* decision — do we produce at the current selling price?

Questions B. and C. that follow apply if the organization is a price leader.

B. Does the organization use a cost-based system of setting its selling price, or does it charge on some other basis, such as what the market will bear?

C. Is the pricing decision a short run one under conditions of idle plant capacity? Or are we thinking longer run, at or near full capacity (and alternative uses of the plant exist)? Naturally, the more complicated the business is, the more we have to refine these questions to suit economic and other conditions.

The following discussion assumes, in general, that we are a price *leader* or organization that is able to set its own selling prices, within limits of course. (We know from economics courses that if our profits are too high we may be inviting other companies to start up businesses to compete with us.) Three situations merit our attention: (1) intermediate term pricing; (2) cost-plus contracts; and (3) short term, idle capacity circumstances.

If competition is *not* a threat in the intermediate term we would try to charge as much as we can ("what the market will bear"). We could perform a cost-volume-profit analysis *if* we have data on what volume we might expect to sell at different prices. If we lack such volume-price data, our selling prices may bear little relationship to cost.

In contrast, if competitors might be attracted if we make "excessive" profits (given the investment risks we are being subjected to), we might try to ascertain what our costs are, and then add a reasonable profit on to our cost to arrive at a selling price. By "reasonable" we mean not enough to invite much competition. What, then, is "cost"? Cost, for purposes of price setting, might include manufacturing, selling and administrative expenditures. Note that this differs from "cost" for financial accounting inventory valuation purposes — which excludes any costs of selling and administration. We might arrive at manufacturing cost by using any one of the combinations displayed in Illustration III, which is explained later. Most cost textbooks describe various manufacturing cost determination methods at length. Selling and administrative costs for a particular product in a multi-product company would tend to be arbitrary allocations. Often these are made, in part, to guess at what competitors might have to incur if they decided to start up to compete with you. Since our costs are determined in an arbitrary manner we must be careful not to attach too much reliability or importance to them. In summary, cost-based pricing in the intermediate term often contains a considerable amount of guesswork because we really cannot be precise in our determination of cost. Too frequently, what appears to be cost-based pricing turns out, on closer examination, to be judgment-based pricing. It may take into account many market factors, such as prices of different, yet substitute, products.

Sometimes, "cost plus" contracts exist. That is, the contractor may agree to charge his cost plus a 15 or so percent profit on top of cost. In such circumstances "cost" must be defined very carefully in the construction contract. Otherwise, endless arguments could ensue over methods of allocating indirect (e.g. computer) costs of manufacturing, selling, and administration. Most cost accounting textbooks explain the different arbitrary allocation methods.

The third major circumstance to consider is pricing in the short term under conditions of idle plant capacity. When competition exists this may be more of an *output* (do I produce at this price?) than a pricing decision. Illustration II lists the accounting techniques that might be useful in short term pricing/output evaluations. The most sophisticated of those listed are under C: contribution margin analysis and differential or incremental cost and revenue analysis. Contribution margin analysis focuses on variable revenues and costs. (Contribution margin equals revenue less variable manufacturing, selling, and administrative costs.) Differential cost analysis takes into account variable revenues and costs and those fixed costs that increase as a result of the extra production output.

Theoretically (when the term variable cost means "variable with output"), only variable costs ought to be incurred under conditions of idle capacity. Thus, contribution margin analysis should answer the question of what price to sell at to recover those variable costs that increase in order to produce in the short term. Hence, if someone offers to buy a product for $1 per unit that has variable manufacturing, selling, and administrative costs of 90 cents per unit, a contribution margin of 10 cents per unit exists. The price could be dropped to just above 90 cents per unit, and a contribution margin would still exist.

Why is direct costing under column B in Illustration II? Direct costing is defined as variable manufacturing cost (i.e., variable or direct material, direct labour, and variable manufacturing overhead). Variable selling and administration is not included in the cost figure. Thus, direct costing is an incomplete cost for purposes of setting short term selling prices, unless there are no variable selling and administration costs for this order.

In a somewhat similar vein, break-even or cost-volume-profit analysis is in column B for *multi-product* companies because it is a crude analysis. Arbitrary allocations of total plant cost to each individual product would be needed to try to obtain the profit, at different volumes, for one particular product. In short, this would be a rough and ready computation. However, in a one product company, where arbitrary allocations are not necessary, break-even and cost-volume-profit analysis would be a sophisticated technique. It would be helpful to management in situations where price setting is crucial to the success of the organization.

In summary for pricing, we must first estabish whether we have the freedom to set selling prices, or are really only engaged in "produce or not" at the market price (i.e., output decisions.) Next, we have to ascertain whether the prices are market-based or cost-based. Then if cost based, we have to look at the time period (such as intermediate or short term) and whether the plant has idle capacity and might have to use contribution margin accounting. Naturally, other possible circumstances exist. Thus, we again encounter the theme of different costs for different purposes.

3. Output or Production. The similarities between output and pricing decisions are noticeable when we look at columns B and C of Illustration II. Many of the accounting techniques are the same for both evaluations.

Some output evaluations can occur before the manufacturing process commences. That is, the volume of production may be decided by doing a cost-volume-profit analysis, using different possible qualities of direct material or different skills of labourers. But, after production occurs, costs must be collected and compared to budgets to ascertain where the variances arose. In setting budgets we must ask whether unit labour costs will drop as workers become familiar with their tasks (i.e., learning curve effects). In analyzing variances that we have initially derived to conduct performance evaluations, we may discover efficiencies or inefficiencies that bear on output, and perhaps pricing evaluations.

After studying Illustration II and a strong cost accounting textbook it should become obvious that many of the management accounting techniques in columns B and C are useful for more than one evaluation. In a course stressing a decision orientation we have to try to locate the overlaps and not give in to some cliché such as "they are all interrelated."

4. Financing Requirements. The important difference between financing (and investing) and the previous three evaluations is that refined or *sophisticated* financing or investing techniques involve *cash* — and not some form of accrual "cost." If accrual cost figures have to be used in financing-investing evaluations, the technique is obviously a crude one that ought to appear under column B in Illustration II.

Financing decisions often are tied to income tax implications and various forecasts of interest rates, inflation, currency translation rates, and so forth. The management accountant's role is one of trying to ascertain the amount, timing, and uncertainty of cash inflows (receipts) and outflows (disbursements). A computation of funds flow from operations, using accrual accounting, may be too crude and *cash* flows will have to be estimated.

5. Investment and Disinvestment. Most cost accounting textbooks point out the limitations of basing capital budgeting decisions on non-discounting techniques. However, rough or crude techniques may be as good as refined ones when information about the future is unavailable or unreliable.

Once the investment has been made it has to be monitored by post audits to see whether projections in the capital budget tie into actual cash receipts and disbursements. Also, when difficulties arise, differential or incremental cost/revenue analysis is needed to decide whether it would be wise to dispose of the asset. (Will *overall* profit increase if we dispose of the asset?)

6. External Reporting.

There are many different users of financial or external accounting reports. Thus, the distinction between column B and C techniques may be a little foggy because what suits one user may be unsuitable to another. Those who are trying to predict (future) cash flows probably would want segment information, profit forecasts, and current cost information. In contrast those who merely want some record of the past for a scorekeeping function could be satisfied with consolidated GAAP statements (even though we have put them in the B column).

In preparing the financial statements of a company that manufactures one or more products, we must have one or more methods of accumulating the costs of work in process and finished goods and the cost of goods sold. This is where Illustration III fits in. As with Illustration II, Illustration III has its limitations, but it also has some definite strengths.

Every inventory cost accumulation system (for costing work in process and finished goods inventory) has to have *three* parts: column A, column B, and column C. The term "job order," for example, is merely a one third description. It does not tell you what choice has been made in columns B and C. A full description may be job order — standard costs — direct costing.

A company might select any combination of items in columns A, B, and C. To understand applications and a decision orientation we must therefore focus on why a company would choose one particular combination over another. Before we proceed, a couple of generalizations (which have some exceptions) are useful. The first generalization is that the higher the number (or the lower we proceed down the column on the page), the more sophisticated is the technique. Hence, we probably would not choose the higher number for inventory costing purposes alone, but would want it because it helps us in other management evaluations.

Standard costs serve as an example. Currently attainable standards would be useful to compare to actual costs/revenues to obtain performance appraisals for help in deciding what corrective action is needed. Standards that are not currently attainable but will be after a learning period of several months could be useful in price setting. Which standards do we pick — (currently attainable, or attainable in the intermediate term?) We have to ascertain crucial success/failure factors before we can answer. Is performance appraisal more important than price setting? (Maybe we need two standards if both judgments are important.) Then we may use the *one* standard for inventory costing (unless it is materially different from actual and would not be acceptable to independent auditors).

The second generalization is that the lower the number in the column, the less the bookkeeping or upkeep costs. (An exception would be out-of-date standards — which do not require dollars to update them — that might be less expensive than actual costs.) Thus, a company that has no need for information for performance appraisal, pricing, and similar evaluations would tend to use a process-actual-absorption (A1, B1, C1) cost accumulation system. A process system usually is cheaper to maintain than is a job order one, which requires job cost cards, time reports by job, and so forth. Similarly, the determination of cost variability is expensive and is not necessary when absorption costing and one manufacturing overhead rate is employed.

In learning a decision orientation it is often useful to ask yourself who might choose a particular technique (i.e., type of company? for which decisions?). For instance, who might use an "A3, B2, C1" system?

One company that might use an "A3, B2, C1" is an automobile repair firm. You might leave your car at the firm at 8 A.M. and hope to pick it up at 5 P.M. The firm needs some way of invoicing (price setting) you at 5 P.M. It cannot say "come back to collect your car on the tenth of next month after the bookkeeper has closed the books and determined actual costs." Thus, it employs a predetermined system of arriving at estimated "manufacturing" or shop overhead (e.g., estimated shop overhead divided by estimated direct labour hours equals $x per direct labour hour). It might even combine the overhead rate ($x) with a profit element.

The firm would need a job order (A3) system to keep track of the repair costs of each automobile. The actual costs of material (e.g., spark plugs) and the actual labour (e.g., mechanic's time) plus predetermined overhead (B2) are charged to the job. Whether we include or exclude fixed manufacturing overhead is dependent on competition. If competitors are full costing then so would we.

Who might use an "A3, B4, C2" system? The company would probably need job order costs to help in pricing or output decisions. Standards, if currently attainable, would be useful for performance appraisal. Direct costing might help in short term pricing or output decisions (as a step towards contribution margin analysis). If the company is in Canada, direct costing might prove useful in lowering taxable income and income taxes.

In summary, we have to tailor our manufacturing cost accumulation system to crucial success/failure factors for the company and decisions needed to help ensure success. In a multi-product company we could have several different accumulation systems because circumstances (e.g., competition or manufacturing methods) could vary.

7. Income Taxation. Profit-seeking enterprises have to file financial information with tax authorities. This information could vary from what is used for external reporting purposes. Management accounting techniques may be of assistance in helping to postpone tax payments.

8. Other Evaluations. Most of the recurring types of evaluations can be fitted into one or more of the foregoing seven categories. (This is merely a "catch-all" for those who wish to expand their linkage of techniques and decisions.)

Summary

It is possible to pass some management or cost accounting courses and not know how the subject's content might be used in real life. One way of helping to make your course as practical as possible is to develop decision orientation frameworks, such as those described in the foregoing material. The ideal is to develop your own linkage of decisions and accounting techniques. While you are doing this, Illustrations I, II, and III should prove useful.

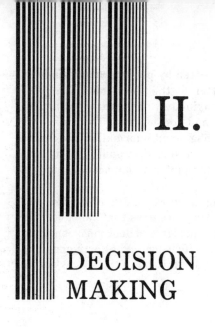

II.

DECISION
MAKING

The first article that has been reprinted, "Simon says . . . Decision making is a 'satisficing' experience," provides background for the decision orientation theme of this book. Herbert A. Simon was awarded the 1978 Nobel laureate in economics for his "pioneering research into the decision-making process within economic organizations." In granting the 1978 Nobel in economics the Swedish Academy of Sciences stated that business economics and administrative research "are largely based on Simon's ideas," many of which were published in the 1940s and 1950s. Simon makes many comments in this article/interview that students of management accounting have to think about and integrate into their analytical thought processes. These include the concept of satisficing, role of external vs. internal (management accounting) information systems, artificial intelligence, group vs. individual behaviour, and organizations of the future. An obvious question to ask ourselves is how many (and which) techniques that we are currently studying in management accounting are likely to survive the next 20 years?

The next article, "Individual Differences and MIS Success: A Review Of The Empirical Literature," follows up on a few of the ideas touched upon by Simon. Management accounting may be viewed as being a portion of a management information system (MIS). What factors lead to a successful information system or cause a system to be unsuccessful? The author, Robert W. Zmud, reviews some of the behavioural research on MIS. One reason for including this article in the book is to illustrate the complexities of the problem and to point out some challenges and interesting research possibilities.

The third article, "Framework for Analysis," takes a more practical look at the design of information systems. The author, a well-known writer, compares and contrasts management control with other types of control and planning systems.

Whereas the first three articles were written by persons who, primarily, are academics, the fourth article was written by the president of a large organization, The Pillsbury Company. (Approximately one-third of the articles in this book were written by executives and consultants.) The author explains the need for, and some uses of, a management information system in a large company. He also discusses several criticisms of accountants and their systems. Of special interest is the flour milling information network and the interrelationships.

The final article in this section is "Management Misinformation Systems." Although the themes may seem obvious, they are ones that cannot be forgotten when we are working with a systems design and decision orientation. The system has to help improve economy, efficiency and effectiveness, especially in those contexts or functions that are critical to the success of the organization.

1

Simon says . . .
DECISION MAKING
IS A 'SATISFICING'
EXPERIENCE

JOHN M. ROACH*

The 1978 Nobel laureate in economics, Herbert A. Simon, sees further automation of decision-making processes as vital to changing needs of organizations and society. He regards "attention" as one of management's scarce resources and points out that coming combinations of management information systems should focus on "quality" rather than quantity of data. Will the corporation be managed by machines?

ONE DAY back in the mid-1950s, Dr. Herbert A. Simon was working in his study near the campus of Carnegie Institute of Technology (now Carnegie-Mellon University) trying to find an appropriate term for what he wanted to say. Eventually he plucked an obscure verb — *to satisfice* (satisfy) — from the Oxford English Dictionary. He used it to help explain a concept of economic decision making that, whether they realize it or not, business organizations and their managers use every day in both run-of-the-mill and complex problem situations. And last month, two decades later, Simon's concept of "satisficing" became a major factor in the Swedish Academy of Sciences' decision to award him the 1978 Nobel prize in economics for his "pioneering research into the decision-making process within economic organizations."

Simon had previously enunciated advanced views on the complexities of organizational decision making in his now classic thesis, *Administrative Behavior,* published in 1947. And what he was trying to say that afternoon

* Reprinted, by permission of the publisher, from *MANAGEMENT REVIEW,* January 1979
© 1979 by AMACOM, a division of American Management Associations. All rights reserved.

in Pittsburg several years later — and did say in subsequent editions of his book — was that while Economic Man, that elusive "maximizer" of traditional economic doctrine, invariably "selects the best alternative from all those available to him," his cousin, Administrative Man (the real-life manager), "satisfices — looks for a course of action that is satisfactory or good enough."

Traditional economic doctrine holds that organizations always make key decisions on the basis of information that maximizes their results — that is, get the best possible price, the best possible share of market, and maximum profit. But in the "real world," this just doesn't happen, Simon explained in an interview with *Management Review* following announcement of his Nobel award — even with the help of today's sophisticated computer-based decision aids.

"Satisficing is intended to be used in contrast to the classical economist's idea that in making decisions in business or anywhere in real life, you somehow pick, or somebody gives you, a set of alternatives from which you select the best one — maximize," Simon said. "The satisficing idea is that first of all, you don't have the alternatives, you've got to go out and scratch for them — and that you have mighty shaky ways of evaluating them when you do find them. So you look for alternatives until you get one from which, in terms of your experience and in terms of what you have reason to expect, you will get a reasonable result."

But satisficing doesn't necessarily mean that managers have to be satisfied with what alternative pops up first in their minds or in their computers and let it go at that. The level of satisficing can be raised — by personal determination, setting higher individual or organizational standards, and by use of an increasing range of sophisticated management science and computer-based decision-making and problem-solving techniques.

"As time goes on, you obtain more information about what's feasible and what you can aim at," Simon said. "Not only do you get more information, but in many, if not most, companies there are procedures for setting targets, including procedures for trying to raise individuals' aspiration levels. This is a major responsibility of top management."

The Carnegie-Mellon economist/scientist warns, however, that one organization doesn't necessarily become better than another just by setting higher aspiration levels for its managers and workers. Recalling the old saying that "If wishes were horses, beggars would ride," he stressed that the main problem is to get the organization to work "very hard and tight" against realistic objectives: "You can destroy morale and suffer a real boomerang effect . . . if you set objectives unrealistically high."

Simon, a member of the Carnegie faculty since 1949, is a multidiscipline scholar — social science, computer science, operations research, statistics, philosophy of science — and now holds the Richard King Mellon Chair in computer science and psychology. Virtually his entire academic career of some 40 years (he is now 62) has been focussed on research into organizational and individual decision-making and problem-solving concepts and techniques — in effect, maintaining a lifelong effort in identifying and improving "how to decide what to do." And he is openly optimistic about prospects for improvement of our decision-making capabilities.

In citing Simon's work in organizational behaviour and decision making, the Swedish Nobel award group took special note of his rejection of the "assumption made in the classic theory of the firm as an omniscient, rational, profit-maximizing entrepreneur." Modern business economics and administrative research "are largely based on Simon's ideas," the Swedish Academy said.

Author of a dozen books and hundreds of articles covering the full range of his academic interests, Simon wrote a lead article, "Management by Machine," that appeared in the November 1960 issue of *Management Review*. Reflecting his intense interest in the expanding capabilities of computer science, the article opened with these eye-catching predictions:

> During the next 25 years, the job of manager will undergo some major changes as machines take over more and more of the activities that now seem too complex and "high level" ever to yield to automation. The chances are strong that, even before this decade is over, machines will be able to perform any function in the organization — and this includes the "thinking" and "deciding" tasks that are the basis of the manager's job.
>
> This doesn't mean that executives will become obsolete. But the business organization in 1985 will be a more highly automated man-machine system, and the nature of management will naturally be conditioned by the nature of the system being managed. . . .

The timetable laid out in this forecast era of new decision-making capabilities appears to have slipped — but only slightly — from the schedule Simon envisioned on the pages of MR more than 18 years ago. He points out now, however, that machines already have taken over many of the "thinking and deciding" tasks of workers and managers. And he suggests that society in general and managers in particular can expect even more sophisticated advances in the decision-making capabilities of man-machine complexes.

Simon rejects suggestions that companies will actually be "managed" by computers. Nonetheless, he stresses that the decision-making powers of machines are advancing steadily with the development of ever more sophisticated computer and related software systems, further refinements in operations research and other management science techniques. He also cites expanding capabilities in the fields of artificial intelligence and cognitive science — both activities concerned with programming computers to do humanoid things.

In spelling out his expectations of future advances in management decision-making processes in his discussion with MR, the Nobel laureate pointed to:

• Development of a second generation of management information systems that will be much more oriented toward decision-making activities.

Managers, he said, really need systems "more oriented toward data that come into the organization from the environment rather than information generated inside the organization."

• The movement of large artificial intelligence programs out of the R&D phase into specific applications of professional-level tasks. As examples of what's ahead in this line, he cited INTERNIST, a computer-based medical diagnosis program and DENDRAL, a Stanford University computer program that identifies molecules from mass spectogram data — formerly a month-long job for a single researcher.

• Increasing use of robotry in industry with the development of new sensing devices and related decision-making hardware.

Other highlights of the interview follow:

What Simon Says about Management and the Science of Decision Making

Under your concept of "satisficing" as a decision-making procedure, how do you know when you've assembled a sufficient range of alternatives from which to select a course of action? You have used the term "aspiration level" in connection with the satisficing process. Is a manager's aspiration level the ultimate criterion?

Simon: If you look at this concept from an evolutionary standpoint, you'll determine that any organism that's going to survive in a world that has its ups and downs is going to have to set targets that are realistically related to its environment. It must be prepared to lower those targets — at least, within limits — when the environment gets tougher, and it has to be prepared to raise those targets if the environment becomes more benign. That's what I mean by "aspiration level." And that, I believe, is the way targets get fixed in business decision making.

For example: How do we know what profit we're going to try to make this year and what sales we're going to shoot for. Well, we look at last year's profits and last year's sales, take a squint at the business situation as best we can — but through very clouded glasses — and then we add a little optimism or pessimism — which says something about us — and we set some targets. Some companies, of course, try to improve their accuracy with the aid of some sophisticated forecasting and other analytical techniques, but in general, businesses go through this routine every quarter and every year.

As time goes on, of course, you obtain more information about what's feasible and what you can aim at. Not only do you get some information, but in many, if not most companies, there are procedures for setting targets, which include procedures for trying to raise individuals' aspiration levels. This is a major responsibility of top management.

Furthermore, you have the whole question of what new alternatives we can discover that we haven't thought of before — what new opportunities we can find — and increasingly in our kind of world, we begin to institutionalize the process of looking for them. We don't leave them to chance; we say we're going to set up a particular part of the business, decide whose job it is to find new alternatives, and determine whether we are able to raise our aspiration levels. That's what research and development is all about. Also, there are many other business functions that look for new gaps that the organization can move into.

In an organization that's operating effectively, there is continual movement, a continual assessment of what's possible, and a continual attempt to try to widen what's possible.

In a sense, then, one of the ways to direct and improve the quality and evolution of an organization is by influencing the aspiration level against which satisficing is measured. Organization A can be better than Organization B if it has measured a higher satisfying criterion in its structure.

With an important qualification! You know the old saying: If wishes were horses beggars would ride. I can't just say that next year I'm going to make a million bucks and since I have that aspiration, I'm going to make it. The problem is how to get that organization to work very hard and tight against realistic operations. You can destroy morale and get a real boomerang effect with a collapse of aspirations if you set objectives unrealistically high. But it's a real-life matter for managers to decide what those levels ought to be.

When we discuss satisficing, aren't we really talking about a decision-making criterion that is more applicable at one organizational level than at another? That is, haven't we, in effect, defined a continuum of a decision-making criterion function that ranges from a kind of optimization or maybe even maximization at the bottom to a satisficing criterion at higher levels? Doesn't the actual decision-making format depend to some degree on the domain of the decision as well as the quality of the data?

Consider a linear programming situation where you have a very complex situation. One way you use optimizing techniques is to try to carve out a simplification of the situation or an approximation of it. Then you can take the simplified model of the situation, apply some sharp mathematical tools, and optimize within the model.

What I'm saying is, one way of satisficing is to simplify the situation as much as you need to in order to be able to apply your optimizing tools; in effect, you're pretending that that's the real situation. As you suggest, you array decisions as a function of level and complexity, moving from very great difficulties in anything approaching maximization at top levels to more and more possibilities as you move down to concrete operations.

You have stated that many of the central issues of our time are "questions of how we use limited information and limited computational capacity to deal with enormous problems whose shape we barely grasp." But you also suggest that we live in a world where attention is a major scarce luxury — that "we cannot afford to attend to information simply because it is there." How do we cope with this problem?

You can discuss this problem at various levels of the organization — a person can do much to improve his system of setting priorities to improve his managerial style. But in terms of wider organizational issues, I believe this question focuses sharply these days on the kinds of information systems you deal with in a company.

After the first wave of enthusiasm for management information systems (MIS), a great deal of disappointment developed. Many of those systems were built on the idea that you could gather up all the important records that were lying around, stuff them all into a computer, and print out some papers, which you could then put on managers' desks — all good information that they didn't have before.

But if you start the other way around and ask what decisions have to be made, what issues an organization should be alerted to promptly, and what information you want to forget, then you start designing an information system, not just in terms of information you happen to have available, but in terms of need for information.

I think the next generation of information systems is likely to be much more realistic. In any event they will start with the concept of performing a decision-making job, planned with the realization that the aim of an information system is to conserve attention, not simply to flood people with data that, in some wild way, might have some potential use for them. It's a matter of directing the attention of people to important, priority matters but at the same time conserving attention.

What other changing dimensions in information technology do you foresee over the next decade?

The pacemaker here, of course, is the computer — the more bangs for a buck that we get out of it every year. Second, but coming much more slowly, I regret to say, is the software technology associated with computers.

As for the second generation of management information systems . . . in addition to the decision-making capabilities I mentioned previously, we also have a great need for a process much more oriented toward information that comes into the organization from the environment rather than information generated inside the organization. In any event, I think we're getting the software technology now to deal with that.

There is absolutely no excuse for a computer to have to learn how to scan print — although by now I think we know reasonably well how to do that. There is absolutely no reason why almost every piece of paper that's produced in our society shouldn't be produced in machine-readable form at the same time it's produced in man-readable form. There's going to be a major shift, and you can see it beginning now. Take the securities industry — computers increasingly have available the same set of numbers and financial reports that the analysts have.

And in computer software, there's a growing sophistication in our ability to model various parts of the business environment — strategic planning made on the basis of being able to simulate various situations, to run off scenarios, to try alternatives, and to do that kind of thinking and planning that we increasingly need.

Twenty years ago you were forecasting that over the next 25 years, the job of the manager would undergo major changes, with machines taking over more and more of the activities that at the time seemed too complex and high level ever to yield to automation. You also foresaw changes in the general occupational profile, with organizations operating with a much higher ratio of machines to men than was characteristic of the late 1950s and early 1960s. As we all know, some of these forecast changes have occurred; others have been slower to take shape. What's ahead now?

The kinds of trends we've been seeing are very likely to continue.

First, there will be a continued increase in service occupations that have nothing much to do with automation. What happens there depends on consumption, on income, and on what things have greater elasticities of demand.

As for the clerical workforce, we're getting to the point where maybe an awful lot of things that can be squeezed out by, at least, our present forms of automation already have been squeezed out. Most of the office factories — the long lines of desks — that you used to see are gone. Now you see more of the secretarial and administrative types. Thus we are going to see more and more people in so-called service or face-to-face people kinds of occupations.

The question of skills is a tough one. But to illustrate a point, consider what percentage of people in our society drive automobiles well enough to get and maintain licenses. About 95 percent. Now run down the list of principal occupations and ask yourself what percentage of the workforce exercises skills on the job that are higher than the skills required to drive an automobile. My guess (and the personnel people I've tried it on haven't been outraged by it) is that 40 percent is a generous estimate. Some 60 percent are using in their work today lower skills than they use in driving back and forth to their jobs. This doesn't sound to me like a world in which there's a major problem with the unskilled, especially since skills are rising in the population.

So when you look at the figures showing much higher unemployment among the unskilled than among the skilled, you should also look at two other things. One is minimum wages, which may make people unemployable in an economy at a given time at what happens to be a minimum wage in that economy. Secondly, you have to look at the whole employment process. I don't care what the skills are. Trot out a whole population full of Ph.D.s if you think that's a high skill — or expert billiard players — and in that society you have some percentage of people unemployed. You'll always find that the unemployed ones are the least skilled of that group, no matter what group it is for all sorts of good reasons.

What I'm really saying is that although there certainly are problems of giving unskilled people an opportunity to make a contribution to society and to earn a reasonable standard of living in that society, I don't think that one should look at automation or technological change in general as a major factor in those problems. I don't see it as a major issue.

And the major issue is . . .?

The major issue is, first, what we feel about degrees of equality or inequality in our society and how much we're willing to let differences in productive capacity reflect themselves in standards of living. That's a decision we make all the time in every society. And second, what really are the potentialities and capacities of the people who are the less productive members of our society? For example, there's an awful lot of useful, productive things that an illiterate person can do. We might have questions about whether the productivity of the work he can do is high enough so that you would be willing to let him live on the income he can produce in that society. The minimum wage laws, for example, are arguments that we are not always willing to leave that test to the market. Welfare systems and guaranteed income schemes are ways of dealing with the fact that in our society, some people may be very much more productive than others, and we're not willing to let that be the sole determinant of income distribution.

In other words, increases in technology do not make it more and more of a villain in economic society.

It certainly does not make it a villain with respect to the viability of the unskilled. As a matter of fact, in my city, trash collectors, whom I don't want to call either skilled or unskilled, are in great demand, and I think probably come dearer than assistant professors . . . and you know, I don't see anything wrong with that.

On several occasions you have posed the question, "Will the corporation be managed by machines?" What is the shape of the future for managers?

Of course, the answer I gave (in *The New Science of Management Decision,* Prentice-Hall) was that the corporation wouldn't be managed by machine — although I predicted it *could* be in perhaps a shorter time span than I would right now. But the main argument of the book was based on a very classical proposition of economics — the doctrine of comparative advantage. I argued that you had to look at not merely what a machine could do, but at the things that machines are relatively good at — computers and factory automation — compared to people.

When computer development really got going after World War II, most people thought that computers could do the sorts of things that blue collar people do and perhaps some routine clerical duties, but that the higher things of the mind were beyond them. I think that our experience in the field of artificial intelligence over the last 20 years has been a little different from that — computers can and do perform far more complicated and even creative tasks.

The area in which the human being retains his largest comparative advantage, I believe, is in coordination of a pair of eyes, a mind, and a set of hands in dealing with an external environment. (For example, writing a computer program to simulate a college professor is a lot easier than writing programs to simulate a bulldozer driver.) Thus we've progressed much more rapidly with programming the kinds of things the central nervous system does than we have with the things the sensory organs do. So if you ask in what kinds of occupations in society is interaction with the environment crucial, you find, for example, a good many blue collar occupations that are largely concerned with the interactions of people with people. You can cite the salesman role, if you want, but even in instances like that you always have to think of the possibility of things being done in a different way than in the past.

My favorite example for this point is the old-fashioned family physician. What was his most needed skill and what did he spend the largest number of hours a week doing? The answer: driving a horse. But, as you know, that got automated pretty fast.

The conclusion I reached was that for the visible future — which is never really very long — the computer was going to reduce the number of people in white collar, well structured jobs and in factory and assembly-line operations. In management, I felt it probably was going to reduce somewhat the number of middle-management people who were making day-to-day management decisions. But beyond that, I didn't see that it was going to make drastic changes in the work force.

As it turned out, many changes have occurred in the clerical area, and we have seen much change in the functions of middle management. But change has come more slowly with respect to factory automation, except in a few continuous process industries. Of course, we also have seen advances in the use of numerical control in activities such as machine tools and related operations, and now robotry is advancing very rapidly. In fact, for the next five or ten years robotry is probably going to be one of the areas of rather rapid change in factory operations of a more discrete kind where it has not been applicable previously because of the need for more sophisticated sensing and grasping devices.

For the past 20 years or so you have been concentrating on psychological studies designed to help understand how the human mind works. What specific tools in this area are available now and what's coming in the future that will help managers in their decision-making responsibilities?

Research on problem solving began as a natural continuation of the work we'd been doing on decision making. It became evident that there was a need to take a more fundamental and microscopic look at decision making, and problem solving is a good part of that.

First, by getting a better understanding of human problem solving, we developed some ideas about how to enlarge the range of operations research (OR) tools so that today we have not only some optimization techniques but also the so-called "heuristic search" — rule-of-thumb type — techniques.

Second, there is an increasing number of books and university courses on problem solving, and I believe that others outside the university setting — the Kepner-Tregoe organization is one example — are working well within this tradition. The people doing this work are drawing on some very old and classical ideas (we didn't invent the subject), but they are also drawing more and more on the psychological literature that's been turned out in the last couple of decades of research.

Third, we are seeing some large artificial intelligence programs that do professional-level tasks, though so far they are just getting out of the R&D phase into some specific applications — but mostly in fields other than management. For example, the University of Pittsburgh medical school has INTERNIST, a computer-based medical diagnosis program developed by Dr. Jack Meyers of the medical school and a computer scientist, Dr. Harry Pople. The system is used for diagnosing in the area of internal medicine, and it has reached the point at which physicians are beginning to consult it to check their own judgment and to see whether it thinks of something that they didn't.

Stanford University has a computer program called DENDRAL that identifies molecules by analysis of mass spectogram data. Formerly, a chemist had to take a month out of his life to do one of these analyses.

In the management field there was some early movement in this direction in an artificial intelligence program that made investment decisions. It could take a trust agreement and make a set of decisions that simulated very closely the decisions that would be made by a bank trust officer. Now there is a wide range of computer aids in the investment field that, I believe, are partly a byproduct of that kind of research. The money manager now has at his computer console a lineup of analyses that represent the kinds of rules of thumb that one uses in decision making in that business. It would not be a difficult programming job to automate a large percentage of those decisions.

It sounds like INTERNIST and DENDRAL are at the cutting edge of exciting developments in the artificial intelligence field. Is there anything like them on the horizon in the management area?

INTERNIST and DENDRAL certainly illustrate the level that the technology has reached, but I can't cite clear-cut examples in the management area now because there hasn't been enough R&D in management fields. Moreover, it's astonishing to me how little R&D is going into these types of efforts over all — and especially management.

Who, for example, has mounted sizable efforts on this problem in business corporations — not counting the non-profit organizations that may have research projects? Xerox has a big R&D effort on this now, and I guess IBM is somewhat cranked up on some aspects of it. A number of Japanese companies have been concentrating mostly on the robotry and pattern recognition aspects. But the amount of commercial R&D in the whole area of artificial intelligence/decision making is very tiny, and most of the work that has been done has been supported by grants from DARPA (Defense Advanced Research Projects Agency) unit in the Defense Department. Probably less than $20 million a year.

There's some reason for this situation, of course. Another old saying goes, "Be not the first by whom the new is tried. . . . " Also, corporations can't afford to do too much of the basic research, which then is appropriated by industry generally. For this reason, then, one of the roles the government has to play in our economic society is a major one in developing new technology — as it has with nearly every major technology we have.

Are there any significant differences in the effectiveness of group vs individual decision making?

Sure, there are differences, but when I think about that aspect, I need a finer classification because there are many aspects of group decision making. Take, for example, the Japanese *ringi* system. When you talk about the so-called bottom-up decision-making process, in one very real sense, that's group decision making. Somebody has a notion that he thinks should be pushed. He develops a document or two on it, begins to circulate it around the organization, drinks tea with a lot of people, and after a while, a consensus begins to develop. I don't know how this is actually tested, but when the man feels that he has a consensus, he develops a formal document and sends it around, and everybody puts his stamp on it.

Is that group decision making? I don't know how many people are in the room.

On the other hand, you have the American system, operating in an organization that resembles a hierarchy. Somebody has an idea that he tries on a few people. After a while, maybe a document goes up the line, and at some point, the boss approves it. In many ways, it looks different, but at the same time, there's a lot of consultation — sometimes a meeting, a few people talking, somebody shipping a memo to somebody else who comments on it or takes a piece of it and works it out.

There's very little individual decision making in any organization I know about — that is, the sense of one person going off by himself, kicking the idea around from ground level, finishing it, and then saying, "This is the way we're going to do it." But when you get down to the question of how you actually do group decision making, you run into issues like whether you get people around a table and what do you talk about. Another big point is who you get around the table.

Then the concept of satisficing applies to the group as it does to the individual?

I think so. If you just look at the flow of decisions, the flow of problem solving that takes place during the decision process, and take the names off the pieces of it so it's an abstract thing, I don't think the structure is terribly different from individual decision making.

When we're making a complex decision individually, we also divide it into pieces, work on one and then another, and then we've got to put them together again. Somewhere, at some point, you're a committee of the whole, yourself. So if you look at the problem abstractly, the similarities are much more visible than the differences for complex decisions.

In your discussions of the science of management decisions, you have expressed the view that organizations will generally retain their traditional hierarchical structures. Does the matrix structure fit this pattern?

The matrix situation, if I understood if correctly, is not very different from the notion that Frederick Taylor had about functional foremanship and his general notion that unity of command was only an illusion. The matrix organization is a legitimization of the idea that decision premises have to come from several sources. It makes a task force idea workable by signaling that it's not an "illicit" way of doing business in an organization.

The matrix is a great step of progress, in which somebody invented a label (though it's more than that, of course) that made legitimate the fact we all knew before — but sort of felt ashamed of — that there is no unity of command, and can't be, in a complex organization and that because of the distribution of expertness, commands have to flow from a number of directions.

Aren't we saying then, in effect, that in those situations we do not have a pure hierarchical structure, that it is something different from what we heretofore assumed to be the preferred structure?

I think the change in our perceptions is greater than the change in reality. In a study of the controllership function back in 1953, we found that most of the problems in defining the role of the factory controller involved defining what his relative responsibilities were to the controller's department and to the factory manager. And that was difficult to do at the time because it was felt to be illegitimate for him to be responsible for both.

The matrix idea has helped us (1) to recognize the commonness of the situation by bringing it out into the open and (2) to develop a set of more or less common understandings of how you deal with it and that people can live with multiple authority relations.

What we have then is a very dynamic hierarchical structure, in which the nature of the hierarchy shifts as the problem changes and the kind of expertness that is required for proper relationships also shifts.

It's fair to say then that if you look at almost all business organizations today, there still is a fall-back hierarchy. When it comes to a clinch, the manager still knows who his boss is.

Perhaps some will tend to identify an organization structure as an administrative hierarchy for taking certain personnel oriented decisions and a functional heirarchy that is business-problem related. But what makes the former particularly important is that it's inevitable that a man looks at his career, more often than not, in terms of the administrative hierarchy.

You stated recently that it is "commonplace to observe that economics has traditionally been concerned with what decisions are made rather than how they are made." You have also argued that there is an urgent need to enlarge the established body of economic analysis to encompass the procedural aspects of decision making rather than adhering entirely to the concerns of substantive rationality. Can you then suggest what such economists or economic analysts should specifically utilize from other sciences that would be useful in providing greater assistance to the business community and its needs for work-a-day economic intelligence or know-how? Would we then have better economic forecasts — that is, more accurate predictions of business cycles and economic blips in the road ahead for business decision makers?

There are a number of answers to that. One is that there have been other fields whose concern has been to build actual decision procedures for solving problems, such as operations research. Actually, I think economics learned a great deal — for example, in linear programming — that has had a major impact on economic theory. But now we have the field of artificial intelligence coming along which provides procedures for solving problems covering a wider range than you can handle with, say, OR techniques. I think economists need to learn something about AI. Also there is a subarea within computer science now called "computational complexity," where there have been efforts to apply some of these ideas to economic theory. Then, of course, over the psychological side, having an understanding of how people do change their targets and to respond to environmental events is important in understanding things like the phenomenon of inflation.

As for getting better economic forecasts and analyses more useful to business, I guess the cautious way to put it is that if we are going to have any chance of getting better forecasts, we are going to have to look at what is known throughout the social sciences and about how people's expectations are formed and how they change. We can't do this in a vacuum without looking at those types of business and consumer behaviors. Likewise, we need to borrow some of the techniques of other social sciences for getting at these behaviors.

Take marketing as an example. I think there has been an increasing impact both of psychological theory and of techniques for getting data about people's marketing behavior. One shouldn't give the impression that none of these data has contributed to business cycle forecasting. But over all they have never had a very enthusiastic reception in economics.

In your writings on decision making, you have described yourself as a technical radical, an economic conservative, and a philosophic pragmatist. How do these terms shape your concept of the present and future processes of management decision making?

By technological radical, I meant that from the beginning I've been unable to see what the ultimate limits of computers are in terms of the range of human functions that they will be able to perform. The early line about computers was that they were dumb beasts that did only what you programmed them to do. That's true, but sometimes you can program them to do surprising things. And that's where the technological radicalism comes in — a real belief that the computer is a powerful general purpose device that, as we learn how to use it, is going to be able to perform a wider and wider range of human functions.

By economic conservative, I meant that I believed that the real limiting factor on the rate at which the use of the computer organizations would be extended was that you have to embody them in capital — steel, wires, glass, and what-not — and that for a long time to come, there might be a lot of fancy things you can do with a computer, but the question is: Which of these things will pay? After all, you can also hire people to perform many of these functions, and it isn't always clear how rapidly changeovers to computers will occur.

By philosophic pragmatist, I mean that I just can't get very excited about arguments about computers and "free will." I'd just like to see what we can do with computers; such philosophical questions will settle themselves in the long run.

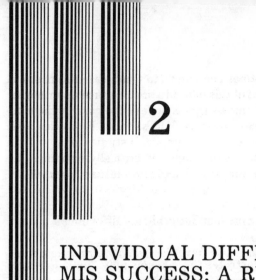

2

INDIVIDUAL DIFFERENCES AND MIS SUCCESS: A REVIEW OF THE EMPIRICAL LITERATURE

ROBERT W. ZMUD*

Of the numerous factors believed to influence MIS success, the area of individual differences has by far been the most extensively studied. This paper synthesizes the findings of empirical investigations of the manner in which individual differences impact MIS success. Suggestions are made regarding those aspects which would benefit most from future research.

1. Introduction

Many factors are believed to impinge upon the success experienced by organizations regarding their development of management information systems (MIS). Although clearly not exhaustive, the following typifies the variety of issues addressed by both academics and practitioners [23], [54], [64], [70]: organizational characteristics, environmental characteristics, task characteristics, personal characteristics, interpersonal characteristics, MIS staff characteristics, and MIS policies.

Those factors generating the largest amount of research activity have involved the influence of individual differences upon MIS design, implementation, and usage. While researchers from a variety of disciplines have shared a common interest in examining the effect of a number of cognitive, personality, demographic, and situational variables upon information processing

* Reprinted by permission. "Individual Differences and MIS Success: A Review of the Empirical Literature" by R. Zmud, *Management Science*, Volume 25, #10, October 1979, pp. 966-975. Copyright © 1979 The Institute of Management Sciences. The author is an academician.

and decision behavior, no attempt has been made to synthesize this material as it relates to MIS. It is the intent of this paper to provide such a synthesis.

The paper is organized around a model that is believed to portray the manner in which individual differences influence MIS success. First, the basic elements of the model are introduced. Then, empirical studies involving the various model elements and their relationships are critically examined. Finally, the implication of these findings and needs for future research are discussed.

2. A Model Illustrating the Impact of Individual Differences upon MIS Success

Figure 1 shows a model which illustrates the manner individual differences are believed to influence MIS success. Two distinct paths are conceptualized. An upper path finds individual differences amplifying or dampening limitations in human information processing and decision behavior, which in turn impose or suggest MIS design alternatives directed toward motivating or facilitating MIS usage. A lower path reflects the impact of individual differences upon the attitudes held by potential MIS users and upon the tendencies for MIS users to involve themselves in the MIS development effort. These paths can thus be characterized as representing the *cognitive* and *attitudinal* influences of individual differences upon MIS success. Two relationships are depicted in Figure 1 as dotted lines. These lines represent research studies bypassing the upper and lower paths described above. The remainder of this section more completely describes the model elements.

Figure 1. Impact of Individual Differences upon MIS Success.

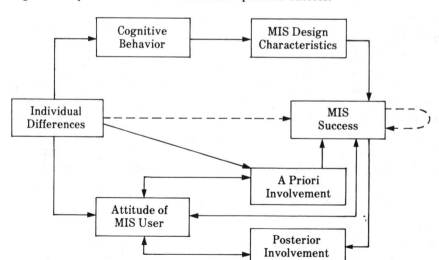

Individual Differences
The individual differences believed most relevant to MIS success are grouped into three classes: cognitive style, personality, and demographic/situational variables.

Cognitive styles represent characteristic modes of functioning shown by individuals in their perceptual and thinking behavior. While such behaviors are dependent on task and situational elements [16], many individuals exhibit pervasive tendencies toward particular cognitive behavior and consistent individual differences can be observed. Although the cognitive style construct is acknowledged to be multidimensional, the number of such dimensions and the relationships between dimensions are not clear. Most MIS-related research, however, has focussed on three dimensions [9]. The *simple/complex* dimension [95] pertains to structural characteristics of perception and thinking and has been operationalized as three distinct properties: differentiation, i.e., the number of elements sought and assimilated in cognition; discrimination, i.e., the assigning of slightly varying stimuli to the same or different categories; and integration, i.e., the number and completeness of rules used in cognition. The *field-dependent/field-independent* dimension (low analytic/high analytic) was initially conceptualized as an ability to disembed a context field in perception but has since been broadened to reflect whether an individual is bound by external referrents or can make use of internal referrents in structuring cognitions [116]. The *systematic/heuristic* dimension reflects whether an individual utilizes abstract models and systematic processes in cognition or whether the approach taken is based more on experience, common sense and the practicalities of a situation [46], [121].

Personality refers to the cognitive and affective structures maintained by individuals to facilitate their adjustments to the events, people and situations encountered in life [38]. Personality variables believed to strongly impact MIS success include locus of control, dogmatism, ambiguity tolerance, extroversion/introversion, need for achievement, risk taking propensity, evaluative defensiveness, and anxiety level [54].

The demographic/situational variables cover a broad spectrum of personal characteristics [54]. Both general intellectual abilities and a knowledge of specific content areas are believed to influence MIS usage, as have attributes such as sex, age, experience, education, professional orientation, and organizational level.

Cognitive Behavior
Cognition refers to the activities involved in attempts by individuals to resolve inconsistencies between an internalized conceptualization of the environment and what is perceived to be actually transpiring in the environment. While not directly oriented toward MIS, three distinct research areas have evolved. Information processing theory is concerned with explaining the types of memory structures utilized in cognition and how data is perceived,

organized and retrieved in terms of these memory structures [10], [89]. Artificial intelligence is concerned with replicating how problem situations are represented and resolved in human cognition [81]. Behavioral decision theory is concerned with describing the ways in which beliefs and values are incorporated into the decision making process [102]. The most relevant aspects of these research areas to MIS success involve the uncovering of human limitations in cognition, which then become critical elements to be supported by a computer-based MIS.

MIS Design Characteristics

The perspective adopted of a MIS is that its organizational role is to support decision making activity [37]. The design characteristics of concern can be broadly classified as belonging to three groups: the information received, the decision aids provided, and the delivery system which serves as the interface between the MIS user and a computer-based MIS.

Information has value only when it reduces the uncertainty that pervades decision making [52]. When designing the information component of a MIS, a number of factors need to be addressed, including the source, timeliness, level of aggregation, completeness, accuracy, reliability, validity, frequency, and currentness of information [37], [119].

Decision aids are provided to overcome limitations inherent in human cognition and to ensure that available information is sensed and used. While numerous decision aids can be identified, most fall into the categories of analytic models [50] or display enhancements [106]. With both categories, the intention is to increase the comprehensibility of information.

The convenience and ease of use of a MIS are considered as important to MIS usage as is the quality of information received [83]. Delivery system factors cover a broad range of items ranging from technical issues such as man-computer response times [75] and query languages [70] to human factors issues [20] and organizational issues such as the adequacy of training provided MIS users [123] and the relationships existing between MIS users and the MIS staff [30].

Attitude of MIS User

Organizational members possess preconceived attitudes, i.e., beliefs, values and expectations [111], regarding the role of MIS within the organization. These attitudes have been seen to be expressed toward perceptions of the capabilities of and need for a MIS, perceptions of the organizational environment for MIS, perceptions of the MIS staff and the need for user interaction with this staff, and perceptions toward organizational change in general [40], [92], [98].

A Priori Involvement

The implementation stages that precede the introduction of a MIS into an organization, i.e., project initiation, feasibility study, requirements analysis, system design, and system development, provide numerous opportunities for user involvement [30], [55], [62], [107], [123]. *A priori* involvement includes all active contributions by potential MIS users toward this effort.

Posterior Involvement
The opportunities for users to contribute toward MIS success also exist after implementation [55]. It is the exception rather than the norm if no modifications are required once a MIS has become operational and users gain experience with it; and, as all organizations undergo continual change, even a well-designed MIS would benefit from periodic adjustments to ensure it remains compatible with user requirements [60]. *Posterior* involvement thus refers to all active contributions by actual MIS users once a MIS has been introduced into the organization.

MIS Success
Evaluation of MIS success is a complex and perplexing issue [34], [53]. While it is easiest to simply examine actual usage, success ultimately depends on how well the MIS has, in fact, supported decision making. Thus, user satisfaction with a MIS and user performance with a MIS become important valuation measures. All three of these success variables are considered.

3. Results from Empirical Studies

Empirical research is surveyed and evaluated in the context of the model presented above. Not all these studies directly relate to MIS; however, as the intent of the paper is to synthesize a number of interdisciplinary studies that touch upon issues related to MIS design, both studies oriented specifically toward MIS and studies oriented toward information processing and problem solving behavior are included.

The discussion that follows is organized around the relationships displayed in Figure 1. In general, these relationships should be considered as associative, rather than causal, in nature.

Individual Differences — Cognitive Behavior
Information requirements of decision makers are dependent upon task, situational and individual factors [16], [71], [109], and the role of individual differences is quite clear. A decision maker's information requirements to a large extent are based upon the individual's "world-view," which is totally reflective of the individual. Depending upon the scope of a MIS, one may design for the individual [50] or for a group of individuals [2]. The objective of this aspect of MIS research on individual differences is to locate the critical individual differences and determine how best to design a MIS for individuals so characterized.

Cognitive Style. In contrasting the information processing behaviors of simple and complex individuals, complex subjects have been found to search for [95], [49] and use [95], [100], [112] more information, to prefer aggregate rather than raw data [2], and to use more rules [42] when integrating information. A slightly different outcome, however, found that complex subjects used more complex, but less simple, information [26]. Regarding their decision making behavior, complex subjects have been found to generate more decision alternatives [42], [100] resulting in greater flexibility [13], [99] but less confidence [100] and more decision time [26].

In contrasting the decision behavior of field-dependent and field-independent individuals, field-independent subjects have been found to seek more information [36], to prefer detailed, aggregate, quantitative reports [2], [7], [24], [67], and to require more decision time [7]. Another finding indicated that when a mismatch existed between field-dependency/field-independency and report format, subjects tended to request additional reports [7].

In contrasting the decision behavior of heuristics and systematics both consistent and inconsistent findings have been observed. Systematics have been seen to consistently prefer more quantitative information [46] and require more decision time [77], [78], [113] than heuristics. However, systematics have been found to prefer more [39], [77], [113] and less [3], [86] information and to prefer aggregated [3] and raw [5], [86], [105] data when compared with heuristics. One study does suggest possible explanations for these inconsistencies [8]: systematics with access to decision aids requested less information than heuristics while systematics without decision aids requested more information than heuristics; and, heuristics with low task knowledge requested the most information.

Finally, a related issue involves individual perceptions of cognitive styles. The systematic and complex styles have been perceived as being more potent than the heuristic and simple styles [120]. While highly speculative at best, it would appear that such perceptions would have a long-term impact upon MIS design.

Personality. Greater information search activity has been observed for subjects possessing an internal locus of control [58], [84], a low degree of dogmatism [56], [61], and high risk-taking propensity [110]. Low dogmatic subjects have also been characterized as more deliberate [61] and less confident [110] decision makers.

Evidence is also available regarding other personality variables. Extroverted subjects were found to more quickly retrieve information stored in their own minds and to retain information better over short intervals, but not for long intervals when compared with introverts [31]. Subjects classified as being intolerant of ambiguity were found to prefer concrete stimuli and to perceive more information as being valuable [21].

Demographic and Situational. Subjects with higher general intelligence have been observed to process information faster, select information more effectively, retain information better, make decisions faster [110], and to better organize information in their minds [45]. Subjects with higher quantitative abilities make more use of short-term memory but less use of long-term memory than do subjects with lower quantitative abilities [45], and subjects with greater verbal abilities possess enhanced short-term memory when compared with subjects with lesser verbal abilities [44].

Experienced decision makers were shown to select information more effectively but to integrate it less effectively and to be more flexible but less confident [110]. Three factors related to experience are task knowledge, age, and management level. Subjects possessing a high level of task information were observed to engage in less information search [8]. Older subjects were found to engage in more information search [108], to select information more effectively and be more flexible [110], to require more decision time [108], [110], and to exhibit depressed long-term memory capabilities [31]. Subjects in higher management levels, however, were found to require less decision time [108].

Cognitive Behavior — MIS Design Characteristics

The limitations [74] and other peculiarities of human cognition provide numerous opportunities for MIS designs to aid the user in task accomplishment. The studies undertaken that indicate areas for computer-aided support are broadly categorized as involving information or decision aid considerations.

Information. While search activity [59], decision accuracy [1], [25], [59], [103], and decision confidence [103] all increase as the quantity of relevant information increases, it has become generally acknowledged that humans do not understand their own information requirements. They often demand too little or too much information [6], [94] and have been observed to prefer more information than economically justified [26] as well as using less information than their own prior expectations [113]. A major role of a MIS, thus, is to both select and filter appropriate information elements for the decision maker.

The inclusion of irrelevant information in a report has been found to degrade performance [17], [29] and should be avoided. Redundancy, in the form of contextual or elaborative information, is desirable as it aids the user in recognizing, evaluating, and remembering critical information [25], [43], [76], [91], [103]. Overredundancy, however, can hinder information processing when capacity limitations are reached [43].

A related consideration is the order of information presented. When information quantities prohibit presenting all information at once, care must be taken to minimize primacy or recency effects [6], [94].

Decision Aids. Humans have been found to be slow in initiating action [114], to delay too long when making decisions [41], [94], and to be reluctant to change prior decisions [94], [114]. Decision performance would benefit, thus, from decision aids that direct, to a certain degree, a decision maker's behavior.

Humans are also typically unable to make full use of provided information, particularly when it is multidimensional [94] or if it must first be stored in memory, inferred from a report, or otherwise transformed [101]. Humans develop and consider too few alternatives [96] and often accept the first alternative that makes sense [114]. It has been consistently observed the simple models and decision rules are extremely good predictors of human decision behavior [18], [102]. Such models have tended to outperform man [35] even when model parameters are arrived at in an *ad hoc* manner [19]. As decision makers apparently develop effective strategies but fail to use them, it might be beneficial to have these strategies automatically invoked by a MIS.

Probabilistic analysis appears extremely uncomfortable for most individuals. Humans tend to be reluctant to work with probabilistic data [18], to systematically violate the rules of rational decision making [79], [102], and to exhibit difficulties in weighing new evidence as it affects a decision situation [6], [12], [72], [103]. The provision of probabilistic aids would appear to be a necessity in most situations.

MIS Design Characteristics — MIS Success

As indicated in the previous section of this paper MIS design attributes were classified as belonging to three groups: information needs, decision aids, and delivery system components. Studies have been undertaken to examine aspects of each of these design areas with regard to MIS success.

Information.   User satisfaction with a MIS has been shown to be positively related to the degree to which information needs are perceived to be met [4], [93] but to be negatively related to the amount of information being received [62]. Also, a group of MIS users receiving an unalterable report were less satisfied than another group receiving reports which could be modified [28].

Decision Aids.   The availability of quantitative models has resulted in improved decision performance [8], [15], [104] but was found to lengthen decision time [8], [15] and decrease confidence [15]. Graphical reports have been shown to result in better performance than tabular reports [8], [96] and were preferred when compared with tabular or bar chart reports [119]. Color-coded graphics have improved performance [96], a single multi-line graph resulted in better performance than multiple single-line graphs [97], and format improvements were observed to be positively associated with increased MIS usage [32].

Delivery System.   Management personnel have proven to be very intolerant of poor MIS-user interface designs [14], [28]. Ease of use and favorable user interfaces have both been positively associated with MIS satisfaction [4], [64].

On-line usage, as opposed to batch usage, has resulted in faster and more consistent performance [23], [85], [90] and a higher degree of user satisfaction [62], [64], [90] but only when the MIS is accessible and reliable [90]. With on-line usage, CRT terminals were observed to result in better performance [57] and higher user satisfaction [48] even though users took longer and made more errors [57] than did typewriter-like terminals. A study contrasting the concerns of on-line versus batch users uncovered some interesting differences [92]: while batch users emphasized access time and MIS availabilities with regard to data and decision aids, on-line users stressed response time, training, and their relations with the MIS staff.

Other studies have underscored the importance of response time to on-line MIS usage. Delays longer than 10 seconds, irregular delays, and uncertain delays in the flow of communications from a MIS to a user have consistently been shown to lower user satisfaction [75], [82], [90], [93]. Enforced delays in the communication flow from a user to a MIS were observed to improve performance but to lower satisfaction [11].

A related delivery system feature is the query language provided users to communicate with a MIS. Vocabulary enhancements have been positively associated with increases in MIS usage and satisfaction [32].

Two organization-oriented delivery system attributes are user compatibility with the MIS staff and the quality of training provided users. Both factors have been demonstrated to be positively associated with higher user satisfaction [4], [93]. While management personnel are often too busy to attend formal training sessions [14], it is possible to provide self-teaching through the MIS. Such a strategy has, in fact, been shown to result in better user performance than traditional training sessions [51].

Individual Differences — MIS User Attitudes
Extroverted, perceptive individuals were found to possess more positive attitudes toward MIS [117] while males [69], older individuals [64], [80], and less educated individuals [66] were observed to exhibit less posititive attitudes.

Individual Differences — A Priori Involvement
Cognitive differences between MIS users and MIS designers have been suggested as a major deterrent to effective user involvement in MIS design [30], [122]. Differences have been observed between designers and the MIS user for both cognitive style and self-image [33].

MIS User Attitude — A Priori Involvement
One study has uncovered a positive association between MIS attitude and a priori involvement [62].

A Priori Involvement — MIS Success
A priori user involvement in MIS design has consistently been observed to be positively associated with user satisfaction with a MIS [22], [30], [47], [62], [68], [107]. A related finding was that ineffective user-designer communication during design was negatively associated with satisfaction [30]. The results of studies examining the association between a priori involvement and MIS usage, however, have not been consistent: while one study did uncover a positive association [107], two others have found no association [68], [53].

MIS User Attitude — MIS Success
Preconceived attitudes toward MIS are associated with MIS usage to a much greater extent than MIS satisfaction. Usage has been positively associated with attitudes regarding the potential of a MIS [53], [63], [66], [87],

[88], the urgency of MIS [87], [88], the extent of top management support for a MIS [63], [64], [68], [87], and the quality of the MIS staff [68], [87]. Regarding MIS satisfaction, only a positive association with attitudes of top management support [64], [66] and mixed results regarding MIS potential [66] have been observed.

Posterior Involvement — MIS Success
The results of a single study indicate the existence of a negative association between *posterior* involvement and MIS satisfaction [62]. Apparently, MIS users involved in this modification effort tended to be those dissatisfied with the MIS.

Posterior Involvement — MIS User Attitudes
No empirical studies have been reported.

Individual Differences — MIS Success
A number of research studies have directly examined the impact of individual differences upon MIS success. These results will be reported regarding MIS usage, MIS satisfaction, and or decision performance via a MIS.

MIS *Usage.*   Systematics have been observed to utilize a MIS more [62] and less [92] than heuristics. Subjects with greater risk-taking propensities utilized a MIS less [110]. Individuals characterized by more education [62], longer tenure in an organization [62], [63], [64], [115], and a greater degree of organizational success [62] were seen to utilize a MIS less, while individuals with higher task knowledge and those of a professional status tended to use a MIS more [115]. Findings regarding organizational level, however, have been mixed [27], [28], [62], [68].

MIS *Satisfaction.*   Systematics were seen to exhibit less satisfaction with a MIS than heuristics [64]. Individuals characterized by more education [65] and longer tenure [62], [64], [68] tended to be less satisfied with a MIS but individuals shown to have achieved greater degrees of organizational success tended to be more satisfied [65].

Decision Performance.   Systematics [77], [78], [86] and field-independents [7] have been observed to perform better when using a MIS than, respectively, heuristics and field-dependents. While risk taking propensity was shown to be positively associated with better performance, need-for-achievement was seen to be characterized by a non-linear association, with individuals possessing moderate need-for-achievement performing best [118]. A complex association was uncovered in a study examining evaluative defensiveness and anxiety [118]. Here, individuals with a high evaluative defensiveness under conditions of debilitating anxiety performed best while individuals with a high evaluative defensiveness under conditions of facilitating anxiety performed worse. Both general intelligence level [110] and quantitative ability [15] were positively associated with performance. Results of studies examining tenure [62], [108] and education level [62], [113] were mixed.

MIS Usage — MIS Success
Consistently positive associations have been observed between MIS usage and MIS satisfaction [4], [62], [64], [65], [68], [92], [107], [113].

4. Discussion of the Empirical Results and Suggestions for Future Research

The model presented as Figure 1 is used as a structure for evaluating the research already undertaken and for indicating those areas about which least is known. In addition to focussing upon the cognitive and attitudinal influences of individual differences upon MIS success, the interaction of these two elements will also be explored.

Cognitive Influences
A large number of studies have addressed the impact of individual differences upon information processing and decision behavior. As might be expected, the strongest associations have been observed with regard to the personal characteristics that directly relate to individual perception and structuring of environmental stimuli, i.e., cognitive styles and related personality constructs that construct and sustain an individual's "world view." While fewer studies have focused upon affective personality variables and upon demographic attributes, these individual differences have also been associated with distinct cognitive behaviors. What is not clear is whether the influence of noncognitive individual differences directly influences cognitive behavior or moderates the relationships between cognitive styles and cognitive behaviors. Studies investigating this issue are needed.

A related concern is that many of the studies reported were not conducted in a MIS context; and, many of the MIS-based studies were of a laboratory nature and/or utilized students as subjects. The replication of these studies in *real* MIS environments would be beneficial.

The variations in cognitive behaviors attributable to individual differences as well as the documented limitations inherent to human information processing and decision behaviors provide ample opportunities for designers to provide MIS that extend the decision making capabilities of organizational members. Although some research in this direction has been pursued, much remains unknown as to how best to support the individual decision maker *throughout* the entire decision process: problem finding, problem structuring, solution generation, analysis, and choice. Past studies have primarily addressed issues of information presentation. Future studies would benefit from the adoption of a decision support system, rather than an information system, perspective.

Finally, it is becoming increasingly realized that cognitive behaviors are dependent on contextual, i.e., task and environmental, factors as well as individual differences. In order for the results of research studies to be interpretable and generalizable, experimental designs for individual difference research must incorporate relevant contextual variables. To neglect to do so will result in ambiguous, inconsistent, and, possibly, meaningless findings.

Attitudinal Influences

While a number of studies clearly indicate that the attitudes and *a priori* involvement of MIS users are positively associated with MIS success, very few studies have examined the influence of individual differences upon either user attitudes toward MIS or user involvement in MIS design efforts. That such associations do exist is apparent from the number of studies indicating a strong association between individual differences and MIS success. Little is known regarding the characteristics of individuals who tend to possess negative attitudes or who tend to disassociate themselves from MIS design activities. Such knowledge would enable organizations to focus educational and promotional efforts upon those user groups most likely to inhibit MIS success.

A number of other potentially beneficial research avenues suggest themselves given the paucity of empirical studies evident with respect to the relationships denoted as the lower path of Figure 1. First, it seems intuitive that a relationship would exist between MIS attitude and user involvement. Only a single study touched upon this issue, and then only as a small part of a very broad investigation. Second, an interesting outcome observed was that MIS-user *attitudes* are associated with MIS usage while MIS-user *involvement* is associated with MIS satisfaction. Apparently, the relationship between attitudes, involvement, satisfaction, and usage is quite complex. Again, no studies have investigated this issue. Third, little attention has been given to *posterior* involvement. As software maintenance costs typically exceed software development costs, it would seem that the role of the user in specifying MIS modifications and enhancements is crucial. When do users get involved? What type of users get involved? How can users be motivated to become involved?

The Cognitive-Attitudinal Interface

An important research area involves the relationship between user attitudes toward MIS and MIS design characteristics, particularly with regard to delivery system components. It seems apparent that the attributes of most delivery system components, i.e., query languages, response times, the physical interface, training, organizational arrangements between users and the MIS staff, etc., would directly reflect user attitudes. No studies, however, have been uncovered that examine this issue.

5. Conclusion

This analysis of the empirical literature regarding the influence of individual differences upon MIS success indicates rather clearly that individual differences do exert a major force in determining MIS success. It is just as apparent, however, that much remains unknown regarding the specific relationships involved and the relative importance of individual differences when contrasted with contextual factors. With organizations committing an increasing portion of their MIS efforts toward the utilization of the computer to *actively* support decision making, the potential payoff from further research investigating the relationships between MIS success and the personal charcteristics of MIS users is high.

References

1. ADAMS, J.R. and SWANSON, L.A., "Information Processing Behavior and Estimating Accuracy in Operations Management," *Acad. Management J.*, Vol. 19 (1976), p. 98-110.
2. BARIFF, M.L. and LUSK, E.J., "Cognitive and Personality Tests for the Design of Management Information Systems," *Management Sci.*, Vol. 23 (1977), p. 820-829.
3. BARKIN, S.R. and DICKSON, G.W., "An Investigation of Information System Utilization," *Information and Management*, Vol. 1 (1977), pp. 35-45.
4. BARRETT, G.V., THORNTON, C.L. and CABE, P.A., "Human Factors Evaluation of a Computer-Based Information Storage and Retrieval System," *Human Factors*, Vol. 10 (1968), pp. 431-436.
5. BARRETT, M.J., "Information Processing Types and Simulated Production Decision Making," MISRC Working Paper 73-02, University of Minnesota, 1973.
6. BEACH, B.H., "Expert Judgement about Uncertainty: Bayesian Decision Making in Realistic Settings," *Organizational Behavior and Human Performance*, Vol. 14 (1975), pp. 10-59.
7. BENBASAT, I. and DEXTER, A.S., "Value and Event Approaches to Accounting: An Experimental Evaluation," *Accounting Review.*, Vol. 54 (1979), pp. 735-749.
8. − − −and SCHROEDER, R.G., "An Experimental Investigation of Some MIS Design Variables," *MIS Quart.*, Vol. 1, No. 1 (1977), pp. 37-49.
9. − − −and TAYLOR, R.N., "The Impact of Cognitive Styles on Information System Design," *MIS Quart.*, Vol. 2, No. 2 (1978), pp. 43-54.
10. BITHER, S.W. and UNGSON, G., "Consumer Information Processing Research: An Evaluative Review," Working Paper No. 25, College of Business Administration, Pennsylvania State University, 1975.
11. BOEHM, B.W., SEVEN, M.J. and WATSON, R.A., "Interactive Problem − An Experimental Study of 'Lockout' Effects," *Proceedings*, AFIPS Spring Joint Computer Conference, Vol. 38 (1971), pp. 205-210.
12. BRIGHTMAN, H.J. and URBAN, T.F., "The Influence of the Dogmatic Personality upon Information Processing: A Comparison with a Bayesian Information Processor," *Organizational Performance and Human Behavior*, Vol. 11 (1974), pp. 226-276.
13. BRUNER, J.S. and TAJFEL, H., "Cognitive Risk and Environmental Change," *J. Abnormal and Social Psych.*, Vol. 62 (1961), pp. 231-241.
14. CARLSON, E.D., GRACE, B.F. and SUTTON, J.A., "Case Studies of End User Requirements for Interactive Problem Solving Systems," *MIS Quart.*, Vol. 1, No. 1 (1977), pp. 51-63.
15. CHERVANY, N.L. and DICKSON, G.W., "An Experimental Evaluation of Information Overload in a Production Environment," *Management Sci.*, Vol. 20 (1974), pp. 1335-1344.
16. − − −and − − −, "On the Validity of the Analytic-Heuristic Instrument Utilized in 'The Minnesota Experiments': A Reply," *Management Sci.*, Vol. 24 (1978), pp. 1091-1092.
17. COFFEY, J.C., "A Comparison of Vertical and Horizontal Arrangements of Alphanumeric Material," *Human Factors*, Vol. 3 (1961), pp. 93-98.
18. CONRATH, D.W., "From Statistical Decision Theory to Practice: Some Problems with the Transition," *Management Sci.*, Vol. 19 (1973), pp. 873-883.
19. DAWES, R.M., "The Robust Beauty of Improper Linear Models in Decision Making," paper presented at Division V, American Psychological Association Meeting, San Francisco, August 1977.
20. DeGREENE, K.B., "Man-Computer Interrelationships," in K.B. DeGreene (ed.), *System Psychology*, McGraw-Hill, New York, 1970.
21. DERMER, J.D., "Cognitive Characteristics and the Perceived Importance of Information," *Accounting Rev.*, Vol. 48 (1973), pp. 511-519.
22. DICKSON, G.W. and POWERS, R.F., "MIS Project Management: Myths, Opinions and Reality," *California Management Rev.*, Vol. 15 (1973), pp. 147-156.
23. − − −, SENN, J.A. and CHERVANY, N.L., "Research in Management Information Systems: The Minnesota Experiments," *Management Sci.*, Vol. 23 (1977), pp. 913-923.
24. DOKTOR, R.H. and HAMILTON, W.F., "Cognitive Style and the Acceptance of Management Science Recommendations," *Management Sci.*, Vol. 19 (1973), pp. 884-894.

25. DORRIS, A.L., SADOSKY, T.L. and CONNOLLY, T., "Varying Data and Information in a Decision Making Task," *Ergonomics*, Vol. 20 (1977), pp. 643-649.
26. DRIVER, M.J. and MOCK, T.J., "Human Information Processing, Decision Style Theory, and Accounting Information Systems," *Accounting Rev.*, Vol. 50 (1975), pp. 490-508.
27. DUNLOP, R.A., "Some Empirical Observations on the Man-Machine Interface Question," in C.H. Kriebel, R.L. Van Horn and J.T. Heames (Eds.), *Management Information Systems: Progress and Perspectives*, Carnegie Press, Pittsburgh, 1971.
28. EASON, K.D., "Understanding the Naive Computer User," *Computer J.*, Vol. 19 (1976), pp. 3-7.
29. EBERT, R.J., "Environmental Structure and Programmed Decision Effectiveness," *Management Sci.*, Vol. 19 (1972), pp. 435-445.
30. EDSTRÖM, A., "User Influence and the Success of MIS Projects," *Human Relations*, Vol. 30 (1977), pp. 589-607.
31. EYSENCK, M.W., *Human Memory: Theory, Research and Differences*, Pergamon Press, Oxford, 1977.
32. FERGUSON, R.L. and JONES, C.H., "A Computer Aided Decision System," *Management Sci.*, Vol. 15 (1969), pp. B550-B561.
33. GINGRAS, L. and McLEAN, E.R., "A Study of Users and Designers of Information Systems," Information Systems Working Paper 2-79, Graduate School of Management, UCLA, 1979.
34. GINZBERG, M.J., "Finding an Adequate Measure of OR/MS Effectiveness," *Interfaces*, Vol. 8, No. 4 (1978), pp. 59-62.
35. GOLDBERG, L.R., "Man Versus Models of Man: A Rationale, Plus Some Evidence, for a Method of Improving on Clinical Inference," *Psychological Bull.*, Vol. 73 (1970), pp. 422-432.
36. GOODENOUGH, D.R., "The Role of Individual Differences in Field Dependence as a Factor in Learning and Memory," *Psychological Bull.*, Vol. 83 (1976), pp. 675-694.
37. GORRY, G.A. and SCOTT MORTON, M.S., "A Framework for Management Information Systems," *Sloan Management Rev.*, Vol. 13, No. 1 (1971), pp. 55-70.
38. GOUGH, H., "Personality and Personality Assessment," in M.D. Dunnette (Ed.), *Handbook of Industrial and Organizational Psychology*, Rand-McNally, Chicago, Ill. 1976.
39. GROCHOW, J., "Cognitive Style as a Factor in the Design of Interactive Decision Support Systems," Unpublished Ph.D. Dissertation, MIT, 1973.
40. GUTHRIE, A., "Middle Managers and MIS: An Attitude Survey," *J. Economics and Business*, Vol. 26 (1973), pp. 59-66.
41. HAMMER, C.H. and RINGEL, S., "The Effects of Amount of Information Provided and Feedback of Results on Decision Making Efficiency," *Human Factors*, Vol. 7 (1965), pp. 513-519.
42. HARVEY, O.J. and SCHROEDER, H.M., "Cognitive Aspects of Self and Motivation," in O.J. Harvey (Ed.), *Motivation and Social Interaction*, Ronald Press, New York, 1963.
43. HSIA, H.J., "Redundancy: Is it the Lost Key to Better Communication?" *Audio Visual Comm. Rev.*, Vol. 25 (1977), pp. 63-85.
44. HUNT, E., FROST, N. and LUNNEBORG, C., "Individual Differences in Cognition: A New Approach to Intelligence," in G.H. Bower (Ed.), *The Psychology of Learning and Memory*, Academic Press, New York, 1973.
45. — — and LANSMAN, M., "Cognitive Theory Applied to Individual Differences," in W.K. Estes (Ed.), *Handbook of Learning and Cognitive Processes*, Lawrence Erlbaum Associates, Hillsdale, N.J., 1975.
46. HUYSMAN, J.H.B.M., "The Effectiveness of the Cognitive Style Constraint in Implementing Operations Research Proposals," *Management Sci.*, Vol. 17 (1970), pp. 92-104.
47. IGERSHEIM, R.H., "Managerial Response to an Information System," *Proceedings*, AFIPS National Computer Conference, Vol. 45 (1976), pp. 877-882.
48. JONES, C.H., HUGHES, J.L. and ENGVOLD, K.J., "A Comparative Study of Management Decision-Making From Computer Terminals," *Proceedings*, AFIPS Spring Joint Computer Conference, Vol. 36 (1970), pp. 599-605.
49. KARLINS, M., "Conceptual Complexity and Remote Associative Proficiency as Creativity Variables in a Complex Problem Solving Task," *J. Personality and Social Psych.*, Vol. 6 (1967), pp. 264-278.
50. KEEN, P.G.W. and SCOTT MORTON, M.S. *Decision Support Systems: An Organizational Perspective*, Addison-Wesley, Reading, Mass., 1978.
51. KENNEDY, T.C.S., "Some Behavioral Factors Affecting the Training of Naive Users of an Interactive Computer System," *Internat. J. Man-Machine Studies*, Vol. 7 (1975), pp. 817-834.

52. KING, W.R. and EPSTEIN, B.J., "Assessing the Value of Information," *Management Datamatics*, Vol. 5, No. 4 (1976), pp. 171-180.
53. – – – and RODRIQUEZ, J.I., "Evaluating Management Information Systems," *MIS Quart.*, Vol. 2, No. 3 (1978), pp. 43-51.
54. KLAUSS, R. and JEWETT, J., "Issues and Methodology for MIS Research," paper presented at Joint TIMS/ORSA Meeting, April 1974.
55. KLING, R., "The Organizational Context of User-Centered Software Designs," *MIS Quart.*, Vol. 1, No. 4 (1977), pp. 41-52.
56. LAMBERT, Z.V. and DURAND, R.M., "Purchase Information Acquisition and Cognitive Style," *J. Psych.*, Vol. 97 (1977), pp. 3-13.
57. LANCASTER, F.W. and FAYEN, E.G., *Information Retrieval On-Line*, Melville, Los Angeles, Calif., 1973.
58. LEFCOURT, H.M., "Recent Developments in the Study of Locus of Control," in B.A. Maher (Ed.), *Progress in Experimental Psychological Research*, Academic Press, New York, 1972.
59. LEVINE, J.M., SAMET, M.G. and BRAHLEK, R.E., "Information Seeking with Limitations on Available Information and Resources," *Human Factors*, Vol. 17 (1965), pp. 502-513.
60. LIENTZ, B.P., SWANSON, E.B. and TOMPKINS, G.E., "Characteristics of Application Software Maintenance," *Comm. ACM*, Vol. 21 (1978), pp. 466-471.
61. LONG, B.H. and ZILLER, R.C., "Dogmatism and Predecision Information Search," *J. Appl. Psych.*, Vol. 49 (1965), pp. 376-378.
62. LUCAS, H.C., Jr., *Why Information Systems Fail*, Columbia University Press, New York, 1975.
63. – – –, "Behavioral Factors in System Implementation," in R.L. Schultz and D.P. Slevin (Eds.), *Implementing Operations Research/Management Science*, American Elsevier, New York, 1975.
64. – – –, *The Implementation of Computer-Based Models*, National Association of Accountants, New York, 1976.
65. – – –, "The Use of an Interactive Information Storage and Retrieval System in Medical Research," *Comm. ACM*, Vol. 21 (1978), pp. 197-205.
66. – – –, "Empirical Evidence for a Descriptive Model of Implementation," *MIS Quart.*, Vol. 2, No. 2 (1978), pp. 27-52.
67. LUSK, E.J., "Cognitive Aspects of Annual Reports: Field Independence/Dependence," *J. Accounting Res.*, Vol. 11 (1973 Supplement), pp. 191-201.
68. MAISH, A.M., "A User's Behavior Toward His MIS," *MIS Quart.*, Vol. 3, No. 1 (1979), pp. 39-52.
69. MANN, F.C. and WILLIAMS, L.K., "Observations on the Dynamics of a Change to Electronic Data Processing Equipment," *Administrative Sci. Quart.*, Vol. 5 (1960), p. 217-256.
70. MARTIN, J., *Design of Man-Machine Dialogues*, Prentice-Hall, Englewood Cliffs, N.J., 1973.
71. MASON, R.O. and MITROFF, I.I., "A Program for Research on Management Information Systems," *Management Sci.*, Vol. 19 (1973), pp. 475-487.
72. – – – and MOSKOWITZ, H., "Conservatism in Information Processing: Implications for Management Information Systems," *Decision Sci.*, Vol. 3 (1972), pp. 35-54.
73. MILLER, D. and GORDON, L.A., "Conceptual Levels and the Design of Accounting Information Systems," *Decision Sci.*, Vol. 6 (1975), pp. 259-269.
74. MILLER, G.A., "The Magical Number Seven, Plus or Minus Two: Some Limits on Our Capacity for Processing Information," *Psychological Rev.*, Vol. 63 (1956), pp. 81-97.
75. MILLER, R.B., "Response Times in Man-Computer Conversational Transactions," *Proceedings, AFIPS Fall Joint Computer Conference*, Vol. 33 (1968), pp. 267-277.
76. MITROFF, I.I., NELSON, J. and MASON, R.O., "On Management Myth-Information Systems," *Management Sci.*, Vol. 21 (1974), pp. 371-382.
77. MOCK, T.J., "A Longitudinal Study of Some Information Structure Alternatives," *Data Base*, Vol. 5 (1973), pp. 40-45.
78. MOCK, T.J., ESTRIN, T.L. and VASARHELYI, M.A., "Learning Patterns, Decision Approaches, and Value of Information," *J. Accounting Res.*, Vol. 10 (1972), pp. 129-153.
79. MOSKOWITZ, H., "An Experimental Investigation of Decision Making in a Simulated Research and Development Environment," *Management Sci.*, Vol. 19 (1973), pp. 676-687.
80. MUMFORD, E. and BANKS, O., *The Computer and the Clerk*, Routledge and Kegan Paul, London, 1967.
81. NEWEL, A. and SIMON, H.A., *Human Problem Solving*, Prentice-Hall, Englewood Cliffs, N.J. 1972.

82. NICKERSON, R.S., "Man-Computer Interaction: A Challenge for Human Factors Research," *Ergonomics*, Vol. 12 (1969), pp. 501-517.
83. PAISLEY, W.J., "Information Needs and Uses," *Annual Rev. Information Sci. and Technology*, Vol. 3 (1968), pp. 1-30.
84. PHARES, E.J., *Locus of Control in Personality*, General Learning Press, Morristown, N.J., 1976.
85. PROKOP, J.S. and BROOKS, F.P., "Decision Making with Computer Graphics in an Inventory Control Environment," *Proceedings*, AFIPS Fall Joint Computer Conference, Vol. 37 (1970), pp. 597-607.
86. RITTENBERG, L.E., "Information Processing Types and Simulated Production Decision Making: A Comparison of Two Methods of Classification," *Proceedings*, AIDS National Meeting, Vol. 5 (1973). p. 271.
87. ROBEY, D., "Attitudinal Correlates of MIS Use," *Proceedings*, National AIDS Meeting, Vol. 10 (1978), pp. 170-172.
88. − − − and ZELLER, R.F., "Factors Affecting the Success and Failure of an Information System for Product Quality," *Interfaces*, Vol. 8, No. 2 (1978), pp. 70-78.
89. RUMELHART, D.E., *Human Information Processing*, Wiley, New York, 1977.
90. SACKMAN, H., "Advanced Research in Online Planning," in H. Sackman and R.L. Citrenbaum (Eds.), *Online Planning: Towards Creative Problem Solving*, Prentice-Hall, Englewood Cliffs, N.J., 1972.
91. SARBIN, T.R., TAFT, R. and BAILEY, D.E., *Clinical Inferences and Cognitive Theory*, Holt, New York, 1960.
92. SCHEWE, C.D., "The Management Information System User: An Exploratory Behavioral Analysis," *Acad. Management J.*, Vol. 19 (1976), pp. 577-590.
93. − − −, WIEK, J.L. and DANN, R., "Advanced Marketing Information Systems: An Empirical Investigation of System User Problems," *Proceedings*, AIDS National Meeting, Vol. 6 (1974), pp. 356-359.
94. SCHRENK, L.P., "Aiding the Decision Maker − A Decision Process Model," *Ergonomics*, Vol. 12 (1969), pp. 543-557.
95. SCHROEDER, H.M., DRIVER, M.J. and STREUFERT, S., *Human Information Processing*, Holt, New York, 1967.
96. SCHULTZ, H.G., "An Evaluation of Formats for Graphics Trend Displays," *Human Factors*, Vol. 3 (1961), pp. 99-107.
97. − − −, "An Evaluation of Methods for Presentation of Graphic Multiple Trends," *Human Factors*, Vol. 3 (1961), pp. 108-119.
98. SCHULTZ, R.L. and SLEVIN, D.P., "Implementation and Organizational Validity: An Empirical Investigation," in R.L. Schultz and D.P. Slevin (Eds.), *Implementing Operations Research/Management Science*, American Elsevier, New York, 1975.
99. SCOTT, W.A., "Cognitive Complexity and Cognitive Flexibility," *Sociometry*, Vol. 25 (1962), pp. 405-414.
100. SEIBER, J.E. and LONZETTA, J.T., "Some Determinants of Individual Differences in Predecision Information-Processing Behavior," *J. Personality and Social Psych.*, Vol. 2 (1965), pp. 736-740.
101. SLOVIC, P., "About Man's Ability to Process Information," *Oregon Research Institute Res. Bull.*, Vol. 12 (1972).
102. − − −, FISCHKOFF, B. and LICHTENSTEIN, S., "Behavioral Decision Theory," *Annual Rev. Psych.*, Vol. 28 (1977), pp. 1-30.
103. − − − and LICHTENSTEIN, S., "Comparison of Bayesian and Regression Approaches to the Study of Information Processing in Judgement," *Organizational Behavior and Human Performance*, Vol. 6 (1971), pp. 649-744.
104. SMITH, H.T. and CRABTREE, R.G., "Interactive Planning: A Study of Computer Aiding in the Execution of a Simulated Scheduling Task," *Internat. J. Man-Machine Studies*, Vol. 7 (1975), pp. 213-231.
105. STABEL, C., "The Impact of a Conversational Computer System on Human Problem Solving Behavior," Working Paper, Sloan School of Management, MIT, 1973.
106. STEWART, T.F.M., "Special Report on Terminals," in I.L. Auerback (Ed.), *Best Computer Papers*, Petrocelli/Charter, New York, 1975.
107. SWANSON, E.B., "Management Information Systems: Appreciation and Involvement," *Management Sci.*, Vol. 21 (1974), pp. 178-188.
108. Taylor, R.N., "Age and Experience as Determinents of Managerial Information Processing and Decision Making Performance," *Acad. Management J.*, Vol. 18 (1975), pp. 74-81.

109. — — —, "Psychological Determinants of Bounded Rationality: Implications for Decision Making Strategies," *Decision Sci.*, Vol. 6 (1975), pp. 409-429.
110. — — — and DUNNETTE, M.D., "Relative Contribution of Decision-Maker Attributes to Decision Process," *Organizational Behavior and Human Behavior*, Vol. 12 (1974), pp. 286-298.
111. TRIANDIS, H.C., *Attitudes and Attitude Change*, Wiley, New York, 1971.
112. TUCKMAN, B., "Personality Structure, Group Composition and Group Functioning," *Sociometry*, Vol. 27 (1964), pp. 469-487.
113. VASARHELYI, M.A., "Man-Machine Planning Systems: A Cognitive Style Examination of Interactive Decision Making," *J. Accounting Res.*, Vol. 15 (1977), pp. 138-153.
114. VAUGHAN, W.S., Jr. and MAVOR, A.S., "Behavioral Characteristics of Men in the Performance of Some Decision Making Task Components," *Ergonomics*, Vol. 15 (1972), pp. 266-277.
115. WERNER, D.J., "A Study of the Use of an Experimental Information System in a Medical Environment," *Management Information*, Vol. 3, No. 3 (1974), pp. 133-142.
116. WITKIN, H.A., OLTMAN, P.K., RASKIN, E. and KARP, S.A., *A Manual for the Embedded Figures Test*, Consulting Psychologists Press, Palo Alto, Calif., 1971.
117. WYNNE, B.A., "Cognitive Bases for Man-Machine Decision Information System User Attributes," *Proceedings*, Northeastern AIDS Meeting, Vol. 4 (1975), p. 62-67.
118. — — — and DICKSON, G.W., "Experienced Managers' Performance in Experimental Man-Machine Decision System Simulation," *Acad. Management J.*, Vol. 18 (1975), pp. 25-40.
119. ZMUD, R.W., "An Empirical Investigation of the Dimensionality of the Concept of Information," *Decision Sci.*, Vol. 9 (1978), pp. 187-195.
120. — — —, "Perceptions of Cognitive Styles: Acquisition, Exhibition and Implications for Information System Design," *J. Management*, Vol. 5 (1979), pp. 7-20.
121. — — —, "An Information Processing Conceptualization of the Systematic-Heuristic Cognitive Style," Working Paper, Department of Information Systems, Georgia State University, 1979.
122. — — — and COX, J.F., "The Implementation Process: A Change Approach," *MIS Quart.*, Vol. 3, No. 2 (1979), pp. 35-43.
123. — — — and CAIN, D.D., "Conceptual Framework and Systems Analyst Job-Fit," Working Paper, Department of Information Systems, Georgia State University, 1979.

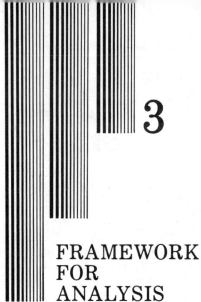

FRAMEWORK FOR ANALYSIS

ROBERT N. ANTHONY*

"Planning and control systems" is usually used as a generic term. However, this article points out that there are many different planning and control processes in business, and suggests a classification of them, which can serve as a framework for analysis.

Since dogs and humans are both mammals, some generalizations that apply to one species also apply to the other. It is for this reason that some new surgical techniques can be tested on dogs before being risked on humans. But dogs and humans differ, and, unless these differences are recognized, generalizations that are valid for one species may be erroneously applied to the other. For example, canine behavior can be largely explained in terms of conditioned reflexes, but human behavior is much more complicated. Similarly, some generalizations can be made about the whole planning and control process in a business; however, there actually are several quite different types of planning and control processes, and mistakes may be made if a generalization (principle, rule, technique) valid for one type is applied to the other.

The purpose of this article is to suggest a classification of the main topics

* From *Management Services* (March-April 1964), pp. 18-24. Reprinted by permission of the Editor. At the time of writing, the author was a professor at Harvard University.

This article is based on research done for the Division of Research at the Harvard Business School and financed by The Associates of the Harvard Business School. Both the professional and financial aspects of this support are gratefully acknowledged. For an expanded treatment of the subject see Robert N. Anthony, *Planning and Control Systems: A Framework for Analysis* (Boston: Harvard Business School, Division of Research, 1965).

or "species" that come within the broad term, Planning and Control Systems, and to suggest distinguishing characteristics of each. Hopefully, this will lead to a sorting out and sharpening of principles and techniques applicable to each species.

The particular classification chosen has been arrived at after careful analysis of how well various alternatives match statements made in the literature and, more important, what is found in practice. It is, however, tentative. Better schemes may well be developed, and we expose this one primarily in the hope that discussion of it will lead to agreement on *some* scheme, not necessarily this.

In this article, we shall focus on a process labeled *management control.* We shall describe its main characteristics, and distinguish it from processes labeled *strategic planning* and *technical control.* (Two other processes, *financial accounting and information handling,* are also relevant, but space does not permit a dicussion of them here.)

Obviously, we do not assert that these processes can be separated by sharply defined boundaries; one shades into another. Strategic planning sets the guidelines for management control, and management control sets the guidelines for technical control. The complete management function involves an integration of all these processes, and the processes are complementary.

We do assert that the processes are sufficiently distinct so that those who design and use planning and control systems will make expensive errors if they fail to take into account both the common characteristics of a process and the differences between processes. This article will deal with these similarities and differences and point out some of the errors that are made when they are not recognized.

Management Control

Management control is the process of assuring that resources are obtained and used effectively and efficiently in the accomplishment of the organization's objectives.

Management control is a process carried on within the framework established by strategic planning. Objectives, facilities, organization, and financial factors are more or less accepted as "givens." Decisions about next year's budget, for example, are limited by policies and guidelines prescribed by top management. The management control process is intended to make possible the achievement of planned objectives as effectively and efficiently as possible within these "givens."

The purpose of a management control system is to encourage managers to take actions which are in the best interests of the company. For example, if the system is structured so that a certain course of action increases the reported profits of a division, and at the same time *lessens* the profits of the company as a whole, there is something wrong. Technically, this purpose can be described as *goal congruence.*

"Total" System Necessary

Psychological considerations are dominant in management control. Activities such as communicating, persuading, exhorting, inspiring, and criticizing are an important part of the process.

Ordinarily, a management control system is a *total* system in the sense that it embraces all aspects of the company's operation. It needs to be a total system because an important management function is to assure that all parts of the operation are in balance with one another, and, in order to examine balance, management needs information about each of the parts.

With rare exceptions, the management control system is built around a *financial* structure; that is, resources and outputs are expressed in monetary units. Money is the only common denominator by means of which the heterogeneous elements of output and resources (e.g., hours of labor; type of labor; quantity and quality of material; amount and kind of products produced) can be combined and compared. (Although the financial structure is usually the central focus, nonmonetary measures such as time, number of persons, and reject and spoilage rates are also important parts of the system.)

The management control process tends to be *rhythmic;* it follows a definite pattern and timetable, month after month and year after year. In budgetary control, which is an important part of the management control process, certain steps are taken in a prescribed sequence and at certain dates each year; the dissemination of guidelines, the preparation of original estimates, the transmission of these estimates up through the several echelons in the organization, the review of these estimates, final approval to top management, dissemination back through the organization, operation, reporting, and the appraisal of performance. The procedure to be followed at each step in this process, the dates when the steps are to be completed, and even the forms that are to be used can be, and often are, set forth in a manual.

Interlocking Subsystems

A management control system is, or should be, a *co-ordinated, integrated* system: that is, although data collected for one purpose may differ from those collected for another purpose, these data should be reconcilable with one another. In a sense, the management control system is a *single* system, but it is perhaps more accurate to think of it as a set of interlocking subsystems. In many organizations, for example, three types of cost information are needed for management control: (1) *costs by responsibility centers,* which are used for planning and controlling the activities of responsible supervisors; (2) *full program costs,* used for pricing and other operating decisions under normal circumstances; and (3) *direct program costs,* used for pricing and other operating decisions under special circumstances, such as when management wishes to utilize idle capacity. ("Program" is here used for any activity in which the organization engages. In industrial companies, programs consist of products or product lines, and "product costs" can be substituted in the above statements.)

Line managers are the focal points in management control. They are the persons whose judgments are incorporated in the approved plans, and they are the persons who must influence others and whose performance is measured. Staff people collect, summarize, and present information that is useful in the process, and they make calculations which translate management judgments into the format of the system. Such a staff may be large in numbers; indeed the control department is often the largest department in a company. However, the significant decisions are made by the line manager, not by the staff.

Strategic Planning

Strategic planning is the process of deciding on changes in the objectives of the organization, in the resources that are to be used in attaining these objectives, and in the policies that are to govern the acquisition and use of these resources.

The word *strategy* is used here in its usual sense of deciding on how to combine and employ resources. Thus, strategic planning is a process having to do with the formulation of long-range, strategic, policy-type plans that change the character or direction of the organization. In an industrial company this includes planning that affects the objectives of the company; policies of all types (including policies as to management control and other processes); the acquisition and disposition of major facilities, divisions, or subsidiaries; the markets to be served and distribution channels for serving them; the organization structure (as distinguished from individual personnel actions); research and development of new product lines (as distinguished from modifications in existing products and product changes within existing lines); sources of new permanent capital; dividend policy; and so on. Strategic planning decisions affect the physical, financial, and organizational framework within which operations are carried on.

Irregular in Nature

Briefly, here are some ways in which the strategic planning process differs from the management control process.

A strategic plan usually relates to some part of the organization, rather than to the totality; the concept of a master planner who constantly keeps all parts of the organization at some coordinated optimum is a nice concept but an unrealistic one. Life is too complicated for any human, or computer, to do this.

Strategic planning is essentially *irregular*. Problems, opportunities, and "bright ideas" do not arise according to some set timetable, and they have to be dealt with whenever they happen to be perceived. The appropriate analytical techniques depend on the nature of the problem being analyzed, and no overall approach (such as a mathematical model) has been developed that is of much help in analyzing all types of strategic problems. Indeed, an overemphasis on a systematic approach is quite likely to stifle the essential element of creativity. In strategic planning, management works now on one problem, now on another, according to the needs and opportunities of the moment.

The estimates used in strategic planning are intended to show the *expected* results of the plan. They are neutral and impersonal. By contrast, the management control process, and the data used in it, are intended to influence managers to take actions that will lead to *desired* results. Thus, in connection with management control, it is appropriate to discuss how "tight" an operating budget should be: Should the goals be set so high that only an outstanding manager can achieve them, or should they be set so that they are attainable by the average manager? At what level does frustration inhibit a manager's best efforts? Does an attainable budget lead to complacency? And so on. In strategic planning, the question to be asked about the figures is simply: Is this the most reasonable estimate that can be made?

Strategic planning relies heavily on *external information,* that is, on data collected from outside the company, such as market analyses, estimates of costs and other factors involved in building a plant in a new locality, technological developments, and so on. When data from the normal information system are used, they usually must be recast to fit the needs of the problem being analyzed. For example, the current operating costs of a plant that are collected for measuring performance and for making pricing and other operating decisions usually must be restructured before they are useful in deciding whether to close down the plant.

Communications Are Limited

Another characteristic of the relevant information is that much of it is imprecise. The strategic planner estimates what *will* happen, often over a rather long time period. These estimates are likely to have a high degree of uncertainty, and they must be treated accordingly.

In the management control process, the communication of objectives, policies, guidelines, decisions, and results throughout the organization is extremely important. In the strategic planning process, communication is much simpler and involves relatively few persons, indeed, the need for secrecy often requires that steps be taken to inhibit communication. (Wide communication of the *decisions* that result from strategic planning is obviously important, but this is part of the management control process.)

Strategic planning is essentially applied economics, whereas management control is essentially applied social psychology.

Both management control and strategic planning involve top management, but middle management (i.e., operating management) typically have a much more important role in management control than they have in strategic planning. Middle managers usually are not major participants in the strategic planning process and sometimes are not even aware of the fact that a plan is being considered. Many operating executives are by temperament not very good at strategic planning. Also, the pressures of current activities usually do not allow them to devote the necessary time to such work. Currently, there is a tendency in companies to set up separate staffs which gather the facts and make the analyses that provide the background material for strategic decisions.

Exhibit 1. Some Contrasts

	Strategic Planning	Management Control
Person primarily involved	Staff and top management	Line and top management
Number of persons	Small	Large
Mental activity	Creative; analytical	Administrative; persuasive
Variables	Complex; much judgment	Less complex
Time period	Tends to be long	Tends to be short
Periodicity	Irregular, no set schedule	Rhythmic; set timetable
Procedures	Unstructured; each problem different	Prescribed procedure, regularly followed
Focus	Tend to focus on one aspect at a time	All encompassing
Source of information	Relies more on external and future	Relies more on internal and historical
Product	Intangible; precedent setting	More tangible; action within precedent
Communication problem	Relatively simple	Crucial and difficult
Appraisal of soundness	Extremely difficult	Much less difficult

These and other differences between management control and strategic planning are summarized in Exhibit 1, above.

Strategic planning and management control activities tend to conflict with one another in some respects. The time that management spends in thinking about the future is taken from time that could otherwise be used in controlling current operations, so in this indirect way strategic planning can hurt current performance. And, of course, the reverse also is true.

More directly, many actions that are taken for long-run, strategic reasons make current profits smaller than they otherwise would be. Research and some advertising expenditures are obvious examples. The problem of striking the right balance between strategic and operating considerations is one of the central problems in the whole management process.

Consequences of Confusion

Following are statements illustrating some of the consequences of failing to make a distinction between strategic planning and management control.

"We should set up a long-range planning procedure and work out a systemized way of considering *all* our plans similar to the way we construct next year's budget." (A long-range plan shows the estimated consequences over the next several years of strategic decisions already taken. It is part of the management control process. Although it provides a useful background for considering strategic proposals, it is not strategic planning. Strategic proposals should be made whenever the opportunity or the need is perceived in a form that best presents the arguments.)

"The only relevant costs are incremental costs; pay no attention to fixed or sunk costs." (This is so in strategic planning, but operating managers are often motivated in the wrong direction if their decisions are based on incremental costs; for example, in intracompany transactions.)

"We may be selling Plant X some day. We should therefore set up the operating reports so that management will have at its fingertips the information it will need when it is deciding this question. For example, we should show inventory and fixed assets at their current market value." (Operating reports should be designed to assist in the management of current operations. Special compilations of data are needed for such major, nonroutine actions as selling a plant. Collection of such data routinely is both too expensive and likely to impede sound operating decisions.)

"Our ultimate goal is an all-purpose control system — integrated data processing — so that management will have all the data it needs for whatever problem it decides to tackle. We should collect data in elemental building blocks that can be combined in various ways to answer all conceivable questions." (This is an impossible goal. Each strategic proposal requires that the data be assembled in the way that best fits the requirements of that proposal. No one can foresee all the possibilities. The "building block" idea is sound with limits, but the limits are not so broad that all problems are encompassed.)

"All levels of management should participate in planning." (All levels of management should participate in the planning part of the management control process, but operating managers typically do not have the time, the inclination, or the analytical bent that is required for formulating strategic plans. Furthermore, such plans often must be kept highly secret.)

Technical Control

Technical control is the process of assuring the efficient acquisition and use of resources, with respect to activities for which the optimum relationship between outputs and resources can be approximately determined.

The definition of technical control refers to outputs and resources. *Outputs* are the accomplishments of the organization, what it does, and *resources* are the inputs which the organization consumes. For a whole business, the outputs are the goods and services sold, which are measured by revenues earned, and the inputs are costs and expenses incurred. In rough terms, "outputs" equals "results," and "resources" equals "cost."

One of the important tasks in an organization is to seek the *optimum* relationship between outputs and resources. For some activities, this optimum relationship is fairly easy to establish: To manufacture a given part should require such-and-such labor, a certain sequence of machine operations, and so on. For other activities, there exists no "scientific" (even in the loose sense of this term) way of establishing the optimum relationship; for these activities, decisions as to what costs to incur depend on human judgment.

The term "managed costs" is a descriptive one for those types of resources for which an objective decision as to the optimum quantity to be employed cannot be made. An important management function is to make judgments as to the "right" amount of managed costs in a given set of circumstances. These are, by definition, subjective judgments.

Management control applies to the whole of an organization, and to any parts of the whole in which managed costs are significant. Technical control applies to those activities, and only to those activities, in which there are no significant elements of managed cost. Or more simply, in the management control process, management judgment is an important element; in the technical control process, the technique itself is dominant.

As an example of technical control, consider inventory control. If the demand for an item, the cost of storing it, its production cost and production time, and the loss involved in not filling an order are known or can be reasonably estimated, then the optimum inventory level and the optimum production schedule can both be calculated, and reasonable men will agree with the results of these calculations.

In other than exceptional circumstances, these calculations can determine the actions that should be taken. Management intervention is necessary only when these exceptional circumstances arise.

Some Areas Can't Be Measured

By contrast, consider the legal department of a company. No device can measure the quality, or even the quantity, of the legal service that constitutes the output of this department. No formula can show the amount of service that should be rendered nor the optimum amount of costs that should be incurred. Impressions as to the "right" amount of service, as to the "right" amount of cost, and as to whether the relationship between the service actually rendered and the cost actually incurred was "right" are strictly subjective. They are judgments made by management. If persons disagree on these judgments, there is no objective way of resolving the disagreement. Yet the legal department as a part of the whole organization must be controlled; the chief counsel must operate within the framework of policies prescribed by top management. The control exercised in this situation is management control.

Examples of activities that can be subjected to technical control are: automated plants, such as cement plants, oil refineries, and power generating stations; the direct operations of most manufacturing plants (but often not the overhead expense items); production scheduling; inventory control; the "order-taking" type of selling activity; and order processing, premium billing, payroll accounting, check handling, and similar paperwork activities.

Example of activities for which management control is necessary are: the total activities of most manufacturing plants, which include such "judgment" inputs as indirect labor, employee benefit and welfare programs, safety activities, training, and supervision; most advertising, sales promotion, pricing, selling (as distinguished from order taking) and similar marketing activities; most aspects of finance; most aspects of research, development, and design; the work of staff units of all types; and management activity itself.

The control appropriate for the whole of any unit which carries on both the technical and the management types of activities is management control. The control of the whole accounting department is management control even though technical control is appropriate for certain aspects of the work, such as posting and check writing.

Some people believe that the distinction between the two classes of activities described above is merely one of degree rather than of kind; they say that all we are doing is distinguishing between situations where control is "easy" and "difficult," respectively. We think the distinction is more fundamental than that, and hope this will be apparent from the following brief list of characteristics that distinguish management control from technical control.

Management control covers the whole of an organization. Each technical control procedure is restricted to a subunit, often a narrowly circumscribed activity.

Just as management control occurs within a set of policies derived from strategic planning, so technical control occurs within a set of well-defined procedures and rules that are derived from management control.

Control is more difficult in management control than in technical control because of the absence of a "scientific" standard with which actual performance can be compared. A good technical control system can provide a much higher degree of assurance that actions are proceeding as desired than can a management control system.

Rules Can Be Programed

A technical control system is a *rational* system; that is, the action to be taken is decided by a set of logical rules. These rules may or may not cover all aspects of a given problem. Situations not covered by the rules are designated as "exceptions" and are resolved by human judgment. Other than these exceptions, the application of the rules is automatic. The rules can in principle be programed into a computer, and the choice between using a computer and using a human being depends primarily on the relative cost of each method.

In management control, psychological considerations are dominant. The management control system at most assists those who take action; it does not directly or by itself result in action without human intervention. By contrast, the end product of an inventory control system can be an order, or a decision to replenish a certain inventory item, and this order may be based entirely on calculations from formulas incorporated in the system. (The formulas were *devised* by human beings, but this is a management control process, not a technical control process.)

In consideration of technical control, analogies with mechanical, electrical, and hydraulic systems are reasonable and useful, and such terms as feedback, network balancing, optimization, and so on, are relevant. It is perfectly appropriate, for example, to view a technical control system as analagous to a thermostat which turns the furnace on and off according to its perception of changes in temperature. These analogies do not work well as models for management control systems, however, because the success of management systems is highly dependent on their impact on people, and people are not like thermostats or furnaces; one can't light a fire under a human being simply by turning up a thermostat.

A management control system is ordinarily focused on a financial structure, whereas technical control data are often nonmonetary. They may be expressed in terms of man-hours, number of items, pounds of waste, and so on. Since each technical control procedure is designed for a limited area of application, it is feasible to use the basis of measurement that is most appropriate for that area.

Approximations Meet Data Needs

Data in a technical control system are in real time and relate to individual events, whereas data in a management control system are often retrospective and summarize many separate events. Computer specialists who do not make such a distinction dream about a system that will display to the management the current status of every individual activity in the organization. Although this *could* be done, it *should* not be done; management doesn't want such detail. Management does not need to know the time at which lot No. 1007 was transferred from station 27 to station 28; rather, it needs to know only that the process is, or is not, proceeding as planned, and, if not, where the trouble lies.

Similarly, technical control uses exact data, whereas management control needs only approximations. Material is ordered and scheduled in specific quantities, employees are paid the exact amount due them, but data on management control reports need contain only two or three significant digits and are therefore rounded to thousands of dollars, to millions of dollars, or even (in the U.S. Government) to billions of dollars.

A technical control system requires a mathematical model of the operation. Although it may not always be expressed explicitly in mathematical notation, there is a decision rule which states that given certain values for parameters $a, b, \ldots n$, action X is to be taken. Models are not so important in management control. In a sense, a budget or a PERT network are models associated with the management control process, but they are not the essence of the process.

The formal management control *system* is only a part of the management control *process,* actually a relatively unimportant part. The system can help motivate the manager to make decisions that are in the best interests of the organization, and the system can provide information that aids the manager in making these decisions; but many other stimuli are involved in motivating the manager, and good information does not automatically produce good decisions. The success or failure of the management control process depends on the personal characteristics of the manager: his judgment, his knowledge, his ability to influence others.

Technique Is All-Important

In technical control, the system itself is a much more important part of the whole process. Except in fully automated operations, it is an exaggeration to say that the system *is* the process, but it is not much of an exaggeration. The technical control system ordinarily states what action should be taken; it makes the decisions. As with any operation, management vigilance is required to detect an unforeseen "foul-up" in the operation, or a change in the conditions on which the technique is predicated. And management will be seeking ways to improve the technique. In general, however, the degree of management involvement in technical control is small, whereas in management control it is large.

As new techniques are developed, there is a tendency for more and more activities to become susceptible to technical control. In the factory, the production schedule that was formerly set according to the foreman's intuition is now derived by linear programing. And, although not too long ago it was believed that technical control was appropriate only for factory operations, we now see models and formulas being used for certain marketing decisions, such as planning salesmen's calls and planning direct mail advertising. This shift probably will continue; it is a large part of what people have in mind when they say, "Management is being increasingly scientific."

Following are statements illustrating the consequences of failing to make a distinction between management control and technical control:

"Computers will make middle management obsolete." (Although computers can replace human beings in technical control, they are not a substitute for the human judgment that is an essential part of the management control process.)

"Business should develop a management control system like the SAGE and SAC control systems that work so well for the military." (The military systems mentioned are technical control systems. They are not related to the management control problem in the military, let alone that in business.)

"The way to improve the management control process is to develop better management decision rules." (This implies that mathematics, rather than human beings, is the essence of management control.)

"Transfer prices should be calculated centrally." (This gives no recognition to negotiation and the exercise of judgment by divisional managers.)

"If you follow the planning and control techniques described in this book, your profits are a near predictable certainty." (This implies that the technique, rather than the quality of management, is the principal determinant of success.)

Summary

We have described several subsystems that come under the general heading, "planning and control systems." Although related to one another, they have different purposes and different characteristics; different ways of thinking about each of them are therefore required. Generalizations about the whole area are, if valid, so vague as not to be useful. By contrast, useful generalizations, principles, and techniques can be developed for each of the subsystems. Mistakes are made when those valid for one subsystem are applied to another.

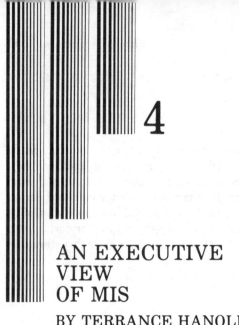

4

AN EXECUTIVE VIEW OF MIS

BY TERRANCE HANOLD*

Theoreticians may debate the topic fruitlessly, but a management information system has become an absolute necessity for successful operation of a large and complex business enterprise

Whether there can be a management information system was once a matter of great debate. And there were signs for a time that exhaustion had settled the issue. The debate had been prolonged but hardly profound, so we were grateful for the respite. But recently the charge that MIS is a mirage has once more been raised in the *Harvard Business Review.*

Truth, it seems, is always on the scaffold and Error on the throne.

Scholars, too, I suppose are human. At least the claims of charity require this assumption. But where the rest of us rely simply on blunt assertion to support our biases, they with greater guile clothe their prejudices in the guise of reason.

The classical and perhaps the deadliest weapon they employ for the subversion of truth is the scholastic debate. Even lower in bad eminence is the scholastic spurious debate, where he picks an absent opponent, often unnamed and always unaware of the contest, sets all the terms of the argument, imposes all of the assumptions employed and, if he is worthy of his PhD, demolishes his adversary with considerable ease. This, of course, is the favorite strategy of those who write business review articles.

It is a despicable, villainous device.

Let me advise you in confidence that this is exactly what I now propose to do myself.

As the description of the system he proposes to disprove, my anonymous antagonist (John Dearden, Herman Krannert Professor of Business Administration at Harvard University, "MIS Is a Mirage," *Harvard Business Review*, January-February, 1972, p. 90) quotes the following:

> "A management information system is an organized method of providing past, present and projection information related to internal operations and external intelligence. It supports the planning, control and operational function of an organization by furnishing uniform information in the proper time-frame to assist the decision making process." (Walter J. Kennevan, "MIS Universe," *Data Management*, September, 1970.)

Whether or not acute analysis might modify it in part, this is a competent and sufficiently extensive description of a management information system.

How does a scholar go about its destruction? His first effort at discreditation is to describe it as "grandiose." Aside from the charge itself, he offers nothing but ridicule to support the description. Then to give it a character it does not claim, he attributes to the definition the universal dimension of a *total* management information system. Quite clearly, the author of the statement makes no such claim of universal content, and it is certainly not fairly subject to attack on that score. It includes only information capable of systematic collection and of organized processing and presentation in a business environment.

The next means of establishing the proposition that MIS is a phantasmagorical mirage is the attempted demonstration by logic rather than by evidence that the creation of a *total* management information system is beyond the capability of man.

He declares the fact that certain rival business schools now offer MS and PhD degrees in management information systems. Such persons, he says, "must clearly be technicians and would have little impact on most of the information supplied to management, particularly at upper levels." Since the author is engaged in the manufacture of Masters of Science and DBAS, his authority on this point far exceeds mine, and I must accept his estimate of their fundamental incompetence to create a useful product. So this category of potential inventors of an MIS is by concession disqualified.

In order to disqualify the rest of the world, he imposes on us his assumptions that the creator of a management information system must be a specialist, that he must attack the information system as a whole, and that the systems approach must be used in making that attack. This, of course, indulges in the contradictory assumptions (1) that management is incapable of participating effectively in the designation of the content and methodology of an information system and (2) that anyone outside of management would be incompetent to define what management needs. By this system of logic, he attempts to disqualify that part of the world other than doctors of philosophy from competence in this field.

But the only person unequivocally excluded by this misshapen logic is my anonymous antagonist himself. The willful logic of small minds is hardly the proper test of the fact or possibility of an MIS. The best evidence, I think, follows from experience. With this beginning I should like to describe how an MIS comes into being, where its direction and control are properly lodged, and why it is essential to a modern business organization of scale.

Information is at the core of my subject. Hence a few minutes' reflection on the nature of information is an unavoidable inconvenience.

Information has to do with the communication of knowledge inspired by observation — with the interchange of thoughts and ideas proceeding from experience. A more expansive definition embraces knowledge derived from study or instruction as well. So the contributions of the schools are under no ban of exclusion from information if we take a generous view.

Information is different in kind from data. Information has the attribute of communication which data does not have. In the context of business, data is merely the digital shadow of haphazard events indifferently recorded. It enters our data bank in the accidental series of occurrence in time. And even that degree of order is indifferently observed. Each bit is a meaningless fragment in itself, and the mass communicates nothing.

Yet information begins with data. Data is transformed into information through the infusion of purposeful intelligence. Thus information is data refined by intelligence so that it communicates meaning or knowledge, and in the course of communication will inform one or more parties to the interchange with ideas or conclusions.

Further, the quality of the information resulting from this alchemy can be of several degrees, depending upon the sophistication of the intellectual tools applied to the data and to the nature of the actions which the information process must support.

In the ordinary affairs of life, data is transformed into information on an extemporized basis. We make no pretense at a systematic collection of relevant data, nor do we pretend to apply consistent principles, values or methods to its treatment. Thus when eggs are on the breakfast menu, my wife may advise their rejection today because the cholesterol level revealed in my annual physical report is at the top of her consciousness: tomorrow, under the same circumstances, she may insist that I have them because eggs and grapefruit have a tempering effect on my weight.

But in a business context, information must be developed in systematic fashion if it is to merit a confidence level warranting immediate credence and use. Our initial statement of meaning emphasized that information is the *communication* of knowledge. Credibility is at the heart of communication, and the speed with which information is communicated determines its worth.

I neither deny the value nor decry the use of intuitive rather than systematic information in the critical case. It is occasionally an essential exercise of business expertise. Mutations in corporate practice are as necessary as in the realms of nature when environmental adaptation requires it. But it has an infrequent place in the continuing conduct of a business. And it is legitimate for use in the exceptional case only after the systematic information has been examined and found not quite adequate.

Business information, then, requires the systematic collection of data and its systematic processing according to a series of intellectually valid methods. The output of the system will communicate knowledge which will dictate or assist the selection of action decisions in fields to which the data and the methods are relevant.

Managerial Information. Now, let us consider the nature of *managerial* information. Is managerial information a subclass of business information? We may at least assume that to be the case for the purpose of inquiry. And it is certainly true that, as there is a hierarchical difference between data and information, so there are hierarchical differences between the several levels of business information and between the information systems which serve them.

Information Systems. The definition of a management information system raises the fiercest disputations vented since the Diet of Worms. As an honorary founder of the Society for Management Information Systems, I follow its proceedings with the closest attention. Since the scope of its function obviously depends upon a definition of such systems, it is an area of principal controversy among certain of our members.

After much informal debate and a few unilateral pronouncements by our more authoritative fellows, a formal colloquium on the subject was arranged. For eight hours the subject was collectively threshed. Each participant assailed every definition proposed, including his own, from id to ibidem. None received acceptance by vote, consensus or extrasensory perception.

So the field is free to each to adopt his own as long as he agrees to impose it on no one else. Perhaps the humanistic approach suggested by Bishop Walton in opening one of our annual sessions is the most appropriate for group therapy. He said, by way of paraphrase, "It is almost impossible to define an information system, but it is easy to recognize one." So I shall describe a managerial information system as I see it.

An information *system* defines the data needed to generate the information required to serve a specific business function. It employs a data collection system; a data transmission system; a data storage system; a data retrieval system; an appropriate array of intelligence infusion systems, which are usually described as software or application programs and which employ the principles and methods of the function or discipline served; and an information communication system.

MIS Described. As distinguished from an *information* system, I conceive a *management* information system to consist of a *cluster* of business information systems. MIS is a symbol rather than a descriptive name, which designates an integrated complex of information systems of such a variety and sophistication and interrelationship as experience qualified by rational assessment determines to be essential or useful to the general or executive management of the business enterprise.

These are ordinarily conceived to be strung on an electronic network with a myriad of mind-boggling devices. For any particular information system, it may be demonstrated that there is no need for a computer or random access files or remote terminals or any of the other electronic gear that decorate our offices and inflate our equipment accounts. The span and effectiveness of the information system justify its name, not the apparatus which serves it.

But the conduct in concert of a complex of information systems is in practical terms impossible without a computer.

The Accounting Information System. Accounting supplied the first business information system, I suppose. Accounting defined the data needed to generate the information required for its purpose as that data relating to the assets and liabilities of the firm and to transactions affecting those assets and liabilities. It collected the data needed by the accounting system through the day book, gave it order by processing it through the journal, and meaning and relationship by transferring these entries to the ledger according to the shifting principles and prejudices of the profession. Accounting communicated the resulting information through the balance sheet, profit and loss statement and supplementary schedules.

From the accountant's viewpoint, only the compulsions of time have made a transfer from manual to mechanical to electronic methods tolerable. As far as he is concerned, no change in the accounting information system has occurred in consequence of this shift in tools. Taken by itself, an accounting system is an accountant's information system and not a managerial information system. Only as it becomes entwined in a complex of several information systems does it become a part of a whole deserving that cachet.

Accounting and MIS. An MIS dealing with numbers of information systems as an integrated complex can hardly be established or operated or utilized by management unless they are all threaded together on a computer-directed network. And if it is to succeed, the threading must somehow be directed by the management, not by accountants or systems types or other functionaries. Let me try to illustrate this point by a scatter of examples from one of our businesses — our flour milling enterprise.

Each car of wheat received at one of our flour mills results in an entry which discloses the cost per unit, an official classification, an official grade, a total weight, a protein analysis, a bin location in our elevator where it is stored, a freight transit credit in most cases and several other bits of data. All of these pieces of data are collected in our central data bank.

In the course of processing this data, we derive an inventory of our wheat. Since each shipment loses its identity in the bin in which it is placed, the inventory of each bin is an average of the type, grade, protein, cost and so forth of its contents. We derive accounts payable in favor of the seller. A transit credit account and other fascinating offal of the milling accounting process also result. So by processing this data into like or related classes, we begin its transformation into information.

Concurrently, it is hoped, sales of flour are being made. As orders are received, they are scheduled for production. The central production department allocates orders among the mills by means of a program which employs inventory data, data respecting the location of each mill, the character of wheat supply tributary to each mill, the delivery point of the order, the availability of transit billing suitable for application to its further shipment, the specifications of the flour ordered, the capacity and load balance of our mills and so on. This determination rests on data which have reciprocal as well as consecutive relationships and hence are handled best through computer-administered programs. These programs employ raw data from the data bank, as well as information derived from the accounting system. So information at one level of use is merely data at the next.

On receipt of its production schedule, the wheat committee at the mill uses another computer program to determine the optimum cost and quality of wheat mixes to be used to produce these orders. It is based on data respecting its wheat inventories and the array of orders directed to be placed on the mill. It also uses subjective data in our data bank respecting many functional characteristics of various types of wheat, their several milling qualities, yield and so forth. This program, of course, serves also to indicate the specified order in which these shipments will be manufactured.

The wheat procurement department is advised of the planned depletion of stocks by kind, grade and amount. So having a view both of the kinds and qualities of wheats consumed, of the future orders received or anticipated for milling at that location and the destination points, it makes plans for purchasing wheats in the market of the predicted type, grade, protein, origins, destinations, etc. Again, in making this decision, accounting information is used in combination with a great deal of historical crop and sales data.

Through these processes, an immense amount of market data accumulates respecting the total and seasonal uses of present and potential customers by product and by delivery point. Employing models of several kinds, the marketing department can determine the most profitable mix of products to sell, to whom and at what destinations and by sales periods. In consequence, it is able to assign specific targets by time period, by customer and by product.

Finally, the general management in flour milling is able to make medium term forecasts, taking into account estimates of wheat supplies by origin, type, cost, estimates of the effect of these elements on prices, margins, volumes and product mix by market area. By varying the data and assumptions, they derive alternative strategies to fit changes in wheat supplies, transportation costs, competitive action and other contingencies. Necessary capital investments, distribution networks, sales force assignments and personnel requirements are also indicated.

What we see here briefly and simplistically is the transformation of data to information for use in immediate departmental actions through the injection of the functional intelligence of that department. As each informational component is successively woven into other data processed through further functional methods and intellectual disciplines, we ultimately reach a system complex and a volume and variety of informational flows which begin to match the needs of the general or executive management. Only at that point do we begin to justify the label of a managerial information system.

The structure begins with the primitive selection and abbreviated classification of data according to the accounting dictate. Accounting is first concerned with an orderly record of every item and movement and transformation of firm assets and of every contract and obligation of the firm which may enhance or diminish those assets.

This is first-level knowledge of critical importance which is not diminished by its position in the managerial scale, but it hardly rationalizes or utilizes all of the data in the bank, nor does it apply all of the talents, such as procurement, production, finance and marketing, that the development of managerial information requires.

Information begins with data, but it is data infused with an organizing and purposeful intelligence. The initial intelligence applied to data is that of accounting, but a whole array of disciplines is introduced into the process as it proceeds to managerial use. The base of the data during these successive processes is perpetually expanding in both detail and extent.

Thus, information is data infused or refined by intelligence so that it communicates meanings not immediately reflected by the data alone. When information is communicated, it informs either or both of the parties involved. But the nature of the information conveyed will differ according to the function of the person informed and according to the point in the informational hierarchy from which he derives his information.

We have arrived at the conclusion that accounting produces an information system almost adequate for accountants. We have found that an accounting system is not an MIS because it is not designed to develop the data or to communicate the information required by the multiplying disciplines which must today feed business management. That system is designed to collect only such data as accountants deem relevant to their function and to put that data in such order, to marinate the data in such values and principles, and to subject the data to such procedures as are embraced in their particular functional philosophy.

These are not conclusions comfortable to accountants. In my defense may I be permitted to say that in my view Karl Marx somewhat overstated the case when he described accountants as "jackals of capitalism."

Disappointment is the product of expectation. As I remember it, 20 years ago the accounting profession felt it had the key to dominance in business decisions. It appeared to sprout from the revelation by our outside auditors of the breakeven chart. From the ranges of results it displayed we could readily select the proper sales and cost levels we ought to obtain, garlanded with an attractive return on investment. And these results could be neatly battened down and guaranteed by a set of controls derived from the DuPont chart room and administered by the accounting department.

Controls could forestall all mishaps and assure a golden future. And obviously the controller would be suitably adorned with dignities and powers and a seat at the right hand of the chairman almighty.

But something unfunny happened on the way to the board room. A number of analyses have since been made, and there are several nominees for the blame. And, of course, there is blame enough so that it may be distributed lavishly among them. Charity forbids that they be singled out. Collectively we may designate them as the inciters of the knowledge revolution.

Technology made huge additions to the stock of data which could be made into business information. Computers performed its transformation at speeds and costs which made it economically useful. Computers also gave entry into the office of the "science of abstraction — mathematics" in a multitude of applications. This led to the professionalization of the established branches of business and to the invasion of the counting room by a host of new sciences and professions. Both the effect and the cause of this change from skill-centered craftsmen who knew their job to knowledge-centered professionals who knew their world was the transition of the business information base from a transaction record to a data file enormously wider in scope.

So business has advanced to the statistical analysis of the present and the mathematical computation of the future, while the controller was left to this arithmetical accounting of the past. Sic Transit Gloria.

What Now? Fifteen years ago the controller had the only rational and continuing information system in the firm. Today every department in the firm is developing a business information system suited to its function. And the general and executive managements are securing, by accretion if not by design, a management information system which is the composite sum of the lot, plus the contribution made by executive management themselves as required by their own functions.

Can the controller recapture the information monopoly he once embraced? Can he again become the croupier of the only game in town? I think not.

Each information system requires of its governor expertise in the function or discipline it serves. And an information system forms an organic union with those it serves. As Professor Whisler puts it, "Older technologies are extensions of man's hand and muscles and were his tools and servants, while modern information technology is an extension of man's brain and is his partner — or even his master." No manager can afford to tolerate an interloper here. He must establish his own direct, continuing, reciprocal, interacting involvement in the system, subject to no man's leave of hindrance and certainly subject to no man's control.

For these reasons, Pillsbury's corporate policy obliges each of its operating firms "to obtain full utilization and value from Pillsbury's Business Information System." to ensure this result, the policy provides that "the

General Manager must assume responsibility for the definition of the information and processing requirements of his" operation. "A senior professional from the corporate department will be attached to the (firm) to serve as the General Manager sees fit in helping him to define his subsystem's requirements."

This same concept is carried to the corporate level. Our policy states that "Certain affairs of The Pillsbury Company are inseparable from its Executive Office. Among them is the Pillsbury Business Information System. Without immediate control of the design and operations of this system in its entirety, the Executive Office cannot effectively function. It is for this reason that PBIS reports directly to the Executive Office.

What Next?   What becomes of "managerial accounting for decision making" in such an environment? How am I to deal with a letter from a young and ambitious member of the controller's group who expresses his point of view by this textbook quotation: ". . . it is felt that an accountant's role should not be confined to merely dealing with historic systems, data and controls. Along with looking at the past and present, he must also look to the future of the company which he serves. Nor should he be narrowly viewed as a corporate policeman, but more as an objective viewer of the corporate reality (performing an evaluative-mirroring function). While he may not be the supplier of answers, he can at least help to raise relevant questions and identify problem areas."

These phrases have a singing quality which appeals without persuading. It is the accountant's instinct to coach the manager respecting the decisions he makes, and at the end of the year, it is his function to sit in judgment on the results of those decisions. You and I understand the game, but the lads who are answerable to the world for the published results do not.

They think it indecorous for a man to urge a decision while uncommitted to its consequences. And they think it indecent, to put the matter in its politest terms, for him later to publish, underline and critique these consequences when they prove unfavorable, while hiding under the flag of neutrality that his accounting title gives him.

The burden of management is to influence the future favorably, and even predictably. A leading partner of one of the principal public auditing firms remarks that in the torment of change which tosses all enterprises today, "Success in committing resources to profitable opportunities is being measured less and less adequately by focusing on profits achieved . . . The concepts proposed in this discussion are based on the firm conviction that generally accepted accounting principles, as they are now constituted, and the management accounting practices that result from them, are inadequate — that they cannot respond to the forces of society which are, today, calling for meaningful information."

As a remedy he proposes a scheme of "entrepreneurial accounting" — a scheme for reflecting the future profitability of a firm — which would alter accounting concepts long in fashion, but would do little to enlarge the basis of judgment or the area of certainty for a manager required to deal with "problems (which) have been exponentially expanded."

We are dealing, of course, with the ancient urge toward aggrandizement of function which is neither foreign nor peculiar to accountants. And the supporting rationale is seductive. Accounting has honorably assisted the decisional processes of management in the past — why not enlarge its dominion so that it embraces the whole information structure on which managers depend?

A computer environment does add a favorable time dimension to accounting information which suits it to use in the arena as well as in the postmortem parlor. This new dimension offers accountants the temptation to float widely over the whole informational range. But they enlarge their span of activity at the peril of loss of stature and effectiveness which depends on their respectful obedience to the limits of their professional domain.

Accountants have the capacity to convert accounting data into accounting information because their professional training qualified them to infuse that data with accounting intelligence. Outside their field they become mere data gatherers, for their training gives them no special competence to convert data into the marketing, production, procurement or other information systems which ultimately fuse into an MIS. If they attempt an indiscriminate power of dictation in areas outside their own field, they lose their professional identity and become simply computer systems technicians.

Worse, they become a well-meaning but formidable obstruction to the creation of the end they say they desire — a true MIS — for they deter the entry of the variety of talents, disciplines and intelligences necessary to that end. The fact is that no single function or discipline can furnish a sufficient information base for management. That is why we have kept our information systems free of the grasp of any one function. Thus, we have enabled our managers to draw the informational output of every function freely into its channel. Each functional information system is the responsibility of the functional manager in matters of design, structure and purpose. The MIS is the responsibility of the general and executive management.

Also at the heart of the matter is the distinctive character of the accounting function. Here we come to the point of division. MIS is essentially an operative system completely enmeshed in the management function. Accounting, control and audit are essentially an evaluative system — a system for evaluating management's performance *and hence necessarily outside of the management function.*

Accounting's prime concern was once with the form of the entry. Today its first test must be with the clarity of the disclosure. Its function was once private and procedural. It is now professional, charged with a public trust. Recognition of this obligation will be a business landmark in the 1970s. The primacy of their fiduciary duty will preclude conflicting postures, such as are implied by "managerial accounting," or entangling alliances with management which their dominance over MIS would create.

The accounting fraternity is under a fiduciary obligation to the board of directors, to the owners, and to the public to furnish such performance evaluations of the firm and its management. The success of an accounting information system is measured by the support it furnishes to the discharge of this mission. Happily, the better the accounting information system serves this end, the more useful are its inputs to the MIS, because they more faithfully reflect professional accounting intelligence.

Not only must these evaluative judgments be made free of bias, they must be free of the suspicion of bias which comes from a compromising involvement in the operative management function. The fiduciary obligation must rest on the internal staff as well as on the outside auditors. For I cannot conceive, looking to the future, how an outside auditor can certify financial statements prepared by a staff whose interests are conflicting and whose loyalties are divided.

It has been argued that thus limited the accountant's role is simply demeaning. In my opinion, the inputs we get from men who maintain a position of professional integrity are of the ultimate value in the heat of time-pressed indecision. In my opinion the counsel of those who rightly maintain the posture of counselor will be of highest worth to those who have the burden of management in this decade. Those who counsel on the basis of professional principles profoundly understood and respected have a value beyond measure. And their value is the greater because they counsel rather than control, because they reason rather than rule.

A great profession is one whose practitioners think greatly of their calling. Perhaps the privilege of a prideful self regard, justly entertained, is the greatest reward that any future employment can offer.

The Financial Officer. One of my associates has pointed out an uncomfortable omission in my argument which requires a further point to be made. In an accountant's working day role, accounting may be "merely a subset of the substance of his function." It does not recognize "the double identity of a controller, as chief accountant and as finance officer." And my friend puts into place the proper recognition of the critical leadership and contributions which our divisional controllers have made to the development of our MIS, not only in the areas dealing with the hard facts of the past, but in the systems designed to "record, process and evaluate the *uncertain future* of an *uncertain world.*"

He also establishes the interesting proposition that certain of our accountants took the initiative in developing tools for *decision* making in the managerial world of *uncertainty,* and that their example finally led to the "emancipation" of these "managerial functions from the traditional controller's control." So we attain again unto the revealed truth that decisions pertaining to the uncertain present and the unseen future are the prerogatives of management, not the controller.

But there are some decisional areas often managed by accountants which are beyond the areas of transaction records, control mechanisms, and evaluative measurements and judgments of management. These are the functions of the finance officer.

To adopt my associate's conclusions, "A clear distinction is needed between the controller as an accountant and the controller as a finance officer. The function of finance is distinctly a managerial function dealing with uncertainty, as much as the other functions (marketing, production, etc.). The finance officer has to deal with the timing of finance decisions, the choice of sources of financing, the control of liquidity, the estimation of future shortages or surpluses, and predicting future interest rates. His information system is distinguishable and separate from the accounting system. However, there is a tendency for finance officers and chief accountants to be identical and drawn from the accounting profession.

As in all cases where an absolute line of division is wished for, there is a band of overlap. At the operational levels in the firm these may be both necessary and extensive. But at the senior policy levels it is undesirable and in my judgment will not long be tolerable.

Theoretically, as my friend supposes, the fiduciary character of the controller has always existed. But the focus of responsibility continually shifts with the scale and mission of our institutions and with the ideals and objectives of our society. So the fiduciary nature of the controller's function has advanced from an occasional aspect to the dominant character of his function. (Walter F. Frese and Robert K. Mautz, "Financial Reporting By Whom?" *Harvard Business Review*, March-April, 1972.)

Hence, while the financial office is derived from the accounting functions, it has attained a status and character distinct from that of the controller. Prediction is the dominant contribution of the financial officer, who is preoccupied with the acquisition and allocation of resources by the firm; while designation and measurement is the prime concern of the controller who accounts for the inventory and evaluates the benefits of the corporate resources.

Finance by its nature adheres to management. The controller by his function must be allied to ownership and its representatives, the board of directors.

The Imperative Necessity for MIS. I must now return for a closing session with my anonymous adversary. He contends that a series of business information systems, each oriented to a particular function or operation, must result in an MIS which is "uncoordinated, and therefore inefficient and unsatisfactory." Because of the vast differences which necessarily exist between these several systems created for accounting and control, for production and distribution, for marketing, etc., he contends that expertise in one area is of little value in another. It follows he thinks that since one man cannot master the design of every system, there can be no single homogeneous MIS embracing them all.

If we followed the same logic we must also conclude that there cannot be a firm of size or complexity because no one man has the talent to master every function and operation necessary to the accomplishment of its mission. Consequently, according to his test, no one is qualified to manage it in total. Perhaps we have inadvertently stumbled upon the flaw in the system! But the fact is that we do have the executive office, and it is required to oversee the total effort of the firm. And it must have an MIS to get the job done.

The key to MIS is an integrated data base, not a universal genius expert and omniscient in everything. As we have noted, each of the functional systems utilizes data and output from other systems as well as data inputs from sources peculiar to its function. From these materials it generates information suited to the performance of its particular function. And this information also feeds back into the data base where it is available as data for all of the other business systems.

It follows that if our functional information systems cover the operations of the firm with reasonable sufficiency, there is information in the data base adequate to support an executive management information system. Some further data will be needed, of course, because executive management considers a different opportunity horizon and a different time span than does operating management. But with this modest qualification the material is at hand to do the job.

And the job is no more complex — indeed, it is less so — than the problem of creating the several operating systems. The critical problem to the construction of an MIS is the integrated data base itself. This requires first a unified communication system through which the system data must flow, it requires rapidly expanding data file facilities, and it demands a data coding and addressing scheme which makes all the data in the bank reasonably available (hopefully randomly and instantly available) to every system in the firm.

The real obstacle to MIS in most firms is the structure of the data files themselves, and the means in hand for accessing them. Without adequate methods and structures here the problem of system interfaces — which means people interfaces — becomes the condition precedent to performance. And a guarantee of unsatisfactory performance. My anonymous antagonist says that this is a matter to be solved by eduction, but as you will recall he disqualified B school products as a solution much earlier in the game. So he is bucking the problem to some other branch of learning when he takes this exit. And indeed he closes his article in a state of hopelessness.

"Management must always operate with insufficient information . . . In many areas the truth of these statements is becoming more salient because while the role of management is becoming more complex, the new information technology is not helping significantly . . . The problems of control in decentralized companies are much more difficult than they were ten years ago — increases in size, complexity, and geographical dispersion have made control much more difficult. Yet the new information technology has been of little help in this area, simply because the problems of controlling decentralized decisions do not lend themselves to computerized or mathematical solutions . . . part of our information crisis results from the nature of the present business environment. We shall simply have to live with it."

This is a perfect demonstration of the absolute necessity of MIS, and a complete admission of the impossibility of reaching it through his approach. He has discredited people interfaces as a means of establishing data flows between related information systems. He has failed to see either the necessity or feasibility of avoiding this impediment by an integrated data base.

For we shall not reach the MIS we need for the management of the enterprises we have created through the scholastic logic bequeathed us by a medieval heritage. We shall reach it by the perceptive application of the information technology which daily experience teaches us, if we are disposed to learn.

5

MANAGEMENT MISINFORMATION SYSTEMS

RUSSELL L. ACKOFF*

Five assumptions commonly made by designers of management information systems are identified. It is argued that these are not justified in
many (if not most) cases and hence lead to major deficiencies in the resulting systems. These assumptions are: (1) the critical deficiency under
which most managers operate is the lack of relevant information, (2) the
manager needs the information he wants, (3) if a manager has the information he needs his decision-making will improve, (4) better communication between managers improves organizational performance, and (5) a
manager does not have to understand how his information system works,
only how to use it. To overcome these assumptions and the deficiencies
which result from them, a management information system should be im-
bedded in a management control system. A procedure for designing such
a system is proposed and an example is given of the type of control system which it produces.

The growing preoccupation of operation researchers and management scien-
tists with Management Information Systems (MIS's) is apparent. In fact, for
some the design of such systems has almost become synonymous with operations research or management science. Enthusiasm for such systems is
understandable: it involves the researcher in a romantic relationship with
the most glamorous instrument of our time, the computer. Such enthusiasm
is understandable but, nevertheless, some of the excesses to which it has led
are not excusable.

* From *Management Science*, Vol. 14, No. 4 (December 1967). Reprinted by permission of
The Institute of Management Sciences. The author is a professor.

Contrary to the impression produced by the growing literature, few computerized management information systems have been put into operation. Of those I've seen that have been implemented, most have not matched expectations and some have been outright failures. I believe that these near- and far-misses could have been avoided if certain false (and usually implicit) assumptions on which many systems have been erected had not been made.

There seem to be five common and erroneous assumptions underlying the design of most MIS's, each of which I will consider. After doing so I will outline an MIS design procedure which avoids these assumptions.

Give Them More

Most MIS's are designed on the assumption that the critical deficiency under which most managers operate is the *lack of relevant information.* I do not deny that most managers lack a good deal of information that they should have, but I do deny that this is the most important information deficiency from which they suffer. It seems to me that they suffer more from an *overabundance of irrelevant information.*

This is not a play on words. The consequences of changing the emphasis of an MIS from supplying relevant information to eliminating irrelevant information is considerable. If one is preoccupied with supplying relevant information, attention is almost exclusively given to the generation, storage, and retrieval of information: hence emphasis is placed on constructing data banks, coding, indexing, updating files, access languages, and so on. The ideal which has emerged from this orientation is an infinite pool of data into which a manager can reach to pull out any information he wants. If, on the other hand, one sees the manager's information problem primarily, but not exclusively, as one that arises out of an overabundance of irrelevant information, most of which was not asked for, then the two most important functions of an information system become *filtration* (or evaluation) and *condensation.* The literature on MIS's seldom refers to these functions let alone considers how to carry them out.

My experience indicates that most managers receive much more data (if not information) than they can possibly absorb even if they spend all of their time trying to do so. Hence they already suffer from an information overload. They must spend a great deal of time separating the relevant from the irrelevant and searching for the kernels in the relevant documents. For example, I have found that I receive an average of forty-three hours of unsolicited reading material each week. The solicited material is usually half again this amount.

I have seen a daily stock status report that consists of approximately six hundred pages of computer print-out. The report is circulated daily across managers' desks. I've also seen requests for major capital expenditures that come in book size, several of which are distributed to managers each week. It is not uncommon for many managers to receive an average of one journal a day or more. One could go on and on.

Unless the information overload to which managers are subjected is reduced, any additional information made available by an MIS cannot be expected to be used effectively.

Even relevant documents have too much repetition. Most documents can be considerably condensed without loss of content. My point here is best made, perhaps, by describing briefly an experiment that a few of my colleagues and I conducted on the OR literature several years ago. By using a panel of well-known experts we identified four OR articles that all members of the panel considered to be "above average," and four articles that were considered to be "below average." The authors of the eight articles were asked to prepare "objective" examinations (duration thirty minutes) plus answers for graduate students who were to be assigned the articles for reading. (The authors were not informed about the experiment.) Then several experienced writers were asked to reduce each article to two-thirds and one-third of its original length only by eliminating words. They also prepared a brief abstract of each article. Those who did the condensing did not see the examinations to be given to the students.

A group of graduate students who had not previously read the articles were then selected. Each one was given four articles randomly selected, each of which was in one of its four versions: 100 per cent, 67 per cent, 33 per cent, or abstract. Each version of each article was read by two students. All were given the same examinations. The average scores on the examinations were then compared.

For the above-average articles there was no significant difference between average test scores for the 100 per cent, 67 per cent, and 33 per cent versions, but there was a significant decrease in average test scores for those who had read only the abstract. For the below-average articles there was no difference in average test scores among those who had read the 100 per cent, 67 per cent, and 33 per cent versions, but there was a significant *increase* in average test scores of those who had read only the abstract.

The sample used was obviously too small for general conclusions but the results strongly indicate the extent to which even good writing can be condensed without loss of information. I refrain from drawing the obvious conclusions about bad writing.

It seems clear that condensation as well as filtration, performed mechanically or otherwise, should be an essential part of an MIS, and that such a system should be capable of handling much, if not all, of the unsolicited as well as solicited information that a manager receives.

The Manager Needs the Information That He Wants

Most MIS designers "determine" what information is needed by asking managers what information they would like to have. This is based on the assumption that managers know what information they need, and want it.

For a manager to know what information he needs he must be aware of each type of decision he should make (as well as does) and he must have an adequate model of each. These conditions are seldom satisfied. Most managers have some conception of at least some of the types of decisions they must make. Their conceptions, however, are likely to be deficient in a very critical way, a way that follows from an important principle of scientific economy: the less we understand a phenomenon, the more variables we require to explain it. Hence, the manager who does not understand the phenomenon he controls plays it "safe" and, with respect to information, wants "everything." The MIS designer, who has even less understanding of the relevant phenomenon than the manager, tries to provide even more than everything. He thereby increases what is already an overload of irrelevant information.

For example, market researchers in a major oil company once asked their marketing managers what variables they thought were relevant in estimating the sales volume of future service stations. Almost seventy variables were identified. The market researchers then added about half again this many variables, performed a large multiple linear regression analysis of sales of existing stations against these variables, and found about thirty-five to be statistically significant. A forecasting equation was based on this analysis. An OR team subsequently constructed a model based on only one of these variables, traffic flow, which predicted sales better than the thirty-five-variables regression equation. The team went on to *explain* sales at service stations in terms of the customers' perception of the amount of time lost by stopping for service. The relevance of all but a few of the variables used by the market researchers could be explained by their effect on such perception.

The moral is simple: one cannot specify what information is required for decision-making until an explanatory model of the decision process and the system involved has been constructed and tested. Information systems are subsystems of control systems. They cannot be designed adequately without taking control in account. Furthermore, whatever else regression analyses can yield, they cannot yield understanding and explanation of phenomena. They describe and, at best, predict.

Give a Manager the Information He Needs and His Decision-Making Will Improve

It is frequently assumed that if a manager is provided with the information he needs, he will then have no problem in using it effectively. The history of OR stands to the contrary. For example, give most managers an initial tableau of a typical "real" mathematical programming, sequencing, or network problem and see how close they come to an optimal solution. If their experience and judgment have any value they may not do badly, but they will seldom do very well. In most management problems there are too many possibilities to expect experience, judgment, or intuition to provide good guesses, even with perfect information.

Furthermore, when several probabilities are involved in a problem the unguided mind of even a manager has difficulty in aggregating them in a valid way. We all know many simple problems in probability in which untutored intuition usually does very badly (e.g., what are the correct odds that two of twenty-five people selected at random will have their birthdays on the same day of the year?). For example, very few of the results obtained by queuing theory, when arrivals and service are probabilistic, are obvious to managers; nor are the results of risk analysis where the managers' own subjective estimates of probabilities are used.

The moral: it is necessary to determine how well managers can use needed information. When, because of the complexity of the decision process, they can't use it well, they should be provided with either decision rules or performance feed-back so that they can identify and learn from their mistakes. More on this point later.

More Communication Means Better Performance

One characteristic of most MIS's which I have seen is that they provide managers with better current information about what other managers and their departments and divisions are doing. Underlying this provision is the belief that better interdepartmental communication enables managers to coordinate their decisions more effectively and hence improves the organization's overall performance. Not only is this not necessarily so, but it seldom is so. One would hardly expect two competing companies to become more cooperative because the information each acquires about the other is improved. This analogy is not as far-fetched as one might at first suppose. For example, consider the following very much simplified version of a situation I once ran into. The simplification of the case does not affect any of its essential characteristics.

A department store has two "line" operations: buying and selling. Each function is performed by a separate department. The Purchasing Department primarily controls one variable: how much of each item is bought. The Merchandising Department controls the price at which it is sold. Typically, the measure of performance applied to the Purchasing Department was the turnover rate of inventory. The measure applied to the Merchandising Department was gross sales; this department sought to maximize the number of items sold, times their price.

Now by examining a single item let us consider what happens in this system. The merchandising manager, using his knowledge of competition and consumption, set a price which he judged would maximize gross sales. In doing so he utilized price-demand curves for each type of item. For each price the curves show the expected sales and values on an upper and lower confidence band as well. (See Figure 1.) When instructing the Purchasing Department how many items to make available, the merchandising manager quite naturally used the value on the upper confidence curve. This minimized the chances of his running short which, if it occurred, would hurt his

Figure 1. Price-demand curve

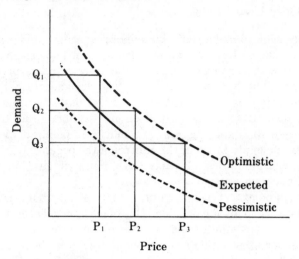

performance. It also maximized the chances of being over-stocked but this was not his concern, only the purchasing manager's. Say, therefore, that the merchandising manager initially selected price P_1 and requested that amount Q_1 be made available by the Purchasing Department.

In this company the purchasing manager also had access to the price-demand curves. He knew the merchandising manager always ordered optimistically. Therefore, using the same curve he read over from Q_1 to the upper limit and down to the expected value from which he obtained Q_2, the quantity he actually intended to make available. He did not intend to pay for the merchandising manager's optimism. If merchandising ran out of stock, it was not his worry. Now the merchandising manager was informed about what the purchasing manager had done, so he adjusted his price to P_2. The purchasing manager in turn was told that the merchandising manager had made this readjustment, so he planned to make only Q_3 available. If this process — made possible only by perfect communication between departments — had been allowed to continue, nothing would have been bought and nothing would have been sold. This outcome was avoided by prohibiting communication between the two departments and forcing each to guess what the other was doing.

I have obviously caricatured the situation in order to make the point clear: when organizational units have inappropriate measures of performance which put them in conflict with each other, as is often the case, communication between them may hurt organizational performance, not help it. Organizational structure and performance measurement must be taken into account before opening the flood gates and permitting the free flow of information between parts of the organization. (A more rigorous discussion of organizational structure and the relationship of communication to it can be found in Reference 1, page 88.)

A Manager Does Not Have to Understand How an Information System Works, Only How to Use It

Most MIS designers seek to make their systems as innocuous and unobtrusive as possible to managers lest they become frightened. The designers try to provide managers with very easy access to the system and assure them that they need to know nothing more about it. The designers usually succeed in keeping managers ignorant in this regard. This leaves managers unable to evaluate the MIS as a whole. It often makes them afraid to even try to do so lest they display their ignorance publicly. In failing to evaluate their MIS, managers delegate much of the control of the organization to the system's designers and operators who may have many virtues, but managerial competence is seldom among them.

Let me cite a case in point. A Chairman of the Board of a medium-size company asked for help on the following problem. One of his larger (decentralized) divisions had installed a computerized production-inventory control and manufacturing-manager information system about a year earlier. It had acquired about $2,000,000 worth of equipment to do so. The Board Chairman had just received a request from the Division for permission to replace the original equipment with newly announced equipment which would cost several times the original amount. An extensive "justification" for so doing was provided with the request. The Chairman wanted to know whether the request was really justified. He admitted to complete incompetence in this connection.

A meeting was arranged at the Division at which I was subjected to an extended and detailed briefing. The system was large but relatively simple. At the heart of it was a reorder point for each item and a maximum allowable stock level. Reorder quantities took lead-time as well as the allowable maximum into account. The computer kept track of stock, ordered items when required and generated numerous reports on both the state of the system it controlled and its own "actions."

When the briefing was over I was asked if I had any questions. I did. First I asked if, when the system had been installed, there had been many parts whose stock level exceeded the maximum amount possible under the new system. I was told there were many. I asked for a list of about thirty and for some graph paper. Both were provided. With the help of the system designer and volumes of old daily reports I began to plot the stock level of the first listed item over time. When this item reached the maximum "allowable" stock level it had been reordered. The system designer was surprised and said that by sheer "luck" I had found one of the few errors made by the system. Continued plotting showed that because of repeated premature reordering the item had never gone much below the maximum stock level. Clearly the program was confusing the maximum allowable stock level and the reorder point. This turned out to be the case in more than half of the items on the list.

Next I asked if they had many paired parts, ones that were only used with each other; for example, matched nuts and bolts. They had many. A list was produced and we began checking the previous day's withdrawals. For more than half of the pairs the differences in the numbers recorded as withdrawn were very large. No explanation was provided.

Before the day was out it was possible to show by some quick and dirty calculations that the new computerized system was costing the company almost $150,000 per month more than the hand system which it had replaced, most of this in excess inventories.

The recommendation was that the system be redesigned as quickly as possible and that the new equipment not be authorized for the time being.

The questions asked of the system had been obvious and simple ones. Managers should have been able to ask them but — and this is the point — they felt themselves incompetent to do so. They would not have allowed a hand-operated system to get so far out of their control.

No MIS should ever be installed unless the managers for whom it is intended are trained to evaluate and hence control it rather than be controlled by it.

A Suggested Procedure for Designing an MIS

The erroneous assumptions I have tried to reveal in the preceding discussion can, I believe, be avoided by an appropriate design procedure. One is briefly outlined here.

1. Analysis of the Decision System

Each (or at least each important) type of managerial decision required by the organization under study should be identified and the relationships between them should be determined and flow-charted. Note that this is *not* necessarily the same thing as determining what decisions *are* made. For example, in one company I found that make-or-buy decisions concerning parts were made only at the time when a part was introduced into stock and was never subsequently reviewed. For some items this decision had gone unreviewed for as many as twenty years. Obviously, such decisions should be made more often; in some cases, every time an order is placed in order to take account of current shop loading, under-used shifts, delivery times from suppliers, and so on.

Decision-flow analyses are usually self-justifying. They often reveal important decisions that are being made by default (e.g., the make-buy decision referred to above), and they disclose interdependent decisions that are being made independently. Decision-flow charts frequently suggest changes in managerial responsibility, organizational structure, and measure of performance which can correct the types of deficiencies cited.

Decision analyses can be conducted with varying degrees of detail, that is, they may be anywhere from coarse- to fine-grained. How much detail one should become involved with depends on the amount of time and resources that are available for the analysis. Although practical considerations frequently restrict initial analyses to a particular organizational function, it is preferable to perform a coarse analysis for all of an organization's managerial functions rather than a fine analysis of one or a subset of functions. It is easier to introduce finer information into an integrated information system than it is to combine fine subsystems into one integrated system.

2. An Analysis of Information Requirements

Managerial decision can be classified into three types:

(a) Decision for which adequate models are available or can be constructed and from which optimal (or near optimal) solutions can be derived. In such cases the decision process itself should be incorporated into the information system thereby converting it (at least partially) to a control system. A decision model identifies what information is required and hence what information is relevant.

(b) Decisions for which adequate models can be constructed but from which optimal solutions cannot be extracted. Here some kind of heuristic or search procedure should be provided even if it consists of no more than computerized trial and error. A simulation of the model will, as a minimum, permit comparison of proposed alternative solutions. Here too the model specifies what information is required.

(c) Decisions for which adequate models cannot be constructed. Research is required here to determine what information is relevant. If decision-making cannot be delayed for the completion of such research or the decision's effect is not large enough to justify the cost of research, then judgment must be used to "guess" what information is relevant. It may be possible to make explicit the implicit model used by the decision-maker and treat it as a model of type (b).

In each of these three types of situation it is necessary to provide feedback by comparing actual decision outcomes with those predicted by the model or decision-maker. Each decision that is made, along with its predicted outcome, should be an essential input to a management control system. I shall return to this point below.

3. Aggregation of Decisions

Decisions with the same or largely overlapping information requirements should be grouped together as a single manager's task. This will reduce the information a manager requires to do his job and is likely to increase his understanding of it. This may require a reorganization of the system. Even if such a reorganization cannot be implemented completely what can be done is likely to improve performance significantly and reduce the information loaded on managers.

4. Design of Information Processing

Now the procedure for collecting, storing, retrieving, and treating information can be designed. Since there is a voluminous literature on this subject I shall leave it at this except for one point. Such a system must not only be able to answer questions addressed to it; it should also be able to answer questions that have not been asked by reporting any deviations from expectations. An extensive exception-reporting system is required.

5. Design of Control of the Control System
It must be assumed that the system that is being designed will be deficient in many and significant ways. Therefore it is necessary to identify the ways in which it may be deficient, to design procedures for detecting its deficiencies, and for correcting the system so as to remove or reduce them. Hence the system should be designed to be flexible and adaptive. This is little more than a platitude, but it has a not-so-obvious implication. No completely computerized system can be as flexible and adaptive as can a man-machine system. This is illustrated by a concluding example of a system that is being developed and is partially in operation. (See Figure 2.)

Figure 2. Simplified Diagram of a Market-Area Control System

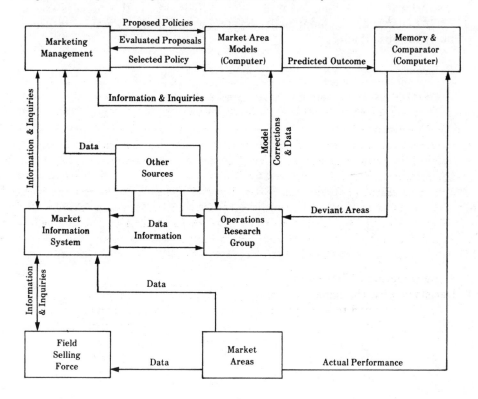

The company involved has its market divided into approximately two hundred marketing areas. A model for each has been constructed as is "in" the computer. On the basis of competitive intelligence supplied to the service

marketing manager by marketing researchers and information specialists he and his staff make policy decisions for each area each month. Their tentative decisions are fed into the computer which yields a forecast of expected performance. Changes are made until the expectations match what is desired. In this way they arrive at "final" decisions. At the end of the month the computer compares the actual performance of each area with what was predicted. If a deviation exceeds what could be expected by chance, the company's OR Group then seeks the reason for the deviation, performing as much research as is required to find it. If the cause is found to be permanent the computerized model is adjusted appropriately. The result is an adaptive man-machine system whose precision and generality is continuously increasing with use.

Finally, it should be noted that in carrying out the design steps enumerated above, three groups should collaborate: information systems specialists, operations researchers, *and managers.* The participation of managers in the design of a system that is to serve them, assures their ability to evaluate its performance by comparing its output with what was predicted. Managers who are not willing to invest some of their time in this process are not likely to use a management control system well, and their system, in turn, is likely to abuse them.

Reference

1. Sengupta, S.S., and Ackoff, R.L., "Systems Theory from an Operations Research Point of View," *IEEE Transactions on Systems Science and Cybernetics,* Vol. 1 (Nov. 1965), pp. 9-13.

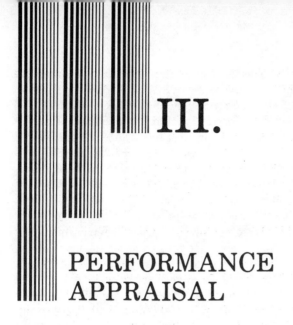

III.

PERFORMANCE
APPRAISAL

Several generalizations about performance appraisal systems can be stated. Performance appraisal or evaluation systems are useful for coordinating employee efforts and communicating with them in a manner that promotes motivation. To be effective the systems must exist in advance of actual activity (e.g., before manufacture of a product). Evaluation systems are also needed to ascertain what actually happened, through comparing actual to a standard or budget. With information about recent variances, managers might take steps to try to avoid future, unwanted variances.

The difficult part of management accounting comes after we learn the generalizations. How do we get the performance system to operate in practice. The first two articles, by Robert N. Anthony and Raymond Villers, provide interesting examples and offer advice. In "Cost Concepts for Control," Anthony explains the communication, motivation, and performance reporting aspects of performance/control systems using some easily-grasped examples. He also works with the themes of this book, illustrating why searching for one "best" method is usually fruitless.

"Control and Freedom in a Decentralized Company" explains how a responsibility accounting system might have to be designed in a few illustrated circumstances. The author, Villers, addresses several key operational points, such as how responsibility passes from one person to another, and the benefits and limitations of different systems that try to strike a balance between control and a manager's operational freedom. The three case studies, especially the one involving the purchasing agent, are worth reading several times.

The third article, "Dysfunctional Consequences of Performance Measurements," is an interesting reminder of the strengths and limitations of control systems of varying complexity. The themes reinforce Anthony's comments about the "wisdom" of searching for one best way.

"Divisional Performance Measurement: Beyond an Exclusive Profit Test" serves as a good reminder of the possible limitations of portions of the analytical framework that we have used in Section I. The author, Lee D. Parker, probes the subject of goals and goal congruence. The article overlaps the ideas expressed by other authors in this section of the book, especially regarding motivation, control, and autonomy. But, somewhat different interpretations from those of some other authors are expressed.

The final article in this Section, "Profit Centers, Transfer Prices and Mysticism," like the previous one, examines divisional performance measurement techniques. The author, M.C. Wells, attempts to sort some myths from practical realities. He also examines the role of transfer prices for different management decisions and not just for performance appraisal.

In total, the five articles provide useful guidance for applying management accounting techniques listed in many cost and managerial accounting textbooks.

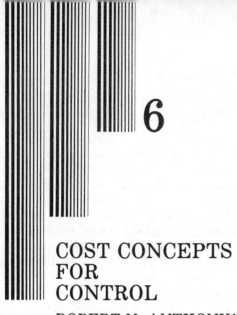

6

COST CONCEPTS FOR CONTROL

ROBERT N. ANTHONY*

The framework your Cost Concepts Committee used to state concepts relating to control is somewhat unconventional, and some background about our deliberations may help to explain why we finally decided on this framework. Initially, we attacked the problem by examining various types of cost constructions that are used for control purposes, in an attempt to find criteria for determining which of these was, in some sense, the "best". We had lots of possibilities: actual costs, basis standard costs, normal capacity costs, current budgeted costs, attainable costs, systems that prorated all overhead, systems that prorated no overhead, and many more. In the course of our long discussions, one committee member would explain and uphold a technique that he had seen used effectively in some company, and another member would counter with a description of a completely different system that he had observed being used with apparently equal effectiveness in another situation. Although we tried very hard to do so, however, we could find no objective way of generalizing on which type of cost system was "best" for control purposes.

We eventually concluded that an attempt to find objective means of differentiating among the various control systems in current use was not feasible

* From *The Accounting Review* (April 1957), pp. 229-34. Reprinted by permission of the Editor. At the time of writing, the author was a professor at Harvard University.

This paper was one of three presented by members of the Committee on Cost Concepts and Standards at the annual meeting of the American Accounting Association, Seattle, August 31, 1956. It relates to the "Tentative Statement of Cost Concepts Underlying Reports for Management Purposes" published in the April 1956 issue of *The Accounting Review*.

and that our failure to find such criteria indicated that we probably were not approaching the problem properly. The plain fact is that competent managements use a variety of cost constructions for control purposes, and each may find merit in its own system. It is also true that a system that works well in one company may not work at all in another company; even though the two companies have substantially similar control environments. It therefore became apparent that any attempt to define concepts in terms that implied that one of these systems was inherently good and all others inherently poor, or less good, was bound to be fruitless.

This conclusion led us to attack the problem in quite a different manner. We asked ourselves: "What does the control process actually consist of?" Most authorities agree that control, in the sense in which it is used in business management, has to do with the attempts of one person to direct or influence the actions of other persons. This personal, human element in the process came to be the focus of our thinking.

Although the management control process is often compared with mechanical or electrical control devices, such as the thermostat, such an analogy is apt to be quite misleading. A thermostat reacts to stimuli in a definite, predictable fashion. When the temperature rises to a certain point, the furnace is shut off. Human beings, on the other hand, do not behave so predictably; human reactions to a stimulus are much more complicated, and human control systems cannot be so easily or so precisely designed as mechanical or electrical ones. If, for example, my wife tells me the room is too warm, my reaction may be (and after years of training, usually is) to open a window or to take some other steps to cool it; but, occasionally, I may procrastinate and do nothing, or I may even argue that the room is not too warm anyway.

Thermostats do not argue, they do not procrastinate, they do not resent being told what to do, they do not do what they think is best. In short, they are not human.

A management control system, which does involve human beings — indeed, whose only purpose is to influence the action of human beings — is therefore fundamentally different from mechanical or electrical controls. It follows that our attempt to examine a system in terms of its mechanics — the methods of setting standards, of prorating overhead, and so on — was bound to fail because it missed the main point entirely. And as soon as we considered the management control process as something that basically involved people and the reactions of people, it became evident that there were some useful things that could be said about the role of cost information in this process.

We ended up by grouping the control concepts under three headings, closely related to human reactions and stated in terms of the purposes for which cost information is used in the control process. These are: (1) to communicate information about approved plans, (2) to motivate people, and (3) to report performance.

Communication

With respect to the communication of plans, we had in mind primarily the approved budget, which is the end result of the planning process discussed in another section of the Tentative Statement of Cost Concepts. The approved budget is a communication device in that it tells each unit of the organization something about what management expects it to do during the budget period and also shows the unit how its work fits in with the overall activity of the organization. In addition to the budget, plans and objectives are also communicated by cost standards.

Any means of human communication inevitably raises the problem of semantics. We are all increasingly aware of the fact that the recipient of a communication rarely, if ever, understands precisely what the author intended to say. This is as true with cost information as it is with any other language, and we therefore call attention in our report to the necessity of obtaining common agreement and understanding throughout the organization as to the precise meaning of the budget figures and cost standards used in that company.

Motivation

Our second heading, costs as a motivating device, relates to what is, perhaps, the most important purpose of all; but it is also the most difficult one to state in writing. Let me try an example in an attempt to show how cost construction can motivate people, that is, how they can influence the actions that people take. I choose, because it concerns all of us who are teachers, the prosaic matter of controlling the costs of mimeographing or other duplicating work. Visualize a school in which the administration recognizes the necessity for having its faculty generate a certain amount of mimeographing work but which recognizes also that funds available for this and other purposes are not limitless. How can control be exercised over the amount of funds spent for mimeographing and the manner in which the work is done? Of the many ways of solving this problem, I shall mention only enough to indicate how the cost system can help, in various ways, to motivate the people involved.

One possibility is to have no formal control at all. This is a common practice. When a school chooses to follow it, it presumably relies on custom, informal conversations, or perhaps even warnings of one kind or another, to keep the cost of duplicating work from becoming exorbitantly high. The fact that schools that follow this practice do not use costs as a control device in this area illustrates the point that cost control is by no means the only possible type of control.

Another possibility is to set up a budget for each department or other organizational unit in the school. Perhaps there will be an item in this budget for duplicating work, or alternatively the budget may specify an overall amount for the total needs of the department, of which duplicating work is but one element. These two types of budgets can motivate the department head quite differently. The first tells him that he is permitted to incur a certain amount of cost for duplicating work, considered by itself; the second tells him that he has certain funds with which to run his department, and it is up to him to decide whether his needs for duplicating work are more important than other possible ways of spending his departmental funds.

Now let us go a step further. How shall we define the "cost" of duplicating work? Shall we charge the department head with the labor cost of the girl in his own department (or a girl in some other department whose services he may borrow) who cuts the stencils? If we do, we remove any incentive for him to use his own or borrowed help, and we shall therefore expect that he will normally send the work to the central duplicating staff, rather than ask his own people to do it. Shall we charge him for the cost of this central staff? If we do not, there is no reason why he should not use it, whether his need is justified or not, and we therefore encourage thoughtless use of its facilities. If we do charge him, we may encourage him to go outside the school for his duplicating work if he can find an outside party who will do it at a lower cost. Perhaps this is what we want him to do. On the other hand, we may prefer that he have the work done inside. If so, maybe we should charge him only for the direct cost of the central staff, which will set up a differential against outside work.

I could introduce many other ramifications, but I hope I have said enough to demonstrate that to the extent that cost constructions are involved in this problem, the decision as to what type of cost should be used is arrived at, not by trying to find the true, objective cost of duplicating — if there is such a thing — but rather by using cost constructions that are calculated to motivate the department head to act as the administration wishes him to act.

The foregoing situation may be somewhat trivial. To show that similar considerations are involved in a factory problem, let us look briefly at the problem of the control of maintenance and repair costs. The maintenance function is that of keeping the buildings and equipment in good operating condition. This is partly the responsibility of the operating department foremen, who can influence the amount of required maintenance work by the care they give to their equipment.

There are at least a dozen ways in which the costs of the maintenance department can be charged to the several operating departments, and each gives a different "message" to the foremen as to how they should view their responsibility for maintenance. Here are a few of the possibilities and the implications that are likely to be conveyed by each.

Method No. 1: Do not charge any maintenance costs to the operating departments

Message: The operating foreman has no responsibility for maintenance costs. He requests the maintenance department to do the work that he thinks should be done, and the maintenance department has the responsibility for doing it. The maintenance department is implicitly responsible for the condition of the equipment.

Method No. 2: Prorate total maintenance costs to the operating departments on the basis of the number of direct labor hours incurred in each department

Message: Maintenance costs in total are expected to vary proportionately with plant activity. However, the foreman of each department has no direct responsibility for maintenance work, and the maintenance department, as in the first method, has full responsibility. The operating foreman is told his "fair share" of total maintenance costs incurred.

Method No. 3: Charge departments for each job they have done at a prescribed amount for each type of job

Message: The foreman is responsible for situations that create the need for maintenance work, such as machine breakdowns. The maintenance department is responsible for the cost of doing a given maintenance job. The foreman therefore need not be concerned with the efficiency with which the maintenance men work since he will be charged a prescribed amount for each job no matter how much is actually spent in doing the job.

Method No. 4: Charge each department for maintenance work at a prescribed hourly rate for each hour that a maintenance man works in the department

Message: The foreman is responsible both for situations that create the need for maintenance work and for the time taken by the maintenance people to do the work. Presumably, he has some control over the work of the maintenance men. He may, in some situations, even be authorized to hire outside maintenance people if he believes that they will do the work less expensively than the rates charged by the maintenance department.

None of the above methods is necessarily better than the others. Depending on what management wishes to accomplish, any one of these methods, or other methods not listed, or some combination of them, may be best for a given company. The problem is to decide what direction the motivation should take and then to select a method that influences the foremen to act in this manner.

In essence, the Committee concluded that the method of constructing costs for control purposes is governed by management policy, that the costs system should be designed to help carry out that policy, and that rigid mechanical rules are therefore not applicable.

So far, I have discussed only the basic idea of motivation. Our statement of cost concepts ideally should go considerably beyond this basic idea and list specific points that can be used as guides in constructing costs used for control purposes.

Frankly, we have made only a small beginning in this direction. We do emphasize the necessity for relating costs to personal responsibility, which is the "responsibility center" or "activity center" concept that has been written about extensively in recent years. We attempt to be fairly specific about what, as a practical matter, is meant by personal responsibility since there are few, if any, cost elements that are completely and solely the responsibility of a single person. But we do not feel sure enough of our ground to make very many generalizations in this area. The topic is one which is of great concern to people in practice, but it is also one on which, for some reason, not much has yet been written. We therefore simply cannot find many points that are sufficiently well substantiated to warrant including them in the Tentative Statement. This is one of the areas in which our statement is indeed extremely tentative, and with the passage of time, I think many specific and useful points can be added to this section of the statement.

Before leaving this subject, I want to mention briefly two other points that trouble some with whom we have discussed this section of the Tentative Statement.

One is the fact that, people being the way they are, not everyone is motivated identically by the same stimulus. That this is so is undeniable. Nevertheless, there must be some common patterns of human behavior that apply to large numbers of people. To go back to the example of the faculty members and the duplicating work, there undoubtedly are some faculty members who will not order too much duplicating work no matter how much leeway they are given, and there probably are some who will, in one way or another, obtain too much no matter how tight the control system is. But these groups must constitute only a minority, for if most people were in the first group, controls would be unnecessary; and if most were in the second group, controls would be impossible.

The second point is that to some people the very attempt to describe costs in terms of human relations smacks of trickery, of attempting to fool people. I think this feeling arises from the implicit assumption that there must be some objective way of defining cost, and as we emphasize in the introductory section of the Tentative Statement, this simply is not so. Perhaps it is sufficient to say here that any attempt to use costs to trick or mislead the organization is likely to be self-defeating, in that it will motivate people in quite a different direction from what is intended.

Reporting

We come now to the third area, costs as a basis for reporting and appraising performance. In this area, we first must face a familiar paradox, which can be stated as follows: Cost reports describe what has already happened;

therefore they cannot be used to control events, since no one can alter or undo what has already been done; therefore, a control report cannot really control anything.

One explanation of this apparent paradox is obvious, namely, that cost reports provide the basis for actions such as praise, criticism, or suggestions for change, all designed to improve *future* performance. We think, in addition, there is another, more subtle way in which cost reports influence performance, and indeed influence the very performance being reported on. Advance knowledge of the fact that a report on performance is going to be prepared can be an important stimulus to good performance on the part of the person being judged. I think this is well illustrated by our process of grading students, for it is doubtful that we would willingly undertake the grading drudgery unless we believed that the fact that students knew they were eventually going to be graded had in some way influenced the work they did during the year.

In the Tentative Statement, we list some concepts that are relevant to the reporting area, including methods of constructing and using standard costs, the idea of management by exception, the important point that control systems are likely to be ineffective unless the people involved believe that the standards are reasonable and equitable, the use of return on investment as an overall yardstick of performance, and so on. I think these are adequately stated in the report, and I will therefore not elaborate on them here.

Conclusion

This, then was our approach to enumerating and defining the concepts relevant to costs for control. Our framework was the *purpose* for which costs are used. In such a framework, we recognized that human reactions and motivations were dominant considerations. Our problem thereupon became not strictly an accounting problem, such as the construction of a set of financial statements, nor an accounting-economics problem, such as that discussed in the planning section of the Tentative Statement. Rather, it was a problem involving both accounting and psychology, the study that deals with human reactions.

Your committee is not made up of psychologists; in fact, its members are somewhat skeptical of some of the psychological patter. We are convinced, however, that approaching the control problem in terms of human motivation — subjective though this approach is, and different though it may seem from the customary language of debit and credit — is much more fruitful than an attempt to define "true" costs, or to say whether ideal standards are better than normal standards, or any other mechanical approach.

The usefulness of such an approach becomes apparent when the concepts are applied to a practical control problem. Without such an approach, one can easily become immersed in pointless arguments on such matters as whether rent should be allocated on the basis of square footage or cubic footage. There is no sound way of settling such disputes. With the notion of motivation, the problem comes into clear focus: What cost constructions are most likely to induce people to take the action that management desires? Answering this question in a specific situation is difficult, and very little in the way of guides towards a specific answer will be found in our statement. But, at least, we think the concepts suggested here describe what the accountant is trying to do.

And as time goes on, we expect that out of experience, and discussions like the one we have today, more specific statements will evolve, so that eventually principles will be developed in the control area comparable with those developed over the years in the financial accounting area.

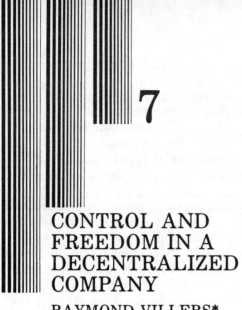

7

CONTROL AND FREEDOM IN A DECENTRALIZED COMPANY

RAYMOND VILLERS*

... Control is not by itself a hindrance to individual freedom. Rather, control is in fact a prerequisite to decentralization, and without decentralization there can be no real freedom.

Industrial management today faces a strange dilemma. Half a century of experience has shown conclusively that planning and control are the basic requirements of economical manufacturing. But a decade or so of intensive research in human relations shows with equal conclusiveness that our large organizations and our methods of planning and control are, more often than not, antagonistic to good human relations, so essential to the successful management of an industrial enterprise. Reliable studies indicate that our methods of planning and control may even tend to deprive the members of our industrial organizations of one of man's basic needs — a sense of purposeful and worthwhile accomplishment.[1]

Practical Problem

Planning and control are nevertheless as necessary today as ever; large organizations are here to stay — and will continue to develop further. The practical problem, therefore, "is that of building large organizations and of

* From *Harvard Business Review* (March-April 1954), pp. 89-96. © 1954 by the President and Fellows of Harvard College; all rights reserved. The author was a business consultant when this article was written.

[1] See, for instance, Chris Argyris, "The Impact of Budgets on People," *Harvard Business Review* (January-February 1953), p. 97.

retaining, at the same time, the quality and strength of small, well-integrated work groups."[2] How can this be done?

An increasing number of companies are endeavoring to find the answer in a policy of decentralization of decision-making; that is, they are trying to spread the responsibility for final decisions. The methods followed in implementing this policy vary greatly from one company to another. Some companies have decentralized along geographical lines, others by products manufactured, others by management functions, and so on; sometimes these various factors are combined.

In every case, however, certain functions or activities are kept centralized. At General Motors, for instance, the divisions are decentralized both geographically and by products, but the financial and legal functions have remained centralized. At Koppers, where decentralization is also the general rule, the purchasing function is centralized for most products. And in many other companies the personnel function has remained centralized.

Regardless of the specific approach used, all companies face the same two major obstacles to success in their efforts:

1. The difficulty of decentralizing down to a sufficiently small unit. (The decentralized unit of a large corporation is generally of substantial size, often including many plants and several thousand employees. There is little or no decentralization *within* such a unit.)

2. The difficulty of controlling the decentralized unit. (Simplified controls, such as those based essentially on the well-known criterion of "return on investment," often prove to be deceptive and can be applied successfully only to decentralized units of substantial size.)

Useful Concept

It is the purpose of this article to describe the concept of centralized planning and control associated with decentralized authority and responsibility which management can use to overcome these obstacles. This concept reconciles the organization's need for coordinated action with the legitimate aspirations of individuals; and it is applicable to large, small, and medium-size companies alike. Although it is comparatively new, it has gained increasing acceptance in recent years, no doubt due in large part to the results it has secured.

After a brief description of its basic features, three case studies will show how it works in the hands of executives who are under pressure to solve everyday business problems. This will give us a realistic idea of the difficulties and the benefits which can be expected when the concept is applied.

Four Essential Features

There are four essential features of the concept of centralized planning and control in conjunction with decentralized authority and responsibility:

---

[2] Burleigh B. Gardner and David G. Moore, *Human Relations in Industry* (Chicago: Richard D. Irwin, Inc., 1950), p. 402.

Management must functionalize planning and control, centralizing it in a separate department.

Management must make a precise determination of the lines of authority and responsibility.

Management must define clearly the methods by which the various division and department heads can participate in planning.

Management must develop methods of control which are adapted to the need of coordinated action in a decentralized organization.

Now let us examine these points in a little more detail.

Centralized Control

In the process of planning and controlling the complex activities of such specialized departments and functions as purchasing, marketing, engineering, personnel, accounting, and so on, modern management has developed techniques which have themselves become so complex that they have to be handled by specialists. When this need is recognized, general management retains the full responsibility for high policy decisions, for giving directives, for rewarding or penalizing; but the technical activities involved in planning and control are entrusted to a specialized department. Some companies call it the "control department," others the "administrative controls department," and still others merely extend the regular duties of the controller's office to include the new function.

Although the details vary greatly among individual companies, a planning and control department usually has these general functions:

1. It collects the data necessary to general management at the time decisions of high policy are being made — sales estimates, marketing policy, size of inventory, level of employment, financing needs, and so on.

2. It translates high policy decisions into specific assignments. The department heads who receive such assignments are given an opportunity to express their views and may under specified conditions request a change in the scope or the timing of the assignments.

3. It compares the quantity, quality, timing, and costs of actual performance with the specifications in the assignment, and prepares managerial reports based on the comparison. The reports are addressed to the department which has received and accepted the assignment, as well as to executives at high levels of management who are responsible for coordinating action in the organization. Under this centralized approach, in turn, such reports can be kept together in an up-to-date "control book."

Lines of Authority

The translation of high policy into specific assignments for departments or individuals obviously means that someone must make decisions with respect to lines of authority and responsibility. The planning and control department is *not* responsible for decisions of this sort. Rather, they should be made by the top operating executives in the form of permanent operating procedures for the whole organization.

Much has been said about the dangers of specialization. The reader is no doubt familiar with the picture often presented of the conditions prevailing in the average modern plant where no member of management supervises a wide variety of jobs but instead each is restricted to a narrow field of activity. Instead of being left alone with a crew of men as in the "good old times" (which incidentally were not very pleasant times in terms of human relations), the modern foreman sees his activity limited by many specialists — the engineer, the inspector, the personnel director, and so forth. He tends to feel like a small cog in a big wheel.

To some extent this picture is true. Supervisors do often feel frustrated in this way. But in another respect it is misleading. The popular assumption about the cause of the dissatisfaction is not justified. It is not specialization so much as the *lack of communication* that causes supervisors to feel the way they do.

Moreover, it is futile to try to solve the problem by turning the clock back. Specialization is the unavoidable consequence of our industrial civilization. It will get us nowhere to be nostalgic; rather, we must think in terms of constructive adjustment to the needs of today's industrial life. Most certainly we should not ignore the human problem, but we should consider it in the light of the requirements of modern industry.

In sum, we do not need to be afraid of drawing lines of authority and responsibility to meet the needs of specialization if at the same time we keep the lines of communication between the various functions wide open. Then each specialist can visualize in its proper perspective the part he plays in the whole organization, even though his field of authority and responsibility is clearly and, if need be, narrowly defined. Instead of feeling like a cog in a wheel, he can feel like a member of a team — a specialized but eminently useful member.

Participation in Planning

The specialist's feelings of being part of a team are reinforced if he is called upon to participate in the planning of his activities and is given complete independence of action within his field of specialization. These purposes are served and encouraged within the framework of planning and control when the following principles are observed:

1. The planning and control department acts as a service department only. It does not issue orders, but simply translates general decisions into specific assignments. It does not tell each department *how* a certain goal should be reached but defines *what* should be accomplished and *when* it should be done, in order to implement decisions of policy made at a high management level.

2. These specific assignments are initially *proposals.* In actual practice they take the form, for example, of a schedule of material requirements addressed to the purchasing department, or of a schedule of production of finished items addressed to the plant superintendent, or of a schedule of preparation of blueprints for tools addressed to the manager of the tooling department.

Each department manager who receives such an assignment has the privilege of declining it for any valid reasons, such as that the time allowed is too short or the quality is unobtainable. If the department concerned cannot agree with planning and control on a substitute assignment, the matter is referred to a higher level of management as in the case of any controversy between departments in a well-managed organization.

3. To expedite matters and avoid unnecessary meetings, it has been found advantageous to establish the general rule that if the department head who receives the assignment raises no objections to it within a given period, say three or four days, he becomes fully responsible for the performance. At the same time he and his associates are free to choose their own ways and means as long as the goal assigned is reached at the right time, at the right cost, and in accordance with the terms of the assignment or standard specifications.

Methods of Control

The risk involved in the foregoing practices is obvious. A department or an individual is entrusted with a given assignment and left alone in accordance with the principle of decentralization of authority and responsibility. That is fine if he succeeds, but what happens if he fails? Obviously, this is a crucial question.

A partial answer is that the members of the organization should be given the proper training and should have opportunities to develop their ability to handle responsibility. If they can judge wisely what assignments they can fulfill and what they cannot, failures to perform will be rare. Furthermore, they can be asked to give a warning as soon as they have a serious reason to doubt that they will be able to perform as expected. Through this procedure the damaging consequences of an eventual failure can be minimized.

Nevertheless, it is a fact that failure will occur from time to time. A policy of decentralization of authority, based on the concept that individuals may be entrusted with the full responsibility for certain assignments, is acceptable only if the risk entailed by failure is not of excessive magnitude. It is essential, therefore, for control to be exercised at such frequent intervals as is necessary to prevent excessive damage in the case of a failure to perform. This means that there is a limit to how far decentralization can go. To illustrate:

If new tools are required for a certain production run six months hence, the assignment issued to the tool engineer might be broken down into these five stages:

1. Preliminary report and proposed design
2. Cost estimate
3. Blueprint and ordering of materials
4. Test run
5. Delivery of tools to tool room

The planning and control department assigns a deadline to *each* of these steps, using the final deadline set up by top management for a guide, and allowing for a certain safety cushion in the timing. If a delay occurs in the test runs, for instance, it is reported immediately. Proper managerial action by a higher authority can be taken in time to prevent the whole production program from being jeopardized because tools are not available.

Finally, it is in some cases possible and desirable to evaluate in dollars and cents the consequences of a failure to perform. If, for instance, an undue delay occurs in the delivery of materials, the cost of this delay, in terms of dollars of direct labor representing the time lost in the plant, may be recorded in a special report which reflects the responsibility of the purchasing agent in the matter.

Three Case Studies

Now let us turn to three actual cases[3] which illustrate, in narrative form, some of the difficulties and advantages of applying the concept of planning and control associated with decentralized authority and responsibility.

Plant Superintendent

This is the case of a plant superintendent in a plant employing over 700 workers.

Prior to the creation of a planning and control department, the organization of planning was very much neglected. The plant superintendent was accustomed to regulating production on the basis of orders received by the company from its customers and of indications given to him in an informal way by the sales department. He would request the services of the maintenance department when needed; his assistant would keep an eye on the materials in the warehouse; he would anticipate his needs in personnel in time of seasonal peaks and give instructions for future hiring to the personnel department; and so forth. While he complained about being forced into such an exhausting activity, and while he was sincere in his complaint, he actually found it gratifying in many respects.

Then a planning and control department was established. He learned that in the future this department would tell him what items should be produced and when, and that no longer would he have responsibility for materials, tools, personnel, and so on. Instead, he would merely have to requisition from the warehouse; tools would be ready for use the day an item was scheduled for production; and personnel needs would be anticipated on the basis of future production programs without requiring his intervention. Quite naturally, he felt as if he had been demoted.

It soon became apparent that his area of authority had in fact decreased; to this extent his first reactions were confirmed. Granted, his authority was

---

[3] Adapted from the author's book, *The Dynamics of Industrial Management* (New York: Funk & Wagnalls Company, 1954).

more clearly defined. But he was no longer negotiating with the sales department about a rush order, or with the tooling department about urgent requirements, or with the purchasing department about needed materials. He was told what to produce and when.

Yet if his authority had decreased in *surface*, it had increased in *depth*. He soon noticed that, within his own field of responsibility, he had more stature as a manager than before. No one at a higher level would suggest to him that he should, for instance, instruct his foremen to watch more carefully the quality of production or the productivity of their workers — subjects which had in the past been a frequent source of controversy between him and his vice president. He was shown the results obtained in his plant in more detail than he had ever known in terms of cost, rejects, sales returns, absenteeism, turnover, and so on; but this was information rather than interference, for it was left to him to improve the situation, as needed, in his own way.

In turn, he learned to apply similar principles in his relationships with his foremen; and, thanks to the planning and control department, he had more data with which to control their performance objectively.

After about a year this plant superintendent came to the conclusion that he had gained in independence of action and that his real responsibility had increased. He concentrated willingly and with sincere satisfaction on his newly defined assignment. In retrospect, that things turned out this way seems to be due in large part to two factors, which experience indicates are essential to the successful centralization of planning and decentralization of responsibility:

1. Centralized planning was limited to a service activity; it did not operate as an order-issuing agency.

2. Informal relationships developed between specialized functions — e.g., between the plant superintendent and the head of the tooling department — which made it possible for them to work together despite the fact that neither had authority over the other.

Purchasing Agent

In this case (all names disguised), Richards was the purchasing agent in a highly centralized company, the Rigid Corporation. The president of the company was in the habit of checking every move of his executives. He would call Richards at any time of the day, and sometimes in the evening at his home: "Have you written to the supplier about that problem we discussed this morning?" Or, "Don't write; go and see him." Or, "Don't tell him this; rather, take it from that angle. . . ." He would also make remarks implying that his executives were not punctual, such as, "I called you half an hour ago, but you had not yet arrived."

Richards' salary was good and his job secure, but after ten years he finally decided that the situation was hopeless, and he quit at the first opportunity. He went to the Hart Manufacturing Company as purchasing agent. His predecessor there had been transferred prior to his arrival and was not available to instruct him about the details of his new job.

The Hart Manufacturing Company had been reorganized two years before. A planning and control department had been created, and a policy of decentralization of authority had been adopted. Having served as an advisor to the company, the writer was asked to initiate Richards. The initiation went much as follows:

> From what you tell me, I would say that you will find that the methods of management at the Hart Manufacturing Company are almost exactly the opposite of those you were used to at the Rigid Corporation. You will find that no one here will check how you are doing your job.
>
> Ralph, whom you met this morning, is the head of the planning and control department. He will tell you what materials are needed for production and when. Every six months he will give you a general purchasing program and you will place the orders. You get the specifications from the engineering department. You select the suppliers yourself. You decide yourself about what prices you want to pay.
>
> You will find that for most materials used we have standard prices. The variance between the price you pay and the standards are carefully followed up by Ralph's department and reported both to you and to your vice president, who keeps in touch with the market and will step in if he feels that the prices you are paying are too high. Incidentally, if you find a way of getting lower prices, he will step in, too — to congratulate you.
>
> But, in any case, he will step in *after* you, under your own responsibility, have placed the purchase order, not before — unless you turn to him for advice, which you may do at any time. In some exceptional cases, he may take the initiative; but you will find this a very rare occurence.
>
> For planning purposes the weeks of the year are designated by consecutive numbers. Every week you will receive a release schedule which will tell you what materials, on order but not yet delivered, are needed for production during each of the following eight weeks. As you know, we are short of materials. [This was a few months after the outbreak of the war in Korea.] This release schedule is therefore a very important matter. Check it carefully when you receive it. If you do not call Ralph within a few days after you received it, you are considered as having accepted it.
>
> It then becomes your responsibility to supply the materials on time. Any delay will disrupt production. The cost of the disruption will be evaluated by the planning and control department and will be charged against your department.

At this point, Richards asked two questions and received the following answers:

Question: You know how suppliers are. They may say "yes" and yet they don't deliver. They may just say "perhaps." What do you want me to tell

Ralph, when I receive his release schedule, in a situation where I am 50-50 sure?

Answer: Your position is fully appreciated. But you must realize that, in the whole organization, you are *the one* who is in the best position to evaluate the situation. Now, someone has to take responsibility. As you know, a plant cannot have a "perhaps" production schedule or "perhaps" tools on hand or a "perhaps" machine setup. It has to be "yes" or "no." Sometimes we will be disappointed. Everyone agrees that it can happen that you will say "yes," and yet the material will not be there on time. But that doesn't lessen your responsibility.

The real issue is how often it will occur and what the damage will be. At the end of the year, two accounts will tell the whole story. The price-variance account will show how active you have been in getting good prices. The time-lost account will show how reliable your deliveries to the production department have been.

In addition, of course, we expect that your materials will be up to specifications — and that you will not systematically protect yourself by refusing to accept Ralph's release schedules.

Question: What do I do if I think that I cannot get the material on time?

Answer: You call Ralph and tell him so. Nine times out of ten, even more often than that, you will settle the matter between yourselves by changing the production schedule. Your release schedules are issued weekly for an eight-week period. As a rule, this gives you at least four weeks' advance notice, inasmuch as we avoid changing the coming four weeks unless it is absolutely necessary. Now, if you and Ralph cannot see eye to eye, the matter will have to be referred to the executive committee, but you will find that Ralph is pretty good at solving problems.

By the way, let me make this clear to you. Ralph is no more your boss than you are his. If the foreman of the tool room needs to purchase anything, you know that he is not permitted to go and buy it outside. He must send *you* a requisition. Now, this does not make you his boss. You are the head of another service department. The release schedule he sends you is a service he renders to you and to the whole organization. It is important for you to understand the spirit in which his department functions.

You will find that the control you are submitted to is very detailed, but it is objective. You receive an assignment. You may accept it or reject it. But if you accept, you must perform. There is no excuse for a failure — no argument, either. If you fail, the damage is evaluated. We all make mistakes. The important point is to avoid making too many mistakes and also to understand fully that this extensive control is the necessary balance to the great freedom of action you are being given.

No one will ask you at what time you arrive in your office, why you did not show up last Thursday, or whether you have neglected to write to this or that supplier. You are your own boss as far as your function is concerned.

Failure and Resentment. About three months elapsed. Richards was delighted. A new life had started for him. He felt like himself again — no fears, a real feeling of independence. He worked harder than ever, but he worked really for himself.

During Week No. 24 he was advised that Part No. 1234 — a critical part — would be needed for assembly on Tuesday morning, Week No. 32. He found that the regular supplier could not deliver. He called everywhere, finally found a supplier in the Middle West, and accepted the commitment.

He followed up by mail. Yes, the supplier assured him, the part would be ready. The matter was so important that on Thursday of Week No. 31 he checked by phone. Yes, the shipment had left on time. Richards was reassured and did not check further. But on Tuesday of Week No. 32 the part was not in the warehouse. Inquiry revealed that the shipment had been misdirected by the railroad company and was still in Chicago.

The writer was asked to "arbitrate" the case and decided that the time lost in the plant should be charged to the purchasing department. Certainly the plant manager could not be asked to underwrite a loss due to failure of delivery over which he had no supervision.

Richards listened attentively and smiled politely as the decision was explained. But obviously he felt that an injustice had been committed; he was bitterly disappointed. He said that he thought he had done all he possibly could. It did no good to remind him that he had performed very well in the past and would certainly perform well again in the future.

From that point on Richards' attitude was changed.

New Understanding. Some time later, while teaching his course in industrial engineering at Columbia University, the writer was describing to his students the advantages of centralizing planning and control in conjunction with decentralizing authority and responsibility. In all fairness to the students, he felt they should be told that at least in one specific case the plan had not worked well. He invited Richards to come as a guest lecturer and present the other side of the picture. Here is what happened:

Class time was 9.00 a.m. Shortly before, Richards entered the writer's office. He was smiling and looking forward to the chance to let off steam. "Don't hesitate to tell them how you feel," he was told. "Don't beat around the bush."

Richards smiled; he certainly would take full advantage of the opportunity. He said he would tell them he liked the idea in general, but that you should not go too far with it. Suddenly he stopped talking and looked worried.

"May I use your phone to place a long-distance call to the office?" he asked. "I just forgot to tell them I would not be in today."

It was the writer's turn to smile. "I should like to ask you one question. In your previous job, at the Rigid Corporation, would you have forgotten to tell them that you were not coming?"

"Certainly not," he said. "I would have requested permission three weeks in advance, and most probably the permission would have been refused."

The suggestion was made: "Why don't you tell that to the class, too?"

Richards' face changed. He was obviously thinking deeply. "Oh," he said, "I think I see the point."

The session in class was rather different from what had been expected. The students were surprised to hear a guest lecturer who, contrary to their expectation, was not at all critical of the concept they were studying!

Plant Variance

In a certain organization, objections were being made to a report which the planning and control department was putting out.

This report was a weekly analysis of the variance between the actual direct labor payroll in the assembly department and what the payroll would have been if all goods had been produced at standard cost. The planning and control department was in charge of assigning to each department concerned the responsibility for a portion of the variance. The maintenance department would be responsible for breakdown, the purchasing department for lack of material, the sales department for rush orders, the plant management for time lost and so on. Virtually the whole variance could thus be accounted for.

The cost of this report was considered excessive by some executives. It required, at that time, almost the whole attention of two clerks and about eight hours of IBM equipment. For a certain period, the report was issued without bringing any return; and some executives remarked sarcastically, "What is the use of knowing where we are losing money if we lose it anyway?"

After a few months, however, their attitude changed. The first beneficial effect of the report was that it eliminated a source of friction that had for years cast a shadow over the relationships between sales and production, namely, requests for rush orders. It is the rare executive who is not familiar with this kind of problem.

The sales department requests a rush production. The plant scheduler argues that it will disrupt his production and cost a substantial though not clearly determined amount of money. The answer coming from sales is: "Do you want to take the responsibility of losing the X Company as a customer?" Of course the production scheduler does not want to take such a responsibility, and he gives up, but not before a heavy exchange of arguments and the accumulation of a substantial backlog of ill feeling.

Analysis of the payroll in the assembly department, determining the costs involved in getting out rush orders, eliminated the cause for argument. Henceforth, any rush order was accepted with a smile by the production schedulers, who made sure that the extra cost would be duly recorded and charged to the sales department — "no questions asked." As a result, the tension created by rush orders disappeared completely; and, somehow, the number of rush orders requested by the sales department was progressively reduced to an insignificant level.

Even more spectacular was the virtual total elimination of a "plant variance" of almost $1,000 a week. Everyone in the organization knew that the labor expense in the assembly department was much higher than the standard; but the causes were so numerous and their relative impact so undetermined that every executive or supervisor was sincerely convinced that he was *not* the one who could help. But when the head of the assembly department was shown that $1,000 a week was attributable to time lost in his department, he realized that this was really his responsibility. So he reorganized entirely his procedures of job assignment and made it a point every week to study the payroll analysis report at a meeting he held with his foremen.

After six months the plant variance had virtually disappeared. The savings resulting from that factor alone more than compensated for the cost of the whole analysis.

Conclusion

As the foregoing cases indicate, neither specialization nor control presents insurmountable obstacles to the free development of human personality in our modern industrial organizations. It is true that specialization narrows the *area* of responsibility of each executive, but it does not necessarily lessen the *depth* of his authority. Within his field, he may have more responsibility and leeway than his predecessors of earlier years. Much the same applies to control. Contrary to a widespread prejudice, born of the many abuses that have been committed in the past, control is not by itself a hindrance to individual freedom. Rather, control is in fact a prerequisite to decentralization, and without decentralization there can be no real freedom.

The high-ranking executive who is responsible for the operations of large sections of an industrial organization and who is not in a position to make use of effective controls, tends to be tyrannical because he is worried. He will give much greater independence to his subordinates if he knows that their mistakes will be detected before any irreparable damage results. That is a key function of the concept described in this article — centralized planning and control in conjunction with decentralized authority and responsibility.

This concept is not, however, a substitute for good management. It is only a tool of management. Like any other tool, it may be misused; and precisely because it is effective, it may become dangerous. It may become an instrument of oppression if excessive emphasis is placed on "control"; or it may become the source of serious disruptions if, on the contrary, "decentralization" is overemphasized.

At the same time, experience shows that this concept, if applied with skill and moderation, provides a solution to the strange dilemma in which industrial management finds itself today. Management can use the concept to reconcile the technical necessity for planning and control with the pressing need for good human relations in industry.

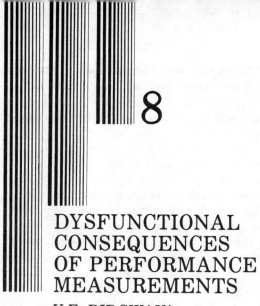

8

DYSFUNCTIONAL CONSEQUENCES OF PERFORMANCE MEASUREMENTS

V.F. RIDGWAY*

There is today a strong tendency to state numerically as many as possible of the variables with which management must deal. The mounting interest in and application of tools such as operations research, linear programming, and statistical decision-making, all of which require quantifiable variables, foster the idea that if progress toward goals can be measured, efforts and resources can be more rationally managed. This has led to the development of quantitative performance measurements for all levels within organizations, up to and including measurements of the performance of a division manager with profit responsibility in a decentralized company. Measurements at lower levels in the organization may be in terms of amount of work, quality of work, time required, and so on.

Quantitative measures of performance are tools, and are undoubtedly useful. But research indicates that indiscriminate use and undue confidence and reliance in them result from insufficient knowledge of the full effects and consequences. Judicious use of a tool requires awareness of possible side effects and reactions. Otherwise, indiscriminate use may result in side effects and reactions outweighing the benefits, as was the case when penicillin was first hailed as a wonder drug. The cure is sometimes worse than the disease.

It seems worthwhile to review the current scattered knowledge of the dysfunctional consequences resulting from the imposition of a system of performance measurements. For the purpose of analyzing the impact of performance measurements upon job performance, we can consider separately single, multiple, and composite criteria. Single criteria occur when only one

* From *Administrative Science Quarterly* (September 1956), pp. 240-47. Reprinted by permission of the Managing Editor. The author was a professor when this article was written.

quantity is measured and observed, such as total output or profit. Multiple criteria occur when several quantities are measured simultaneously, such as output, quality, cost, safety, waste, and so forth. Composite criteria occur when the separate quantities are weighted in some fashion and then added or averaged.

Single Criteria

A single criterion of performance was in use in a public employment agency studied by Peter M. Blau.[1] The agency's responsibility was "to serve workers seeking employment and employers seeking workers." Employment interviewers were appraised by the number of interviews they conducted. Thus the interviewer was motivated to complete as many interviews as he could, but not to spend adequate time in locating jobs for the clients. The organization's goal of placing clients in jobs was not given primary consideration because the measurement device applied to only one aspect of the activity.

Blau reports another case in a federal law enforcement agency which investigated business establishments. Here he found that work schedules were distorted by the imposition of a quota of eight cases per month for each investigator. Toward the end of the month an investigator who found himself short of the eight cases would pick easy, fast cases to finish that month and save the lengthier cases till the following month. Priority of the cases for investigation was based on length of the case rather than urgency, as standards of impartiality would require. This is one of many instances in which the existence of an "accounting period" adversely affects the overall goal accomplishment of the organization.

Chris Argyris also reports this tendency to use easy jobs as fillers toward the end of a period in order to meet a quota.[2] In this case, a factory supervisor reported that they "feed the machines all the easy orders" toward the end of the month, rather than finish them in the sequence in which they were received. Such a practice may lead to undue delay of the delivery of some customers' orders, perhaps the most profitable orders.

David Granick's study of Soviet management reveals how the attention and glory that accrue to a plant manager when he can set a new monthly production record in one month leads to the neglect of repairs and maintenance, so that in ensuing months there will be a distinct drop in production.[3] Similarly, the output of an entire plant may be allowed to fall off in order to create conditions under which one worker can make a production record, when the importance of such a record is considered greater than overall plant production.

[1] Peter M. Blau *The Dynamics of Bureaucracy* (Chicago, Ill.: U. of Chicago Pr., 1955).
[2] Chris Argyris, *The Impact of Budgets on People* (Ithaca, N.Y.: Cornell U., 1952).
[3] David Granick, *Management of the Industrial Firm in the U.S.S.R.* (New York: Columbia U. Pr., 1954).

Joseph S. Berliner's report on Soviet business administration points out sharply how the accounting period has an adverse effect upon management decisions.[4] The use of monthly productions quotas causes "storming" at the end of the month to reach the quota. Repairs and maintenance are postponed until the following month, so that production lags in the early part of the month, and storming must again be resorted to in the following month. This has impact upon the rate of production for suppliers and customers who are forced into a fluctuating rate of operations with its attendant losses and wastes.

Standard costs as a criterion of performance are a frequent source of dissatisfaction in manufacturing plants.[5] The "lumpiness" of indirect charges that are allocated to the plants or divisions (indirect charges being unequal from month to month), variations in quality and cost of raw materials, or other factors beyond the control of the operating manager, coupled with inaccuracies and errors in the apportionment of indirect charges, cause distrust of the standards. A typical reaction of operating executives in such cases seems to be to seek explanations and justifications. Consequently, considerable time and energy is expended in discussion and debate about the correctness of charges. Only "wooden money" savings accrue when charges are shifted to other accounts and there is no increase in company profits. It should be pointed out, however, that having charges applied to the proper departments may have the advantage of more correctly directing attention to problem areas.

Granick discusses two measures of the success of the Soviet firm which have been considered and rejected as overall measures by Soviet industrial leaders and economists.[6] The first, cost-reduction per unit of product, is considered inadequate because it does not provide a basis for evaluating new products. Further, variations in amount of production affect the cost-reduction index because of the finer division of overhead costs, quality changes, and assortment. The second overall measure of a firm's performance, profitability, has been rejected as the basic criterion on the grounds that it is affected in the short run by factors outside the control of management, such as shortages of supplies. Profitability as a measure of success led to a reduction in experimental work and deemphasized the importance of production quantity, quality, and assortment. Neither cost-reduction nor profitability was acceptable alone; each was only a partial index. The Soviets had concluded by 1940 that no single measure of success of a firm is adequate in itself and that there is no substitute for genuine analysis of all the elements entering into a firm's work.

Difficulties with single criteria have been observed in operations research, where one of the principal sources of difficulty is considered to be

[4] Joseph S. Berliner, "A Problem in Soviet Business Management," *Administrative Science Quarterly*, 1 (1956), pp. 86-101.
[5] H.A. Simon, H. Guetzkow, G. Kozmetsky, G. Tyndall, *Centralization vs. Decentralization in Organizing the Controller's Department* (New York, 1954).
[6] Granick, *op. cit.*

the choice of proper criteria for performance measurement.[7] The difficulty of translating the several alternatives into their full effect upon the organization's goal forces the operations researcher to settle for a criterion more manageable than profit maximization, but less appropriate. The efficiency of a subgroup of the organization may be improved in terms of some plausible test, yet the organization's efficiency in terms of its major goal may be decreased.

In all the studies mentioned above, the inadequacy of a single measure of performance is evident. Whether this is a measure of an employee at the working level, or a measure of management, attention is directed away from the overall goal. The existence of a measure of performance motivates individuals to effort, but the effort may be wasted, as in seeking "wooden money" savings, or may be detrimental to the organization's goal, as in rushing through interviews, delaying repairs, and rejecting profitable opportunities.

Multiple Measurements

Recognition of the inadequacies of a single measure of success or performance leads organizations to develop several criteria. It is felt then that all aspects of the job will receive adequate attention and emphasis so that efforts of individuals will not be distorted.

A realization in the employment office studied by Blau that job referrals and placements were also important led eventually to their inclusion in measuring the performance of the interviewers.[8] Merely counting the number of referrals and placements had led to wholesale indiscriminate referrals, which did not accomplish the employment agency's screening function. Therefore, to stress the qualitative aspects of the interviewer's job, several ratios (of referrals to interviews, placements to interviews, and placements to referrals) were devised. Altogether there were eight quantities that were counted or calculated for each interviewer. This increase in quantity and complexity of performance measurements was felt necessary to give emphasis to all aspects of the interviewer's job.

Granick relates that no single criterion was universally adopted in appraising Soviet management.[9] Some managers were acclaimed for satisfying production quotas while violating labor laws. Others were removed from office for violating quality and assortment plans while fulfilling production quotas. Apparently there is a ranking of importance of these multiple criteria. In a typical interfirm competition the judges were provided with a long list of indexes. These included production of finished goods in the planned assortment, an even flow of production as between ten-day periods and as

---

[7] Charles Hitch and Roland McKean, "Suboptimization in Operations Problems" in J.F. McCloskey and Flora F. Trefethen (eds.), *Operations Research for Management* (Baltimore, Md., 1954).

[8] Blau, *op. cit.*

[9] Granick, *op. cit.*

between months, planned mastery of new types of products, improvement in product quality and reduction in waste, economy of materials through improved design and changing of technological processes, fulfillment of labor productivity tasks and lowering of unit cost, keeping within the established wage fund, and increase in the number of worker suggestions for improvements in work methods and conditions and their adoption into operation. But no indication of how these indexes should be weighted was given. The preeminence of such indexes as quantity, quality, assortment of production, and remaining within the firm's allotment of materials and fuels brought some order into the otherwise chaotic picture. The presence of "campaigns" and "priorities" stressing one or more factors also has aided Soviet management in deciding which elements of its work are at the moment most important.

Without a single overall composite measure of success, however, there is no way of determining whether the temporarily increased effort on the "campaign" criteria of the month represents new effort or merely effort shifted from other criteria. And the intangibility of some of these indexes makes it impossible to judge whether there has been decreased effort on other aspects. Hence even in a campaign period the relative emphases may become so unbalanced as to mitigate or defeat the purpose of the campaign.

The Soviet manager is working then under several measurements and the relative influence or emphasis attached to any one measurement varies from firm to firm and from month to month. Profits and production are used, among other measurements, and these two may lead to contradictory managerial decisions. Granick hypothesizes that some managers have refused complicated orders that were difficult to produce because it would mean failure to produce the planned quantities. Acceptance of these orders would have been very profitable, but of the two criteria, production quantity took precedence.

Numerous American writers in the field of management have stressed the importance of multiple criteria in evaluating performance of management. Peter Drucker, for example, lists market standing, innovation, productivity, physical and financial resources, profitability, manager performance and development, worker performance and attitude, and public responsibility.[10] This list includes many of the same items as the list used by Soviet management.

The consensus at a round-table discussion of business and professional men[11] was that although return on investment is important, additional criteria are essential for an adequate appraisal of operating departments. These other criteria are fairly well summed up in Drucker's list above.

Thus we see that the need for multiple criteria is recognized and that they are employed at different levels of the organization — lower levels as in the

---

[10] Peter F. Drucker, *The Practice of Management* (New York: Harper & Row, 1954).
[11] William H. Newman and James P. Logan, *Management of Expanding Enterprises* (New York: Columbia U. Pr., 1955).

employment agency, higher levels as considered by Granick and Drucker. At all levels these multiple measurements or criteria are intended to focus attention on the many facets of a particular job.

The use of multiple criteria assumes that the individual will commit his or the organization's efforts, attention, and resources in greater measure to those activities which promise to contribute the greatest improvement to over-all performance. There must then exist a theoretical condition under which an additional unit of effort or resources would yield equally desirable results in over-all performance, whether applied to production, quality, research, safety, public relations, or any of the other suggested areas. This would be the condition of "balanced stress on objectives" to which Drucker refers.

Without a single over-all composite measure of performance, the individual is forced to rely upon his judgment as to whether increased effort on one criterion improves over-all performance, or whether there may be a reduction in performance on some other criterion which will outweigh the increase in the first. This is quite possible for in any immediate situation many of these objectives may be contradictory to each other.

Composites

To adequately balance the stress on the contradictory objectives or criteria by which performance of a particular individual or organization is appraised, there must be an implied or explicit weighting of these criteria. When such a weighting system is available, it is an easy task to combine the measures of the various subgoals into a composite score for over-all performance.

Such a composite is used by the American Institute of Management in evaluating and ranking the managements of corporations, hospitals, and other organizations.[12] These ratings are accomplished by attaching a numerical grade to each of several criteria, such as economic function, corporate structure, production efficiency, and the like. Each criterion has an optimum rating, and the score on each for any particular organization is added to obtain a total score. Although there may be disagreement on the validity of the weighting system employed, the rating given on any particular category, the categories themselves, or the methods of estimating scores in the A.I.M. management audit, this system is an example of the type of over-all performance measurement which might be developed. Were such a system of ratings employed by an organization and found acceptable by management, it presumably would serve as a guide to obtaining a balanced stress on objectives.

A composite measure of performance was employed in Air Force wings as reported by K.C. Wagner.[13] A complex rating scheme covering a wide

---

[12] *Manual of Excellent Managements* (New York, 1955).
[13] Kenneth C. Wagner, "Latent Functions of an Executive Control: A Sociological Analysis of a Social System Under Stress," *Research Previews,* Vol. 2 (Chapel Hill: Institute for Research in Social Science, March, 1954), mimeo.

range of activities was used. When the organizations were put under pressure to raise their composite score without proportionate increases in the organization's means of achieving them, there were observable unanticipated consequences in the squadrons. Under a system of multiple criteria, pressure to increase performance on one criterion might be relieved by a slackening of effort toward other criteria. But with a composite criterion this does not seem as likely to occur. In Wagner's report individuals were subjected to tension, role and value conflicts, and reduced morale; air crews suffered from intercrew antagonism, apathy, and reduced morale; organization and power structures underwent changes; communications distortions and blockages occurred; integration decreased; culture patterns changed; and norms were violated. Some of these consequences may be desirable, some undesirable. The net result, however, might easily be less effective over-all performance.

These consequences were observable in a situation where goals were increased without a corresponding increase in means, which seems to be a common situation. Berliner refers to the "ratchet principle" wherein an increase in performance becomes the new standard, and the standard is thus continually raised. Recognition of the operation of the "ratchet principle" by workers was documented by F.J. Roethlisberger and William J. Dickson.[14] There was a tacit agreement among the workers not to exceed the quota, for fear that the job would then be rerated. Deliberate restriction of output is not an uncommon occurrence.

Although the experiences reported with the use of composite measures of performance are rather skimpy, there is still a clear indication that their use may have adverse consequences for the over-all performance of the organization.

Conclusion

Quantitative performance measurements — whether single, multiple, or composite — are seen to have undesirable consequences for over-all organizational performance. The complexity of large organizations requires better knowledge of organizational behavior for managers to make best use of the personnel available to them. Even where performance measures are instituted purely for purposes of information, they are probably interpreted as definitions of the important aspects of that job or activity and hence have important implications for the motivation of behavior. The motivational and behavioral consequences of performance measurements are inadequately understood. Further research in this area is necessary for a better understanding of how behavior may be oriented toward optimum accomplishment of the organization's goals.

---

[14] F.J. Roethlisberger and William J. Dickson, *Management and the Worker* (Cambridge, Mass: Harvard U. Pr., 1939).

9

DIVISIONAL PERFORMANCE MEASUREMENT: BEYOND AN EXCLUSIVE PROFIT TEST

LEE D. PARKER*

The measurement of divisional performance in decentralised companies has come to be generally practised by means of a single index of divisional profitability. Accountants have traditionally been placed in the position of designing or adopting a measure of division performance which best 'represents top management objectives'.[1] This has been seen to be best represented by some form of divisional profit index in accordance with accountants' concentration upon the profit goal of the firm.[2] Divisional performance measurement literature has therefore concentrated upon the development and use of a single index of divisional success couched in terms of profit. Alternative indices of divisional profit which have become generally accepted include:

1. Division Net Profit
2. Division Controllable Profit
3. Division Contribution Margin
4. Return on Investment
5. Residual Income[3]

---

* From *Accounting and Business Research* (Autumn 1979). Reprinted by permission of the editor and author, a senior lecturer at Monash University.

[1] C.T. Horngren, *Cost Accounting: A Managerial Emphasis,* Prentice-Hall, 4th Edition, 1977, p. 709.
[2] G. Shillinglaw, *Managerial Cost Accounting,* Richard D. Irwin, 4th Edition, 1977, p. 777.
[3] C.L. Moore and R.K. Jaedicke, *Managerial Accounting,* South Western Publishing Company, 4th Edition, 1976, pp. 517-520.

This approach to divisional performance measurement is based to a large degree upon accountants' acceptance of the concept of goal congruence which for instance Horngren[4] defines as achieved when a corporate accounting system specifies goals and subgoals to encourage behaviour such that individuals accept top management goals as their personal goals. This paper extends the argument against the validity of this goal congruence concept to argue that the current accounting approach to divisional performance measurement is biased, narrow and unrealistic in view of the range of objectives towards which any one division strives. This argument is further extended to consider the single divisional profit index as an instrument of top management control and the conflicts with divisional autonomy which that may involve. The alternative presented by this paper therefore is a return to the development of multiple measures of divisional success criteria of a quantitative and qualitative type.

Goal Congruence Questioned

The arguments against the efficacy of the goal congruence concept can be summarised as follows.[5] Accountants' belief in their responsibility for encouraging goal congruence among managers has its origins in part in their unitary view of the business enterprise. On the other hand many organisation theorists hold a pluralist view of the business enterprise[6] in that it is comprised of a coalition of individuals and groups who cooperate to go some distance towards achieving their separate objectives. It can therefore be argued that a company is a coalition of which top management is only one part, where a whole range of aspirations are continually juggled and balanced.

The difference between the unitary and coalition views of the firm is largely attributable to the progression of concepts of the firm developed from the classical economic and management schools around 1900 to 1939 to the more behavioural perspective of the modern organisation theorists around 1940 to 1970. The classical unitary view emanated from the works of such writers as Max Weber[7] and Frederick Taylor,[8] while the behavioural perspective can be assembled from the works of a considerable body of researchers such as Mayo, Merton, Selznick, Maslow, Gouldner, Simon and

---

4 C.T. Horngren, *op. cit.*, p. 151.
5 For a fuller discussion of this view refer to L.D. Parker, 'Goal Congruence: A Misguided Accounting Concept', *Abacus*, June 1976, pp. 3-13.
6 Refer to A. Fox 'Industrial Relations: A Social Critique of Pluralist Ideology' in *Man and Organization*, J. Child (ed.), George Allen and Unwin, London, 1973, pp. 185-199.
7 Refer for instance to M. Weber, 'Legitimate Authority and Bureaucracy', reprinted in *Organization Theory*, D.S. Pugh (ed.), Penguin 1971, pp. 15-29.
8 F.W. Taylor, *The Principles of Scientific Management*, New York, 1913.

March, McGregor, Argyris, and Tannenbaum.[9] The classical economic/ management theories of the firm are built upon the principles of division of labour, chain of command, line and staff structure and span of control.[10] The firm is viewed as an entrepreneur who seeks to maximise the firm's profit by rationally deciding upon courses of action with full knowledge of available alternatives.[11] This classical perspective is limited, however, by its concentration upon the formal structure of organisation and by its neglect of individual personality, informal groups, intrafirm conflicts and decision processes.[12] The modern organisation theory approach, however, focusing primarily on human organisation and relying more upon empirical research data, investigates strategic parts of the organisation's subsystems, their interrelatedness, and their goals.[13] The frame of reference adopted is described as behavioural and it argues that:

1. The firm of itself does not act. Only its personnel act.
2. Behaviour is conditioned by personality as well as environmental factors.
3. Behavioural processes of organisation members are a function of their cognitions, perceptions, beliefs and knowledge.
4. Rewards or goals are often complex.[14]

In seeking to promote goal congruence (rather than a looser form of co-ordination for instance) through divisional performance measurement, accountants are adhering to a predominantly classical view of organisations. (This will be demonstrated further in this paper with reference to the accounting literature on divisional performance measurement.) Their perspective of divisional performance measurement would be more amenable to modification if they incorporated more of the modern organisation theory views into their thinking. In this way, the divisionalised firm could be considered in terms of the goals, motivations and decisions of its participants who form a bargaining, equilibrium-seeking, decision-making system.[15]

---

[9] Refer for instance to E. Mayo, *The Social Problems of an Industrial Civilisation*, Harvard, Boston, 1945; R.K. Merton, 'Bureaucratic Structure and Personality', in *A Sociological Reader on Complex Organisations*, A. Etzioni (ed.), Holt Rinehart and Winston, 1970, pp. 47-59; P. Selznick, 'Foundations of the Theory of Organisations', reprinted in *Systems Thinking*, F.E. Emery (ed.), Penguin Modern Management Readings, 1969, pp. 261-267; A.H. Maslow, *Motivation and Personality*, Harper, New York, 1954; A.W. Gouldner, *Patterns of Industrial Bureaucracy*, Free Press, Glencoe, Illinois, 1954; J.G. March and H.A. Simon, *Organizations*, Wiley, New York, 1958; D. McGregor, *The Human Side of Enterprise*, McGraw-Hill, New York, 1960; C. Argyris, *Integrating the Individual and the Organisation*, Wiley, New York, 1964; and A.S. Tannenbaum, *Social Psychology of the Work Organisation*, Tavistock, London, 1966.
[10] W.G. Scott, 'Organization Theory: An Overview and an Appraisal', in *Organisations: Structure and Behavior*, Vol. 1, 2n Edn, J.A. Litterer (ed.), Wiley, New York, pp. 16-17.
[11] J.W. McGuire, *Theories of Business Behavior*, Prentice-Hall, Englewood Cliffs, NJ, 1964, pp. 19-20.
[12] W.G. Scott, *op. cit.*, pp. 16-17.
[13] *Ibid.*, pp. 21-25.
[14] J.W. McGuire, *op. cit.*, pp. 27-28.
[15] M. Schiff and A.Y. Lewin, *Behavioral Aspects of Accounting*, Prentice-Hall, Englewood Cliffs, NJ, 1974, pp. 4-5.

Organisation and administrative theorists have further recognised that a single dominant enterprise goal is unlikely to be discovered and have argued for the simultaneous existence of a whole range of corporate goals some of which may even conflict.[16] It is arguable, for instance, whether an organisation can be conceived as having 'a goal'. An individual can be approached to determine his goals, but an organisation cannot be approached in the same way.[17] Instead, the 'coalition' view of the organisation allows the recognition of organisational goals which reflect the demands of an often conflicting coalition. Thus Schiff and Lewin[18] point out that these goals need not be internally consistent with each other, that they may vary in terms of prescription of action and measures of success and that they are the outcome of bargaining processes. This state of affairs reflects the fact that individuals provide the organisation with goals and skills.[19] The composition of an organisation's 'goal set' at any point of time will then reflect the bargaining power and position of its subcoalitions and the extent of consensus reached.[20] Empirical evidence for the existence of an organisational 'goal set' and some determinants of its components has been available as far back as 1959.[21]

The economic model of profit maximisation which is usually utilised in accountants' treatment of goal congruence as the predominant goal of the firm has also been questioned from time to time.[22] Its assumptions of the rational decision-maker is at odds with the perspectives adopted by psychologists, sociologists and anthropologists and its assumption of certainty about future outcomes has been criticised as being unrealistic. The observed tendency of individuals to adopt satisficing behaviour[23] provides further doubt as to the ability of companies to act as true profit maximisers. Huff and McGuire[24] point out that empirical studies as far back as 1939 have indicated that businessmen do not even know how to begin, in the uncertain

---

[16] Refer to C. Perrow, *Complex Organizations. A Critical Essay*, Scott Foresman, Glenview, Illinois, 1972, pp. 160-163 and R.L. Smith, *Management Through Accounting*, Prentice- Hall, Englewood Cliffs, NJ, 1962, pp. 228-229.
[17] D. Silverman, *The Theory of Organisations: A Sociological Framework*, Heinemann, London, 1970, p. 9.
[18] M. Schiff and A.Y. Lewin, *op. cit.*, pp. 5-7.
[19] R.D. Lansbury and P. Gilmour, *Organisations: An Australian Perspective*, Longman Cheshire, Melbourne, 1977, p. 83.
[20] M. Schiff and A.Y. Lewin, *op. cit.*, p. 7.
[21] Refer to a study conducted by J.K. Dent, 'Organizational Correlates of the Goals of Business Management', *Personnel Psychology*, 1959, pp. 365-393.
[22] Refer to J.W. McGuire, 'The Finalité of Business', in *Management and the Behavioral Sciences*, M.S. Wadia (ed.), Allyn and Bacon, Boston, 1968, p. 383 and M.F. Cantley, 'The Choice of Corporate Objectives', *Long Range Planning*, September 1970, pp. 36-42.
[23] C. Perrow, *op. cit.*, p. 149.
[24] D.L. Huff and J.W. McGuire, 'The Interdisciplinary Approach to the Study of Business', reprinted in *Management and Organizational Behavior Theories: An Interdisciplinary Approach*, W.T. Greenwood (ed.), South Western Publishing Co., Cincinnatti, Ohio, 1965, pp. 94-95. They cite the empirical studies of R.L. Hall and C.J. Hitch, 'Price Theory and Business Behavior,' *Oxford Economic Papers*, May 1939 and R.A. Lester, 'Shortcomings of Marginal Analysis for Wage-Employment Problems', *American Economic Review*, March, 1946.

real world, to maximise profits. Indeed goals have been likened to rationalisations of prior actions[25] which raises the question as to whether a goal is a means to an end rather than an end in itself.

An alternative view of corporate functioning therefore emerges. The company may be viewed as a coalition in which participants continually bargain for the composition of a set of corporate goals which continually change in response to the bargaining process and in response to personnel entering and leaving the company. That is to say, accountants must recognise that goal setting is essentially a human-political process. Top management's long term goals may not be shared by division managers. Goals are formulated by individual personnel, groups, departments, divisions etc., so that corporate goals may be at least in part formulated in response to pressures from all levels of the organisational hierarchy. This observation leads Leavitt *et al*[26] to argue that organisational goals are set to a large extent through internal negotiation among organisational subunits. Corporate goals therefore become a set of short term stabilisers for expectations derived from a whole range of individual and group activities.[27] Should accountants come to recognise the 'goal set' as a realistic view of corporate goal structure then they are still faced with the task of defining whether it includes policies, strategies, goals, forecasts and tactics. Even so, the 'goal set' has been implicitly recognised by many management writers in their descriptions of corporate objectives such as market standing, productivity, profitability, staff development, labour relations, public image, social responsibility, technical leadership, etc.

Goal congruence as a concept for application in both centralised and divisionalised companies appears to be of doubtful relevance. Modern organisation theory would appear to suggest that accountants' encouragement of congruence between divisional and corporate goals is both unnecessary and misdirected. This view would furthermore argue that only loosely coordinated divisional operations may be quite tolerable and indeed the best that can be hoped for in many decentralised organisations. Even when some operations are coordinated, the goals of different divisional groups may be far from reconciled or congruent. Instead, a divisionalised company is likely to accommodate a whole range of (sometimes inconsistent) goals, generated by a variety of individuals and groups, continually being modified, and being reviewed in terms of satisfactory rather than maximum performance. Nevertheless accountants continue to pursue goal congruence in their construction of divisional performance measures. It is to the effects of this approach upon divisional performance measurement that this paper now turns.

---

[25] K.E. Weick, *The Social Psychology of Organizing*. Addison-Wesley, Reading, Mass., 1969, pp. 8, 37-38.
[26] H.J. Leavitt, W.R. Dil, H.B. Eyring, *The Organizational World*, Harcourt Brace Jovanovich, New York, 1973, pp. 23-25.
[27] Refer to C. Perrow, *op. cit.*, p. 162 and R.M. Cyert and J.G. March, *A Behavioral Theory of the Firm*, Prentice-Hall, Englewood Cliffs, N.J., 1963, pp. 4-43, 83-127.

Goals in Traditional Divisional Performance Measurement

Classical management assumptions about corporate goals have been seriously questioned and yet traditional accounting thought has continued to
subscribe to those assumptions. These appear to be largely unrealistic and
yet they are still in evidence in accounting texts dealing with divisional
performance measurements. Even so, accounting writers sometimes unwittingly make contradicting statements or indeed deliberately point out con-
tradictions which have become evident to them. Horngren for instance
makes two potentially contradictory claims on one page,

> Keep in mind that an organization is a group of individuals seeking to
> achieve some common goals. . . .
>
> Each member has objectives of his own, often not coinciding with
> those of the organization.[28]

The first statement merely expresses the classical management assumption
while the second statement implies a coalition view of the company which
appears to refute the assumption in the first statement. Solomons'[29] view
of divisional and corporate goal-setting is similarly classical. He defines success in divisional performance merely as success in earning a profit and
appears to base his complete examination of divisional performance upon
this one premise.

Amey[30] has also taken a relatively classical view of the corporate objectives in his treatment of divisional performance. While considering profitability to be the key indicator of business success he does recognise the
possibility of multiple objectives but still sees them only in the context of
economic success and economic efficiency. Indeed quite early in his study, he
recognises the possibility of multiple corporate objectives other than profit
and rate of return but chooses to ignore them in his economic efficiency
calculations.

On the one hand Amey[31] advances convincing arguments for the probability that profit satisficing is an aim of companies rather than profit max-
imising, since it reduces the risk of close substitutes appearing, reduces the
risk of large established companies entering the industry and reduces the
risk of governmental anti-monopoly legislation. On the other hand he suggests that whatever the company's overall objective is (and most organisation researchers would claim that there is more than just one), the first two
elements for economic efficiency should be retained — maximum physical

---

[28] C.T. Horngren, *Cost Accounting: A Managerial Emphasis,* Prentice-Hall, 1972, 3rd edition, p. 697.
[29] D. Solomons, *Divisional Performance: Measurement and Control,* Irwin, Homewood,
Illinois, 1965, pp. 60, 238.
[30] L.R. Amey, *The Efficiency of Business Enterprise,* George Allen and Unwin, 1969,
pp. 3-4, 15.
[31] *Ibid.,* pp. 152-154.

productivity and minimum unit cost. Presumably Amey has recognised the possible existence of the 'goal set' but has then chosen to ignore it. For the purposes of fairly assessing divisional performance, it is difficult to see how it can be ignored. Furthermore given the unlikely existence of the single, profit-maximising corporate and divisional goal, and given the suggested weaknesses in the concept of goal congruence, these observations might cause accountants to wonder whether the continued attempts to refine divisional profit measures are really likely to be useful or relevant to the needs of the modern corporation.

The Manager or the Measure

Horngren identifies one of the causes of dysfunctional decision making in decentralised companies as being:

> a lack of harmony or congruence between the overall organizational goals and the individual goals of the decision makers.[32]

The accountant's task of persuading (by measurements or any other means) managers to give up some of their personal objectives in favour of some officially pronounced top management goals may be quite difficult and misdirected in any case. ROI, for instance, may induce certain behavioural responses in managers but are hardly likely to cause them to alter their desires, needs and philosophies. Top management goals, furthermore, may bear little resemblance to the real company goal set generated from all levels of management, unions, interest groups and individual employees.

The prime importance of divisional managers' own objectives is recognised by Moore and Jaedicke[33] when they support Dean's argument that the selfish interests of division managers can be aligned more closely with company (top management) goals by allowing transfer prices to be determined by negotiation and by allowing divisional managers recourse to markets outside the company. Whether negotiation could fulfil such an aim is debatable. Nevertheless the argument does recognise the direct effects on company operations which divisional managers' objectives can have. What the argument above also demonstrates about traditional management accounting thinking is its preoccupation with refining measures for directing employee behaviour to suit top management ends. This is even more amply demonstrated by Tomkins' statement that:

> When examining operating decisions, it was generally assumed that delegation of the decision-making process to divisions was desirable

---

[32] C.T. Horngren, 3rd edition, *op. cit.*, p. 694.
[33] C.L. Moore and R.K. Jaedicke, *Managerial Accounting,* South Western Publishing, 1972, p. 556, supporting J. Dean, 'Decentralization and Intracompany Pricing' *Harvard Business Review,* 1955.

provided that a suitable technical procedure was available for simultaneously achieving maximization of both corporate objectives and divisional objectives.[34]

Given the fickle nature of human behaviour and the range of ever changing corporate goals, that ultimately suitable technical procedure may in fact never be found. Tomkins[35] does concede the possibility of deliberate self-interest in division managers. The remedy, he suggests, lies in a 'good performance evaluation and reward procedure'. Given the questionable validity of the goal congruence concept, that procedure may be too narrowly based and largely misdirected. Furthermore, such an obvious 'carrot and stick' philosophy may cause division managers to ignore top management goals to an even greater extent.

It is therefore quite possible that accountants may have placed too much emphasis upon refining divisional profit measurement techniques for influencing manager behaviour rather than trying to serve managers with information which better relates to the real multiple corporate goals to which they themselves contribute. In his discussion of divisionalisation of investment decisions, Tomkins[36] takes a small step in this direction when he wonders if there should be less emphasis placed upon the search for overall corporate models and divisional submodels and more time given to the investigation of the optimal degree of independence as suggested by some organisational theorists. This would seem to be a reasonable approach in view of the arguments against goal congruence and would seem to be closer to the spirit and intention of divisionalisation. It should involve the discarding of the directive attitude of accounting measurement and the new concentration upon the autonomous behaviour and aims of the full spectrum of corporate personnel.

The Inadequate Divisional Profit Test

If accountants recognise that the performance of divisions can only be judged in relation to the whole corporate 'goal set' then they must be prepared to reject any divisional profit measure as the sole test of performance. Yet the profit test is still receiving major emphasis in the accounting literature. Horngren[37] sees Return on Investment or Residual Income as the quantitative measure best representing top management objectives. Shillinglaw[38] argues that profit-centre decentralisation assumes that the performance of

---

[34] C. Tomkins, *Financial Planning in Divisionalised Companies*, Accountancy Age Books, Haymarket Publishing Co., 1973, p. 143.

[35] *Ibid.*, pp. 6-7.

[36] *Ibid.*, pp. 153-154.

[37] C.T. Horngren, 3rd Edition, *op. cit.*, pp. 698-699.

[38] G. Shillinglaw, 'Divisional Performance Review: An Extension of Budgetary Control', in *Contemporary Cost Accounting and Control*, G.J. Benston (ed.), Dickenson Publishing Co., Belmont, California, 1970, p. 305.

the profit-centre manager is gauged by his reported profit. Divisional accountability[39] is thus treated primarily in terms of the amount of income produced and top management's assessment is again based upon these questionable premises of the primacy of the company profit goal and its accompanying managerial goal congruence.

Solomons[40] claims that the term 'divisionalisation' adds to the term 'decentralisation' and the concept of 'delegated profit responsibility' and continues to narrow the accounting perspective of divisional performance measurement in accordance with the classical management perspective:

> Third, since the principal objective of divisional management is the long run maximisation of the division's contribution to the profitability of the corporation as a whole, there is . . . a readily available measure of divisional success in the form of profit contribution.[41]

The mere availability of the profit contribution measure does not automatically imply that it is appropriate or sound yet Solomons advocates the restriction of divisional autonomy should the profit test prove difficult to apply. Any tendency for accountants to preserve measurement techniques that are inappropriate to company activities must risk the eventual bypassing of the accounting system by management altogether, in favour of a broader, possibly more qualitative means of divisional performance measurement.

Moore and Jaedicke[42] do realise that profit as an index of division performance may be inadequate. They feel that it does not account for a division manager's ability to build good customer relations, to secure employee loyalty etc. (even that list is narrow in perspective). Again, however, they return to traditional thinking in looking to the further refinement of profitability index measures. It hardly seems a logical step for accountants to further refine a measure which they consider to be unrepresentative of the total situation. In many firms, however, Caplan[43] argues that profitability is the only criterion that receives serious attention, whereas he suggests that business organisations should try to develop the best possible set of goals and criteria and that in evaluating performance against those criteria, they should remember that the process itself is imperfect. He cites the general empirical findings that single criterion indexes of performance overemphasise that single factor (such as return on investment) to the exclusion of other important factors and that the more pressure that is related to return on investment, the more managers concentrate on that index instead of making decisions that benefit the whole organisation.

---

[39] G. Shillinglaw, 'Toward a Theory of Divisional Income Measurement', in *Contemporary Issues in Cost Accounting*, H.R. Anton and P.A. Firmin (eds.), 2nd edition, Houghton, Mifflin & Co., Boston, 1972, pp. 463-464.
[40] D. Solomons, *op. cit.*, p. 3.
[41] D. Solomons, *op. cit.*, p. 9.
[42] C.L. Moore and R.K. Jaedicke, *op. cit.*, p. 544.
[43] E.H. Caplan, *Management Accounting and Behavioral Science*, Addison-Wesley, Reading, Mass., 1971, pp. 103-108.

The prospect for the further development of, say, return on investment, as a single criterion of divisional performance, should advisedly be considered by accountants as limited. Not only does an undue concentration upon it risk the difficulties outlined by Caplan, but as Hopwood argues, 'beyond some point the search for technical perfection is doomed to failure'.[44] The question of divisional performance measurement is both technical and behavioural. Important aspects may be ignored if accountants focus only upon technical issues.

Top Management Control

Why should accountants continue to subscribe to the goal congruence concept when its foundations have been subject to so much criticism? One possible reason might be their belief that it serves as a convenient vehicle for top management to exercise ultimate authority and control over all corporate personnel and operations. Indeed it could be argued that the accounting literature concerned with divisional performance measurement does assume the right and ability of top management to control total activity in the company.

Evidence for this underlying assumption in the accounting approach to divisional performance assessment appears fairly readily within the accounting literature. Arrow[45] claims that top management's enforcement rules should encourage the lower level manager to maximise top management goals after which he is rewarded and for this reason top management must have a way of measuring performance. Should accountants offer return on investment as the measure of divisional performance for Arrow's stated purpose, they may be merely acting as tools of, albeit thinly veiled, top management attempts to achieve overall corporate control. Organisation theorists would claim that such complete control is not possible (and to the average accountant, the union presence might be the most immediately tangible evidence for that view).

Horngren, too, suggests that:

> The optimal amount of decentralization is the amount that attains top management's overall objectives most efficiently and effectively.[46]

and that

> The aim is to get a system that will point the managers toward the top management goals. . . . In addition, incentives must be provided that will spur managers towards those goals.[47]

---

[44] A.G. Hopwood, *Accounting and Human Behaviour*, Accountancy Age Books, London, 1974, p. 3.
[45] K.J. Arrow, 'Control in Large Organizations', *Management Science*, April 1964, p. 400.
[46] C.T. Horngren, 3rd Edition, *op. cit.*, p. 693.
[47] *Ibid.*, p. 697.

In doing this, he opts for only one measure and then suggests that accountants concentrate upon defining the measure, measuring components, applying standards and timing feedbacks. Henderson and Dearden[48] argue for a divisional control system which carries out two functions:

(1) Motivates division managers to make the same decisions that top management would have made if the company were not divisionalised.

(2) Provides top management with a means of evaluating the effect of division managers' decisions upon the company.

In seeking to improve top management control over divisions, Solomons[49] claims that in the more 'successful' divisionalised companies, divisions are still allowed freedom in their daily operations but are strictly called to account for the results of their operations. This is a somewhat contradictory statement since any 'calling to account' must immediately increase top management control over divisions and therefore may reduce their autonomy.

Moore and Jaedicke[50] add to this view of divisional performance measurement as the means of perpetuating top management control by claiming that top management has no choice but must seek the most 'effective' control device. For this purpose they suggest that accounting measurements are most useful because they allow management by exception. Amey[51], too, demonstrates this bias when he claims that the decentralisation of responsibility is controlled mostly by the use of accounting measurements which are highly centralised. Furthermore, he sees decentralisation of authority and responsibility being related more to the control rather than the planning function of management. He cites one of the conditions laid down by the National Association of (Cost) Accountants of America for effective divisionalisation of profit responsibility as being 'centrally established and administered policies to co-ordinate divisional operations in the interests of the company as a whole'.[52] This effective centralised control of divisions is more specifically supported by Amey[53] when he recognises and approves the predominance of centralised asset control in divisionalised companies. This attitude is further demonstrated by Tomkins[54] when he suggests that top management may not be prepared to delegate decisions of 'great importance' (however defined). In general this accounting belief in top management control over divisions is best demonstrated by Shillinglaw[55] and Villers,[56] who treat measures such as 'return on investment' as simpli-

---

[48] B.D. Henderson and J. Dearden, 'New System for Divisional Control', in *Contemporary Cost Accounting and Control,* G.J. Benston (ed.), *op. cit.,* p. 337.

[49] D. Solomons, *op. cit.,* p. 15.

[50] C.L. Moore and R.K. Jaedicke, *op. cit.,* p. 565.

[51] L.R. Amey, *op. cit.,* pp. 116-120.

[52] *Ibid.,* p. 120.

[53] *Ibid.,* p. 129.

[54] C. Tomkins, *op. cit.,* pp. 143-144.

[55] G. Shillinglaw, 'Divisional Performance Review: An Extension of Budgetary Control', *op. cit.,* p. 305.

[56] R. Villers, 'Control and Freedom in a Decentralized Company', in *Topics in Managerial Accounting,* L.S. Rosen (ed.), McGraw-Hill, Toronto, 1970, p. 186.

fied top management controls over profit-centre managers. They are the means by which answerability is exacted.

The systems view of organisational activity would offer an alternative approach to the emphasis upon accounting controls over divisions.[57] In this view, organisational events have multiple causes generated by long cause-effect chains and any one management action may have second and third level effects beyond any immediate consequence. A systems oriented manager would therefore allow organisational subsystems to adjust when disturbed rather than immediately intervening with a proliferation of controls. Accountants and management of divisionalised companies may have been too eager to adopt the latter course of action to date.

Further evidence of the tight control which top management has retained in divisionalised companies despite the apparent granting of autonomy is provided by a survey of UK companies conducted by Tomkins.[58] In the majority of cases examined, a heavy emphasis upon relatively detailed budgetary control over divisions was discovered (in 42 out of 51 cases, in fact). When asked how often divisions reported to head office, 46 respondents (out of 53) replied that they reported monthly or even more frequently (this involved assessment of divisional profit components). From this Tomkins concluded that divisional autonomy did not appar to be as great as he had at first assumed.

What can be concluded from all of these observations?

(1) It appears probable that top management may often attempt to retain maximum control over company activities while overtly granting autonomy under the guise of divisionalisation.

(2) Accountants have assumed that this should be so and that really top management is the sole originator of overall corporate goals.

(3) Accordingly accountants have concentrated upon developing divisional profit measures which have often been used to enhance top management command over corporate affairs.

(4) The concept of goal congruence may have served as a convenient justification for this bias in accounting activity.

This state of affairs has left accountants with a seemingly insoluble problem in the shape of:

The Control-Autonomy Conflict

... it is clear that in the control of the typical organization, perfect decentralization is not possible because of the limitations on enforcement rules associated with uncertainty and risk aversion.[59]

---

[57] D.N. Duncan, 'Training Business Managers in General Systems Concepts', in *Man in Systems*, M.D. Rubin (ed.), Gordon and Breach Science Publishers, New York, 1971, pp. 300-303, 310-311.

[58] C. Tomkins, *op. cit.*, pp. 157-158, 166-167.

[59] K.J. Arrow, *op. cit.*, p. 407.

Top management and accountants might take this to mean that in any conflict between top management control and divisional autonomy, autonomy must be expensed to preserve control. Moore and Jaedicke[60] point to the conflict when naming the two main advantages of a decentralised company as being delegation of decision-making responsibility to levels lower than top management and motivation of managers in relation to the company's profit objectives. This action, they say, creates the problem of controlling and evaluating division management. There lies the conflict. Independence is apparently granted while control is actually retained, mostly via accounting measurement systems. Moore and Jaedicke further imply that when greater freedom has been granted to division managers, profit control is rendered necessary.

In his discussion of means of attaining optimal corporate effects from divisional decisions, Tomkins really highlights the conflict between control and autonomy:

> If the reader is dissatisfied and feels that no ideal tool has been supplied for providing simultaneously both divisional autonomy and overall optimization of performance, perhaps he should be reminded that he is probably seeking something which cannot exist.[61]

From his examination of divisional transfer pricing models he concludes that most either allow divisional autonomy and thereby risk corporate non- optimality, or require full information to be transmitted to head office or require a lengthy calculation process which may emphasise 'the supervision and watchfulness of the head office'. Once again the emphasis tends to fall upon the accountant's view of the necessity of centralised control of divisions for the maximisation of corporate profitability.

What might be concluded here is that accountants have probably recognised the conflict between control and autonomy in divisional performance measurement but have only considered it from one viewpoint. They appear to have seen the problem as being one of designing accounting measurements which retain maximum top management control of a company while still endeavouring to provide divisions with some feeling of autonomy. Possibly, in the conflict between divisional control and divisional autonomy, accountants have been only too eager to sacrifice the latter. 'Pseudo Participation' was a phrase coined by Argyris[62] denoting the apparent granting by management to employees an effective voice in decision-making while actually taking no notice of their views. This was found in cases to incur hostile and disruptive reactions from employees. Accountants might risk the same fate if divisional personnel perceive them to be encouraging pseudo-divisionalisation.

---

[60] C.L. Moore and R.K. Jaedicke, *op. cit.*, pp. 542-543.
[61] C. Tomkins, *op. cit.*, p. 104.
[62] C. Argyris, *The Impact of Budgets on People*, Controllership Foundation, 1952.

As Hofstede[63] argues, since control and autonomy can either coexist or conflict, their simultaneous maximisation is unlikely. Companies can at best hope to attain an optimal balance between the two. Decentralisation therefore may be seen as one attempt to do this. Furthermore, it must be remembered that Tannenbaum[64] has demonstrated that the total amount of control in an organisation does not have a rigid, finite limit. The total amount of control can be increased. Increases in the amount of autonomy allowed to divisions will not therefore automatically reduce total existing control. Contingency theory, with its roots in the systems perspective of organisations, is of further assistance here when it emphasises that an organisation should be designed to suit its environment. In this framework, Lawrence and Lorsh[65] argue that the more certain the environment, the less centralised an organisation can be. In the former situation, coordination can be achieved through the organisational hierarchy while in the latter situation (an unstable environment) it must be carried out at lower organisation levels where the required knowledge and information are available.

A Revised View of Divisional Performance Measurement

The arguments advanced in this paper have a range of implications for the assessment of divisional performance by accountants. Much of the divisional performance literature appears to be based upon a simplistic, unrealistic view of corporate and divisional goals and has often subscribed to the concept of goal congruence while conceding the power of corporate personnel's self-interest. Given the existing range of changing corporate and divisional goals, the divisional profit test taken by itself is inadequate as a measure of any division's progress towards the attainment of the corporate 'goal set'. Its perspective is far too narrow. If accountants wish to claim that they serve the creators of company goals, they should turn their attention to providing performance measures for divisional self-assessment since much of the corporate 'goal set' appears to be generated from the actions of divisional personnel as well as higher management. Furthermore, attempts by accountants to further refine divisional profit measures have been somewhat misdirected, given the need for additional measures of divisional performance.

An alternative approach to divisional performance measurement which accountants might adopt for the benefit of the decentralised company as a whole could be described as follows:

---

[63] G.H. Hofstede, *The Game of Budget Control*, Tavistock Publications, London, 1968, pp. 13-14.
[64] A.S. Tannenbaum, 'Control in Organization', in *Control in Organizations*, A.S. Tannenbaum (ed.), McGraw-Hill, 1968, pp. 3-23.
[65] P. Lawrence and J. Lorsch, *Organization and Environment: Managing Differentiation and Integration*, Harvard University Graduate School of Business Administration, Division of Research, Boston, 1967.

(1) Discard the belief that accounting measures should be used to promote goal congruence among division managers.

(2) Recognise the need to preserve some degree of autonomy in divisional operations.

(3) Review the possible methods of assessing divisional performance with a view to accounting for the needs and objectives of all levels of management above and within each division.

(4) Move beyond the single divisional profit-based index to provide an expanded number of measures of divisional performance which account for a broader range of success criteria.

Accordingly accountants ought to be able to bring their expertise to new areas of division performance and to further develop measures for these. Further attention could usefully be paid to the development of divisional productivity indices, projected monetary benefits of the maintenance of certain market positions, costs versus benefits of product development, division social accounts for social responsibility, and human resource accounting for aspects such as personnel development, employee turnover, accident frequence, etc. Accounting has done much to facilitate the assessment of divisional profitability and has the resources to be of similar service for assessment of other aspects of divisional performance.

All of these proposals may require a considerable change in the basic attitudes of many accountants toward their role and towards the rights of corporate personnel. Goal congruence appears to have been used as a justification by accountants for their active promotion of maximum top management control over divisional affairs while ostensibly granting divisional autonomy. Accountants may have viewed divisional personnel as objects to be constrained by the use of accounting measures. This would appear to contravene directly their officially pronounced role of serving line departments. Rather, consideration should be given to redesigning the system to serve a broader spectrum of divisional personnel as well as higher management. In today's society many corporate activities have been the subject of public scrutiny and are being adjusted accordingly. Prime examples include employee participation in decision making, the reporting of financial information to employees, increased provisions for employee safety and welfare and the growth of various forms of social responsibility reporting. Accountants have always professed their prime aim as being that of serving information users. In present day society, the identity and needs of those users has expanded and it is in this context that this paper has advocated the redesign of the divisional performance measurement system to serve divisional as well as higher managements.

This proposal does not therefore hinge on any contention of the author's as to what he thinks the modern corporation should be like. It rests upon observations of what corporations have become and what society expects of them. Corporations have been recognised as a coalition of individuals and groups working towards a range of continuously changing goals which originate from their own desires rather than being handed down by some authority. In addition, these corporations now operate in a social and political climate which is causing them to offer lower level employees a more powerful role in daily operations, more rights and more access to corporate information, while at the same time providing the public with more information about the effects of their operations upon society at large and responding to social pressure for changes in policy when required. The expansion of accountants' service from top management to include lower levels of management at division level therefore represents a response to society's present view of what corporations ought to be like and to the observations of organisation researchers as to what corporations are in fact like.

What of the divisional performance measurement system itself? Further investigation into the appropriate degree of divisional independence is required along with the development of measures for divisional self-assessment. Resulting benefits to the company may in fact outweigh the cost of non-optimal corporate decisions made at division level. Finally the diminishing influence of the goal congruence concept would seem to call for a reduction in accountants' emphasis upon the divisional profit test and its incorporation with other performance measures relating to other aspects of division operations. By way of suggestion, accounting researchers could begin to consider some specific performance criteria for different aspects of divisions operations as outlined below. As should become evident, considerable scope exists for the future development of the composite set of divisional performance indices.

In the first instance, the financial management of divisions might be reflected upon more fairly than by a single probability index by such information as:

(1) Stock and asset turnover statistics,
(2) Gearing ratios,
(3) Fixed asset statistics such as age of classes of equipment, depreciation policies, levels of maintenance expenditure, etc., and
(4) Major sources and applications of funds.

Productivity of a division is admittedly difficult to measure. A rough guide might be profit before interest and tax per employee although such a figure would have to be related to the capital intensiveness of the division's operations and other salient factors. Further refinement of productivity measures calls for further enlightened effort by accounting researchers.

A division's marketing strategy could usefully be assessed with reference to such measures as:

(1) Its achieved volume of sales.
(2) Its current share of the market.

(3) Its estimated product mix related to average contribution margins attained.

(4) Sales effort, efficiency and consumer response ratios such as sales/visits, selling expenses/sales, visits/days, and sales/orders.[66]

Any divisional research and development might be scrutinised by measures such as expenditure percentage of sales, expenditure per employee, actual versus planned cost for progress actually achieved, actual versus planned progress, anticipated excess cost for complete projects, estimated project benefits achieved etc. No single one of these measures could be used in isolation as an accurate representation of a division's research and development effort but some combination could present a reasonable overall impression. A product-line matrix of total research and development effort (in £s or %s) could be designed for two groups of categories such as:

(1) Cost reduction, product improvement, new product design.

(2) General research, applied research, project development.[67]

Some elements of social responsibility accounting might be further developed and applied as divisional performance measures. This again would be a reflection of the variety of goals contained in the division/company 'goal set'. Such measures might take one of the following forms:

(1) Social responsibility budget.

(2) Narrative social responsibility report.

(3) Outlay cost social responsibility report.

(4) Cost-benefit social responsibility report.[68]

Of course much more developmental work is required of accounting researchers in this area.

Employee related information could also be usefully included in this broadened scheme for divisional performance measurement. This would justify continued efforts by accounting researchers in developing means of accounting for company human resources. Accidents occurring in a division could be reflected by measures such as:

(1) Number of accidents causing lost time.

(2) Hours lost as a percentage of hours worked.

(3) Injury costs (developed from tables of hospitalisation costs, convalescence costs, worker compensation costs, and insurance premium increases).

---

[66] Refer for instance to G. Shillinglaw, *Managerial Cost Accounting,* 4th Edition, Richard D. Irwin, Homewood, Illinois, 1977, pp. 295-317.

[67] Refer for instance to G. Shillinglaw, *Managerial Cost Accounting,* 4th Edition, pp. 744-765. A. Matz and M.F. Usry, *Cost Accounting: Planning and Control,* South Western Publishing Co., Cincinnatti, Ohio, 1976, p. 502.

[68] Refer for instance to L.D. Parker, 'Accounting for Corporate Social Responsibility: The Task of Measurement', *Chartered Accountant in Australia,* October 1977, pp. 5-15.

The prevalence of industrial disputes within a division could be reflected by its number of working days lost in a year, hours lost as a percentage of hours planned, and lost contribution margins. Divisional human resource management might also be related to the average staff turnover rate for a period such as 6 months or a year. This could also be presented in monetary terms if average human resources of the division were valued in some way (e.g. on a basis of recruiting, acquisition, training, formal and informal development activities).

In Conclusion

The above range of divisional performance measures is not an all-inclusive list and may not all be appropriate to each division. Nevertheless they demonstrate a range of possible goals, criteria and related activities which a single profit-based index fails to reflect. At any rate the adoption by a company of an expanded range of divisional performance measures may serve to identify potential long term operational problems in the short term before they actually eventuate so that ex ante corrective or preventative action can be taken. It must also be remembered that it is primarily the division which is being assessed by itself and higher management through these measures and that a division manager could control some components of these measures only to a certain degree. A division cannot be evaluated upon aspects of its operations which are beyond its control. Furthermore accountants should recognise the necessity of combining both qualitative and quantitative approaches to divisional performance measurement. A balanced view of divisional operations is unlikely to result from excessive reliance upon one particular approach only.

Finally some reference must be made to the potential problem of information overload which might result from the adoption of a range of divisional performance measures. Such a problem could most likely be averted by the presentation of the complete group of detailed measures to division managers for their own autonomous use in managing division operations and of a summarised group to higher management for their broader policy purposes. These difficulties in measurement and presentation however are essential aspects of a broadened scheme of divisional performance measurement which, formidable though they may seem, must be confronted by accountants if they are to render the measurement of divisional performance more realistic.

This paper therefore argues for the future development of a matrix of divisional performance measures both by area of operation (financial, market, employee, social etc.) and by degree of divisional controllability. A composite mix of quantitative and qualitative indices is required for balanced assessment of divisional performance. It is a critical problem which urgently awaits the attention of accounting researchers.

10

PROFIT CENTERS, TRANSFER PRICES AND MYSTICISM

M.C. WELLS*

Two recent articles[1] attack the myth that profit centers and transfer prices can help in inducing managers of semi-autonomous divisions of companies to work in the best interests of the firm as a whole, and in controlling what they do. Both discard fictitious transfer prices and propose instead that divisions be charged the marginal or incremental costs of a contemplated action. They also suggest that a system of budgets should be used to control the actions of managers, and that managers are unlikely to be induced to work towards organizational objectives by any other means.

It is not suggested that profit centers and transfer prices are of no use where divisions are autonomous and trade freely in the market place. In that case, where a company

> can be logically broken down by type of business instead of functional activity (manufacturing, marketing, and so forth), a profit-center system is appropriate. And, when appropriate it has [amongst others] the following advantages:
>
> The manager is motivated to maximize the return on his investment, and thus contribute to the profit goals of the company. (In other words, his goals are consistent with those of the company.)

---

* From *Abacus*, Vol. 4, No. 2 (December 1968), pp. 174-81. Reprinted by permission of the Editor. The author is an academic in Australia.

[1] Bruce D. Henderson and John Dearden, "New System for Divisional Control," *Harvard Business Review* (September-October 1966), p. 144; and Billy Goetz, "Relevant Transfer Prices," *The Accounting Review* (July 1967), p. 435.

A profit-center manager can be evaluated on the basis of his profit performance.[2]

We will contend that, while incremental costs may be proper data to be used when allocating company resources, there is *no* situation, in the circumstances described, in which *any* form of transfer price is useful or meaningful. This view is reinforced by the conclusion that if profit centers are to be eliminated as proposed by Goetz, or amended as proposed by Henderson and Dearden,[3] then *all* forms of transfer prices must be dealt with in the same way.

Transfer Prices

Transfer prices have been described as: "the net value per unit that records the transaction for the purposes of operating statements,"[4] the "pricing [of] the goods and services that are exchanged between . . . divisions within the firm,"[5] "the intra-company charges at which goods or services are 'sold' by one organizational unit to another in the same company" (Goetz). There are differences of terminology in these descriptions — the value of a transaction, the price of an exchange, and the charge for a sale. And subtle differences in the terms used can easily lead to confusion. But there is a central idea common to these descriptions. It is the representation in monetary terms of a movement of goods from, or the rendering of a service by, one division or department to another within the same company. The monetary amounts proposed vary from cost or cost-plus through market or negotiated prices to marginal or incremental costs. Yet the proposals are all in respect of a change within the company.

By means of a "reasonably believable specific case," Goetz illustrates his contention that "relevancy and goal congruence demand that incremental costs be used as transfer prices." The incremental costs of a proposed activity are found by "budgeting the present mix, budgeting the contemplated mix, and subtracting the total of the second budget from the total of the first." The example involves four divisions, *A, B, C* and *D. D* hires a computer from a manufacturer for $4,000 per week, plus $50 per hour for each hour in excess of 40 per week. Divisions *A, B* and *C* have the following jobs done on the computer: *A,* 15 jobs of one hour each; *B,* one job of 15 hours; and *C,*

---

[2] John Dearden, "Computers: No Impact on Divisional Control," *Harvard Business Review* (January-February 1967), p. 100.

[3] Henderson and Dearden propose that the divisional contribution be the mainstay of the control system. They reject the conventional concept of profit when they dismiss return on investment as a valid control device. The difference of approach is that Henderson and Dearden's "contribution" requires the assumption of revenue for each division, whereas it is here suggested that nothing is achieved by pricing interdivisional transfers.

[4] J. Dean, "Decentralization and Intracompany Pricing," *Harvard Business Review* (July-August 1955), p. 66.

[5] J. Hirshleifer, "On the Economics of Transfer Pricing," *Journal of Business* (July 1956), p. 172.

2 jobs of six hours each. A total of 42 hours' usage at a cost to the company of $4,100.

Assuming that all these jobs are at present being done on the computer, the transfer price for each division is the saving in cost from discontinuing any one job or package of jobs. Accordingly "Division D should charge Division A $50 for each of Division A's 15 jobs, or $100 for any package of two or more (or even all 15) of these jobs . . . Division B $100 for its one 15-hour job, and Division C $100 for each of its two jobs, or for a package of the two." In each case the proposed charge is the reduction in the weekly hire of the computer which would result from discontinuing job or jobs concerned.[6]

Marginal Cost Variations

	Div. A Hrs.	Div. B Hrs.	Div. C Hrs.	Total Usage Hrs.	Total Cost $	Difference Between Present and Contemplated Mix $
Present usage:	15	15	12	42	4100	—
Contemplated usage:	14	15	12	41	4050	50
	13	15	12	40	4000	100
	12	15	12	39	4000	100
	15	0	12	37	4000	100
	15	15	6	36	4000	100
	15	15	0	30	4000	100

On the further assumption that identical services are available outside the company for $120 per hour, it is also shown that transfer prices derived from market prices or traditional cost accounting procedures may encourage managers "to make decisions inimical to the welfare of the company."[7]

This example leads one to conclude that, in the circumstances described, anticipated incremental costs may be useful and valid data when deciding whether to have a job done outside the company or on the company's own computer. They cannot, however, be described as "the unique correct transfer price here, and everywhere in intra-company transfers." In this case, the assumptions are unusually restrictive — no allowance is made for progressive changes and, as Goetz points out in a different context, the transfer price to one division may be changed by the unilateral decision of another division. That is, the proposed transfer price to Division A is $50 per one-hour job; but if two jobs are discontinued, the incremental saving from

---

[6] The transfer prices are shown in the last column of the table.

[7] The charge to Division C, at market prices will be $1,440 for 12 hours' usage. If Division C's two jobs are worth $650 and $300 respectively to the firm, it will pay Division C to discontinue both. In that event, the company will discontinue jobs worth $950, and will save only $100 in computer hire cost (see footnote 6). Similar argument is used in respect of traditional cost accounting methods. The argument is not disputed.

subsequently discontinuing a third job is zero. Does the transfer price to Division *A* then become zero? Assuming no further jobs are available, will it remain zero? Is the manager acting in the best interests of the firm if he discontinues two jobs so that he can obtain the other 13 for nothing? Similarly, when one division withdraws 2 hours of usage, does the transfer price to the other divisions also fall progressively to zero? Can it be $100 for Divison *B* in one period, $50 the next, and perhaps zero the next, depending on the actions of Divisons *A* or *C*? These questions are not answered by Goetz, but a positive answer is implied by his example.

Increasing use of services is also dealt with. It is assumed that the computer is acquired when the weekly load has accumulated to 30 hours' usage. The weekly hire cost is then $4,000, or $133.3 per hour. This is presumably the transfer price for that first package of jobs. A further 10 hours of usage can now be added at no incremental cost, and accordingly, no charge to the other divisions, until 40 hours' usage per week is reached. From then until 168 hours' usage per week is reached, the incremental cost is $50 per hour. If the value of the jobs warrants it, a second computer will then be acquired at an incremental cost of $2,000,[8] and this cost will be shared by the package of jobs put on it at that time. Now, depending upon when it happens to be discovered, the transfer price for a one-hour job may be either $133 per hour, $0, $50, or some other amount as a part of the package of jobs which incurs the incremental cost of $2,000. If this is the case, the transfer price is in no way related to the benefit to the firm of having the job done, nor does it assist in allocating company resources. It is simply a function of the order in which jobs are discovered.

There are two further questions which may be raised: Which divisions should have access to company resources, and why is it necessary to charge divisions for the use of those resources?

Divisional Allocations
The proposed charges are inequitable as between divisions. For a package deal, Division *C* is charged $100 for 12 hours' usage while Divisions *A* and *B* are charged the same amount for 15 hours' usage. On an individual job basis Division *A* is charged at the rate of $50 per hour while Divisions *B* and *C* are charged $6.6 (15 hours for $100) and $16.6 (6 hours for $100) respectively. In the absence of any special features, such charges are unlikely to lead to harmony between divisional managers. Yet if the company is to make the best use of its resources, then they should be allocated in order, according to the extent that the anticipated increment to costs of using the resources are exceeded by the anticipated benefits. This is the same problem as that encountered in investment decisions generally. Its solution requires the determination of a "shadow price," the maximum amount a firm might be expected to pay for a resource in any given circumstance. It repre-

---

[8] $4,000 weekly hire for the new computer minus $2,000 saved by transferring 40 hours of overtime from the first to the second computer.

sents the "economic value per unit of scarce resource" — the extent to which expected incremental benefits exceed expected incremental costs for the firm as a whole.[9]

Both Hirshleifer[10] and Henderson and Dearden (p. 149) have pointed out that sub-optimal decisions may result if the likely effects of a contemplated action are not assessed for the firm as a whole. And, even if the alternative with the highest shadow price is not adopted because of some special or non-quantifiable factors, the shadow price is still relevant to the decision as an indication of the opportunity cost to the firm of the course of action adopted. But it must be stressed, this does not require that divisions be subsequently charged for the use of those resources. Neither has it anything to do with managerial evaluation. The actions of managers are controlled and evaluated *after* the resources have been allocated. They relate to the use actually made of those resources, and the costs incurred in employing them. In both cases, an anticipated result of action is compared with an actual result. In neither case is this facilitated by transfer prices.

Divisional Evaluation

Goetz states that his proposals imply that financial responsibilities centers, or profit centers, "have no validity, are worse than useless, wherever one organization subdivision does work for another; that divisional managers cannot be evaluated in terms of 'profits' made by their division." Similarly, Henderson and Dearden state: "It is our conviction that R.O.I. for divisional performance evaluation can be so misleading that it is destructive" (p. 144). If these suggestions are correct, if profit centers are not helpful for these purposes, then what relevance have transfer prices of any sort? If it is not intended to calculate a "profit," why is there a need to charge divisional managers at all for the use of company resources?

The example referred to above, which is given under the heading "Decisions to Make, Buy, Change, or Discontinue," demonstrates that incremental costs are appropriate here. But they have nothing to do with transfer prices. The decisions referred to all involve parties that are *external* to the firm and, under the proposed system, no transfer price is charged unless there is a transaction with an outside party which gives rise to an incremental cost. Yet according to the descriptions of transfer prices given earlier, they are only in respect of an *internal* movement of goods and services. They are a necessary requirement of profit centers. The whole purpose of transfer pricing is to enable a divisional "profit" to be determined. If profit

---

[9] D.W. Miller and M.K. Starr, *Executive Decisions and Operations Research* (Prentice-Hall, Englewood Cliffs, 1960), p. 404. See also W. Beranek, *Analysis for Financial Decisions,* (Irwin, Homewood, 1963), pp. 91-92. I am grateful to Mr. G. McNally of the University of Canterbury, New Zealand, for bringing this point to my attention. He does not necessarily agree with any other views expressed.

[10] J. Hirshleifer, "Economics of the Divisionalized Firm," *Journal of Business* (April 1957), pp. 96-108. The examples demonstrate the dangers of unilateral decisions by divisional managers where the firm manufactures or markets competing rather than complementary products.

centers are dismissed as having "no validity," and as being "worse than useless," then surely transfer prices must be dismissed in like terms!

It is widely recognized that the evaluation of divisional managers requires a clear definition of their individual responsibilities.[11] Managers can only be held responsible for the use of those factors over which they exercise control. This requires that it be possible to trace each item of cost to the manager responsible for incurring it. Transfer prices do not satisfy this test. They are necessarily imposed (except under Dean's proposals where they would be negotiated); and the internal profit measures which their use makes possible suffer from the well-known problems of arbitrary allocations of overhead, or the difficulties of defining an investment base.

Financial responsibility centers are not the same as profit centers. The former imply responsibility for certain identifiable items of a financial nature. The latter are defined by Dean in terms of the responsibility of divisional managers for economic performance, taking the "basic goal" as profits.[12] This definition incorporates two distinct attributes from which may be derived two different, but operationally meaningful, concepts. These are responsibility centers, where a given level of management can be held responsible for certain operations, costs, etc.; and profit centers where, in addition to these, the "basic goal is profits." But divisional profits can only be measured if the division is an autonomous economic entity and does not contribute goods or services to other divisions of the company, nor draw goods, services, capital or knowledge from them. If these conditions are not satisfied, some allocation of either or both costs and revenues will have to be made before the "profit" can be determined. This conflicts with the concept of traceability. It prevents the evaluation of the manager's discharge of his responsibilities.

"Properly Conceived System of Budgetary Control"

For the purposes of controlling the use of a firm's resources, and of evaluating the performance of divisional managers, it has been suggested that a system of budgetary control based upon responsibility centers will provide the necessary data. It can also be used, it is said, to induce managers to work towards the achievement of company goals (Goetz). Henderson and Dearden have developed a three-tier system for these purposes, comprising a contribution budget, a fixed- and managed-cost budget, and a capital budget. This system provides a satisfactory method of guiding and controlling divisional managers; and because the budgets are linked, it also provides for an overall assessment of plans and intentions. But in both cases the authors propose the abolition of profit centers while retaining transfer prices. This conflict seems to stem from the view that budgets are necessarily in monetary

---

[11] See, for example, C.T. Horngren, *Cost Accounting, A Managerial Emphasis* (Prentice-Hall, Englewood Cliffs, 1967), p. 266. Horngren quotes from John A. Higgins, "Responsibility Accounting," *The Arthur Andersen Chronicle* (April 1952).

[12] Dean, "Decentralization and Intracompany Pricing," p. 67.

terms and that, to be included in a division budget, any item must be expressed in monetary terms.[13] This is a conventional view. It is also an unnecessary restraint to impose on a budgetary system.

Usually, a divisional manager will have no control over, nor any interest in, the costs previously incurred in obtaining or producing the goods transferred to his division. His concern is with the costs of further treatment of the goods. The receiving manager should therefore account for the quantity of goods received, and the costs incurred subsequently in his division. The despatching manager will have previously accounted for his costs in a similar manner. Performance may then be judged by comparing processing costs incurred with expected processing costs; the quantities processed with the quantities expected to be processed in a given time; and the general costs of each department with the expected general costs. Processes and departments may be judged to be economical or efficient without recourse to a profit test.

Budgets prepared in this way, incorporating quantities and monetary amounts, each in its proper place, are related directly to the things under the control of divisional managers. They also remove the need for any form of transfer pricing in internal reporting.

External Reporting

There may be some situations in which divisional transfers seem to be required to be expressed in monetary terms. These are reporting to external parties, and the calculation of income tax liability. In both cases, goods transferred from one division to another are usually valued at "cost or market." This has the appearance of transfer pricing. However, the object is not divisional evaluation, but the determination of the results and position of the firm as a whole.

If the proposals of Goetz and of Henderson and Dearden are adopted, the internal records of the firm will be of little help in the preparation of external reports, and they may be confusing. But if quantitative budgets and traceable costs are used, the same inputs will serve both internal and external reporting requirements. Only a two-way classification of costs is required — as to responsibility centers and as to products.

If some of the recent suggestions on external reporting were to be adopted, the need to express transfers in monetary terms would disappear entirely.[14] If replacement prices or current exit prices were used to value

---

[13] Goetz accepts the usefulness of quantitative budgets, and suggests that they provide "a less debatable measure of efficiency than dollar cost, at least when the latter is contaminated by doubtful allocations or transfer prices." That being so, why not dismiss the need for transfer prices entirely?

[14] See, for example, G.J. Staubus, *A Theory of Accounting for Investors* (University of California Press, Berkeley and Los Angeles, 1961); R.T. Sprouse and M. Moonitz, *A Tentative Set of Broad Accounting Principles for Business Enterprises* (A.I.C.P.A., 1962); R.J. Chambers, *Accounting Evaluation and Economic Behavior* (Prentice-Hall, Englewood Cliffs, 1960).

inventories, then only quantities of inventories at each stage of production would need to be recorded. The monetary amount of inventories on hand would be obtained by multiplying those quantities by the relevant prices. Also, the costs of constructing or acquiring fixed assets would be irrelevant for these purposes. The monetary amount for external reporting would be the asset's current price.

Conclusion

A good deal of accounting, as currently practised, has a mystical quality. Depreciation methods, inventory valuations, arbitrary distinctions between capital and revenue, overhead allocations, and joint product costing are examples of accounting procedures that fall into this category. So also do profit centers and transfer prices. Revenue which is not revenue, transfer prices which are not prices, and profit centers which do not earn a profit, are mystical inventions. They are fictions which cannot serve as a basis for action.

It is here contended that the notion of transfer prices is a corollary of the notion of profit centers. If, as has been suggested, the notion of profit centers is unnecessary, the need for any form of transfer price is also eliminated. The usefulness of incremental costs and revenues for certain decisions is not denied. In the example quoted, decisions of the "make, buy, or discontinue" variety were considered. For investment decisions generally, incremental costs, or shadow prices, are relevant. But such choices do not require the use of transfer prices. Three descriptions of these were quoted. They all referred to an internal exchange of goods and services, and not to a transaction which involved parties external to the firm.

We noted that Goetz dismisses the concept of profit centers and responsibility centers, and, with Henderson and Dearden, proposes instead a system of budgetary control. We distinguished profit centers from responsibility centers and concluded that the proposed system of budgetary control requires only the latter. It does not follow, as Henderson and Dearden suggest, that goods being transferred from one responsibility center to another need be charged at their marginal cost. Only the quantity of goods transferred need be recorded. Divisional and other managers are "charged" only with costs which are incurred on their initiative. Costs can then be compared with budgeted figures for the purposes of evaluating managers and inducing them to work towards the general goals of the firm.

The conventional needs for external reporting were considered. Costs must be traced for external reporting to products, as they are for internal reporting to responsibility centers. But we noted that the adoption of recent proposals for external reporting might remove the need for product costing and thus, also, the need for the pricing of transfers. But the arguments for and against these proposals are beyond the scope of this paper.

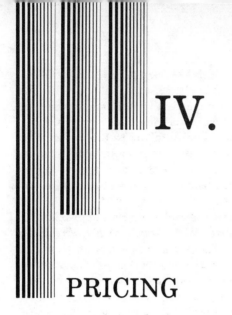

IV.

PRICING

Section I sets forth several possible situations where management accounting figures potentially are, and are not, useful for price setting. Most of the articles in Section IV illustrate applications, or misapplications, of several of the management accounting "pricing" technques noted in Section I and in other textbooks. The purpose of these types of articles is to help provide some practical illustrations that students can relate to as they are learning a decision orientation. Little in the way of *new knowledge* is provided in these articles; but much long-lasting assistance is given for developing diagnostic, judgmental, analytical, evaluative, and similar skills.

"Pricing for Profit in the Printing Industry" seems, at the outset, to be a textbook application. However, the author proceeds to fit in practical realities and difficulties, objectives, and motivational considerations. Of special interest is the interrelationship of various management and management accounting procedures and techniques.

The second article, "Anyone for Widgets?", has to be viewed as a classic. Throughout, the author humorously addresses the important theme that different costs and revenues (management accounting techniques) are needed for different purposes or management decisions. In particular the author, Howard C. Greer, contrasts the cost information required for two different decisions: pricing and inventory valuation (i.e., financial accounting/external reporting). We could add another comparison — pricing versus performance appraisal — and related management accounting techniques of tight versus currently-attainable standard costs. The latter may be useful for performance appraisal purposes but not be what Greer has in mind for pricing. Under what circumstances might Greer object to the use of currently attainable standards?

"Accounting Logic?" is also a classic which has been printed under different titles and variations in wording. It is largely self-explanatory and shows the dangers of choosing inappropriate management techniques for the decisions: pricing, disinvestment, and profit computation (inventory valuation). It also brings up an important issue — what you might be told by an inexperienced accountant who might have a different decision in mind than the one for which you desire to use the information. Users of accounting information have to know the assumptions made by preparers; otherwise misinformation and poor decisions could result.

"The Price of a Flight" provides a realistic example of costing problems in the airline industry. The first question we must always ask is "*Why* do we want to know about cost data?" Which *judgment(s)* do we wish to make? When we have responded to this first question we then have to look at the *facts* — such as those noted early in the article: type of plane, time of year, number of passengers, and so forth.

"Product Contribution Analysis For Multi-Product Pricing" ties several management accounting concepts together, especially contribution margin analysis, cash flow discounting, and return on investment. The author, a controller at the time of writing, was required to resolve pricing issues for his employer, a paper products company.

"Is Your Cost Accounting up to Date?" was written by management consultants to remind companies that their management accounting system must change whenever *managerial judgments* or *facts* change. Trade-offs among judgments, assumptions about expected facts, and many other cost-benefit considerations are built into information systems. Monitoring is necessary to ensure that useful information is generated by a system and the authors list several factors that have to be watched closely. These authors also stress the theme, "before redesigning a cost accounting system, management must identify the objectives of the new system." The authors do not give a high priority to price setting. Why?

11

PRICING FOR PROFIT IN THE PRINTING INDUSTRY

DAVID K. HARDER*

When the printer establishes a sales volume projection to incorporate into his profit plan, he must realize that volume by itself will not counter the low profit margins that are characteristic of the printing industry.

Most commercial printers operate in a job shop environment and compete for virtually every order with competitors who, like themselves, are operating with low profit margins.[1]

For a printer to price his product successfully in a competitive marketplace, he must have knowledge of his costs, market demand, competitive prices and their reaction to price variations. We present here an application of contribution theory which provides the printer with the tools he needs to arrive at the best pricing decisions, taking into account the variables of each situation.

Current Pricing Methods Invalid

Printing industry trade associations strongly advocate the use of marked-up facility hour costs as the primary method of pricing. These hour costs are constructed so as to be all-inclusive or fully absorbed with the arbitrary allocations of overheads and other indirect costs. As a pricing tool, this method should force all jobs estimated to carry their fair share of overhead and, if anticipated facility usage is achieved, the profits realized will be equal to the total of mark-up margins of all hours sold.

---

* From *Management Accounting* (May 1979). Copyright © 1979 by The National Association of Accountants. All rights reserved. The author is a vice president of finance.

[1] Industry statistics indicate that, for 1977, the average printing company earned less than 5% net before taxes on sales and returned less than 8% on gross assets.

In a competitive marketplace, however, the use of full hour costs as a basis for pricing has proven to be less than ideal. In practice, a routine pricing decision would work like this.

First, a prospective job is "estimated" to determine what conversion facilities need to be used and what special order materials and services need to be added to produce the job. From a table or list of production standards, the time resources necessary to convert the product are accumulated for each required production center.

Next, the time required in each production center is extended at the full hourly rate and then totaled. Raw material costs and other special expenses not included in the hourly rates are then added to the conversion total. Now the total job cost is ready to be marked-up to arrive at a selling price.

From this point a variety of things over which the printer has little control can happen in a competitive situation. Specifically, at the extremes, if the prices are too high, orders are lost, and if prices are too low, the orders are booked. Neither situation is healthy, and price retaliation is often considered by the printer who constantly loses orders, thereby increasing the chances that the entire market will be unprofitable for all printers.

The marked-up full cost formula approach to pricing (price = full cost + profit) is invalid because the nonprice factors of the marketplace are not considered. The acceptance and rejection of prices in the marketplace are based on a constantly changing set of circumstances, none of which is particularly sensitive to an individual printer's profit expectations or projected facility utilization. Therefore, because the printer must be sensitive to the marketplace, his formula for price success must become: market − his costs = profit.

For the printer who desires to achieve a better understanding of the results of his pricing decisions, the contribution theory offers an interesting and useful set of tools to embark on a pricing-for-profit program. As the first hurdle, he must break away from the traditional industry trade association costing and pricing methods and objectively establish the necessary environment within which the program can evolve.

The next point that needs to be made is that pricing must not be reduced to a strict formula but should be dynamic and made with full knowledge of the four basic factors that affect profit: cost, volume, efficiency, and price.

Each pricing decision should be made objectively so as to take the best advantage of each situation. This will allow the printer to select the best product mix at the proper volume and price to yield the desired profit.

Information Needed for a Pricing System

In essence, several things need to be accomplished before a pricing system can be installed. First of all, there must be accurate production standards and a budget or overall profit plan. The elements of cost must then be identified and classified according to their behavioral characteristics. Those costs that vary directly with volume are called variable costs. Those costs

Pricing-For-Profit Terminology

Selling Price. The price at which a given order is actually sold.

Full. Industry-accepted definition of hourly costs constructed to recover (hypothetically) all costs through a series of allocations, unitizations, and charges to individual facilities.

OOP. Direct costs comprised only of elements that vary directly with volume, such as direct conversion costs, DOAs and sales commissions.

DOA. Direct order additives, including items such as paper, ink, film, plates, services or supplies purchased specifically for an individual job, and commission paid for selling the order. (DOAs should never be discounted regardless of pricing method used.)

Period Costs. Costs that do not vary directly with volume — such as rent on machinery, taxes, insurance and depreciation.

Contribution. The difference between selling price and OOP costs.

Profit. The remaining balance after total OOP costs and total period costs are deducted from total selling prices at the end of any specified time period. Contribution − period costs = profit.

PV. The ratio between selling price and contribution dollars.

TCPH. Target contribution per hour based on facility usage and use of the elements of capital.

CRO. The conversion ratio of total OOP costs used to determine the utilization of facilities.

Facility Hour. The unit of time measurement available for sale in any given area.

CPV. Contribution based on conversion only.

MPV. Contribution based on DOAs only.

CPH. Contribution measured as an amount per facility hour or contribution per hour.

OSP. The selling price that would recover target profit based on OOP conversion cost dollars. OSP equals OOP plus CPH.

CCPH. The same as CPH, except that it refers to contribution from just conversion sales as opposed to DOAs. Conversion contribution per hour.

TSP. The target selling price of each facility that would return the desired rate of return consistent with the employment of capital. OOP plus TCPH.

Break Even. The sales volume that equals OOP plus period costs. Profit = 0.

Register. A summary of orders booked in a period that accumulates the pricing elements of each order and reports on the quality and results of pricing.

---

that do not vary with volume are called fixed costs, which are a function of time and are referred to as period costs.

The variable costs have to be identified with a salable production facility and a per hour rate determined for each. This rate will necessarily include all payroll costs, including fringe benefits, and overhead costs directly traceable to specific production centers. Finally, the elements of capital should be identified with each production center in order to determine investment per facility.

As we will later demonstrate, management's choice of a value determinant (historical cost, appraisal value, replacement cost, and so forth), ultimately will affect the determination of target selling prices based on desired return on investment.

Once the OOP conversion hour rates (see terminology) have been established and the period costs have been properly classified, the ingredients are ready to be combined into a dynamic pricing system. When the printer establishes a sales volume projection to incorporate into his profit

Table 1 OOP Cost Worksheet

Mfg. center	Standard chargeable hours	Annual labor cost	Annual repairs & maint.	Annual direct power	Annual direct supplies	Overhead directly identifiable	Total direct cost	OOP cost per/hr	Value
Camera	3,500	48,000	2,100	400	3,500	2,700	56,700	16.20	280,000
Stripping	4,250	60,000	400	—	4,000	3,600	68,000	16.00	20,000
Platemaking	4,900	70,000	3,500	600	18,000	6,200	98,300	20.10	160,000
Press #1	3,120	90,000	5,000	700	15,000	8,400	119,100	38.20	80,000
Press #2	3,120	128,000	4,000	900	12,000	6,500	151,400	48.50	150,000
Press #3	3,120	130,000	4,000	800	12,000	6,500	153,300	49.10	175,000
Press #4	4,680	447,000	9,000	2,700	26,000	11,600	496,300	106.00	410,000
Press #5	1,560	45,000	2,500	600	3,500	3,000	54,600	35.00	50,000
Folders	3,300	40,000	1,700	300	1,000	950	43,950	13.30	60,000
Cutters	4,680	57,000	2,200	300	1,000	950	61,450	13.10	110,000
Stitcher	4,680	68,000	2,600	400	4,500	1,900	77,400	16.50	175,000
Handling	12,070	110,000	1,000	—	5,500	3,000	119,500	9.90	20,000
Totals		1,293,000	38,000	7,700	106,000	55,300	1,500,000		1,690,000

plan, he must realize that volume by itself will not solve the problem of low profit margin. In effect, increased volume may introduce specific elements of period or fixed costs that cannot be eliminated easily in periods of low volume.

Let's assume the hypothetical printing company data in Table 1 for developing our pricing system. Notice that each production center has a developed OOP/hour cost that contains only directly identifiable conversion costs that tend to vary directly with sales volume. What these OOP hour costs reflect, then, is a theoretical pricing floor. As a matter of routine, facility hours should never be sold below this floor.

The second basic element of OOP costs are the DOAs that will have to be estimated for each job and they will vary widely as a percentage of total OOP costs because of the specifications of individual orders. Commissions offer a somewhat greater problem because of the dynamics of the pricing system and several strategies may have to be explored before deciding what best suits the needs of individual companies. We will return to this third element of OOP costs later.

Establishment of a Profit Plan

As shown in Table 2, our objective for the upcoming year is predicated upon achieving $4,366,324 in sales. Our operating plan also indicates that we expect our DOAs to represent 37% of our sales volume. Although our main business is conversion, we must keep in mind that DOAs are an element of capital employed in the operation and that they will be handled, stored, financed, conditioned, and insured. Accordingly, they should be marked-up reasonably to the customer. Therefore, in the example, we are assuming

Table 2 Financial Operating Plan

1. Total projected sales	$4,366,324
2. Cost of sales:	
3. Direct order additives	1,615,540
4. Selling price of DOA's (3)×110%	1,777,094
5. DOA contribution	161,554
6. Conversion selling price (1)-(4)	2,589,230
7. OOP costs (Table 1)	1,500,000
8. Conversion contribution	1,089,230
9. Total contribution	1,250,784
10. Period costs	912,784
11. Target operating profit	338,000
Target PV (9) ÷ (1)	.2865
Target CPV (8) ÷ (6)	.4203
Target MPV (5) ÷ (4)	.0909
Target CRO (7) ÷ (3) + (7)	48.0000
Target ROI−20% on total investment of $1,690,000	

that the DOAs mark-up will average 10%. This amount should be segregated from the total sales figure, leaving the figure that represents conversion sales.

Basic contribution theory tells us that contribution is the result of subtracting OOP costs from selling price, and that PV is arrived at by dividing contribution by selling price. Subsequently, profit is the result of deducing period cost from contribution. From our profit plan in Table 2, we can identify contribution as coming from two sources: 1) DOAs and 2) Conversion.

Figure 1
Average Monthly Revenue and Expense Relationship

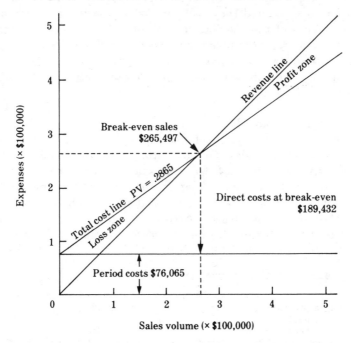

Target profit = sales × PV − period costs

From these data, we can determine statistically the break-even characteristics of our profit plan. Figure 1 illustrates graphically the average monthly revenue and expense relationships of our company. These are very important as a measuring device to monitor the results of P-F-P, i.e., volume, price, cost, and efficiency. It is advisable to maintain a monthly contribution register that indicates progress to break-even on a daily basis.

Figure 2 illustrates graphically the target pricing characteristics of our company as they relate to the financial operating plan. Line A²-B-C represents the theoretical target pricing line ranging from a PV of .0909 at zero CRO to the .42 PV at 100 CRO. The corresponding points on the graph are

Figure 2
Target Pricing Characteristics of the Company

A¹-B-C TSP line per marketing plan

A²-B-C TSP line per financial operating plan

TSP per $100 of OOP at various CRO (Conversion Ratio of OOP)

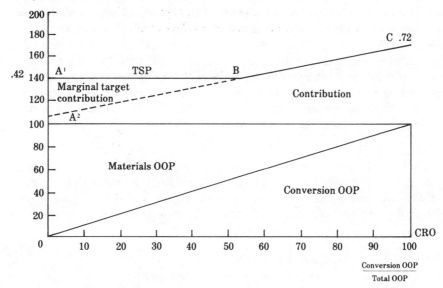

calculated using the formula OOP ÷ 1-PV. Therefore, OSP at 0 CRO is $110, and OSP at 100 CRO is $172. Line A¹-B extends from 48 CRO to zero CRO at a fixed PV (.2865). This line represents the emphasis that must be placed on the need to sell conversion, as opposed to selling DOAs. The less value added to DOAs by the conversion facilities, the less desirable those orders are generally. To achieve the desired company profit goals, we must achieve an average PV of .2865. Low CRO orders challenge the company's abilities to achieve those goals because of the low value added appeal of those orders. To encourage high PV or high CRO orders or both, the target pricing plan should tend to flatten out at target CRO. A creative sales compensation package should support and complement this policy. Our pricing plan then, as plotted on the graph, is line A¹-B-C. Table 3 expands upon how OSP is developed as a function of OOP costs.

The formula can be applied to each element of CRO to arrive at a mark-up table to be used in quickly referencing OSP when we know both the OOP and CRO. It is important to keep in mind that the pricing of orders still has as its basis the estimated production requirements of each individual order extended at the OOP per hour rate.

OSP has thus far been used as a synonym for TSP and applied to conversion cost as a constant factor. Although this method will theoretically achieve the desired results, it suffers from many of the same shortcomings as the Full + Mark-up type of pricing. What we have established to this point, however is a better understanding of the cost-price relationship, an improvement of pricing strategies, the establishment of a theoretical "price floor" (equal to OOP), and an expansion of the knowledge base for improved management decisions.

Depending on the level of complexity of the individual organization, management may desire to experiment with only the pricing tools developed to this point. Experience has proved that systems of this kind tend to evolve gradually at about the same rate that management can absorb the techniques and dynamics of P-F-P. It is, therefore, very important that sufficient backtesting be performed and critically analyzed to determine what is actually happening to pricing quality, product mix, volume, efficiency, and profits, and what adjustments, if any, need to be made before going ahead.

Pricing for ROI

In order for the printer to make a profit, contribution dollars must be booked in an amount greater than period costs. Therefore, the primary objective of P-F-P is to book contribution dollars first to recover the imaginary pool of period costs and second to accumulate period profits. In a competitive

Table 3 OSP as a Function of OOP Costs

Materials/conversion	A	B	C
1. Materials OOP	0	52	100
2. Conversion OOP	100	48	0
3. Total OOP	100	100	100
4. Target CPV	.42	.42	.42
5. Conv. OSP $\left(\dfrac{\text{Line (2)}}{\text{1-Line (4)}} \right)$	172.41	82.76	0
6. Target MPV	.09	.09	.09
7. Mtls. OSP $\left(\dfrac{\text{Line (1)}}{\text{1-Line (6)}} \right)$	0	57.20	110.00
8. Target PV	.2865	.2865	.2865
9. Total OSP $\left(\dfrac{\text{Line (3)}}{\text{1-Line (8)}} \right)$	140.15	140.15	140.15
10. Line (5) + line (7)	172.41	139.96	110.00
11. Formula applicable	B	A or B	A
12. OSP applying formula	172.41	140.15	140.15
13. Contribution at OSP	72.41	40.15	40.15
14. PV at OSP	.42	.2865	.2865

A—Extreme—0 Materials; 100% conversion at OOP
B—Target—52% Materials; 45% conversion at OOP
C—Extreme—100% Materials; 0 conversion at OOP
Formula "A"—If conversion ratio of OOP (CRO) is less than 48; price CPV and PV to force MPV
Formula "B"—If CRP is greater than 48; price CPV and MPV to force PV

marketplace, there generally will be a sufficient number of potential orders to be estimated and priced. Every one of these potential orders is different and would use resources and production facilities differently, thereby having varying degrees of contribution potential for the eventual winner of the bids. Because a printing company the size of our example may have 200 or more jobs of different sizes in various stages of production at any one time, the opportunity to analyze a sufficient number of jobs priced with P-F-P methods is ample. The objective is to test the marketplace with jobs priced to maximize contribution dollars. It must be emphasized, however, that regardless of how sophisticated a pricing system is, there is no assurance of the acceptance of those prices in the marketplace.

OSPs arrived at by formula, without regard to facilities investment, can result in a very unpredictable situation. For example, the formula arrives at OSP by an average mark-up of OOP costs determined by the level of CRO. But, when a job that uses low capital-intensive facilities is priced, it will still be required to carry the same level mark-up of OOP as a job using high capital-intensive facilities. What happens in these situations is simply that the inexpensive jobs tend to be over-priced and the expensive jobs underpriced. That means profitable work tends to be driven away and less profitable work tends to be attracted in competitive situations.

What needs to be developed next is a TSP for each salable production facility based on some measure of investment in that facility. For our example, we have determined our total investment to be $1,690,000 (Table 2), calculated by production center, as shown in Table 1. As mentioned earlier, this value determination can be accomplished or arrived at through a variety of acceptable methods. Table 4 demonstrates the differences in facility target selling prices when calculated for OSP (level mark-up of OOP) as compared to the TSP (return-on-investment) calculation.

When applied to a pricing situation (See Table 5, example 1), the extensions using TSP rates are considerably higher than if OSP rates were used. In another pricing situation using less capital-intensive facilities (Table 5, example 2), the TSP extension is lower than the OSP extensions. The results of pricing for ROI as opposed to level mark-up of OOP are to assign higher prices for work produced on high capital-intensive facilities and lower prices to work produced on lower capital-intensive facilities.

Thus far, we can conclude that the goal of P-F-P is to maximize period contributions, thereby offering the greatest opportunity to achieve the desired ROI. When production facilities are operating at or near capacity, however, the pricing decision takes on an added dimension. Now, in addition to PV, CPV, CRO, TSP and contribution dollars, CPH has to be considered. If we make the selection among orders of equal contribution dollars when production facilities capacity is becoming scarce, we should give CPH more emphasis than when capacity is readily available. If facility hours were limited or scarce, and not all of the potential orders could be booked and produced, we would have to make our pricing decision on the basis of what combination

Table 4 Differences in Facility Target Selling Prices

Manufacturing center	Facility hours	OSP method			TSP method			
		OOP cost	Mark-up factor	OSP	Investment	Contribution as % of invest.	Target CPH	(OOP + CPH) TSP
Camera	3,500	16.20	1.74	27.93	280,000	180,464	51.56	67.76
Stripping	4,250	16.00	1.74	27.59	20,000	12,890	3.03	19.03
Platemaking	4,900	20.10	1.74	34.66	160,000	103,122	21.05	41.15
Press #1	3,120	38.20	1.74	65.86	80,000	51,561	16.53	54.73
Press #2	3,120	48.50	1.74	83.62	150,000	96,677	30.99	79.49
Press #3	3,120	49.10	1.74	84.66	175,000	112,790	36.15	85.25
Press #4	4,680	106.00	1.74	182.76	410,000	264,251	56.46	162.46
Press #5	1,560	35.00	1.74	60.34	50,000	32,226	20.66	55.66
Folders	3,300	13.30	1.74	22.93	60,000	38,671	11.72	25.02
Cutters	4,680	13.10	1.74	22.59	110,000	70,898	15.15	53.27
Stitchers	4,680	16.50	1.74	28.45	175,000	112,790	24.10	40.60
Handling	12,070	9.90	1.74	17.07	20,000	12,890	1.07	10.97
					1,690,000	1,089,230		

Table 5 Two Pricing Situations

Example 1

	Req. hrs	OOP	OSP	TSP
DOA's		1,600.00	1,760.00	1,760.00
Camera	15	243.00	418.95	1,016.40
Stripping	6	96.00	165.54	114.18
Platemaking	5	100.50	173.30	205.75
Press #4	18	1,908.00	3,289.57	2,924.28
Folders	6	79.80	137.58	150.12
Cutters	12	157.20	271.08	639.24
Stitcher	4	66.00	113.80	162.40
Handling	6	59.40	102.42	65.82
Total conversion			2,709.90	4,672.24	5,278.19
Total OOP		4,309.90		
CRO		63		
TSP total			6,432.24	7,038.19
Contribution			2,122.34	2,728.29
PV at target			.3299	.3876

Example 2

	Req. hrs	OOP	OSP	TSP
DOA's		1,600.00	1,760.00	1,760.00
Camera	4	64.80	111.70	271.04
Stripping	25	400.00	689.55	475.75
Platemaking	10	201.00	346.60	411.50
Press #1	36	1,375.20	2,370.70	1,970.28
Folders	16	159.60	275.14	400.32
Cutters	4	52.40	90.34	213.08
Stitcher	8	132.00	227.56	324.80
Handling	32	316.80	546.14	351.04
Total conversion		2,701.80	4,657.73	4,367.81
Total OOP		4,301.80		
CRO		63		
TSP total			6,417.73	6,177.81
Contribution			2,115.93	1,826.01
PV at target			.3297	.2980

of orders is most advantageous. In these instances, PV is not a determining factor in the decision regarding which jobs to book.

Sales Compensation

To encourage salespeople to go after the kinds of jobs that are most profitable for the company, a complimentary commission policy should be implemented based on contribution dollars, not total sales dollars. This commission plan should stimulate profitable sales by rewarding the booking of high PV jobs with a premium commission. One approach is to slide the commission factor based on the over- or underachievement of target PV on a job-by-job basis, paying a higher percentage of contribution if a PV greater than target PV is booked and, inversely, a lower percentage of contribution if a PV less than target is booked.

Keep Pricing Plan Flexible

What we have covered in this article are only some of the variables that must be considered when using P-F-P techniques in actual pricing situations. The pricing plan must not be too rigid, but should be flexible enough to take advantage of each situation. Therefore, pricing in a competitive marketplace should be assigned a level of importance and consideration consistent with a company's desire to achieve an adequate return on its investment.

12

ANYONE FOR WIDGETS?

HOWARD C. GREER*

"The standard cost employed for price-figuring, for inventory valuation
and for efficiency measurement should be the smallest outlay conceivable
under the best imaginable conditions — the shining target at which
every arrow should be aimed."

The Waxahatchie Widget Company was started a couple of years ago by an
acquaintance of mine who lives down our street a little way. In true neigh-
borly spirit, the proprietor, knowing my background, decided to sponge off
me for some free professional advice (easy thing to do — I'm not too busy,
always flattered when someone seeks my counsel).

"Starting a little manufacturing business," he confided modestly one
autumn afternoon, when we were seated side by side at a high school football game that wasn't very exciting. "Thought maybe you could tell me what
I need in the way of a cost system."

The facts were simple. He had rented a small shop building, and installed
two widget-making machines, each with a capacity of 500 widgets an hour.
Operating 40 hours a week, for 50 weeks in a year, a machine could turn out
one million widgets. Labor and material costs would run ten cents per
widget. Other factory expenses were expected to total about $300,000 a
year.

"That's an easy one," I told him. "Running at capacity, your plant can
make two million widgets a year, at a total cost of $500,000. That's 25 cents
each. How much can you sell them for?"

* From *The Journal of Accountancy* (April 1966), pp. 41-49. Reprinted by permission of the
Editor. Copyright 1966 by the American Institute of Certified Public Accountants, Inc.
At the time of writing the author had both a business and academic background.

He wasn't sure — thought he should estimate his cost, then add a percentage for overhead and profit, see what he'd have to charge for them. I shook my head in irritation.

"Come now," I protested. "That's the worst way in the world to establish a selling price. Question is, what are widgets *worth*?" When he looked puzzled, I went on impatiently: "What can a buyer afford to pay for a widget? What's its value to him — materially, commercially, psychologically? That isn't necessarily a function of its cost — it may be much more, or much less, depending on a lot of things."

When he continued to frown uncertainly, I prodded some more.

"Anything similar on the market now?"

"Helox makes one something like it that sells for 35 cents."

"Good," I said. "Try 35 cents for yours. At that price you'll have ten cents per unit for overhead and profit, total $200,000 a year, *if* you can run full blast and sell the entire output."

He looked uncomfortable. He said he probably couldn't do that well, not in the first year, anyhow. And his unit cost per widget was sure to be higher than 25 cents.

"Correction," I told him cheerfully. "You may *spend more money* than that, but it won't be for the widgets; it'll be for owning a plant you're not operating at capacity. In other words, any excess expenditure, over 25 cents per widget, will not be a production cost; it will be an outlay for idle machine time. Expenditures like that add no real value to your product; they're just unabsorbed burden, which is an operating expense, not a product cost element."

He looked really mystified now. "What's unabsorbed burden?" he asked, feebly.

"Absorbing" the "Burden"

"It's like this," I explained. "In owning those two machines you are, in effect, buying yourself 4,000 hours of potential machine time, for a total of $300,000. That's $75 for one machine-hour, in which you can turn out 500 widgets. That figures out at 15 cents each. Thus you 'absorb' factory expense at that rate. Operating at full capacity will 'absorb' the entire 'burden.' Operating at a lesser rate will leave part of the burden 'unabsorbed.' Call it 'idle machine expense,' if you like; whatever you call it, recognize it as a *loss,* not an outlay that makes your product any more valuable, to you or anyone else."

"All the accountants treat it that way?"

"Unfortunately, no," I conceded promptly. "A lot of them will tell you to use so-called *actual* cost in your figuring and price-setting. They'll claim you've got to recover all your expenses in your price, no matter how excessive those expenses may be. They say that the *standard* cost should be the expectable *average* cost, or the cost attainable under *normal* operating conditions ('normal' presumably being 'typical' past experience, good, bad or indifferent as it may have been)."

"That's bad?" my listener inquired, with challenge in his tone. "I've always been told it was dangerous to base prices on costs attainable only under *ideal* conditions, which may never be actually experienced. That's what ruins the market," he added, piously, "people trying to steal business by selling below cost." He'd obviously been absorbing some good old fundamentalist hellfire-and-damnation cost-price indoctrination from some source.

I wasn't having any, so I said, "Do you want advice, or are you just trying to promote an argument? I give advice free; if I have to argue, I charge for my time.

"Here's my advice, based on long experience and careful study. Set your price at what the traffic will bear; that is, at whatever figure will get you enough orders to keep those machines busy. And don't louse up your bookkeeping with any elaborate computed *expectable* costs or *average* costs or *normal* costs or any other artificial and meaningless derivatives of arithmetical accounting procedures. They won't disclose a single useful piece of financial information, or lead you to a single sound business decision."

"You think my cost-plus-profit approach to pricing is wrong, then?" he asked dubiously.

"Completely," I insisted. "Pricing comes first, costing second. Find out what you can safely charge for your product, then under what conditions you can keep your costs within that available price. Start thinking about how much money you can make, at any given price level, if you can operate at capacity, with maximum efficiency and minimum waste of material, labor and machine time.

"Next, find out at the end of each period, how far you missed (and may go on missing) the minimum operating cost you know is attainable under ideal conditions. Then determine in what respects your expenses are too high (variance over standard). Then concentrate on what can be done to eliminate, or reduce, such variances (overexpenditures) in your future operations." I paused, having run out of breath.

He stared at me meditatively. "You make it sound easy," he began.

"So who said it was easy?" I countered, indignantly. "It's damn difficult, for almost everyone. But I'll tell you this: If you don't have the *ideal* constantly and clearly before you, and don't regularly measure and explain your failures to attain it, you'll never come close to getting the most out of your business. Content yourself with being *normal,* and you'll wind up normally unsuccessful."

Over the next few months I saw my friend only once in a while, never more than briefly. On one occasion he mentioned that they'd got the factory running satisfactorily, that they'd priced the widgets at 40 cents, and were developing some business. It was a year later that we first had an opportunity for a more extended discussion.

I asked him how things were going. He said they'd completed their first fiscal year, had sustained a small loss, but were optimistic about the future.

"How much business you do?" I queried. "Let's see: If I remember, you said your plant could turn out a couple million units in a year's time. You make that many?"

"Lord no," he said. "Takes a while to get started, plantwise and market-wise, too. We hit about a million total production. Not bad for a beginning!"

"Sell 'em all?" I inquiried (I had a feeling he hadn't).

"Shipped 600,000 units," he declared firmly, inviting congratulation.

"H-mm," I said, pulling out a pencil and an old laundry bill with some blank space on the back of it. "By my figuring, that would put you pretty deep in the red." I made marks on the paper, while he glowered at me. After a moment, I read him the results.

"Sales of 600,000 units at a standard margin of 15 cents each (40-cent selling price minus 25-cent standard cost) would give you a gross margin *at standard* of $90,000. Producing at only half capacity, you'd be on the hooks for around $150,000 of unabsorbed burden, leaving you a $60,000 loss at that stage. Then you must have had some selling and administrative expense; how much?"

"About $30,000," he muttered.

"Deficit of $90,000 for the year," I concluded. "That the way you figure it?"

"Not at all!" he declaimed indignantly. "Not over a third that much — just about the amount of the overhead expense, in fact —." He glared at me. I looked skeptical.

Year-End Inventory

"My auditors worked up the figures," he explained. "Had 'em in because the bank insisted." He paused. "Conn, Ventional & Co., CPAs — You know them, I'm sure."

"Very highly respected firm," I agreed. "What did they tell you?"

"Said that if a million units cost $400,000 to make, that was 40 cents a piece; since that was the average selling price, it gave us a break-even at the gross margin line, and our loss would be only the amount of the general overhead expenses. About $30,000, as I told you. Not too bad."

"H-m-m," I said again. "In other words they valued the ending inventory at 40 cents (average manufacturing cost), despite the fact that the selling price is only 40 cents —."

"Oh, no," he interrupted. "We've raised the selling price; it's going up to 50 cents next week."

"Wait a minute!" I said. "Though you sold only a third of your potential output last year at a 40-cent price, and have competition at a 35-cent figure, you're now going to try a 50-cent tag and hope to increase your volume at that level?"

"The auditors said we'd have to!" he responded, a little sulkily. "They pointed out that with the factory cost running 40 cents we can't possibly make any more money unless we get at least 50 cents for the widgets." He looked challenging again. I reminded myself that C.V. & Co. were getting a fee, and I wasn't, which automatically made their opinion worth a lot more than mine, and why should I argue about it anyhow?

"Irrefutable logic!" was the most appropriate comment I could offer. He shot me a suspicious glance, but I contrived to look bland and concurring, and happily escaped any further contention.

Breaking Even

Another year went by before the subject came up again. We got hemmed into a corner at a neighborhood cocktail party; we had to discuss something, and my curiosity got the better of my judgment. I remarked that he must have completed his second fiscal year, and how had things come out?

"A little better," he said, but without notable enthusiasm. "We about broke even."

"Business picked up, eh?" I encouraged.

"Well, no, as a matter of fact it didn't," he rejoined. "Our sales were only 400,000 units, and we had to cut our factory production back to 800,000 units. Gave us quite a year-end inventory, but the results don't look too bad." He was obviously unhappy, worried.

I delved into my memory for the figures we'd discussed at our last meeting. A light began to glimmer faintly in the background of my consciousness.

"Hold the phone!" I said. "I'll tell you how it went."

A Shortage of Working Capital

"A year ago," I told him, "you wound up with an inventory of 400,000 units, valued at 40 cents each. This past year you sold 400,000 units at 50 cents each. Using the time-honored first-in-first-out philosophy, you assumed it was the previous year's production you sold; hence your accounts show a gross margin of ten cents per unit, or $40,000 in all; this covered your S&A expense, and made your P&L account come out even at the end of the year."

He nodded confirmation. I pulled out my trusty pencil and paper.

"In this same period," I continued, "you produced 800,000 widgets, at a cost of — let me see: labor and materials, $80,000 — factory expenses, $300,000 (he interrupted to say they'd pared expenses down to $280,000, so I made the correction) — okay, total $360,000. That's 45 cents per unit for the new production —" I folded up the paper. "So you put the 800,000 new units into the year-end inventory at that figure, $360,000, and everything came out ginger-peachy." When he seemed not to share my enthusiasm, I asked what was wrong.

"Nothing, except we're fresh out of cash," he answered resentfully. "How come the accountants tell us we're making money — or at least not losing any — and still I'm constantly adding to my loan at the bank? I don't get it."

"That, my boy," I assured him, "is what is technically known as a shortage of working capital!"

"Don't kid about it," he begged. "This is serious."

I dropped my facetious manner and assured him I could understand his concern.

"What's next year look like?" I inquired. He brightened a little.

"Well, we've got a budget," he assured me. "The auditors helped me set it up. . . ."

"Starting with another price increase, no doubt, to justify the 45-cent cost you've got against your inventory —"

"That's right," he conceded. "The new price will be 60 cents. We're going to tell the trade we've got a *new improved* article. We expect to double our advertising appropriation, hire another salesman, offer prizes to clerks in dealers' stores —"

I interrupted him. (I'd heard this story before, too many times.)

"This actually a new-type widget you're offering?" I inquired.

"Well, no, not really," he confessed. "We're putting it in a larger package, and it will carry a picture of a bathing girl holding a widget —. We need a little sex appeal, our ad man says — and it will give us a talking point —"

"How many you think you can sell?" I asked.

"The quota is set at 800,000," he answered defiantly.

"The exact quantity now on hand," I noted. "What will your production be?"

"We'll have to cut back on it, the bank says; I'm figuring on about 600,000, but it depends on how the sales go —"

"Yes, and on how liberal the bank will be with further loans," I reminded him.

I got out the pencil and paper again. The figures were easy to assemble. "With sales of 800,000 units, at a margin of 15 cents each (60-cent price minus 45-cent inventory cost), you'll have $120,000 margin for overhead and profit; you can spend up to $80,000 for advertising, selling and general activities, and still come up with a $40,000 net income. Enough to erase your deficit, give you a little surplus."

"That's what the auditors said," he confirmed.

"And your inventory at the end of next year will be 600,000 units, having a production cost of $330,000 (55 cents each), and you'll value them in your balance sheet at that figure; then all you have to do is jack up the selling price to maybe 75 cents for the following year —."

"Aw, cut it out!" my friend protested. "I'm bleeding already; don't use sandpaper on me." He looked almost desperate. "Look, I haven't any claim on your sympathy, and even less on your time, but would you go over this with me in detail and show me just where I've gone wrong on this thing?"

"Sure," I answered, mollified by this appeal to my better nature. "Let me have a copy of the figures as you now have them set up; I'll study them a little, and give you my interpretation. If you think it will help you any — "

The results of my efforts are shown in the accompanying analysis, which I took over to his house the next evening. I laid the sheet on the table before us, exposing only the figures in the first four columns, Sections I and II (page 166).

"Let's take a piece at a time," I suggested. "Here's a summary of your results, per books, for the past two years, plus your forecast for the present year. As you told me, your books say you lost a little money in 1963, broke even in 1964, and expect a modest profit in 1965 — enough to give you a small surplus (accumulated earnings, the accountants call it nowadays) at the end of the year."

"Uh-huh," he agreed gloomily. "What's wrong with it? The auditors say the statements have been prepared in accordance with generally accepted accounting principles. That means they're okay, doesn't it?"

"Let's skip that issue for the moment," I told him hastily. "The calculations are in conventional form, if that's what they're saying. But they embody a philosophy that is basically fallacious, no matter how much support it has in textbooks or in practice.

"It's like this," I continued. "First, your 1965 forecast is absurdly optimistic, but that isn't the primary fallacy — you're merely projecting into the future the erroneous concepts of the past."

"Like what?" he protested. "Be explicit, huh?"

The Idle Widget Machine

"The basic philosophical weakness," I responded, "lies in the assumption that any money spent in the course of production activity constitutes a *cost of the goods produced.* In 1963, for example, you spent $400,000 making a million widgets, so they tell you the things cost 40 cents a piece."

"Well, didn't they?" he complained. "Why not?"

"Because," I explained. "Out of the $300,000 you spent for factory expense, only about half was spent on *making widgets;* the other half was spent on maintaining an idle widget machine, which *made nothing. Widget-making* actually got the benefit of maybe 2,000 hours of machine time (worth, on an expenditure basis, say, $150,000). *Making nothing* consumed the other 2,000 machine-hours; that time was wasted, unused, and its expense was a *loss,* not a *cost* of *anything.*"

"But the factory is all one facility," he objected, "including my standby equipment — You can't split it out that way — "

"You're going at it backward," I corrected him. "Try it the other way around. Actually, the only costs you can assign specifically and incontrovertibly to a single item of product are those charges (in this case materials and direct labour) which relate directly and exclusively to that one item. When you start applying *indirect* charges, like machine-time expense, to

Waxahatchie Widget Company
Actual and Prospective Results— Years 1963-65
(all amounts in Ms—000 omitted)

	Company Results and Forecast				Greer Forecast	
Section	1963	1964	1965	Three Years	1965	Three Years
I Quantities (units)						
Beginning inventory	–	400	800	–	800	–
Manufactured	1,000	800	600	2,400	400	2,200
Total	1,000	1,200	1,400	2,400	1,200	2,200
Sold	600	400	800	1,800	200	1,200
Ending inventory	400	800	600	600	1,000	1,000
II Manufacturing costs (company)						
Materials and labor	$ 100	$ 80	$ 60		$ 40	
Factory expense	300	280	270		260	
Total	$ 400	$ 360	$ 330		$ 300	
Manufacturing costs per unit						
Materials and labor	$ .10	$ .10	$ .10		$ .10	
Factory expense	.30	.35	.45		.65	
Total	$ .40	$ .45	$ .55		$ .75	
Results (company)						
Sales revenue	$ 240	$ 200	$ 480	$ 920	$ 120	$ 560
Cost of goods	240	160	360	760	90	490
Gross margin	$ –	$ 40	$ 120	$ 160	$ 30	$ 70
General expense	30	40	80	150	80	150
Profit (loss)	$(30)	$ –	$ 40	$ 10	$(50)	$(80)
Results per unit						
Sales revenue	$ .40	$ .50	$ .60		$ .60	
Cost of goods	.40	.40	.45		.45	
Gross margin	$ –	$ .10	$ .15		$ .15	
General expense	.05	.10	.10		.40	
Profit (loss)	$(.05)	$ –	$ .05		$(.25)	
III Manufacturing costs (Greer)						
Total outlay	$ 400	$ 360	$ 330		$ 300	
Product value-standard	250	200	150		100	
Burden variance	$ 150	$ 160	$ 180		$ 200	
Results (Greer)						
Sales revenue	$ 240	$ 200	$ 480	$ 920	$ 120	$ 560
Cost of goods – standard	150	100	200	450	50	300
Margin – standard	$ 90	$ 100	$ 280	$ 470	$ 70	$ 260
Burden variance	150	160	180	490	200	510
Margin – actual	$(60)	$(60)	$ 100	$(20)	$(130)	$(250)
General expense	30	40	80	150	80	150
Profit (loss)	$(90)	$(100)	$ 20	$(170)	$(210)	$(400)
IV Inventory value						
Company accounts	$ 160	$ 360	$ 330		$ 570	
Standard	100	200	150		250	
Difference	$ 60	$ 160	$ 180		$ 320	

units of product, you're in the realm of theory. You have to start making assumptions — "

"So why not assume that *all* the expense incurred applies to *all* the product made," he interjected triumphantly. "What's wrong with that for an assumption?"

"It's unrealistic," I assured him confidently. "If a machine operated *one day*, and stood idle for the *next 364*, would you assess the *whole year's* machine-time expense against that one day's production?"

"But it's not like that," he started to object.

"And, extending the assumption," I went on, "if the machine continued idle throughout the *entire following year*, would all *that* expense also be part of the cost of that *one day's production*? And so on?"

"You're making it ridiculous," he protested.

"It is ridiculous all right," I fired back at him. "But I didn't *make* it so; it just *is*."

He digested that for a moment or two. "All right, so what makes sense?" he asked finally.

Production and Waste

"Charge each unit of product with machine-time expense proportionate to the amount of machine time actually employed in making that unit of product, and only that much. In other words, you can properly 'absorb' in product cost the expense of actual machine-time usage, and nothing more. When the machine isn't working, it creates no value, and it's delusive to pretend in your accounts that it does. You've got to distinguish between *production* and *waste*, or your whole business philosophy goes to hell, and your profit with it."

"Are you arguing for what the accountants call 'direct costing'?" he inquired.

"Far from it," I assured him. "The direct costing advocates have a still different philosophy, and it's even nuttier than that of the conventional accountants."

He was shaking his head. "I'm confused — " he protested.

"So who isn't?" I retorted. Could I sort it out for him, he asked.

"Well maybe," I rejoined, not too hopefully. "It goes this way. In dealing with fixed (i.e., nonvariable) factory indirect expense, the conventional accountants say that *all* of it is part of product cost, while the direct costers say that *none* of it should be so treated."

"None of it?" he repeated. "If it isn't a product cost, what is it?"

"Point remains obscure," I acknowledged. "Apparently it's just an unallocable operating loss of some sort. A *period* cost, the boys call it. Sun goes down, you're out-of-pocket the amount of a day's outlay for insurance, property taxes, depreciation, supervision, *et al.* You spent the money, but it didn't do any good, create any value; it just ran down the drain. The direct-costers would say your widgets cost only ten cents each, since that's all you can trace specifically to individual product items — "

He looked incredulous, but chose to skip over that. "Repeat your contention again, will you?" he requested.

Cost and Loss

"It's not a *contention*," I insisted. "It's a statement of fact. Fixed expense — machine-usage expense, for example — is a *cost* to the extent that the facilities are actually *employed* in *production of marketable goods;* it's a *loss* to the extent that facilities are *idle,* or are turning out *defective goods, scrap, waste,* and so on." I paused to let it sink in. "There are some fringe issues, of course, like how to estimate maximum potential output, how to deal with shutdowns for normal maintenance, things like that, but the principle is as I stated it."

"And we'll run off the track if we do violence to this sacred principle of yours?"

"You already have," I insisted. "Look at your figures for 1963. They told you that widgets cost 40 cents each, so you charged off the ones sold at that cost; then you inventoried the ones on hand at the same figure; then you put the price up to cover your excessive cost; then in 1964 you repeated and magnified the error by imputing a 45-cent cost to a big year-end inventory; now in 1965 you propose to aggravate the situation further by raising — "

"How would you have done it?" he demanded.

"Like this," I told him soberly, exposing the lower half of the analysis (Sections III, IV, page 166). "You won't be happy with this showing, but it's closer to the realities of the situation. A fair 'standard' cost for your widgets was about 25 cents each (ten cents labor and material plus 15 cents absorbed burden), just as I told you it would be before you started up. Sales of 600,000 units at 40 cents each gave you a (properly calculated) earned gross margin of $90,000. Against this you had $150,000 of unabsorbed factory expense, plus $30,000 of general expense, for a loss of $90,000. The second year your sales volume was down a third in units, but down only $40,000 in money; with a higher selling price you racked up an actual increase in margin over a fair standard cost (it went up to $100,000), but your unabsorbed burden went up an equal amount (to $160,000), and your general expenses were higher, so you had a loss of $100,000 to add to the $90,000 deficit from 1963."

"It can't be!" he objected frantically. "How can there be that much difference?"

"It's in the inventory valuation, of course," I explained soberly. "Look at Section IV here, and you'll see where it shows up. Those 800,000 widgets you had on hand at the end of 1964, valued at a so-called *actual average cost* of 45 cents each, were in fact properly chargeable with no more than a *fair standard cost* of 25 cents each; the 20 cents difference, on 800,000 units, comes to $160,000. That's the exact difference between your book loss of $30,000 and my recomputed loss of $190,000."

"But that's not fair!" he objected. "Nobody's plant is busy 100 per cent of the time."

Would the Auditors Approve?

"Unproven, and probably untrue," I retorted. "Some plants even run over-time. Here's another slant on it. Let's suppose one of your two machines was located here, and the other in some distant place, like Arkadelphia, Arkansas, for example; then suppose you had made all the widgets here, incurring factory expense of, say, $160,000, and kept the Arkadelphia plant shut up tight for the entire year, with standby expenses of another $120,000. . . ." I paused to let it sink in. "Would you claim that the Arkadelphia expense should be added to your expense here, in arriving at your average widget cost? And would your auditors have approved it if you had?"

He got the point all right, but he wouldn't admit it, even to himself. He had to go back to his bankers, he said, and he couldn't very well give them my figures; he'd told them a different story, and now he was stuck with it. He was really low.

To cheer him up I pointed out that if he could sell widgets for 60 cents, he'd do well to buy 'em from Helox for 35 cents, shut his plant down, and get rich on the jobbing profit — maybe even get Helox to buy his plant, if they needed more capacity or would like to get rid of competition. He just gave me an indignant look, and I decided to make my departure before I affronted him further.

I don't know what his banker told him, but I later heard indirectly that he'd obtained some additional capital from a "friendly source" (a rich brother-in-law, to be exact). I consoled myself with a pious hope that they would both awake to the facts of life before going around on that carousel many more times.

* * * * *

Now you may think, gentle reader, that I made all this up, but if so you do me an injustice. What I have presented in the foregoing is a fictionalized, but essentially factual, account of the experience of a company with which I recently had a fairly close association, now terminated by mutual consent. For illustrative purposes, I have resorted to some minor exaggeration and oversimplification in presenting the calculations, and I have excluded some extraneous factors in the situation, but otherwise this account of the basic philosophical conflict involved is starkly realistic.

I emerged from this encounter bruised and somewhat chagrined; it's never pleasant to give sound advice and have it ignored, or to see people fail in well-meant endeavours that might have been successful. I grieved over my friend's disappointment (despite the fact that he's just made a killing in a big real estate deal, and needs widgets like I need another fifteen grand-children).

Under such circumstances, I usually go back to my raspberry patch, which is quite a solace in times of sorrow. Fruit growing, however, presents a few problems of its own. It takes me 20 minutes to pick a pint of berries; the grocery will pay me only 50 cents for them; after deducting the cost of the box, and mileage to the store, this leaves me less than $1.50 an hour for my time; when they put the minimum wage up to that figure, I won't be able to pay myself that much, and I suppose I'll have to go out of the raspberry business, too.

But, since the California climate is pleasant, and my health is good, and I'm mellowing a little in my old age, I would probably have forgotten my irritation with my friend Wax (or, perhaps I should say, with his auditors, who were, in my opinion, primarily to blame for his fiasco), if I hadn't run head-on into the same problem just a few weeks later.

The Whole — More Than the Parts

The Q Company, a client of mine, was being taken over by the Z Company, a big outfit with which I also had some contacts. These folks were about to publish a consolidated income statement for a recently concluded fiscal year (one of these "pooling-of-interests" deals). The preliminary draft came my way, and I observed with considerable surprise that the combined net income figure was substantially greater than the sum of the two constituent net income figures which had been in my hands previously.

"Hmph," I remarked thoughtfully to the unclad young woman portrayed on the Playboy calendar which ornaments my desk. She continued to smile agreeably at me, but without offering any comment.

After a bit I phoned the Q Company finance officer, an old and valued friend.

"Ever hear of the whole being greater than the sum of its parts?" I asked him.

"I know just what you mean," he responded promptly. "Embarrassing, isn't it?"

"It would sure embarrass me," I informed him. "What happened?"

"Well, it's in the inventory, of course" (his unhappy sigh carried over the microwaves all the way from New York). "We always used those fine tight standard costs you helped us set up years ago — "

"I well remember," I assured him, "how tough it was to get them adopted, and how enthusiastic all the plant managers were about them after they'd been used a while — "

"Still feel the same," he told me emphatically; "wouldn't change for anything. Our people are unanimous in saying that the strength of our business has been in hammering away at unfavorable cost variances, squeezing them down, then tightening the standards again. You know. But," he sighed again, "we're told that Big Daddy doesn't do it that way, so now we can't do it that way any more."

"What the hell!" I demanded furiously. "What difference does it make to Z Company?"

Operating Results

"Seems their auditors (auditors again!) insist that the only proper cost standard is one derived from *average actual experience* under *normal operating conditions*. . . . "

"Don't tell me," I interrupted, in disgust. "Q Company had an unfavorable cost variance last year; you initially wrote it off to P&L; then the auditors came in and made you reinstate the part of it they claimed was related to the closing inventory —"

"Little matter of a million-and-a-half iron dollars added to consolidated profit," he confirmed glumly, "which, frankly, I don't think we earned." I asked if he'd told his bosses so.

"Oh, yes, but they said there was a tax problem involved. Z has always used average costs, and the auditors say they're afraid their position will be jeopardized if a subsidiary deviates —"

"Taxes, schmaxes," I retorted, rudely. "When they tell you to do something stupid they always lay it onto IRS or SEC or FTC or some government agency or other. Income taxes should *never* be mixed into measurements of *operating results*, under *any* conditions, and it's dangerous to let your evaluation of management performance get fouled up by any of today's hocus-pocus on taxes."

"Matter of great concern to us here," he said seriously. "We know how to run this business and to make money at it, and we'll go on doing so if we can stick to sound costing principles, but if we get to adulterating our standards to reflect every freak change in the tax laws, I don't know where we'll wind up." He sounded depressed. I was, too.

"Nothing *you* can do, I suppose," he ventured, hesitantly, after a pause.

"If you mean go argue with the auditors, the answer is an emphatic *no*," I assured him. "What was it old John Sharp Williams, of Mississippi, said when he resigned from the United States Senate, years ago? 'I might as well be a hound-dog and bay the moon, as spend my days exhorting my colleagues here' — something like that. I know just how he felt."

"Well, you're lucky; you've retired," he said enviously.

"Why do you suppose I retired early? You'll be smart to do likewise."

"Don't just desert us," he pleaded. "You ought to try to help us out."

"Okay," I responded. "I'll write a letter to the American Institute of Certified Public Accountants about it."

He snorted. "They plainly don't think the subject is of much importance," he pointed out. "In that 469-page *Inventory of Generally Accepted Accounting Principles* this entire problem is casually dismissed in about three scattered sentences."

I reminded him that the subject is lucidly and completely discussed, at some length, in Kohler's *Dictionary for Accountants,* but that didn't cheer him greatly. "So who reads a dictionary?" he complained. "Takes something livelier than a definition to get people interested. Why don't you write an article about it for *The Journal of Accountancy*? They might even print it."

*   *   *   *   *

So I did, and here you have it (or as much of it as may have survived the blue pencil of an amused but scandalized editor and his "technical advisers"). I hope only that they have preserved, for your edification, a full expression of the two major concepts which this fable seeks to formulate.

1. The *cost* reflected in an inventory valuation, and in any price-cost margin computation, must not be more than the sum of those elements of outlay which constitute identifiable and measurable contributions to value-creation; namely, (1) expenditures for materials and services applicable specifically and exclusively to the production of the article concerned, plus (b) such portion of expenditures for ancillary mechanical and administrative activities and services as may be ascribable solely to the productive function involved, excluding costs of maintaining facilities and organization not fully and efficiently employed, along with all wastes and losses which are patently avoidable under optimum manufacturing conditions.

2. The *price* at which an article is offered for sale should be that which (a) reflects its potential use-value in the hands of the buyer, with due regard for its quality, reputation, attractiveness and availability, and (b) promises to generate a sufficient volume of business to ensure adequate utilization of those facilities which the producer may choose to (or be compelled to) employ in its production, with due regard for competitive pressures, alternative usage, etc.

With this important corollary:

The "standard" cost employed for price-figuring, for inventory valuation and for efficiency measurement should be the smallest outlay conceivable under the best imaginable conditions — the shining target at which every arrow should be aimed. Surprising how soon you can start hitting the bull's-eye, if you never let it out of sight.

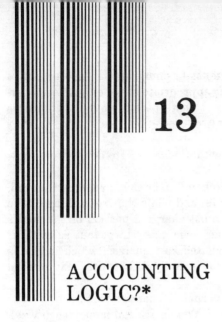

13

ACCOUNTING LOGIC?*

The Scene: A small coffee shop deep in the jungle of accounting logic.

The Time: Today — and tomorrow — if you aren't careful.

The Cast: Joe, owner and operator of a small coffee shop in the jungle; an accounting-efficiency-expert.

As the curtain rises, we find Joe dusting his counter and casting admiring glances at a shiny new rack holding brightly coloured bags of peanuts. The rack is at the end of the counter. The shop itself is like all small coffee shops in the jungle of accounting logic. It is a clean, well-lighted joint patronized by the neighbourhood residents and an occasional juvenile delinquent. As Joe dusts and admires his new peanut rack, he listens almost uncomprehendingly to the reasoning of the accounting-efficiency-expert. (AEE)

AEE: Joe, you said you put in these peanuts because people ask for them, but do you realize what this rack of peanuts is *costing* you?

JOE: It'sa not gonna cost. 'sgonna be a profit. Sure I hadda pay $25 for a fancy rack to holda bags, but da peanuts cost 6¢ a bag and I sell'em for 10¢. Figger I sell 50 bags a week to start. It'll take 12½ weeks to cover da cost of da rack. After that I gotta clear profit of 4¢ a bag. Da more I sell, da more I make. Easy money.

AEE: That is an antiquated and completely unrealistic approach, Joe. Fortunately, modern accounting techniques permit a more accurate picture which reveals the complexities involved.

JOE: Huh?

* Author unknown

AEE: To be precise, those peanuts must be integrated into your entire operation and be allocated their appropriate share of business overhead. They must share a proportionate part of your expenditures for rent, heat, light, equipment, depreciation, decorating, salaries for waitresses, cook —

JOE: Da cook? What's he gotta do wit'da peanuts? He don't even know I got 'em.

AEE: Look, Joe, the cook is in the kitchen, the kitchen prepares the food, the food is what brings people in, and while they're in, they ask to buy peanuts. That's why you must charge a portion of the cook's wages, as well as a part of your own salary to peanut sales. This sheet contains a carefully calculated cost analysis which indicates the peanut operation should pay exactly $1,278 per year toward these general overhead costs.

JOE: Da peanuts? $1,278 a year for overhead? That'sa NUTS!

AEE: It's really a little more than that. You also spend money each week to have the windows washed, to have the place swept out in the mornings, keep soap in the washroom and provide free cokes to the police. That raises the total to $1,313 per year.

JOE: *(Thoughtfully)* But da peanut salesman said I'd makea money — put 'em on da end of da counter, he said and get 4¢ a bag profit —

AEE: *(With a sniff)* He's not an accountant. Do you actually know what the portion of the counter occupied by the peanut rack is worth to you?

JOE: Ain't worth nothing — no stool dere — just a dead spot at da end. No room to put in a stool, causa waitress musta walk dere.

AEE: Modern management accounting permits no dead spots. Your counter contains 60 square feet and your counter business grosses $15,000 per year. Consequently, the square foot of space occupied by the peanut rack is worth $250 per year. Since you have taken that area away from general counter use, you must charge the value of the space to the peanut division of your company.

JOE: Division? ..... You mean I gotta add $250 a year more to da peanuts?

AEE: Right. That raises their share of the general operating costs to a grand total of $1,563 per year. Now then, if you sell 50 bags of peanuts per week, these allocated costs will amount to 60¢ per bag.

JOE: *(Incredulously)* What???

AEE: Obviously, to that must be added your purchase price of 6¢ a bag, which brings the total to 66¢. So you see, by selling peanuts at 10¢ per bag, you are losing 56¢ on every sale.

JOE: Something'sa crazy!

AEE: Not at all! Here are the figures. They prove your peanut operation cannot stand on its own feet.

JOE: *(Brightening)* Suppose I sell lotsa peanuts — thousand bags a week 'stead of fifty?

AEE: *(Tolerantly)* Joe, you don't understand the problem. If the volume of peanut sales increased, your operating costs will go up — you'll have to handle more bags, with more time, more general overhead, more everything. The basic principle of accounting is firm on that subject: "The bigger the operation the more general overhead costs must be allocated." No, increasing the volume of sales won't help.

JOE: Okay. You so smart, you tell me what I gotta do.

AEE: *(Condescendingly)* Well — you could first reduce operating expenses.

JOE: How?

AEE: Take smaller space in an older building with cheaper rent. Cut salaries. Wash the windows biweekly. Have the floor swept only on Thursday. Remove the soap from the washrooms. Cut out the cokes for the cops. This will also help you decrease the square-foot value of your counter. For example, if you can cut your expenses 50%, that will reduce the amount allocated to peanuts from $1,563 down to $781.50 per year, reducing the cost to 36¢ per bag.

JOE: *(Slowly)* Thatsa better?

AEE: Much, much better. However, even then you would lose 26¢ per bag if you charge only 10¢. Therefore, you must also raise your selling price. If you want a net profit of 4¢ per bag you would have to charge 40¢.

JOE: *(Flabbergasted)* You mean even after I cut operating costs 50%, I still gotta charge 40¢ for a 10¢ bag o' peanuts? Nobody's that nuts about nuts! Who'd buy 'em?

AEE: That's a secondary consideration. The point is, at 40¢, you'd be selling at a price based upon a proper evaluation of your then reduced costs.

JOE: *(Eagerly)* Look! I gotta better idea. Why don't I just throw da nuts out — put 'em in da ash can?

AEE: Can you afford it?

JOE: Sure, all I got is about 50 bagsa peanuts — cost about three bucks — so I lose $25 on da rack; I'm outa dis nutty business and no more grief.

AEE: *(Shaking head)* Joe, it isn't that simple. You are IN THE PEANUT BUSINESS! The minute you throw those peanuts out, you are adding $1,563 of annual overhead to the rest of your operation. Joe — be realistic — can you afford to do that?

JOE: *(Completely crushed)* It'sa unbelievable! Last week I wasa make money. Now I'm ina trouble — justa because I think peanuts onna counter isa gonna bring me some extra profit — justa because I believe 50 bags of peanuts a weeks isa easy.

AEE: *(With raised eyebrow)* That is the reason for modern cost studies, Joe — to dispel those false illusions.

14

THE
PRICE
OF A
FLIGHT

DANIEL PÉRUSSE*

Just how much does it cost to put a plane into the air? That was the innocent question I asked some Air Canada people, on the 38th floor of Place Ville-Marie in Montreal, one fine morning last September.

There wasn't one simple answer, but dozens. And a few questions too: "That depends. What kind of a plane are you talking about? A Boeing 747? A Lockheed 1011? A DC-9? And where's it going? To Gander? Frankfurt? Miami? Carrying passengers or cargo? Day or night? How many flight attendants? Is it returning the same day? Full or empty? Will it be flying over the ocean? Over military zones?"

All right, I get the picture. It's complicated. You can't calculate the cost of operating a jumbo jet as you can a moped. "In fact," says David Giles, Manager, Facilitation and User Charges Administration, "if I'm asked how much it costs the company to send one of its planes to any given place, not counting the cost of fuel, I need the following information: the time of year, the day of the week, the time of day, the type of plane, the number of passengers, how long the plane will be on the ground — among other essential data."

Not to mention fuel. Because where fuel is concerned it's simpler, isn't it? The farther you go the more you burn, the more you burn, the more it costs, right? Yes, except that it depends on where you buy it. Fuel costs less in Canada, so that for domestic flights, 26 percent of Air Canada's bill goes for fuel. If we're talking about transatlantic flights it's 33 percent.

---

* The author is a journalist. Originally published in *en Route* (March 1983).

A detail, you say? Yes — a $10 million detail! When we talk about airplanes and fuel we're talking millions — millions of dollars, millions of litres, millions of kilometres. Air Canada poured 1,991,800,000 precious litres down the gullets of its thirsty aircraft in 1981. A $567 million fill-up! To make some comparisons, the 1,536,400,000 litres per year purchased here by Air Canada could fuel all the cars in Montreal for a year. Or send three million cars all the way across the country at once. A Boeing 747, the thirstiest of the big carriers, gulps down 9,200 litres during takeoff alone: That's enough to keep your car running for five years.

At this rate, the airlines must make fuel, like coffee, good to the last drop, and they're doing everything they can to eke out those last drops. In terms of fuel consumption, enemy number one is weight: Dropping 45 kilos means a saving of almost two kilos of fuel per hour. That was translated recently into lighter carpets for the cabins of the Air Canada fleet, because when you carry enough fabric to cover two football fields, lighter material meant 681,900 fewer litres at the pump — at a saving of $225,000.

Other fuel-saving measures have included streamlining of traffic flow (to reduce time in holding patterns and on the ground), improving reservation efficiency (to reduce numbers of empty seats) and monitoring fuel efficiency through computerized navigation aids. At 885 kilometres per hour, even a slight reduction in speed is enough to save thousands of litres of fuel. But big problems require drastic measures, and last fall Air Canada took on two of the brand-new Boeing 767s, a generation of aircraft which are at least 27 percent more efficient than the older models.

Despite all these measures, Air Canada still spends $1.64 million *a day* on fuel. That's $68,000 an hour, $19 a second or $36,000 just to send a 747 from Montréal to Paris. In a Lockheed 1011, Halifax is $20,000 away from Vancouver, Miami is $10,000 from Toronto. Since the 1973 oil crisis, the cost of jet fuel has increased sevenfold.

But there's another, larger cost: personnel. Air Canada's 23,000 employees receive $773 million annually in salaries and social benefits; that's 35 percent of the company's operating costs.

Indirectly, this sum helps determine the cost of flying a plane. More precisely, the flight staff alone (1,862 pilots and 3,400 flight attendants) accounts for $210 million per year — plus $30 million for hotel rooms and living expenses when they're away from base.

Once they're on board, passengers don't just admire the passing clouds. In 1981, 13 million Air Canada passengers consumed two million steaks, 25 million eggs, 150,000 chickens, 50,000 meat pies, 180,000 sausages, 54,360 kilos of carrots and 63,420 kilos of peas. A $71-million grocery basket! Plus $9 million for dishes, glasses and serviettes.

And that's not all. From takeoff to landing, in the air and on the ground, airline companies must pay certain 'user charges' for their planes, similar to tolls and parking expenses for a car. There are airport charges for landing, takeoff, safety installations, navigation aids, air traffic control, communications, radar, weather forecasting. There's a charge for the use of airways, runways and parking areas. Not to mention security and baggage handling. And the unkindest cut of all: there's even an add-on charge for filling up with fuel.

"These costs vary tremendously from country to country," says Ronald Pelletier, User Charges Representative. "For instance, European countries are grouped together under Eurocontrol. In 1981 they imposed route charges of one billion dollars on the member airlines of IATA (International Air Transport Association)."

For Air Canada that meant $12 million. As well, some countries demand payment simply for flying over their territory. It's a question of 'sovereign air space.' An Air Canada flight from Toronto to Frankfurt must dish out $3,000 to fly over Ireland, England, France, the Netherlands, Belgium and Germany.

The costs for flying over Europe, calculated according to the weight of the aircraft and the distance covered, are among the highest in the world. For example, 1,000 kilometres of German air space costs a 747 $1,935; in Belgium and Luxembourg, $1,575.

Europeans are past masters at calculating these fees. There's even a tax on the noise made by planes. At Charles-de-Gaulle airport in Paris, the fee is three francs per passenger for any sort of plane. The Swiss tax only the DC-8, the noisiest plane of all. In Germany they're logical: Each airplane produces its own noise, so each has its 'price,' while in England the larger, quieter aircraft are given discounts.

However, as Ronald Pelletier explains, "For Air Canada, London's Heathrow Airport has one of the highest levels of charges in the world. During the peak period, in summer, it costs $11,397 to land a 747. At Tampa, Florida, the cost is only $111."

Thus a flight will cost more to certain places, on certain dates, at certain hours. An airplane that lands in Paris at night, for example, must pay its share for lighting the runway beacons. And if the weather takes a turn for the worse, any unfortunate aircraft grounded in the fog will have to lay out additional money to pay for the fog dissipators.

In London, taking off one minute earlier may make a difference of $5,000, if it means a shift into a peak period.

Air Canada pays some $220,000 per day for such charges, twice as much as four years ago. And that doesn't include airport passenger taxes, taxes on fuel, property and sales tax. These account for $100 million paid annually to the three levels of government.

Every day, Air Canada's 36 DC-9s, 14 DC-8s, 38 B-727s, 18 L-1011s, four B-747s and two 767s carry more than 30,000 passengers over 120,000 kilometres all over the world.

Each of these 16,500 seats represents an investment of $190,000. And the fleet, which depreciates at the rate of $130 million annually, must be maintained and upgraded. In addition to annually painting about 15 airplanes, over the next few years Air Canada will trade in its old airplanes for new ones, at the cost of $4.5 billion. A single Boeing 767 rings in at $54 million. By the end of this year, $35 million will have gone to rejuvenating the airline's 36 DC-9s.

But all these seats have to be sold. "It's like a huge inventory," says Guy Chiasson, Vice-President of Marketing. "And the product is perishable: an empty seat costs almost as much as one that's occupied, but it doesn't bring in anything. We have to ensure that every plane is filled to capacity."

To reach 70 percent of capacity, Air Canada calls on, in addition to its own services, more than 23,200 travel agents around the world. And these people don't donate their services: Commissions on sales are more than $140 million. With competition on most of its lines, Air Canada must also advertise its wares: $20 million is spent every year on publicity. One million dollars is needed just to produce the brochure listing flight schedules. And $200,000 in stamps to send them out.

To sum up: Fuel, personnel, airport and airway charges, food purchases, maintenance, tie-ups (inactive aircraft) and sales commissions account for $2 billion a year.

But the story doesn't stop there: Bills have to be paid. Eighty percent of receipts are from ticket sales. Rates vary according to destination. In Canada, the company determines a basic price which is always the same, regardless of destination. To this is added an amount calculated according to distance: the 'average price per kilometre.' The result is that a passenger flying directly from Halifax to Vancouver will pay exactly the same amount as another who makes a stopover in Montreal or Edmonton. For the company, though, it's not the same: The more stopovers, the costlier the flight. Don't forget that each stop involves paying the costs of landing, takeoff, air traffic control and fuel.

What are Air Canada's other sources of revenue? Charter flights ($33 million), transporting merchandise ($225 million), service contracts to other carriers ($146 million). The company is also selling its technological expertise, not only in maintenance and ground assistance, but in data processing as well. ReserVec, Air Canada's computerized reservation system, handles 200,000 transactions an hour at peak periods. Buyers include travel agents, other airline companies and Via Rail.

Despite the hundred or so strikes that annually paralyze the aviation world, despite the fact that 95 percent of its operations are carried out between the 45th and 55th parallels, under the world's worst meteorological conditions, Air Canada's punctuality record is one of the best in the industry. That's because, at $4,000 a minute, for passengers and company alike, time is money.

15

PRODUCT CONTRIBUTION ANALYSIS FOR MULTI-PRODUCT PRICING

WILLIAM S. KALLIMANIS*

Pricing in a multi-product firm can mean the difference between profit and loss. Yet, there is no agreement as to how prices should be set. Prices may be set on a cost plus a percentage markup, or what the market will pay, or what the industry leader will set as a price. All these and myriads of possible combinations fail to get into the heart of the problem of providing management with relevant data regarding a pricing decision. Nor do they show management the economic consequences of a pricing decision.

Price is influenced by the supply, quality, state-of-the-art, usefulness of the product and competition, whether we consider identical or substitute products. The price is also influenced by its stage in its life cycle. In this paper I propose to deal with the problem of pricing products on the basis of contribution, within competition and production constraints, and with the proper consideration of income flow over the estimated life cycle of the product.

The product life cycle, although its length will vary by product and industry, consists of the following stages: development, introduction, growth, maturity, decline and phase-out. For pricing decision purposes it is also important to recognize management's objectives during any given stage.

During the *product introduction* period, for example, one might use either a saturation or skimming price. Price reduction will be necessary to discourage competition or to meet it during the *growth* stage. Finally, when the product reaches *maturity* the price can be further reduced by passing along manufacturing savings to customers during the *decline* phase while

---

* From *Management Accounting* (July 1968), pp. 3-11. Reprinted by permission of the National Association of Accountants. The author was a controller when this article was written.

preparing to bow out of the market or to start a new cycle with its replacement.

General Analysis

What has briefly been described in the previous paragraph is known as marketing strategy. Marketing strategy and pricing policy, however, can be rather meaningless without reliable quantitative measures on which to base decisions. To measure the consequences of any marketing strategy it is necessary to anticipate prices, demand, and variable costs at several desirable volume levels. These data are used to calculate gross contribution at each level projected, both for the new and for the old products being replaced.

Assume, for example, the general contribution statement for a company's sales mix to be as follows:

Contribution Analysis   12-31-83

	($ millions)	%
Net sales	40	100
Variable cost	24	60
	—	—
Contribution	16	40
Period costs	8	20
	—	—
Taxable income	8	20
Tax at 50%	4	10
Net income	4	10

The most significant item in this statement is the 40 per cent contribution. This means that with our present prices and sales mix, every time a $1.00 sale is made, the company has 40 cents remaining for payment of its period costs and contribution to profit.

Although the general contribution statement is useful, it cannot be used for management decisions because it does not show product contribution or the specifics of sales mix. We may prepare a more useful form to reveal contribution by individual product as in Exhibit 1. This statement reveals a wide range of percentage contribution rates among products:

Product	Contribution%
A	40%
B	45
C	35
D	70
E	65
F	30
G	50
H	21
Overall	40%

Exhibit 1   Comparative Contribution Statement ($ Millions)

	Total Amount—%	Products A Amount—%	B Amount—%	C Amount—%	D Amount—%
Sales	$40.00 — 100	$24.00 — 100	$1.00 — 100	$1.40 — 100	$ .60 — 100
Variable Cost	24.00 60	14.40 60	.55 55	.91 65	.18 30
Contribution	$16.00 40	$ 9.60 40	$ .45 45	$ .49 35	$ .42 70

	Products E Amount—%	F Amount—%	G Amount—%	H Amount—%
Sales	$2.00 — 100	$3.00 — 100	$4.00 — 100	$4.00 — 100
Variable Cost	.70 35	2.10 70	2.00 50	3.16 79
Contribution	$1.30 65	$ .90 30	$2.00 50	$ .84 21

A more meaningful way of comparing the revenue and contribution of products is to rank them according to the dollar magnitude of individual products:

Rank According to Magnitude of Revenue

Product	Revenue Each	Cum.	Percentage Each	Cum.	Rank
A	$24.00	—	60.0	—	1
G	4.00	$28.00	10.0	70.0	2
H	4.00	32.00	10.0	80.0	3
F	3.00	35.00	7.5	87.5	4
E	2.00	37.00	5.0	92.5	5
C	1.40	38.40	3.5	96.0	6
B	1.00	39.40	2.5	98.5	7
D	.60	40.00	1.5	100.00	8
Total	$40.00		100.00		

Rank According to Magnitude of Contribution

Product	Contribution		Percentage		Rank	%
	Each	Cum.	Each	Cum.		
A	$ 9.60	—	60.0	—	1	60
G	2.00	$11.60	12.5	72.5	2	
E	1.30	12.90	8.2	80.7	3	
F	.90	13.80	5.5	86.2	4	
H	.84	14.64	5.3	91.5	5	40
C	.49	15.13	3.1	94.6	6	
B	.45	15.58	2.8	87.4	7	
D	.42	16.00	2.6	100.0	8	
Total	$16.00		100.00			100%

We can now prepare a comparative ranking schedule:

Product	Rank	
	Contribution	Revenue
A	1	1
G	2	2
E	3	5
F	4	4
H	5	2
C	6	6
B	7	7
D	8	8

Note that Product H ranks No. 2 in sales revenue but falls to No. 5 in dollar contribution toward period costs and profit.

The management's objectives will dictate which ranking is most significant. That is, if the short-term objective is to raise revenue, the revenue ranking will be important. If the management wishes to increase earnings per share, however, the contribution ranking would be more significant. In either case, the reliance on one at the sacrifice of the other would be detrimental to the firm.

Another point is also significantly illustrated by this analysis. We note that Product A contributes 60 per cent and the other seven products contribute only 40 per cent of the total dollars contributed. Consequently the decisions one must make regarding Product A could and will vary greatly from those made about products B through H:

Product		Contribution
A		60%
G	12.5	
E	8.2	
F	5.5	
H	5.3	40%
C	3.1	
B	2.8	
D	2.6	
Total		100%

Recognizing the heavy dependence on Product A, the management will attempt to control its manufacturing costs and to maintain volume at highest contribution level while planning to systematically phase out and replace it.

Management can now strategically plan and influence the cost, price and volume, as well as mix structure of the remaining seven products in order to improve contribution and, consequently, profit. Simulation methods may here be helpful.

Price Volume Contribution Simulation

Let us assume that the relevant prices are $40, $38 and $42, and that the variable cost per unit remains unchanged within this range of prices and demand. Question: Which of these alternatives is most desirable from the economic point of view?

Before this question can be answered, we would need to simulate a separate income statement for each price; then compare their contribution flows and present values in the following manner:

1. Simulate contribution for each price:

A. Unit price $40:

			Demand by Year					
			1	2	3	4	5	Total
Volume (units)			8,000	10,000	13,000	8,000	5,000	44,000
	Unit Price Amount	%						
Sales	$40	100	$320K	$400K	$520K	$320K	$200K	$1,760K
Variable cost	24	60	192	240	312	192	120	1,056
Contribution	$16	40	$128	$160	$208	$128	$ 80	$ 704

B. Unit price $38:

			Demand by Year					
			1	2	3	4	5	Total
Volume (units)			12,000	13,000	10,000	8,000	5,000	48,000
	Unit Price Amount	%						
Sales	$38	100	$456K	$494K	$380K	$304K	$190K	$1,824K
Variable cost	24	63	288	312	240	192	120	1,152
Contribution	$14	37	$168	$182	$140	$112	$ 70	$ 672

C. Unit price $42:

			Demand by Year					
			1	2	3	4	5	Total
Volume (units)			6,000	8,000	10,000	8,000	6,000	38,000
	Unit Price Amount	%						
Sales	$42	100	$252K	$336K	$420K	$336K	$252K	$1,596K
Variable cost	24	55	144	192	240	192	144	912
Contribution	$18	45	$108	$144	$180	$144	$108	$ 684

2. Recap of the contribution flows:

	Contribution by Price/Year			Difference over	
	Index Price	Alternative Prices		Index Price	
	$40	$38	$42		
Year	(1)	(2)	(3)	4(1-2)	5(1-3)
1	$128K	$168K	$108K	($40)	$20
2	160	182	144	(22)	16
3	208	140	180	60	20
4	128	112	144	16	(16)
5	80	70	108	10	(28)
Total	$704	$672	$684	$24K	$12K
Volume (Units)	44,000	48,000	38,000	(4,000)	6,000

At the $38 price, in order to maintain the contribution flow of the desired index, the company should sell 1,500 $\left(\frac{\$24K}{\$16} \text{ contribution/unit} \right)$ more units, or a total of 45,500. At the $42 price, the company must sell 750 $\left(\frac{\$12K}{\$16} \text{ contribution unit} \right)$ more units, or a total of 44,750 to recover the difference in contribution flow.

3. Present value of contribution flow:

Although a recap of contribution is useful, the analysis is far from being complete because the flows under each price have different patterns over the life cycle of the product, hence different present values. For example, at the $40 price the contribution peaks out during the third year; at the $38 price the contribution begins high, peaks during the second year, then goes down. Finally, at the $42 price the flow starts out slow, peaks out during the third year, then levels off.

For long-range planning purposes then, we should convert to estimated current value as illustrated in Exhibit 2. Question: Which of these alternatives is most desirable? To answer this question we need to ask two other questions: (a) Which of the three volumes can best fit in the projected production load? and (b) Which of the contribution flows has the greatest present value?

Exhibit 2   Contribution Flows by Year and Price

Year	Present Value Factors 15%	$40 Index Price		$38		$42	
		Amount	P.V. Amt.	Amount	P.V. Amt.	Amount	P.V. Amt.
	1	2	3 (1×2)	4	5 (1×4)	6	7(1×6)
1	.870	$128K	$111K	$168K	$146K	$108K	$ 94K
2	.756	160	121	182	138	144	109
3	.658	208	137	140	92	180	118
4	.572	128	73	112	64	144	82
5	.497	80	40	70	35	108	54
Total		$704K		$672K		$684K	
			$482K		$475K		$457

If the answer to the question (a) is: the company cannot accommodate larger production loads without increasing the cost (manpower and equipment), the choice would then be the $42 price. The sales force should devote additional effort to selling the additional units needed to recover the contribution difference between the index price and the decision price. This concentration of sales effort should be made early in the product life cycle, in order to bring the present value of the contribution in line with that of the index price.

If production is not a critical problem (capacity is adequate to facilitate a slight increase in production load), the $40 index price is the most favorable alternative. This is shown by the fact that present value of the contribution flows is largest at $482,000. On the other hand, if production capacity is not a problem and the objective is to penetrate the market, the best alternative would be the $38 price, which has a present value contribution flow of $475,000. This is only $7,000 less than the maximum present value at the $40 price. Management should also try to increase sales by the number of units necessary to recover the difference in present value of contribution flow.

Operational and Strategic Analyses

So far the discussion has centered around one product. In the remainder of this paper the group of reports presented deal with the evaluation of the economic consequences of a pricing decision for multiple products. These reports have been grouped in two categories:

1. Operational analysis.
2. Strategic planning.

Operational analysis refers to an analysis of present potential, such as unit, product and product line contribution.

Unit Contribution Analysis is the master file, in which all relevant data pertaining to a product are kept. This master file is used to extend units sold or forecast, to arrive at product contribution data. (See Exhibit 3.)

Product contribution analysis is a list of products sold, ranked according to the dollar magnitude of their contribution. From this report a marketing manager can readily see that there are a myriad of other analyses which can be designed to measure salesman, region and customer contribution performance. We are not here concerned with these added possibilities for analysis. Exhibit 4, however, shows the significance that the information can take when presented in a combined revenue and contribution schedule.

The management planning committee, having the standard file of relevant product information, the actual history of sales and the product contribution can now think in terms of how to develop pricing strategy. To aid the committee in this task, two additional reports are needed: (1) product life cycle analysis and (2) strategic analysis.

Product life cycle analysis is intended to give the management planning committee a complete history of relevant facts about the product, such as prices, quantity sold, revenues and contribution, from the date of product introduction to date of decision. (See Exhibit 5 on page 189.)

Strategic analysis. The management committee, having the basic data on a product master file, knowing the current contribution picture and product life cycle, can then consider the consequences of possible price changes on the profitability of the company. The purpose of strategic analysis is to provide management with a measurement of economic consequences for each given price decision or strategy (Exhibit 6, page 190).

Using the original pricing structure, it is anticipated that Product A's sales will increase by 20 per cent and that the remainder will have a 10 per cent gain. The revenue to be generated from the additional sales is $6,400,000 (forecast $46,400,000 − $40,000,000 last year's sales) and the contribution will be increased $2,560,000 (forecast $18,560,000 − $16,000,000 last year).

Exhibit 3   Unit Contribution Analysis (Standard File)

Product	Price	Std. Hours	Material Amt.	Material % Total Var. Cost	Labor Amt.	Labor % Total Var. Cost	Var. Burd. Amt.	Var. Burd. % Total Var. Cost	Total Amount	Unit Contribution Amount	Unit Contribution % of Price
D	$60.0								$18.0	$42.0	70%
E	20.0								7.0	13.0	65
A	40.0								24.0	16.0	60
G	40.0								20.0	20.0	50
B	10.0								5.5	4.5	45
C	14.0								9.1	4.9	35
F	30.0								21.0	9.0	30
H	40.0								31.6	8.4	21

Exhibit 4

Products	Revenue	Variable Costs	Margin	Contribution Amount	Contribution % of Total	Contribution Accum. %	Contribution Rank	Revenue % of Total	Revenue Rank
A	$24.00	$14.40	40%	$ 9.60	60.0	—	1	60.0	1
G	4.00	2.00	50	2.00	12.5	72.5	2	10.0	3
E	2.00	.70	65	1.30	8.2	80.7	3	5.0	5
F	3.00	2.10	30	.90	5.5	86.2	4	7.5	4
H	4.00	3.16	21	.84	5.3	91.5	5	10.0	2
C	1.40	.91	35	.49	3.1	94.6	6	3.5	6
B	1.00	.55	45	.45	2.8	97.4	7	2.5	7
D	.60	.18	70	.42	2.6	100.0	8	1.5	8
Total	$40.00	$24.00	40%	$16.00	100.0			100.0	

Exhibit 5 Product Life Cycle Analysis

Product	Month	Day	Price	Quantities Volume Each	Quantities Volume Cum.	% Each	% Cum.	Revenue Amount 000's Each	Revenue Amount 000's Cum.	% Each	% Cum.	Variable Cost Amount 000's Each	Variable Cost Amount 000's Cum.	Contribution Amount Each	Contribution Amount Cum.	% Each	% Cum.
Z	June 65	1	$50	1,000		1.17	—	$ 50	$ —	1.30	—	$ 30	$ —	$ 20	$ —	1.56	—
		2		1,200	2,200	1.41	2.58	60	100	1.56	2.86	36	66	24	44	1.87	3.43
		3		1,500	3,700	1.76	4.34	75	185	1.95	4.81	45	111	30	74	2.34	5.77
		4		2,000	5,700	2.34	6.68	100	285	2.60	7.41	60	171	40	114	3.12	8.89
		5		3,000	8,700	3.52	10.20	150	435	3.90	11.31	90	261	60	174	4.67	13.56
⁓	⁓	⁓	⁓	⁓	⁓	⁓	⁓	⁓	⁓	⁓	⁓	⁓	⁓	⁓	⁓	⁓	⁓
	Jan 67	16	40	4,800	55,300	5.63	64.84	216	2648	5.62	68.69	144	1659	72	989	5.61	77.02
		17		4,400	59,700	5.16	70.00	198	2846	5.15	74.04	132	1791	66	1055	5.14	82.16
		18		3,600	63,300	4.22	74.22	162	3008	4.22	78.26	108	1899	54	1109	4.21	86.37
		19		3,900	67,200	4.57	78.79	156	3164	4.06	82.32	117	2016	39	1148	3.04	89.41
		20		3,700	70,900	4.34	83.13	148	3312	3.85	86.17	111	2127	37	1185	2.88	92.29
		21	35	3,000	73,900	3.52	86.65	120	3432	3.12	89.29	90	2217	30	1215	2.34	94.63
		22		2,400	76,300	2.81	89.46	96	3528	2.50	91.79	72	2289	24	1239	1.87	96.50
		23		1,800	78,100	2.11	91.57	72	3600	1.87	93.66	54	2343	18	1257	1.40	97.90
		24		2,000	80,100	2.34	93.91	70	3670	1.82	95.48	60	2403	10	1267	.78	98.68
		26	30	1,500	81,600	1.76	95.67	53	3723	1.39	96.86	45	2448	8	1275	.62	99.30
		27		1,000	82,600	1.17	96.84	35	3758	.91	97.77	30	2478	5	1280	.39	99.69
		28		500	83,100	.59	97.43	18	3776	.49	98.26	15	2493	3	1283	.23	99.92
		29		200	83,300	.23	97.46	7	3783	.18	98.44	6	2499	1	1284	.08	100.00
		30		2,000	85,300	2.34	100.00	60	3843	1.56	100.00	60	2559	—	1284	—	100.00
	Total			85,300		100.0%		$3,843.		100.0%		$2,559.		$1,284.		100%	

Exhibit 6   Strategic Analysis

Forecast at Present Prices I

Product	Price	Anticipated Volume	Amount Revenue	Variable Cost	Anticipated Contribution Amount	% of Total Contribution	Cumulative Percent	Rank
A	$40.00	72,000	$28,800K	$17,280K	$11,520	62.08	—	1
G	40.0	110,000	4,400	2,200	2,200	11.85	73.93	2
E	20.0	110,000	2,200	770	1,430	7.70	81.63	3
F	30.0	110,000	3,300	2,310	990	5.33	86.96	4
H	40.0	110,000	4,400	3,476	924	4.98	91.94	5
C	14.0	110,000	1,540	1,001	539	2.90	94.84	6
B	10.0	110,000	1,100	605	495	2.67	97.51	7
D	60.0	11,000	600	198	462	2.49	100.00	8
Total		743,000	$46,400K	$27,840	$18,560	100.00		

Exhibit 7   Strategic Analysis

Product	Revised Price	Anticipated Volume	Anticipated Revenue	Contribution Amount	% of Total Contribution	Cumulative Percent	Revised Rank	Prior Rank
A	$40	72,000	$28,800	$11,520	59.94	—	1	1
G	42	100,000	4,200	2,200	11.45	71.39	2	2
E	20	110,000	2,200	1,430	7.44	78.83	3	3
F	34	105,000	4,200	1,365	7.10	85.93	4	4
H	38	130,000	4,940	1,092	5.68	91.61	5	5
C	14	100,000	1,680	588	3.06	94.67	6	6
B	10	130,000	1,300	585	3.04	97.71	7	7
D	60	10,500	630	441	2.29	100.00	8	8
Total		757,500	$47,950	$19,221	100.0			

Question: What would happen if the management committee decided to change prices as indicated by Strategy Y below?

Strategy "Y" Change Price — Primary Effects

Product to be Changed	Current Price	Proposed Price	Change in Vol.	Change in Rev.	Change in Contribution
F	$30	34	− 5,000	$900K	+$375
H	40	38	+20,000	+540	+ 168
G	40	42	−10,000	−200	-0-
			5,000	$1,240K	$543

It is anticipated, that by increasing the price of Product F to $34 instead of $30, Product G to $42 instead of $40, and dropping Product H's price to $38 instead of $40, the company will gain $543,000 in contribution. In addition to these primary effects, there will also be secondary consequences:

Secondary Volume Effects (Gained and Lost Contributions)

Products with Secondary Qty. Changes	Price	Change in Volume	Change in Revenue	Change in Contribution
C	$14.0	+10,000	$140 K	$49 K
B	10.0	+20,000	200	90
D	60.0	− 500	− 30	− 21
		29,500	$310	+$118

The result of the secondary consequences is favorable. That is, the net results will further increase contribution (by $118,000). The next step is to combine the changes and prepare a revised forecast of contribution (Exhibit 7, page 190).

Looking at the revised forecast, one can see a summary of the economic consequences of Strategy Y. That is, the volume will go up by 145,000 units, the revenue will increase $1,550,000 and the contribution will be raised by $660,000. This technique is repeated for as many feasible strategies as possible and then summarized according to management objectives and in order of magnitude of:

1. Liquidity
2. Earnings per share
3. Manufacturing output (compared to physical constraints)
4. Maximize revenue
5. Maximize contribution
6. Maximize profit

7. Return on investment (net present value)
   a. % return on gross sales
   b. % return on net sales
   c. % return on capitalization
   d. % return on assets employed

Summary

What is really significant in a pricing decision is neither cost nor price but rather the present value of the contribution that the product makes toward the recovery of period costs and profit over each product's life cycle. The simulation of price-cost-volume-contribution by life cycle yields consequences which can be anticipated and used in strategic planning geared toward achieving a specific corporate objective.

16

IS YOUR COST ACCOUNTING UP TO DATE?

A revised system can be a tool for
sharpening your company's competitive edge

ROBERT G. EILER, WALTER K. GOLETZ, AND DANIEL P. KEEGAN*

Greater competition, inflation, and increased outside attention to interim reporting all make a good cost accounting system more important than ever. Nevertheless, many companies have not changed their systems in recent years to reflect current conditions and to give an accurate picture of individual product costs. Since cost accounting bears on financial reporting, manufacturing processes, cost control, and product pricing, redesigning a cost system is not easy. But new computer and material control systems can facilitate the process. These authors point out how companies can use the more accurate information that an up-to-date system provides to formulate strategy and thus improve their competitive position.

Three years ago, when a $500-million division of a large company experienced an unexpected inventory adjustment, corporate management dispatched the internal auditors to determine what had happened. The auditors issued a report explaining in technically correct terms, that much of the inventory adjustment was due to poor but unreported product yields, delayed recognition of manufacturing variances, and routine deferral of several

* The authors are members of the management advisory services staff of Price Waterhouse. Reprinted by permission of the *Harvard Business Review*. From *Harvard Business Review* (July/August 1982). Copyright © 1982 by the President and Fellows of Harvard College; all rights reserved.

other types of variances (such as material substitutions) in work in process that showed up only at physical inventory time. Their report did not say that the underlying cost accounting system was at fault; there were plenty of procedural findings to explain the inventory adjustment.

The next year, the same division achieved only 60% of its profit plan, and managers decided that shrinking margins caused by intensely competitive pricing were the culprit. They also believed that the attention devoted to the previous year's inventory adjustment had confused the real issue: what had been considered an accounting problem was really a fundamental business problem. Once again the inventory was adjusted but, while significant in absolute terms, the adjustment was minor in relation to the division's overall profit problems.

Exhibit Symptoms of an Aging Cost System

Visible to top management	Inventory adjustments	Delays in getting answers to fundamental business questions concerning costs
	Large variances	
	Unsatisfactory knowledge of product profit margins	Audit reports citing poor inventory controls
Less visible, but easily detected	Inability to find someone in middle management who can explain, in depth, how the cost system works	Production decisions that are often based on capacity absorption considerations
	Awkward transfer pricing	Large accounting staffs that often perform "special analytic studies"
	Great relief when a physical inventory does not result in adjustment	Too much aggregation of general ledger data
	Lack of interest on the part of plant management in the budgeting process	
Visible only through detailed analysis	Poor analysis of manufacturing variances	Unclear separation of direct and indirect charges
	Little integration of manufacturing and cost systems	Little or ineffective use of predetermined budget allowances
	Incorporation of "factors" in product cost buildups and inventory entries	Control methods not extended to indirect departments
	Improper naming of cost elements, e.g., everything received in the plant is "material"	Improper identification of correct bases for overhead absorption
		Grouping of dissimilar variances

The term "shrinking product margin" began to take on special meaning. Subtraction of division costs from division revenues did indeed result in a smaller profit margin. Revenues, however, had been relatively constant. It was cost that had changed dramatically. The market had resisted cost pass-throughs, and furthermore, because of the way the cost accounting system had been developed, it was difficult to associate the increased costs with any one product line, much less with specific products. Therefore, the company could not accurately assess profitability by product, product line, customer, or geographic territory without a great deal of analytic work.

Unfortunately, just when the company most needed a well-designed cost system, the existing system proved quite inadequate. While the other divisions were not experiencing exactly the same profit problems, it appeared that their cost systems would not provide details on product profitability either.

Through the years we have learned a few unmistakable signs of a cost accounting system that is in trouble (see the *Exhibit*). The most obvious and the one that causes most companies to scurry is the symptom just mentioned — a large, unexpected inventory adjustment. Other symptoms, however, should be just as alarming to top management. These include high overhead rates, large manufacturing variances, and accounting staffs that always seem to be performing "special analytic studies" of cost. A particularly frustrating sign that cost accounting does not provide needed information is delays in getting answers to fundamental business questions, especially concerning product margins.

More subtle symptoms include plant managers' lack of interest in the budgeting process, the incorporation of "factors" into product cost buildups and inventory entries to prevent an inventory adjustment, complex and misunderstood transfer pricing, and little integration of cost and manufacturing systems. Before we explore these symptoms, let's first see why cost accounting is in the spotlight.

New Importance of Cost Accounting

Several factors now cause managers to turn their attention to cost accounting. A primary reason is increased competition, which leads to more frequent review of pricing. If promised quality and delivery are satisfactory but price can be improved, a customer will seek alternative suppliers. A seller who can aggressively price incremental business will gain a toehold with the customer.

Sharp-penciled pricing requires rapid access to current information about costs — from raw material all the way through the product's bill of material. Once-a-year product cost buildups are highly unsatisfactory, especially with double-digit inflation.

In addition, the indirect costs associated with the manufacturing process — energy, equipment maintenance, quality assurance, and data processing — often rise more rapidly than direct product costs. Furthermore, direct labor, which has traditionally absorbed this overhead, is becoming an increasingly unsatisfactory determinant. Many of these indirect costs are disproportional to the direct labor used. As a result, companies have extremely high burden rates, and these rates tend to confuse rather than explain the reasons for increased product costs.

New control systems unlock many opportunities for cost accounting improvement. Some U.S. companies are spending large sums to develop integrated manufacturing control systems. Even smaller companies can now afford computer-based systems that would have been impractical a decade ago, combining materials requirements planning, production scheduling, and shop floor control through on-line terminals. Information on purchases received, material movements, completed operations, amount of scrap bills of material for the product, work-in-process quantities, and other information traceable by computers are precisely the data on which an advanced cost system should be established.

Today's pace of change is often so overwhelming that the validity of a basic assumption of cost theory has diminished. Traditional cost accounting systems assume a certain amount of stability — at least through the budgeting period, which is usually one year. The possible requirements to publicly discuss the adequacy of internal accounting control brings new urgency to the problem of cost accounting. Because of the cost accounting system's key role in inventory valuation and cost-of-sales determination, companies can no longer ignore deficiencies in their cost systems. With attention being focused on public disclosure of interim results and business segment data, the traditional escape hatch of taking an annual physical inventory to correct the accounts is no longer satisfactory.

How a Cost System Goes Awry

The following scenario describes the failure of a hypothetical company's cost accounting system. Most cost systems have probably gone through some of these stages.

A manufacturer has a cost accounting system that has evolved through the years, but it was originally designed to meet the needs of a much simpler organization. The company began many years ago with one plant manufacturing variations of a single product. Overhead was a small portion of total costs, and it was convenient, therefore, to absorb the overhead on the basis of labor dollars. The plant then became unionized and adopted an incentive payroll system; there was no great need for information concerning labor efficiency because workers were paid only for what they produced, and dollars went into inventory on the basis of such figures.

As the company grew larger, additional product lines came into existence and new plants were opened. In time, Plant B uses Plant A's semifinished products and Plant C receives the resulting component for final assembly and shipping. All items Plant C receives are considered to be direct material, and because each of the plants is still a profit center, an interplant markup is included in product costs and eliminated in consolidation. Since the eliminations can be done only at an aggregate level, it is always difficult to determine the correct cost and profitability of items produced sequentially in different plants.

Overhead becomes a bigger and bigger portion of product costs. It is budgeted at a plantwide level and applied on direct labor at a rate of 400% or higher. At this rate, an incremental dollar of direct labor will cover $4 of overhead costs without changing the burden proportion. Each year, however, the direct labor base seems to shrink as a part of product costs, and the burden rates creep up. Adding to the difficulty, a new piece of capital equipment simultaneously increases overhead and decreases the contribution of direct labor. Products not produced on this piece of equipment absorb the additional overhead.

To compound planning and control problems, the cost accounting system is based on process costing concepts, and in the next stage the company becomes a job shop. When there were only a few products with minor variations, a process cost accounting concept might have been completely satisfactory. But new product lines demand large inventories of semifinished products. Measurement points at raw material requisitioning and final shipping only are no longer adequate. There are too many operations and inventory stocking levels in between.

In companies like this, plant personnel spend a great deal of time preparing manual reports (or developing computer systems) concerning each production stage. These reports have long recognized the change in product characteristics, but the cost accounting system never formally reflects that information. Plant managers have no faith in the data provided by cost accounting since it often differs greatly from what they know about operations from daily reports.

Revising the System

It is easy enough to see that the cost systems of many companies may no longer be adequate. Timely knowledge of current product cost is an important element in the planning and control process, especially in an era of rapid change. Fixing an obsolete cost system, however, is not a simple task. No other system has such a pervasive effect on a company. Cost accounting is based on budgets and forecasts; it is entwined with the material control systems; it provides information for financial reporting; it influences pricing and marketing strategy; and it is the source of information for make-or-buy decisions, certain capital expenditure decisions, and performance measurement decisions. Revising the system often takes several years of attention and a good set of blueprints.

Aims of the System

Before redesigning a cost accounting system, management must identify the objectives of the new system. These should include:

Accurate product costing. The overriding focus of a revised system should be product costing standards that closely approximate actual costs. This objective should take precedence over any other system goal. This effort will require concentration on that somewhat mystifying pool of costs called overhead. Managers should no longer be satisfied to "just get it into inventory." Overhead costs should be associated with the right products in the right proportions.

Cost control. The revised system should provide exception information to be used in controlling costs. Elements of cost should be analyzed at different volume levels to separate those that are controllable in the short run from those that are not. The revised system should embody flexible budgeting techniques to extensively monitor both production and service departments. As a by-product of such an analysis, it becomes possible to separate variable costs from those that are assumed to be relatively fixed over a fairly broad range of production volume. This information can help managers make decisions.

Physical control. Many managers find, often the hard way, that a cost system will not be successful if they don't enforce reporting disciplines. You may well conclude that raw material, intermediate stock, and finished goods should be segregated, behind fences, from work-in-process inventory. The stockrooms should be accessible only to material handlers who have inventory custodial responsibilities.

Identifying variances. Companies that are building new material control systems probably can gather data concerning actual labor, actual material consumed, and so on at the operational level. This information, flowing directly from shop-floor data collection, is captured primarily to permit monitoring of production status. In addition, however, these data can be measured against standards maintained in computer-based engineering files to reveal variances in actual operations.

It will then be possible to pinpoint problems in detail, and because the calculations will be a by-product of routine production monitoring, the information will be fresh when reported. Such up-to-date information can especially benefit companies trying to determine whether least-cost manufacturing processes are being used.

Integrity of inventory accounts. Before a new cost system can come into existence, the company should ensure proper income measurement. In many companies this can be done only by taking a physical inventory and pricing it. Since plant cost accountants constantly fear that the year-end inventory will uncover many surprises, they may hedge the year-end results by incorporating judgmental factors into product cost buildups and interim financial statements. Sometimes these factors are proper; more often they are not. One objective of the new system should be their elimination.

Management information. Managers may disagree about the proper conceptual basis of a revised system. Some may be proponents of absorption costing and others, equally vocal champions of direct costing. Elements of both probably can be effectively incorporated into a well-designed cost system. In such a case, profitability reporting would consist of a hybrid concept in which variable material, labor and overhead costs would be subtracted from revenues, showing a contribution margin by product, product line, and customer.

Fixed costs, however, would flow through the accounts and be incorporated in the inventory balances. Consequently, marginal contribution profitability reports could be brought back to an absorption costing basis by calculation of the increased or decreased fixed costs in inventory. In fact, certain traditional absorption cost variances, such as fixed spending and volume variances, could be computed very easily with the new system.

Providing this hybrid type of financial reporting is relatively easy. It supports profitability analysis well at different volume and mix levels, and it also supports pricing strategy. Marginal contribution reporting is another aid to management decision making.

How to Start

Cost accounting lies at the heart of the management process. Knowledge of product cost is necessary for competitive positioning. An organization that does not take a long, hard look at its cost system runs the risk that its competitors might.

If a review of a company's cost accounting system reveals the symptoms shown in the exhibit, what should managers do?

Step 1:
Diagnostic Review

Since few companies examine their cost accounting frequently and since cost accounting transcends organizational boundaries, it is usually necessary to create a diagnostic team, which will report to executive management. One iconoclast, or at least someone who does not understand all of the cost accounting actions that have been taken in the past, should be on the team.

The team should first determine whether the symptoms of an inadequate cost system represent small problems that can be quickly remedied or more pervasive problems requiring significant work. The latter case is much more likely. The team should also identify short-term "fixes" that are needed and decide if the existing system can weather a few more years. Its conclusion on this subject is very important because installing a new system is not easy.

Step 2:
System Blueprint

In the unhappy case where it is found that the existing system makes little sense for the company, the team should establish a system blueprint. Here it is important to separate "what we want to do" from "how we are going to do it."

The system blueprint should outline the major features the revised system will include, illustrated with pro forma reports, information flows, and sample economic transactions. The blueprint should be bold in its approach. It should tackle the issues identified during the diagnostic phase, and it should show how the revised system will simplify operational decision making.

Experience indicates a number of desirable features for revised cost systems that seem to fit all companies. These general features include:

Integration with material control systems. An effective cost accounting system must be integrated with the material control systems. A company that is planning to install a materials planning and control system has no opportunity to upgrade cost accounting without a large incremental cost. A well-functioning material control system provides most of the data needed for cost accounting. Unfortunately, planners far too often ignore cost accounting needs when the material system is being installed; perhaps worse, companies must then use the existing cost accounting system with the new material system.

Expansion of inventory accounts. The raw material, work-in-process, and finished goods control accounts that have served companies well over the years should usually be expanded dramatically in the new system. Because of the computer base, the volume of entries takes on much less importance than it did previously. Control accounts with names such as "material received," "work-in-process — center Z," and "distressed stock — location 21" might all be found in the general ledger.

Flexible budgeting. Both production and service departments should be under flexible budgeting control. Fixed and variable rates should be determined, and budgeted expenditure levels should be based on some type of activity measurement, such as production volume. In most companies, the cost of utilities, maintenance, material handling, and stock-keeping is much greater than direct labor.

Overhead cost identification. Direct labor alone is seldom a satisfactory basis for overhead allocations. Overhead amounts should be incorporated within product costs in a precise manner. The bases for allocation could include planned inspections, machine hours, job orders produced, setups required, the value of material received or staged, and intermediate product movement. A well-constructed product routing sheet helps to identify the proper basis for incorporating overhead costs into product costs. Expenses that can be identified, such as research and development or marketing costs, should also be associated with individual products or product lines.

Integrating budgeting, standards development, and actual expenditures. Estimates of expenditures in the form of budgets are an important element of a well-functioning cost system. These budgets should be used to develop standards for each product. Actual expenditures should be accumulated, compared, and reported on a basis consistent with these budgets and standards. Modern systems should give the manager the ability to explain in some detail why differences exist between the budgeted and the actual expenditure.

Cost estimating. Estimating cost will be simpler if the revised system (computer based) can maintain three levels of standard product costs. The first standard, established at the time of the annual budget revision, is used to value inventory and cost sales during the fiscal year. The second should be based on the most current material costs, labor standards, production methods, and bills of materials. These current standards represent the approximate cost of turning out products today if there were no intermediate items in inventory; they are often a more useful basis for decision making than the more traditional information obtained by allocating variances to product lines.

A third and final level should be provided within the system to allow simulations of future product costs based on forecast increases in labor rate or material costs. Most up-to-date material control systems have features designed to assist in materials requirements planning and make computation of these three types of product costs relatively simple.

The structure and complexity of the product directly affect the type of cost system that an organization should have. Certain product-dependent characteristics a company should consider include:

Total manufacturing time. A product that has many levels of subcomponents and that requires a considerable amount of manufacturing time presents special cost accounting problems. Techniques must be established to prevent surprises that may emerge when the job order is closed or when physical inventory is taken.

Types of material loss. A cost accounting system must effectively address elements of production that lead to material losses: lost or scrapped units, component scrap, test failures, start-ups, yield loss, atmosphere loss, or other unique loss. The system in this area must be tuned to support the company's product-costing and cost-control objectives.

Product technology. The timing and frequency of new products and engineering changes will have an impact on the cost system. The system must thus be responsive to the dynamics of the product and production process. Out-of-date bills of materials and routings will only diminish the integrity of the cost accounting system.

Finally, certain features of cost systems depend on organizational considerations. A good example is transfer pricing. The extent of intercompany component transfers and the way the company evaluates manufacturing operations both influence the complexity of a cost system. If each plant (or division) is to remain a profit center, a margin in excess of cost will be built into the transfer price. The margin, of course, must be eliminated by accounting procedures prior to the determination of corporatewide profits.

Often, communication failure and misinformation result from awkward or poorly designed transfer pricing, leading to internal bickering or bad judgments concerning the true source of profits. For these reasons, many companies prefer a transfer price based strictly on cost, with no profit margin.

Step 3:
Check Against Corporate Goals
Knowledge of costs has a broad effect on an organization. The way the system measures and reports performance and profits can be a strong force for changing management style. Therefore, executives should see and understand the blueprint. If it is not consistent with corporate strategy, it should go back to the drawing board.

Step 4:
Detailed Design
A number of important matters must still be considered before an implementation plan can be prepared. Now data processing, cost accounting, and material control specialists come to the fore. They should help to translate the blueprint into a series of construction specifications. They must answer such questions as: Will new computer hardware be needed? How will the material control system be changed? What is the timing of accounting journal entries? How will current product cost information be communicated? Will additional budgeting be required?

Step 5:
Implementation Planning
Even though the system blueprint should encompass the whole company, actual implementation is a step-by-step process that usually starts out as a prototype at one location. The system can then be fairly rapidly implemented throughout the organization. A detailed implementation plan and a trial run save a great deal of backtracking.

Executives will want to review a summary of the plan so that they know one exists. They should also have some curiosity about the cost of this endeavor. And most important, executive interest shows intent.

Tying System to Economics
The successful cost system will support the economics of your business. Cost accounting is no more than the thread that ties together an organization's economic plans and events. Developing such a system requires broad perspective and keen insight on the part of planners. This is why commitment and involvement of top management are so important.

In designing a cost control system, managers should take into account:

Shape of cost curve. While most companies see their costs rise with sickening regularity, the costs of some products, notably electronics, are falling. In fact, many industries try vigorously to reduce product costs. To do this, it is extremely important to separate carefully the effects of volume and performance on product costs. In a purely mechanical sense, if volume increases and fixed costs remain the same, product cost falls, yet the reasons behind this product cost reduction have little relation to the effect of better purchasing, labor reductions, or improved engineering design.

Cost proportions of product. Knowledge of product cost proportions should also direct control efforts. In many companies, although direct labor represents less than 10% of product cost, it receives a great deal of attention by industrial engineers, factory supervisors, and labor negotiators. Purchased material may represent 50% or more of product costs, but many companies consider purchasing activity routine. Investment to control this activity or to provide better information for purchasing decision making may not seem promising. But a shift of attention will benefit the company.

Knowledge of product cost proportions from the beginning to the end of the production process and understanding of the fixed cost implications of seemingly unimportant decisions can help management avoid costly mistakes. For example, a local plant management that had previously obtained a component from a "cousin" plant for a transfer price of $8.00 decided to purchase the part from outside, where the price was $7.50. However, $1.50 of the $8.00 internal cost was fixed cost that had been assigned to the component. Adding that fixed cost to the $7.50 price meant that the company would, in effect, be paying $9.00 for the outside component, unless there was some way to eliminate the fixed cost.

Executives in certain companies would argue that the buy-rather-than-make decision was correct and that the only way to enforce fixed cost control is to permit decisions like this. The point becomes even more dramatic if an entire product line is to be abandoned. On balance, however, the cost system should not encourage such potentially costly actions.

We have already mentioned the third cost component, overhead. Usually, dictates of management control overhead. But this technique seems to be working poorly.

Product acquisition strategy. For competitive reasons, many organizations are purchasing items that they previously manufactured. In such a case, once again, a direct-labor-based overhead distribution technique becomes a company villain. The products that are *not* purchased absorb the costs of the purchasing department and of receiving, receiving inspection, and stocking. As a result, the cost system shows that it is better to buy than to make. Like a snowball gaining momentum as it rolls downhill, internally manufactured components become more costly.

Companies that routinely purchase items for further fabrication or assembly into final products must, at a minimum, establish a purchased item overhead pool and allocate acquisition and stocking costs to the appropriate items. In other words, the cost system should show the economic reality of operating decisions.

Competitive Importance

From a study of up-to-date material control and profitability reporting systems in several *Fortune* "500" companies and many smaller companies, the one overwhelming conclusion we have reached is that, in American industry, knowledge of individual product costs is a strategic matter that companies must address to maintain their competitive position. The design and installation of an up-to-date cost system are not trivial undertakings, but if your cost system creaks each time the company moves, action is indicated.

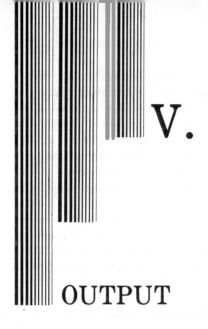

V.

OUTPUT

The "output" category has been used in this book to include a variety of decisions, but mainly focuses upon the quality and quantity of goods or services that are required. Some of the articles overlap into performance appraisal and inventory costing for external reporting and income taxation purposes.

The author of the first article, William J. Vatter, has made many contributions to managerial and cost accounting. The title, "Tailor-making Cost Data for Specific Uses," well describes the contents. Particular attention should be given to Vatter's observations about (1) seeking simple answers and (2) undeserved respect for numbers.

"The Fable of the Accountant and the President" shows how a combination of certain *facts,* a particular *management evaluation,* and an unsuitable management evaluation technique can spell "disaster." If management has idle capacity (fact), and desires information for performance appraisals (management evaluation) — specifically a bonus tied to income, and uses absorption costing (technique), then the income and bonus can be manipulated by increasing output. Many more similar combinations of facts-evaluations-techniques are ineffective, or misleading, as authors such as Vatter have pointed out.

"The Chop Suey Caper" humorously addresses a troublesome point in managerial accounting — allocations of costs that are common to more than one product or service or department/segment. How should the common costs be split up and charged to each product/service/segment? Is there a so-called right way? In general, for some decisions, cost allocations can result in the compilation of misleading information. However, allocations often are needed for inventory valuations and for pricing cost-plus contracts, and may apply in a few restricted performance appraisal circumstances where significant influence exists. In most financing-investing evaluations allocations can be avoided by focusing on incremental cash flows. When we are using a decision orientation theme considerable attention has to be given to what we mean by "cost allocations" and when they make sense.

"For Direct Costing in the Steel Industry" is another of the actual world examples that were chosen to help in learning how to tailor management accounting techniques to specific decisions. The author outlines some of the issues that have to be faced. Why does the company want direct costing figures?

"Formal Decision Making under Uncertainty: A Structure" specifically addresses problems of coping with an uncertain future. More attention is given to this issue in Section VIII, "Information Economics." This article examines the use of subjective probabilities. Would Vatter agree with Chesley's quantification?

The final three articles in this section on Output might well have been included in earlier sections but have been delayed to this point because they help to integrate decisions and accounting techniques. The first of the three, "Cost Information and Competitive Strategy: Lessons from Japan" outlines the vital role that cost figures can play in management decisions. The author, a specialist in Japanese management, explains the need to have reliable cost figures if a company is to be competitive in world markets. He stresses the importance of collecting costs in particular ways (by markets as well as products) for performance appraisal, pricing and output judgments. To be competitive cost trends must be known and costs must be lowered.

The next article, "Control Systems Supporting Economy, Efficiency and Effectiveness" is written from a public sector or government viewpoint. The late author is the former Auditor General of Canada, a somewhat equivalent position to the head of the Government Accounting Office (GAO) in the U.S. Given that governments often do not have a bottom line "profit test" for many of their programs how does one judge their performance? How does the taxpayer obtain information to assure himself/herself that "value for money" is being received? This article is an excerpt from the official annual report that is sent by the auditor general to elected federal officials. Evaluations of the type described (economy, efficiency, systems to measure effectiveness) require a multi-disciplinary "audit" team, not just accountants.

The final article, "The Stressful Effects of Budget Cuts in Organizations" presents a behavioural view of cost cutting. Accountants may think in terms of cost cutting and tight budgets, and being highly competitive in the short run. Yet, the author points to probable declines in productivity that could surround the uncertain environment that accompanies cutbacks. The article serves as a good reminder of the communication and personnel strategy that is necessary when cuts are made. Hoped-for benefits may not be received if morale of survivors drops.

17

TAILOR-MAKING COST DATA FOR SPECIFIC USES

WILLIAM J. VATTER*

Costs and cost data are important — not only to accountants who record and report such data, but also to a large number of other people. The greatest number of those interested in cost data are the people who share in some fashion in the task of management. As should be the case with any product or service, the demands of those people who use the results of cost analysis and cost accounting must and will be served. Just as soon as cost accounting is found inadequate for the needs it is supposed to meet, just as soon as cost accounting does not provide the data which management must have, cost accounting will either change to meet those needs or it will be replaced with something else.

The significance of cost data with regard to various problems of accounting, management and economic policy is a vitally interesting subject. It is a subject which deserves more attention from cost accountants everywhere. There is, however, a great deal of confusion and misunderstanding as to just how cost data are related to managerial and other decisions. To avoid this confusion and misunderstanding, it is essential to recognize that cost data must be treated differently when they are to be used for different purposes.

Two Human Failings Cloud the Situation

It is a natural human trait to seek simple answers to our problems. One is often impressed with the confidence that people have in simple solutions. We are constantly seeking the one factor that will serve as the answer to a

* From *N.A.(C.)A. Bulletin,* 1954 Conference Proceedings. Copyright 1954 by the National Association of Accountants. Reprinted by permission of the National Association of Accountants. The author had a distinguished career as an academic.

whole group of puzzles. We search for the key log in the jam, the straw that broke the camel's back — the philosopher's stone! Not that there is anything wrong with the simple answer if it really fits the problem. The trouble is that, in our zeal to get the one true and simple answer, we frequently overlook the real nature of the problem.

Worse, when we are faced with a complex problem that demands more careful analysis than we are willing to give, we get "practical" about it — that is, we assume away some of the issues, simply because we do not know how to deal with them, or because we are unwilling to take the trouble to learn what we ought to know. The world, and each of our respective businesses, is so full of problems that it is not uncommon to find those problems solved by the most convenient means — which is to ignore them! We want simple answers and we get simple answers, even if they must be made simple by ignoring the questions!

A second natural human trait is the tendency to revere mathematics. A quantitative answer is somehow more appealing and more convincing than a nonnumerical one. Numbers convey a kind of meaning which is less likely to be misunderstood, because everybody has learned to count in the same way. However, we often go too far in our dependence upon the objectivity of numbers. We impute to numerical calculations a reality and a dependability which they may not in fact have. The fact is that numerical data can be manipulated in many ways, all of which are entirely correct arithmetically and many of which may be valid for certain circumstances. Sometimes, however, there may be little validity in the calculations, because they do not apply to the situation. Yet it is surprising how often people will believe that a given calculation is correct, merely because it is arithmetically consistent — it can be checked against the rules of arithmetic.

I have no real quarrel with the emphasis on figures to deal with complex managerial problems. Indeed, I have a healthy respect for those who tackle the problems of the real world which I avoid by my being a college professor. I do not wish to suggest that management should operate by guesswork or intuition or that the patterns of cost analysis developed by accountants and applied by you to the problems of business should be scrapped. I merely wish to point out that sometimes the ground rules may be more important to playing a game than is the method of keeping score. Even in keeping score, it is reasonably helpful to know what game is being played!

I am certain that the two human traits I have mentioned, the search for the simple answer and the reverence for mathematics, can cause a lot of trouble for cost accountants. Cost figures may actually be misleading if they are computed to fit one purpose and used for another purpose. The validity and results of a business decision may often be traced to the way in which costs were marshalled in tackling the problem.

Figures on the Family Car

The methods of assembling and applying cost information to the solution of business problems depend upon the specific purpose or use to be made of the figures. Data which may have one meaning under one set of circumstances will have an entirely different meaning under other conditions. Let me illustrate this by a very simple and common case, the family car. The data are those which could have come from your personal records — if you are accountant enough to keep such records, which I am not! The questions I shall ask are those which have actually been asked in recent months by my own family. I am fairly sure that these same questions have arisen in your own case. The data are as follows:

Annual Cost of Operating the Family Car

Fuel (720 gallons at 29 cents)	$208.80
Lubricating oil and additives	30.00
Chassis lubrications	16.50
Inspections and maintenance	35.00
Washing and polishing	28.50
Licenses, city and state	26.50
Garage rent (less portion applicable to storing furniture, etc.)	126.06
Public liability & property damage insurance (net after dividend)	67.80
Depreciation $2,500 - $900 \div 4 =$	400.00
Personal property taxes (Valuation $200)	8.00
Total	$947.16

Per mile, for 10,800 miles, 8.77 cents

These figures presumably answer the question of how much it costs to drive a car per year. However, the only reason for wanting to know that is to be able to make a better decision with regard to some proposed action. The question of whether one can "afford" a car is too vague and meaningless to warrant much discussion here. I can assure you (from my own experience in selling cars) that the reasons for automobile ownership are far removed from any questions of economy or cost, in the great majority of cases.

Suppose the car is now in service and the question is raised to whether it should be used in preference to other transportation for a business trip of, say, 1,000 miles. Looking at the items in the cost schedule, it appears that the cost of fuel, lubrication, and perhaps some of inspection and maintenance, are relevant to the decision. These are costs that would be increased if we drove the car the extra distance, whereas washing and polishing, licenses, garage rent, insurance, depreciation, and property taxes would be irrelevant to the decision because they would be the same in total, whether or not the proposed trip is made. If (as some folks do) we trade cars often enough so that we do not purchase tires, it could well be argued that nothing should be shown for this item, since it is covered by depreciation. But, if we do not trade often enough to be able to overlook tire replacements, these should be about one-fourth cent per mile. Thus we have a per mile estimate of roughly three cents a mile as out of pocket cost to be considered in this situation. However, there probably should be something added to cover the extra *collision* risk (which presumably we are carrying without an insurance contract) and there may be other items, such as extra meals, bridge tolls, overnight lodging, etc., to take into account. Evidently what it costs to drive a car depends upon what you intend doing with it.

Some of you may say, "That's easy — it is the variable costs that are important anyway. Fixed costs are the ones to ignore!" Do not be too sure about that, either. If the question is asked as to whether or not the family should operate two cars instead of one, so that the use of the car by one person does not leave the rest marooned, the answer is to be found in a quite different way.

The variable costs, those which increase in total with the number of miles driven, are, in this case, quite irrelevant, unless the two cars in question have very different operating characteristics. These will be the same for either car for any given number of miles. If the total mileage for two cars is more than for one, then the variable costs are relevant, but only for the additional mileage. The fixed costs are really the important ones for this question. To acquire a second car will double the washing and polishing, the licenses, garage rent, insurance, depreciation, and perhaps more than double the personal property taxes. Worse yet, there should also be added the investment aspect of the transaction. Whether or not interest is a cost, it must certainly be taken into account when a decision involves tying up funds for such a purpose. Small wonder that the second car is often a smaller and less expensive vehicle. My own is a jalopy in the strict sense of that term!

All of this may raise another question — whether it is really wise to own a car in the first place. There are other means of transport — livery, taxicab, and car rental services would insist that at least there is something to be said for their side of the case. How could we use the figures given to establish an answer to this kind of question?

If we should give up automobile ownership, the costs shown in the schedule would be saved, except for the item of depreciation. This is ordinarily computed on the difference between original cost and ultimate trade-in value at the end of the intended service-life. In this case, the figures are a new cost of $2,500 three years ago, an expected trade-in at the end of four years at $900. The difference of $1,600 is spread over four years. Will this $400 per year be saved by disposing of the car? The car in question actually has a present market value of $800. If it is used for another year, it will bring only $600. The relevant depreciation for this purpose is only $200 for the next year, regardless of the other figures. But we should also include interest on the $800 present market value. If we had no car, the money could be put to work. What it would earn is what we lose by keeping the car.

There are perhaps other cost items that should be included. What about the dry-cleaning bills arising from walking three blocks in the rain to get the car from a parking space, while taxicabs roll past the door of the theatre? Or how about the suit that was ruined changing a tire just after leaving a friend's home at 12.30? Indeed, there are costs that do make a difference and there are computations other than the ones shown in the schedule. My illustration may seem biased against car ownership, but that is because I have not mentioned other, perhaps more important, factors than those included in the costs. My wife and I have two cars and I am sure we could not get along without both of them. She will not let me use hers, and I am too lazy to walk, even to the drugstore!

The question of whether or not one can really afford to operate a car may have strange implications. One member of our faculty (not an accountant nor in the business school) once asked what could be done about the very high cost of operating his car, which he figured at some sixteen cents per mile. The reply given him (by one who was something of a practical joker) was, "You don't drive the car enough for it to be efficient — hire a boy to drive it around the block for several hours each Saturday. That will get your cost down." I am sorry to report that the professor was stopped from this endeavor only by vigorous persuasion on the part of a more kindly colleague!

Business Needs Which Call for Tailor-Made Costs

Directing our attention more specifically to the subject of costs for special purposes in business situations, the first question to be raised is, "What is the nature of these different situations in which costs should be tailor-made?" I think the broad classification involved here is a four-fold one:

1.   Measuring income.
2.   Control of cost incurrence.
3.   Overall planning.
4.   Decision-making in specific situations.

Measuring Income

In terms of financial reporting — that phase of accounting directed toward informing the employees, investors and the public of the financial activities and results of operations — the prime function of cost data is to measure the expense flow. The trouble encountered in this field is the fact that cost data are related to income in many different ways.

First, there are two or more basic approaches to the problem with respect to how price-fluctuations should affect income. Much has been said and done about this. We have had proposed various types of "lifo," related methods, and index numbers. Some still hold the view that good old "fifo" or "average" cost is to be desired. Many of you, I suspect, prefer standard cost pricing for inventories, with variances carried into the operating statement for the year. Some prefer to prorate some, or even all, standard cost variances to achieve a more conventional cost calculation for inventories and factory costs of goods sold. To prorate variances, however, is to me even more than a compromise. It is an admission that conventional accounting for purposes of measuring income is different from the meeting of managerial needs by the collection of cost-variance data.

What is true of prices can be true of other things, not only in terms of compromise methods but in the pattern of conflicting objectives. The whole concept of matching costs with revenues can be viewed in at least two ways. When production fluctuates from month to month in order to keep in step with market demand, there is a problem as to how fixed costs shall be dealt with in the computation of inventories (i.e., as to how costs shall be assigned against a fluctuating revenue). Usually, this problem is solved by some pattern of normalization, an allocation of fixed costs levelling the otherwise awkwardly fluctuating inventory costs which would become high when production is low and low when production is high.

Along with this, comes a closely related problem as to what is meant by the "normal" output level. In standard cost theory, idle capacity cost is regarded as the cost of subnormal activity. Thus, costs of manufacturing may include costs that are not costs of product. There are costs of not producing, as well as costs of production.

In any event, the figures now to be presented are simple only because I have made them so. If this were a year-end statement, the proration of unabsorbed burden (or indirect costs) and/or the reallocation of variance would yield the results shown, only if all the possible patterns of accounting were to be realigned to the notion of total average annual cost. This is, of course, impossible, not only because cost accountants differ in their attitudes toward the handling of variances and under-absorptions, but also because the ordinary situation is too complex to permit such prorations on any but the simplest bases. Generally, as I suggested earlier, we solve complex problems by being practical. We force our problems to be simple.

In this instance, if we assign four-fifths of the manufacturing cost against the revenue for this period in the example given, the net income is conventionally established at $35,000. However, this calculation satisfies only those of us who are concerned about matching cost dollars with revenue dollars, all costs assumed to "rank abreast!" The statement appears below.

Measuring Income

Sales 80,000 units at $5......		$400,000
Manufacturing costs (100,000 units)		
Direct costs	$200,000	
Variable indirect	150,000	
Fixed indirect.....	50,000	
Total	$400,000	
Less inventory (1/5)	80,000	320,000
Gross margin.....		$ 80,000
Selling costs.....	$ 30,000	
General administration.....	15,000	45,000
Net operating margin (before income tax).....		$ 35,000

There are some who think that the matching process is a matching of revenues for a period with costs assigned to that period. On this basis, fixed costs have no relevance whatever to products or to inventories. They should be "expended" in that period when they appear as costs of being in business. Thus, the inventory would be one-fifth of variable costs only, or $10,000 less, and the net margin would be only $25,000. This view really arises from recognition of managerial aspects of accounting. Whether "direct" or variable costing is right or wrong is a matter of purposes and situations. My only point here is to make it clear that, even for purposes of measuring income, there are different kinds of costs and different ways of handling cost data.

Cost Control

The second broad purpose that cost data are made to serve is the managerial objective of placing responsibility for the incurrence of cost. This phase of cost-analysis is not the same thing as the computation of unit cost for products and services. One of the major tasks of accounting, from the managerial viewpoint, is the tracing of costs to the making of decisions. If decisions which are made can be identified with their cost, good decisions can be distinguished from bad ones; we may not only learn from our mistakes but we may find those mistakes through analysis of costs associated with decisions.

For control purposes, bases of distribution, methods of cost reapportionment, and allocations by means of burden or indirect cost rates, are all likely to be irrelevant and useless. Worthy and estimable as such cost calculations may be for other needs, they simply do not apply, for the most part, to cost control in the sense we use the term. What is essential to cost control is "activity accounting" (to borrow a phrase from Eric Kohler). Costs must be related to the things being done, and this is largely a matter of setting costs against decisions.

To attempt cost control only by the use of unit costs seems to me to overlook the prime purpose of control, which is to see that the various levels of decisions that have to be made in a business are harmonious. The salesman who merely sells as much as he can of everything, the machine tool hand who merely minimizes scrap losses, the engineer who designs the most durable mechanism — may each be working against, rather than for, the satisfactory and profitable performance of the enterprise functions. The organization and planning devices that are used to specialize managerial and other skills are and should be supplemented by functional, departmental, and operational-activity classifications of cost. The classifications should follow the levels of responsibility. Costs over which a factory manager or superintendent has jurisdiction should be charged at that level. Those that are associated with other levels of authority or delegated functions should be so charged. Thus, it is doubtful whether, from this viewpoint, machinery depreciation, building maintenance, and a number of other costs should even appear at the level of a manufacturing department foreman, or an operating cost center in the product-costing sense of that term.

Yet, in the patterns of cost incurrence that are associated with given activities, care must be taken to remove the effect of variables which have no direct connection with the activity being costed. An illustration is afforded by the first of the two tables next shown. Changes in cost as here portrayed would seem to show this year's operations less efficient and more costly than last year's. This is true, but it is irrelevant if the price shifts are beyond the control of the department head. A more careful comparison, making allowances to be sure that price changes do not affect the comparability of data, yields a quite different result. The two sets of figures appear below:

Cost Control and Price Shifts

	This Year	Last Year
Direct labor	$28,000	$24,000
Direct materials.	50,000	36,000
Indirect labor	10,000	8,000
Supplies	6,000	4,000
Power	2,800	3,000
Totals	$96,800	$75,000

Last Year Adjusted to Current Costs

	This Year	Last Year
Direct labor (up 20%)	$28,000	$28,800
Direct materials (up 40%)	50,000	50,400
Indirect labor (up 20%).	10,000	9,600
Supplies (up 40%)	6,000	5,600
Power	2,800	3,000
Totals	$96,800	$97,400

This kind of difficulty may, of course, be met by other means. But if real control is to be had by fixing responsibility for decisions, the irrelevant variables must be ruled out. This same kind of analysis requires adjustment of costs when standard conditions obtain with respect to equipment, materials or men. Proper adjustments are not always obvious or easy to make, but they must be made if the objective of cost control is to be attained.

Overall Planning

Much of what has been said about cost control applies equally well to the planning of costs. The attempt to forecast what costs should be and then to make them behave the way they should is the nearest business administration has ever come to a scientific or logical pattern. The attempt to forecast results and then to test these forecasts in experience is the pattern of scientific advance. Startling discoveries may arise when the reasons for failure are sought. Research — at the level of pure theory, or in the more mundane realms of product testing and development — can teach us much about management. It is important that the forecasts be sound and that proven hypotheses be employed, but every hypothesis has its limits. When I was a student in college chemistry, water was simply H_2O. Now, they tell me, there are nine kinds of water, each with properties and a formula of its own.

This same kind of thing is true of costs and cost behavior. Economists and cost accountants have never understood each other in this area, partly because they do not understand themselves. Let me illustrate. Every cost is a variable cost, and every cost is also a fixed cost over some range. The only difference is the size of the step. In theory, every plant can be expanded. Therefore, fixed costs may jump as we move from a high level of activity to a larger plant or a new set up of machinery, or another layout. We are frequently plagued by costs which jump at certain crucial points. These semifixed costs are merely smaller editions of the broad-scale fixed costs. Even so-called variable costs have their own little step-patterns. Raw materials and direct labor are acquired and applied in units that are least theoretically unreducible. One more unit of such costs (however small) is a step in the cost pattern.

There are several other observations which need to be made about costs for planning. One is that costs always look different in different circumstances. Increases in volume will always elicit more prompt expansion of staff than will be found feasible in terms of contraction, for the same amount of reduction in volume. Part of this is because of uncertainty and the desire to maintain continuity of operations. But part of it is the human desire to cling to what is, since we know not what should be!

Another observation is that costs need better classification than they are ordinarily given, and more study should be allotted to the problem of cost behavior. We should not wait for statisticians and economists to do such work for us. I have been much amused to see accountants striving desperately to perfect a formula to forecast travel costs as a percentage of sales, when it is clear that the factors governing the costs are not sales dollars or tonnage. Even more disturbing is the fact that, once a formula is set, the cost never falls below that formula. Strong pressure may keep it from rising, but it will not go any lower than we have said it should be!

Still one other point may be made on the planning aspect of costs. Rate of activity is often (and I think wrongly) taken as output or capacity or some related concept. Costs for planning and control purposes are related to decisions. Decisions have to do with inputs, not outputs. It would be better to talk and think about break-even charts, budgets, and other planning devices in terms of the input factors which must be controlled, rather than the output bases on which we can write up our post-mortems!

Decision-Making: The Special Order, Choice of Output Level

There is a great variety of cost situations in which the question of relevance must be asked again and again. It must be checked and rechecked, for cost data have a way of remaining mute and unchanged under differing conditions. The right cost for one purpose may be the misleading cost for another. A few illustrations may serve to point up these problems. I shall touch only briefly on each of the illustrations. Still, and even though these illustrations are not exhaustive, I think they will serve to present the general areas of importance, and the essential cost data, that are relevant to some specific decisions.

The data presented below this paragraph are directed to the question of whether or not a special order should be accepted. This order is special in that it is entirely unrelated to any other existing plans or commitments of the firm. The question in this case is whether or not the firm should accept an order for 1,000 units of this product at a price of $5 per unit. The figures follow:

The Special Order

Revenue (20,000 units)		$140,000
Factory costs (20,000 units)		
Variable	$92,000	
Fixed	18,000	110,000
Gross Margin		$30,000
Selling cost variable	$ 20,000	
Administration, fixed	16,000	36,000
Loss		$ 6,000

It will be seen that the total factory costs applicable to 20,000 units is $110,000, which is $5.50 per unit. The offer seems unattractive, until it is recognized that acceptance of the order will leave fixed costs unaffected. Thus, the relevant factory cost is $92,000 variable costs, or $4.60 per unit. Each additional unit produced will increase factory cost by $4.60. Thus, the acceptance of this order will tend to reduce a present loss by adding $5,000 to revenue and only $4,600 to factory costs. However, the selling costs are also variable. We have been assuming tacitly that they were fixed or, at least, would not be increased by the acceptance of the order under consideration. However, these selling costs might include packing, shipping or handling charges that would be increased if this order is accepted. The answer must be found by establishing which costs may be expected to increase if the order is taken and by how much. Only by such an approach can an intelligent decision be made.

Another question is choice of a level of output. The figures below show data regarding a loss-product. The selling price is set by competition and the market at $4.50. As can be seen there is no hope of making a profit, since the average unit cost is, even for the highest output level, $5.51. However, the question here concerns the level at which the loss will be least. These are the data:

Level of Output — Price Given

| | Rate of Production and Sale | | | |
	10,000	11,000	12,000	13,000
Factory cost, variable....................	$37,000	$40,800	$44,600	$48,400
Factory cost, fixed.......................	9,000	9,000	9,000	9,000
Selling cost, variable....................	6,000	6,600	7,400	8,200
Administration, fixed....................	6,000	6,000	6,000	6,000
	$58,000	$62,400	$67,000	$71,600
Average unit cost.......................	$5.80	$5.67+	$5.58+	$5.51−
Average variable unit cost...............	$4.30	$4.31	$4.33	$4.35

The answer seems obvious. The unit cost is least at the 13,000 unit level. This should be the point of lowest loss. But these total average unit figures are not relevant and the decision suggested by the falling average unit costs is wrong. For, if we analyze the *changes* in cost associated with the *changes* in output (differential cost), it will be seen that, to produce 11,000 units, involves costs of $62,400. This, compared with the cost of producing 10,000 units ($58,000), shows a differential of $4,400, or $4.40 per unit. With a price of $4.50, the deficit is reduced by $100 if the rate of operations is raised to 11,000 units. However, when we compare the cost at 11,000 units with that for 12,000 units, the differential is $4,600 or $4.60 per unit. There is a disadvantage of 10¢ per unit or $100 in the move from 11,000 to 12,000 units. A similar situation is found in the differential cost between 12,000 and 13,000 units. Hence, the firm will minimize its loss by expanding to 11,000 units, but not beyond.

It should be noted that total average unit cost is irrelevant for this purpose. It should also be pointed out that even average-*variable*-per-unit cost does not reflect the cost situation properly. There is no safe way to approach the cost angles of special orders or output variations except to consider variable costs only, and then at the indicated levels. Indeed, it is possible to go further than this. In any situation involving price or output variations, the only relevant costs are those variable costs associated with the proposed changes.

Decision-Making: Make or Buy, Sell or Process Further

A frequently raised question, and one that deserves attention, is whether to make or buy an item. The illustrative data are given below:

Unit Cost of Part 17-432

Direct labor (current cost)...........	$ 7.00
Direct materials (current cost).......	8.00
Variable indirect cost...............	4.00
Fixed indirect cost.................	3.00
	$22.00

Quotation is $20 each.

Unit Costs Relevant to Make
or Buy Decision

Direct labor.......................	$ 7.00
Direct materials...................	8.00
Variable indirect cost..............	3.50
Total............................	$18.50

We see the costs of producing a certain part which can be purchased for $20 per unit. First, it should be noted that the earlier comments about currentness of costs are applicable here, as elsewhere. The data given seem to indicate that the item in question should be purchased, since the cost of production is $2 more than the quotation. However, the data as shown are misleading. If only the variable costs are considered (since the fixed costs will be the same whether we make or buy the item) the relevant costs are only $19 per unit.

But there is another angle. It is important that only escapable or avoidable costs should be recognized in a calculation such as this. It has been suggested that variable costs do not always behave as expected. Sometimes, they do not fall when activity is reduced. Hence, a more relevant figure may be had by including in the tabulation only those costs which could be saved if the part were not manufactured, in this case $3.50 variable cost per unit. If it were possible to reduce fixed costs by the decision to purchase this part, that portion of the fixed cost which could be saved by purchase is a relevant cost of continuing to produce the item. As for the situation here described, the decision should be to make this part.

The problem to be approached in the question of sales versus further processing is typical of many industrial situations. The alternative often exists of selling a given item at a given stage of completion or of processing it further to sell at a higher price. For instance, pork may be cured, smoked, canned, etc. Metals may be fabricated to different degrees. Other products may be delivered to the market in various forms. Management must decide for the particular firm how far processing will be carried toward the completely finished state. What costs apply to such decisions and how are they to be dealt with?

The data below refer to operations on two products which are produced jointly. The question raised is whether Product B should be sold as such or processed further to make Product C. The figures involved are:

Costs of carrying on the joint process $36,000
Output of A, 10,000 lbs., price $3.00 per lb., sales value $30,000
Output of B, 10,000 lbs., price $1.50 per lb., sales value $15,000
10,000 lbs. of Product B × $16,000 additional processing will yield 8,000 lbs. of Product C, unit price $4.

The question immediately arises as to the cost of Product B. This can be established conventionally in at least two ways. If the joint costs are divided on the basis of weight, the cost of 10,000 lbs of Product B is $18,000. This, added to the cost of further processing gives a total cost of Product C as $34,000. Since the sale of the latter will bring only $32,000, it does not appear advantageous to carry on the additional processing. However, if the joint costs are divided on the basis of sales value, the cost of Product B is only $12,000 (one-third of $36,000) and the total cost of producing Product C is $28,000, which would indicate a margin of $4,000 to be gained by the additional processing.

Obviously, something is amiss here. The cost allocations give entirely in-consistent results. One or both of them must be wrong. There is no way to establish the correctness of either of these methods of cost allocation. The really important thing to see is that cost allocation between Products A and B is, for the purpose at hand, irrelevant. The way to approach the problem is to take the price of Product B and the revenue to be had from its sale as the cost of putting it into further processing. For that is precisely what is given up when Product B is subjected to further processing. The alternative or displacement cost is the relevant cost in this situation. The calculations would then be:

Displacement cost of putting Product B into further processing	$15,000
Additional costs of carrying on the production of Product C	16,000
Total cost of Product C	$31,000
Revenue from sale of Product C ($8,000 × $4)	$32,000
Advantage in further processing	$ 1,000

The validity of this approach may be established by comparison of the total costs and revenues for each of the alternative actions:

Sell Product B Without Further Processing		Additional Processing — Sell Product C, Instead of Product B	
Sales of Product A	$30,000	Sales of Product A	$30,000
Sales of Product B	15,000	Sales of Product C...............	32,000
Total revenue................	$45,000	Total revenue................	$62,000
Costs before splitoff..............	$36,000	Costs before splitoff..............	$36,000
		Additional processing	16,000
Total costs..................	$36,000	Total costs...................	$52,000
Net margin..................	$ 9,000	Net margin..................	$10,000

The reader may perhaps feel that this situation has been forced by the use of a joint product illustration. This is not the case. The same approach would be indicated if Product A did not exist. The data relevant to the question of further processing must include the revenue foregone by not selling the output at the earlier stage of operations. The costs up to that point — unless they can be altered by the decision to process further — are irrelevant and should be ignored.

It is also worth noting that the joint cost situation is a great deal more common than it is ordinarily supposed to be. Most firms, for one reason or another, have joint costs of producing the various products. For example, to which product should the costs of personnel management be charged? The answer is really that personnel management costs apply to all products in a joint cost sense. Many service department costs are joint costs in this same way. In fact, it is really an unusual situation which does not reflect some elements of the joint cost problem. What has been said earlier in this discussion about the costs of not producing, the costs of being in business, the costs of inefficiency, etc., are cases in point.

The real problem of cost accounting from this viewpoint is not so much the working out of "bases for distributing" joint costs but of establishing when and how much cost is relevant to a given question.

Decision-Making: Selection, Replacement of Equipment

Enough has already been said to cast some doubt on the too-ready acceptance of unit costs as a means of making managerial choices. However, one other area should be explored. Below are shown the data concerning two pieces of equipment which can be employed to carry on a specified operation, with outputs as stated:

Annual Costs

	Machine A 80,000 units	Machine B 100,000 units
Direct labor...............................	$ 6,400	$ 7,000
Direct materials	8,000	9,000
Variable indirect........................	4,000	6,000
Fixed indirect	2,400	3,000
	$20,800	$25,000
	26¢ each	25¢ each

The unit cost comparison on the basis of the data is favorable to the larger machine. This advantage *might* apply to other levels of output but it might not. The relative proportions of fixed and variable costs have an important effect on the responsiveness of unit costs to shifting volume, and it is a dubious calculation which does not take this into account. If the data are set up for the operation of Machine B at a level of 80,000 units, we could have:

Direct labor..................................	$ 5,800
Direct materials	7,500
Variable indirect.............................	4,900
Fixed indirect	3,000
Total......................................	$21,200 per unit 26.5¢

The reason for the higher cost at 80,000 volume is not merely the presence of fixed costs. It has been suggested that variable costs may or may not be proportionate to volume of output, or even to the level of input. To make judgments of the sort here under discussion, it is necessary to know something more about cost behavior than the simple dichotomy of variable and fixed costs.

Further, it should be noted that investment is reflected in these figures only by depreciation charges. This is inadequate if the amount of investment is substantial. Whether or not accountants believe that interest is a cost of manufacture is not really important in this situation. What is important is that the relative investment must be measured in making the decision between these machines. Needless to say, the situation should be studied with full recognition of income tax effects and with some regard for those risks of obsolescence, supercession and inadequacy that are not considered in the usual accounting depreciation charge. That is, there should be a careful judgment as to the capital recovery situation in regard to the rate of technical progress and possible market shifts. Cost figures need to be tailored to fit such a situation, so that they reflect, as best they can, the factors that are relevant to the decision.

To make even more clear that the cost data employed for management purposes must be fitted to the use to be made of them, consider the question of replacement. To make matters more concise, let us assume that the company already owns five machines of Type A considered above. The question is raised as to whether these should be replaced by four Type B machines. This situation is purposely constructed to remove the cost fluctuation at varying volume. It is assumed that 400,000 unit capacity is needed now and in the future. Since Machine B is obviously superior to Machine A on a cost comparison basis, why not replace these machines?

The usual pattern of reluctance to replace centers around the unabsorbed book value of the old machines. But this is irrelevant for, whether or not the old machines are replaced — and regardless of their book value — the write-off is whatever it is. It is of *no* consequence, except as a tax saving.

One real confusion in the data lies in the fact that the cost attributed to the old machines (now in service) includes depreciation, which is also irrelevant since it is not a part of the data for decision. If the cost of an A-type machine is $10,000 and the use-life for depreciation is 10 years, then, for five machines now in service, there has been included in cost $5,000 for the year. This penalizes machines now owned with a cost that cannot be saved (since there is assumed no trade-in value). This cost should be removed.

	Keep 5 A's	Buy 4 B's
Direct labor	$ 32,000	$ 28,000
Direct materials	40,000	36,000
Variable indirect	20,000	24,000
Fixed indirect	12,000	12,000
	$104,000	$100,000
Less sunk-cost	5,000	
	$ 99,000	$100,000
Add interest, insurance and property taxes on additional investment (10%)		5,600
Total	$ 99,000	$105,600

Also, there should be charged in the schedule of cost for the four B-type machines, not only 10 per cent depreciation on their assumed $56,000 total investment, but also interest, insurance, and property taxes on this additional investment. A more relevant comparison is thus the one shown at the bottom of page 220.

It should also be noted that the effect of income taxes needs to be considered, both with regard to the savings or extra costs, and the obsolescence write-off, also if new machines are acquired. It should also be observed that the depreciation charge on the new machine is minimal and should probably be higher for this situation.

A word may be necessary as to the charge for interest, insurance and property taxes. It may be objected that these should be based on average rather than total investment. The reason for showing them as a percentage of total investment is that the superiority of the new machines is being tested on the basis of the first year of operation, i.e., in comparison with the current-year outlook for the machines now in service. To base investment charges on average investment is to assume too much about the problematical future. The advantage in the new equipment — if there is one — should be obvious in the initial year and it should be sufficient to cover the investment charge for that year.

Conclusion

These are not all of the situations that could be described. All of the problems of tailor-making cost data have not been presented here. What I have tried to do is to make it clear that the use to be made of cost data governs their content and that cost data must be tested for relevance before they can be relied upon in management decision-making.

Cost accountants must not only be aware of these distorting influences in the data with which they work but must also be willing and able to analyze data in whatever patterns may be necessary to get proper perspective and to present the basic information that management needs. It is not enough to present all of the data, leaving the interpretations to the readers of reports. The responsibility of the cost accountant is to learn the uses that are to be made of his cost data, and to make certain that the data are used as they should be, and to see that relevant and irrelevant data are handled properly, so that management may rely on the figures for what they purport to be — bases for decision.

The acceptance and discharge of this responsibility does not involve any shift in principles, abandonment of extant methods or other disturbances. Rather, such an approach to the cost accountant's job will develop a more essential and fruitful relationship between managers who need information about their business and the cost accountants who can supply such information. By this means cost accountants can assume a rightfully deserved place in the productive efforts of industry. They can establish themselves as contributors to the attainment of progress.

18

THE FABLE OF THE ACCOUNTANT AND THE PRESIDENT*

Act I:

Once upon a time a company was operating at a loss. Although its plant had a normal capacity of 30,000 widgets, it was selling only 10,000 a year, and its operating figures looked like this:

Price per unit	$	1.00
Total fixed cost	$ 6,000.	
Fixed manufacturing cost per unit	$	.60
Variable cost per unit	$	.65
Total unit cost		1.25
Total manufacturing cost	$12,500.	
Cost of closing inventory	$	0.
Cost of goods sold	$12,500.	
Sales revenue	$10,000.	
Operating loss	$ 2,500.	

---

* Source unknown.

Act II:

Then one day a bearded stranger came to the board of directors and said "Make me president, pay me half of any operating income I produce, and I'll make you all millionaires."

"Done," they said.

So the bearded stranger set the factory running at full capacity making 30,000 widgets a year. His figures looked like this:

Total fixed cost	$ 6,000.
Fixed manufacturing cost per unit	$ .20
Variable unit cost	$ .65
Total unit cost	$ .85
Total manufacturing cost	$25,500.
Cost of closing inventory	$17,000.
Cost of goods sold	$ 8,500.
Sales revenue	$10,000.
Operating income	$ 1,500.

"Pay me," said the bearded stranger. "But we're going broke," said the directors.

"Oh!" said the stranger. "You can read the income figures, can't you? You have never been more profitable!"

Act III:

But just as everything seemed lost, an accountant in gleaming eye shade charged into the room. "Hold," he cried. "I have just changed to the system called VARIABLE COSTING. We charge only variable manufacturing costs to inventory. So now the figures look like this:

Variable cost per unit	$ .65
Cost of manufacturing 30,000 units	$19,500.
Cost of closing inventory	$13,000.
Variable cost of goods sold	$ 6,500.
Sales revenue	$10,000.
Contribution margin (here's where the trick comes in; we'll explain later)	$ 3,500.
Total fixed costs	$ 6,000.
Operating loss	$ 2,500.

So the bearded stranger was foiled and the directors are back looking for a way to earn income — and to sell off the inventory the stranger left them with.

19

THE CHOP SUEY CAPER

HOWARD C. GREER*

This fable was written to demonstrate the elusiveness of the concept of divisional net profits. The article has been edited, with permission, to delete some references to specific divisional net profit measurement difficulties. Readers may thus concentrate on the message the author also conveys about the usefulness of cost allocation for some types of management decisions.

At the door to the supermarket my shopping cart collided with another. Its chauffeur proved to be Hal Hobbs, a neighbor and long-time business acquaintance. On recognizing me, he beamed.

"Aha!" he exclaimed cheerily. "Most appropriate! I need a chain-store expert, I meet one at the chain-store."

"This is a gag?" I inquired, suspiciously. "I'm no expert on chain stores, or much of anything else, for that matter."

Hal looked offended. "You wrote a book," he protested.

"Forty years ago!" I reminded him. "And not a very good one."

"Yeah, but you were in the meat business for years . . . ran a big packing company, had a chain of food stores as an appendage. . . ."

"An experience I'd like to forget," I interrupted hastily. "Results of that food-chain venture hardly qualify me as an expert. . . . "

Hal was undaunted. He grinned. "Okay, so you know the wrong answers; maybe you can help me find the right ones." He gestured to a nearby bench. "Come on, sit down a minute. I need some advice."

---

* From *The Journal of Accountancy* (April 1968), pp. 27-34. Reprinted by permission of the author and editor. Copyright 1968 by the American Institute of Certified Public Accountants, Inc. At the time of writing the author had both a business and academic background.

I sighed, followed him slowly. Hal is worse than the Ancient Mariner, and I saw that I was in for it. We sat down. "What do you care about chain stores?" I demanded. "You're a banker."

"Bankers get mixed up in every kind of business," he assured me. "Right now, I've got a little chain of stores around my neck." He looked grieved.

"Lucky you!" I commiserated. "Which one?"

"Call themselves Mack's Markets. Ever heard of 'em?"

"They got a store in Danville?" I queried doubtfully. "Think I've seen it."

"Yup," he responded. "That one, and four others — Concord, Pittsburg, Antioch and Brentwood. Small operation; annual volume around $5 million. . . . "

"Annual profit around nothin'," I guessed shrewdly, "or you wouldn't be worried."

"Just about nothin'," he confirmed glumly. "They barely broke even last year, and it frets the stockholders."

"Of whom you're one?" I hazarded. "Or did you make 'em a loan?"

"Neither," he responded. "But almost as bad — there's some of the stock in one of our trusts, and the beneficiary is unhappy about it."

"Sell it," I advised promptly, but he shook his head, said it wasn't that easy.

I didn't ask him to explain; I knew he would, regardless.

"It's like this," he went on, pleased to have a captive audience. "Old man Mack, now dead, had this food store in Antioch, where the warehouse and office are still located. Not a bad little operation: he lived over the store, did most of the work himself, made a fair living out of it — you know how it is." I nodded understandingly.

"Getting older, he began worrying about what would happen to the business if he died. One-man show, might fold if he weren't around. Figured a little chain of stores like his would have a better chance of survival than one standing alone. Talked to a couple of other store-owners similarly situated — and it wound up with their putting three units together, with Mack's as the nucleus. Later they took in a fourth — the one in Danville — eventually opened a new one — the so-called Eastside store in East Pittsburg — made it five altogether."

"Either too many or not enough," I commented sagely. He shrugged.

"Anyhow, in due course Mack died, like he thought he would. Left his stock in the enterprise in trust with our bank, benefit of his widow. Didn't leave much else, so she needs the income it should provide."

"And it doesn't provide any; she can't understand why, and you're in the grease."

He nodded gloomily. "Hell of it is," he added, "I can't understand why either."

I chuckled grimly. "This is where I came in," I told him. "Let me guess. Taken individually, each of the stores makes some money; taken collectively, they show up with no profit. That about the way it goes?"

"Right!" he confirmed, slapping my shoulder, "I knew you were the expert."

"My diagnoses are infallible," I assured him. "I don't even have to see the patient. Only thing I'm short on is effective remedies." But he ignored that latter remark.

"Look," he said, squinting thoughtfully. "Would you go over the figures with me some day when you're not too busy — wise me up a little on how to interpret them? I'm no accountant, you know —."

I'm a sucker for such appeals; told him sure, any time; wound up with a promise to join him for an afternoon session with some of the company officials, couple of days later. Smart off and you get involved; it's just that easy.

Hal was back in his customary good spirits when I presented myself at his office, around noon on the appointed day. He bounced out of his chair, grabbed my arm and propelled me toward the door.

"Let's go to lunch, huh?" he boomed cheerfully. "Like Chinese food? Place nearby has the best in town. Want you to try it." I could have told him that a hamburger and milk would suit me better, but he gave me no chance to express a preference.

"Try the chop suey," he insisted, when we were seated in the restaurant, amid some pseudo-oriental decor and a pervasive odor of soy sauce. "It's real good."

I tried the chop suey. It *was* real good. I'd have preferred a hamburger.

"We'll drive out to Antioch," Hal told me blandly after lunch in his best take-charge manner. "That's their head office. Sam Stone, the general manager, is away, but Fred Fain, the treasurer, is the man I want you to meet; he puts the figures together. And he has rounded up the five store managers. Some of them are former owners of the individual stores. Each of them has his own interpretation of the results, and I want you to hear them." He chuckled maliciously. "Then you can tell me who's right, and I'll know where the trouble lies." That he expected to stump me, the expert, was all too plain.

Now, I'll tell it just like it went, altering only the names (to protect the innocent) and the figures (which have been freely rounded to simplify the presentation). You'll get the essentials of the picture just as I did, and you can expert your own way to a conclusion.

'We assembled in a bare little conference room, in the combined warehouse and office over the Antioch store, where the cheerful clang of the cash registers from the floor below happily punctuated the debate. Hal introduced me to the treasurer, Fred Fain, and the five store managers, whom we can call Art Ash (Antioch), Bill Budd (Brentwood), Cap Clay (Concord), Dan Dow (Danville) and Ed Eck, (East Pittsburg). The store managers regarded me dourly; they had evidently encountered experts before.

"Okay, Fred," Hal instructed. "We want to look at those two statements you made up. First pass around copies of the company's income account for last year, the way you made it up for the directors; we'll go over that; then later you can give them the analysis you put together for me, on the basis of the store managers' interpretations."

Fain dutifully passed out copies of his statement, which (appropriately amended to emphasize the salient features) looked about as shown in Exhibit A.

Exhibit A
Mack's Markets, Inc.

Income Statement — Year 1967
(amts. in Ms-000 omitted)

Store Unit	Sales Revenue	Product Cost	Gross Margin	Store Expense	Profit Contribution
A	$1,400	$1,120	$ 280	$140	$140
B	1,200	960	240	130	110
C	1,000	800	200	120	80
D	800	640	160	110	50
E	600	480	120	100	20
All	$5,000	$4,000	$1,000	$600	$400

Overhead Expense	
Warehouse and Delivery	$250
General Office	150
Total	$400

Operating Result
Gain (Loss) — —

Hobbs gave me a moment to digest the figures (the others, I judged, had seen them before).

"See, like I told you," he grumbled. "Gross, $5 million; net, zero. All the stores show a profit, taken individually; the bunch of them show no profit, taken collectively. All they earn at the local level is eaten up by the warehouse and general office expense."

"Do away with the warehouse and general office," I suggested.

"That's the way it used to be," Art Ash put in plaintively. "Old man Mack and I ran this little old store, right here in this one building, with no frills or trimmings — made a little money every year, got along okay." Ash looked aggrieved.

"Yeah, but you were the one came to see me in Brentwood," Bill Budd reminded him, "and told me some mass purchasing power would cut our merchandise costs enough to cover any general overhead a chain might run up." Budd looked aggrieved, too.

"Hold it," I interrupted, lifting an admonitory palm. "Don't take my suggestion seriously till we dig into this a little further. First, let me read off these figures, and see if we're agreed on what they indicate. Follow me through the analysis, and stop me if I get anything wrong."

They all picked up Fain's tabulation, and I continued.

"Your stores do varying amounts of business, as is to be expected, considering location, established patronage, competition and other factors. You all earn a gross margin of around 20 per cent on your sales revenue. Your store operating expenses diminish with diminished volume, but not proportionally, which is also to be expected. Your store profit thus dwindles from 10 per cent in Store A down to just over 3 per cent in Store E. . . ."

"We're just getting started," Ed Eck protested. "Give us a little time."

"I'm not criticizing," I told them. "I'm just reading the figures; the explanations can come later. Point is, the average store profit is only 8 per cent on sales, the general overhead runs 8 per cent on sales, and that leaves you collectively nowhere."

That went unchallenged. Hobbs cleared his throat.

"My idea," he put in, "was we should try to find out which units, if any, are returning less than their fair share of general overhead, so we'll know where our trouble lies."

I grinned cynically. "All you have to do then, is agree on how much overhead each store should absorb. That should be easy."

"You think so?" Hall queried morosely. "Okay, Fred, show him the figures."

The treasurer passed around another sheet, with a flock of numbers on it which looked about like those presented in Exhibit B (page 229).

"Let me explain," Fain cautioned us, "that these aren't any of them net profit figures for which I'm prepared to take any responsibility. I have simply broken down the results the way each of the store managers thought it should be done, then racked them all up on this one page so they can be easily compared." He paused. The men were all diligently studying the tabulation.

"You'll observe," Fain went on, "that the store profit figures are identical in all the cases; only the overhead distribution differs. For each manager, there is a pair of columns (four for Dow) expressing his views on a fair allocation of overhead among the stores, with the resultant net profit contribution of each, thus calculated.

"There wasn't room for 'em all in parallel across an 8½-inch sheet, so you'll find Ash, Budd and Clay in the upper half of the page Dow and Eck in the lower half." He turned to me, with a sardonic grin. "If I had known we were going to have an expert with us, I'd have provided space for him, too, after listening to our ideas, he could quick give us the right answer, and we'd have it on file for future reference."

"Skip me, pal." I urged him. "Let them talk, and I'll just listen."

Hobbs took command. "Okay, Art, you're first on the list; you tell us how you see it." Ash grumbled that a guy whose name began with A was always first on every list, but in this case he didn't mind.

"Very simple," he said, spreading his palms. "We got $400,000 general overhead, and five stores; that's $80,000 a piece. A store is a store is a store; we all benefit alike from being affiliated; we should each bear an equal share of our joint burden. That way," he consulted his figures, "looks like Antioch and Brentwood make some money. Concord breaks even, and the other two stores, being newer and smaller, run a loss that eats up the profits." He leaned back, complacently.

"Well, that's one man's opinion," Hobbs observed cheerfully. "Bill Budd, here, seems to have a different one."

Exhibit B
Mack's Markets, Inc.

Alternative Computations of Net Profit for Each Store Unit
(amts. in Ms — 000 omitted)

Store Unit	Store Profit	Ash Version Ovhd.	Ash Version Net	Budd Version Ovhd.	Budd Version Net	Clay Version Ovhd.	Clay Version Net
A	$140	$ 80	$ 60	$112	$ 28	$170	$ (30)
B	110	80	30	96	14	110	–
C	80	80	–	80	–	60	20
D	50	80	(30)	64	(14)	50	–
E	20	80	(60)	48	(28)	10	10
All	$400	$400	–	$400	–	$400	–

Store Unit	Store Profit	Dow Version W&D	Dow Version G.O.	Dow Version Comb.	Dow Version Net	Eck Version Ovhd.	Eck Version Net
A	$140	$ 90	$ 42	$132	$ 8	$150	$(10)
B	110	75	36	111	(1)	110	–
C	80	50	30	80	–	80	–
D	50	15	24	39	11	50	–
E	20	20	18	38	(18)	10	10
All	$400	$250	$150	$400	–	$400	–

Overhead Allocation Bases

Ash	—	Uniform flat charge to each store
Budd	—	Charge proportionate to sales volume
Clay	—	Incremental cost, with rental adjustment reflected in overhead distribution
Dow	—	Measure service charge for warehouse and delivery; sales volume for general office
Eck	—	Historical expense increases for store units added

"Not too different," Budd countered, with a judicial air. "The general facilities benefit all of us — presumably — and we should all bear a liberal share of the burden. It might be more realistic, though, to recognize differences in store size in spreading the overhead cost. The larger stores do impose more burden on the central office and warehouse, perhaps somewhat in proportion to their relative volume." He glanced around, soliciting concurrence.

"In my analysis," he pointed out, "I've assigned the overhead expense on that basis, Stores A and B still show in the black, and Stores D and E in the red, but the differences are less than in Art's figures."

"Okay, Bill," Dan Dow interjected in some impatience. "You recognize the principle, but you don't apply it correctly. The individual stores should be charged with central facility expenses in proportion to their individual usage of those facilities. That may be, but isn't necessarily, in proportion to their volume."

He addressed himself to Hobbs, enlisting his support.

"Like in Danville," he went on, "we don't make too much use of the central warehouse or require many deliveries from it. We're in a different area; we can pick up a lot of our fresh produce locally, and do; we're right on the route followed by trucks from warehouses of grocery manufacturers in Hayward and San Leandro — they go right by our door and can drop off our consignments, without their going out to Antioch and back. . . ."

Ash, Budd and Fain all wanted to interrupt him, but he waved them down.

"Let me finish, will you?" he demanded. "We don't object to carrying our share of general office expense, but we see no justice in tagging us with maintenance of storage facilities we hardly use, and operation of trucks that come down to Danville only once a week. Charge us with warehouse and delivery expense in proportion to our call on those services, and you come up with figures that show our store is the most profitable one in the bunch!" He sat back grinning.

They all wanted to talk. Fain managed to get the floor.

"Look, Dan," he protested. "Maybe you do get direct delivery on a lot of your stuff, but it's the big jag of product that goes to the warehouse that secures a quantity discount on your purchases which you wouldn't otherwise get. Your expense might be less, but your margin would be less, too. . . ."

Dow grumbled something about taking his chances on that, but Budd didn't let him finish.

"Maybe you only get one delivery a week from the warehouse, but look how far it is to Danville. Take truck cost per mile, and divide it into the small tonnage you receive, and your supposed saving will vanish."

"Truck delivers Pittsburg and Concord on its way down to Danville," Dow pointed out. "The additional cost of the run to Danville is nominal. . . ."

Eck wanted to say something on that subject, but Clay cut him off.

"If you're going to figure it that way," he observed sardonically, "Antioch store shouldn't be charged any delivery expense at all. Store is right here in the warehouse; Art's stock clerk needs anything, he comes up to the second floor with a hand truck, helps himself, takes it down in the elevator. Stuff never sees a delivery truck. How come you didn't include that saving in your figure, Art?"

"I probably should have," Ash conceded. "Especially since my store expense is inflated by the cost of getting the stuff out of the warehouse. Every time my stock boy goes upstairs, he takes half-hour off for a smoke in the washroom, and another half-hour leaning over that jill in the low-cut blouse that keeps Fred's stock records for him. . . ."

"There's another point," Fain interposed patiently. "Fact that the warehouse is close to one of the stores is a *warehouse-and-delivery* expense saving, not a *store* expense saving. If we move the warehouse somewhere else, like we've been talking about, it would change the delivery pattern. Should we then consider the savings attributable to individual store location?"

"Depends on where you put the warehouse," Dan Dow rejoined promptly. "Locate it back of my store in Danville, and we'll lick the pants off all the rest of you."

"Let me talk a minute, will you?" Ed Eck interjected plaintively. "To my mind you're going at this all wrong. My store is new and still small, and all such apportionments of overhead expense are bound to make it look bad. No chain would ever start a new store if its results were to be judged that way."

"How do you think they should be judged?" Hobbs asked him.

"By how much the added unit contributes in direct store profit, and how much *increase* there is in general expense with one more unit in the chain." When Fain growled, "Who knows?" Eck retorted firmly, "I do," and pointed to the figures under his name.

"I went back and dug up the expenses you could reasonably consider related to warehouse, delivery and general office functions, and calculated the approximate annual amounts by which they increased as each new unit was added to the chain. For Antioch alone they were $150,000; when Brentwood came in they went up $110,000; Concord added $80,000, Danville $50,000. . . ."

"And Eastside only $10,000," Ash hooted derisively. "So actually your little operation is the only one makes any profit at all!"

"Results for the whole chain were $10,000 better with my store included than they would have been without it," Eck insisted stubbornly. "When we started you didn't add a foot of warehouse space, or an hour of delivery time (truck always took a full day for the Concord delivery, now drops off for us on the way and still gets done in a day's time). You've got maybe one more clerk in the general office, and that's the whole damn overhead related to the Eastside store."

"Where'd you get your figures?" Fain demanded suspiciously "Not from me."

"Hell, man, they're mostly in the annual reports," Eck retorted, impatiently. Then he grinned. "Besides, I got a girl friend works in your accounting department. . . . She helped me with them a little." Fain scowled.

"Well, Ed had a point," Hobbs agreed, pacifically. "In fact, everyone seems to have a point, except Cap Clay here." He slapped the Concord manager's knee. "Cap don't say nothin', but he must know somethin'." He ran his eye over the sheet of figures once more. "Funny thing, Cap," he went on. "There's only one point on which all your colleagues are agreed — namely, no matter how you slice it, Concord comes up with no profit. You confirm that?"

Clay bestirred himself, laid aside the pipe he'd been smoking and sat forward in his chair, his expression one of tolerant amusement.

"You know what these rascals have done to me?" he inquired. "They have stolen out of the Concord results the single most important profit-contributing element in the whole damn operation, and let the other stores get the benefit in their showing."

"How'd they do that?" Hobbs asked him.

"By adjusting the store rental charges from *actual amounts paid* to the *theoretical* rental value of the premises, as calculated by some real-estate appraisal outfit." I glanced at Fain for confirmation; he looked resentful.

"You see," Clay went on, "store chains are only ostensibly in the food business; what they're actually in is the real estate business. Their success, if any, lies chiefly in the management's astuteness in selecting up-and-coming store locations, getting into them at just the right time, at an economical rental, so they can capitalize on a surge of business when it develops."

The others were restive, but no one challenged him.

"I got started with the Concord store, on my own, years ago when Concord was just a little village. I got a long-term lease, with renewal options, at a very favorable figure, and our results naturally benefited accordingly."

"That was all reflected in the stock you got when you came into the combine," Fain reminded him.

"Sure it was," Clay agreed. "But you then threw all the properties into a realty company and let them charge each store the rent your expert figured it should pay, based on current conditions."

"Realty company merely breaks even," Fain insisted.

"Sure, but since Concord has grown a lot, my location now figures to be worth a lot more money, so you charge me more rent. In Antioch, on the other hand, where the building is old and the location deteriorating you use the gain from my — ahem — foresight — to offset the effect of old man Mack's poor judgment in taking a long-term lease on this building at a high rental." He snorted. "Actually, I'm paying about $20,000 a year of rent that ought to be charged to Art Ash, or to the warehouse. Correct for that, and apply Ed's theory on incremental expense, and you'll easily establish which store makes the most profit." Clay picked up his pipe leaned back, and relapsed into triumphant silence.

Hobbs turned to me with an expression compounded of amusement and frustration. "See how it goes?" he inquired helplessly. "You got any ideas?"

"Come on, expert," Ash needled me. "You give us the answer, huh?"

"Well," I told him, with what I hoped was a placatory smile, "if all we're talking about is how to apportion overhead expenses, to get some measurement of each store's profit contribution, I've got a method that's just as good as any suggested so far, and probably just as defensible."

I ran my eyes over the group. "Okay, let's have it," Fain urged.

"Compute each store's percentage of total store profit, then distribute the overhead on those percentages. Like an income tax, sort of. Ability to pay. You know."

There was a moment's silence, while one or two pencils were busy.

"That way," Dow blurted finally, "no store would show a profit, or a loss."

"Right you are," I confirmed heartily. "And I'll take that for an answer as readily as any of the others."

"Hmm!" Fain volunteered, after a moment's silence. "I think you're on my side. I tell them it's pointless to make *any* distribution of the general overhead —."

"Not pointless, perhaps, but a bit dangerous. These several allocations all bring out factors of significance, but if you publish the results for individual stores, calculated on any basis, someone is bound to get a wrong impression, maybe jump to a wrong conclusion."

"My expert!" Hobbs groaned. "All he tells us is we've all got the wrong answer. . . ."

"Not the wrong answer, the wrong question," I interrupted.

"Which is?"

"How to make money in a chain of stores," I retorted promptly. "And the answer doesn't lie in juggling overhead distributions."

They all wanted to talk, but Hobbs said he'd heard enough, and anyway it was time for a drink, and he and I would stop for one on the way home. The meeting broke up. Everyone but Fain seemed glad to have me leave.

Hal, however, hadn't abandoned his argument. When we were seated a few minutes later, in a plushy cocktail lounge he had selected for us, he resumed the attack.

"Let's get back to business," he insisted briskly, when the drinks were before us. "You're an expert, and I put a simple question: in a chain of stores, how do you determine which ones are profitable and which aren't? Are you telling me there isn't any answer?"

"Not any *one* answer," I responded, "that reflects all aspects and all points of view. On a store-by-store basis each one of these makes a profit contribution; collectively, these contributions aren't big enough to carry the general overhead. How much each store *should* contribute can be debated endlessly, but the debate isn't likely to improve your profit."

"You cost men are supposed to know how to allocate costs," he complained.

"We do," I assured him. "We know a lot of ways, and each one serves *some* purpose, but not *every* purpose. You've had a classic case presented this afternoon, with the usual contrasting alternatives — flat charge per unit vs. a sales-dollar percentage, assumed service availability vs. measured service usage, average overall cost vs. observed incremental expense, actual rentals paid vs. imputed rental value. They're all valid concepts, and each has some limited usefulness. But trying to evaluate the enterprise on a unit-by-unit basis won't lead you to a helpful conclusion. You can't judge the whole just by its parts."

"Why not?" he demanded. "That's all it is, just a bunch of parts —."

"Far from it," I countered quickly. "The fact of the *composite* is normally — and probably in this case — more important than facts about the *constituent elements.*" When he still looked dissatisfied, I fished for an analogy.

"Look," I urged. "A multi-unit business — any multi-unit business — is like that chop suey we had for lunch. Its success lies in a judicious blending of diverse elements.

"When you savor chop suey, you don't try to tell yourself what share of your pleasure derives from the tidbits of pork, the bean sprouts, the water chestnuts, the soy sauce, and other items you fortunately can't even identify. You wouldn't particularly enjoy any one of those items if you were to consume it individually. It's because Lee Fong, out in the kitchen, knows how to *mix* them that you get a tasty meal."

I paused, took a pull at my drink. "Ditto the chain store business," I added, sagely, "or, for that matter, almost any other."

Hobbs was shaking his head. "You've got to have good component elements, or the mixture won't be any good."

"True enough," I agreed. "All I'm saying is you shouldn't let your evaluation of the *mixture* lead you into mis-evaluation of its *individual elements*." I emptied my glass. "Like with your food stores," I added, pressing the point home. "You may have units that are individually okay, just combined in the wrong mix."

We discussed this aspect for a while, but Hobbs couldn't get his mind off the overhead expense distribution problem.

"I shouldn't argue with an expert," he said finally, "but it still seems to me that accountants should be able to develop a scientific formula, taking into account all the factors you've mentioned. . . ."

"Oh, sure!" I agreed, as patiently as I could. "You can be scientific as hell, and some companies try to be. My point is: it just doesn't do you any good."

When he kept on looking unconvinced, I continued.

"Let me give you a prize example, taken from the railroad business, with which I have had a longtime connection." Hal interrupted me to order another round of drinks, then let me resume.

"Long years ago," I told him, "the Interstate Commerce Commission prescribed an accounting formula for determining the respective results of the carriers' freight and passenger operations. It is an excellent formula, both scientific and sensible; it would be hard to find a ground for criticizing it.

"Now this same formula has been applied by *every* passenger-carrying railroad, in *every* year, for at least a quarter century, and the results have been incorporated annually in its big ICC Form A report, with copies freely available to anyone interested. That should be authoritative enough, don't you think?" Hobbs nodded agreement.

"So what happens? In the two decades during which I have actively followed the matter, I doubt that a month has gone by without some public discussion of whether certain passenger trains lose money and, if they do, how much. Usually it's in connection with a hearing on a railroad petition to discontinue one or more trains, sometimes in a freight-rate controversy.

"Does the argument proceed on the basis of the ICC reports? Indeed not. Witnesses by the score get up and challenge the validity of the figures, and their views are sympathetically reported in the public press. Newsmen comment that the railroads "claim" they lose money on passenger service, the phrase clearly employed in disparagement of the rail spokesmen's credibility — ."

"In spite of all that," Hal objected, "isn't the SEC now proposing that the results of all these new "conglomerate" corporations be reported on a divisional basis? So we can all find out which part of their business is producing how much profit, and so on?"

"Right you are," I confirmed gloomily. "It has been suggested that the Accounting Principles Board of the American Institute of CPAs (the practitioner's association) should come up with a recommendation on how such reporting should be done. I don't envy them the job!"

"Don't you believe investors should have the protection of complete information on how their funds are being administered?"

"Ah, nuts!" I exclaimed inelegantly. "Granted your premise, I'll contend that anything investors are told about divisional results in a complex enterprise is quite as likely to mislead as to educate them. Outsiders can't possibly comprehend the nuances of corporate policy, or the exigencies of managerial decisions—. Even boards of directors have trouble with questions like that —."

"Might discourage conglomerate formation," my friend murmured.

I snorted. "If it would, I could almost be for the idea, regardless of its patent philosophical defects. But look at the problem realistically. What can you do about divisional reporting for a conglomerate?" I ticked off the points on my fingers.

"One: You can prescribe a detailed and rigid formula for analyzing the results, applying it to *every* enterprise, in *every* accounting period, regardless of the nature of the business or its changing circumstances and component elements. All that will get you is a rash of criticism and a spate of controversy over the propriety of the accounting determinations and their validity in their application to the instant case. Result will be an obfuscation that the average investor will find it impossible to penetrate." I took a breath.

"Two: You can let each company establish its own pattern, altering it from year to year as management deems appropriate. Result, of course, will be complete noncomparability in reports of different companies, and from year to year in reports of the same company — and who'll be able to learn much from that?"

Hobbs was still dubious. "It's this general overhead allocation that's bugging you?" he inquired. "They could establish a basis —."

"Look," I demanded once more. "How you going to distribute a holding company president's salary over results of an insurance business, an airline, a meat packaging enterprise and a machinery manufacturer? And what will you do with research and development expense when you don't know what your research will uncover, or which unit may benefit? And who should be charged how much for corporate image-adornment expense?". . . .

Hobbs, I could sense, was in somewhat the mood of the little boy who halted his father's discursive response to a casual question by saying: "Well, thanks, but I didn't really want to know that much about it." I could see him telling himself that it would be a long time before he again invited a dissertation from an accounting expert.

In any case, I hope he doesn't call on me again soon. I'm not all that fond of chop suey.

20

FOR DIRECT COSTING IN THE STEEL INDUSTRY

JOHN E. TREACY*

We did observe that physical fluctuations within a department or function are more pronounced than that of its itemized expenses.

The steel industry, because of the nature of the product, is burdened with high fixed expenses. These high costs, and the relationships between the various processes in a steel plant, make it difficult to develop meaningful cost allocations. Although the products are controlled with detailed refinement through chemistry and metallurgy, the production processes are essentially bulky and crude, and most operations are plagued with problems of balancing the capacities of related processes. The result is a burdening of a product and inventory with high fixed costs. This leads one to wonder whether there may be ways of eliminating some of the meaningless and uncontrollable data that results. One possibility which suggests itself is the substitution of direct costing in place of absorption costing which is currently in use.

In order to understand the problem more clearly, it is necessary to focus on two issues: the nature of fixed and variable manufacturing costs, and the relation of direct costing and absorption costing to the basic premise of accounting. The basic objective of accounting is to provide information about the properties of the business entity to the many individuals having varying interest in the entity. A discussion of cost variability generally assumes that

* From *Management Accounting* (June 1977). Copyright © 1977 by The National Association of Accountants, New York. All rights reserved. The author is a Manager of Accounting at International Harvester.

the costs are totals for some period of time. There is the assumption that variable costs are variable in total over a period of time, and that fixed costs are fixed in total for some period of time. The time factor is important. If there was no time factor there would be no such thing as a fixed cost, and over a long enough period of time all costs would be variable. This statement implies that costs are not inherently fixed or variable but are classified as such by the users of cost data.

Absorbed Costs

Our particular plant is a fully integrated steel making facility. (Exhibit 1 is a display of a process flow chart.) The basic production facilities include a coke plant, sintering plant, blast furnaces, basic oxygen furnaces, continuous castings machine, blooming mill, billet and bar conditioning, hot bar mills, and cold drawing and turning mills. The auxiliary departments include metallurgical and chemical laboratories, handling and loading, steam power, electrical and mechanical engineering, production control, industrial relations, and accounting. In all, there are 15 producing facilities and 34 different auxiliary departments. Each month, individual total costs are determined for all auxiliary departments, which are in turn allocated to the primary producing departments.[1] Each primary producing department's total cost is determined and a cost per ton of product for the department is established. This product is then, in effect, sold to the next using or processing department. All costs are actual and fully absorbed.

Changes in production volume have a marked effect on individual department unit costs. They tend to pyramid as the product of one department becomes the raw material of the next. In the coke plant and blast furnaces, for example, it is not practical to shut down a part of the furnace or any part of a battery of ovens. Therefore, labor costs, which would ordinarily be considered highly variable, are relatively constant. These fixed expenses become a substantial part of the total operating cost for the department, and the variations in unit costs resulting from volume changes are very pronounced.

Normal Capacities

Our approach to the problem was to first develop some understanding of the relationships between capacities of related facilities. We attempted to determine normal capacities and then to define the elements of fixed and variable costs for each operation. In this way we would be able to develop a cost per unit that would represent a fixed overhead rate.

Conceptually, there are a number of ways of measuring and stating exactly what is meant by capacity. Our study considered two types. The first is

---

[1] Historically, our steel plant has operated with a process type cost system. During periods of extremely high or low production this cost policy has resulted in wide fluctuations of unit costs.

called rated capacity, which is the rate of production that would result if the equipment were operated continuously at the maximum output for which it was designed. Such a level of activity can be sustained for only a comparatively short period of time since limiting conditions are always present. The second type is called practical attainable capacity. This is the capacity that can be sustained with full practical utilization of the equipment under operating conditions. To determine the practical attainable capacity, we must first reduce the rated capacity to allow for unavoidable operating interruptions such as maintenance, repairs, set-ups, and operator personal time. Production lost due to such causes is usually estimated on the basis of past experience modified by expected future changes.

In order to utilize the concept of capacity in our direct costing consideration, it is necessary to define "scheduled production." Scheduled production is the output currently planned or scheduled for a given unit of equipment or production center. By comparing production currently scheduled with practical attainable capacity as defined above, we can bring out the full extent to which existing physical capacity could be utilized and provide a measure of the capacity not being utilized as well. For our application, a level of 80 percent of rated capacity was deemed to be a practical attainable production capacity.

Separation of Costs

Our second task was the separation of fixed and variable costs by department, the development of some substantiation for such separation relative to volume levels, and the determination of a unit cost. In this case, the unit cost would be a cost per ton. Because the task separating our cost into fixed and variable categories was quite difficult, sometimes arbitrary and very time consuming, it will be described here only briefly. The details of such distribution are not too important. What is important, is that the costs can be separated between the two categories, and that there is an element of change or crossover at various levels of production.

In order to simplify our task, the cost separation was limited to the 15 primary production departments. Each producing department was considered individually, and by reference to historical costs for a twelve month period, a per-unit (ton) overhead cost, representing a fixed unit cost, was developed. The twelve month figures were analyzed by cost elements such as: producing labor, premium pay, vacations and holiday maintenance materials, electric light and power, lubricants, tools and miscellaneous supplies, refractories, etc., to determine the range of the individual cost elements at various production levels. The cost elements were then segregated as to fixed and variable, and unit percentages were established representing the fixed portion of the total unit cost. While the dollar amounts will change, the percentage relationships of the unit cost at levels of production remain constant.

Exhibit 1   Process Flow Chart

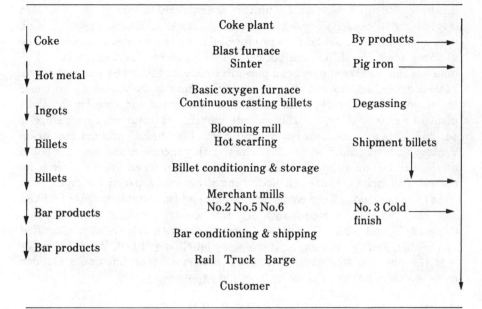

Exhibit 2   Volume Variance Write-Offs

Department	1 Capacity 80 percent	2 Actual production	3 2−1	4 Variance dollars/ton	3×4 Variance write-off
Coke plant	45,000	43,000	2,000	$ 9.50	$19,000
Sinter plant	13,200	12,000	1,200	4.00	4,800
No. 1 Blast furnace	26,400	26,000	400	6.40	2,560
No. 2 Blast furnace	21,600	21,000	600	6.25	3,750
No. 3 Blast furnace	33,600	35,000	+1,400	5.60	+7,840
Pig machine	12,160	12,000	160	1.35	216
B.O.F. molten steel	83,200	80,000	3,200	4.60	14,720
B.O.F. ingots	71,820	70,000	1,820	3.80	6,916
Continuous casting	9,100	9,000	100	18.60	1,860
Blooming mill	48,000	49,000	+1,000	9.80	+9,800
Billet conditioning	53,300	53,000	300	3.80	1,140
No. 2 Mill	16,000	15,000	1,000	25.00	25,000
No. 5 Mill	16,000	16,500	+ 500	28.00	+14,000
No. 6 Mill	15,100	14,000	1,110	30.40	33,744
No. 3 Mill	4,000	5,000	+1,000	40.70	+40,700
Total				(Negative)	$41,366

Note: Volume variance is not calculated when idle expense for a department is being generated. If idle expense is generated for only part of a month, the variance for the operating part of the month is calculated using the following formula.

$$\left[\frac{(\underline{\hspace{1cm}})}{\substack{\text{Week(s)}\\\text{operating}}} \div 4.286\right] \times \left[\underset{\text{Above}}{(\underline{\hspace{0.8cm}}\atop(1))} - \underset{\text{production}}{(\underline{\hspace{0.8cm}}\atop\text{Actual})} - \underset{\text{Above}}{(\underline{\hspace{0.8cm}}\atop(3))}\right]$$

Exhibit 2 illustrates a sample month with each of the producing departments represented. Column 1 indicates the capacity in tons at an 80 percent level of "rated capacity" or what we call "practical attainable capacity." Column 2 indicates the actual tons produced during the month. Column 3 is the variance tons, the difference between the 80 percent level and actual. Column 4 is the fixed cost overhead per-unit (ton) established by our cost segregations described above. Column 3 times Column 4 is the variance tons times the fixed overhead rate. Note that it shows a minus variance for the Coke plant of $19,000. Also, for this sample month, the total minus variance is $41,366. This amount does not become part of individual product cost or inventory, it is instead a write-off to the monthly income statement. As noted on the exhibit, no volume variances are calculated when idle expense is incurred. The formula is used to modify the 80 percent capacity tonnages.

At the conclusion of our cost segregations and the establishment of a fixed unit cost, we felt a reasonably accurate separation had been reached. Generally, items which fluctuated substantially with volume were classified as variable, and the remaining items were labelled as fixed. We did observe that the physical fluctuations within a department or function are much more pronounced than that of its itemized expenses.

Tax Reporting Is a Problem (in the U.S.)[2]

Unfortunately, the legal aspects as to the tax status of direct costing are still unclear. Neither the Internal Revenue Code nor the Income Tax Regulations is specific on acceptable costing methods (although Reg. 1.471-2 indicates some unacceptable methods). Reg. 1.471-3 defines the cost of manufactured merchandise as: ". . . raw material cost plus direct labor expenditure plus those indirect expenses incident to and necessary for production." There is, however, not a word in the regulation that identifies the "indirect expenses" as fixed or variable, or both. Hence, there should be room for argument within the language used. It is quite possible that one or more costing methods could be specified, since regulations do require a taxpayer to take inventories and prescribe the basis on which they are to be taken.

Conclusion

Our specific recommendation for implementing direct costing is now under study by our corporate management. While management concurs with the benefits to be derived in favor of internal control, there still remains the problem of external reporting and comparability with previous historical costs. It is very possible that we will end up with a dual set of records, as a compromise, until the whole issue is more clearly defined by the accounting profession.

---

[2] Direct costing is acceptable for Income Tax purposes under some conditions in Canada.

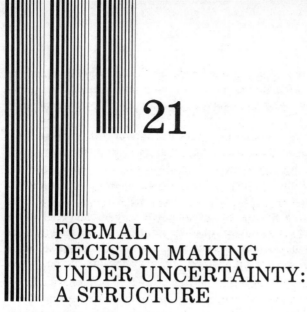

21

FORMAL
DECISION MAKING
UNDER UNCERTAINTY:
A STRUCTURE

G.R. CHESLEY*

Accountants increasingly are being challenged to make their information relevant to decision makers. Clark (1923) long ago suggested the need for "different costs for different purposes." He spelled out a set of typical problems which should have different definitions of cost in order to make the number relevant to the problem. More recently this concept of relevance was used as a primary standard in guiding the development of accounting practices (Committee to Prepare a Statement of Basic Accounting Theory, 1966).

Increasingly, professional examinations are reflecting a trend toward consideration of formal decision-making procedures. This trend parallels the trend within various organizations toward the use of these procedures (Brown, 1970). In order to serve these various functions, it is important for the accountant to understand the basic structures of some of the more formal approaches to decision making.

This paper presents the structure and conceptual framework for one of the most widely used approaches to decision making under uncertainty. The nature and components of this approach are described together with the data requirements and solution approaches. It is important, however, to note carefully the assumptions of the analysis so that more complex approaches can be attempted when the need arises. Edwards and Leitch (1975) provide an application of the approach to investment analysis using a tree

* Reprinted from an article appearing in *Cost and Management* (July/August 1978), by permission of The Society of Management Accountants of Canada. The author is an academician.

design to analyze a sequential situation. Product selection questions, advertising decisions, exploration decisions, and inventory decisions are some common problems which lend themselves to analysis using the approach presented.

Accountants as analysts or as interpreters of the work of other analysts will find the method used in these situations important to understand because of its wide-ranging applications. Extensions of the general method presented are numerous but one important to practitioners and researchers alike is the concept of the value of information (e.g., Feltham, 1972).

The presentation begins with a classic problem which assumes the environment is known. Next, an element of uncertainty is introduced into the problem to demonstrate how it can be resolved. The solution approaches to the uncertainty case are presented followed by a discussion of the nature and source of the information required.

The Certainty Problem

A classic problem faced by commercial concerns is the one which asks "Which product should be sold?" To illustrate this product mix question, a manufacturing concern will be used. Assume that product one, called x_1, has a contribution margin (selling price minus variable expenses) of \$2 per unit. Product two, called x_2, has a \$3 contribution margin per unit. Symbolically, a concern would sell quantities of the two products so as to maximize its contribution margin, that is

$$\text{Maximize: } 2x_1 + 3x_2. \qquad 1$$

If the concern could sell only one of the two products, or if it wanted to decide which product it should promote, then it would sell all that is possible of x_2. This solution assumes no other restrictions on the firm are present.

Sometimes, however, the concern is constrained to a certain amount of, say, manufacturing time. Assume that 100 hours of machine time are all that is available and that four hours are required to produce x_1 and twelve hours are required to produce x_2. Then if $\leq$ can be used to mean less than or equal to, the symbolic representation of the constraint is

$$4x_1 + 12x_2 \leq 100 \qquad 2$$

which says the total hours required $(4x_1 + 12x_2)$ must be less than or equal to the 100 hours available. With the constraint included, we have the classic linear programming problem

$$\begin{aligned} &\text{Maximize: } 2x_1 + 3x_2 \\ &\text{Subject to: } 4x_1 + 12x_2 \leq 100. \end{aligned} \qquad 3$$

A two-product problem can be solved quickly with a piece of paper. When more products and constraints are introduced, a solution technique called the simplex method can be applied to determine the optimal product mix.

The solution of the example presented can be obtained by computing the contribution per hour of constraint, that is

for x_1, \$2 ÷ 4 hours = \$.50 per hour and
for x_2, \$3 ÷ 12 hours = \$.25 per hour.

The optimal solution is to select the product with the largest contribution per unit of the constraining factor (hours), namely x_1. The company would then sell all it can manufacture of x_1, that is 25 units. Only 25 units are possible because each unit takes four hours and only 100 hours are available.

It is important to notice that all the numbers in the linear program are assumed to be known with certainty. In addition, the problem assumes that the numbers can be multiplied by or divided into the unknowns and added to or subtracted from the other products under consideration. Notice also how the constraint changed the solution from an intuitive one to a not so intuitive answer.

The Introduction of Uncertainty

Let us suppose the company were faced with the possibility of a price increase in product x_2, say of \$6. This would increase the contribution margin to \$9 from the original \$3. The new linear program would be

Maximize: $2x_1 + 9x_2$
Subject to: $4x_1 + 12x_2 \leqslant 100.$ 4

The solution is 8⅓ units of x_2. This solution, obtained in the same way as before, is optimal only if the price increase is in effect. Maybe the company must decide what to manufacture before it knows for sure the selling price. If this is the case, it is faced with uncertainty in the selling price and thus the amount it should manufacture. Should it be 8⅓ units of x_2 or 25 units of x_1?

Structure of the Uncertainty Problem

For brevity, let us define two symbols, s_1 for the no increase case and s_2 for the increase. Often the term, states of nature, is applied to the uncertainty elements. The company has two actions open to it if it wishes to sell these products, namely a_1, to produce the 25 units of x_1, or a_2, to manufacture 8⅓ units of x_2. The next step is to determine the contribution earned under each state for each action. For example, if no price increase occurs and 25 units of x_1 are made and sold, then \$2(25) or \$50 contribution is made. If the price increases but 25 units of x_1 are sold, \$50 contribution is also earned. If 8⅓ units of x_2 are sold and no price increase happens, then \$3(8⅓) or \$25 of contribution occurs. If, however, the price increases, then \$9(8⅓) or \$75 results. Table 1 summarizes these facts.

As is evident from Table 1, one must be able to specify the unknown states. Two were used here but more can be used as needed. The more states specified the more data required. Next the alternative actions must be specified which again can be more than two. Corresponding to each act and each state, a payoff must be specified in order to complete the decision table. Each payoff is assumed to be known with certainty.

Table 1   Decision Table

	s_1 No Price Increase	s_2 Price Increase
a_1 Mfg. 25 x_1	$50	$50
a_2 Mfg. 8 1/3 x_2	$25	$75

Solution Approaches

The first approach to selecting the appropriate action is to see if the payoffs for a given action exceed the payoff for all other actions for every state. If this occurs, then of course that action should be taken since it dominates all the rest in terms of payoffs. Unfortunately, not all problems have dominant actions.

A second approach to selecting an action is called the minimax or the maximin solution. Since profits are positive in the example problem, the optimal action is the one with the maximum minimum payoff. The minimum payoff for action one is $50 while for action two it is $25. Thus action one has the maximum of these minimum payoffs. This solution approach is termed ultraconservative because it selects according to the worst possible outcome.

A third solution approach is called the Laplace principle or the principle of insufficient reason. This approach assumes each state has an equal probability of happening or is equally likely to occur. In the two-state example, .50 chance is assigned to s_1 (the no increase case) and .50 is given to s_2. If three states were present, then $\frac{1}{3}$ chance is assigned to each. The next step in this approach is to multiply each probability by each payoff for each action, that is

a_1 .50(50) + .50(50) = \$50

a_2 .50(25) + .50(75) = \$50.   5

The method indicates it does not matter which action is taken since the expected payoff is the same for each action. The question which arises with this approach is: "Why were equal probabilities assigned to each state?" If the probabilities are known, then they should be used. If they are not known, it is inconsistent to assume they are equally likely.

Two other approaches, one called the Hurwicz method and the other called minimax regret, will not be discussed since they either tend to give answers similar to one or the other of the previous methods or their ideas can be analogized to the approach which follows.

Decision Analytical Approach

The decision analytical approach to the previous problem is very similar to the Laplace approach. However, instead of assuming that each state is equally likely, a probability must be assigned to each chance. Before the concept of probability is discussed, an arbitrary probability will be assigned to each state to illustrate the methodology.

Assume the probability of no increase, $p(s_1)$, is .30; $p(s_2)$ is then .70. With these probabilities, the expected payoff for each action is computed as follows:

for action 1   .30(50) + .70(50) = 50, and
for action 2   .30(25) + .70(75) = 60.   6

For the probabilities given, action two is the optimal action.

Probabilities

Probabilities constitute a formal approach to representing the uncertainty involved in a given situation. They have certain basic mathematical properties which permit a series of manipulations to be made upon them. In addition to these purely mathematical properties, probabilities have an empirical interpretation which is useful in characterizing different applications of the mathematical properties.

The relative frequency concept of probabilities is the one most frequently encountered in statistical sampling applications and statistics courses. If one flipped a fair coin indefinitely and in a consistent manner and recorded the occurrence of a head, heads would tend to appear in all flips with a frequency approaching one-half. This long-run approaching concept in mathematics is called a limit. The relative frequency concept, then, characterizes a probability as the limit of the occurrence of an event in a series of identical trials.

But, how does one determine the probability of an event when the situation does not involve a long-run series of repeated trials? This question is, of course, faced by many decision makers.

To answer this question, the concept of personal or subjective probabilities was developed as another empirical interpretation. Subjective probabilities, while having all the usual mathematical properties, represent numbers between zero and one which reflect an individual's or group's beliefs in the occurrence of given events. In essence, whenever an auditor assumes that a given probability distribution represents the amounts he is auditing, he has determined a personal probability distribution. This conception of probability has all the desirable properties of personal experience and also all the associated limitations.

Depending on the problem and the experience of the person expressing the probability, these probabilities may be easy or difficult to obtain. Various questioning methods are available to assist the businessman in expressing his probabilities (Chesley, 1975). For example, the person could be asked directly: "What is the chance that the price increase will occur?" Alternatively, a series of questions could be asked to try to close in on the person's feelings, for example: Is the chance of the price increase ten per cent, twenty per cent, or fifty per cent? In my own research, I have elicited these probabilities from various persons with differing levels of statistical sophistication in a situation involving the probabilities of various reported outcomes of a manufacturing process.

Payoffs

In the previous examples, dollar profits were used in the decison table. Very often this is sufficient but other payoff definitions such as utilities are possible and should be used in certain cases. Let us now explore the nature of the assumption required to use profits and one means of testing the appropriateness of this assumption.

To explore this question, the reader should answer honestly the following question: What amount of money would you take to be indifferent between this amount and a fair lottery with .50 chance of $25 and a .50 chance of $75? An answer less than $50 characterizes a person as a risk-averter. An answer of more than $50 characterizes the respondent as a risk-liker. Only if the answer is $50 (the expected value) does the selection of actions according to the largest expected profit, as was previously shown, necessarily result in a selection which is consistent with the risk attitudes of the decision maker.

A utility function, denoted u( ), is the concept which is used to convert preferences of individuals or groups into numbers so that these preferences can be mathematically manipulated. A set of relatively straightforward assumptions underlies this function. As long as these assumptions hold and an individual is able to answer questions of the type asked of the reader, a utility preference function can be constructed. This function, if it is correctly specified, permits the selection of actions which are consistent with the feelings of the decision maker toward how he values risk. To illustrate how this concept of a payoff is used, let us take the previous problem and assume u($50) is .40, u($75) is .70 and u($25) is .15. The action that should be selected is the one with the largest expected utility, namely

for action one   .30(.40) + .70(.40) = .40 and
for action two   .30(.15) + .70(.70) = .535.   6

In this example, action two has the largest expected utility. Table 2 shows the decision table with the utility numbers inserted.

Table 2 Decision Table Using Utilities

	s_1 No Price Increase	s_2 Price Increase
a_1 Mfg. 25 x_1	u($50) = .40	u($50) = .40
a_2 Mfg. 8 1/3 x_2	u($25) = .15	u($75) = .70

Most individuals and organizations have been found to be risk-averse. However, when decision problems faced by a decision maker have dollar payoffs which are relatively small in terms of those decisions he has faced or in terms of the total resources available to him, he may be willing to be risk-neutral and accept expected values or profits as his decision criterion. For example, the problem used for illustration purposes would be small to any organization of reasonable size so a decision maker for that organization should be risk-neutral for this problem solution. This fact may enable one to avoid the necessity of scaling a utility function although the exercise is usually worth the effort in terms of the insights provided to the decision maker.

Conclusion

The analysis of decisions is a wide-ranging undertaking consisting of situations where it may be assumed the factors involved are known with certainty and also situations where certain attributes are considered to be uncertain. A linear program illustration which assumes certainty was presented and used to examine a way of structuring a wide range of decision problems involving uncertainty about what will happen when an action is taken. The objective of this type of problem structuring is to permit a component-by-component consideration of the question and perhaps the selection of the appropriate action consistent with the preferences of the decision maker.

The structure of the uncertainty problem involves the specification of the uncertain states, the assignment of probabilities to those states, the definition of the possible actions available, and the specification of the payoffs associated with each action and each state. Methods for selecting actions were also presented. Some brief examples of how to obtain the data for these problems were given, although a full discussion of the methods is beyond the scope of this paper. Applications of the approach presented and a further discussion of methods of obtaining the data can be found in Winkler (1972) or Raiffa (1968).

The method described will facilitate the structuring of many problems which would be very confusing if approached on an unstructured basis. The approach permits an uncluttered consideration of the components of decision problems. The action selection methods, even in the face of uncertainty, provide a powerful approach for obtaining decisions.

References:

Brown, R.V., "Do Managers Find Decision Theory Useful?", *Harvard Business Review*, May-June 1970, pp. 78-89.

Chesley, G.R., "Elicitation of Subjective Probabilities: A Review," *The Accounting Review*, April, 1975, pp. 325-337.

Committee to Prepare a Statement of Basic Accounting Theory, *A Statement of Basic Accounting Theory*, American Accounting Association, 1966.

Davidson, S., "Old Wine Into New Bottles," *The Accounting Sampler*, edited by T.J. Burns and H.S. Hendrickson, 2nd edition, 1972, pp. 193-201, reprints a review of J.M. Clark, *Studies in the Economics of Overhead Costs*, The University of Chicago Press, 1923.

Edwards, J.D. and Leitch, R.A., "Sequential Financial Analysis: Decision Trees," *Cost and Management*, January-February 1975, pp. 23-28.

Feltham, G.A., *Information Evaluation*, American Accounting Association, 1972.

Raiffa, H., *Decision Analysis: Introductory Lectures on Choices Under Uncertainty*, Addison-Wesley, 1968.

Winkler, R.L., *Introduction to Bayesian Inference and Decision*, Holt, Rinehart and Winston, 1972.

22

COST INFORMATION AND COMPETITIVE STRATEGY: LESSONS FROM JAPAN

CHARLES J. McMILLAN*

Introduction

In recent years, the subject of organizational productivity and economic performance has received a great deal of managerial attention. In the aftermath of the 1973 and 1979 oil shocks, Western countries have all experienced slower economic growth, but productivity has grown less in North America than all other countries.[1] In a comparative sense, the emerging countries of Southeast Asia have grown the fastest, with Japan being the centre of the new technologies and the main competitor to the U.S. and Canada in export markets.

As Scott notes, "This new industrial competition is the most important challenge facing the entire North Atlantic area, whether economic growth recovers somewhat in the 1980s, the traditional industrial nations will continue to lose industrial jobs unless they respond to it."[2]

This new era of industrial competition raises many questions for North American managers, especially in the way strategic decisions are made and the way competition is understood. Corporate planners, marketing executives, and production engineers all have some understanding of competitor analysis, but the seriousness and completeness of the task are only imperfectly understood. The theme of this paper is that the future world of the new industrial competition, stemming mainly from international forces, elevates the importance of rigorous and conceptually sound competitor analysis for corporate and government strategy. Moreover, the key to undertaking this

---

* Charles McMillan is a Professor at York University in Toronto.

work is information and communication, based on sound accounting systems. For the accountant, this approach to management in the new environment requires an analytical capacity and management role elevated far
above the humdrum of traditional auditing and operations. It requires a pro-
active assessment of future goals and assumptions both about the firm and
its competitors, and a solid analysis of current and future strengths and
capabilities. For the accountant, competitor analysis involves a fundamental
judgement about how information needs to be collected, assessed and
disseminated in a planned and continuous process.

Exhibit 1
Changes in Labor Productivity and Labor Costs of the Manufacturing Industry

(Percentage Changes in Labor Productivity)   (Unit: %)

Year	U.S.A.	Japan	W. Germany	U.K.	France	Italy	Canada	EC
1960 – '80	2.7	9.4	5.4	3.6	5.6	5.9	3.8	5.4
1960 – '73	3.0	10.7	5.5	4.3	6.0	6.9	4.5	5.9
1973 – '80	1.7	6.8	4.8	1.9	4.9	3.6	2.2	4.2
1977	2.4	7.2	5.3	1.6	5.1	1.1	5.1	3.4
1978	0.9	7.9	3.8	3.2	5.3	2.9	3.1	4.1
1979	1.1	8.0	6.3	3.3	5.4	7.3	1.2	5.9
1980	Δ0.03	6.2	Δ0.7	0.3	0.6	6.7	Δ1.4	2.3

Note: 1. The term "labor productivity" means the value of hourly production.
   2. The percentage changes represent the annual average, and they do not necessarily
      accord with individual national statistics.
   3. Percentages given for the EC represent the total EC-9.
Source: U.S. Department of Commerce, Monthly Labor Review.

This paper consists of three parts: the first outlines the nature of competitive analysis in strategic management; the second part provides two examples of how competitive analysis applies to international competition and
productivity; the conclusion cites some examples of how Japanese companies develop reporting systems and speculates on the implications for accounting systems in strategic management.

Competitive Strategy

Exhibit 1 shows the basic objectives of competitive strategy, namely understanding a competitor's current strategy and capabilities and relating these
two basic defensive points to future goals and assumptions about vulnerability and retaliation. Many textbooks treat these issues as an assessment of
competitive strengths and weaknesses and environmental threats and
opportunities, but the true meaning of sophisticated competitive analysis

goes far beyond this view. Historically, military strategists have clearly recognized that frontal attack strategies are both brutal and costly, and may turn into a contest of resources and staying power.[3] An old Chinese saying catches the flavour of the real purpose of competitive strategy:

> To win every battle by actually fighting before a war is won, it is not the most desirable. The highest form of generalship is to conquer the enemy by strategy. The next highest form of generalship is to conquer the enemy by alliance; the next highest form of generalship is to conquer the enemy by battles. The worst form of generalship is to conquer the enemy by besieging walled cities.

The conventional approach to corporate strategy consists of determining the basic goals or ends for the firm and then identifying the means or tactics to achieve the goals or "mission." Goals, mission or strategy are relatively abstract statements of the overall direction of the firm. They are then translated into more specific and operational policies, based around such functions as purchasing, personnel, sales, finance, production, and distribution.

These elements of strategy must be consistent and in tune with the broader environment of the organization, such as industry trends, competitive conditions, political and social values and institutions, and technology. What combines these two basic areas — the goals and policies of the firm and the external conditions in the environment — are the personal values and resources of the organization. Even in very big organizations, but more evidently in small ones, the personal values and decision-making style of the top management shape and influence the strategic direction of the organization.

Competitive strategy builds on this kind of analysis but goes well beyond it to help management understand and assess the environment.[4] Top management in many organizations has found the traditional approach to be less than successful. Not that there has been a shortage of data. Often accountants, marketing specialists, and other staff experts provide an enormous output of information. Unfortunately, even with very sophisticated planning systems, many organizations do not respond to environmental changes with viable long term strategies. Why is this the case? For one thing, there are numerous examples where companies and organizations discover that competitors simply don't play by the traditional rules. The entire Swiss watch industry is a classic example. These thousands of companies not only stayed with traditional mechanical watches, but by missing out on the electronics technology, failed to achieve the economies of scale inherent in electronics. There are countless examples where managers have stayed with the traditional assumptions about how their industry operates, only to see competitors devise novel and often unique approaches to devising winning strategies. Competitors, in other words, can choose the battlefield and thus define the choice of weapons, resources, and timing of the battle.

A second problem is that managers adopt what are essentially static assumptions of the external environment. As noted at the beginning of this article, the new world of international competition makes the competitive environment much larger in scope, more complex in diversity, and much longer in time than a purely domestic approach. Canada and the U.S. have been viewed by most managers as essentially closed economies, with the international dimension viewed as quite secondary to domestic considerations. Yet it is the international dimension that will, in the future, determine the underlying cost structures through competitive pressures, scale economies, new technologies, and the like. Accountants have a major role to play in two respects: in alerting managers to the environmental forces introducing change to the organization, and designing information systems capable of providing data which is timely, relevant, and strategic.

A third problem is that good competitive analysis requires a judicious blend of hard data in the form of numbers and facts, and of creative thinking using hunch, intuition, common sense, judgement, and experience. Some research shows that these differences reflect right and left side of the brain considerations.[5] Accountants, for example, do typically focus on rational and logical forms of information gathering and number crunching. Yet behind the numbers may be a serious weakness in judgement or experience. The challenge is to bring these elements together. As the next section illustrates, the Japanese have concentrated on doing precisely that in their approach to competitive analysis.

Exhibit 2   The Components of a Competitor Analysis

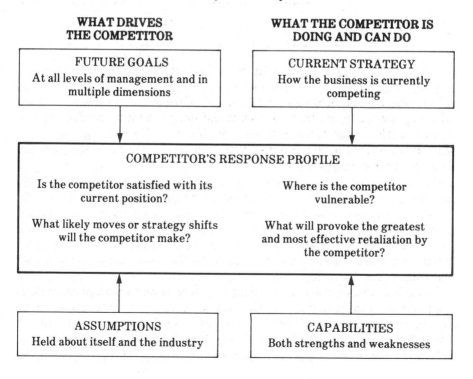

Applying Competitive Analysis

Competitive analysis is fundamentally an approach for applying resources to gain a sustainable competitive advantage. Good competitive analysis requires not only solid information but also a capacity to identify and comprehend relationships. Like a chess game, early moves determine the subsequent configuration of players and the ability to anticipate events and their consequences.

Porter has identified three generic strategies based on an implicit two by two matrix; first, strategic advantage — perceived uniqueness as against low cost and, second, strategic target — industry-wide versus a particular niche.[6]

Exhibit 3 Three Generic Strategies

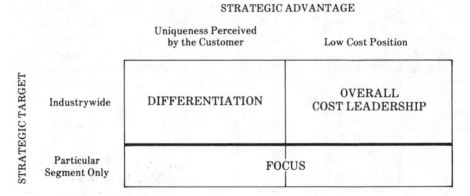

The first strategy, product differentiation, involves designing or marketing products which are recognized as unique by customers (Rolls Royce or Mercedes in cars or Chivas Regal in Scotch whiskey). There are many ways of achieving differentiation, such as brand names, quality, product innovation, superior sales force, service, and the like. The aim is to develop customer loyalty and reduce sensitivity to price as a means of insulating the business from competitive rivalry.

The second strategy, focus, is similar to the first, but concentrates the business on a particular niche or segment. The real contrast is with the third strategy, namely, cost leadership. The aim is to generate high profit margins relative to competitors by achieving lower production and distribution costs. Low cost leadership is maintained by reinvesting in new equipment, new work methods, and new facilities. The strategic target is mainly on costs rather than prices.

In each of these strategy possibilities, there is an important technology component, such as developing the technology through innovation, or imitating technology through buying, or "Me — too." As shown in Exhibit 4, the differences among the strategies require a "package" of strategic moves which entails quite a sophisticated understanding of the technological

Exhibit 4
Illustrative Links between Technological Leadership/Followership and the Generic Strategies

Strategy	Technological Leadership	Technological Followership
Overall cost leadership	First mover on lowest cost product or process technology	Lower cost of product or process through learning from leader's experience
Overall differentiation	First mover on unique product or process that enhances product performance or creates switching costs	Adapt product or delivery system more closely to market needs (or raise switching costs) by learning from leader's experience
Focus — lowest segment cost	First mover on lowest cost segment technology	Alter leader's product or process to serve the particular segment more efficiently
Focus — lowest segment differentiation	First mover on lowest cost segment technology performance needs, or in creating switching costs	Alter leader's product or process to performance needs of particular segment or create switching costs

dimension. This technological component pervades the entire decision-making process. As Skinner notes, "corporations producing products or services must make decisions on their technology when they design products; plan services, choose equipment and processes; and devise operating facilities, distributing, and information systems."[7]

From a theoretical perspective, these points are hardly novel. Yet in practice, there is a large gap across many companies. Consider two examples, one from a production perspective, one from a marketing perspective. What both have in common is an intelligent appreciation of how accounting information is critical to effective decision-making. The first example is the experience curve. The second is market segmentation.[8]

Experience Curves.

Experience curves have a variety of names — learning curves, experience curves, progress cost functions — and a long history. The first English literature reference dates to 1938 when Wright reported his observations on aircraft manufacturing. He notes that as the quantity of units manufactured doubles, the number of direct labour hours it takes to produce an individual unit decreases at a uniform rate. Today, the progress cost curve or experience curve is a staple diet in all textbooks on organization strategy and books on strategic marketing.

Experience curve phenomena are related to but distinct from economics of scale and technological advances. Moreover, they tend to vary by product and sector. For example, U.S. research revealed that the experience effect was about twice as great in assembly (26%) as in machining (14%), because assembly work involved greater complexity and uniqueness. Studies carried out on a number of Japanese industries point to the fact that various firms in such industries as colour television, motorcycles, jewelled watches, cameras, small cars, and steel have superior records of accumulating experience and gaining lower cost. The actual rate of decline is product specific, from about 12% in automobiles and 15% in colour television to as much as 40-50% in semiconductors and integrated circuits.

As shown in Exhibit 5 for Japanese motorcycles, experience curves are plotted with cumulative output in physical volume on the horizontal axis and cost or price per unit of a product on the vertical axis. If the data are plotted on a linear scale, there is a logarithmic decline, and if the relationship is plotted on a double logarithmic scale (indicating percentage change as a constant distance on either axis) there is a straight line, constant relationship between experience and cost. As a management tool, the curve is not an automatic or purely engineering phenomenon: experience effects must be planned. For one thing there is a learning by doing effect wherein tasks carried out the first time take longer than with experience, such that unskilled labour takes more time than skilled and experienced workers. Feedback and scientific work study are part of this process. There must be a major managerial effort to reduce costs by work layout improvements, better supervision, product design simplification and more rationalized purchasing, inventory control, and scheduling. There also must be a recognition that experience curve effects may not apply to all products in the same way (e.g., semiconductors versus T.V. assembly), in all situations (e.g., when raw materials account for a significant percentage of value added), or where technology changes, as when transistors replaced vacuum tubes or when micro circuits replaced mechanical parts in adding machines and calculators.

Exhibit 5   Japanese Motorcycle Industry: Price Experience Curves (1959 - 1974)

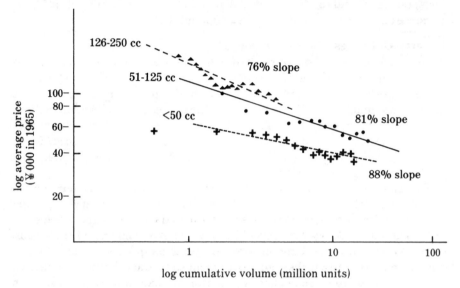

Source: MITI (BCG 1975)

The implications of experience curve analysis for management are many. In the first place, management must recognize its use in planning, and this means that good engineering data are essential. As noted below, the use of experience curves in "design to cost" is meaningless without a solid data basis. In terms of competitive strategy, the experience curve provides a very effective means of linking production strategy to R & D and marketing. Consider the case of pricing. Cost conscious producers may develop a strategy of using different pricing levels depending on the degree of competition and stage of the product life cycle. As shown in Exhibit 6, a firm can adopt a strategy of price exploitation in order to build profit levels but not necessarily to gain market share (assuming competitive conditions). Pricing for market share, by contrast, suggests a strategy of sacrificing profits (and medium term cash flow) to gain longer term market share and improved cash flow. When competition intensifies as a result of the attraction of new entrants due to price exploitation, higher cumulative production can allow for a shift to production based on production costs.

Exhibit 6 Value of Market Share

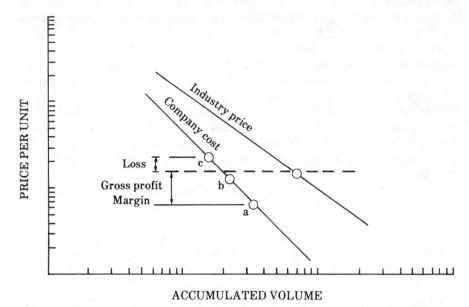

ACCUMULATED VOLUME

Source: Texas Instruments

This analysis corresponds precisely with Japanese manufacturers in scores of products. However, there are other factors which need to be considered. For one thing, a high growth rate requires increases in capital investment for the newest, best practice equipment and processes. Without them, a firm may drop off the experience curve. (Japanese firms making 64K chips are using fourth and fifth generation equipment in the U.S.)[9] Another related issue is the strategic time horizon. Firms emphasizing short time horizons and quick payback periods are likely to forego long term market share and cumulative learning. Such cumulative learning may well mean that, barring some technological breakthrough, a firm which falls behind can never catch up.

Do the Japanese have particular advantages in experience curve application? In theory, the answer must be no. In practice, the answer may be positive, because managerial practice has turned its use into a well defined science. The clear product focus of most Japanese manufacturers and the encouragement through tax incentives of the government have combined with singular attention to world class economies of scale. Plant and equipment, thanks to particular taxation and depreciation laws, are newer in Japan than in the U.S. by a significant margin. Japanese firms like Seiko in watches, Matsushita in televisions, and Kawasaki in motorcycles have effectively used global marketing strategies to develop cumulative experience by shrewd timing of market penetration for new products. Even in a mature industry like cars, Japanese producers have increased production experience at an annual rate of 28%, which allows cumulative experience to double within three years, so that real costs drop 7% per year. The comparable U.S. rate is 3.7% for growth, doubling experience every 18 years, and a real decline in costs of only .6% annually.

The effectiveness of Japanese experience curve practice is indicated in a well-known technique of "design to cost." The particular approach of design to cost is aided by another technique, namely reverse engineering. Instead of designing a product on paper with engineering specifications laid out in blueprints, take an existing product foreign to the firm (e.g., a competitor's), and break it down into component parts and processes. Learn the basic design but improve on it. Reassemble the product based on creative improvements. Reverse engineering and design to cost mean that a particular cost becomes the production constraint, and the manufacturing process is designed to meet that target. This approach is not uniquely Japanese, but it is better understood and more widely practiced there.

Texas Instruments, an American firm whose organizational culture has many parallels to Japanese corporations, has used experience curves for decades. A former TI president, Fred J. Bucy has described the emphasis on the Japanese approach as follows:[10]

> TI is competing head on with the Japanese in several major markets, among them semiconductors (where they have a $300 million government sponsored programme for very-large-scale integration (VLSI) development), calculators, and watches. What is to stop the Japanese from taking over these businesses as they have done in radios, stereos, T.V. sets, motorbikes and steel?
>
> I think the big difference is that TI is the first major non Japanese company they have run into that understands and uses the learning curve. ... The key to using the learning curve is "design-to-cost", where you determine the cost required for the product and the system to manufacture it to hit that cost goal. The effect here is not just spreading overhead over a larger volume of product produced. It also involves constantly forcing manufacturing costs down through design improvements of the product and the production processes.
>
> In Japan, both the government and industries understand this. Most other industries don't. TI has used this concept informally and formally for many years, and this is absolutely mandatory to compete successfully with the Japanese.

To illustrate the impact of successful experience curve application, TI shows three firms in an industry, with current industry price indicated by the horizontal dashed line in Exhibit 6. The three firms have three cost positions depending on accumulated production. Company A has larger market share and higher profit margin, Company C operates at a loss, and Company B is marginal. According to TI's former chairman, "a company participating in a world market has an advantage over a company that builds its production base on a national market, but this advantage can exist only if cost reduction is accepted as the responsibility of the entire organization."

From an accounting perspective, experience curve analysis requires a very careful assessment of relevant costs. Depending on the type of curve, judgements have to be made on the treatment of various kinds of costs — individual items versus shared costs, value added costs versus others such as raw materials. Traditional accounting systems may not disaggregate cost elements in the appropriate way or may allocate costs on the basis of departments or profit centres rather than products. Shared costs in the form of sales forces, research staff, and fixed overhead may be allocated on the basis of percentage of total sales rather than actual costs of resources used. Sometimes costs are not directly comparable, because accounting reports change, tax laws are amended, or whatever. In other words, accountants must become aware of the importance of these production issues in defining and applying experience curve analysis as part of the overall objective of contributing to the organization's competitive analysis and corporate strategy.

Market Segmentation.
In their analysis of Japanese marketing success, Kotler and Fahey[11] make the following argument:

> In market after market, Japanese companies have identified the right segment to enter. One common strategy is to bring out smaller versions of standard products (the Buddhist concept of "small is beautiful" as opposed to the U.S. concept "bigger is better"). Thus Canon and Sharp entered the copying machine market by offering smaller copying machines than Xerox's; Sony and Pansonic entered with smaller radios and television sets; Honda and Yamaha entered with smaller motorcycles. U.S. market leaders prefer to sell larger sized versions of their products (more profit). Harley-Davidson, the leading U.S. motorcycle manufacturers, dismissed the small Hondas pouring into the U.S. as "toys". . . .
>
> All said, Japan's market entry strategy involves segmenting the market, targeting a segment that the competition is not adequately serving, designing the product for that market segment, entering with a low price, offering high quality and service, developing strong distribution, and backing the product with heavy promotion and advertising. This is nothing different than the textbook prescription for good marketing. The only difference is that the Japanese practice these principles thoroughly.

The complexity of modern business, as shown by these case study examples from Japan, requires a very focused understanding of the role of information. When firms like Toyota or Canon or Sharp segment a particular market, they combine not only a shrewd view of the customer but a clear understanding of production costs. To do both, they need good accounting information, product by product, market by market. Curiously, research on American firms shows that information is usually aggregated around very broad product definitions or organizational groupings such as the strategic business unit. However, the way a business is defined and the way a company defines a particular market clearly influence the firm's performance criteria and the significance of particular operating variables.

Abell,[12] for instance, proposes a model of defining a business on the basis of three criteria: 1) customer group served, 2) customer needs served, and 3) technologies employed (ways used to satisfy the need). Just how the firm chooses to define itself impacts on the operations of the company (sales patterns, gross margins, expenses), strategic analysis (research and development) and operational performance (sales per employee, sales per warehouse footage), and these in turn influence the functional roles of purchasing, production, personnel, and marketing. An example of this impact is the computerized scanner business for diagnostic imaging. There are firms which define themselves in terms of customer need (head or body scanning or both), and in terms of technology. EMI, for instance, produces and sells second generation head and body scanners in all major product groups. By contrast, Ohio-Nuclear sells second generation head and body scanners but focuses on the medium sized hospital, while Pfizer sells first generation body scanners but targets large sophisticated teaching hospitals. Depending on which definition is used, each firm faces different decisions on manufacturing, R & D, selling promotion, price, distribution, and service.

The impact of these issues raises many questions for accountants. Information gathered in an organization should be assessed for its use and relevance for strategic and competitive analysis. Managers need much more awareness of the links between operations and strategy and how good, product-based information can have enormous impact on performance.

Many Japanese companies hire accountants who have close first hand working knowledge with production and marketing specialists. Matsushita,[13] for instance, uses its accountants to plan new products, oversee initial production, and schedule the timetable for increased volume. Costs of new products are never mixed with those of old products. As one report noted, "What the head office does insist upon, however, is that the profits of new products not be mixed in the profits of an older product to arrive at a single measure which meets the 10% criterion. Such accounting is coldly vetoed."

Summary and Conclusions

Many writers have attempted to identify the reasons for Japan's very rapid growth and productivity performance over the past decade or more. In scores of products and segments, Japanese companies have picked off their U.S., European, and Canadian competitors. Some people attribute this competitive success to the software management systems of permanent employment, bottom-up decision-making and the like. Others suggest that the Japanese have become the world champion marketers based on the skills at identifying demand for new products. Still other explanations centre on excellent production systems and industrial engineering.

The fact of the matter is that no one explanation provides the answer.

What is common to most of them however is a basic conclusion and lesson for North American managers: the imperatives of having good information systems and detailed performance measurement. At the macro level of society, Japan has probably the best statistical bureau in the world, collecting mountains of information on every conceivable aspect of the global economy and what these imply for Japan.

In the banks and in the large trading houses, there are enormous on-line information systems linking the headquarters in Osaka and Tokyo to the major markets and suppliers of the world. These systems are not put there by accident: the Japanese recognize that the new era of international competition requires the very best intelligence systems to collect, analyze and interpret data.

The same approach exists in the corporation. Managers are trained to use and apply detailed accounting information to improve productivity, develop new products, and study competitors. Firms like Sony and Honda teach their new employees the fundamentals of cost accounting, value analysis and reverse engineering, even if their speciality is marketing, personnel, or production. The average worker is provided with the details of product costs in the most disaggregated form possible so there is intimate knowledge of how specific suggestions can improve quality and cost.

Cultural and institutional differences between Japan and other countries may prevent some specific practices from being applied in North America. However, in terms of other fundamentals, including the use and understanding of accounting information for competitive analysis and strategy, the elements of Japanese practice are eminently feasible and applicable to North American practice. It is up to accountants to see that this is done.

References

1. See, for instance, Edward F. Dernnison, *Accounting For Slower Growth*. Washington: Brookings Institution. Also Economic Council of Canada, *Report* (Ottawa: Information Canada, 1977).
2. Bruce Scott, "Can Industry Survive The Welfare State?" *Harvard Business Review* (September-October 1982), p. 72.
3. For an assessment of applying military strategy to business, see Philip Kotler and Rani Singh, "Marketing Warfare-1980s," *The Journal of Business Strategy*, Vol. 3 (Winter), 30-41.
4. Michael Porter, "How Competitive Forces Shape Strategy," *Harvard Business Review* (March - April 1979), 137-145.
5. Henry Mintzberg, "Planning on the Left Side and Managing on the Right," *Harvard Business Review* (January-February 1976), 49-58.
6. Michael Porter, *Competitive Strategy* (New York: The Free Press, 1980), ch. 2.
7. Wickham Skinner, *Manufacturing In Corporate Strategy* (New York: Wiley, 1978).
8. For an excellent review, see Louis E. Yelle, "The Learning Curve: Historical Review and Comprehensive Survey," *Decision Sciences* 10 (March 1979), 302-328.
9. These and other examples are spelled out in Charles McMillan, *The Japanese Industrial System: Management Strategies For The 1980s* (New York: de Gruyter, 1983), ch. 9.
10. Quoted in *Texas Instruments* case, Manchester School of Business, Manchester, England.
11. Philip Kitler and Liam Fahey, "The World's Champion Marketers: The Japanese," *The Journal of Business Strategy* (Summer 1983), 3-13.
12. Derek Abell, *Defining The Business* (Englewood Cliffs, N.J.: Prentice Hall, 1980).
13. Matsushita Electric, Harvard Business School, Case 9-481-146, 1981.

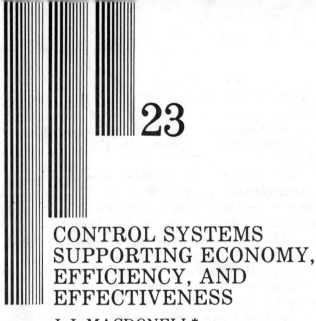

23

CONTROL SYSTEMS SUPPORTING ECONOMY, EFFICIENCY, AND EFFECTIVENESS
J. J. MACDONELL*

I. Prerequisites for Good Management Control Systems

Management control can be exercised effectively only if:

- objectives of the organization, program or activity have been defined as clearly as possible and quantified, where feasible;
- proper planning has been carried out for the achievement of these objectives, including establishing priorities and setting standards for judging performance;
- appropriate organizational arrangements have been made, including clear and fair allocation of responsibilities and resources; and
- adequate processes have been established to monitor performance.

Comprehensive auditing assesses whether these prerequisites exist, including the quality and use of the information produced for management control purposes — its validity, reliability, completeness, relevance, and timeliness — and whether it is transmitted to the most appropriate person or group.

• • • • • •

Audit criteria are developed to reflect as closely as possible the value-for-money expectations of Parliament. Based on its assessment of the audited organization, the Office (of the Auditor General) reports to Parliament the

---

* Reprinted from the *Report of the Auditor General of Canada to the House of Commons* (Fiscal Year Ended March 31, 1979), Chapter 6, "Management Controls", pages 113-114 and 121-123.

degree of management's regard for economy and efficiency, and the adequacy, in the circumstances, of procedures to measure and report program effectiveness.

II. Definitions of Economy, Efficiency, and Effectiveness . . . .

Economy
"Economy refers to the terms and conditions under which the Government acquires human and material resources. An economical operation acquires these resources in appropriate quality and quantity at the lowest cost. If control mechanisms are not in place, programs may be overstaffed or understaffed, or inappropriately equipped in other ways to deliver the expected results."

Efficiency
"Efficiency refers to the relationship between goods or services produced and resources used to produce them. An efficient operation produces the maximum output for any given set of resource inputs; or, it has minimum inputs for any given quantity and quality of service provided. Efficiency is obviously more measurable and more controllable in some situations than in others. The underlying management objective is increased productivity."

Effectiveness
"Effectiveness concerns the extent to which a program achieves its goals or other intended effects. For example: to increase income in a particular area, a program might be devised to create jobs. The jobs created would be program output. This contributes to the desired program effect of increased income which can be mesured to assess program effectiveness. Of course, not all programs are equally evaluable. Also, management procedures for measuring and reporting effectiveness will differ between programs." (Appropriate techniques may not be available, or their high cost might make a thorough evaluation unreasonable.)

• • • • • •

III. Measuring and Increasing Efficiency

Systems purporting to measure efficiency in the Public Service are absent, or for the most part, not used by managers to increase efficiency. Public service managers should monitor their operations and actively seek means of increasing efficiency. This requires, as a minimum, the measurement and reporting of actual operational performance and, more important, identifying and capitalizing on opportunities for increased productivity. But it also requires attention to the major determinants of performance, such as the ability of the work force, work methods and structure, environmental constraints, and motivation.

Relevance and Accuracy of the Measures of Performance

The output must be relevant, comprehensible, and practical to measure, if productivity is to be monitored and improved.

To begin with, output should be well defined and correctly measured. The definitions and measures should be modified to reflect any changes in the nature of the output. Proxy measures should be used only if appropriate. The characteristics of the output, such as quality and level of service, should be specified clearly. Where feasible, the performance reports should include indicators of these characteristics.

Input should be related to the output it produces. Rules for allocating input should be appropriate. Adjustments for significant changes in inventories of work in process should be included in the calculations. Both output and input data should be checked for accuracy and reliability.

Standards

Performance measurement systems and information, to be valid and acceptable for management decisions on productivity improvement, require an adequate base for comparison of observed performance. When it is appropriate to do so, standards should be established by generally acceptable work measurement techniques.

Such standards or bases should be established on a consistent basis from one location to another for decentralized operations. But they should take local circumstances into account so that meaningful inter-regional comparisons of performance can be made.

Actual performance levels should be reasonable in comparison with the related standard or base. When standards have been established by work measurement, the target for an individual should be 100 per cent of standard. Over a period of time, a minimum acceptable group performance should be 80 per cent.

Usefulness of Reports

Performance indicators are of little value if they are unreliable or unrelated to the practical needs of managers. For example, unweighted aggregation of data on significantly dissimilar measures of output should be avoided. Reports should be timely in relation to management needs. They should be summarized and should highlight significant detail.

Productivity Improvement

The primary purpose of performance measurement is to provide information for productivity improvement or for maintenance of prevailing performance levels in the face of changing conditions.

Targets should be set either in terms of absolute performance or as gains over some previous period. Performance data should indicate whether the targets are being met and where corrective action is needed. Where historical comparisons form the basis for reporting efficiency levels, additional analysis should be done to indicate the extent to which productivity improvement opportunities exist.

Increased efficiency should be sought systematically. Recognized techniques, such as work measurement and organization and methods analysis, should be used for this purpose. Where appropriate, mechanization should be considered. All proposed changes should be evaluated before implementation, including consideration of data on past performance.

Performance data should be used to encourage employee groups and managers to improve productivity. The communication to individuals and groups of the performance expected of them is of primary importance.

Productivity data should be used in estimating future resource needs. In the budgeting process, performance data should be used to plan improved ways of delivering programs.

Up-dating Systems

Performance measurement systems have a short life if unadjusted for change. Data collection and analysis routines should be modified to correct identified defects. Computerization or mechanization projects affecting the labour content of an operation should be recognized, and labour productivity indicators revised accordingly. Similarly, performance measurement systems should be modified as necessary to reflect program changes arising from new legislation.

Audit Criteria

To help control the efficiency of work done, performance measurement systems should:

- use relevant and accurate measures of performance;
- compare performance to a standard;
- tailor reports to management needs;
- use performance data to achieve productivity improvement; and
- keep productivity measures and reports current.

IV. Evaluating Effectiveness

Program effectiveness, the achievement of program objectives and other intended effects, is the ultimate issue in value for money. From our research on the state of the art in effectiveness evaluation in Canada and other countries, we developed basic principles. . . .

There is a perception that program evaluation is difficult, expensive and time-consuming. Many managers believe that the effectiveness of their programs cannot be measured. Although there are limitations in what can be measured, practical means are available for at least partial measurement of the achievements of most major programs against stated objectives.

As a general rule, one does not have to approach the limits of the state of the art to plan and carry out useful evaluations. The problem is not so much a lack of technology but failure to apply recognized principles and well tested techniques where appropriate and reasonable.

Measurements of effectiveness that are seriously flawed methodologically are at least useless and perhaps misleading. Decision-makers must have full confidence in the credibility of any analysis before they will give it serious consideration.

Although there will always be elements of subjective judgment in program evaluation, we believe that maximum use should be made of recognized evaluation methodology to measure the impact of government programs. Useful evaluation, however, is dependent on a number of important considerations.

Clearly Specified Program Objective

Value for money implies an ability to ascertain program accomplishments. Within practical limits, program objectives should be specified as clearly as possible to help evaluate effectiveness. Objectives must be specified so that Members of Parliament can seek the answer to this important question: how do I know whether the program is worth its cost?

24

THE STRESSFUL EFFECTS OF BUDGET CUTS IN ORGANIZATIONS
TODD D. JICK*

Signs of the Times

Newspaper headlines proclaiming budget cuts, economic slowdown, and lay-offs have appeared routinely in Western developing countries during the late 1970s and early 1980s. A spirit of austerity has become an integral part of the political and economic environment within which private and public sector organizations operate. And most predictions indicate that this state of affairs will continue well into the 1980s.

Increased efforts to measure efficiency and effectiveness are only one indication of this heightened consciousness. Consider how enriched our vocabulary has become in the area of fiscal analysis. Budgets are said to be filled with the following: fat, padding, cushions, waste tissue, frills, soft spots, and slack. What is to be done with such budgets? Accountants and managers seek opportunities to cut, carve, slice, axe, prune, squeeze, downsize, reduce, streamline, shrink, contract, retrench, trim, lop-off, chop, and slash! Perhaps you are aware of still other such "action verbs."

Few accountants would question the worth and/or necessity of balanced budgets and fiscal responsibility. Few would disagree that cutting costs is a prerequisite of sound management these days and that "what you don't have, you can't spend." And few would disagree that most organizations could use some fiscal pruning. In tough economic times, these rules of thumb are especially prominent and important.

---

* The author is an Associate Professor in the Faculty of Administrative Studies at York University.

And yet, the fiscal benefits of cutback management must also be weighed in relation to their downside human risks and the difficulties in implementing cutbacks. In short, the human impact of budget cuts in organizations also needs to be considered. As jobs, wages, programs and other resources become less secure, the stress of those affected is likely to increase commensurately. Thus, this article is intended to sensitize accountants and managers to the human and organizational *impact* of cutback decisions. It underscores the point that cutback decisions need to be cautiously made and carefully managed in terms of their behavioural effects. Specifically, we will examine four questions:

1. What are the stresses most commonly caused by budget cuts?
2. What are the signs or symptoms of budget cut stress?
3. Why do some individuals experience more stress than others?
4. What can be done to minimize the harmful effects of stress on individuals and organizations in budgetary hard times?

Unfortunately, largely because of the recency of the phenomenon, there has been little systematic research on the stress of budget cuts[1]. This article however will review what is known about how individuals react to both the threat and the reality of such cuts, a relevant problem for accountants and managers who want to manage hard times more effectively and humanely.

Conceptual Framework

We will begin by presenting an overall conceptual framework for the analysis of the factors affecting the way in which individuals perceive cutbacks and respond to them. Figure 1 presents a broad overview of the stress process which will serve as a basis for understanding how budget cuts and stress are related. Based upon some commonly used stress models, stress is portrayed as the result of a "transaction" between an environmental event (e.g., a budget cut) and the perceptions of the affected individual. The objective conditions produce a subjective definition of the situation by the individual, and it is this *perceived* situation which is the primary determinant of the stress response. However, individual responses to environmental demands and to the subjective appraisal of stress will vary as a result of differences in personality, abilities, and coping skills.

Typically, after weeks, months, and even years of rumours, employees are officially informed that budget cuts of X per cent have been mandated by the funding source or by the organization's central budget committee. This announcement represents what we are calling an "environmental demand." The extent of the demand, however, presumably varies — in part because of its objective characteristics (i.e., the extent of the cut, objectively speaking) but also in part because of the interpretation of what that demand signifies for the individual. It is the uncertainty, not knowing whether one has sufficient resources and coping strength to meet future demands, which primarily determines the initial level of experienced stress. This is typically manifest in terms of various adverse behavioural and emotional outcomes.

Figure 1

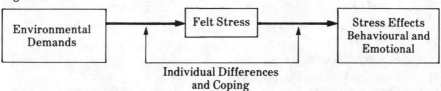

The likelihood that the threat of budget cuts will lead to a state of felt stress is also shaped by various individual differences related to individual vulnerability, preparedness, and coping skills. Thus, for example, individual differences in the number of previous "encounters" with budget cuts, degree of self-perceived power to resist the cuts, coping response repertoires, and tolerance levels of felt stress are all likely to moderate the relationship between objective and felt threat, thereby affecting the degree of experienced uncertainty (as will be discussed later). The next sections will examine more closely the objective conditions under which budget cut stress is most likely and the subjective experience of these stress-producing conditions.

Stress-Producing Conditions: Objective Factors

Budget cuts may take on different shapes and forms, objectively speaking. In the interest of reducing costs, organizations may mandate layoffs, hiring freezes, wage freezes, reductions in work hours, supervisory changes, additional job responsibilities, new spending authorization procedures, etc. Whichever strategy or tactic is chosen, these cuts vary considerably in terms of their likely impact on cost effectiveness and the nature of daily operations.

In addition, the nature of the cuts is likely to impact differentially the likelihood of experienced stress or uncertainty in an organization or organizational unit. Cuts will be more or less stressful to the extent that they embody crisis-like properties. A crisis may be defined as a situation that threatens high priority goals, restricts the amount of response time available, and surprises organization members when it occurs. A crisis is thus viewed as a situation of high severity and high time pressure.

It seems plausible to suggest that the greater the severity and time pressure associated with budget cuts, the greater the likelihood of experienced stress in an organization. As listed in Figure 2, severity and time pressure are each a function of multiple factors. Severity, for example, consists of (a) the size of the cuts; (b) the threat to high priority goals, programs, and organizational survival; (c) the frequency of cuts; (d) the extent or organizational slack or alternate funding availability; (e) the extent of management

Figure 2 Objective Sources of Budget Cut Stress

	DIMENSIONS	
	HIGH SEVERITY	HIGH TIME PRESSURE
C H A R A C T E R I S T I C S	Size of cuts Impact on goals, programs or survival prospects Frequency of cuts Organizational slack availability of alternate funds Extent of management assurances Selective cuts	Forewarning Information clarity Response time Duration of cuts

assurances regarding job security and organizational survival; and (f) the extent to which they are selective or uniform. Research in these areas has generally found that in cases of threatened or actual cuts:

- The greater the size of the budget cuts, the higher the likelihood of experienced stress/uncertainty.
- The greater the extent to which the cuts affect changes in goals, programs or organizational survival, the higher the likelihood of experienced stress/uncertainty.
- The higher the frequency of cuts, the higher the likelihood of experienced stress/uncertainty.
- The less organizational slack and the fewer the opportunities for alternate funding, the higher the likelihood of experienced stress/uncertainty.
- The fewer the management assurances regarding job security or departmental survival, the higher the likelihood of experienced stress/uncertainty.
- The more the cuts are selective rather than uniform, the higher the likelihood of experienced stress/uncertainty (due to more opportunity for inequity).

Partial support for these hypotheses can be found in research which examined the relationship between the severity of cutbacks and the degree of impact on employees[2]. Work-related attitudes, anxiety level, and motivation of employees in organizations which had experienced sporadic or minor layoffs were compared with those for employees in organizations which had layoffs of more than 10% in a two-year period. It was anticipated that the more severe the layoffs, the more dysfunctional the consequences on retained employees. Although results did not provide consistent support for all hypotheses, it was found that there was more unease and anxiety, and less expressed motivation among employees in situations of more severe cutbacks and decline.

The time pressure dimension may be characterized in terms of four factors: forewarning information, clarity, response time, and duration. Forewarning refers to whether there was clear indication that the budget cut was coming and how long a period there was between such information being presented and the event itself. Information clarity refers to the degree of ambiguity in the information available regarding the likelihood of future events. Response time is the time between the occurrence of the crisis event and the point at which responses and changes are made. A funding reduction, for example, may allow several months between official notification of next year's grant and the announcement of a firm budget and related changes to be made. Finally, some cuts are mandated to last longer than others. On the basis of these time pressure dimensions, the following may be hypothesized:

- The less forewarning information of impending budget cuts, the higher the likelihood of experienced stress/uncertainty when the cuts finally occur.
- The lower the information clarity regarding impending budget cuts, the higher the likelihood of experienced stress/uncertainty.
- The lower the response time available between the mandate to cut and the actual cuts, the higher the likelihood of experienced stress/uncertainty.
- The longer the mandated duration of the budget cuts, the higher the likelihood of experienced stress/uncertainty.

This section has suggested that differences in experienced stress and uncertainty due to budget cuts can be understood, in part, on the basis of differences in the objective properties of the cutback situations. Clearly, however, the response to threatened or actual budget reductions is also shaped by the *perceived* severity and time pressure which ultimately produce the degree of experienced stress.

Feelings of Stress

The degree of experienced stress caused by these changes and cuts depends upon the degree of *perceived* uncertainty of outcomes as well as the individual's ability to handle the new demands or conditions. Thus budget cuts are stressful and meaningful only insofar as their importance and uncertainty are acknowledged. Accordingly, the objective severity and suddenness of budget cuts can differ from the perceived severity and time pressure.

What are the most commonly-felt stresses associated with budget cuts? As organizations adapt to leaner times, employees may be subject to multiple sources of stress, including:

(a) *Role Confusion:* What am I supposed to be doing/what is most important "these days"?

(b) *Job Insecurity:* Is my job vulnerable? Am I next?

(c) *Work Overload:* How can I do twice as much work with less support staff or resources?/Increased documentation of all spending activities/more meetings.

(d) *Career Plateauing:* My opportunities for career advancement seem thwarted due to the budget cuts.

(e) *Poor Incentives:* The extra extrinsic rewards for doing my work well are no more.

(f) *Office Politics and Conflict:* Everyone is chiefly concerned with their own personal survival and it can be unpleasant. Conflicts with others are likely to increase as a result of scarce resources.

(g) *Lack of Participation in Decision-Making:* All the budget decisions are made by "them" but I feel I should contribute as well.

(h) *Tense Organizational Climate:* The atmosphere is generally tense and lacking in the good humour of the "good ole days."

(i) *Ideological Disagreement:* I am not pleased with the new direction of my organization. I disagree fundamentally with many of the budget priorities and it makes me question whether I really want to work here.

(j) *Job and Personal Life Conflicts:* I see my family less than ever since the budget cuts and I am more tense when I get home.

Budget cuts will be associated with felt stressors, as those above, to the extent that the cuts evoke apprehension, worry, fear, or anxiety that the disruptions or changes will deny the employee valued outcomes. An individual typically makes a mental calculation regarding the nature of the demands/changes and his/her internal or external resources for coping with the threatening demands.

To illustrate how an individual might respond, consider a letter (Figure 3) which might be sent to employees announcing a consolidation of two departments due to budget restraints:

Figure 3   Letter Announcing Cutbacks

DATE: May 28, 19____.

To: All Employees

I want to take this opportunity to announce to you that we have decided to consolidate X and Y Departments. This consolidation, which has been under consideration for a number of years, will begin on the first of June and will concentrate on administrative and support activities . . .

The consolidation will result in a reduction in force. Normal attrition will account for some of this reduction but the possibility of small target layoffs does exist. Every attempt will be made to provide alternative employment for those who are affected.

I am sure that the merger will raise many questions in your mind. I have asked an Ad Hoc Committee for each department to collect questions for prompt and specific replies. The days ahead are bound to be difficult. I sincerely believe that this consolidation will prove to be in the best interest of our company.

Sincerely,

Vice President Operations

Let us consider the reactions of a "typical" employee with average seniority, dedication, income, and performance history. The cuts, in the form of a consolidation, are likely to be perceived as rather demanding because they may involve "small target layoffs," increasing the job insecurity of the average employee, and because they are imminent. In addition to perceived job insecurity, other perceived demands might include the fear of work overload or impeded performance due to the consolidation of services, changes in work assignments, the prospect of potential conflict and politics with employees over scarce resources, the fear of wage freezes, shrinking promotional opportunities, and insufficient time to implement and absorb the threatened changes.

The magnitude of these demands and the resultant uncertainty, however, depend of course in part on the employee's capacity to successfully utilize various coping resources. For example, the presence of social support and the knowledge of personal stress-management skills might immediately reduce the individual's vulnerability. Similarly, financial savings or the confidence that alternate employment is readily available would cushion the magnitude of the demands. In addition, the employee might be reassured by management guarantees or by powerful coalitions of employees (unions) which could lead a campaign to resist or delay the cuts. In the real case of this consolidation example, however, few of these buffers existed, given the absence of clear management reassurances, a weak union, a tight labour market, and an already stretched pocketbook for most employees.

For many individuals in situations such as the consolidation example, uncertainty of outcomes is likely to be intense. For example, employees may have doubts that they can perform well even if they try to when they perceive themselves to be overloaded, under unrealistic deadlines, and/or in chronic conflict with their peers over scarce resources. Similarly, ambiguous messages may exist regarding the outcomes that will accrue based upon successful performance. When there are threatened or actual cutbacks in jobs, programs, or promotional opportunities, individuals may fear that performing well will not necessarily guarantee job security, may not involve their special abilities and skills, and may not lead to a promotion.

Many employees facing these demands may then feel that unless the situation is altered (either by reducing the cuts or increasing their ability to live with such demands) important areas of their personal and/or professional lives could be adversely affected. The perceived consequences for quality of work life, quality of family life, career prospects, job and economic security, work group relations, personal job standards, and one's performance record intensify the feelings of stress.

In summary, budget cuts can cause considerable fear and anxiety which, if left unattended, can lead to harmful consequences for both the individual and the organization.

Signs of Budget Cut Stress

Faced with such conditions of high threat and crisis, what are the signals which would help you identify an individual who is experiencing stress and uncertainty?

On an individual level, some common strain responses include decreased attention span, a tendency to "live for today," and a reliance upon familiar tried and true responses. Together, these responses are likely to limit a person's ability to think clearly, to weigh problems carefully, and to make sound judgements. Other responses include increased resistance to change, thoughts of quitting, less effort, and less job satisfaction. These are many of the withdrawal symptoms of what is commonly referred to today as "burnout," a mixture of behavioural and emotional reactions signalling fatigue and disillusionment in extreme cases. Federal budget cuts, in the U.S. for example, seem to have played a significant role in a recent increase in federal employees' usage of health services: almost triple the usual number were treated for stress-related symptoms such as dizziness, stomach cramps, diarrhoea, and increased blood pressure.

And there is little doubt that most of these stress responses have adverse effects on productivity.

In Denver, government employees whose staff had been pruned and reorganized were found to be so fearful about their future that productivity suffered. One manager estimated that the atmosphere of "gloom" cost the equivalent of about a month's work per year per employee[3].

Two researchers[4] have predicted different forms of employee response which reflect the varying degrees of cutback severity:

- Under conditions of low uncertainty and few cuts, employees will experience a moderate degree of unease; some will search for another job.
- Under conditions of low uncertainty and high cuts (over 10% in one year, 25% over three years), high seniority employees will attempt to structure layoff rules to protect themselves while low seniority employees and those in low priority programs will leave quietly, protecting their recall rights.
- Under conditions of high uncertainty but low cuts, the most marketable employees will leave.
- Under conditions of high uncertainty and high decline, employee behaviour will be dominated by caution, withdrawal, anxiety, tentativeness, and resistance to change.

A more dynamic model of individual reactions to crisis situations was proposed by other researchers[5]. They describe a four-stage sequence of crisis reactions: shock, defensive retreat, acknowledgement, and adaptation and change. The first phase is characterized by feelings of confusion, inability to fully grasp what's happening, and poor planning of an adequate coping response. The second stage involves clinging to the past, avoidance of reality, denial, rigid thinking, and resistance to change. These two phases have been labelled "the crisis syndrome" for it is at these periods that experienced stress is most intense. Given the recurring quality of many cutback situations, some individuals become "stuck" in crisis syndrome thinking, and become unable to remove the experienced stress entirely. The final two phases involve, first, a period of acceptance of the new situation and then eventual adjustment so that the individual no longer experiences a state of crisis.

Another researcher found some strong empirical evidence of the crisis syndrome as applied to budget cuts per se[6]. In a study of a hospital merger and associated work force reductions, he identified several manifestations of the stress associated with the early crisis phases of shock and defensive retreat. Threatened jobs and general uncertainty were correlated with increases in voluntary resignations, reduced job satisfaction, weakened loyalty toward the organization, various psychomatic and somatic symptoms, and decreased productivity due to reduced effort on the job. There also was evidence of narrow thinking in problem solving situations.

Further confirmation comes from a study of reorganization, pay cuts, and layoffs in the municipal departments of a large California city[7]. Initial reactions were typically characterized by shock and extreme anxiety regarding job security and the continued desirability of a career in the public sector. The shock gave way to feelings of powerlessness and submission. Survey data collected before and after the changes showed a significant increase in turnover intentions and a significant decrease in job participation, pay satisfaction, and intrinsic motivation.

To summarize, the models, empirical findings, and anecdotal evidence suggest that *the experienced stress created as a result of budget cuts will be manifest in terms of well recognized behavioural, psychological, and physiological symptoms.* However, it is unclear which stress conditions lead to which responses. Furthermore, not all individuals will experience increased stress as a result of budget cuts: the degree of experienced stress will vary in part as a result of the degree of perceived crisis. In addition, certain individual characteristics, or coping skills, will moderate the associated strain outcomes.

Individual Differences

Stress research has clearly shown that individuals confront stressful conditions with a variety of behaviours and cognition which can serve to alter these conditions or mediate their impact. Thus individual differences, especially coping skills, serve as critical moderators or mediators of experienced stress. These mediators have been described as the resources, actions, and perceptions mobilized by individuals as they seek to avoid or minimize distress. In the study of hospital cuts, such individual differences in reaction were typical. For example, 54 per cent of employees reported being "worried" when the cuts were announced, while 12 per cent reported feelings of indifference and 4 per cent were "pleased." Variables such as personality, experience, seniority, and occupational level are most likely to shape an individual's assessment of the importance of the cuts and the resources for coping with those demands.

Two related factors which have been predicted to influence the perception of a crisis are expectations and previous experience. In studies of natural disaster situations, any threat "cues" will tend to be interpreted as *un*threatening by those not expecting the disaster, until such interpretations can no longer be made[8]. However, when individuals are expecting the disaster, an apparent over-sensitivity to stress cues develops such that even a minor suggestion of possible threat stimulates emergency-type reactions.

Furthermore, various studies provide support for the hypothesis that decision-makers who have had minimal past experience with budget cuts will be more likely to perceive them as severe crises and thus experience more felt anxiety. In addition, previous experience can affect the likelihood that scarcity of information will be perceived and deemed valid. The following propositions, therefore, seem likely:

- If budget cuts are threatened where there have been no previous cuts, the tendency will be to interpret them as unthreatening until such interpretations can no longer be made.
- Under conditions of recent, but not repeated cuts, individuals will develop an oversensitivity to budget cut threat cues.

However, under conditions of repeated exposure to threat, there will be a selective sensitivity unlike either of the predicted reactions above. In part, this is related to expectations, but it is also a reflection of the amount of knowledge, training, or experience possessed by individuals in similar situations. Thus, one might also hypothesize that:

- Under conditions of repeated exposure to and experience with budget cut threats, individuals will develop a selective sensitivity to warning signals and tend to interpret new information more accurately.

Certain personality moderators have also been identified as being related to the determinants of crisis perceptions, though few have actually been tested in the case of budget cuts. For example, it is expected that personality type of high anxiety, low self-esteem, and Type A (workaholics) will be more likely to perceive budget cuts as severe crises.

Figure 4   Budget Cut Stress: A Summary Diagram of Key Concepts

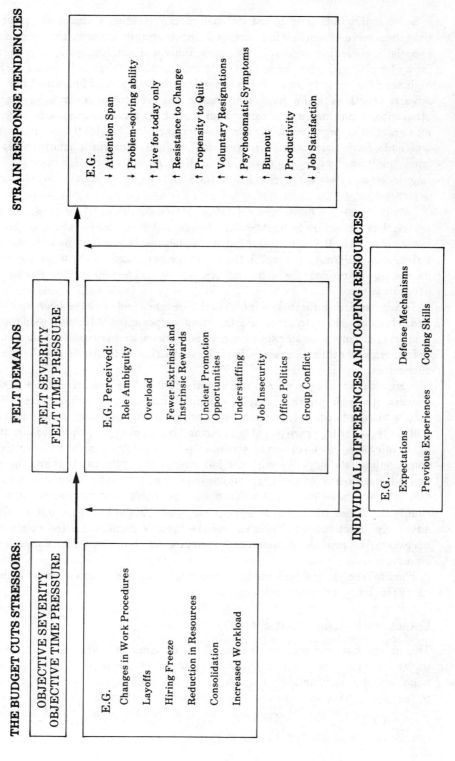

THE BUDGET CUTS STRESSORS:

FELT DEMANDS

STRAIN RESPONSE TENDENCIES

OBJECTIVE SEVERITY
OBJECTIVE TIME PRESSURE

FELT SEVERITY
FELT TIME PRESSURE

E.G.

Changes in Work Procedures

Layoffs

Hiring Freeze

Reduction in Resources

Consolidation

Increased Workload

E.G. Perceived:

Role Ambiguity

Overload

Fewer Extrinsic and
Instrinsic Rewards

Unclear Promotion
Opportunities

Understaffing

Job Insecurity

Office Politics

Group Conflict

E.G.

↓ Attention Span

↓ Problem-solving ability

↑ Live for today only

↑ Resistance to Change

↑ Propensity to Quit

↑ Voluntary Resignations

↑ Psychosomatic Symptoms

↑ Burnout

↓ Productivity

↓ Job Satisfaction

INDIVIDUAL DIFFERENCES AND COPING RESOURCES

E.G.

Expectations   Defense Mechanisms

Previous Experiences   Coping Skills

Some individuals tend to use defense mechanisms as a means of protecting themselves from feeling stressed. Interestingly enough, this became especially evident in research examining individual differences in tolerance for ambiguity and need for security[9]. It was predicted that individuals with high need for security and low tolerance for ambiguity would manifest more adverse reactions to the uncertain threats. The results, however, suggested otherwise: conditions of ambiguity had less effect on individuals who were intolerant of ambiguity and high in need for security. Evidently, individuals who had a basic aversion to threatening ambiguous situations handle ambiguous conditions by denying or distorting their "objective" predicament. This functioned as a defense mechanism in the short run to reduce the level of experienced stress.

Finally, there are numerous individual coping mechanisms for minimizing personal overreaction to unexpected change and uncertainty. These include knowing one's self better, taking a wider perspective (e.g., "in a hundred years, who will know or care?"), time management, and all the physical and mental preparedness which reduces one's vulnerability to stressful pressures.

To summarize, a number of individual difference factors have been identified which are likely to moderate the stress experience. Although evidence is sparse, factors such as experience, expectations, and personality all seem to influence whether a person is likely to feel stress in the context of budget cuts crises.

Figure 4 portrays the way in which individual differences affect the stress process. According to this model, some individuals faced with the same "objective" budget cuts might panic and become highly stressed while others will perceive far less threat and demand and might even find the situation an exciting challenge. Even if the stress is generally felt by most individuals, some individuals will cope with the felt stress more effectively than others and mitigate many of the harmful consequences ("strain response tendencies"). Given these individual differences, it is crucial that managers and accountants either find ways to prevent those budget-cuts which would adversely affect some individuals and the organizations, or, if the cuts are necessary, to provide support and guidance to those who feel excessive stress.

The final section will indicate some recommended stress management techniques for budget decision-makers.

Coping with Budget Cut Stress

This article has reviewed and explored the dynamics of experienced stress under conditions of fiscal cutbacks. As fiscal cuts are perceived to be "at hand" and/or are ultimately realized, many threatened employees are likely to feel and behave in ways that are detrimental to themselves as well as to the functioning of the organization. As stated though, not all individuals will suffer negative stress reactions to budget cuts. One can imagine two individuals hit with the same pattern of cuts, one who ends up limping along wracked with stress, desperately seeking to get out if possible, while the other appears to be maintaining all essential activities or even exhibiting new and original activities while exuding confidence, loyalty, and commitment to the organization. What can be done by managers and accountants to maximize the number of the latter individuals and minimize the former?

The key is to follow *two basic principles of cutback management:*

1. Cuts made on the basis of expedience, convenience, arbitrariness, short-term perspectives, or political interests will exacerbate stress in organizations. Cuts should only be made based on careful priority analysis, rational planning, and both the short *and* long-term view.
2. "It's not what you cut but how you cut it!" The most effective cost reductions and savings can still create negative counter-effects and/or not be implemented as planned if they are decided upon, introduced, and explained in ways unacceptable to employees.

Although "success" stories of well managed budget cuts are far less frequent than tales of demoralized managers and employees, there are certain techniques which work effectively in most situations. They are fashioned after the two principles above and expected to minimize perceived uncertainty and perceived demands:

- MAXIMIZE DOWNWARD COMMUNICATION
  Employees in the dark will become restless, resistant and discouraged. Hold meetings, provide fact sheets, make speeches, and encourage questions. Constantly emphasize the "why" behind all cuts and actions.

- INVOLVE AFFECTED PARTIES AS MUCH AS POSSIBLE
  Involve employees in the cutback decisions where feasible and let them participate in establishing new priorities and long-term planning.

- RE-SHAPE EXPECTATION LEVELS TO SUSTAIN MOTIVATION
  If life in the organization will never be what it once was, say so! But, at the same time, identify new goals which are needed, challenging, yet attainable. Explain what your people are *working for* while they are retrenching.

- BUILD ON READINESS TO MAKE CUTS, NOT RESISTANCE
  For every pound of resistance to cuts, there is almost always at least an ounce of willingness or readiness to try something new or do something better. If people are asked to offer innovative methods that demand less resources, they usually have more than enough to offer.

- PROVIDE OUTLETS FOR STRESS RELEASE
  In stressful times, humour and oddball recreational activities will serve to release pent-up tensions, build group cohesion, and will develop a healthy distance from problems often beyond one's control.

- BE PREPARED TO TAKE SOME GRIEF

  Although often uncomfortable and unpleasant, managers and accountants involved in budget cuts must encourage the voicing of negative, hostile feelings and complaints. Small group, face-to-face interaction characterized by "heat" and anger should also allow for compromises and diffuse angry feelings.

Managing human resources in tough fiscal times is a formidable challenge. You need to exercise astute technical and analytic skills, sensitive people skills, and no small amount of faith in yourself and in your organization to withstand intense pressures. As one observer glibly remarked, "It's just not as much fun managing in a contracting organization as it is in an expanding one."

Yet, organizations that are cutting back — just as individuals who experience crises — sometimes emerge stronger, more self-aware, and more effective in the long-run. The first step in that direction is for accountants and managers to appreciate the people risks and challenges involved in cutback management: to evaluate the effects of cutbacks on individuals over time, the effects of cutbacks on different types of individuals, and the effects of different cutback situtions (i.e., differing degrees of threat) on individuals. This knowledge can then be utilized to develop and apply individual and organizational strategies for managing the challenging demands of hard times.

References

1. Jick, T.D. and V.V. Murray "The Management of Hard Times: Budget Cutbacks in Public Sector Organizations," *Organization Studies,* 1982, 3, 141-170.
2. Blonder, M.D., *Organizational Repercussion of Personnel Cutbacks: Impacts of Layoffs on Retained Employees,* PhD dissertation, City University of New York, 1976.
3. Blundell, W.E., "As the Budget Axe Falls So Does Productivity of Grim U.S. Workers", *Wall Street Journal,* August 17, 1978.
4. Levine, C.H., and C.G. Wolohojian, "Retrenchment, Uncertainty, and Human Resources: Combatting the Discount Effects of a Bleak Future." Paper presented at the Annual Conference of the American Society for Public Administration, San Francisco, 1980.
5. Fink, L., J. Beak, and K. Taddeo, "Organizational Crisis and Change," *Journal of Applied Behavioral Science,* 47/1, 1971, 15-41.
6. Jick, T.D. *Process and Impacts of a Merger: Individual and Organizational Perspectives,* Unpublished doctoral dissertation, Cornell University, 1979.
7. Walsh, J.T., and D.S. Tracey, "Long-Term Organizational Effects of Voter-Mandated Property Tax Relief." Paper presented at the American Psychological Association Annual Meeting, Montreal, 1980.
8. Withey, S.B., "Reaction in Uncertain Threat," in G.W. Baker and D.W. Chapman (Eds.), *Man and Society in Disaster,* New York: Basic Books, 1962, 93-123.
9. Greenhalgh, L. and T.D. Jick, "The Phenomenology of Sense-Making in a Declining Organization: Effects of Individual Difference," Paper presented at Academy of Management Meetings, Dallas, 1983.

VI.

FINANCING, AND INVESTING

Most cost and managerial accounting textbooks give much attention to investing (capital budgeting) evaluations, but often simplify the crucial practical aspects, such as income tax and uncertainty. Similarly, the serious practical issues affecting cash budgeting usually tend to be given short treatment. The first two articles in this section look at some important bread and butter cash flow and liquidity issues.

"Cash Flow Analysis: More Important than Ever" examines several factors that influence an organization's cash flow. The authors are concerned with the need to plan and better control the flow of cash, instead of assuming that it is a residual. They employ a variation of a critical success/failure analytical framework (see Section I) to analyze some "causes" of cash flow variation.

"Identifying and Resolving Problems in Corporate Liquidity" follows up on the previous article. The authors give the results of a liquidity management survey designed to identify signals that indicate pending liquidity problems and how management attempted to resolve illiquidity. Although the results are often not surprising, they help our attempts to develop a decision orientation by strengthening our convictions.

"Strategic Capital Budgeting" is the first of three articles on this topic. The author, Harold Bierman, Jr., is one of the developers of capital budgeting thought. Note his observation, "the frontier of capital budgeting, uncertainty, has tended to resist efforts to find easily computed feasible solutions to accept or reject decisions." He then proceeds to discuss capital allocations in a practical setting.

"Structuring Capital Spending Hurdle Rates" follows up on portions of Bierman's article. The author, Allen H. Seed III, is a business consultant. He provides some practical insights into how companies actually handle investment decisions. The Seed and Bierman articles have some interesting similarities and differences.

"Capital Budgeting Using Terminal Values" explains why it is beneficial to evaluate some investing decisions in terms of future ("terminal") values instead of present values. The author, an academic, is particularly concerned about rates for *reinvestment* of funds generated by projects.

"Anatomy of an Auto-Plant Rescue" looks at the *disinvestment* decision. The article, like many in this book, describes a real situation. Two portions of the article are particularly interesting for students of management accounting: (1) the arithmetic used to back up the initial decision to close the plant, and (2) the company's comparison of what it cost to manufacture in their own plant versus the cost of buying outside the company.

"Recovery Rate and Cash Flow Accounting" has been written by a well-known accounting academician. The article overlaps performance appraisal, investment, and external reporting evaluations. A prime concern of many people is the evaluation of projects *after* the asset/investment has been acquired and is in use. Was the decision to acquire the investment wise? Can we learn anything from the mistakes that we might have made? The author examines a typical accounting problem — cash versus accrual measurements and their interpretation — in an investment setting.

25

CASH FLOW ANALYSIS: MORE IMPORTANT THAN EVER

BRADLEY T. GALE AND BEN BRANCH*

A clear understanding of the link between financial and strategic planning can help managers select the best options for cash use.

You won't find many executives arguing the importance of cash flow to the future success of their businesses, especially as inflation increases the already high cost of capital. Most will admit, however, that they tend only to monitor their cash — that they have few ideas about how to control it or use it to their strategic advantage.

Based on information culled from their extensive data base, Bradley Gale and Ben Branch of the Strategic Planning Institute have found that cash flow can be manipulated and can serve as an effective tool in business strategies. In this article, they demonstrate that a business's competitive position, the growth rate of its market, and its current strategic moves have a predictable effect on cash flow. By understanding how these factors impinge on cash supplies, the manager of a single business unit can evaluate the trade-offs among alternative strategies that use cash. Also, managers of groups of businesses can improve their ability to allocate cash supplies among their individual businesses.

* Bradley Gale is director of research, Strategic Planning Institute. Ben Branch is professor of finance, University of Massachusetts, Amherst and a research associate at SPI. Reprinted by permission of the *Harvard Business Review*. Copyright © 1981 by the President and Fellows of Harvard College; all rights reserved. From *Harvard Business Review* (July/August 1981).

Authors' note: We gratefully acknowledge the contribution of colleagues at the Strategic Planning Institute — Mark Chussil, Donald F. Heany, Sidney Schoeffler, and Donald J. Swire — to the research for this article, and we thank Ruth G. Newman for her editorial guidance.

Managers sometimes think that their strategies are tied to the tail of a very erratic cash kite and that fluctuations in cash supplies are too irregular and unpredictable to manage properly.

In fact, the reverse is true. Cash flow is predictable and manageable. A company's strategy and market position directly affect it. The recognition of this fact is as calming as it is essential — not only to the manager of a single business unit but also to a CEO or group vice president.

The single business unit needs cash to grow, modernize, and finance normal day-to-day operations. But managers must analyze the cash potential of each business unit in order to decide which can be relied on as cash sources and which require heavy investment to grow.

In the 1980s, companies face increasing requirements for funds even as they deplete their resources by allocating more to energy conservation and environmental protection (so-called unproductive uses of cash). Moreover, skyrocketing inflation menaces their cash supplies. And lagging U.S. productivity compounds the problem of cash availability because it underscores the need for many businesses to reindustrialize at great expense.

We have used the PIMS data base (see the ruled insert on p. 291 for a more detailed description of PIMS) to discover some important facts about cash generation and cash use, about how companies use and abuse this vital resource, and about ways in which they can restructure cash flow:

Growth drains cash. Being in a strong market is exciting but keeping up with the fast pace requires cash. Even when real market growth is zero, inflation drains cash.

Calculating net cash flow rates

The cash flow rates shown in the exhibits and dicussed throughout this article are net cash flow as defined here. We have made some basic assumptions about tax rates and interest expenses to help determine net cash flow at the operating business unit level.

We begin by assuming a tax rate of 50% and zero interest expenses. Gross cash flow is calculated as depreciation plus half the cash from pretax, preinterest income.

Net cash flow is gross cash flow minus (1) cash absorbed by increases in average working capital and (2) increases in gross investment in plant and equipment.

The average rate for the PIMS data base is about 4% (four cents of net cash flow for each dollar invested).

See the *Appendix* for guidelines on how to estimate rough cash flow rates that reflect interest expenses and dividend payments.

A **high relative market share generates cash.** But building a future market position requires large expenditures for marketing programs or new product development.

Aggressive asset management is vital to ensure sufficient cash. Increased investment relative to sales can be threatening because it always strains cash supply.

In this article, we examine these findings and their implications for all companies.

Cash Producers versus Cash Users

A large percentage of the businesses we studied consume more cash than they generate; in fact, more than a third have a negative operating cash flow before interest expenses (see *Exhibit I*). After we subtract interest expenses and dividend payments from cash flow, about two-thirds of the businesses are cash drains.

That so many businesses are cash drains suggests that control is a slippery and complex problem. There are wide differences in the *rate* at which particular businesses use or generate cash. For example, 26% generate cash at a yearly rate above 10% of investment. On the other hand, nearly 15% of them *consume* cash at the 10% rate or beyond. Since businesses may show such divergent cash flow results, it is rational to assume that successful cash control demands systematic study and the careful attention of senior management.

Exhibit I   Cash Flow Level of PIMS Businesses, 1970-1979

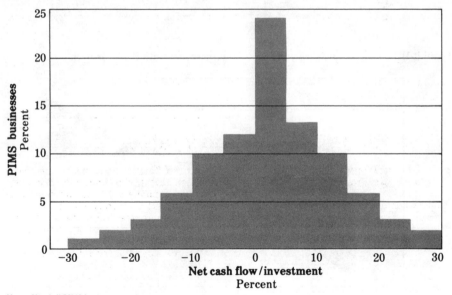

Note: 8% of all PIMS businesses are beyond these bounds.

Businesses in fast-growth markets usually absorb cash unless corporate policy directs that they break even; businesses in slow-growth markets usually throw off cash unless they are allowed to keep and reinvest it.

Cash flow is lowest when sales growth (in current dollars) is rapid (see *Exhibit IIA*). When growth is slow or negative, cash flow is very positive. In fact, at a moderate growth rate, all a company needs is an average ROI to generate positive cash flow (before dividend or interest payments). At rapid growth rates, however, average ROI no longer suffices.

Exhibit IIA   Rapid Growth Drains Cash

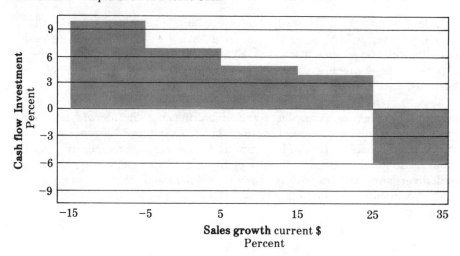

Exhibit IIB   ROI for Break-Even Cash Flow Increases with Sales Growth

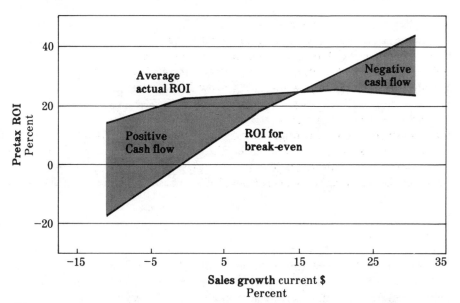

Note:

Break-even ROI (pretax, preinterest) = $2g/(1+g)$, where g is the rate of growth expressed as a decimal. If g =.10, ROI for break-even cash flow rate =.2/1.1=18%. See S.J.Q. Robinson, "What Growth Rate Can You Achieve?" *Long-Range Planning*, August 1979. Also, readers will note that the crossover points between positive and negative cash flow rates shown in *Exhibits*

IIA and *IIB* differ. The ROI for the break-even rate assumes that investment will grow at the same rate as sales over time. But during the 1970s the ratio of investment to sales declined. Because investment did not keep pace with sales, the ROI actually needed to break even during the 1970s was less than that shown in *Exhibit IIB*.

The algebraic relationship between growth and ROI needed to generate a break-even cash flow is positive and dramatic. But the correlation between growth and *actual* ROI is only moderate. When actual ROI exceeds that required to break even (growth rate below 15%), cash flow is positive. When it falls short, cash flow is negative. (*Exhibit IIB* shows ROI needed for a business to finance break-even cash flow at various rates of growth.)

We have observed how cash flow decreases with growth in current dollar sales. Such a decrease depends on growth in real market and selling price, as well as basic market share strategy.

When real market growth is rapid, maintaining share may require considerable cash for working capital and for additional plant and equipment.

Inflation also takes its toll. Although one might expect that a rise in the selling price would generate cash, it generally does not. Indeed, a company finds its cash depleted as rising prices are either accompanied by (or are prompted by) rising costs. In addition, as prices rise, the need of most companies to tie up larger amounts of money in inventory and accounts receivable exacerbates cash requirements.

So cash flow varies *inversely* with both the real market growth rate and the rate of increase in selling prices. Our data base shows that businesses with slow rates of selling-price and real market growth generate an average cash flow rate of 6%, while those with the highest growth in both average only 2%.

One caveat: a low rate of cash flow year after year does not carry the same stigma as recurrently low ROI. Even negative cash flow is not necessarily a serious problem. As long as a business establishes the strategic position required to earn an attractive return, it generates cash when the market ultimately slows down. But, while rapid growth continues, the company may still require additional resources (see *Exhibit III*).

If your business is in a slow-growth market, chances are you find it relatively easy to generate enough cash to meet your needs. But whether your market grows, shrinks, or stands still, a large relative share produces cash.

Large-share businesses in slow-growth markets (called "cash cows" in terminology coined by the Boston Consulting Group) have the highest cash flow, while small-share businesses in rapidly growing markets have the lowest. In our data base, the former generates an average positive cash flow of 9%, while the latter generates a negative 3%. *Exhibit IV* shows cash flow contour lines emanating from an empirical model that captures the joint impact of real market growth and relative market share on cash flow.

These contour lines are smooth and systematic because they represent the *average* cash flow rate for a locus of growth/share positions. But we need to remember that growth and share together account for only about one-tenth of the dispersion in cash flow rates illustrated in *Exhibit I*. An individual business may be above or below the cash flow value on its contour line because several key factors other than growth and share also affect its cash flow rate. *Exhibit V* presents some of the key factors that affect cash generation and cash use. They are selected from a cash flow model that explains about two-thirds of the dispersion in cash flow rates among business units.

Exhibit III   Cash Needs Are Determined by Environment and Strategy

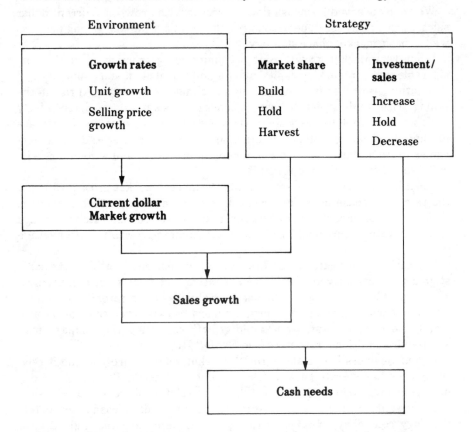

In addition to market growth and share, a change in either market share or investment intensity can affect cash *flow* by influencing cash *use*. As we have seen, businesses often consume cash when attempting to maintain share in a growing market. Gaining or attempting to build share can also be expensive.

In addition to the normal jockeying for market share against domestic competitors, businesses also endure the pressures of world-class competition. Confrontations lead to shakeouts and fewer competitors. By definition, the survivors realize a net gain in share and a drain on their cash supplies.

Whether management decides to build share or capitalize on the business's present position, the decision should be based on the conscious realization of the impact of the decision on cash flow. If a company wishes to strengthen its future market position by increasing marketing expenditures or introducing new products, it will have to withstand higher costs in the short run.

Exhibit IV   Cash-Flow-Rate Contour Lines for the Growth-Share Matrix

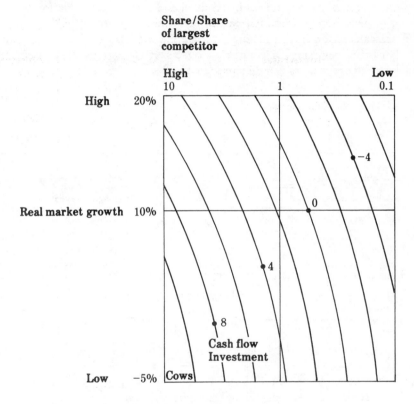

Similarly, managers can generate cash by harvesting the business's present market position, reducing marketing expenditures, and withholding introduction of new products. Those businesses in our data base that aggressively put out a lot of new products and increase marketing expense show a negative cash flow of 4%, compared with a positive 5% for less aggressive companies.

Companies that increase investment intensity usually face a dramatic reduction in their cash flow.

For example, management may decide to boost investment relative to sales and value added in order to push capacity ahead of the market, increase inventories, or liberalize receivables policy. This tactic may be sound, but it will cut into profits and increase the rate of investment buildup, thus reducing cash flow.

More serious may be circumstantial shifts, such as an unplanned rise in inventories or accounts receivable, the need to replace quickly plant and equipment at inflated costs, or a sales slump that reduces capacity utilization.

Although it is difficult to predict when circumstances will force a business to consume cash, world-class competition certainly acts as a catalyst. Foreign competitors with up-to-date technology, plant, and equipment put pressure on executives to reindustrialize, and soaring construction costs hike up the price tag of reindustrialization. Since the stakes are usually high, a miscalculation in the attempt to rebuild a single business unit can cripple an entire company. Without rigorous asset management, the equity built up over 40 or 50 years can dissipate in 2 or 3.

Exhibit V   Summary of Factors Affecting Cash Generation and Use

Cash generation		Cash use	
Factor	Impact	Factor	Impact
Long-run		Real market growth	−
Market share	+	Selling price growth	−
Investment intensity	−	Percentage change in share	−
Short-run		Point change in investment/sales	−
Rate of new product introductions	−		
Marketing expense growth	−		

Aggressive asset management has two principal goals:

- Reduce the amount of cash required to keep pace with growth.
- Reduce excess capital and thereby improve profits.

Managers *can* reduce investment relative to sales without harming (and in fact they may *enhance*) the business's competitive position, but success requires careful strategic planning.

Cash Allocation and Portfolio Balance

A business unit's market environment, competitive position, and strategy all affect its rate of cash flow. In a portfolio context, the multibusiness general manager will want to turn the relationship around to focus on the effects of cash allocation on the strategy of individual business units.

He or she can find the ratio of cash reinvestment by dividing cash used (increase in gross plant and equipment plus increase in net working capital) by cash generated (aftertax income plus depreciation). Businesses with a cash flow rate of zero reinvest as much cash as they generate — i.e., a cash reinvestment ratio of 1.

Businesses in rapidly growing markets usually have cash reinvestment ratios greater than 1, while those in declining or slow-growth markets have ratios much less than 1.

The portfolio of an entire company will balance if the cash used by rapidly growing businesses roughly equals the cash generated by businesses with declining or slow growth. The same balancing effect can be achieved if the company requires each business unit to have a cash reinvestment ratio of 1 (see *Exhibit V*).

This second balancing act may backfire. A business in a rapidly growing market may not keep pace and may be strangled. Its share of the market slips, and it cannot generate cash. If the cash generated by a business supplying a slow-growth market is not invested elsewhere, that business may overinvest in its basic product line. Such a business doesn't compensate for the cash flow needs of the company's high-growth businesses. Instead it becomes investment intensive; profits fall, as does its ability to generate cash.

By understanding that the welfare of the portfolio depends as much on capital allocation among businesses as on project selection within business units, managers can guarantee a more profitable equilibrium between present needs and long-term goals and begin to allocate assets strategically across the portfolio. With the increasing demands of high inflation, lagging productivity, and the need to reindustrialize, only astute companies that understand the link between strategy and cash will survive and prosper.

What is PIMS?

The empirical evidence supporting our findings comes from the data base assembled by the Strategic Planning Institute (SPI), a nonprofit, tax-exempt organization in Cambridge, Massachusetts.

Called PIMS (profit impact of market strategy), the data base includes the business experiences, both good and bad, of more than 1,700 product and service businesses operated by SPI's more than 200 member companies in North America, Europe, and Australia. Each business is defined as a division, product line, or other profit center within its parent company, selling a distinct set of products or services to an identifiable group of customers in competition with a well-defined set of companies.

For each business, the data separate revenues, operating costs, investments, and strategic plans. Before making information in the data base available to member companies, SPI disguises and summarizes the collected data.

SPI collects data not only on traditional balance sheets and income statements but also on each company's market share, investment intensity, productivity, product quality, and unionization.

The data base describes more than 200 such characteristics for each business and, in addition, documents its actions, the market it serves, its competitive environment, and its financial results.

Appendix: Alternative measures of net cash flow rates

So far, we assume that interest expenses are zero. Typically, interest expenses are about 4% of investment (say, the ratio of debt to investment equals .4 and the interest rate equals 10%). Interest expenses are subtracted before taxes. Assuming the tax rate is 50%, we need to adjust our cash flow figures by 2% (.5 of 4%) to reflect interest expenses. Since the average net cash flow rate (preinterest expense) is 4%, the average cash flow rate after interest and taxes (but before dividend payments) would be about 2%.

If dividend payments are about 5% of investment (say, ROI after interest expenses and taxes equals 10%, and half of profits is paid out as dividends), the average net cash flow rate after dividend payments will be about −3%.

The PIMS average for different measures of net cash flow (NCF) rates can be summarized as follows:

The exhibits show NCF rates based on measure (a). To obtain rough NCF rates that reflect interest expenses (b), subtract 2 points from the NCF figures shown in the exhibits.

Simply subtracting an additional five points from after-interest cash flow rates will not yield a good approximation of the true after-dividend NCF rates. The dividend payout ratio usually declines as growth increases, and most of the exhibits show the effects of growth-related factors. In very rapid growth situations, the additional subtraction could be as low as 0 to 2 points. In slow growth or declining environments, it could be as much as 8 to 9 points.

	NCF measure	PIMS average, 1970-1979	Percent of PIMS business with negative NCF rates
a.	NCF rate, assuming interest expense = 0	4%	33%
b.	NCF rate, assuming interest expense = 4% of investment	2%	50%
c.	NCF rate, after interest expenses and assuming dividends = 5% of investment	−3%	67%

26

IDENTIFYING AND RESOLVING PROBLEMS IN CORPORATE LIQUIDITY

JAMES M. JOHNSON, DAVID R. CAMPBELL, AND JAMES L. WITTENBACH*

Over 400 Fortune 1000 treasurers participated in a liquidity management survey conducted by the authors. While it included a wide range of opinion, an overwhelming response pointed to major causes of illiquidity and to actions that would produce a resolution of the problem.

Illiquidity is a problem faced periodically by many large and many more small businesses. Although numerous articles have been written about the subject, little has been known about how executives actually manage liquidity.

To develop a better understanding of liquidity management in practice, the authors reported the results of their survey of Fortune 1000 treasurers in the article, "Problems in Corporate Liquidity" (*Financial Executive,* March 1980). It focused upon the degree of illiquidity experienced by major companies during and since the recession of the mid-1970s, the objectives of liquidity management, and the factors that executives should consider in managing liquidity.

This article is a continuation of the authors' investigation of liquidity management. The purpose is to address the dynamic issues of how executives

* From the *Financial Executive* (May 1982). Reprinted by permission. The authors are academicians at University of Notre Dame.

* EDITOR'S (of the Financial Executive) NOTE: This article is based on a liquidity management survey sent to treasurers of each company in the Fortune 1000, resulting in 418 returned questionnaires (a 41.8-percent response rate). For a complete discussion of the survey methodology, see pages 44-46 in the March 1980 *Financial Executive.*

identify liquidity problems — i.e., what are the important signals, and what measures are taken to *resolve* a condition of illiquidity. The results reported are taken from a survey conducted by the authors.

The Survey

The treasurers were asked to indicate the degree of liquidity problems encountered by their businesses over the past five years and to evaluate the relative importance of numerous liquidity problem awareness and resolution statements. For each of the 17 awareness and 22 resolution items, executives were requested to rate their degree of importance on a scale ranging from one (very unimportant) to five (very important). Executives also were given the option of designating a question as not applicable.

In response to the question of liquidity problem severity, 46 respondents indicated their companies suffered substantial problems; 89 experienced moderate problems, 68 reported few problems; and 215 indicated no liquidity problems were encountered. Those companies experiencing at least a few problems comprise this study (a total of 203 businesses).

The results were examined to determine whether companies which experienced different degrees of liquidity problems responded differently. With only one exception (which will be noted), companies that experienced from substantial to few problems did not respond in a meaningfully different fashion. Accordingly, average responses ranged across the spectrum of degree of liquidity problems experienced.

Identifying the Problems

Executives were requested to rate the importance of 17 factors which could trigger their awareness of a liquidity problem. For the convenience of discussion, the factors have been (somewhat arbitrarily) grouped into three categories: sales and expense control, asset management, and liability management. The results are shown in **Table 1.**

In the area of sales and expense control, it is interesting to note that sales control ("sales orders declining") and expense control ("increased difficulty in controlling expenses") are virtually tied at moderate importance in triggering an awareness of illiquidity. The number one factor of importance in this group is an inability to pass increasing costs along to customers. Two areas, below breakeven sales and difficulty in procuring materials, were rated as least important in flagging liquidity problems. When viewed collectively, the responses suggest that an awareness of illiquidity was brought about by a condition truly described as "stagflation." Although a decline in revenue was evident, the liquidity crunch was attributable to unit costs increasing more rapidly than unit prices — a condition brought about by a slump in demand. By its low ranking, executives apparently felt below break-even volume was a trivial indication of illiquidity, an explanation more symptomatic than problematic.

Table 1 Identifying Liquidity Problems

Factor and group	Average rankings (Unimportant)																							(Important)
	2.0	2.1	2.2	2.3	2.4	2.5	2.6	2.7	2.8	2.9	3.0	3.1	3.2	3.3	3.4	3.5	3.6	3.7	3.8	3.9	4.0	4.1	4.2	4.3
Sales and Expense Control																								
Sales orders were declining												●												
Sales were below break-even volume							●																	
Increased difficulty in controlling expenses										●														
Increasing costs could not be passed on																	●							
Raw materials more difficult to acquire							●																	
Asset Management																								
Daily cash inflows were declining																●								
Cash balances were lower than normal													●											
Accounts receivable increased																	●							
Receivables turnover declined																●								
Inventory turnover declined																		●						
Inventories built up																								●
Working capital declined																●								
Liability Management																								
Debt ratio increased																		●						
Firm was dependent upon one primary source of financing and more funds from such sources became limited					●																			
Firm was funding capital projects with short-term debt which could not be completely converted into long-term funds						●																		
All or most assets were pledged to secure existing debt			●																					
Accounts payable increased						●																		

Executives rated a buildup in inventories as by far the most important signal of liquidity problems in this group. The second most important signal was a decline in inventory turns. These two factors, of course, are not addressing the same issue. One may envision a company which is reducing its inventory levels but still experiences a reduction in turns because sales are dropping at a more rapid rate than the inventory reduction. The fact that executives *simultaneously* gave high ratings to *both* increasing inventory levels and decreasing turns suggests that the decline in product demand was difficult to predict. Had the slump been predictable, one would expect a winding down of production, a concomitant *decrease* in inventory levels, and thus a low rating to have been given to the "inventories built up" factor.

A reduction in daily cash inflows, receivable turns, and working capital levels, along with an increasing level of receivables, were all rated as important signals of liquidity problems. Below-normal cash balances was the factor deemed least important of all asset signals, which indicates that executives attach more importance to the *flow* of cash ("daily cash inflows were declining") than to the *stock* of cash ("cash balances were lower than normal".)

Liability Management

An increasing debt ratio was clearly the most important signal in the opinion of responding executives; all other signals in this group were rated as relatively unimportant. It is reasonable to conclude that an increasing debt ratio is considered a powerful illiquidity signal because the increase *itself* makes it increasingly difficult to tap debt markets for additional financing that may be required.

Resolving the Problems

For the convenience of discussion, measures taken to remedy liquidity problems are grouped into three categories. The results are shown in **Table 2.**

Sales and Expense Control

To control expenses, executives ascribed the greatest importance to greater cost control of overhead. Two moderately important tactics implemented to accomplish this were to examine alternative supply sources and to begin personnel layoffs. It is significant to note that four of the five tactics given low importance ratings could be considered to have substantial detrimental repercussions over time. Delaying new product offerings could compromise a company's image and market position well beyond the delay period, and cutting dividends could affect its cost of financing. A new hire freeze or delay in compensation adjustments might damage morale, adversely affect turnover, or have other undesirable human capital consequences.

Liquidity crunches are predominantly viewed as short-term phenomena, and thus companies tend to adjust to them with flexible or reversible tactics (e.g., layoffs and cost reductions). They are reluctant to tamper with what might be called pipeline processes (flow of new personnel, dividend payments, new product introductions) — activities whose present level, stature, or position take considerable time to achieve and therefore must continue to

Table 2 Resolving Liquidity Problems

Factor and group	(Unimportant) Average rankings (Important)																							
	2.0	2.1	2.2	2.3	2.4	2.5	2.6	2.7	2.8	2.9	3.0	3.1	3.2	3.3	3.4	3.5	3.6	3.7	3.8	3.9	4.0	4.1	4.2	4.3
Sales and Expense Control																								
New product offerings were delayed		●																						
Greater cost control of overhead																		●						
Purchasing agents examined alternative sources of supply										●														
Dividends were reduced	●																							
New hirings were frozen		●																						
Lengthened time for raises				●																				
Personnel were laid off										●														
Operating managers were compensated largely on ability to generate cash inflows			●																					
Asset Management																								
Receivables were trimmed																		●						
Used more rigorous receivables collection policy																		●						
Reduced investment in inventories																								●
Reduced capital expenditures															●									
Plants were closed							●																	
Assets not meeting long-term profit objectives were disposed of												●												
Liquidated certain assets to meet operating/debt service needs							●																	
Educated nonfinancial personnel on significance of asset management																●								
Liability Management																								
Payables were extended										●														
Increased short-term borrowings																		●						
Revolving bank credit arrangements were established													●											
Revolving bank lines were increased										●														
Greater emphasis placed on leasing assets		●																						
Increased long-term borrowings																		●						

be "fed" or suffer potential repercussions far beyond the period during which the action itself was taken.

The most important asset management action taken by executives to resolve illiquidity was to reduce investment in inventories. In fact, this was the most important action taken among all of the three groups. It is appropriate that inventory reductions be given this status because it will be recalled that the number one signal of illiquidity was a buildup of inventory. Also consistent with illiquidity remedies are the high ratings given to trimming accounts receivable and putting in use a more rigorous receivables collection policy.

Moderate importance was attached to educating non-financial personnel on the significance of asset management and on the reduction of capital expenditures. The educational thrust was undoubtedly an important tactic necessary to implement receivables, inventory, and capital expenditure actions taken. Reducing capital outlays represents the most significant pipeline action taken by the companies surveyed to bring liquidity under control.

The three actions considered to be least important in resolving illiquidity should also be considered the most drastic measures proposed: plant closings and two kinds of asset liquidations. The only factor in the study where companies facing different degrees of liquidity problems gave a significantly different response was the "liquidated certain assets to meet operating/debt service needs." Here, companies reporting few liquidity problems gave an average response of 1.8 (an unimportant liquidity remedy). However, companies that faced substantial problems rated it 3.3 in importance. Thus, companies facing the worst liquidity problems were forced to take the most drastic remedial action.

Liability Management

Executives indicated that increasing the level of borrowings, from both short- and long-term sources, was the most important liability management action taken to resolve liquidity problems. This may appear somewhat curious because executives indicated that debt ratio increases were considered an important signal of illiquidity. However, recognizing that a condition of illiquidity can occur fairly rapidly, executives may quite justifiably interpret a rising debt position simultaneously as a sign of, and a cure for, a liquidity shortage. It may be viewed as a sign because it compromises further borrowing and (thus) ideally would not be done. It is also a cure, as in the short run it must be done.

Establishing or increasing bank lines were only of modest importance in resolving liquidity problems, as was extending accounts payable. A shift to leasing was considered by far to be the least significant debt financing action employed. Executives were much more prone to use more financing from traditional sources than to seek out new forms.

Conclusion

In the opinion of surveyed executives, the most important signs of illiquidity were asset-based in general, and an inventory buildup was considered to be the single most important monitoring device. A reduction in inventory turns and an increasing debt ratio were rated second and third, respectively, in importance as signs of illiquidity.

To resolve liquidity problems, reducing inventories was the most important action taken. This, of course, is consistent with inventory buildups being considered the most important sign of a liquidity crunch. Greater cost control of overhead, collecting and trimming receivables, and increasing borrowings were rated next in importance as corrective actions.

In descending order of importance, executives rated the following as being the most important factors in liquidity problem identification and resolution:

- Working capital (inventory most important).
- Overhead costs.
- Debt financing.

27

STRATEGIC
CAPITAL
BUDGETING

HAROLD BIERMAN, JR.*

Business and academic literature has offered well defined and reasonably exact decision rules for allocating capital among investment projects as long as certainty is assumed. If there are accept or reject decisions involving independent investments, both the net present value and the rate of return procedures lead to consistent and theoretically correct decisions. Mutually exclusive investments add some complexities in that internal rate of return has to be used carefully, but the pitfalls in its use are well known and there are ways of avoiding them.

Even the so-called capital rationing problem (there are more investment opportunities than there is cash available) has been solved in the theoretical literature which offers a variety of programming solutions, and if these calculations have too demanding informational requirements or are too complex, there is the index of present value method to offer an approximate workable solution.

But the frontier of capital budgeting, uncertainty, has tended to resist efforts to find easily computed feasible solutions to accept or reject decisions. Each of the suggested solutions (such as simulation, risk adjusted discount rates, or the capital asset pricing model) have real difficulties that have precluded their use with any degree of reliability.

The existence of uncertainty gives rise to strategic capital budgeting.

* From *Financial Executive* (April 1979). Reprinted by permission. The author is an academician.

The Strategy Element of Capital Budgeting

If there were no uncertainty there would be no strategic capital budgeting. A firm would merely accept all independent investments yielding more than the borrowing rate. Uncertainty creates the need to allocate resources to different divisions when the total allocated is less than that requested by a division.

One way of solving the strategic capital budgeting problems that firms face is to eliminate the word "strategic" and declare the strategic problem to be one of the several capital budgeting problems that the business community is familiar with and has dealt with before. The fact, however, that there are several different components of the firm operating in several different industries and geographical areas adds to the complexity of the decision process.

Consider the real world decision maker who understands the theoretical capital budgeting literature, but still has a problem of allocating limited capital among several different countries. Before the advent of the multi-national firm that deals in many different industries, the capital market solved this problem resource allocation. The market test was real to the executive who wanted to expand beyond the capabilities of internally generated funds. If the capital market decided the past performance did not warrant more capital, the decision was firm and appeal was difficult.

It is true that now a conglomerate may raise capital in the market, but that is not going to solve the problem of how much each division should be allocated to invest. That allocation is a managerial decision.

Allocating Resources by Decision

One easy answer to the allocation problem is to say that it does not make any difference which division submits the project, but rather the relevant consideration is desirability of the project itself. A division making zero income may have the best project in the firm, while the divisions making the most profit may not have any additional desirable projects. This certainly can happen and in a world of complete certainty and unbiased investments project analyses, the question of which division originated the project could be ignored, and the profitability of the project itself could be the sole consideration.

But consider the real world where there is gaming by divisional managers, there is uncertainty, and where there is a past history of performance. Assume the division making zero profits has had a long history of submitting projects that are expected to be highly profitable, but unfortunately some unforeseen event always happens that makes the forecasts bad predictors of the future. The actual results tend to be less than that forecasted. Thus, the division earns less than the required return even though a sensible capital budgeting procedure has been in existence.

Bad performance tends to indicate that excessive optimism was contained in the capital budgeting requests in the past, or at least there was poor ability to forecast the future. In like manner, the highly profitable division has tended to more than meet the capital budgeting forecasts of the past. In fact there might well be a situation where the highly profitable division is not submitting enough capital budgeting requests (only the super projects are being submitted; marginally desirable projects are not being submitted).

Now the choice is clearly defined. Do the managers allocating capital look at the present capital budgeting requests and ignore the past history of the division? Obviously, systematic biases in the capital budgeting analyses of the past should not be ignored, but rather they should affect the way in which we evaluate the present proposals.

In allocating capital, should management attempt to evaluate the reasons why past profitable projects (at the time of submission) have turned out to be nonprofitable? The easy answer is, yes. The problem is that this path leads to subjective evaluations based on evidence that is going to be difficult to accumulate.   Managers who are confident of their abilities to identify causal factors and are pleased to have the opportunity of explaining unpleasant and difficult decisions to peers and subordinates would use this procedure. An attempt would be made to identify systematic biases being introduced into the investment analyses and to adjust for these biases. It is consistent with making capital budgeting decisions using the best techniques, with the inputs being improved by the elimination of the observed biases.

The one drawback of the procedure is that it substitutes judgement for historical evidence. Assume a situation where the historical performance of the division has been a disaster, but now reasons for this unfortunate circumstance are being found and it is being said that new investments will be profitable even though past investments were not. Should the hard objective evidence be used or the subjective evaluation of what is going to happen in the future?

Consider the following information contained in the annual report of a Fortune 500 firm. Division A contributed $98,000,000 of operating profit during the year and spent $157,000,000 on capital expenditures. Division B contributed $32,000,000 of operating profit and spend $3,600,000 on capital expenditures. The operating results were not unique to that year, but reflected typical operations. How would you feel if you were the General Manager in charge of Division B?

Obviously, the firm is using subjective evaluations in allocating resources between the two divisions.

An alternative is to substitute the objective evidence for the explanations, and to use the cold hard numbers representing performance instead of the explanations of why the goals were not met. This alternative is obviously less "intelligent" in that it ignores evidence (all the explanations of why the past goals were not met). On the other hand it can be well-defined, predictable, and fair. A manager would know how to get new investment funds. Good performance would lead to additional funds being allocated to the division. Bad performance would lead to a situation where it was extremely difficult to obtain additional resources.

One solution would be to allocate funds based on operating income. Thus Division A would receive

$$\frac{98}{98 + 32} = \frac{98}{130} = .75$$

of the investable funds and Division B would receive .25. An improvement in the allocation results when the operating incomes are charged with a cost for the capital utilized. Table 1 shows the result of applying a capital cost of .05 to the capital utilized.

Table 1   Dollar Amounts in Millions:

	Assets	Capital Cost (.05)	Income After Interest
Division A	2,460	123	−25
Division B	208	10	22

This table clearly indicates that Division A should have to defend its request for capital funds. Given its past performance, it is in an inferior position to Division B in the competition for funds.

Obviously, past performance should not be used as the sole basis of resource allocation, but rather as an important input into the allocation process.

A high level of performance would be a desirable condition for getting extra funds but it would not be a sufficient condition. In addition to performance, the division must have projects that merit investment.

Also, not all the funds would be allocated based on performance. An automatic allocation scheme could lead to a situation where projects meriting attention were ignored because they were housed in a poorly performing division. Thus there would be a two tiered system of strategic allocation.

Some of the funds would be allocated based on performance, but there would also be a review to insure that projects that were desirable from a corporate point of view were also undertaken.

Conclusion

Recognizing the presence of intentional and unintentional biases in preparing capital budgeting requests, these requests cannot be accepted automatically without review for purpose of budget allocation in multidivisional firms. One easy way of adjusting for bias and introducing an objective bias of allocation is to use past performance of the divisions as the basis for the allocation of at least some of the investment funds. Past performance gives some indication of how reliable past capital budgeting requests have been. Past performance, properly measured, is a reasonable indication of the bias present in the capital budgeting requests in the past. The use of past performance as the basis of allocation of at least part of the capital budget is apt to be perceived by managers as being more fair than an allocation entirely based on subjective evaluation of the future.

28

STRUCTURING CAPITAL SPENDING HURDLE RATES

ALLEN H. SEED, III*

The benchmark used by corporate officers to determine the various projects to be undertaken in the coming year is generally the "hurdle rate," or rate of return. Structuring these rates to reflect capital cost, risk, and strategic impact can influence a company's growth and its decisions for the future.

At least once a year, the senior executives and directors of many corporations address the problem of establishing a capital spending budget and selecting the projects that will be undertaken during the following year. The usual practice is for proposals to be submitted up through the organization; top management selects the most promising proposals, and the directors approve the selection. Some projects are selected for economic reasons; other selections are largely based on nonfinancial considerations such as environmental compliance.

Regardless of the common threads of this process, considerable controversy surrounds the appropriate methodology to be applied to the selection.

One of the focal points of this controversy is the determination of capital spending hurdle rates**: Should they even be used, and if so, how should they be calculated?

---

* From the *Financial Executive* (February 1982). Reprinted by permission. The author is a Senior Consultant with Arthur D. Little, Inc.
** A hurdle rate is the rate of return that must be generated by a capital spending project for it to be a desirable economic undertaking. In theory, this is the point where marginal revenue is just equal to marginal cost.

This article explores alternative practices and points of view and suggests a new broad approach that provides a methodology for quantifying the factors that should be considered and one that can be applied in a practical manner to most business situations. The factors are as follows:

1) The cost of capital.
2) The inherent risk of the project.
3) The relative importance of spending for different strategic and tactical purposes.

By using a different debt to equity mix and cost of equity assumptions, it is possible to simulate the cost of capital that would apply in varying financial risk and strategic business circumstances.

The Value of Hurdle Rates

A survey of 136 companies by The Conference Board[1] showed that 62 companies (46 percent) do not specify minimum cutoff rates for their capital investments. These proportions correspond with my own experience. Many companies do not establish capital spending hurdle rates for three reasons:

1) Management wishes to reserve the prerogative of determining which proposals should be accepted and which should be turned down or deferred. They do not wish to discourage the submission of any capital proposals. However, all proposals should be ranked in the order of their desirability.

2) It is difficult to determine what "cutoff" or "hurdle rate" should apply, as risks, capital costs, and strategic considerations vary among projects. Moreover, some projects should be considered on a noneconomic basis.

3) If a hurdle rate is made known to operating management, the figures used in proposals may be "massaged" to pass this rate rather than present the project on an objective basis.

There is merit to the point of view of not using hurdle rates. Good proposals should indeed not be discouraged, particularly those that cannot be supported on strictly a financial basis. It *is* difficult to determine the cost of capital and the impact of risks. Simplistic, arbitrary rates are not a solution either, and operating management *will* tend to play games with capital proposals if hurdle rates are known.

However, not establishing cutoff rates impose some important disadvantages. Operating managers are not informed about the basic economics of the business. The absence of information encourages the submission of proposals that do not support these economics. It is akin to asking managers to prepare budgets without budget guidelines or objectives, or marketing managers to set selling prices without cost information. Each individual is left to his own devices without any common focus or sense of direction. Unofficial yardsticks as to "what will fly" often emerge from this vacuum. Such yardsticks are communicated through the grapevine and are as apt to provide misinformation as they are to constructively assist with the capital spending proposal and selection process.

Single Hurdle Rates

Some companies that use capital spending cutoff rates use single hurdle rates. The underlying concept is that returns from any prospective capital expenditures should exceed this cost if the enterprise is to enhance its overall return to its stockholders. Half of the 74 companies included in The Conference Board study follow this practice; however, this proportion may be on the low side for business in general. The companies that participated in The Conference Board study had a median sales volume of $484 million. Thus, they tend to represent the practices of some of the larger members of the corporate community. An informal study by Samuel L. Hayes, III of Harvard University[2] suggests most companies use a single rate (if any), and the derivation of this rate often does not take inflation into account. Moreover, the process of capital allocation appears to be highly politicized.

Commonly, the hurdle rate is a round number that ends in a zero or five. Some years ago 10-percent returns after taxes were considered to be a satisfactory cutoff for capital expenditures, but more recently 15- and 20-percent cutoff returns seem to be more typical. This rate may be arbitrary, or it may be based on a calculation of the company's cost of capital.

One definition of the cost of capital is that it consists of the risk-free rate of return plus an allowance for risk, inflation, and expenses of marketing and servicing the capital. While this definition seems straightforward on face value, it is fraught with practical difficulties in determining just what this cost is in most enterprises. Consider the elusiveness of the components of this formula: What is the risk-free rate of return in a free capital market? Should the yield of U.S. government securities approximate this value, and if so, why do these yields fluctuate so widely in relation to real or prospective inflation rates? What premium should be assigned for risk? As swings in the stock market have indicated, this factor is also subject to the vagaries of the market and the supply of capital that is available for investment. And what about inflation?[3]

• A practical approach to determining the "cost of capital" (a concept widely used in utility rate making) is to add up the weighted cost of each of its components, debt deferred charges, and preferred and common stock. While each component has an apparent measurable cost, as with the case of the theoretical approach, a problem immediately arises as to what this cost really is. Should debt be valued at its historical cost or a replacement basis? (We suggest the latter.) How should deferred charges be treated; is this free capital and how should it be considered? What is the cost of equity capital; should it be based on present markets, and if so, over what time frame? Should equity costs be based on the market for the company's existing stock or the cost of new stock? And what mix of capital components should be assumed — the present mix or a mix adjusted for the financial norms of the industry concerned? I believe that there are workable solutions to this dilemma, but the fact still remains that one must choose between imperfect alternatives.

There are two reasons for using a single hurdle-rate approach:

• It is relatively easy to understand and apply throughout the organization. More complex multiple hurdle rates contain more variables and hence require heightened understanding and additional analysis.
• All calculations of prospective cash flows from capital spending projects are often rough approximations at best. Why attempt to refine the cost of capital calculation when a rough yardstick will serve in this imperfect environment?

These reasons for a single hurdle rate have appeal; however, they do not reflect the differences in risk that are inherent in certain types of expenditures, nor do they reflect differences in the strategic impact of the cost of capital that is inherent in different types of businesses. These latter differences can lead to significant shifts in capital spending with consequent important strategic and financial consequences to the enterprise.

The Need for Multiple Hurdle Rates

The use of multiple hurdle rates is not new. Several companies use different rates for different types of projects. These rates typically reflect differences in project size, capital cost including business and financial risk, and priorities. What we believe is new, however, is an effective, organized method for linking hurdle rates to the current cost of capital, to risk, and to strategic impact. This approach is not intended as a substitute for sensitivity and risk analysis for major projects. It is a tool that can be readily applied in any organization to help screen proposals and sharpen capital spending decision-making.

Gordon Donaldson prescribes strategic hurdle rates for capital investments related not to the cost of capital but to the actual investment alternatives available to the business.[4] He makes a distinction between tactical and strategic hurdle rates. "The hurdle rate for tactical decisions would be the ROI* standard reflecting the current potential of the profit center based on demonstrated performance. Strategic hurdle rates for any division would be the best ROI performance among other divisions; and for all divisions, the most attractive ROI on new products or markets."

One way of dealing with the issues of relating capital spending with stra-

---

* return on investment

tegic objectives is to ration the amount of capital available to each division or business unit.

Harold Bierman, Jr.[5] suggests that strategic objectives are obtained if past performance is used as a basis for allocation of at least part of the funds available for capital spending. The track record of management is often an important indicator of capital expenditure desirability. All other things being equal, betting on a winning jockey is more productive than betting on losers. The man who has delivered before is most likely to deliver again. However, both of these approaches tend to minimize the importance of cost of capital and the individual contributions that can be derived from specific capital expenditures. Most companies have a wide range of capital spending opportunities available to them, and the challenge is to select amongst these competing opportunities.

Several years ago I was associated with a large packaging manufacturing business that was losing money. One of the actions that led to the subsequent dramatic improvement in profitability of this business was the construction of efficient new plants and the acquisition of high-speed automated equipment. Even in a mature business surrounded with red ink, there are usually a number of opportunities to make judicious capital expenditures where the potential returns exceed the cost of capital. The point is that the cost of capital should be factored into the hurdle rate, and that this rate should be modified to reflect differences in risk and strategic priorities.

As previously implied, there are three dimensions to the multiple hurdle rate structure that I propose:

Base Cost of Capital
Anticipated replacement cost in year of expenditure for normal capital structure for type of company concerned. This element should reflect the current cost of debt and equity based on the existing capital market and anticipated inflation rates. Deferred charges and other "free" capital should be excluded from this calculation.

Risk Adjustment
Normal, above normal, and below normal based on type of proposed expenditure. This element adjusts the pro forma mix of debt and equity to reflect the realities of the financial risk involved.

Strategic Impact
High, medium, and low. This factor reflects the position of the business in its life cycle and can be equated to the relative growth rates (business risk) of the industry served. A "high impact" means that a business is in the ascending part of its life cycle with above-average growth. "Medium impact" means that the industry is near the top of its life cycle with average growth. "Low impact" implies industry maturity with limited expansion potential.

The concept here is that the cost of equity would reflect a different price-earnings (P/E) multiple depending on how the business evolves as a result of the expenditure. For example, a capital expenditure that is designed to help migrate from a low P/E ratio (no growth) business to a higher P/E ratio (growth) business would have a lower cost of equity assigned to it than a capital expenditure that was designed to maintain the status quo. The underlying rationale here is that given a normal financial structure, investors will pay a higher premium for equity in a growth industry, and thus a company's cost of capital stock will decrease as the balance of its portfolio of businesses shifts from a mature to a growth state.

Determining the cost of capital for different strategic purposes does not preclude the need to allocate capital for strategic investments or to evaluate strategic investments in their totality. Most companies find that capital resources are limited, and thus available capital must be allocated to support different strategies as part of the strategic planning process. These requirements, and their associated returns, should be calculated for the strategy as a whole. Spending for fixed assets is ordinarily only part of this investment. However, when the prospective returns for the strategy are quantified, they can be compared with different costs of capital depending on the nature of the strategy.

The first step in quantification is to assign values to the normal (base) case for the industry concerned; the second step is to adjust these values for the variation of each dimension. These amounts may be obtained by analyzing debt-equity ratios, price-earnings ratios, and new issue costs of various types of comparable businesses. Published market values may be adjusted to reflect flotation costs to determine new issue costs. Reasonableness is more important than precision in this instance because the resulting hurdle rates are used as a basis for rough sorting rather than for detailed analysis.

For example, let us assume that the corporation involved is a large diversified manufacturing company. Regardless of its existing financial structure, such a company might be expected to maintain a 1:2 debt/equity ratio. New debt would cost about 12 percent before taxes and 6.5 percent after taxes based on a 46-percent effective tax rate. New equity would cost about 12.5 percent after taxes based on a 8 × P/E ratio. On a weighted basis this works out to a composite after-tax replacement cost of capital of 10.5 percent (0.67 × 12.5 + 33 × 6.5). This becomes the base case (normal risk, medium strategic priority) cost of capital for this corporation.

Values for the risk dimension are determined by modifying the mix of debt and equity to reflect the normal financial structure required to support the type of expenditure to be considered. Lower risk businesses with predictable cash flows (such as real estate and finance companies) typically support debt/equity ratios of 4:1, whereas high-risk businesses are normally entirely financed by equity. Thus, the cost of capital for below-normal risk projects (for medium strategic priority businesses) might be calculated to be 7.7 percent (0.20 × 12.5 + 0.80 × 6.5). The inherent cost of capital for high-risk projects would be 12.5 percent because this type of project should be entirely financed by equity.

Table 1

Strategic Impact	High (12× P/E)	Assumptions:
		  80% debt @ 6.5%
		  20% equity @ 8.3%
		Cost of Capital:
		  6.9%
			Assumptions:
			  33% debt @ 6.5%
			  67% equity @ 8.3%
			Cost of Capital:
			  7.7%
				Assumptions:
				  No debt
				  100% equity @ 8.3%
				Cost of Capital:
				  8.3%

	Medium (8× P/E)	Assumptions:
		  80% debt @ 6.5%
		  20% equity @ 12.5%
		Cost of Capital:
		  7.7%
			Base Case Assumptions:
			  33% debt @ 6.5%
			  67% equity @ 12.5%
			Cost of Capital:
			  10.5%
				Assumptions:
				  No debt
				  100% equity @ 12.5%
				Cost of Capital:
				  12.5%

	Low (5× P/E)	Assumptions:
		  80% debt @ 6.5%
		  20% equity @ 20%
		Cost of Capital:
		  9.2%
			Assumptions:
			  33% debt @ 6.5%
			  67% equity @ 20%
			Cost of Capital:
			  15.5%
				Assumptions:
				  No debt
				  100% equity @ 20%
				Cost of Capital:
				  20%

		Below normal (80/20)	Normal (33/67)	Above normal (0/100)

Degree of Risk
(Debt/Equity)

Values for the strategic impact dimension are determined by adjusting the cost of equity to reflect the P/E ratios of independent companies that are engaged in the industry associated with the strategic purpose of the expenditure. In this instance, it might be reasonable to assume that the corporation's P/E ratio (in today's market terms) will increase from 8 to 12 times if the corporation's strategic objectives are obtained. Conversely, capital expenditures required for low-priority strategies (e.g., to maintain mature businesses) would cause the P/E ratio to slip from 8 to 5 times. In the first instance, the cost of equity would be 8.3 percent after taxes and, in the second instance, the cost of equity would be 20 percent after taxes.

All of these elements can be arrayed in a manageable matrix as illustrated in **Table 1.**

It should be emphasized that the foregoing values are shown for illustrative purposes only. Each organization will have its own notions of relevant debt/equity mixes and the cost of each element of capital. These costs will also change over time to reflect changes in the rate of inflation and the money market. Some organizations may also wish to add a contingency factor to their calculations to offset optimistic projects, allow for the unknown, and partially compensate for limited capital availability.

The matrix of hurdle rates that are developed should be used by all business units of a corporation for all projects that are to be evaluated on an economic basis. Each business unit should be classified by strategic impact, as most of the internal proposals of any business unit will ordinarily fall into the same category. This means that different business units will use different hurdle rates. The effect of this approach is to favor the growth business units (with a lower incremental cost of capital) and penalize the business units in mature industries (with a high incremental cost of capital). However, capital expenditure proposals from business units in mature industries that lead to strategic growth opportunities would be subject to lower (high strategic impact) hurdle rates even though the host business has a low strategic impact. The governing concept is that it is the purpose of the expenditure — not the proposer of the expenditure — that determines the appropriate strategic impact to be selected.

Rates of return using the discounted cash flow or ROI methods may be compared with the appropriate cost of capital contained in the hurdle rate matrix to help ascertain the value of the proposed expenditure. Of these two methods for calculating actual returns, the discounted cash flow method is preferred because it reflects the time value of money. The discounted cash flow rate of return is the discount rate that equates the present value of cash receipts from a capital investment with the present value of the cash outlays made to support the investment. Cash receipts are ordinarily assumed to be the year-by-year incremental profit contribution after income taxes, but before depreciation (cash flow) from the project. Cash outlays should be incremental requirements for working capital as well as capital expenditures.

Hurdle rates can also be used as the discount rate in performing net present value or benefit-cost ratio calculations. The difference between the present value of the outlays and receipts of a proposed investment based on the discount that is applied is the present value of the project. A benefit-cost ratio is determined by dividing the net present value of receipts by the present value of outlays.

Conclusion

Meaningful multiple hurdle rates should be used as benchmarks to help with management decision-making. Executives of many large and medium-size businesses typically consider hundreds of capital proposals each year. These proposals often involve many millions of increasingly scarce and expensive capital and have an impact on the strategic course of the business. Structuring capital spending hurdle rates on a matrix to reflect cost of capital, degree of risk, and strategic impact can help make this process more manageable and can improve the effectiveness of the resultant decisions.

References

1. Patrick J. Davey, *"Capital Investments: Appraisals and Limits,"* The Conference Board, Inc., 1974, P. 6.
2. Samuel L. Hayes, III, "Capital Commitments and the High Cost of Money," *Harvard Business Review,* May-June 1977.
3. Allen H. Seed, III, *Inflation: Its Impact on Financial Reporting and Decision Making,* Financial Executives Research Foundation, 1978.
4. Gordon Donaldson, "Strategic Hurdle Rates for Capital Investment," *Harvard Business Review,* March-April 1972.
5. Harold Bierman, Jr., "Strategic Capital Budgeting," *Financial Executive,* April 1979.

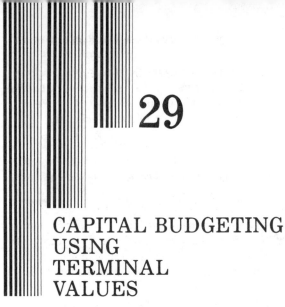

29

CAPITAL BUDGETING USING TERMINAL VALUES
MICHAEL F. VAN BREDA*

Calculating the terminal value of a project makes the comparison of projects much simpler than other methods in current vogue.

Current wisdom has it that to evaluate a capital project one should calculate its net present value. If this is positive, one is advised to invest in the project in the absence of restraining qualitative factors. As an alternative, one is sometimes encouraged to calculate the internal rate of return. If this exceeds the hurdle rate, the project is acceptable — again, all other things being equal. In contrast to the above two methods, one is invariably warned against using the payback method, since this does not take the time value of money into account.

There is a fourth alternative that is used, but rarely stressed in textbooks. Instead of calculating the value of a project as of its start, why not calculate the value of a project as of its close, i.e., its terminal value as opposed to its present value? The advantages of this approach are:

1. It highlights the hidden assumptions in present value and internal rate calculations.
2. It makes the comparison of projects much simpler than any of the methods in current vogue.
3. It integrates very neatly the time value of money concept with the payback method.

---

* From *Management Accounting* (July 1981). Copyright © 1981 by the National Association of Accountants. All rights reserved. The author is an academician.

It should be stressed, however, that this approach introduces no new theoretical concepts.

Present Value Calculations

Consider a simple accept-reject capital budgeting decision involving a project which extends over four years yielding $10,000 at the end of each year. Assume further that the required initial outlay is $23,616 and that the cost of capital is 10%. A simple calculation yields a present value amount of $31,699, while $8,083 is the net present value or NPV. Because the NPV is positive, one is usually advised to accept the project.

As an alternative to calculating the NPV, one can calculate the internal rate of return or IRR. This is the rate which discounts the benefits to the initial cost of the project, i.e., that discount rate which would give a zero NPV. In this case: 25%. If we assume that 10% is the required rate of return or hurdle rate of the company, then we should accept this proposal.

It should be obvious that, if the hurdle rate is less than the IRR, a positive NPV must result when the hurdle rate is used to calculate the NPV. The IRR is merely that rate of interest that drives the NPV to zero. In a sense, it is a special case of the more general NPV calculation. If, for instance, a hurdle rate greater than the IRR were used to discount the benefits, a negative NPV would result.

Because of this relationship between the IRR, the hurdle rate, and the NPV, the methods give identical results for accept-reject decisions, i.e., one would accept the same projects on either criterion. A positive NPV implies an IRR greater than the hurdle rate and vice versa.

Terminal Amount Calculations

There is, however, no reason why one should compare the costs and benefits of a project as of the *outset* of that project. One could do the comparison equally well as of the *end* of the project's life. Table 1 should make the mechanics involved clear. The amount of $46,410 is the *gross terminal amount*[1] or GTA of the project. It is the amount that the benefits would have *accumulated* to if reinvested at the hurdle rate of 10%. To arrive at the GTA, one simply calculates the interest that could be earned over the year from the reinvestment of the accumulated benefits and interest to date.

Against the GTA of $46,410 must be set the *opportunity cost* of the initial investment of $23,616. This is the amount which the initial investment would have earned if invested at the hurdle rate. In this case, it is $10,960 as Table 2 illustrates. Subtracting the initial investment and the opportunity cost of

---

[1] The use of the word "amount" is deliberate. Value has connotations of a measure of utility, which are not implied here at all. It would also be preferable, for the same reason to speak of present amounts, but the term present value is so rooted in the language now that a change in terminology is unlikely. One hopes that the less familiar terminal value will be replaced by the more correct terminal amount.

the investment from the GTA yields the *net terminal amount* or NTA. In this case, NTA is $46,410 less $34,576 or $11,834. In order to decide whether to accept or reject the project one uses the following rule:

Rule I: In accept-reject decisions, if the net terminal amount or NTA is positive, accept the project. Otherwise reject.

In order to justify this rule, note first that, if the NPV of $8,083 is invested at the cost of capital, it yields the NTA of $11,834. A moment's reflection should indicate that this must be so. The NPV is the surplus of benefits over costs calculated as of the start of the project. Investment of the initial surplus must yield the terminal surplus. Thus, if the NPV is positive, the NTA must be positive. Choices based on positive NTA's will be identical, therefore, to choices based on positive NPV's.

Table 1

Year	Balance start of year	10% interest	Receipt end of year	Balance end of year
1	0	0	10,000	10,000
2	10,000	1,000	10,000	21,000
3	21,000	2,100	10,000	33,100
4	33,100	3,310	10,000	46,410
		6,410	40,000	

Table 2

Year	Balance start of year	10% interest	Balance end of year
1	23,616	2,362	25,978
2	25,978	2,598	28,576
3	28,576	2,858	31,434
4	31,434	3,142	34,576
		Less	23,616
(34,576 − 23,626 = 10,960)			10,960

What should also be apparent is that the IRR is that rate of interest that generates an NTA of zero. This conclusion follows from the fact that the NPV invested over the life of the project yields the NTA. If the NPV is zero as a result of discounting at the IRR, then so must be the NTA. See Tables 3 and 4.

The amount of $57,656 is the accumulated value of the benefits from the project when reinvested at 25%, i.e., the cash the business could expect to have in hand at the end of the project's life if the benefits were reinvested at 25%. It is also the amount to which the initial investment of $23,616 would accumulate if invested at 25% compounded annually.

The figure of $57,656 may be interpreted as the total of the project which when subtracted from the GTA yields the NTA of zero. From this we have a second rule for investment:

Rule II: In accept-reject decisions, if the rate of interest that yields a net terminal amount of zero exceeds the hurdle rate or the minimum acceptable rate, accept the project. Otherwise, reject.

Opportunity Costs

If the NPV and NTA calculations yield identical results, why bother with the terminal calculations? The advantages, as we shall see, are several. One should be immediately apparent. The *gross* terminal amount of $46,410 is plainly and simply the gross cash the business could have in hand at the end of the project's life — provided, of course, it paid no interim dividends. No such meaning can be given to a present value. Thus, one reason for doing a terminal calculation is that the results are readily and easily interpreted.

A second advantage of calculating net terminal amounts, as opposed to net present value, is that it highlights that against the benefits to be received from the investment must be set the cost of the next best alternative. In accept-reject decisions the firm has two alternatives. It can bury its cash or invest it in a savings account of sorts. Assuming that this investment pays interest at the required rate of return of 10%, the terminal value of this alternative is $34,576. This option is clearly superior to burying the cash and therefore constitutes the next best alternative to the project.

For the project to be viable, its aggregate benefits must exceed those of the next best alternative. However, because the value of the next best alternative is the opportunity cost of the project, what I am saying is that the gross terminal amount of the project less its opportunity cost must be positive. This is of course a standard economic result — one is advised in economic terms to proceed only when the value exceeds opportunity cost.

The important point here is not the precise definition of opportunity cost, but the distinction between opportunity costs and outlay costs. In other words, when calculating the NTA there are four amounts to consider. In our case, when the firm is assumed to have cash in hand available for investment, only three of these become visible in the later accounting for the project.

Table 3

Year	Balance start of year	25% interest	Receipt end of year	Balance end of year
1	0	0	10,000	10,000
2	10,000	2,500	10,000	22,500
3	22,500	5,625	10,000	38,125
4	38,125	9,531	10,000	57,656

There is first the cash that will be paid out for the project — in our case $23,616. This amount is, of course, highly visible. There are the actual cash benefits that the project will generate — in our case $40,000; these are net benefits, i.e., they are cash revenues less cash costs. Both items are very visible. Then there are the further benefits that the $40,000 will earn through re-investment. Table 1 shows these to be $6,410 under the assumption that the primary benefits are reinvested at the required rate of return of 10%. These figures are also usually visible.

Finally, there is the interest that could have been earned, but wasn't, on the initial investment of $23,616. Table 2 illustrates this option with a total of $10,960 at a rate of 10%. However, unlike the three other amounts, these costs are neither visible in terms of hard cash, nor in the accounts of the firm. In other words, capital budgeting, unlike financial accounting, forces one to take into consideration costs other than simple outlay costs. This factor is inherent in present value calculations; terminal amount calculations do not introduce it as something new. However, what the terminal calculation does do is to highlight the fact that costs other than outlay costs are being used. In other words, we have the three alternatives:

	Proposed project	Simple investment	Do nothing
Terminal "value"	$46,401	$34,576	$23,616
Less: Outlay cost	23,616	23,616	23,616
	$22,794	$10,960	$—0—

The terminal value of the simple investment constitutes in this case the opportunity cost of the project. Thus, restating our analysis we have:

	Proposed project
Net terminal "value"	$22,794
Opportunity cost	10,960
Net terminal amount	$11,834

The net terminal amount of $11,834 is the economic profit earned by investing in the project. The accounting system by contrast would show, typically, only the net cash flow, i.e., $46,410 less $23,616 for an accounting profit of $22,794.

This could lead to a project that is evaluated *ex post* to appear to be more profitable than its *ex ante* evaluation. One way to compensate for this would be to use *residual income*. This technique involves the subtraction from conventional net income of the opportunity cost of capital. In our case, $10,960, to be precise, leaving $11,834 as the residual. This fact alone constitutes a strong argument for the use of residual income in controlling investment centers. Its use ensures comparability between capital planning and capital control.

Table 4

Year	Balance start of year	25% interest	Balance end of year
1	23,616	5,904	29,520
2	29,520	7,380	36,900
3	36,900	9,225	46,125
4	46,125	11,531	57,656

This explicit comparison of benefits against both outlay costs and opportunity costs is especially important when alternative projects are being evaluated and compared. For example, one project might have an IRR of 20% while another has an IRR of 25%. This forecast might suggest choosing the latter project.

However, recall that the IRR is that rate which results in an NTA of zero. The NTA in turn is the GTA less the initial investment, less the interest that could have been earned by the reinvestment of the initial outlay. An IRR calculation assumes that the reinvestment of the benefits and the initial outlay both occur at the IRR, i.e., in one case we are calculating opportunity costs at 20% and in the other at 25%. Clearly this is a logically unsupportable assumption. Other things being equal, one would never invest monies at 20% when a 25% rate of interest exists. The solution is to calculate opportunity costs for each alternative at a comparable rate of interest such as the hurdle rate.

Alternative Projects

For example, consider the case where we have to choose between our first project against a second. Assume that the second requires the same outlay as the first, i.e., $23,616. However, it yields a single benefit only, of $48,970 at the end of the fourth year.

The IRR on the first project has already been shown to be 25%. One can easily show that the IRR on the second project is 20%. The four-year discount factor appropriate to a rate of 20% is 0.482 which multiplied by $48,970 gives $23,616. Subtracting the initial outlay yields an NPV of zero. One might be inclined on this basis to favor the first project since its IRR is five points higher.

It is easy, however, to show that the second project has an NPV of $9,831 at 10%. This amount derives from a four-year, 10% discount factor of 0.683 yielding a present value of $33,447, from which one subtracts the initial outlay of $23,616. Since this NPV is positive, the project is acceptable. Moreover, the NPV of this project is greater than that of the first project, which was $8,083. If we adopt the rule of choosing that project with the highest NPV, then the second project is to be preferred to the first.

Common sense and the NTA calculation demonstrate the basis for the choice. The net terminal amount of the first project has already been shown to be $11,834. Because the investment required is the same for both projects the interest that could have been earned is an identical $10,960 which with the $23,616 yields an identical terminal cost of $34,576. The net terminal amount of the second project is, therefore, $14,349. Clearly what we have done, therefore, is to choose that project with the highest net terminal amount.

The reason for this apparent clash between the IRR approach on the one hand and the NPV/NTA approach on the other lies essentially in different assumptions about opportunity costs or the reinvestment of benefits. At 25% the benefits of the first project will accumulate to $57,656 which greatly exceeds the GTA of the second project which is $48,970. However, at a rate of 10%, the GTA of the first project is only $46,410 and the second project is preferable.

In general, it is appropriate to assume that the benefits from both projects may be reinvested at the hurdle rate. This hypothesis at least assures logical consistency in our assumptions, so:

Rule III: Choose the project (or set of projects) which yields the greatest net terminal amount.

This rule is completely general. It applies equally to situations involving capital rationing and to situations where capital is abundant, but mutually exclusive investments exist. It is a simple, monotone transformation of the rule that management should maximize the value of the firm. Stated otherwise, this rule is identical to the rule that management should maximize net present value or long-run profit.

Its advantage lies in its ease of interpretation, *not* in the fact that it introduces a new theory — which it does not. For instance, in cases like the above, where the initial investment is identical for both projects, the rule implies that one should should choose that project which has generated the most *cash* by the *end* of its life. The gross cash yield from the first project was shown in Table 1 to be $46,410, while the gross cash yield from the second project is $48,970. All other things being equal, the second project is to be preferred.

The rule applies with equal force, and the method with equal insight, to situations involving capital rationing with multiple alternatives. The rule, as it is generally stated, is to allocate the capital budget in such a way as to maximize the total net terminal amount. But, since the capital budget is a fixed amount, this is equivalent in turn to maximizing the total cash to be generated over the life of the project.

Consider, however, what this implies. For an individual, viewing a lifetime of benefits and alternative work possibilities, say, the rule suggests that he or she wishes to leave the largest bequest possible. For a company, the principle implies that it is wholly indifferent to the cash flow pattern and desires only to maximize its cash holding at the end of the project's life. In our example, it implies that the firm can survive without a steady inflow of cash as in the first project, but can afford to wait for the ultimate large inflow to arrive.

When put this way, many feel that this result is not their personal goal, nor is it the goal of their company. In this case, neither a net present value nor a net terminal amount is of any help in choosing a course of action. Both methods assume maximization of end-of-period wealth as the goal of the investor. The terminal calculation does not offer a new goal. What it does is to make the goal implicit in NPV calculations more explicit.

Unfortunately, no general rules can be offered when wealth maximization is rejected as a goal. All one can do is to lay in some detail the nature of the project and leave the individual to apply his or her own judgment to each specific case. Terminal calculations provide an ideal framework for doing just that.

Extensions to Terminal Calculations

Some extensions: Where two mutually exclusive investments are being considered, but the scale of the investment differs, it is sometimes necessary to go one step further. This situation occurs when the net terminal amount of the two projects is identical. For example, consider the two projects A and B:

	Project A	Project B
Gross terminal amount	2,003	43
Original investment	1,600	32
Interest on investment	400	8
Net terminal amount	3	3

Rule III clearly breaks down here. Two possibilities are then open. The first involves calculation of a profitability index:

	Project A	Project B
Profitability index	2,003/2,000 = 1.002	43/40 = 1.075

Now the highest index should be chosen. The argument here is that, given equal net present values or net terminal amounts, one would select that project which makes the most *efficient use* of funds. Another way of viewing this argument is to assume that one could buy 50 of the smaller projects for the same amount as one of the larger projects. On this basis the set of Project B's will yield a GTA of $2,150 (50 × 43) which is clearly superior to $2,003.

The second argument is that, failing this ability to duplicate the smaller investment, one should maximize total cash in hand, assuming that one is using one's own funds. In that case, Project A yields $403 at the end of its life as opposed to the $11 for Project B.

The matter is controversial and may be left moot since the situation is almost certainly no more than an academic exercise. Invariably two projects will have differing NTA's when Rule III applies — regardless of the scale of the investment.

A more common occurrence is for two projects to have unequal lives. Then the terminal calculations enter into their own and are clearly superior to present value calculations even as a conceptual device. The terminal amount calculations force the evaluator to make appropriate assumptions to even out the lives so as to arrive at a common terminal date. This can be either the shorter life with an appropriate assumption about the investment opportunities of the cash spinoff or the shorter project. Unlike with present value calculations, the terminal amount calculations force explicit assumptions. Consider for example the two projects in Table 5 where the required rate of return is 10%.

Table 5

	Life	Investment	Annual cash benefit	NPV	Internal rate of return
Project A	5	$2,864	$1,000	$ 927	22%
Project C	15	5,092	1,000	$2,514	18%

Note first, that by a net present value calculation, the second project is to be preferred. Note next that, by an internal rate of return criteria, the first project is to be preferred. The two criteria conflict and do so because the inequality of lives was ignored. This is not possible with a terminal amount calculation. Using the longer life for illustrative purposes, the NTA of Project C may easily be shown to be $10,504 ($31,773 − $21,269). To calculate the terminal amount of Project A at the end of five years is equally simple. This is $1,491 ($6,105 − $4,614).

For the remaining ten years, however, some very explicit assumptions are forced on us. We could, for example, assume that the $1,491 be reinvested at its own internal rate of 22%. Such an assumption would lead to a net terminal amount at the end of the 15 years of $10,892, making Project A preferable. This is, in fact, precisely the assumption that the internal-rate-of-return criterion makes.

When spelled out this explicitly, it is abundantly clear that this assumption is untenable. Project C's benefits are being reinvested by assumption, at 10% over that period. Why should the cash throw-off of Project A be any different? A more reasonable assumption is a reinvestment at 10%, which yields a net terminal amount at the end of 15 years of $3,867. This result makes Project C clearly preferable.

Obviously, other assumptions are possible. For example, a third project beginning in year six might be available which returns 18% — and so on. The important point is that the terminal calculations literally force one to make assumptions about what one will do with the cash throw-off of Project A at the end of five years. In this sense, it is clearly superior to present value calculations. In fact, it is interesting to note that virtually all textbook authors go over at this point to terminal amounts to explain the apparent conflict between the criteria of net present value and internal rates of return. Why not then concentrate on terminal amounts in the first place?

Capital and Cash Budgets

It has already been stressed that the one advantage of doing a net terminal amount calculation instead of a net present value calculation is that it makes the implicit goal or criterion much more explicit. The NTA approach makes it quite plain that the assumed aim of the investor is to maximize terminal wealth; that is, the accumulated cash from the project less the opportunity cost of the project.

As yet another benefit, the terminal approach enables one to lay the project information out in a thoroughly satisfactory manner when the single maximization goal is deemed inappropriate. It does this by integrating the capital budgeting process with the cash budget of the firm and in a way that makes it simple for management to evaluate. Consider by way of example the layout in Table 6 of the first project.

The last column in Table 6 indicates the cash balance at the end of each year after making allowance for the initial investment of $23,616. It shows the cash in hand from the benefits generated by the project itself and from the interest earned from the reinvestment of those benefits. Not only is this calculation provided for the end of the project, but also for each year of its life.

Such an approach enables management to take into consideration the cash in hand at the end of the project's life — one criterion for evaluating a project. It also enables management to consider the cash flow at each point along the way — a second and usually very important criterion for evaluating a project. This cash flow incidentally, is easily converted into an income flow by simply including the leads and lags in the accrual system. This calculation would enable management to evaluate the impact of the project on the income statements as well.

But, not only does the table provide a full picture of the cash flows associated with the project, it also indicates at what point the receipts alone, and more particularly, the receipts plus interest will exceed the initial outlay. In other words, the *payback period* is readily apparent from the last column of the table. In this case it is somewhere between two and three years that the project's net cash flow turns positive. Thus, the table yields a third criterion that management often uses.

Note, moreover, that the terminal method highlights the assumptions one is making about the reinvestment of benefits. Table 6 assumed that this was occurring at a rate of 10% — the cost of capital. Table 7 makes the more general assumption that the reinvestment rate will vary, perhaps decline.

Of course, varying interest rates can be used with NPV calculations. The difference is that here one can see exactly and explicitly what is being assumed.

Thus far, I have concentrated on actual outlay costs, that is cash revenues and cash expenses that form the net benefits, the interest income received from the reinvestment of that cash, and the initial cash outlay for the capital equipment. The less visible opportunity cost has not been included yet. By extending Table 6 a few more columns, or by providing an additional table, as is done here, one can compare the benefits received from the project with the opportunity cost of that project. Table 8 gives the details.

The opportunity cost in this table is the interest lost by investing in the project rather than say, putting the amount of $23,616 into 10% bonds. The amounts are cumulative and are drawn from Table 2.[2]

The last column indicates the net terminal value at the end of each year. In particular, it yields the net terminal value in the last year. This is the amount that one is assumed to want to maximize when one does terminal amount calculations. It is the amount that figured in Rule III. Thus, the table (or tables as presented here) yields a fourth criterion for management's consideration.

It is worth noting how including the opportunity cost delays the breakeven point in the project. Table 6 shows a negative cash balance of $2,616 at the end of the second year, while Table 8 shows a negative net terminal amount of $7,576. There is an added bonus here from setting the calculations out in this way. One can see not only when cash will breakeven, but also when benefits versus costs will breakeven.[3]

Making Project Evaluation More Explicit

To draw all this together then, the terminal approach introduces no new theory to capital budgeting. In the case of accept-reject decisions, a positive NTA criterion will select the identical projects to a NPV criterion. Where alternatives are available, to choose the project with the highest NTA is identical to choosing the project with the highest NPV. The method does not alter familiar criteria.

What it does do is to present the details of a project or projects in such a way that:

• They can be more easily evaluated by top management;

---

[2] An alternative, but less satisfactory, interpretation of this amount of $10,960 is the cost of finance. Seldom though can financing be tied to a specific project. Better, therefore, to think of it as the benefit foregone by investing in the project. This might, of course, be another project rather than a bond, when cumulative benefits would replace the cumulative interest.
[3] Note that on a full cost-benefit basis at the IRR of 25%, the project does not breakeven until the end of the project's life. This is, of course, definitional — the IRR is that rate that yields a net terminal amount of zero, i.e., allows the project to breakeven only at its end.

- Their impact on the firm's cash flow and income statements can be made more easily apparent;
- All the usually implicit assumptions are made explicit;

Table 8

Year	Gross bal. end of year	Cash outflow	Net cash bal. end of year	Opportunity cost	Net terminal amount
1	10,000	23,616	−13,616	2,362	−15,978
2	21,000	−	− 2,616	4,960	− 7,576
3	33,100	−	9,484	7,818	1,666
4	46,410	−	22,794	10,960	11,834

Table 7

Year	Balance start of year	Interest rate	Interest	Receipt end of year	Balance end of year	Net cash bal. end of year
1	0	−	−	10,000	10,000	−13,616
2	10,000	25%	2,500	10,000	22,500	− 1,116
3	22,500	20%	4,500	10,000	37,000	13,384
4	37,000	10%	3,700	10,000	50,700	27,084

Table 6

Year	Cash bal. start of year	10% interest	Receipt end of year	Cash inflow	Gross bal. end of year	Net cash balance end of year
1	0	0	10,000	10,000	10,000	−13,616
2	10,000	1,000	10,000	11,000	21,000	− 2,616
3	21,000	2,100	10,000	12,100	33,100	9,484
4	33,100	3,310	10,000	13,310	46,410	22,794

- The breakeven or payback period is readily visible; and
- A multi-criteria evaluation is more easily possible.

In brief, the whole theory of the time value of money assumes that one wishes to maximize net terminal wealth.[4] All that net present value does is to discount this goal back to the here and now and label it net present value. This manipulation does not, of course, alter the goal. The aim of maximizing end-of-period wealth may or may not be appropriate. That depends on circumstances. What I suggest is that, by setting the calculations out in investment terms rather than in discounting terms, the maximization goal is made explicit. Moreover, it enables the reader to see the annual gross cash flow picture, the cash breakeven point, and the cost-benefit breakeven point. All these are vital pieces of information which should not be excluded from any project evluation.

---

[4] The only place the terminal method breaks down is when benefits extend to infinity as in the case of a perpetuity. Here again, however, the method forces one to be explicit about one's assumptions. In this case we are assuming an infinite planning horizon. This is an interesting extreme in mathematical analysis, but hardly relevant in real world application, where a five- or ten-year planning horizon is far more appropriate.

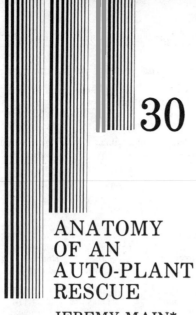

30

ANATOMY
OF AN
AUTO-PLANT
RESCUE

JEREMY MAIN*

One after another the big old Chrysler plants in Detroit shut down. Hamtramck Assembly, Eight Mile Stamping, and Huber Foundry closed in 1980, Lynch Road Assembly and part of Mack Stamping in 1981. It was the same each time. First the rumors on the factory floor. Then the stark announcement of the closing. That was it. Labour and management never tried to work together to keep a plant open. A year ago the familiar rumors flitted through the Detroit Trim plant, which makes seat covers for Chrysler cars. Figures shown to managers said Detroit Trim was hopelessly noncompetitive, and the plant seemed doomed. Surprisingly, not only is the plant still functioning today, but its productivity is up by more than 25% and it has prospects of enjoying prolonged good health.

This time, when the rumors started, the United Auto Workers went to Chrysler's management to find out if they were true, and if so, to see what the union could do to help. And this time Chrysler was responsive. Without any of the belligerent rhetoric that has characterized union-management relations in the auto industry, the two sides worked out an agreement that completely altered the economics of the plant, the way it works, and the way it is managed. By March 1 the plant met the productivity goals Chrysler had set as a condition for keeping it open.

When finally drawn together by a mutual threat, labor and management discovered they both thought the plant's 709 employees, blue- and white-collar alike, were not putting in much of a day's work. Many sewing machine

---

* From *Fortune* (April 4, 1983). © 1983 Time Inc.

operators were finishing their quotas an hour or more before the whistle signaled the end of the day shift at 2:30 P.M. The two sides agreed that the plant's roster could be cut by 25% and the remaining employees given new quotas to keep them busy for a full eight hours — or 7½ hours, to be more accurate, since the eight hours include two 12-minute breaks and a five-minute wash-up period.

Old work rules have been swept aside along with the old work standards. A foreman doesn't have to call a plant electrician to unplug a sewing machine. Anyone can unplug it. Managers now have the flexibility to change job assignments. Work teams are smaller.

The burden isn't falling all on the blue-collar workers, by any means. A large proportion of the managers, foremen, clerks, and skilled tradesmen have been dismissed, leaving those who remain with more to do. Even the number of company-paid union officers at the plant has been cut, from six to four, and one spends more time on plant work than union affairs.

The plant employees, mostly women, aren't exactly happy about the new pace of work. Hunched tensely over their sewing machines and cutters, they grumble they're having trouble meeting the new quotas. But they accept the hard work as the price of keeping their jobs and saving the plant.

While they haven't become bosom buddies, management and labour have achieved a measure of trust and mutual respect that has been conspicuously missing in Detroit. Joe Zappa, 57, president of the once powerful UAW Local 212 that encompasses Detroit Trim, says of Moe Teodosic, 43, the kinetic plant manager, "Without him, we would never have done it." Teodosic says the same of Zappa. Indeed, it almost seemed as if the plant management and union leaders formed an alliance aimed at dragging along their respective constituencies — corporate management and labor rank and file. Managers have learned not to use words like "concession," "featherbedding," or "giveback," and labor leaders are becoming comfortable with words like "productivity" and "competitiveness." Stephen Sharf, 62, Chrysler's executive vice president for manufacturing, still can't resist the occasional reference to featherbedding, and that still annoys Zappa. But Zappa isn't the old fire-eating union boss he was when Local 212 had 12,000 members in 14 plants and he repeatedly won reelection by a wide margin. He's retiring as president, and membership is down to 3,000 dues payers in 11 remaining plants. "Zappa has changed a lot," says Sharf. "We are changing too."

Detroit Trim sits at the edge of the city, right beside I-75, which at this time of year has as much trash as grass along its embankments. A railroad track separates the plant from the Highland Park headquarters of the Chrysler Corp. Teodosic occupies an office big enough for a chairman of the board, but the unhealthy potted plants, the plain furniture, and the view of the parking lot beside I-75 tell the visitor that the chairman of the board is several echelons away.

Detroit Trim is a very ordinary plant, more like a garment factory than a modern auto facility. Most of the sewing is done on machines that are decades old, and there's not a robot in sight unless you count the eight-year-old automatic cutting machine guided by numerical tape. Huge rolls of polyurethane padding, and vinyl and fabric covering materials are delivered to the plant. Devices known as fales machines join the padding and material together and chop them into manageable pieces. These are passed on to sewing machine operators and cutters who build up the seat covers step by step, one adding a welt or reinforcing strip, another a side panel, and so on. The finished covers finally reach the inspectors who count and check them and put them in bins for shipment. Detroit Trim turns out good work. Quality was never a problem.

The plant's survival became doubtful in 1981 when Chrysler switched to a new budgeting system. Instead of creating a budget on the basis of its costs, each plant had to compare its numbers with the costs of buying the same products outside the company. The comparison was disastrous for Detroit Trim. The plant's output would have cost Chrysler $51.5 million for the 1983 model year. A company survey showed that seat covers of the same quality could be obtained for $30.8 million from vendors using non-UAW labor. When Teodosic finished the new budget in October 1981, he says, "the decision was instant. There was no way a company that would have been lucky to make $1 million that year could afford a $20-million drain." People on his staff looked at the figures and thought, as one of them recalls, "It's gone." As it turned out, Chrysler lost $476 million in 1981 on sales of $10 billion. In 1982 it earned $170 million on the same volume.

Chrysler made no announcement of its plans to close Detroit Trim, but it doesn't take long for this kind of information to spread around a factory. Even before the study was finished, Zappa and Helen Armstrong, 48, the sturdy, no-nonsense chairman of the shop committee, were asking Teodosic what was going on. When rumors of a shutdown started circulating, UAW officials took the unusual step of calling top Chrysler executives. Zappa pointed out to Chrysler Vice Chairman Gerald Greenwald, 48, that while he, Zappa, was living on a reduced UAW salary, Greenwald was enjoying a recent promotion and raise. It was his way of saying the workers had made the sacrifices and now needed some consideration. The man above Zappa in the union hierarchy, Ken Morris, 67, director of UAW Region 1B, stepped in to take a major role in rescuing the plant. He urged Marc Stepp, 60, the UAW's vice president for Chrysler affairs, to bypass the usual channels and take the matter up directly with Chrysler's top management. Stepp arranged a meeting with Sharf and Thomas W. Miner, 55, Chrysler's vice president for industrial relations.

The two sides, still hostile and suspicious but subdued, met at Chrysler headquarters on April 2, 1982. Sharf, who had been a tool- and diemaker at Ford before starting the climb that led almost to the top of Chrysler, said to the union people it would be insulting to tell them how much they would have to give up to make the plant competitive. "Go ahead and insult me," said Morris. Sharf pointed out that non-UAW sewing machine operators in the U.S. were making half as much as those in the plant. The discussions didn't get much beyond generalities, but Sharf agreed to offer the UAW a rescue plan.

While the plan — or two plans, as it turned out — was being developed in April and May, Teodosic followed a line of reasoning that led to a crucial conclusion. Teodosic is not at all a typical auto executive. As a 24-year-old he came over from his native Yugoslavia in 1963 to join his father, who had settled in the U.S. after World War II and was working at Chrysler's Jefferson Assembly plant. Teodosic signed up as an unskilled worker on the line, like his father. In his spare time he proceeded first to learn English, then earn a B.A. and finally an MBA at Michigan State University.

His career progressed as rapidly as his education. He became a foreman and kept on rising, so that when his father retired in 1980 it was plant manager Teodosic who handed him his pin. Teodosic hasn't become a smooth, well-nourished auto executive. His gray, three-piece suits are rumpled and his hair sticks out in multiple directions, presumably charged with the same electricity that drives him. He smokes two packs a day and speaks rapidly with strong Slavic intonations in his vowels. His first name, Momcilo, is always shortened to Moe.

Teodosic's crucial study showed that if Chrysler did shut down Detroit Trim it would save nothing like the full $20.7-million difference between vendor costs and plant costs. For one thing, it would not save the salaries of Teodosic and nine members of his staff who run three other plants, including another trim plant outside Toronto. Chrysler would also have to pick up $3.8 million in continuing pension costs included in the plant budget. These and other items Teodosic found represented a total of $9.3 million in annual costs if Detroit Trim were padlocked. Chrysler thus would save not $20.7 million but $11.4 million.

"We hadn't realized this," says Zappa, "and if it hadn't been for Moe we would really have been in trouble." Not only did Sharf accept Teodosic's figures, but he added in something for the fact that a captive plant has advantages. It can be ordered around, and the quality of its work is a known factor. Inner-city jobs were involved too. Therefore, said Sharf, the corporation was willing to swallow $5 million of the $11.4 million if the plant could save the remaining $6.4 million.

On July 13 the company and the plant management each submitted to the union plans for saving Detroit Trim. The plant proposals suggested a series of concessions, notably a $2.25-an-hour cut in base pay. It might seem that a UAW worker, faced with the loss of his job, would be willing to work for $6.84 instead of $9.09 an hour. But such reasoning disregards the realities of the auto industry. The UAW was trying to negotiate a general pay raise and wasn't about to make an exception.

The rank and file wouldn't swallow a pay cut because they knew the plant would have to be kept open until July 1983 to finish the model year. For a

year after that, half the Detroit Trim workers — those with 20 years' seniority or more — would have received 95% of their pay through unemployment compensation and supplementary unemployment benefits. Two years
guaranteed at virtually full pay looked better than an immediate cut. Other
workers would get lesser amounts for shorter periods. Zappa knew the
plant's proposal was unacceptable, but instead of rejecting it noisily as he
might have in the old days of confrontation, he just laid it aside.

The corporation's plan suggested that the workers take possession of the
factory for $1 under an Employee Ownership Plan (OEP) and then bid com-
petitively to supply Chrysler with seat covers. To see how it might work,
Zappa, Helen Armstrong, and other UAW officers visited Hyatt Clark Industries, a former General Motors roller-bearing plant in New Jersey now
owned and run by its workers. The delegation didn't like what it saw at all.
The plant was barely surviving at the time, the workers had taken a cut in
pay, some had been laid off, and the others were working harder than ever.
Even foremen were performing directly productive tasks, a shocking thing
for a good unionist to see. Furthermore, the plant had lost the protection
of the corporate umbrella. It seemed to the UAW group that Hyatt, which
wound up losing $5.5 million in 1982 but may break even this year, rep-
resented the worst possible outcome.

While these proposals were being considered, another crucial contribution
to a solution arrived almost by chance. Charles "Doug" Howell, 63, has made
a career of saving ailing plants, going back to the 1960s when he worked for
the Air Brake Co. and later at Rockwell International. He believes that ulti-
matums and hardball tactics get plants shut down; what keeps plants open
is a willingness to share information, to answer any questions, and to build
trust. As a consultant with Arthur D. Little Inc., Howell happened to be
visiting Chrysler to offer his help on productivity matters. Sharf invited him
to help out with Detroit Trim. Howell suggested that the UAW and Chrysler jointly hire Arthur D. Little to build credibility between labor and management. Both sides agreed, and eventually split ADL's $85,000 fee.

Howell saw that his first task was to check out Chrysler's estimate that it
could buy its seat covers from outside vendors for $30.8 million. "The UAW
thought the quotes were unbelievably low and would be raised as soon as
the plant was closed," says Howell. He established that vendors could indeed supply Chrysler for that unbelievably low price. The UAW believed
him.

It didn't hurt that on their visit to Hyatt the UAW group had heard good
things about Howell's integrity. He had served as Hyatt's interim chief
executive officer for six months after the workers took it over. Once Howell
verified the vendor figures in September, says Teodosic, "the whole labor
attitude changed." Now both parties accepted the same premise: Detroit
Trim had to do a lot to get competitive, or go under.

But since neither of the two plans submitted to the UAW was going to fly,
how was the plant to get competitive? Sharf told the union the only alterna-

tive was an all-out effort to increase productivity, laying some workers off if necessary. The union replied that productivity shouldn't all come out of labor's hide. Howell stepped in as honest broker to say he would make sure management contributed as much as labor, and he added the suggestion that the full-time union staff on the premises, who are paid by Chrysler, be cut.

It turned out that labour viewed the plant much as management did: overstaffed, encumbered by wasteful work rules, and failing to get eight hours' work out of its employees. "This plant was greatly overmanned. Some people were working only three or four hours a day. I've never been overworked here." That's a union official talking — James E. Smith, 39, plant steward for Local 889, which represents salaried workers.

Under Howell's guidance, management and labor set up a rather elaborate participative method for finding the way to greater productivity. Six committees consisting of management, union officials, and rank-and-file workers were set up under the umbrella of a steering committee in September and began discussing the issues exhaustively. The talking dragged but Zappa didn't mind a bit. He was well aware that unless Chrysler soon placed orders with outside vendors, it would have no choice but to rely on Detroit Trim for seat covers for the 1984 model year. A little more delay would buy the plant another year's life, until July 1984.

But Chrysler was watching the calendar too and announced early in October that by December 1 it would have to decide where to place its 1984 orders. Unless agreement was reached by that day, it would close the plant. Since the leisurely participative approach clearly would not meet this deadline, all committees except the steering committee were scrapped. Instead Howell, with the help of two Arthur D. Little colleagues, made a fast study to determine what jobs could be eliminated and how much work standards could be increased.

Howell's recommendations went to the 14-member steering committee, made up of both union and management representatives, which agreed on a new productivity plan on November 8. Total employment at the plant would be cut from 709 to 528. The direct labor force — the production workers on the fales, sewing, and cutting machines — would be reduced by 21%. Salaried workers, including managers, would be cut 25%, and indirect workers — the janitors, tradesmen, and others who maintain the plant and repair equipment — by a whopping 40%. Howell, an old hand at finding fat in factories, wasn't surprised that indirect labor could be cut more than direct, He found, for instance, a welder hired long ago for reasons long forgotten, who had only a few hours' work a week to do. The welder will be laid off and another craftsman trained to weld occasionally.

The plan's premise was that with nearly 200 fewer workers the factory would produce at the October level because individuals would work harder and crews would be reduced. The standards for the daily output at each station — the number of pieces each cutter or sewing machine operator would have to turn out — would rise 15% to 28%. If Chrysler increased its orders for seat covers, fewer direct workers would be laid off. But the number of indirect workers in many categories would not go up again as orders increased. Only two electricians, instead of three as before, would be assigned to back up the day shift, regardless of the size of the shift.

The agreement embodied several principles that would never have been accepted by old-style unions or management. Work rules would be flexible and barriers between jobs would be dropped. If an electrician needed to work on a ladder, it wouldn't take another electrician to hold the ladder — anyone would do. Management and labor would keep each other well informed. "What used to be just their business is now our business," says Helen Armstrong. "We need answers to questions being asked on the floor."

The steering committee became a permanent cost control panel that hunts for ways to improve productivity. Management agreed to reduce the ratio of foremen to workers from 1-to-21 to 1-to-30 and to maintain the new ratio, so that if workers are laid off, so are foremen. "Management doesn't want all those foremen," says Sharf. "If workers came in on time, did their jobs, and paid attention to quality, we could have one foreman to 100 workers."

All the savings embodied in the agreement totaled $5.4 million — $1 million short of the $6.4 million demanded by Chrysler. It was close enough and Chrysler's officers approved it on November 12. On November 18 the rank and file met to hear Zappa give a lucid, resonant history of the whole effort to save the plant. Zappa had no trouble with the little opposition that developed. Even shipping clerk Norman A. Lupo, 38, whom union leaders count on to object to almost anything, confined himself to a mild suggestion that Chrysler promise not to contract out for any seat covers.

Zappa told the workers nothing could be done to change the agreement. "Either you approve it," he said, "or it won't fly and tomorrow the company starts jobbing out." He concluded, "For those of you who criticize everything the company does, here's your golden opportunity to show 'em how to do it. This is the way to go, damn it." The vote was 4 to 1 in favor of the agreement.

One more deadline remained. By March 1 the plant had to prove that the rescue plan could work. Beginning in January one group after another on the floor was given its new work standards. Helen Armstrong was busier than ever, cajoling some workers, encouraging others, sitting down at a sewing machine herself to test a new norm, chasing down rumors, resupplying the washrooms with paper when the reduced janitorial force didn't get around to it. "I've even had my poor church praying for the plant," she says.

"The first week everybody fussed and said it would never work," Mrs. Armstrong relates. "They asked, 'Why did you ever agree to this?' But no one refused to try. The second week they said maybe it will work. A lot of them still haven't made their increases, but they're close to it." Jesse L. Thomas, 30, for example, was asked to raise the number of welts she sews on seat backs from 293 to 376 a day, an increase of 28%. "I can do about seven hours now," she said a few weeks ago, meaning that during the full shift she can finish the equivalent of seven hours' work. "I'm still pushing, but it's not as hard as it was at first." She was up to 330 welts.

Workers to be laid off, or "bumped" in union parlance, were chosen and notified, and jobs reorganized and streamlined. Crews on the big fales machines were cut by one worker. Linda Petro-Ulrey, 33, Detroit Trim's production control manager and the only woman manufacturing executive in Chrysler, is losing six of her staff of 17, who schedule the plant's work. Those remaining are learning new functions so they can switch to where they are needed. "Management can put us anywhere they want," says Jim Smith, the white-collar union steward. "It used to be done, but very rarely. Now it will be the norm." He doesn't mind a bit. He thinks learning new skills makes him more valuable. But one older fellow worker took early retirement rather than face new tasks.

Happily for the rank and file, the big layoffs originally envisioned in the rescue plan never happened. Chrysler's sales picked up, so did the plant's output, from 11,460 pieces daily in the fall to over 14,000 in February (one cover for a seat cushion or seat back counts as a piece). So instead of fewer production workers making the same number of seats, the same number are making more. But the good news is no help to the management and non-production workers whose numbers didn't vary with output. Hardest hit are the skilled tradesmen. They were reduced from 41 to 26 in February. "We've saved the plant but I've lost my job," says Gary Cosby, 40, an electrician whose 18 years' seniority wasn't enough to keep him from being bumped.

The blue-collar workers are still suspicious of management. Says Mrs. Armstrong, "There's a lot of tension out there. The hourlies don't want to see musical chairs. They want to see equality of sacrifice. I am certainly watching but I can honestly say management is keeping to the agreement." Seven out of 26 on the management payroll, not including foreman, have been laid off.

Even before the deadline arrived, it was clear the plant would achieve Chrysler's savings target — which was raised from $5.4 million to $5.9 million as volume increased. Toward the end of February, with four-fifths of the plan in operation, savings were running at an annual rate of $6.4 million — exceeding the improvement the company had insisted on.

Without any of the new paraphernalia of productivity — robots, quality circles, just-in-time inventories — the Detroit Trim plant has achieved extraordinary increases in output mainly by getting a full day's work out of its employees. The typical U.S. factory, in Howell's view, probably has just as much room for improvement. Less labor-intensive plants might not match Detroit Trim's spectacular gains in the output of direct-production workers, but might find equivalent savings elsewhere — in the ranks of managers and indirect workers. Many a plant manager might end up echoing Teodosic, who muses: "To think that a plant that had so much slack in it almost closed down."

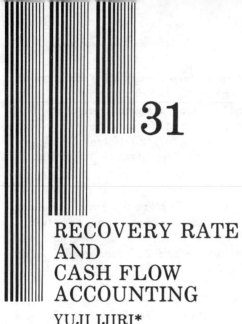

31

RECOVERY RATE AND CASH FLOW ACCOUNTING

YUJI IJIRI*

Evaluation of a company's performance should be based on cash flow, according to the author. One method of making such a measurement, the corporate recovery rate, is discussed here.

There has been a serious discrepancy between the way in which investment decisions are made and the way in which results of the decisions are evaluated.

In investment decisions, the primary factor is cash flow. Such indicators as payback period, internal discounted cash flow (DCF), rate of return, and present value are all based on cash flow. In performance evaluation, emphasis shifts to earnings. Performance of a project is evaluated mostly on earnings and related indicators, such as return on investment. Performance of a division or a corporation, which may be viewed as a collection of projects, is even more heavily based on earnings. Thus, for example, a project is approved on the expectation of earning a 15 percent after-tax DCF rate, but when it comes to performance evaluation, it is reported as having earned a 10 percent return on investment. The two rates are often not reconcilable, and management is left without feedback on whether a project is generating the expected cash flow at the planning stage.

Therefore, either investment decisions should be based on earnings or performance evaluation should be based on cash flow. The choice is rather obvious, because the primary objectives of a business enterprise is cash

* From *Financial Executive* (March 1980). Reprinted by permission. The author is an academician.

flow. Earnings is only a surrogate to represent performance of the enterprise on this cash flow objective. And if earnings do not tell how well a project or a division or a corporation is doing in terms of cash flow, then the concept and measurement of earnings has to be changed.

Over the years, earnings have become extremely complex and moved further away from the notion of cash flow, since many official pronouncements are concerned with methods of handling noncash items. Perhaps the time has come to go back to cash flow and see what can be done without mixing it with a host of noncash items.

The Recovery Rate

It is true that performance of a project cannot be properly evaluated until the project is terminated. For example, actual DCF rate, that is, the rate at which the present value of all cash inflows and outflows becomes zero, cannot be calculated until all cash flows from the project are determined. Project performance, however, has to be evaluated well before the end of the project's economic life. Therefore, some standard methods must be introduced to deal with the uncertainty in future cash flows, in order to make a proper assessment of current project performance.

Unfortunately, the earnings concept is constructed as a residual, after all cash and noncash items are put together. Noncash items, which are relatively "soft" and ambiguous, are mixed with cash items, which are relatively "hard" and objective. Like adding miles to inches, such a mixture has an effect of reducing the reliability of the resulting figure.

Would it not be better to develop an indicator of performance based on cash items only, together with some guidelines on how noncash items may be taken into account? The user of the performance indicator can then apply his own judgment if he wishes to do so.

As one such possibility, consider what may be called the "recovery rate," which is the cash flow in a period divided by the gross investment. For example, if a project has an initial investment of $1,000,000 and an annual cash recovery of $200,000, the recovery rate is 20 percent. (Note that the denominator, gross investment, is not affected by depreciation.)

If annual cash flow is uniform, then the recovery rate is the reciprocal of the familiar payback period, which is five years in the above example. Also, assuming uniform cash flows, the recovery rate is equal to the DCF rate if the project has an infinite life, and is an excellent approximation of the DCF rate if the recovery rate is over 15 percent and the project life is over 15 years, which is perhaps the case in a majority of capital investment decisions.

Corporate Recovery Rate

For each individual project, cash flows fluctuate from year to year, hence the recovery rate does, too. But, what about an aggregate of projects, such as cash flows of a division or a corporation? It seems that the corporate recovery rate may be more stationary than the project recovery rate because ups and downs in the latter are averaged over all projects. If so, recovery rate can be a useful indicator of corporate performance.

It is not easy to calculate a corporate recovery rate from financial statements, since these statements are not oriented toward cash flow. But, some approximations may be made.

The total amount of investment made by the corporation on all projects that are currently under operation may be estimated by "gross assets": total assets plus accumulated depreciation. To reflect the average amount of investment during a year, an average of the beginning and ending gross assets may be used.

(It is true that gross assets do not coincide with gross investment, due to such factors as investments that were expensed, idle assets, and surplus cash. But, roughly speaking, gross assets should provide a reasonable similarity to gross investment in many cases.)

Cash flow from all projects of the corporation, on the other hand, may be approximated by "funds from operations" plus "proceeds from disposal of long-term assets," both of which appear on the statement of changes in financial position. A decrease in total current assets, if it occurs, is added to that sum, since disposals of current assets are not reported separately.

In investment decisions, however, the expected profitability of a project is evaluated independently from the cost of financing the project, hence interest and other finance charges are not deducted from cash flows. Therefore, to make the performance indicator comparable to data used in investment decisions, we must add back the interest expense to the above sum of funds from operations and proceeds from disposal of long-term assets. (Although the use of after-tax interest may be justified, here we use before-tax interest, since the corporation did in fact have available for distribution to shareholders and creditors the amount equal to earnings and before-tax interest.)

Figure I

$$\text{Corporate Recovery Rate} \;=\; \frac{\text{Cash Recoveries}}{\text{Gross Assets}}$$

where

Cash Recoveries = (Funds from Operations)
+ (Proceeds from Disposal of Long-Term Assets)
+ (Decrease in Total Current Assets)
+ (Interest Expense)

and

Gross Assets = (Total Assets) + (Accumulated Depreciation) averaged between beginning and ending balances.

Figure II Corporate Recovery Rates

	1972	1973	1974	1975	1976	1977	1978	Avg.	Corp. DCF Rate	Corp. Payback Period
Alcoa	8.2%	7.8%	9.2%	6.4%	8.4%	8.4%	10.4%	8.4%	5.6%	11.9 yrs.
American Brands	10.2	10.8	11.4	10.5	9.3	10.5	11.1	10.5	8.4	9.5
American Can	6.5	8.0	8.5	8.1	8.4	8.6	8.1	8.0	5.0	12.5
Bethlehem Steel	6.3	7.2	9.0	8.1	7.2	2.4	8.4	6.9	3.3	14.5
Chrysler	9.1	9.6	4.9	2.8	11.3	6.3	9.7	7.7	4.5	13.0
DuPont	10.8	12.7	10.2	9.1	11.3	11.9	12.7	11.2	9.3	8.9
Esmark	8.6	9.5	11.6	11.2	13.9	12.1	11.2	11.2	9.3	8.9
General Electric	9.9	10.1	10.4	10.8	10.7	10.5	11.2	10.5	8.4	9.5
General Foods	12.1	10.8	10.7	11.3	11.2	11.7	9.8	11.1	9.2	9.0
General Motors	14.6	15.2	9.9	12.0	16.1	15.8	16.7	14.3	13.1	7.0
Goodyear	8.4	8.1	7.8	7.1	7.3	8.7	8.7	8.0	5.0	12.5
Gulf Oil	10.7	13.3	12.9	10.5	11.5	8.9	9.8	11.1	9.2	9.0
IBM	18.2	19.0	18.8	18.3	18.7	19.5	19.9	18.9	18.2	5.3
Int'l. Harvester	6.8	7.0	8.1	8.6	9.4	10.4	6.9	8.2	5.3	12.2
Int'l. Paper	8.4	10.5	12.3	13.3	12.0	11.4	11.4	11.3	9.4	8.8
RCA	14.0	13.9	12.0	10.3	13.7	15.1	15.6	13.5	12.1	7.4
Texaco	9.7	12.6	14.2	6.0	8.1	9.9	9.6	10.0	7.8	10.0
Untd. Tech.	7.1	6.7	8.9	8.6	13.0	9.3	9.1	9.0	6.4	11.1
U.S. Steel	4.3	6.3	9.5	7.4	6.4	4.8	5.0	6.2	2.1	16.1
West'ghouse El.	7.7	8.1	6.4	6.7	6.9	6.6	7.3	7.1	3.6	14.1

Thus, we may calculate corporate recovery rate based on the equation in **Figure I.**

Figure II shows corporate recovery rates for some selected corporations, calculated with the formula in **Figure I,** and using data in published financial statements.

Note that the recovery rate is reasonably uniform over the years for many corporations. Apparently, averaging project cash flows helped stabilize the recovery rate.

In **Figure II,** the corporate DCF rate is calculated under the assumption that all cash flows occur at the end of each year. It is this rate, "i," which makes the capital recovery factor $i/(1 - (1 + i)^{-20})$ equal to the average recovery rate. If we take into account that cash flows normally occur throughout the year, the DCF rates for many of the corporations in the figure are increased by approximately one tenth (obtained by changing the numerator "i" of the capital recovery factor by the natural logarithm of $1 + i$). Corporate payback period in the figure is, on the other hand, unaffected by the average life of projects and is determined by taking the reciprocal of the average recovery rate.

These are the terms which businessmen can readily relate to their experience in investment decisions. In particular, corporate DCF rate may be compared to see whether the cash flow of a corporation has been sufficient to cover the cost of capital.

The same analysis of recovery rate may be made for divisions. Divisional DCF rate or divisional payback period may then be determined for divisional performance evaluation. Such indicators of performance can be related more readily with projects that were recently undertaken by the division. For a large project, the project itself may be taken as the accounting unit, and the recovery rate for the project may be determined and compared with original expectations.

ROI vs. Recovery Rate

Undoubtedly, return on investment (ROI) is a more advanced concept than recovery rate, since the former includes adjustments for depreciation and other noncash items both on the denominator and the numerator, whereas the latter does not. The question here is whether such additional adjustments make the indicator more useful for management.

It seems that recovery rate is more easily understandable, intuitively appealing, and less subject to ambiguities, arbitrariness, and potential manipulations than ROI. Needless to say, recovery rate does not incorporate the economic life of a project, while ROI does. But should it really be incorporated?

When it comes to aggregation of information, more is not necessarily preferred to less. Before we add apples to oranges, we must seriously question whether the addition results in clouding what was previously a sharp concept.

The economic life of a project would certainly be a worthwhile concept to incorporate in a performance measure, if it were capable of being measured objectively. Unfortunately, it is in many cases anybody's guess. It is perhaps one of the most uncertain factors in investment decisions. If so, it would perhaps be far better to leave the factor out of the indicator so that the user can fill it in based on his own assessment rather than incorporating it in the indicator based on the accountant's judgment (which is not necessarily better than the user's judgment).

If the basic approach in the above argument for recovery rate is reasonable, we may generalize it to the entire field of accounting.

In the past, development of accounting has been such that more and more factors are incorporated in determining earnings. From a common sense viewpoint, this is certainly an improvement. Yet, the discussion on ROI versus recovery rate casts some doubt on whether or not the user has actually been better off as a result of incorporating more factors into the earnings figure.

Perhaps, it is worthwhile to see what kind of accounting can be developed based on cash flow. At worst, such a "primitive" accounting system can offer a bench mark that may be used to evaluate the contribution of the existing accounting system. More likely, however, is the possibility that a simple accounting system which excludes noncash items can be a satisfactory or even a better means for information and control.

Cash flow accounting has been used before and cash flow statements have been prepared before, eliminating noncash items from income statement. But, there has not been any attempt to develop a structure of cash flow accounting based on fundamental concepts. Some salient features of such a structure are provided below:

Investment cash flows and financing cash flows are reviewed separately. An enterprise is looked at as an entity engaging in investment and recovery and in financing and repayment.

The debit side of a balance sheet accounts for investment cash flows (investment and recovery), while its credit side accounts for financing cash flows (financing and repayment).

Balances on the balance sheet are interpreted as investments yet to be recovered or financing yet to be repaid. The emphasis is more on the cash that was invested and less on the certain types of goods that were obtained in return. Thus, the primary classification on the debit side of the balance sheet is based on the kinds of industries or projects in which investments were made, in a manner similar to identifiable assets in segmented reporting.

Assets classified by their physical properties may be useful for some purposes. But it seems far more important to classify them by the types of projects for which they were acquired.

Note that the historical cost principle is consistent with this view of the balance sheet. Unless assets are converted into cash or a cash equivalent, investment is considered unrecovered and is simply transferred from assets to assets.

A hierarchy of cash flows is created based on delegation of authority. Cash flow from investors to a corporation is an investment cash flow (debit) for the investor, while it is financing cash flow (credit) for the corporation. Cash flow from the corporation to its subsidiary is an investment cash flow for the corporation and is a financing cash flow for the subsidiary. The same chain relationship connects the items on the balance sheet between the subsidiary and one of its divisions, the division and a department, the department and a project, down to the lowest level in the cash flow hierarchy.

The income statement and the statement of changes in financial position (or funds statement) are replaced or at least supplemented by the cash flow statement, which summarizes cash flows during the year for both investment and financing cash flows. To accommodate the need for the conventional earnings measure, at least in transition, noncash items may be added to the cash flow statement to arrive at the earnings figure. But, such noncash items are clearly separated from the cash items included in the cash flow statement as a way of warning the reader that noncash items are generally more ambiguous, arbitrary, and subjective than cash items. Therefore, the reader who wants to substitute figures for these noncash items can do so.

Reporting budgeted or forecasted cash flows in cash flow statements is emphasized, together with some indication of the reliability of the forecasts made in the past by the same enterprise. Conventional classification of assets by the types of assets — for example, receivables, inventories, and fixed assets — is primarily used as a means of estimating the amount and timing of future cash flows. If so, direct forecasts by management familiar with more intricate factors of the management of its business can probably give better data.

Unlike noncash items, many of which are arbitrary and not verifiable, the accuracy of cash flow forecasts during the coming year can be verified a year later. An enterprise which makes a forecast that is consistently more optimistic than indicated by actual cash flows will not only have its forecasts discounted by investors but will also be looked upon as a poor planner.

The effects of inflation may be introduced in cash-flow accounting by means of a general price-level adjustment, using a price index which is indicative of the change in the general purchasing power of money.

Inflation is not just a change in commodity prices. Inflation occurs only when changes in commodity prices are so synchronized that they reduce the general purchasing power of money. Therefore, what needs to be adjusted in a past purchase of a plot of land for $100,000 is not the price of the land but the amount paid some years ago, so that this old cash flow is made comparable to current cash flows in terms of purchasing power.

In the hierarchy of cash flows previously mentioned, the investing side would not care whether the cash given to the lower echelon were invested in marketable securities, inventories, or fixed assets insofar as a certain amount of cash flows back to it. Cash recovery is of primary importance to the investor; the types of assets that are held by the lower echelon are only of secondary concern.

Thus, if we accept the view that cash flows are the key factor in business, general price-level adjustment should be the means of incorporating the effects of inflation, not replacement cost, which attempts to adjust the factor on the wrong side of the transaction.

Conclusion

Complex concepts and systems of information processing are certainly a sign of progress in science. They are, however, not necessarily of value in the art of management. On the contrary, in some areas of management, the virtue of simplicity stands out. Accounting may perhaps be one of such areas because it is a language of business to be used by a large number of people.

Some fundamental change in the direction of accounting is needed. The Financial Accounting Standards Board is in the process of establishing a conceptual framework for financial accounting. In this attempt, the FASB is indicating its willingness to consider a fundamental change in the nature of financial reports. Such an opportunity does not arise frequently. This is the time for us to seriously consider the foundation of business and its objective and then to develop an accounting system that responds to the need for data in business in the simplest and the most straightforward manner. Corporate recovery rate and cash flow accounting are steps toward this objective.

VII.

EXTERNAL
REPORTING
AND TAX

Financial and management accounting overlap in several circumstances. We just saw one possible overlap in the previous article, by Ijiri, where capital investment decisions and *cash* flows (managerial accounting) might be later evaluated, crudely, by financial accounting's *accrual* methods. As well, costing of work in process and finished goods of a manufacturing company and effects of the "cost" on other decisions has received attention from several authors, especially Greer ("Anyone for Widgets"). A third overlap occurs in the field of inflation, or changing price, accounting. Some financial accountants are obsessed with their version of objectivity and verifiability, whereas management needs the best information it can get — "subjective" if necessary.

"How One Financial Officer Uses Inflation-Adjusted Accounting Data" addresses the "changing price" topic overlap. The author ties the figures into judgments about "investment decisions," "pricing," "performance evaluation," and inventory costing.

"A Cash Flow Model for the Future" continues with Ijiri's theme in his Section VI article. The author, an academic, constructs cash basis financial statements using concepts such as contribution margin. Although the approach may seem impractical now, the article helps to focus on areas of difference between advocates of the "cash flow" and "accrual/allocations" schools of thought.

"An Activity Analysis Approach to Unit Costing with Multiple Interactive Products" could have been placed in several different sections of this book. On the one hand the article helps to remind us that many of the techniques described in textbooks are oversimplified. Hence, our learning/education process has to consist of deriving some general concepts or skills (e.g., diagnostic, analytical, judgment) from the textbook examples that we can use in the complex situations. On the other hand the article gives an interesting application of techniques that cross over several disciplines.

Traditional financial accounting articles have not been included in this book because they tend to be covered in financial accounting courses.

32

HOW ONE FINANCIAL OFFICER USES INFLATION-ADJUSTED ACCOUNTING DATA

KENNETH R. TODD, JR.*

A company can seriously misjudge its future performance if it relies sole-ly on historical cost accounting, because internal financial goals for oper-ating managers should be based on data adjusted for inflation.

Over the years, the controllership profession in the United States has played the leading role in using financial data within the corporation to manage operations. Our function has been to "tell it like it is" and to en-sure that the resulting data are used constructively by managers in our com-panies.

The rising rate of inflation over the past decade has eroded the accuracy of traditional performance measures and has implied favorable performance and growth records, both internally and externally, that in no way reflect the underlying economic and physical progress of the company.

Controllers in the U.S. face a formidable challenge in showing how to adapt our internal financial systems so as to avoid this misleading influ-ence of inflation on traditional profitability measurements.

In an inflationary environment, conventional historical accounting data have serious deficiencies for measuring internal operating profit perfor-mance. The accounting deficiencies have always been there; however, the degree of distortion from economic reality has increased measurably in the past decade with the high rate of inflation. These inadequacies essentially arise from matching costs from an earlier period with current revenues.

---

* From the *Financial Executive* (October 1982). Reprinted by permission. The author is Vice President and Controller, American Standard Inc.

This article was adapted from a speech given at an FEI seminar in Chicago, Ill., on April 13, 1982.

Since the mid-1970s, American-Standard has been modifying its financial measurements to eliminate the distortions and inequities of historical cost accounting. We have found that adjustments are necessary to understand and manage our worldwide businesses. The approach is especially suitable for our decentralized structure for managing our operations, which are essentially involved in manufacturing.

It has been said many times that accounting is the language of business used to communicate facts, events, and financial conditions to management and to the public. In a decentralized environment, in particular, it is important that there be a means to communicate goals and results from the top down and from the bottom up.

To communicate well, the internal financial reporting system must be designed to meet the essential responsibilities of corporate management, which include the following:

• Allocation of resources among the units, including capital resources and the time of management.

• Assessment of performance of operating units and operating management.

Corporate management should carry out these functions with an overall financial objective in mind. My company's objective is to attain a real, inflation-adjusted rate of return on assets sufficient to finance and expand our businesses and to offer above-average returns to shareholders. In attaining its objective, management has found it extremely helpful to incorporate inflation-adjusted performance measurements within the internal reporting system. To understand why, one needs to examine these problems with conventional measurements.

Corporate management develops specific goals so that operating management understands what is expected. Typically, these financially based goals include the following:

• Annual growth of "earnings."

• A return on book investment.

Recently, there has been growing debate about the appropriateness of some of the traditional financial goals. Many have pointed out that these goals can represent something far short of real performance in our inflationary environment. Some, such as Robert Cushman of Norton Company, have been extremely blunt about inflation's distorting impact on financial performance. In Norton's 1979 annual report, Mr. Cushman said, "Our growth is deceptive. Since 1971, 79 percent of our gains have resulted from inflation. At the current rate of inflation, Norton can stand absolutely still and become a $2 billion company in 5 years.

"Our financial performance is deceptive. Our 5-year growth in earnings is high by any standard. Yet if we keep this up, if our common stock price stays close to seven times earnings, and if we maintain a 6-percent dividend yield, shareholders will receive only a tiny return in constant dollars. And while our capital budget is now almost equal to our net earnings, it will have a difficult time keeping up with the highly inflated costs of new plant and equipment. The trouble with inflation is that it is an enemy masquerading as a friend. As it balloons our figures it makes us look good. We don't know whether to expose it or exploit it, and we end up doing both.

"So we as a company — and as individuals — must be honest with ourselves and with the public. We cannot accept reality on the one hand and talk a glowing future on the other. When it is inflation that pumps up our figures, we should acknowledge it and fight it. . . ."

The same distortions that can give false comfort in reporting financial results to the public can also lead to internal complacency in judging the performance of operating units. Worse yet, it can lead to wrong decisions. I will try to develop the reasons why we believe internal financial goals for operating managers should be based on data adjusted for inflation. Adopting these modifications gives corporate management the right incentives to encourage maximum asset utilization in its operations and the right tools for better economic decision-making.

Accounting distortions have more than academic interest, because important corporate decisions can be affected. There are at least three areas in which problems can arise if a corporation uses only historic cost accounting information in measuring performance:

Investment Decisions

A company will find that some of its divisions have higher return on book investment than others. This performance criterion is one factor considered in allocating capital resources. A considerable amount of the differences in return on book assets among units, however, can be merely a reflection of when a unit acquired its fixed assets. The unit that acquired its assets in the past at deflated dollars can look very good in today's terms when compared with a unit that acquired its fixed assets recently. It may be that the converse relation is actually true in terms of economic returns on new investments. Then too, units with high returns may be inhibited from making necessary new investments because they will depress the return on historical book assets. The internal accounting system should have incentives for management to make correct capital investment decisions.

By trying to maintain unrealistically high book returns, management can be inhibited from investing in the business. Book returns can lead management into a trap of "milking the business" and shying away from necessary replacements with new and better equipment and facilities.

Pricing

There are many factors influencing the pricing decision, but one key consideration is the cost of production. If the marketing department considers cost as the historical inventory cost, it can be deceived about the current profits generated from pricing decisions. "Frozen" standard costs can be a particularly misleading set of data, however useful for public reporting.

Operating management has to have an incentive to keep its pricing in line with current cost, and one incentive is to measure results using only the current cost of production.

Performance Evaluation

Management must evaluate a unit's performance, relative to both its own goals and to the other units in the corporation. Because of the differences in impact of inflation among units, it becomes difficult to compare operations using only historical cost information. The conventional accounting definition of "income" must be modified when trying to measure the performance of operating units to assure fair comparisons among units and *not* to reward management for inflationary effects.

Comparisons with competitor's financial results is also very difficult when using historical cost information, because inflation magnifies basic accounting policy differences, such as LIFO vs. FIFO inventory accounting and varying depreciation policies. Inflation-adjusted results are much more comparable because many of the distortions are eliminated.

An accounting system has to be designed in such a way that it will produce numbers needed for reporting to the shareholders and to various governmental authorities around the world. On top of these minimum requirements, a system must be added for attaining management's objectives and communicating within the corporation.

The design of the financial measurement system is the key role of the corporate controller. It is a challenge to his ingenuity and creativity to meet the needs in the most cost-effective manner, and no outside body such as the FASB or SEC can tell him how to do it. Measuring internal profits is strictly a consideration for top management and the controller.

Most of the elements of accounting systems designed for public reporting suit internal needs as well. In general, reporting of revenues, current expenses, cash and receivables, and liabilities is much the same for both internal and external purposes; a good match of costs and revenues occurs. However, the accounting system used for many of the other accounts must be modified substantially if the data are to meet management's previously discussed objectives.

Any management system must have a core concept that managers understand. American-Standard has adopted as its basic concept the maintenance of productive capacity — in other words, staying in business. We define operating income as the funds left over and available for expansion of the business after maintaining the productive capacity of our units and providing a minimum return to security holders. A unit at break-even (the minimum level of sustainable performance) has no funds left over for expanding its business or for distribution to other units. It has charged to current operations an amount sufficient to cover the replacement of the fixed assets and current cost of production, but it can only maintain the business at the current level.

With this in mind, four essential modifications will be examined to make the internal accounting systems meaningful, dealing with the following:

Inventory-Cost System

In the primary financial statements, the accounting profession still does not allow the corporation to completely match the current cost of production with current sales. All companies' reported results include an element of "inventory profit." Paper inventory profits arise from matching current revenue with the lower cost of production from an earlier time period and are essentially created by the effects of inflation. Companies using the LIFO system show considerably less inventory profit than companies on FIFO or average cost.

In no way do any of these profits represent performance by management, nor do they represent amounts that could be used by other divisions or distributed to security holders. To stay in business, a company must constantly provide for higher cost of production by matching current costs against comparable sales.

The accounting "profits" from higher inventory values must be retained just to maintain the business on its current level. We have found that it is beneficial to both executives and operating management to keep these paper profits completely out of our units' operating income. In the parlance of FAS 33, they are holding gains that will be realized only on liquidation.

Most manufacturing companies use some type of standard cost system for their inventories. There are varying principles used in standard costing: some favor actual cost at the beginning of the period, while others favor anticipating inflation in the cost of labor and materials. Those companies that freeze their standards to the cost levels that prevail before a year begins may find their standards potentially misleading to the marketing department. Many of our divisions have adopted indexing systems that provide this department with current standard costs adjusted for the impact of inflation.

Severing the Link — Balance Sheet/Income Statement

To get the most out of an internal accounting system, management accountants must sever the traditional link between the income statement and the balance sheet. One accounting principle may be appropriate in measuring income, and the converse may be appropriate in measuring a unit's financial condition. LIFO/FIFO inventory systems are a case in point. Clearly, LIFO matches current cost better with revenue, but the balance sheet result is meaningless, because the LIFO reserve is not a valuation reserve. So we should use FIFO cost for valuing inventories and LIFO for measuring income; the difference between net LIFO value and current cost really should be considered a part of stockholders' equity. Management should be held accountable for the FIFO inventory cost, and income should be measured on current cost of production.

Fixed Assets/Depreciation

The major inflation adjustment of conventional accounting data relates to depreciation, a technique for charging income for capital investments. With a zero rate of inflation, if we allocate the cost over life of the fixed asset correctly, we can achieve an approximate matching of this cost of doing business with revenue and be consistent with what economists would consider depreciation.

However, with inflation running at 10 percent, accounting depreciation differs materially from what economists would recognize as depreciation. Economists know that to stay in business, a company should retain profits at a rate sufficient to have funds on hand for functionally replacing manufacturing equipment and facilities at the end of their useful lives. If the company pays out the difference between historical and economic depreciation as dividends, it will have insufficient funds to replace the asset when needed, and many U.S. industries have done just that. The understatement of depreciation and overstatement of profits is a prime problem of U.S. industry today.

It does not matter that a replacement machine may have additional benefits in terms of lower production costs. Timing is what is critical; those reductions will take place after the investment has been made. What is important is that a company retain from current operations sufficient funds to replace its fixed assets before the fact, and charging income for realistic depreciation is how this is accomplished.

The machine does not literally have to be replaced in kind, because it is usual for technology to improve over time, but it has been our experience that the new equipment requires investment of the same order of magnitude as the replacement value of the old equipment.

Replacement depreciation has been criticized because it is not a precise calculation. Neither, of course, is historical depreciation, because it rests on assumptions concerning the timing of future replacement and the value of existing assets at that time.

The entire concept of depreciation is subject to much misinterpretation by both management and accountants. To understand the value of replacement depreciation, the nature of the profit to be measured should be considered. First, we assume we want to stay in business and that to do so will require spending capital over the years. In other words, capital expenditures are a cost of doing business. If we charge operations only for historical depreciation and pay out the profits as dividends, we will not be able to replace our plant and equipment and will eventually go out of business. By charging replacement depreciation, we are measuring a profit based on cash flows available for distribution.

Many people would like to escape the difficult task of assessing a realistic depreciation charge by looking at other measures such as "cash flow." But the problem can't be finessed so easily; capital investments need to be made just to stay in business.

Should one subtract capital expenditures from "cash flow" in considering what a unit's cash contribution has been? The answer, we believe, is not to use historical depreciation but to use replacement depreciation for measuring the income of internal operations. In this sense, inflation-adjusted profits are more in line with the cash flow of a business, which is one of the fundamental concepts of profit measurement.

Aside from being a better measure of income, replacement cost gives us a relative benchmark for comparison with capital spending plans. Historical depreciation is no longer a measure of whether capital spending is replacing the assets used in the business, but replacement depreciation gives an indication of whether a business is expanding or contracting.

Foreign Exchange Translation Accounting

Inflation's impact on depreciation and on the creation of inventory profits is well known, but the inflationary impact on international operations is more complicated. The differing rates of inflation from country to country create movements in foreign exchange rates.

Management must measure the foreign units on the same basis as domestic units, because management is making the same performance evaluation of both. Thus, it has to deal with their foreign exchange effects. Somehow, the accounting system must isolate foreign exchange effects from other aspects of business performance.

We have concluded that in a relatively stable currency environment, such as Europe, foreign exchange translation gains or losses should be excluded from operations, although normal foreign exchange gains or losses from operating transactions should be included in operating income.

For very soft-currency nations, such as Brazil, the usual dollar foreign exchange loss should be deducted from operating income so that the Brazilian unit has incentive to earn an economic profit. Recognizing the foreign exchange gain or loss on monetary items is akin to including the local currency monetary holding gain or loss of FAS 33 in income. FAS 52 now includes such gains or losses in the determination of income only for hyper-inflationary countries such as Brazil.

The Brazilian economy is an outstanding example of why management must adjust its accounts for inflation. A company can easily find itself out of business if it looks only at cruzeiro income before adjusting for inflation. The point is that a company using local indexes to "adjust for inflation" can end up with substantial losses on a U.S. dollar basis.

By adopting the modifications as described, management can make financial performance measurements more comparable among units and a better indication of a unit's actual cash generation, fostering the stability of measurement in an inflationary climate. Operating units can understand the underlying concept of staying in business as the basis for profit measurement.

The system provides an incentive for better asset utilization and eliminates any semblance of "paper" or "unreal" profits in operating results. The primary performance measurement is "operating income." It forms the basis for the return on net assets (RONA), which is calculated for each operating entity of American-Standard. RONA measures the longer-run profitability of each operation; operating income is a stand-alone figure used to plan and control operations. These numbers are not supplemental, but are part of the basic reporting package.

Operating Income represents the funds available after providing for the replacement cost of a pro-rata share of the productive capacity used; the current cost of inventory items sold; and the minimum return required for security holders (capital charge). In other words, a unit at breakeven has no funds left over for expanding its own business or for distribution to other units. Operating income excludes any upward revaluation of inventories and ignores any actual financing cost that may be on the books of the operation.

Net Assets are all assets of operations less current liabilities that are without financing cost. Inventories are carried at current standard costs and facilities at replacement cost less accumulated replacement depreciation. Use of current values allows return calculations to exclude the distortions caused by historical patterns of when assets were acquired and by differing depreciation policies. The liabilities to be deducted are those that are interest-free and of a nonfinancing nature, such as trade accounts payable and accrued liabilities.

RONA is operating income (before deducting capital charge) divided by net assets on a replacement basis; it measures the long-run profitability of the divisions. New capital expenditures are evaluated using discounted cash flows incrementally, but overall profitability of a unit is a consideration in the capital investment decision.

Inventory Accounting — Cost of goods is on a current cost basis, using standard costs and the immediate recognition of variances from standard. The annual revaluation to current standards is not reflected in operating income but is considered as a corporate item. Units employing average cost accounting remove from operating income the increase in inventory values attributable to inflation.

Replacement of Facilities and Replacement Depreciation — Operating income must include provision for replacing productive assets used in the business. Replacement values are generally computed on a current cost basis using indices acceptable for public reporting of inflation-adjusted results. Other systems have been tried, but the added cost of going beyond an indexing system is not matched by the benefit of more accurate replacement cost. Replacement depreciation is based on realistic estimates of the economic lives of the assets employed. Because of the lag in developing inflation-adjusted fixed-asset data, it is necessary to extrapolate each year's replacement values from data 2 years old, using estimates of the increase in replacement cost over the last two years.

There are a few instances in which replacement depreciation is not used. The exceptions are allowed only when an entire business will be abandoned or a unit's capacity utilization will be substantially decreased.

Capital Charge on Assets

The decision of where to borrow money is made by the corporation; therefore, the capital structure of each unit is not under the control of operating management. Actual interest expense should be considered a corporate item and not part of the operating income calculation. In its place is a capital charge based on the total net assets under the control of each unit.

A charge is recognized each month for the use of net assets by each division. The charge is applied to the replacement values of current assets and is based on the cost of capital to the corporation. The same rate is used for both foreign and domestic operations, because the choice of actual financing of each operation and its capital structure is a corporate decision. Currently, the rate charged is 12 percent of net assets on a current cost basis. The charge represents the opportunity cost of capital to the corportion and an allocation of all corporate charges.

Studies have concluded that the "real" cost of debt has been 1.5 to 3.0 percent per year, and that the "real" return on equity (dividend payout plus capital arising from retained earnings) has been about 6.5 percent, suggesting that equity carries a risk premium over debt of 4-5 percent. The studies have been from the perspective of the security holder. For the stockholder to realize 6.5 percent, the corporation must earn about 12 percent before taxes. With a debt/equity ratio of 20/80, a capital charge of 10 percent would equate to the average real return achieved in recent history by U.S. manufacturing companies. To this 10 percent is added corporate overhead of 2 percent, resulting in the 12-percent capital charge.

The rationale for the rate is that all units should be charged for the "cost of capital" free of inflation in a way consistent with the inflation adjustments incorporated in the rest of the financial reporting system.

A 12-percent charge is applied each month to replacement values of current assets, based on the cost of capital to the corporation. The same rate is used for both foreign and domestic operations and provides a powerful incentive for local managements to manage their assets effectively.

An operating income of zero, after a 12-percent capital charge, represents what in the past has been average industry performance. It is viewed as the minimum acceptable sustainable level of performance. If a company records an average performance, that is, zero operating income, it will be able to sustain real growth of 3-4 percent. Positive operating income implies outperforming the industry average and, of course, higher real growth rates.

Because of computational difficulties, the arbitrary nature of allocations, the conceptual difficulties as to what constitutes a tax expense, and the problems of comparability with competitors, use of pretax operating income in the financial measurement system is preferable to trying to adjust operating profits for taxes paid. As long as pretax benchmarks are kept in mind, the advantages of using pretax operating income far outweigh those of using an arbitrary aftertax approach, which must oversimplify complex interrelationships.

The RONA concept can be related to several measures of importance:

* A company's RONA, and therefore each of its division's RONAs, bears a direct relationship to the potential for expanding productive capacity.
* The division's RONA can be compared with the performance of publicly held companies that show inflation-adjusted results. The pretax inflation-adjusted results all follow similar accounting conventions, so that results on an inflation-adjusted basis are quite comparable.

Management is expected to discuss the trends affecting its business, and this can prove quite difficult in an inflationary environment. Looking at historical sales, we might assume a business is growing, when the underlying trend is actually continued volume decline. The culprit is inflation, as price increases keep the sales trend tilted upward. We now find it most convenient to stay with a constant dollar measurement in looking at financial data over the years; the data are more representative of physical changes in our business units.

Looking ahead, we can consider in each case whether the market will allow recovery of cost increases. Display of data in today's dollars permits discussion of substantive business issues. For sales, for instance, we can observe the overall trend — if down, inquire into the basic market, our market share, and the product mix within the market. The essential point is that showing data in today's dollars gives a better description of the trend than using nominal dollars, and it allows management to discuss more substantive issues.

Conclusion

Inflation complicates the task of using accounting data constructively in running business units. Historical accounting numbers can give false comfort and lead to wrong decisions. Incorporating inflation adjustments requires additional work, but it allows for a system that encourages the generation of real profits in an inflationary environment. At American-Standard, we've found that incorporating these inflation adjustments in our internal measurement system has been well worth the effort.

33

A CASH FLOW
MODEL
FOR THE
FUTURE
WILLIAM L. FERRARA*

A workable cash flow financial reporting system definitely is within reach — but will traditionally conservative accountants buy it?

The economic impact of financial reporting standards plus the notion of a required consistency between decision models and financial reporting are pushing us inevitably toward a greater cash flow orientation in financial reporting. Some accountants still resist this cash flow trend because of the profession's traditionally strong predisposition toward accrual accounting, but the two reasons above may ultimately change their minds.

To illustrate the cash flow concept, I have set up a cash flow counterpart to each of the traditional accrual accounting financial statements. Included are a cash flow version of the income statement, balance sheet, and "funds flow" statement. Attention is given to segments of the firm as well as to the total firm, and appropriate distinctions are made among operating flows, invested capital flows and financing flows.

Yuji Ijiri put the whole issue in perspective when he said:

> There has been a serious discrepancy between the way in which investment decisions are made and the way in which results of the decisions are evaluated.
>
> In investment decisions the primary factor is cash flow . . . In performance evaluation the emphasis shifts to earnings . . . The two . . . are often not reconcilable . . .

---

* From *Management Accounting* (June 1981). Copyright © 1981 by the National Association of Accountants. All rights reserved. The author is an academician.

Therefore, either investment decisions should be based on earnings or performance evaluation should be based on cash flow. The choice is rather obvious, because the primary objective of a business enterprise is cash flow. *Earnings is only a surrogate to represent performance of the enterprise on this cash flow objective. And if earnings do not tell how well a project or a division or a corporation is doing in terms of cash flow, then the concept and measurement of earnings has to be changed.* (Emphasis supplied).[1]

I tend to agree with Ijiri. For example, ". . . before we try to promulgate rules concerning accounting for a specific transaction we ought to understand the decision model and related economic factors behind that transaction. The ultimate . . . should be: Financial reporting practices for specific transactions should be consistent with decision models underlying such transactions."[2]

"Thus, there is really no choice but to convert performance evaluation from accrual accounting to cash flow accounting. Otherwise, we will put managers in the intolerable position of making decisions one way and having their performance evaluated another way."[3]

Because of this dilemma we ought to be somewhat amenable to experimentation with cash flow financial reporting. I have prepared a complete set of suggested cash flow reports, including a revised balance sheet and income statement, which I will explain. At this time, the only thought is that these reports can be a useful adjunct to today's accrual reports. Tomorrow — who knows? Given the number of people concerned about and working on the cash flow ideology, there may be sufficient refinement and unanimity to mandate a greater cash flow orientation in financial reporting.

A Cash Flow Income Statement

Table 1 contains a cash flow counterpart to the accrual income statement. Note that both the total corporation as well as segments of the corporation are included. Also note that the direct costing ideology is included via the distinction between fixed and variable costs. An additional point to note is the distinction between "identifiable costs" and "corporate costs" similar to FAS No. 14, "Financial Reporting for Segments of a Business Enterprise."

A casual scrutiny of Table 1 might suggest that the only adjustment to the accrual income statement is to disregard depreciation as a cost. The following adjustments also ought to be considered, however:

---

[1] Yuji Ijiri, "Recovery Rate and Cash Flow Accounting," *Journal of Accounting, Auditing and Finance,* Summer 1978, pp. 331-348.
[2] William L. Ferrara, "Decision Models, Financial Reporting, Accounting Research and Accounting Education — Some Interactions," *DR Scott Memorial Lectures 1979-80,* School of Accountancy, University of Missouri-Columbia.
[3] William L. Ferrara, "Accounting for Performance Evaluation and Decision-Making," *Management Accounting,* December 1976.

1. Inventories on hand as well as in the hands of customers ought to be valued at variable cost. Thus sales for the period would include only sales for which cash has been collected. Accounts receivable in the traditional sense would become a parenthetical note attached to inventories in the hands of customers valued at variable cost.[4]
2. With regard to payables, Ijiri's "constructive cash flow" notion should be implemented so that assets acquired with debt will be considered to be acquired via a simultaneous cash inflow from borrowing and a cash outflow to acquire an asset. As stated by Ijiri,[5] this should draw a necessary distinction between cash flow accounting (especially as recommended here) and the cash basis of accounting, which is strictly based on cash receipts and disbursements.[6]
3. The distinction between corporate and identifiable fixed costs indicates a strong desire to maintain an allocation-free accounting framework.
4. Certain specific elements of cost ought to be spelled out by giving them line item status within the fixed and variable cost categories. A specific case in point is research and development costs, and perhaps even exploration and drilling costs in the case of natural resource companies.

Cash Flow Invested Capital and ROI

Invested capital on a cash flow basis is illustrated in Table 2. Both property, plant and equipment and working capital are shown at cost. If desired, current assets could be portrayed by including current liabilities among "financing data" (see Table 6). Also, investments in affiliates and unconsolidated subsidiaries could be included at cost, with operating flows included on a constructive or actual cash flow basis in Table 1 and financing flows included among "financing data."

Table 3 shows how one could combine the operating flows of Table 1 and the invested capital of Table 2 into a "return on investment" report by segment and total system. These ROIs are what Ijiri refers to as the "recovery rate." Keep in mind that the "total invested capital — at cost" denominator in the ROI calculation could be based on some form of monthly, quarterly or annual average.

Ijiri used the ROI or "recovery rate" creatively. He first identified the "recovery rate" as the reciprocal of the payback period and then, in effect implicitly assuming the cumulative present value factor is the payback period (stable recovery rate), he estimated the discounted cash flow (DCF) rate or internal rate of return. As he pointed out, this procedure can be done

---

[4] Certain types of income manipulation would be eliminated by this adjustment.
[5] Yuji Ijiri, "Cash Flow Accounting and Its Structure," *Journal of Accounting, Auditing and Finance*, Summer 1978, pp. 331-348.
[6] Some (not the author) might argue for "constructive cash flows" with regard to sales and receivables, which would result in values for inventories in the hands of customers at sales price. This would yield a cash flow concept essentially the same as the more traditional funds flow concept.

easily at the project and corporate level (presumably also the segment level) as long as one is willing to venture assumptions concerning stability of the recovery rate and estimates of the average economic life of projects.[7]

Table 1   Annual Operating Cash Flow Report

| | Total system | Segments | |
		A	B
Sales	$65,000	$35,000	$30,000
Variable costs	29,000	16,000	13,000
Margin over variable costs	$36,000	$19,000	$17,000
Identifiable fixed costs (excluding depr.)	15,000	8,500	6,500
Segment flow	$21,000	$10,500	$10,500
Corporate fixed costs (excluding depr.)	5,000		
Net flow	$16,000		

Table 2   Beginning-of-Year Invested Capital Report

| | Total system | Segment | | Corporate |
		A	B	
Working capital	$ 35,000	$17,000	$13,000	$ 5,000
Property, plant and equipment — at cost	110,000	50,000	40,000	20,000
Total invested capital — at cost	$145,000	$67,000	$53,000	$25,000

Table 3   Annual Operating Cash Flow ROI Data

| | Total system | Segments | |
		A	B
Segment flow	$ 21,000	$10,500	$10,500
Segment capital (at cost)	120,000	67,000	53,000
Segment ROI	17.5%	15.7%	19.8%
Net flow	$ 16,000		
Total invested capital (at cost) — BOY*	145,000		
Net ROI	11.0%		

* Beginning-of-year

---

[7] Yuji Ijiri, 1978, *Op. Cit.*

I am uncomfortable with all this attention to ROI, recovery rate or DCF rate at the project or segment level, however. The strategic planning process seems to require that ROI be considered relevant only at a level of aggregation which may be at the corporate or total system level.[8] In addition, the recovery of invested capital as well as the return on invested capital or ROI must be discussed. Capital recovery must be addressed in any meaningful cash flow system.

Table 4 Annual Capital Charge and Capital Recovery

Net flow		$16,000
Capital charge		
Total invested capital (at cost) — BOY	$145,000	
Less capital recovered — BOY	20,000	
Net invested capital — BOY	$125,000	
Desired ROI	10%	12,500
Capital recovered for the year		$ 3,500

Capital Recovery and Net Invested Capital

A number of authors already have dealt with the issue of discounted cash flow decision making versus accrual accounting for performance evaluation. Their recommended solution was the adoption of annuity depreciation methods which brought the discounted cash flow technology and accrual accounting into agreement. Unfortunately, however, their illustrations essentially were based upon single asset firms and did not describe how the annuity depreciation method could be applied to the normal multi-asset firm.

I also recommend the annuity depreciation method, but only at the corporate or total systems level. This procedure avoids the aforementioned difficulties of ROI at the project and segment level plus the impossible allocation problem with regard to attributing actual cash flows to individual projects and segments.

Annuity depreciation, as defined here, involves the recovery of capital costs rather than allocation per accrual accounting. Annuity depreciation addresses the issue of how much of your investment you have recovered in cash over and above some desired ROI rate.

Table 4 illustrates the calculations involved using the corporate or total systems data of Tables 1 and 2 and a desired ROI of 10%. By combining the invested capital data of Table 2 plus any changes in invested capital during the year and the capital recovery data of Table 4, we can produce an end-of-year invested capital report (Table 5) which shows invested capital at cost as well as net capital recovery to date. Table 5 literally becomes the cash flow version of the asset side of the balance sheet.

[8] See William L. Ferrara, 1980, *Op. Cit.* pp. 17-21.

With regard to capital recovery in Table 4, the determination of a desired ROI rate deserves some mention. Theoretically it should conform to the firm's cost of capital, however determined. Pragmatically it also could be at minimum the prime rate or the prime rate plus a few points to allow for risk. Whichever approach is taken at this experimental stage, data should be detailed enough so that analysts can use their own notion of a desired ROI rate.

A final point to mention with regard to invested capital and capital recovery is the treatment of asset trade-ins and dispositions. Consistent with the cash flow approach and the calculation of capital recovery on a total system basis only, I recommend a treatment similar to composite or group depreciation with no recognition of gains or losses on trade-in or disposition. Assets should be removed from asset accounts at original cost and cash or other value received upon disposition should be removed from the "capital recovery account."

Table 5   End-of-Year Invested Capital Report

	Total system	Segments A	B	Corporate
Working capital — BOY	$ 35,000	$17,000	$13,000	$ 5,000
± Increases or decreases	3,000	1,000	2,000	-0-
Working capital — EOY*	$ 38,000	$18,000	$15,000	$ 5,000
Property, plant and equipment — BOY	$110,000	$50,000	$40,000	$20,000
± Increases or decreases	25,000	5,000	15,000	5,000
Property, plant and equipment — EOY	$135,000	$55,000	$55,000	$25,000
Total invested capital (at cost) — EOY	$173,000	$73,000	$70,000	$30,000
Capital recovered — BOY	$ 20,000			
± Increases or decreases	3,500			
Capital recovered — EOY	$ 23,500			
Net invested capital — EOY	$149,500			

* End-of-year

Equity or Financing Data

Table 6 presents the equity side of the cash flow balance sheet. Note that it is in agreement with Table 5, which pointedly illustrates that assets can still equal equities in a cash flow framework.

The statement of equity or long-term financing consists of both a long-term debt element and a stockholders' equity element. Stockholders' equity, as illustrated, is composed of "paid-in capital" and "retained capital charges," which is the sum of annual capital charges shown in Table 4 less interest and dividends. A favorable balance in both retained capital charges and capital recovered to date would indicate that the firm's cash flows have been sufficient to earn a desired ROI rate in excess of dividends and interests, which is as it should be if a stockholder hopes to ultimately receive a capital gain on his investment.

As is the case in accrual accounting, "gains or losses" on capital stock transactions would be confined to the paid-in capital account(s). Gains or losses on long-term debt, however, would be regarded as adjustments of interest costs previously included in the determination of retained capital charges.

Table 6   End-of-Year Long-Term Financing Data

Long-term debt − BOY	$ 50,000
± Increases or decreases	10,000
Long-term debt − EOY	$ 60,000
Stockholders' equity	
Paid-in capital − BOY	$ 40,000
± Increases or decreases	10,000
Paid-in capital − EOY	$ 50,000
Retained capital charges − BOY	$ 35,000
± Capital charge for the year	12,500
− Interest	(5,000)
− Dividends	(3,000)
Retained capital charges − EOY	$ 39,500
Stockholders' equity − EOY	$ 89,500
Total long-term financing − EOY	$149,500

Table 7   Annual Cash Flow Summary

	Total system	Segments A	Segments B	Corporate
Cash inflows				
Operations	$16,000	$10,500	$10,500	$(5,000)
Invested capital				
Reduction in working capital	-0-	-0-	-0-	-0-
Sale of property, plant and equipment	-0-	-0-	-0-	-0-
Long-term financing				
Sale of debt	10,000	-0-	-0-	10,000
Sale of stock	10,000	-0-	-0-	10,000
Total inflow	$36,000	$10,500	$10,500	$15,000
Cash outflows				
Invested capital				
Increase in working capital	$ 3,000	$ 1,000	$ 2,000	-0-
Purchase of property, plant, and equipment	25,000	5,000	15,000	5,000
Long-term financing				
Retirement of debt	-0-	-0-	-0-	-0-
Retirement of stock	-0-	-0-	-0-	-0-
Interest	5,000	-0-	-0-	5,000
Dividends	3,000	-0-	-0-	3,000
Total outflow	$36,000	$ 6,000	$17,000	$13,000

Annual Cash Flow Summary

A summary of all cash flows is contained in Table 7. Note that the cash flows are categorized into operating, invested capital, and long-term financing flows. This summary is the cash flow counterpart to the "funds statement" of traditional accounting.

Now that the complete cash flow package has been discussed and illustrated, let us consider how one might evaluate the progress of the firm and its segments using such cash flow concepts.

Performance Evaluations at the Segment Level

At the segment level, cash flow evaluations could proceed via the Ijiri ROI approach discussed earlier although segment ROIs present a host of difficulties. First there is the problem of allocating corporate costs and corporate assets to segments in order to make segment ROIs comparable to corporate ROIs. But allocations become arbitrary, so it is best to avoid them — thus making segment ROIs free of allocations.

Second, even allocation-free segment ROIs are questionable in the context of the strategic planning process. Strategic planning addresses a portfolio of segments wherein one measures "cash in vs. cash out." Segments in which we invest cash — cash users — are potential high growth segments in which one hopes to obtain a high market share by investing heavily in research and development, advertising and promotion, and facilities. The payoff in such expenditures is in the future when the segment no longer needs expenditures because growth has peaked and the former cash user becomes a cash generator. This cash generator then becomes the source of cash for new cash users as the process of corporate life continues to spawn new segments to replace the old and dying which, interestingly, provide the sustenance (cash) to develop the new and growing.

Table 8   Some Typical Ratios

Net flow percentage	×	Net invested capital turnover	×	Financial leverage	=	Return on stockholders' equity
$\dfrac{\text{Net flow}}{\text{Sales}}$	×	$\dfrac{\text{Sales}}{\text{Net invested capital}}$	×	$\dfrac{\text{Net invested capital}}{\text{Stockholders' equity}}$	=	21.3%
$\dfrac{16{,}000}{65{,}000}$	×	$\dfrac{65{,}000}{125{,}000}$	×	$\dfrac{125{,}000}{75{,}000}$	=	21.3%

The use of ROI at the segment level would make a cash-using segment look bad and a cash-generating segment look extremely good. In such a case, ROI (and even accrual income) may force such a short-range view onto management that cash users may never be turned into cash generators and our old and dying cash generators may be viewed as such high "profit" producers that they deserve all of our investable resources.

At the segment level, evaluations should be in terms of cash in vs. cash out as shown in the segment columns of Table 7. Furthermore, the segment operating flows ought to be spelled out in sufficient detail that such items as research and development and advertising and promotion are line items. Then one can evaluate a cash user in terms of how well it is proceeding on the road to becoming a substantive cash generator. Similarly, one then can evaluate a cash generator in terms of how effectively cash is being generated. In both cases, five years of historical (budgeted vs. actual) data plus five years of projected data in terms of cash flows and market share should be the predominant means of evaluation.

Cash Flow Performance Evaluations at the Total System Level

At the total system or corporate level, financial evaluations could be generated by Ijiri's ROI approach, especially if one could empirically rationalize an average corporate recovery rate and an average economic life for capital expenditure projects.[9]

The system I have described, however, seems intuitively preferable because it allows for both a return of capital (capital recovery) and a return on capital (capital charge or desired ROI). The main difficulty is with regard to determining the desired ROI rate. At this stage I would recommend the prime rate or the prime rate plus, say, 2% in order to judge whether or not the total system is yielding a return that a stockholder should regard as the minimum and still be able to cover interest and dividend payments.[10]

Additional aspects of the evaluation scheme could be an ROI based on the net flow ($16,000) of Table 1 and the net invested or unrecovered capital at the beginning of the year, shown in Table 5 ($125,000), which is $16,000/$125,000 or 12.8%. This scheme could be refined further by a return on stockholders' equity of Table 6, which is $16,000/$75,000 or 21.3%. Actually, using the net flow of Table 1 and other data from Tables 1, 5 and 6, one can generate all the typical ratios of accounting as shown in Table 8. One also could use average balances rather than beginning or end-of-year balances.

Our financial evaluation now relates to capital charges being able to consistently cover interest and dividend payments by some norm amount and the steadiness (and perhaps increase) of the components of and total return

---

[9] Through the use of cash flow projections for, say, the next five years, one even could use Ijiri's system to project the upper limit to the corporate DCF rate.
[10] The prime rate should be before tax as we are concerned about a before-tax return to the stockholder. Somewhat related is my preference to treat income taxes as corporate costs because of a desire to avoid allocations.

on stockholders' equity. Ideologically we have retained a good deal of traditional accounting. The main substantive change is to a cash flow system.

Cash Flow and Inflation Accounting

The cash flow system just described should make it much easier to account for the ravages of inflation. All assets are dated and carried at original cost, and capital recovery, financing data and operating flows are dated. The net result, then, is an ability to speak of net invested capital or assets as the unrecovered price level adjusted historical cost in terms of cash flows. Even the gain or loss on monetary items should present no difficulty.

Because we speak of *unrecovered cost* rather than *value*,[11] we have no problem with general price level indices vs. specific price level indices vs. replacement cost vs. current value. Staying strictly with the notion of cash flows and the hopeful recovery of more than was invested, we can focus our attention on the general level of prices and cash flow measured in terms of general purchasing power.

The case has been made for a greater cash flow orientation to financial reporting, which, again, moves us toward the basic objective of business — cash flow and recovering more than was invested. A consistency between decision models and financial reporting also is attained.

The cash flow system described contains the cash flow counterpart to all the financial reports of traditional accounting. A complete set of cash flow ratios was described for the corporate or total system level while reports were designed to fit the strategic planning process at the segment level. Even inflation accounting was accommodated.

Now we need some empirical experimentation designed to address the real-world applicability of the system. Given the number of accounting academicians and practitioners involved in exploring the cash flow ideology, I am convinced that a workable cash flow financial reporting system is within reach, and it may very well be quite similar to the one I described.

---

[11] I favor *unrecovered cost* rather than *value* because I am very concerned with accountability, auditability and objectivity. Nonetheless, it is not too difficult to appreciate at least some aspects of the arguments put forth by those who favor a *value* approach.

34

AN ACTIVITY ANALYSIS APPROACH TO UNIT COSTING WITH MULTIPLE INTERACTIVE PRODUCTS

HIROYUKI ITAMI and ROBERT S. KAPLAN*

Average variable costs are not directly defined for multiple products produced in complex production settings. An activity analysis model can be used for basic cost measurement and for building a linear programming model of manufacturing operations. The model can then be used not only to compute the optimal production plan and associated marginal costs but also to assign average costs to final products. The activity analysis framework enables many overhead costs, such as maintenance, overtime, shift premiums, and indirect labor and materials, to be treated within the model. Thus, they are absorbed directly into the cost of final products rather than allocated indirectly through an overhead charge.

Three average costing methods based on sacrifice value (marginal costs) and benefit value (marginal revenue) of products are considered. The method based entirely on the market value of products has less desirable properties than allocation methods which use the dual variables (marginal costs) from the programming model. Another benefit is that various cost allocation methods using input-output analysis can be considered as special cases of average costing methods presented in this paper.

* Reprinted by permission from *Management Science* (Volume 26, #8, August 1980, pp. 826-839). Copyright © 1980, The Institute of Management Sciences. The authors are academicians.

1. Introduction

Most traditional cost accounting treatments of product costing deal with extremely simple production processes (Horngren [3, Chapters 4, 9, and 10]); (Shillinglaw [9, Chapters 4-7]). A product is assumed to be produced from a unique set of material and labor inputs and processed in a straightforward way through a sequence of machines or departments. In such cases, it is not hard to estimate the variable costs of production and the only controversial issue is whether fixed costs, associated with using the capacity resources of the firm, should be unitized and counted as part of the product's costs. In many situations, however, the production process is far more complicated. A firm may have different types of machines, each capable of producing the same product. Each machine type may require different amounts of input material, labor quantity and quality, and machine time to produce the same output. Another complication arises with joint products in which a common input factor yields many different types of output in fixed proportions. Also different products may compete for scarce machine time so that an opportunity cost is incurred any time a product is processed on the machine. Finally, many components of variable overhead, such as electricity, maintenance, supervision, and overtime, may be more accurately traced to use of specific resources rather than varying proportionately with some aggregate level of activity such as direct labor costs or machine hours. For these more complicated and generally more realistic production situations it is not possible to compute a unique variable cost associated with each output product.

Even if unique variable costs could be computed, they would be misleading because of the constrained and interdependent production processes. The objective is not to maximize sales of high contribution margin products but rather to maximize sales of products which have the maximum contribution margin per unit of scarce resource consumed. With many scarce resources in a department, such profitability measures are not easily computed. While in principle we could envision solving large linear programs describing the firm's production possibilities each time product costs or optimal product mixes were needed, in practice there may be implementation issues caused by a variety of factors which would make such a scheme impractical.

In this paper we develop a model for deriving product costs for such complex production processes. A production planning model (PPM) which generates optimal production schedules based on the different production activities and processes is assumed. Various average cost schemes are derived from the production model and their properties investigated. Thus one objective of this paper is to compute a figure which, taking into account the nature of the production opportunities, can be viewed as the "average" variable cost of each product. Such a figure may enable managers to get a better feel for the cost and hence the profitability of various products without having to get immersed in complex production models. In effect, we are attempting to generate summary cost data which we believe can provide useful information for managers. The information is useful in the sense that a manager can treat the average cost data using simplified decision models rather than having to be concerned with the full complexity of the production and sales opportunity set.[1]

Besides this admittedly imprecise motivation for a simple aggregate cost figure, there are other reasons for deriving average variable product costs. Firms which attempt production smoothing throughout the year will occasionally be producing in excess of immediate sales requirements. Thus there is a need to compute a cost figure for inventory valuation and income measurement purposes. If some or all of the products in a department are sold on a "cost-plus" pricing basis, there is an obvious need to compute product costs. An advantage of the proposed scheme is that many costs such as overtime, shift premiums, maintenance, and traceable utility charges, which usually are included in a general factory overhead category, can be accounted for directly.

The increased intrusion of government, regulatory agencies, and private anti-trust cases into what were formerly the internal affairs of a company creates an external demand for defensible product-line cost information. The pricing policies and product line profitability of many firms have come under close scrutiny by legislators, regulators, and the general public. There appears to be an increasing demand for firms to cost-justify their price increases. Federal Trade Commission requirements for very detailed product-line reporting may require computing individual product costs. Such a computation is not trivial when products in different reporting categories share the same production facilities or are derived from common input materials. Finally, in conspiracy, price discrimination and price-fixing litigation, a great deal of attention is paid to *the* costs of producing various products. In all these situations, investigators are unlikely to be dissuaded from their search by protestations that product costs are hard to measure or indeterminate. Thus a variety of internal and external forces may be operating which makes the computation of a reasonable and defensible average variable cost figure a useful exercise. We will examine some of the possibilities in the remainder of this paper.

Before introducing the basic production model, we should indicate that we will work with a deterministic environment in which technology parameters, production constraints, and sales opportunities are known for certain. A simpler production environment but with demand and production parameter uncertainty is discussed in Itami [5] where the emphasis is to determine the value of timely information. Ultimately, these two approaches could be synthesized to demonstrate the value of providing approximate cost data derived from a simple aggregate and deterministic production model to a manager attempting to optimize profits in the presence of demand or production uncertainty. This possibility will be discussed later, but

---

[1] Our approach is similar in spirit to the use of an average cost-based transfer price scheme for divisional autonomy as developed in Ronen and McKinney [8].

for the analytic development in this paper we will restrict ourselves to a deterministic setting that will highlight the issues involved when attempting to compute average variable costs in a multi-product, multi-resource production environment.

2. Activity Analysis Model

We assume that the firm's production possibilities can be described by a sequence of activities. An activity is an operation or transformation of a set of inputs into one or more outputs. Activities include acquisitions of commodities and services from other entities, internal operations within an entity, and dispositions of commodities and services out of the entity or their transformation into monetary items. Cost measurement is done on the basis of activities not on the products or services produced by these activities.

Each activity is defined by a set of relations which relate the amount of inputs consumed to the amount of output produced by the activity. An activity might be the operation of a particular machine which, for each hour of operation, uses a given amount of raw material and labor to produce a given amount of one or more products. The firm makes choices among a number of activities and operates the selected activities at given levels in order to achieve a profit-maximizing or cost-minimizing schedule. With this view of production, the quantities of inputs and outputs of the firm are determined by the levels of the activities (see Koopmans [6] and Staubus [10] for extensive treatments of activity analysis and activity costing).

Initially, we assume that the production department is given an $m \times 1$ vector, $\bar{\mathbf{x}}$, of demands for outputs. Its objective is to meet the demanded production at minimum cost. The department has n activities which convert input factors into outputs. Let z_j be the level of activity j ($j = 1, \ldots, n$). For each activity j, there is a set of coefficients p_{ij}, $i = 1, \ldots, m$, where p_{ij} is the amount of output i produced by each unit of operation of activity j. If $\mathbf{z}$ is the $n \times 1$ vector of activity levels, and $\mathbf{P} = |p_{ij}|$ is the $m \times n$ Production Rate Matrix, then $\mathbf{Pz}$ is the vector of outputs. To satisfy the demand constraints, $\mathbf{Pz} \geqslant \bar{\mathbf{x}}$.

The firm has k capacity resources (machine time, floor space, scarce raw materials) which cannot be increased in the short run and each unit of activity j uses up b_{ij} units of resources i, $i = 1, \ldots, k$. Therefore, if $\mathbf{B} = |b_{ij}|$, and $\mathbf{d}$ is the $k \times 1$ vector of available capacity resources, we have $\mathbf{Bz} \leqslant \mathbf{d}$. For input, or variable, resources, let a_{ij} be the amount of input i, $i = 1, \ldots, l$, used by each unit of operation of activity j so that, with $\mathbf{A} = |a_{ij}|$, $\mathbf{Az}$ is the $l \times 1$ vector of inputs used when operating at activity level $\mathbf{z}$. If $\mathbf{c}$ is the $1 \times l$ vector of unit input prices for the l variable input factors, the variable cost of operating at level $\mathbf{z}$ is given by $\mathbf{cAz}$.

We summarize the above discussion in the following Production Planning Model (PPM):

$$\min \theta = \mathbf{cAz}$$
$$\text{s.t. } \mathbf{Pz} \geqslant \bar{\mathbf{x}}, \qquad\qquad \text{(PPM)}$$
$$\mathbf{Bz} \leqslant \mathbf{d},$$
$$\mathbf{z} \geqslant \mathbf{0}.$$

For later reference, we present the dual to PPM:

$$\max \mathbf{v\bar{x}} - \mathbf{wd}$$
$$\text{s.t. } \mathbf{vP} - \mathbf{wB} \leqslant \mathbf{cA},$$
$$\mathbf{v}, \mathbf{w} \geqslant \mathbf{0}.$$

The dual vector $\mathbf{v}$ represents the shadow prices associated with having to meet the specified production goal of $\bar{\mathbf{x}}$ and the vector $\mathbf{w}$ represents the shadow prices of the k capacity resources.

To illustrate these points, consider a department with two output products, three production activities, and one supporting activity called maintenance. There are six inputs: labor and materials for Product 1; labor and materials for Product 2; labor and materials for maintenance. The cost vector, $\mathbf{c}$, for these inputs is given by

$$\mathbf{c} = (1, 2, 2.5, 1, 1.2, 1).$$

The input usage matrix, A, is given by

$$A = \begin{bmatrix} 2.5 & 4 & 0 & 0 \\ 5 & 8 & 0 & 0 \\ 0 & 0 & 1 & 0 \\ 0 & 0 & 1.5 & 0 \\ 0 & 0 & 0 & 1 \\ 0 & 0 & 0 & .2 \end{bmatrix}$$

Each column in A represents an activity and each row represents a variable input factor. The variable costs of operating the four activities are given by the vector $\mathbf{cA} = [12.5, 20, 4, 1.4]$.

The production rate matrix, P, is given by

$$P = \begin{bmatrix} 1 & 1 & -0.5 & 0 \\ 0 & 0 & 1 & 0 \end{bmatrix}.$$

The three production activities do not have joint products but the third activity requires 0.5 units of product 1 to produce 1 unit of product 2. The fourth column has two zeroes since the maintenance activity does not produce any outputs.

We assume that the desired output from the department is 100 units of product 1 and 200 units of product 2. The demand constraints are therefore:

$$
\begin{bmatrix}
1 & 1 & -0.5 & 0 \\
0 & 0 & 1 & 0
\end{bmatrix}
\begin{bmatrix}
z_1 \\ z_2 \\ z_3 \\ z_4
\end{bmatrix}
\geq
\begin{bmatrix}
100 \\ 200
\end{bmatrix}.
$$

The constraints imposed by the capacity resources on the levels of the activities are given by $\mathbf{Bz} \leq \mathbf{d}$:

$$
\begin{bmatrix}
1 & 1.5 & 0 & 0 \\
2 & 1 & 0 & 0 \\
0 & 0 & 1 & 0 \\
0.1 & 0.15 & 0.05 & -1
\end{bmatrix}
\begin{bmatrix}
z_1 \\ z_2 \\ z_3 \\ z_4
\end{bmatrix}
\leq
\begin{bmatrix}
350 \\ 300 \\ 300 \\ 20
\end{bmatrix}
$$

The first three rows correspond to the use of three machines and the fourth row determines the maintenance requirement. The department is budgeted 20 units of maintenance activity supplied at zero incremental cost. Essentially, this represents a fixed cost associated with a minimal standby maintenance capability. Operation of each activity generates a linear demand for maintenance. If this demand exceeds the 20 unit allotment, additional maintenance is supplied at an incremental cost determined by elements in the $\mathbf{c}$ and $\mathbf{A}$ matrices. This constraint illustrates how overtime or other semivariable overhead costs are treated in PPM. In general, there is no requirement that the $\mathbf{B}$ matrix be square.

The objective of the department is to select optimal levels of its four activities to minimize variable costs, $\mathbf{cAz} = 12.5z_1 + 20z_2 + 4z_3 + 1.4z_4$, subject to the above two sets of constraints.

The PPM determines the optimal production plan for any given (feasible) demand of final products, $\bar{\mathbf{x}}$. The general structure of PPM encompasses a wide variety of production possibilities including joint products, intermediate products, and overtime (see Itami [5, pp. 75-76]). Thus the activity analysis model, PPM, provides a general setting for describing the firm's production opportunities. While the linearity assumption within each activity may seem restrictive, decreasing returns to scale caused by use of less efficient labor and capital or multiple shift operation are easily incorporated by defining separate activities for each class of labor, capital, and shift operation. Using a well-known result from linear programming theory, the minimum total cost, θ^0, in PPM will be a convex, piece-wise linear, increasing function of $\bar{\mathbf{x}}$, the production goal. Therefore, the marginal costs of increasing production will not be constant as traditionally assumed in the cost accounting literature. Rather, marginal costs will be increasing step functions of output volumes.

Costs, in PPM, are not directly associated with the vector of final products, $\bar{x}$. Cost measurement is done at the activity level with the following chain: activity operations $(z) \rightarrow$ inputs used $(Az) \rightarrow$ cost charges for inputs used (cAz) (Staubus [10]). In this paper we derive both marginal costs and average variable costs for final products for the primal and dual solutions to PPM.

3. Marginal Costs

The solution to PPM and its dual yield the optimal activity levels, z^0, the minimum variable cost $\theta^0 = cAz^0$, and the two vectors of dual prices v^0 and w^0. The vector v^0 represents the marginal costs of changing the requirements vector $\bar{x}$. That is

$$v^0 = \partial \theta^0 / \partial \bar{x}$$

as long as the optimal basis does not change for incremental changes in $\bar{x}$. Any particular component, v_j^0, is a nondecreasing step function of $\bar{x}_j$, implying that marginal costs are nondecreasing with output. The nonlinearities in this system arise from the capacity constraints on activity levels.

Solving our numerical example yields the optimal solutions:

$$\theta^0 = 4071,$$
$$z = [100, 100, 200, 15]^T,$$
$$v^0 = [27.78, 17.96],$$
$$w^0 = [0, 7.57, 0, 1.4].$$

The marginal costs of producing an additional unit of products 1 and 2 are 27.78 and 17.96 respectively. The marginal cost of product 1 exceeds the direct variable costs (12.5, 20) of either of the two activities producing it because of capacity constraints.

The marginal costs for products (v^0) and fixed resources (w^0) can be used for pricing, make versus buy, and capacity expansion decisions. But if the marginal product costs are used for valuing the final products, the imputed cost of these goods will usually exceed the variable input costs of producing these goods even before any overhead is allocated. By the dual theorem of linear programming:

$$\theta^0 = cAz^0 = v^0\bar{x} - w^0d.$$

As long as there is at least one scarce resource, so that $w^0d > 0$, the variable input costs, cAz^0, will be less than the sum of the marginal costs of the final products, $v^0\bar{x}$. For the remainder of the paper we will assume that the cost of total products $(\bar{x})$ valued at their marginal cost (v^0) exceeds the total cost of activities $(\mathbf{c}\mathbf{A}\mathbf{z}^0)$; i.e., that $\mathbf{w}^0\mathbf{d} > 0$. In our numerical example, the marginal costs exceed the total input costs by \$2299 $(\mathbf{w}^0\mathbf{d} = 300(7.57) + 20(1.4))$.

Thus marginal costs can give a somewhat distorted picture of the underlying profitability of the department. In an extreme case, we could have a process in which $n - 1$ units of output are produced on a standard low cost activity and the last unit requires the use of a high cost activity. If all units are "costed" on a marginal cost basis, the entire production run would be allocated costs as if it were produced solely on the least efficient activity used. While such marginal cost information is useful for considering the effects of contracting for additional sales or expanding production capacity, it overstates the average cost of producing a given quantity of output. Also, marginal cost valuation of output would not provide a good indication as to whether the most efficient activities were used to produce the output. If, because of production inefficiencies, only $n - 3$ units are produced on the standard low cost activity (instead of $n - 1$ units), then 3 units instead of 1 must be produced with the high cost activity. In this case, marginal costs are unaffected by the production inefficiency and hence do not provide a good basis for control. In contrast, the average cost of production would increase when 2 additional units were produced with the high cost activity and would signal the potential cost inefficiency. In the rest of this paper, we consider schemes for developing average variable product cost information.

4. Standard Average Variable Costs

Variable product costs would be uniquely determined if there were separate and independent production activities for each product. This situation does not occur in general so that computing unit costs in a multi-process multi-product setting will involve difficulties analogous to those encountered when computing standard costs with joint products.

Let s denote a $1 \times m$ vector of average unit costs (to be determined). Since physical identification of total variable costs with products on a product-by-product basis is impossible in our situation, it is natural to try to base costing or valuation of products on some "values" related to these products. Value has a dual nature, i.e., we can talk of benefit value and sacrifice value (Ijiri [4, Chapter 2]). Benefit value is perhaps best represented by some measure of market values (e.g., marginal revenue) of products. The simplest situation occurs when we assume a vector, q, of (constant) selling prices for each final product. For sacrifice value, we use the measure already developed in the PPM of marginal cost, $\mathbf{v}^0$.

The three average product costing methods we shall present in this section are special cases of a general formula relating s to benefit values and sacrifice values,

$$\mathbf{s} = \alpha\mathbf{v}^0 + \beta\mathbf{q},$$

where α and β are scalars or weights.[2] Different average product costs are determined by varying the values of α and β.

We impose one requirement on α and β so that the resulting s will represent "standard product costs." We require that the total cost of final product, valued at average unit costs, be equal to the minimum variable cost of the input factors used in their production; that is the imputed costs of the final products just equal the minimum cost of activities necessary to achieve the desired output. Formally, we state this requirement as:

$$s\bar{x} = cAz^0 \equiv \theta^0. \tag{R}$$

In joint product costing, a common costing method is to make product costs proportional to the market price (or net realizable value after further processing). A rationale given to this alternative is to make product costs reflect the revenue-generating power of each product (Horngren [3, Chapter 16]). In the above general formula for s, this method is equivalent to setting $\alpha = 0$ and determining β from (R):

$$s = k_1 q$$

where

$$k_1 = \beta = \theta^0/q\bar{x}.$$

We call this procedure Marginal Revenue (MR) costing. Note that under this procedure average costs bear little relation to production costs.

An alternative allocation assigns average costs so that they are proportional to the marginal costs of each product, v^0. Formally, we set $\beta = 0$ in the general formula and determine α from (R). Namely,

$$s = k_2 v^0$$

where

$$k_2 = \alpha = \theta^0/v^0\bar{x}.$$

We call this procedure Marginal Cost (MC) costing.

---

[2] This formula can also be used for average costing of products whose interaction may or may not be represented in the activity analysis framework. Writing a marginal cost vector and a marginal revenue vector of multiple products as MC and MR respectively, the formula is

$$\text{Average cost} = \alpha\ MC + \beta\ MR.$$

The three costing methods presented in this section are applicable in this generalized situation. The properties of these methods to be presented in this section will also hold in general. Thus, this section presents, in a sense, a general approach to average product costing in an interactive multiproduct situation. This general formula is merely a simple linear combination of marginal cost and marginal value, where linearity is assumed for simplicity.

A third alternative takes a position in between the above two extremes. As a simple approach for combining sacrifice value and benefit value in a single measure, we adopt a normalizing condition:

$$\alpha + \beta = 1.$$

The resulting s is:

$$s = k_3 v^0 + (1 - k_3)q$$

where

$$k_3 = (q\bar{x} - cAz^0)/(q\bar{x} - v^0\bar{x})$$

when $q\bar{x} \neq v^0\bar{x}$. (If $q\bar{x} = v^0\bar{x}$, the condition $\alpha + \beta = 1$ becomes incompatible with (R).) We call this procedure Equivalent Profitability (EP) costing for reasons to be given shortly. In essence, the contribution margins $(q - s)$ under this average costing are indicative of overall profitability.

Properties of Average Costing Methods

Some immediate properties of the three average costing procedures follow. For MR costing, it is easy to show that

$$s_i/s_j = q_i/q_j$$

or

$$(q_i - s_i)/(q_j - s_j) = q_i/q_j.$$

Thus, for MR costing, the ratio between the average costs of any two products equals the ratio between the two market prices. This ratio also equals the ratio of the contribution margins of the two products (since costs are proportional to prices). This is a well-known result for the relative market value method for joint product costing.

For MC costing, we have that

$$s_i/s_j = v_i^0/v_j^0.$$

Thus, average costs ratios under MC costing equal marginal cost ratios.

For EP costing, we have that

$$(q_i - s_i)/(q_j - s_j) = (q_i - v_i^0)/(q_j - v_j^0)$$

This means that ratios of product contribution margins under EP costing, $(q - s)$, equal the ratios of marginal contributions margins $(q - v^0)$. As a corollary of this property, the percentage of total contribution margins attributed to a product with EP unit costs equals the percentage of contribution margin when valuing products at marginal costs.

From these immediate properties of the three costing methods, we can conclude that average costs under MC and EP costings have some information content with potential relevance to manufacturing and product mix decisions. MR costing seems to give the least information content. We shall elaborate on these preliminary conclusions in the next two sections where we investigate various properties of the three costing methods in depth.

Returning to our numerical example from the previous section we obtain the three cost allocations shown in Table 1, assuming the market price vector, $q = (28, 20)$.

Table 1   Average Costs in Numerical Example

Method	k	Average Cost Vectors
MR	.599	(16.77, 11.98)
MC	.639	(17.75, 11.48)
EP	6.347	(26.60, 7.05)

First, note that MR and MC average costs are almost the same. This occurs because the price vector, $q = (28, 20)$, is close to the marginal cost vector, $v^0 = (27.78, 17.96)$.

Also notice from Table 1 that the EP method assigns relatively high average cost to product 1 and relatively low average cost to product 2. This assignment is due to the low margin of price over marginal cost for product 1 $(28 - 27.78 = 0.22)$ as compared to the higher margin for product 2 $(20 - 17.06 = 2.04)$. The margin of price over average cost is only 1.4 for product 1, but 12.95 for product 2. Thus, EP costing clearly identifies that, on an incremental basis, product 2 is far more profitable than product 1 and it would be better to expand product 2's sales rather than product 1's. In an extreme case, it is possible for a product to receive a negative average cost under EP costing, making the contribution margin greater than the selling price. This may be considered as a form of subsidy to the product to make it look more profitable because of its overall favorable effect on the company. Such a situation can occur when there are market dependencies (such as complementary products) or production interdependencies (joint costs). Negative average costs could not arise for either MR or MC costing.

As one can see from this example, EP average costs offer useful information on the marginal profitability of each product at any given output volume, $\bar{x}$. Without knowing the full complexity of production interdependencies, the sales manager, for example, can now have an indication of which product is more profitable for incremental sales. Furthermore, EP average costs have additional nice properties when $\bar{x}$ is determined from another linear programming model which describes the firm's complete sales and production opportunities.

Additional Properties

We now consider additional properties of the average costing models. We show that the average costs under EP costing do not alter the relative profitability of products in an overall product mix optimization mode. In other words, under EP costing, the sales optimization model will give the same optimal solution as the global production-sales optimization model. Finally, we shall investigate the properties of MC and EP costs in some special cases. This discussion will also indicate the wide applicability of PPM and its associated costing methods.

Decision Similarity with EP Costing.   Assume that the firm has the following global linear programming model for its entire operations (sales and production) to maximize total contribution margin. We call it (G):

$$\max qx - cAz$$
$$\text{s.t. } Pz \geqslant x,$$
$$Bz \leqslant d,$$
$$Hx \leqslant h,$$
$$x, z \geqslant 0.$$

Here x represents sales or product mix variables. The constraints $Hx \leqslant h$ represent, for example, market conditions on maximum sales of products, minimum sales requirements from policy considerations and any sales interdependencies among products. We further assume that the demanded output level, $\bar{x}$, in PPM arises from the optimal solution x^0 from the above global model.

We show that EP costing allows a sales optimization model to be solved without explicit production considerations to give the same x^0 as from (G). Consider a product mix sales model (S):

$$\max (q - s)x,$$
$$Hx \leqslant h, \qquad\qquad \text{(S)}$$
$$x \geqslant 0,$$

where s is some vector of average variable costs. We can think of supplying a salesman with cost information s and having him determine an optimal product mix based on his knowledge of sales opportunities. For future reference, the dual linear programs of (G) and (S) are as follows and denoted by (G_D) and (S_D) respectively.

$$\min wd + uh$$
$$\text{s.t. } v + uH \geqslant q, \qquad\qquad (G_D)$$
$$vP - wB \leqslant cA,$$
$$v, w, u \geqslant 0;$$
$$\min uh \qquad\qquad (S_D)$$
$$\text{s.t. } uH \geqslant q - s.$$

We now show that when s is computed using the EP method, the globally optimal solution is optimal to the simplified sales model (S), subject to one mild condition. We formally state and prove this property of EP costing in:

PROPOSITION 1. *Assume* $(\bar{x}, z^0)$ *is the optimal solution in* (G), *that* (v^0, w^0, u^0) *is the optimal solution in* (G_D). *If*

(i) $k_3 = (q\bar{x} - cAz^0)/(q\bar{x} - v^0\bar{x}) > 0$ *and*
(ii) $s = k_3v^0 + (1 - k_3)q$,
then $\bar{x}$ *is optimal in* (S).

PROOF.   Clearly $\bar{x}$ is feasible in (S) and the objective value of (S) for $\bar{x}$ is $(q - s)\bar{x}$. Let

$$u' = k_3u^0.$$

The vector u' is a feasible solution to (S_D) since

$$u'H = k_3u^0H \geq k_3(q - v^0) = q - s$$

and

$$u' = k_3u^0 \geq 0.$$

The objective value of (S_D) for u' is

$$
\begin{aligned}
u'h &= k_3u^0h \\
&= k_3u^0h\,\bar{x} && \text{(complementary slackness in (G))} \\
&= k_3[(q - v^0)\bar{x}] && \text{(complementary slackness in } (G_D)\text{)}. \\
&= (q - s)\bar{x}.
\end{aligned}
$$

Thus, we have feasible solutions $(\bar{x}, u')$ for (S) and (S_D) and their respective objective values are equal. By the duality theorem of linear programming, $\bar{x}$ is optimal for (S) and u' is optimal for (S_D).

Note that in Proposition 1 we have a condition on k_3 to be positive. This implies that both $q\bar{x} - cAz^0$ and $q\bar{x} - v^0\bar{x}$ are of the same sign. This seems to be a mild condition since $q\bar{x} - cAz^0 > 0$ (positive profit) is the usual case we would like to consider and then $q\bar{x} - v^0\bar{x} > 0$ implies (through complementary slackness) that $u^0h > 0$. The last inequality implies that the sales constraints are, on balance, restrictions on profit. On the other hand, $u^0h < 0$ will occur, for example, when the sales constraints are mostly minimum sales requirements (thus making many components of h negative). When such restrictions are so strong that $u^0h < 0$ the condition $k_3 > 0$ requires $q\bar{x} - cAz^0 < 0$, or that the total contribution margin has to be negative, too.

The unit contribution margin vector, $(q - s)$, under EP costing also keeps the optimality of $(\bar{x}, z^0)$ invariant in yet another production and sales planning model. Consider a modified global model where no explicit charge is made for activity costs and cost is charged on the product basis through the average costs s. We call this model (G'):

$$
\begin{aligned}
\max \ (q - s)x, & \\
Pz \geq x, & \\
Bz \leq d, & \qquad (G') \\
Hx \leq h, & \\
x, z \geq 0. &
\end{aligned}
$$

PROPOSITION 2.   *If $(\bar{x}, z^0)$ is optimal in (G), it is also optimal in (G').*

PROOF. (G') is a more restricted problem than (S) since two extra sets of constraints have been added without changing the objective function. Therefore, the optimal objective value of (G') cannot be greater than the optimal objective value of (S). But $(\bar{x}, z^0)$ is feasible in (G') since it is feasible (and optimal) in (G). The objective value of $(\bar{x}, z^0)$ in (G') is $(q - s)\bar{x}$ which is equal to its upper limit, the optimal value of (S). Thus, $(\bar{x}, z^0)$ is optimal in (G').

This proposition, along with Proposition 1, further indicates that EP costing yields product costs that are consistent with the sales and production planning models of the firm.[3]

The various linear programming models we have formulated provide alternative decentralization schemes. For example, assume that the firm has solved some global problem to arrive at the demanded production requirement $\bar{x}$ in PPM. The production department must then select an optimal set of activities, z, to meet this production constraint. Thus, PPM involves decentralization by assigning quantity rather than price guidelines. The sales model (S) allows for decentralization of the sales department with a pricing guideline; the sales department selects an optimal product mix given a transfer price s (computed from EP costing) for the outputs of the manufacturing process.[4] These schemes are consistent with the production department being run as a cost center and the marketing department as a profit center. A minimal information set for the planning department of a combined production and marketing department (e.g., a decentralized division) is the full set of constraints, and the market price and EP average cost

---

[3] It is possible for (S) to have alternate (including an infinite number of) optimal solutions one of which is the globally optimal solution. This occurs frequently in decomposition problems using linear programming. The decentralized model (S) is equivalent to one of the subproblems which arise from decomposing (G) into two subproblems. See Baumol and Fabian [1] for a discussion of decomposition and nonunique optimal solutions.

[4] The basic idea of obtaining invariant optimal decisions after product costing is related to the concept of sterilizing cost allocations in Thomas [11].

vectors, q and s, as shown in model (G '). This model can be solved without knowing the resource costs of the activities, z.

One of the obvious criticisms of this type of scheme is that to obtain EP average costs, s, we have to know $\bar{x}$ which is assumed here to be given by the global optimization model. A natural question to ask is why we need cost information s after we have already solved for the optimal production and sales plan from the global model. One possible answer is that external factors, as described in the introduction, may require the derivation of average product costs. In this case, EP costing will give product costs which are consistent with the firm's optimal decision.

Another, perhaps more positive, answer is that the EP costs could be valuable for the firm's (decentralized) decisions even when the global model is not solved first. Suppose that $\bar{x}$ is obtained from the global model assuming the standard conditions for the sales and production opportunities and cost coefficients. The resultant EP costs may be called the standard EP costs. These costs can be used in the decentralized sales decision making with the positive assurance that under the standard conditions, the decision is precisely a global optimum. For repetitive sales decisions, in which the environment will vary randomly from the standard conditions, the decentralized sales decision will be nonoptimal in a precise sense. But it may be argued that unless the actual environment is radically different from the standard one, the decentralized decision would not be too far from the true optimum or at least EP costs would give valuable information on product profitability. Thus, having the standard EP costs (or even a set of standard EP costs for a set of different standard environmental conditions) could serve a purpose similar to the role of ordinary standard costs in cost accounting. This issue, however, is speculative and is open to further research.

Special Cases of PPM. First, consider when the firm is operating below capacity. If the demanded output level $\bar{x}$ can be produced without reaching the limit in any scarce resource (i.e., the case where all the constraints $Bz \leqslant d$ will be satisfied as strict inequalities), then $w^0d = 0$. In that case, one can easily verify that for both MC costing and EP costing,

$$s = v^0.$$

With no effective scarce resource constraints, the firm has a linear production function with constant prices for inputs. Then, the total cost function becomes a linear function and the average costs must equal marginal costs. In this situation, though, MR average costs need not equal marginal costs, certainly another undesirable feature of this method.

Another special case of interest is when P (the production rate matrix) has an inverse and thus we can solve $Pz = \bar{x}$ for z as

$$z = P^{-1}x.$$

Then, clearly, the total variable cost function becomes a linear function of the output $\bar{x}$,

$$cAP^{-1}\bar{x}.$$

There exists no choice problem of alternative production processes. All the cases of variable cost allocation using input-output analysis (Feltham [2], Livingstone [7]) can be considered examples of this special case. Solving PPM becomes a question of checking the feasibility of a given $\bar{x}$. If it is feasible, v^0 should be equal to cAP^{-1}. Furthermore, in this case $w^0d = 0$ so that, again,

$$s = v^0 = cAP^{-1}$$

for both MC and EP costing. Of course, this is not the case for MR costing except by coincidence.

Finally Itami [5, pp. 82-87] has shown how MC average costs can be used constructively as standard costs to motivate the manager to use the most efficient set of activities to produce the desired mix of products, $\bar{x}$.

5. Summary

Average variable costs are not directly defined for multiple products produced in complex settings. The activity analysis approach can be used for basic cost measurement and for building a linear programming model of manufacturing operations. The model can then be used not only to compute the optimal production plan and associated marginal costs but also to assign average costs to final products. Three average costing methods based on sacrifice value (marginal costs) and benefit value (marginal revenue) of products have been considered. The method based entirely on the market value of products has less desirable properties than allocation methods which use the dual variables (marginal costs) from the programming model.

Use of the activity analysis framework yields some additional benefits. One is its versatility to have many overhead costs, such as maintenance, overtime, shift premiums, indirect labor and materials, treated within the model. Thus, they are absorbed directly into the cost of final products rather than allocated indirectly through an overhead charge. Another benefit is that various cost allocation methods using input-output analysis can be considered as special cases of average costing methods presented in this paper.

References

1. BAUMOL, W.J. and FABIAN, T., "Decomposition, Pricing for Decentralization and External Economies," *Management Sci.*, (Sept. 1964), pp. 1-132.
2. FELTHAM, GERALD A., "Some Quantitative Approaches to Planning for Multiproduct Systems," *Accounting Rev.* (January 1970), pp. 11-26.

3. HORNGREN, CHARLES T., *Cost Accounting: A Managerial Emphasis*, 4th ed., Prentice-Hall, Englewood Cliffs, N.J., 1977.
4. IJIRI, YUJI, *The Foundations of Accounting Measurement*, Prentice-Hall, Englewood Cliffs, N.J., 1967.
5. ITAMI, HIROYUKI, *Adaptive Behavior: Management Control and Information Analysis*, Studies in Accounting Research No 15, Amer. Accounting Assoc., 1977.
6. KOOPMANS, TJALLING (ed.), *Activity Analysis of Production and Allocation*, Wiley, New York, 1951.
7. LIVINGSTONE, JOHN L., "Input-Output Analysis for Cost Accounting, Planning and Control," *Accounting Rev.* (January 1969), pp. 48-64.
8. RONEN, JOSHUA and McKINNEY, GEORGE, "Transfer Pricing for Divisional Autonomy," *J. Accounting Res.*, Vol. 8 (1970), pp. 99-112.
9. SHILLINGLAW, GORDON, *Managerial Cost Accounting*, 4th ed., Irwin, Homewood, Ill., 1977.
10. STAUBUS, GEORGE J., *Activity Costing and Input-Output Accounting*, Irwin, Homewood, Ill., 1971.
11. THOMAS, ARTHUR, *The Allocation Problem: Part Two*, Studies in Accounting Research No. 10, Amer. Accounting Assoc., 1973.

VIII.

INFORMATION ECONOMICS

This final section of the book is a "short course" in topics associated with the field of decision-making under conditions of uncertainty. Article 21, "Formal Decision Making Under Uncertainty: A Structure" introduced some of the basic concepts. The two articles in this section are in the nature of brief teaching notes, to help supplement material that is in some cost and managerial accounting textbooks. The author is covering several topics, and their interrelationships, in a compact manner. Consequently, the material may be perceived as requiring greater concentration than was needed for several articles in the previous sections.

In viewing the material, readers ought to bear the main theme of this book in mind: for which decision situations might the techniques or concept prove useful? Also, under what circumstances, and for which decisions, would each particular concept or technique be invalid? It is too easy to exert considerable effort learning how the technique works, and then avoid thinking about sensible applications for management. The author helps the reader commence the "application" process of learning, but does not have sufficient space to continue this educational path.

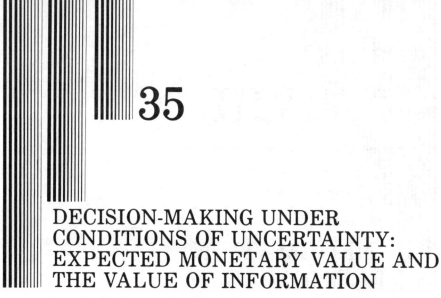

35

DECISION-MAKING UNDER CONDITIONS OF UNCERTAINTY: EXPECTED MONETARY VALUE AND THE VALUE OF INFORMATION

ANTHONY A. ATKINSON*

1. Introduction

In this article, decision-making is defined as the choice of a single course of action from a set of mutually exclusive courses of action. Approaches to decision-making are many and varied. Decision-making has been defined by some as a science and by others as an art which is incapable of representation by rules.

The purpose of this article is to describe a formal and normative approach to decision-making. Whether this decision model is descriptive of practice is neither considered nor relevant here. The question of relevance and validity of this model is an issue of individual choice which is left to the reader.

This article begins with a discussion of a structured approach to decision-making. After a brief consideration of the issues concerning decision-making under conditions of certainty, the discussion turns to consider an axiomatic model of decision-making in the presence of uncertainty. After illustrating this model with an example, issues relating to information and its value are raised.

*School of Business Administration at Dalhousie University.

This article will serve as little more than an introduction to this area for the novice and as a review for those previously exposed to this literature. Throughout this article, references are made to supplementary material for the reader wishing a complete treatment of these issues.

2. A Formal Process of Decision-Making

Churchman, Ackoff, and Arnoff [1957] have described decision-making as the following multi-step process:

(i)   Identify problem
(ii)   Specify objectives
(iii) Develop a criterion function
(iv)   Determine the possible alternative courses of action
(v)   Specify outcomes of the alternative courses of action
(vi)   Use the criterion function to rank the action alternatives
(vii) Choose the preferred course of action.

While this paradigm is quite general, we will restrict our attention in this article to an economic perspective and confine the discussion to issues surrounding the maximization of profit and return. Thus our concern here is to determine a preferred course of action when the stated objective is to maximize profits.

Throughout this article we will make use of the following two examples to illustrate the ideas being developed.

Case 1:
A manufacturer is considering the production and sale of a new product. Manufacturing and sales constraints will limit the sale of the new product to 10,000 units.

The incremental fixed costs related to this project are $25,000 and the selling price per unit is expected to be $20. The variable, or incremental, manufacturing and selling costs per unit total $17.00. If the new product is not produced the facilities will be rented for $1,000.

Case 2:
A manufacturer is considering the production and sale of a new product. There are no incremental fixed costs associated with this product and the variable cost per unit to manufacture this product is $2.00. The anticipated price for this product is $10 less one-hundredth of one cent for every unit sold. Throughout the development of Case 2 we will use elementary techniques from differential and integral calculus. If you are not familiar with these methodologies, simply ignore the discussions of Case 2 (which are self-contained so as to preserve continuity of the main text).

Using the approach proposed by Churchman, Ackoff, and Arnoff let us consider each of these problems.

Step	Case 1	Case 2
(1) Identify problem	Whether or not to develop the new product	How many units to manufacture and sell
(2) Specify objective	Maximize profits	Maximize profits
(3) Develop criterion function	Profit (P)=Revenue−Cost	Profit (P) = Revenue − Cost
(4) Alternative courses of action	Action i) Do not develop product Action ii) Develop product	Choose production and sales (x). There are infinitely many courses of action
(5) Specify outcomes	Action i) P = $1000 Action ii) P = (20−17)(10,000)−25,000 = $5000	$P = (10-.001x)\,x - 2x$
(6) Rank alternatives	(A) Action (i) with a profit of $5000 (B) Action (ii) with a profit of $1000	$\dfrac{dP}{dx} = 8-.002x$
(7) Choose action	Implement new product	x = 4000 Produce and sell 4000 units

Note that the results reproduced in the above table depend crucially on the economic criterion of profit maximization which we have assumed.

To demonstrate the effect of an alternative criterion consider Case 2. Suppose that, in addition to maximizing profits, the decision-maker is interested in status. Suppose, further, that status is represented, for the decision maker, by amount of production. This decision-maker has two objectives.

(i)   Profit $P = (10-.001x)\,x - 2x$
(ii) Status   x

These objectives are conflicting. Suppose that the decision-maker decides to develop an overall criterion function by weighting profit by 5 and status by 1. The criterion function becomes

$$C = 5P + x = (41 - .005x)x$$

and the optimal output is 4100 units. Comparing this solution to the solution above provides an indication of how the solution is sensitive to the criterion assumed.

With the above discussions and examples of decision-making under conditions of certainty in place we now raise the issues of uncertainty.

3. Uncertainty

Few decisions undertaken in the business world are contemplated under conditions of outcome certainty. Whether the decision is a bet on a horse race, a medical diagnosis, a jury verdict, a move in checkers, a football play, or the development of a new product, uncertainty is usually associated with the outcome of the decision. Questions inevitably surround every decision: will the operation be successful? Is the defendant guilty? Will the checkers or football play or new product be successful?

In order to develop a decision-making calculus to cope with conditions of uncertainty we will need to be specific about how we propose to deal with uncertainty.

Following a seminal treatise by Knight [1933], it became fashionable to distinguish between risk and uncertainty. Knight defined risk as "a quantity susceptible of measurement" and uncertainty as an "unmeasurable" quantity. In other words, when probabilities can be assigned to possible outcomes we are dealing with risk. When we are unable or unwilling to quantify our feelings about the likelihood of outcomes, we are dealing with uncertainty. While this is a traditional distinction, it is no longer popular, given the advent of Bayesian analysis which assumes that prior probabilities can be assigned to all outcomes. We will return to this issue below. At this point it is sufficient to point out that we will require that decisions be made under conditions of risk, using Knight's terminology, and we will not distinguish between the terms risk and uncertainty.

4. Decision-Making Under Uncertainty

Decision-making under uncertainty is characterized by uncertainty over the outcome of a given course of action. To develop these ideas, we will make use of some standard terminology.

(i) **Action:**   An action is a decision implemented by a decision-maker.

(ii) **State:**   A state is an event, outside the control of the decision-maker, which is subject to uncertainty.

(iii) **Outcome:** An outcome is the consequence or payoff which accrues to the decision-maker. The outcome is determined jointly by the action taken and the state which obtains.

Given any action-state pair the decision-maker can specify what outcome will occur. Uncertainty about outcomes exists because of uncertainty over which state will occur.

To focus this terminology, and to expand Case 1 above, suppose that variable cost is not known for sure. Variable cost is expected to be either $15.00 or $19.00. Suppose in Case 2 above that variable cost is not known for sure. Variable cost is expected to fall between $1.00 and $3.00 with all possibilities on this interval equally likely. We can now illustrate the above terminology using the two sample problems.

	Case 1	Case 2
ACTION	Units of production (x)	Units of production (x)
STATE	Variable cost (c)	Variable cost (c)

STATE

		C=15	C=19	
	x = 0	1000	1000	
OUTCOME ACTION				(10 −.001x)−cx
	x = 10,000	25,000	−15,000	

When facing decision-making under conditions of uncertainty our initial task is to develop a systematic approach to characterizing and dealing with uncertainty. The most successful and widely advocated approach is the expected utility hypothesis which has as a special case, the expected value hypothesis. We will turn to consider the expected utility hypothesis below but first we will briefly consider some alternatives.

One of the difficulties of discussing alternatives to the expected utility hypothesis is that few alternatives are rigourously stated. Thus approaches based on whimsy, experience, or some individual's personal and unarticulated decision calculus are not discussed here. This does not imply the irrelevance or inferiority of these approaches but rather that the lack of documentation renders the discussion of such methodologies impossible.

There are three methodologies, which have been developed in game theory, each of which provides an alternative to the expected utility hypothesis. Each of those is discussed briefly so that efficacy of the expected utility hypothesis can be related to some alternative. These alternative methodologies are: (i) the minimax criterion, (ii) the maximin criterion and (iii) the Hurwicz criterion.

In each of the methodologies the decision-maker begins by specifying the utility outcome associated with each action state pair.

In this article we will confine our attention to the expected value hypothesis, thus utility is defined directly in terms of profit.

Using the minimax criterion, the decision-maker chooses the action which minimizes the maximum payoff. In Case 1, the maximum payoff from choosing x = 0 is $1000 and from choosing x = 10,000 is $25,000. Thus the action promising the minimum maximum return is x = 0.

Using the maximin criterion, the decision-maker chooses the action which maximizes the minimum payoff. In Case 1, the minimum payoff from choosing x = 0 is $1,000 and the minimum payoff from choosing x = 10,000 is −$15,000. Thus the action promising the maximum minimum return is x = 0.

Note that in *this* case, the maximin and minimax criteria chose the same action. In the following problem, the minimax choice is Action 1 and the maximin choice is Action 2.

STATES

		1	2	3
	1	100	200	500
ACTION	2	400	700	300
	3	600	100	400

The Hurwicz criterion assigns an index to each action. The decision-maker begins by choosing an pessimism-optimism index (a). This index assumes a value between zero and one and reflects the personal attributes of the decision-maker. That is, there is no such thing as a correct pessimism-optimism index.

The decision-maker then determines the lowest (l) and highest (h) utility numbers associated with each action. Each action's index (I) is computed as follows

$$I = al + (1-a) h$$

The action with the highest index is chosen. Suppose that the decision-maker chooses an optimism-pessimism index of 0.4. The index for each of the three actions introduced in the above problem are:

(i)   Action 1:   (.4)(100) + (.6)(500)   = 340
(ii) Action 2:   (.4)(300) + (.6)(700)   = 540
(iii) Action 3:   (.4)(100) + (.6)(600)   = 400

With a pessimism-optimism index of 0.4, the decision-maker chooses action 2.

Note that if the pessimism-optimism index is one, the decision-maker chooses the action with the maximum minimum return. This is the maximin criterion. If the pessimism-optimism index is 0, the decision-maker chooses the action with the maximum maximum return. Thus the decision-maker's cautiousness is directly related to the value of the pessimism-optimism index chosen.

There have been numerous objections to these criteria. It is neither the purpose, nor within the scope of this article, to discuss these here. However we do note, in passing, a major objection to these approaches is their failure to consider, in any systematic way, the decision-maker's prior beliefs about which state will occur.

To illustrate this point, recall that any one of these criteria is only appropriate if there exists uncertainty about which state will occur.

Suppose that, in Case 1, uncertainty exists but that the decision-maker believes that there is only one chance in one billion that the variable cost per unit will be $19.00. Are the minimax or maximin criteria which both pick $x = 0$ reasonable? Most people believe not and argue that a mechanism which considers the strength of prior beliefs is required. We turn then to consider the expected utility hypothesis.

5. Expected Utility Hypothesis

The expected utility hypothesis evolved through the writings and contributions of many authors. The first complete exposition of the modern theory of utility is attributed to Von Neumann and Morgenstern [1944]. Savage [1954] synthesized the Bayesian concept of subjective probability with Von Neumann and Morgenstern's utility theory to develop a theory which is currently used, almost exclusively, in theoretical work. This is the methodology which we now describe.

Expected utility theory is an axiomatic system. Certain axioms or postulates of behaviour are described. From these axioms a formal, robust, and powerful decision-making calculus is developed. If one accepts the behavioural axioms, then the theory is a normative theory describing how decisions should be made. For this reason, a considerable amount of interest and effort has been directed towards understanding these axioms which we now consider briefly.

The postulates of Savage which serve as the basis for the modern treatment of utility theory are both abstract and obtuse and have been simplified and restructured by Luce and Raiffa [1957] into an alternative and comparable axiomatic system. Demski [1972] summarized Luce and Raiffa's system into the following essential axioms which we now discuss.

First we require that the decision-maker's beliefs can be expressed using the normal probability calculus. There are three critical assumptions here:

Axiom 1:   The probability assigned to any state is non-negative.
Axiom 2:   The probability assigned to the set of all states is 1.
Axiom 3:   The probability that two, independent, states simultaneously occur equals the sum of their individual probabilities of occurring.

These are the three axioms of a probability measure. If we accept these three axioms all of probability theory follows. For a comprehensive discussion and treatment of modern probability theory the interested reader is referred to Parzen [1960]. Less formal treatments are found in most statistics texts. See, for example, DeGroot [1975].

In addition to requiring a consistent treatment of probability, we require the decision-maker to exhibit certain personal preferences. First we will state each assumption and discuss its meaning. Then we shall discuss the significance of each assumption.

Axiom 1: The decision-maker can rank any pair of outcomes or actions and all rankings are transitive.

This axiom implies two things. *First* that any pair of outcomes, no matter how diverse, can be ranked in terms of preference. The decision-maker cannot claim that any relevant outcome is incomparable. *Second,* we require that rankings be transitive. That is, if outcome 1 is preferred to outcome 2 and outcome 2 is preferred to outcome 3 then outcome 1 is preferred to outcome 3.

Axiom 2: When faced with two lotteries each with the same outcomes and each promising a non-zero probability of receiving one of two outcomes, the decision-maker will choose the preferred lottery solely on the basis of which lottery provides the largest chance of receiving the preferred outcome.

Consider the following situation:

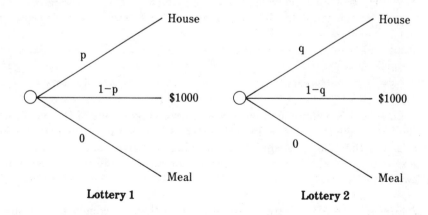

The decision-maker has ranked the alternatives as follows:

(i) House   (ii) $1,000   (iii) meal

In this case, Lottery 1 provides:

(i)   p   probability of winning a house
(ii)   1−p probability of winning $1000
(iii) 0   probability of winning a meal.

Lottery 2 provides:

(i)   q   probability of winning a house
(ii)   1−q probability of winning $1000
(iii) 0   probability of winning a meal.

Axiom 2 states that Lottery 1 will be preferred to Lottery 2 if, and only if, p is greater than q. Alternatively, Lottery 2 is preferred to Lottery 1 if and only if, p is less than q.

Axiom 3:   The form of uncertainty facing the decision-maker is irrelevant. All that matters is the probability of obtaining each outcome.

Consider the following two Lotteries

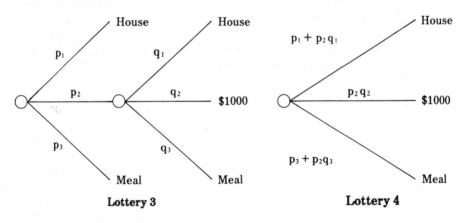

Lottery 3 is a compound lottery with two stages. One of the outcomes of the first stage is a lottery. In both lotteries the eventual outcomes are identical and the prior probability of obtaining any given outcome is the same. Axiom 3 states that the decision-maker should be indifferent between these two lotteries.

Axiom 4:   Given a lottery promising one of two outcomes, there is always an intermediate value such that, for some probability of obtaining each outcome, the decision-maker is indifferent between facing this lottery and receiving the intermediate value.

Consider the following lotteries where the decision-maker ranks the outcomes in the following order: (i) house, (ii) $1000, (iii) meal.

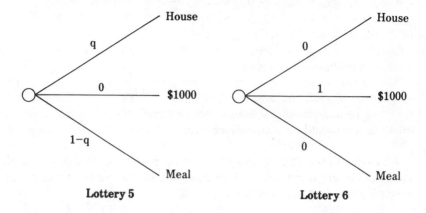

Lottery 5   Lottery 6

Lottery 5 promises a house with probability q and a meal with probability 1−q. Axiom 4 asserts that there exists some value of q such that the decision-maker will be indifferent between Lottery 5 and Lottery 6.

With this axiomatic structure, utility theory shows that there exists a utility function, defined over all actions and outcomes with the following properties:

(i) The utility function will assign real numbers to actions in such a way that ranking actions by their utility numbers will result in the same ranking as the decision-maker's preference ranking.

(ii) The real numbers assigned to each action will be the utility number assigned to each outcome multiplied by the probability of that outcome occurring summed over all outcomes.

This is the expected utility hypothesis. If the utility function has as its only component, and is linear in, profit, then the expected utility hypothesis takes on a special form, the expected value hypothesis. We will concern ourselves exclusively with the expected value hypothesis for the remainder of this article. Before we turn to develop the methodology more fully, we will discuss, briefly, the preference axioms described above.

6. The Axioms of Preference

Since the axioms of preference described above lead unambiguously to an unequivocal process of decision-making, these axioms have attracted considerable attention and discussion. The importance of the criterion is that, if accepted, decision-making can be programmed once the decision-maker determines the relevant parameters.

There have been two approaches to examining or critiquing the preference axioms: (i) descriptive validity and (ii) reasonableness. As we discuss
the axioms below, we will alternate between these two types of criticisms.

(i) Axiom 1

Of all the axioms of preference, Axiom 1 has received the most criticism for
both its realism and descriptive validity.

The axiom requires two characteristics of preference. First, that the
decision-maker can, and will, rank all outcomes. This precludes the possibility of the decision-maker rejecting any outcome as incomparable. This seems
innocuous, in itself, but combined with Axiom 4 a powerful implication is
derived. We return to this issue below.

The second requirement is that preferences are transitive. This has been
attacked as not being descriptive of individual behaviour. Transitivity requires a consistency which some experimenters suggest is not characteristic
of most individuals. One such experiment, which has been widely discussed
and interpreted was conducted by Allais [1953].

Allais presented the following alternatives to subjects:

In alternative 1, the decision-maker is offered a choice between $1,000,000
(Action 1) with certainty or the following Lottery (Action 2).

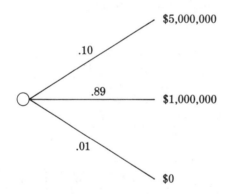

In alternative 2, the decision-maker is offered a choice between two lotteries.

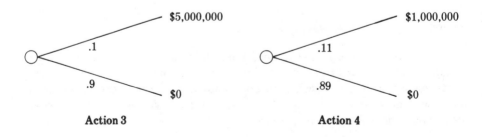

At this point you might decide which action you would choose if confronted with alternative 1 and which action you would choose if confronted with alternative 2.

Consider a hypothetical decision-maker who wishes to subscribe to the axioms underlying utility theory. Given this, we can use a utility function to assign numbers to outcomes to predict which action the decision-maker will choose.

Suppose the utility function assigns the following numbers to outcomes. (Since utility is an ordinal measure only, it is without loss of generality that a utility number of 0 is assigned to the outcome 0.)

Outcome	Utility Number
$5,000,000	a
$1,000,000	b
$ 0	0

Note that consistency requires that a is greater than b and b is greater than 0. The expected utilities of each of the actions are as follows

a_1	b
a_2	$.1\,a + .89b$
a_3	$.1\,a$
a_4	$.11\,b$

The choice of action made by the decision-maker will be as if the decision-maker chose the action with the highest expected utility.

In alternative 1, the expected utility of a_1 is greater than the expected utility of a_2 if, and only if, the ratio b/a is greater than 10/11.

In alternative 2, the expected utility of a_4 is greater than the expected utility of a_3 if, and only if, the ratio b/a is greater than 10/11.

The ratio b/a represents the personal risk-taking attributes of decision-makers and may vary over time and between decision-makers. However, the example is constructed so that the consistent decision-maker will exhibit one of the following preference pairs:

Either	(i)	a_1 to a_2 and a_4 to a_3
or	(ii)	a_2 to a_1 and a_3 to a_4
or	(iii)	indifference between choosing between
		a_1 and a_2
		a_3 and a_4.

Several experimenters, beginning with Allais, have discovered many subjects who prefer a_1 to a_2 and, simultaneously, prefer a_3 to a_4. This was taken, by Allais, as a refutation of the expected utility hypothesis.

This conclusion is only appropriate if the theory is to serve as descriptive of all decision-making behaviour. Other authors notably Savage [1954] and Raiffa [1968] have interpreted expected utility theory as a normative theory of how people should make decisions. Their response to Allais is to point out that intransitivity is inconsistent behaviour which ought to be modified.

This article will not consider the philosophical issues surrounding descriptive and normative theories. We will content ourselves here with presenting a consequence of intransitive preferences which has been used to convince people that intransitive preferences should be modified. The argument takes the form of demonstrating that there are riskless arbitrage opportunities available to extract wealth from people exhibiting intransitive preferences.

Consider an individual who has evaluated three paintings; a_1, a_2, a_3. The individual prefers painting a_1 to painting a_2 and painting a_2 to painting a_3. This we will denote as a_1Pa_2 and a_2Pa_3. Transitivity requires that a_1 be preferred to a_3. Suppose however that the decision-maker prefers a_3 to a_1.

Let us endow our decision-maker with painting one and three cents. Since painting three is preferred to painting one, the decision-maker will trade painting one for painting three. In addition, since the decision-maker strictly prefers painting three to painting one, the decision-maker will be willing to pay some additional amount to make the trade. Suppose this amount is one cent. (The amount is irrelevant as long as it is positive.) Once the trade is concluded the decision-maker is left with painting three and two cents.

Since painting two is preferred to painting three and painting one is preferred to painting two it can be seen that two more trades will return painting one to our decision-maker. He now has his original painting but has squandered three cents. Note that these are not transaction costs but losses resulting directly from intransitive preferences.

Using sequences of trades, we can extract with no risk, real assets from such a person. For this reason, many theoreticians view intransitivity as inconsistent behaviour.

(ii) Axiom 3

Axiom 3 has beef interpreted as the "no utility in gambling" axiom. This means that the decision-maker's attitude towards a gamble is dependent solely upon the risk involved and not the form of the gamble.

Consider the following alternatives: in alternative 1, the decision-maker faces a 2/3 chance of winning $5 and a 1/3 chance of losing $5. In alternative 2, the decision-maker faces a 1/3 chance of winning $5 and a 2/3 chance of facing the following lottery. Toss a fair coin: win $5 if heads occurs and pay $5 if tails occurs.

An individual who subscribes to the axioms of expected utility must consider the alternatives above as equal since the risk is identical in both cases. However, someone who experiences a thrill (or pain) from gambling may seek (or avoid) alternative 2 because of the multiple gambles. This preference is not admissible under the axioms of utility.

(iii) Axiom 4

In itself, Axiom 4 is little more than a continuity assumption required to insure that the criterion of utility maximization behaves in predictable ways.

Luce and Raiffa [1957, p. 27], however, have pointed out a disconcerting implication of axiom 1 and axiom 4 acting jointly. Consider the following example used by Luce and Raiffa. "It is safe to suppose that most people prefer $1.00 to $0.01 and that to death. Would, however, one be indifferent between one cent and a lottery involving $1.00 and death, that puts any positive probability on death." If the decision-maker defers, for any probability, then either axiom 1 or axiom 4 are violated. In this case, expected utility theory can be rescued by resorting to a system of multi-dimensional utility. We will ignore such a development to concentrate on ventures having only monetary outcomes.

7. The Expected Value Hypothesis

As mentioned above, a special case of the expected utility hypothesis, the expected value hypothesis, occurs when the utility function is linear in and a function of only monetary outcome.

An individual whose preferences for monetary outcomes can be described by a function which is linear in those outcomes is said to exhibit risk-neutrality. Discussion of risk behaviour which is not risk-neutral is deferred to the subsequent article. In this article we will thus refer to expected utility as expected value but it is understood that this reflects only a special case of utility theory.

Let us return to cases 1 and 2 above to illustrate the expected value calculation.

(i) Case 1

Suppose the decision-maker assigns the following prior probabilities to each of the mutually exclusive and exhaustive states:

State (Variable Cost)	Probability
$15	.3
$19	.7

The expected value of the two actions are computed as follows:

action $x = 0$: $1000 (.3) + (1000)(.7) = \$1000$
action $x = 10{,}000$: $25{,}000 (.3) + (-15{,}000)(.7) = \$-3000$.

Again, note that the expected value of each action is found by weighting each outcome by its probability and summing over all outcomes.

In this case, based on prior beliefs concerning outcomes, the decision-maker would choose no production.

It is left as an exercise for the reader to verify that the decision-maker will prefer production (x = 10,000) if, and only if, the prior probability that variable cost will be \$15 is greater than 0.4.

(ii) Case 2

In case 2 expected value is computed as follows:

$$EV = \int_{1.00}^{3.00} [(10 - .001x)x - cx] \; f(c)dc$$

which is simply the continuous case analog of weighting each outcome by its associated probability.

To find the optimal course of action, we find the first derivative of expected value with respect to the number of units.

$$\frac{dEV}{dx} = (10 - .002x) \int_{1.00}^{3.00} f(c)dc - \int_{1.00}^{3.00} cf(c)dc$$

Since $\int_{1.00}^{3.00} f(c)dc$

represents the sum of all assigned probabilities f(c) this must equal 1 (probability Axiom 2).

$\int_{1.00}^{3.00} cf(c)dc$ is simply the expected value

of random variable c which is \$2.00.

Thus $\dfrac{dEV}{dx} = (10 - .002x) - 2 = 8 - .002x$

Since $\dfrac{d^2EV}{dx^2} = -.002$

it follows that $8 - .002x = 0$ gives a maximum implying the optimal production (x*) is 4000.

There is an important rule implied in this example. Whenever the decision-maker is risk-neutral the occurrence of the uncertain parameter can be replaced by the variable's expected value. The distribution of the variable is irrelevant to a *risk-neutral* decision-maker. All that matters is the mean of the distribution.

8. Opportunity Loss and the Value of Perfect Information

An important consequence of making decisions in the face of uncertainty is that, ex post, we will often decide that we would have done things differently *if* we had known *in advance* which of the uncertain states would occur. This idea is captured by the notion of opportunity loss which we now develop.

Each action/state pair has an opportunity loss associated with it. The opportunity loss is computed as follows. For each state determine the action with the highest payoff. Subtract the outcome from every other action associated with this state from the highest payoff. Repeat this procedure for each state.

(i) Case 1
Following the above algorithm, we can compute the following table of opportunity losses.

		STATE	
		VC=15	VC=19
ACTION	x = 0	24,000	0
	x = 10,000	0	16,000

Thus the opportunity loss is $16,000 when the decision-maker undertakes to produce the new product and the variable cost is $19.00. By definition, the optimal course of action, given any state, has, associated with it, an opportunity loss of zero.

(ii) Case 2
For any realization of variable cost (c), the firm's return (P) is given by

$$P = [(10-c) - .001x]x$$

where x is output. Optimal output (x*), when decisions are made with c known, is given by

$$x^* = \frac{(10 - c)}{.002}$$

Substitution for x* in the profit function gives optimal profit (P *)

$$P^* = \frac{(10 - c)^2}{.004}$$

Recall that the optimal decision for the risk-neutral decision-maker who is facing uncertainty is

$$x^* = \frac{(10 - \bar{c})}{.002}$$

where $\bar{c}$ is the expected value of variable cost.
The consequential return, given any realization of c, is

$$P = \left[(10-c) - .001 \left(\frac{10 - \bar{c}}{.002} \right) \right] \left(\frac{10-\bar{c}}{.002} \right)$$

and the opportunity loss is

$$OL = \frac{(10 - c)^2}{.004} - \frac{(10 - c)(10 - \bar{c})}{.002} + \frac{(10 - \bar{c})^2}{.004}$$

$$OL = \frac{1}{.004} (\bar{c} - c)^2.$$

The opportunity loss, in a real sense, presents the opportunity lost by the decision-maker when making decisions in the presence of risk. If the decision-maker made decisions under certainty, the opportunity loss would always be zero.

It is a trivial algebraic exercise to demonstrate that maximizing expected value is equivalent to minimizing expected opportunity loss. (Both amounts sum to the same value for all actions. This sum is the expected return over repeated trials if decisions are made with perfect information.) Consequently, ranking actions by minimizing expected opportunity loss is equivalent to ranking actions by maximizing expected value.

(i) Case 1
Expected opportunity loss

$$x = 0: \quad (.3)(24,000) + (.7)(0) = \$7,200$$

$$x = 10,000: \quad (.3)(0) + (.7)(16,000) = \$11,200$$

(ii) Case 2
Expected opportunity loss is given by

$$EOL = \int_1^3 \frac{1}{.004} (\bar{c} - c)^2 f(c)dc$$

$$EOL = \frac{\text{variance } c}{.004} = \left(\frac{(3-1)^2}{12} \right) \left(\frac{1}{.004} \right) = 83.3$$

Recall, that the expected opportunity loss represents the difference in expected return between making decisions with complete information and making decisions under conditions of uncertainty. Thus the expected opportunity loss represents the decision-maker's expected gain if perfect information is received *before* the decision is made. The expected opportunity loss associated with the optimal course of action is called the expected value of perfect information and represents the maximum amount that the decision-maker would be willing to pay for perfect information about which state will occur. This algorithm thus provides us with a methodology to value information.

This algorithm has been criticized in that the expected value of information depends upon:

(i)   The risk preferences of the decision-maker.

(ii) The prior beliefs of the decision-maker. For example, if we denote by p the probability that the decision-maker assigns to variable cost being $15, the expected value of perfect information is

24,000 p   if p is 0.4 or less

16,000 (1-p) if p is 0.4 or greater.

(iii) The outcomes.

Thus, valuing information using this methodology is very context specific. To review this concept reconsider case 1. Based on the decision-maker's prior information the optimal course of action is to not undertake production of the new product. The decision-maker expects that there is a probability of 0.70 that, after the uncertainty is resolved, the decision not to invest will be the preferred decision. Alternatively, the decision-maker expects that the probability is 0.30 that, after the uncertainty is resolved, the decision not to invest will not be the preferred decision and the decision-maker will suffer an opportunity loss of $24,000. The expected opportunity loss is thus $7200 (24,000 × .3).

Thus, if the decision-maker were to receive perfect information about what the variable cost will be, the decision-maker would reduce the expected opportunity loss from $7200 to $0. Consequently the decision-maker would be willing to pay up to $7200 for this information.

9. Sample Information

With the concept of expected opportunity loss we have a way of valuing perfect information. This is of limited use however, since we can seldom obtain perfect information. We now turn to develop a way to value information which causes us to revise our beliefs about which state will occur but not to the extent of knowing, for sure, which state will occur.

Before we consider this task, we will first introduce two notions:

(i) A graphical way to depict decision-making under uncertainty.

(ii) A way to revise prior beliefs when sample, or imperfect, information is received.

(i) Graphical Representation of Decision-Making under Uncertainty

We will outline here a method of depicting decision-making under uncertainty which has been described by Raiffa [1968]. The methodology is commonly referred to as a decision tree.

The graph depicts the sequence of events taking strict care to preserve the time sequence. Two symbols are used to denote nodes:

☐ refers to a decision point

◯ refers to a point where some uncertainty is realized.

Using this methodology we would denote Case 1 as follows:

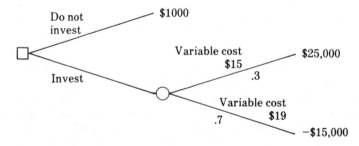

Note the following:

(i) At each decision node, all decisions possible at that node are shown.

(ii) At each chance node, all state realizations possible at that point are shown.

(iii) The utility associated with the outcomes of each action/state pair are noted at the end point of that branch.

(iv) The order of presentation is critical and follows the actual temporal sequence. In the above case, the decision is taken first and then uncertainty is realized.

Once the graph of the decision problem is completed, it can be used in a systematic way to discover the optimal course of action. The methodology which is used is *averaging out* and *folding back*. This is done as follows.

Beginning at the end of each branch, work your way back through the tree computing the expected utility of each lottery. The expected utility of the lottery is shown above the chance node. Then the optimal course of action is chosen based on the highest expected utility. Courses of action which are rejected are so signified by denoting the action with the following mark // across the alternative.

The completed analysis for Case 1 would appear as follows:

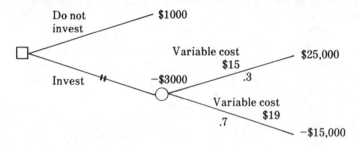

To further illustrate this technique, consider the following completed analysis for a more complex problem.

A decision-maker faces the choice of one of three courses of action: a_1, a_2, or a_3. If action a_1 is chosen there is a certain payoff of $5000.

If action a_2 is chosen, the immediate outcome depends on which one of two possible states (s_1 or s_2) occurs. If s_1 occurs then the decision-maker must choose between one of two courses of action: a_4 or a_5. If action a_4 is chosen, the outcome depends upon which one of two possible states (s_3 or s_4) occurs. If s_3 occurs the outcome is $10,000, if s_4 occurs the outcome is $5000. If action a_5 is chosen the outcome is $8000 with certainty. If action a_2 is chosen and s_2 occurs the payoff is −$2000.

If action a_3 is chosen the outcome depends upon which one of three possible states occur (s_5, s_6, or s_7). If s_5 occurs, the payoff is $10,000. If s_6 occurs, the payoff is −$5000. If s_7 occurs, the payoff is $8000.

The prior probabilities assigned by the decision-maker to the states are

s_1	.8
s_2	.2
s_3	.4
s_4	.6
s_5	.2
s_6	.1
s_7	.7

If the decision-maker adheres to the expected utility hypothesis and, further, is risk neutral, the graphical analysis would be as follows:

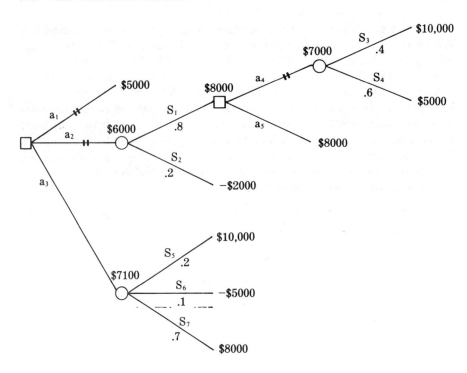

(ii) Joint and Conditional Probabilities and Bayes' Rule

In order to develop the notion of the value of imperfect, or sample, information we will require the concepts of joint and conditional probability. As with
all of the discussions of statistical methodologies in this article, the discussion here is superficial, intuitive, and incomplete. The interested reader is
referred to any probability or statistics text for a complete treatment.

Consider two events, A and B. The complement of A is (not A), denoted $\bar{A}$,
and the complement of B is (not B), denoted $\bar{B}$. We have the following table of
joint probabilities.

	A	$\bar{A}$
B	w	x
$\bar{B}$	y	z

That is, the probability of events B and A occurring simultaneously is w. We write

p(A ∩ B) = w

to denote the joint probability of A and B. The probability of A is given by w+y and the probability of B is given by w+x. Since A and Ā and B and B̄ are mutually exclusive, probability Axiom 2 requires that w+x+y+z = 1.0.

Now suppose we know that B has occurred. This is information affecting our beliefs about A and will cause us to revise our beliefs about A.

Consider the following *Venn* diagram.

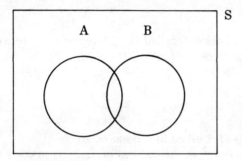

The box represents the sample space or all possible events. The probability that S occurs is 1.00. If we like, we can construct the box so that it has an area of one. Thus, circle A will have an area of w+y. Not A, the area outside the circle A, will have an area (probability) of x+z.

Similarly, circle B will have an area of w+x and the area outside circle B will be y+z.

Think of inference in the following way. Someone will throw a dart at the box denoting the sample space. The dart will certainly land inside the box. You have assigned a *prior* probability of w+y that the dart will land in circle A and a probability of w+x that the dart will land in circle B.

The probability of A and B occurring jointly is depicted by the intersection of circles A and B.

We can thus further specify the diagram as follows

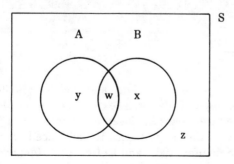

Suppose that you have a bet on your prediction of whether or not the dart lands in A. The dart has been thrown, outside your range of vision and now you must announce whether or not the dart landed in circle A.

Suppose further that before your prediction is announced, your agent surreptitiously signals to you that the dart landed in circle B.

This is news. The possible area where the dart can land has just shrunk from S down to circle B. Making the assumption that it is equally possible for the dart to have fallen anywhere in circle B, we can conclude that the probability that the circle has fallen into area A is the following:

$$\frac{\text{Ratio of the area common to A and B}}{\text{Area of B}} = \frac{w}{w + x}$$

We write the new probability which is called the posterior probability (it is the probability posterior to the receipt of information) as

$$P(A|B) = \frac{P(A \cap B)}{P(B)}$$

That is the revised probability of A given that B has occurred.

This is the essence of information in the context of decision-making under conditions of uncertainty. Information causes a decision-maker to revise prior beliefs about state probabilities. Since decision-making is conditional upon beliefs, information has the potential to be valuable because it can alter the preferred course of action.

We have developed intuitively the rule

$$P(A|B)P(B) = P(A \cap B)$$

Similarly we can show $P(A \cap B) = P(B|A)P(A)$

Thus we have

$$P(A|B)P(B) = P(B|A)P(A)$$

and

$$P(A|B) = \frac{P(B|A)P(A)}{P(B)}$$

The last formula has a special place in inference and decision-making. This formula is called *Bayes' Rule.* Bayes' Rule can be extended to multiple states and, in some cases, the procedure works in closed and usable form for continuous distributions. However, these are topics for advanced treatments (see for example, Raiffa and Schlaifer [1961] and DeGroot [1970]) and are not considered here.

The relationship $P(B|A)$ when A is the object of inference and B is the sample information is called the likelihood or, more generally, the likelihood function.

Let us illustrate these concepts by returning to Case 1.

Suppose, in Case 1, that the decision-maker can commission an accounting study which investigates what the variable cost will be. Let us use the following notation.

A_1	Variable cost is $15
A_2	Variable cost is $19
B_1	Accounting study says cost will be $15
B_2	Accounting study says cost will be $19.

The study has the following characteristics: if variable cost will be $15 there is a probability of 0.8 that the study will say the cost will be $15 and a probability of 0.2 that the study will erroneously conclude that the cost will be $19. If variable cost will be $19 there is a probability of 0.9 that the study will say that the cost will be $19 and a probability of 0.1 that the study will erroneously conclude that the cost will be $15.

The study is expected to cost $4000. Should the study be undertaken?

We begin our analysis by coding the likelihood information as follows:

$$P(B_1|A_1) = 0.8 \qquad P(B_1|A_2) = 0.1$$

$$P(B_2|A_1) = 0.2 \qquad P(B_2|A_2) = 0.9$$

Now let us compute the probabilities of receiving each signal using the conditional probabilities

$$P(B_1) = P(B_1|A_1)P(A_1) + P(B_1|A_2)P(A_2)$$

$$P(B_1) = (0.8)(.3) + (0.1)(.7) = 0.31$$

$$P(B_2) = P(B_2|A_1) + (A_1) + P(B_2|A_2)P(A_2)$$

$$P(B_2) = (.2)(.3) + (.9)(.7) = 0.69$$

Alternatively since B_1 and B_2 are mutually exclusive and exhaustive of the sample space we could have found $P(B_2) = 1 - P(B_1)$.

We are now ready to compute our posterior probabilities

$$P(A_1|B_1) = \frac{P(B_1|A_1)P(A_1)}{P(B_1)} = \frac{(.8)(.3)}{(.31)} = \frac{24}{31}$$

$$P(A_2|B_1) = 1 - \frac{24}{31} = \frac{7}{31} \text{ OR } \frac{(.1)(.7)}{.31}$$

$$P(A_1|B_2) = \frac{P(B_2|A_1)P(A_1)}{P(B_2)} = \frac{(.2)(.3)}{.69} = \frac{6}{69}$$

$$P(A_2|B_2) = 1 - \frac{6}{69} = \frac{63}{69} \text{ OR } \frac{(.9)(.7)}{.69}$$

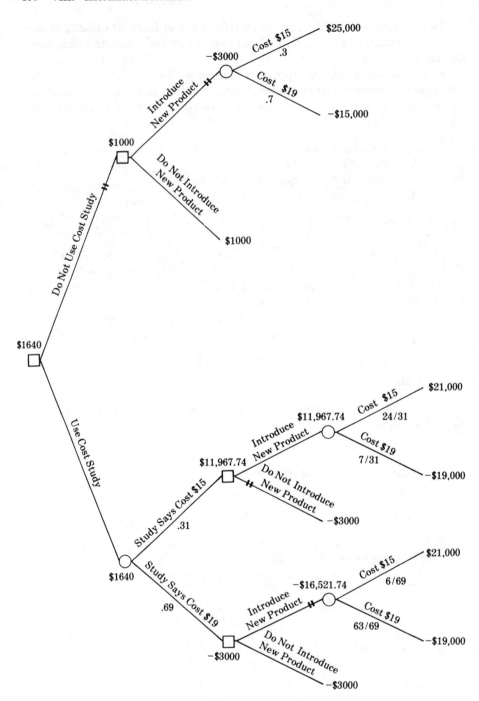

We can now summarize our information on a decision graph and determine our optimal course of action. Note that the cost of the accounting study is deducted from all branches which follow the receipt of sample information. Note also that the probability assigned to the variable cost is conditional on the result of the accounting study.

The graphical analysis indicates that the optimal course of action is to conduct the cost study. If the study predicts that the variable cost of the new product will be $15 then the new product should be implemented. If the study predicts the variable cost of new product will be $19 then the new product should not be undertaken. This situation where the optimal course of action is conditional upon the information signal is a necessary condition for information to have value.

Note that the expected value of the decision to undertake the study is $1640. Without the study the expected value is $1000. Thus the *net* expected benefit of the study is $1640−$1000 = $640. Recall that this is, indeed, the net expected benefit since we have already considered the study cost explicitly by deducting it from the outcomes following the cost study. The gross expected benefit of the study is $640 + $4000 = $4640. This is less than the expected value of perfect information ($7200) which we computed above because the imperfect information will sometimes result in opportunity losses.

10. Conclusion

In this article we have reviewed briefly the following topics:

(i) Decision-making concepts
(ii) The axiomatic systems of probability and preference underlying expected utility theory
(iii) The expected value hypothesis
(iv) The value of perfect information
(v) Decision trees
(vi) Bayes' Rule
(vii) The value of sample information.

The purpose of the review is two-fold. For those who have been exposed to this material this article should serve as a review of the primary topics. For those for whom this material is new, hopefully, this article will serve as a motivation to explore these topics more fully. This article is too superficial and brief to serve as a treatment of these topics. Because of this, we conclude by providing a brief and selective review of the material in this area.

(A) *Probability*
    (i) Drake [1967]: an introductory treatment
    (ii) Parzen [1960]: a standard reference text

(B) *Utility*
   (i)   Demski [1972]: a brief review of concepts
   (ii) Von Neumann and Morgenstern [1944]: the first complete development of modern utility theory
   (iii) Savage [1954]: the standard reference for the axioms of utility
   (iv) Luce and Raiffa [1957]: a discussion of Savage's proposals and an alternative, equivalent, axiomatic system.

(C) *Decision Theory and Value of Information*
   (i)   Raiffa [1968]: an informal, easy-to-follow introduction
   (ii) Winkler [1972]: an introductory treatment
   (iii) Raiffa and Schlaifer [1961]: a rigorous treatment
   (iv) DeGroot [1970]: a rigorous treatment

Problems

1. Consider the following payoff table.

	S_1	S_2
a_1	10	-5
a_2	1	15

If the decision-maker is risk-neutral and believes that the probability of s_1 is 0.6, show that the optimal course of action is a_2 and the expected value of perfect information is $5.40.

2. A risk-neutral street vendor stocks two products. Each day the vendor packs one of the two products in his cart and sets out. The payoff to the vendor depends upon the product stocked and whether the weather is warm or cool. The vendor believes that the probability is 0.3 that the weather will be cool tomorrow. If product 1 is stocked, the vendor's payoff is $150 if the weather is cool and $20 otherwise. If product 2 is stocked, the vendor's payoff is $-$10 if the weather is cool and $100 if the weather is warm. Show the following:

(i)   The optimal course of action is to stock product 2
(ii) The expected value of perfect information is $48.00.
(iii) The vendor will prefer product 1 only when $P(s_1)$ is greater than $1/3$.

3. An oil company holds the rights to drill for oil on a piece of land. If oil is found, the net payoff is expected to be $20,000,000. If no oil is found, the

net loss will be $5,000,000. The company's senior geologist believes that the probability is 0.3 that oil will be found. The company has been offered $2,000,000 for its rights.

If the company makes decisions on the basis of maximizing expected value, show that the minimum price the company would sell its rights for is $2,500,000.

4. A company operates an automated line which fills milk cartons. The line foreman suspects with probability 0.3 that the machines are out of adjustment and are overfilling each carton by 3 millilitres.

The machines are scheduled for regular maintenance in one week and at that time they will be completely overhauled and adjusted. The foreman is wondering if a partial adjustment should be made now. The regular maintenance will be performed in one week, regardless of what is done now.

The cost to the company of shutting down the line and resetting the machines is $8000. The cost of overfilling, if that is occurring, will be $20,000 over the period of the next week. Show that the optimal course of action is to leave the machine unadjusted.

5. *This problem requires elementary differentiation.*
A risk-neutral newsboy buys papers for $c apiece and sells them for $p apiece. Any papers unsold at the end of the day can be sold to a recycling plant for $s apiece. All orders must be placed daily before 10:00 a.m. which is before daily demand is known.

Demand (x) is a random variable which is, to the newsboy, defined by a probability density function f(x).

(i) Show that the optimal quantity to stock (q) is found by

$$F(q) = \frac{p - c}{p - s}$$

where F(q) is the probability that demand is less than or equal to q. That is, the newsboy will order a sufficient quantity of papers such that the probability of a stock-out is

$$1 - \frac{p - c}{p - s}$$

(ii) Show that the expected value of the optimal order policy given in (i) is

$$(p - s) \int_{0}^{q} x\, f(x) dx$$

(iii) Show that the expected value of perfect information is

$$s \int_0^q x\, f(x)dx + p \int_q^\infty x\, f(x)dx - c\bar{x}$$

where $\bar{x}$ is expected demand.

6. Return to the data in question 2 above. Suppose that the street vendor is thinking about consulting George the gypsy for a weather forecast. George's forecasts are correct 90% of the time. Show that the maximum that the vendor would be willing to pay for one of George's predictions is $34.

7. Return to the data in question 3 above. Suppose the oil company can perform a seismic test. The existence of the test and its results will be known only to the company. The test has three possible outcomes: good, fair, poor. The likelihood function relating underlying states to test-outcomes is as follows:

Underlying State	Probability Test Outcome		
	Good	Fair	Poor
Oil	.7	.2	.1
No oil	.1	.3	.6

The test will cost the firm $2,000,000. Show that the *net* value of the test information is $790,000 and that the optimal course of action is to perform the test and:

(i)   drill if the test says good
(ii)   sell if the test says fair
(iii) sell if the test says poor

8. Return to the data in question 4. Suppose the company can test the fill amount of the machines by removing random cartons from the assembly line and measuring their contents. The cost of the test is $2000. The test will indicate the fill level is improper 20% of the time when it, in fact, is correct and will indicate the fill level is proper 30% of the time when it, in fact, is improper. Show that the net value of the test is −$600 and that the optimal course of action is not to perform the test.

Bibliography

Allais, Maurice. "Le comportement de l'homme rationnel devant le risque: critique des postulates et axioms de l'ecole americaine," *Econometrica*, Volume 21, 1953, pp. 503-546.

Churchman, C.W., R.L. Ackoff, and E.L. Arnoff. *Introduction to Operations Research*, Wiley, New York, 1957, Chapter 5.

DeGroot, M.H. *Optimal Statistical Decisions*, McGraw-Hill, New York, 1970.

DeGroot, M.H. *Probability and Statistics*, Addison-Wesley, Reading, 1975.

Demski, J.S., *Information Analysis*, Addison-Wesley, Reading, 1972.

Drake, A.W., *Fundamentals of Applied Probability Theory*, McGraw-Hill, New York, 1967.

Knight, F.H., *Risk, Uncertainty and Profit*, Houghton Mifflin Company, Boston, 1933, pp. 19-20 and Chapter 7.

Luce, R.D., and H. Raiffa, *Games and Decisions*, Wiley, New York, 1957.

Parzen, E., *Modern Probability Theory and Its Applications*, Wiley, New York, 1960.

Raiffa, Howard., *Decision Analysis: Introductory Lectures on Choices Under Uncertainty*, Addison-Wesley, Reading, 1968.

Raiffa, H., and R. Schlaifer, *Applied Statistical Decision Theory*, Division of Research, Graduate School of Business Administration, Harvard University, Boston, 1961.

Savage, L.J., *The Foundations of Statistics*, Wiley, New York, 1954.

Von Neumann, John, and Oskar Morgenstern, *Theory of Games and Economic Behavior*, Wiley, New York, 1944.

Winkler, R.L., *Introduction to Bayesian Inference and Decision*, Holt, Rinehart and Winston, Inc., New York, 1972.

36

DECISION-MAKING UNDER CONDITIONS OF UNCERTAINTY: RISK AVERSION, GROUP DECISION-MAKING, AND AGENCY THEORY

ANTHONY A. ATKINSON*

1. Introduction

The process of a systematic approach to decision-making under conditions of uncertainty has been defined by many writers over the last forty years. Beginning with Von Neumann and Morgenstern [1944] and followed by Savage [1971] an axiomatic system of decision-making, called utility theory, has been developed.

A special case of utility theory, the expected value hypothesis has become widely known and used. This application, as well as the foundations of utility theory, have been described in an accompanying article which appears in this volume. In this article, we will begin by considering the issues of risk aversion. We will then turn to issues of valuing information when the decision-maker is risk averse.

Following the discussion of risk-aversion, we will take up two separate, but related, topics: group decision-making and the risk-sharing value of information. The latter topics represent natural extensions of decision-making under uncertainty and underlie, to some extent, agency theory which is the utility based approach to organization design and control.

When dealing with risk-averse utility, it is inevitable that a minimum amount of algebra is required. The amount of notation employed here is minimal. The reader may skip over any mathematical development since all ideas developed in this article are described both intuitively and algebraically.

*School of Business Administration, Dalhousie University

2. Expected Utility Theory

Expected utility theory is a systematic treatment of decision-making under conditions of uncertainty. The contribution of utility theory is that it shows that if an individual subscribes to a set of assumptions, or axioms, concerning coding probabilistic beliefs and expressing preferences then the following two results obtain:

(i) there exists a real valued function (a utility function) which assigns numbers to outcomes in such a way that ranking outcomes by these numbers will result in the same ranking chosen independently by the decision-maker;

(ii) ranking actions by expected utility will result in the same ranking of actions chosen independently by the decision-maker.

This does *not* mean that decision-makers construct utility functions or compute expected utilities. What is implied is that the behaviour of individuals who subscribe to the axioms of expected utility can be modeled by the expected utility paradigm.

The most well known application of the expected utility criterion is the expected value hypothesis. The expected value hypothesis predicts that the decision-maker will choose the course of action which has the highest expected value. The utility function which is consistent with this behaviour has wealth as its only argument and, further, is a linear function. This linearity, in turn, implies that the decision-maker is indifferent to risk or risk-neutral. That is, the decision-maker requires no compensation for undertaking risk, all that matters is the expected value of the gamble.

This assumption of risk neutrality has been the object of considerable discussion. In fact, the impetus to develop utility theory was prompted by the dissatisfaction with the attributes of risk-neutrality.

Before we consider how expected utility theory handles risk aversion we first consider the attributes and properties of risk aversion.

3. Risk Aversion

There are many phenomena in our society which dispute risk-neutrality as a reasonable portrayal of decision-making behaviour in the face of uncertainty. State lotteries, insurance, diversification of portfolios (both in a security and a business operation sense), and buying or selling futures contracts are all instances of behaviour which is inconsistent with the expected value hypothesis.

Lotteries have associated with them a negative expected value since transactions cost and the organizer's share cause less to be paid out than is taken in. Lotteries typify a common attribute of gambling. In a lottery the gambler willingly seeks out a gamble with a negative expected value where there is a small chance of a large gain and a large chance of a small loss.

Insurance is the antithesis of gambling. When voluntarily buying insurance, the insured willingly seeks out a gamble with a negative expected value where there is a small chance of a large loss and a large chance of a small loss.

In the case of gambling, the gambler pays more than the expected value for the lottery ticket. In the case of insurance, the insured pays more than the expected loss to avoid a gamble. The gambler exhibits risk-seeking behaviour, the insured, risk-averse behaviour. These are fundamentally different types of behaviour and most people would not be too surprised to see both behaviours being simultaneously exhibited by the same individual. Friedman and Savage [1948] have given considerable thought to this issue.

It is useful to develop a graphical representation of utility. For this purpose we will require a two-coordinate graph. On the horizontal axis we will represent wealth, on the vertical axis, utility. Consider the following three utility graphs.

In all three figures, the utility function is increasing in wealth reflecting the assumption that more wealth is always preferred to less.

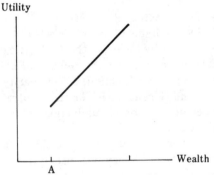

Figure 1

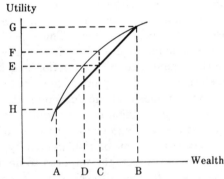

Figure 2

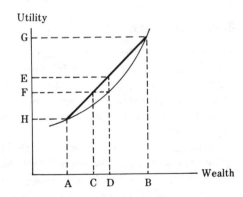

Figure 3

In Figure 1, the utility function is linear in wealth. In Figure 2, the utility function is concave in wealth. We will see, below, that a concave utility function characterizes risk aversion. In Figure 3, the utility function is convex in wealth.

In Figure 2, consider the line segment joining any two points, A and B, on the utility function. Suppose the decision-maker faced the following gamble involving A and B.

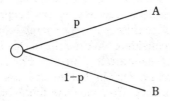

If p=1 we have A and if p=0 we have B. The line joining A and B represents the expected value of this lottery for values of p varying from 1 to 0.

Suppose we fix p at a particular value and determine that C is the expected value of the resulting lottery, that is C=pA+(1−p)B. We have already defined a risk-averse decision-maker as someone who values a lottery at less than its expected value. Suppose the decision-maker values the lottery as D. We can thus conclude that the expected utility of the gamble is E, where E=p(H)+(1−p)G. Note however that the utility associated with the expected value of the gamble is F which is greater than E. Thus the arc defining expected value will always lie to the right of the function defining expected utility. The definition of a concave function is that any point on the arc defined by any two end points will always be greater than any linear combination of the end points. Thus concave utility functions are associated with risk aversion. The reader who is familiar with statistics should note that the above result can be established using Jensen's inequality which states that, for a concave function f(x) and the expectation operator E,

$$Ef(x) < f(E(x)).$$

Thus, there is a value RP such that

$$Ef(x) = f(\bar{x} - RP).$$

Where $\bar{x} = Ef(x)$

In a similar way, using Figure 3 we can show that risk seeking behaviour implies a utility function which is convex in wealth.

These are, admittedly, simple utility functions. Friedman and Savage [1948] have argued, using a casual empiricism, that individuals exhibit utility

functions which are concave over low values of wealth, convex over intermediate values, and concave over higher values.

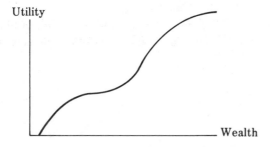

Swalm [1966] conducted an analysis of the risk-taking behaviour of executives and described the observed utility functions as characteristically
S shaped.

Notwithstanding the empirical evidence, both casual and experimental,
which suggests that utility functions are neither strictly (always) concave
nor strictly convex, most of the theoretical literature has concentrated on
utility functions which are concave. We will concentrate on risk aversion in
this article by arguing, without justification, that most business decisions
reflect risk-aversion and thus this is the relevant behaviour to discuss.

4. Evidence of Risk Aversion

There are two types of evidence offered in support of the hypothesis that
risk-aversion is characteristic of decision-making in the presence of uncertainty:

(i)   by argument
(ii) by market evidence.

While there are many instances of each type of evidence the most widely
discussed argument is that due to Bernoulli [1954] (and subsequent embellishments) and the most widely discussed market evidence is that due to
Markowitz [1952]. We will discuss each of these in turn.

(i) Bernoulli and the St. Petersburg Paradox

In 1738, Daniel Bernoulli, a Swiss mathematician, wrote what has become a
classic paper in the area of utility theory. Bernoulli argued that, in effect,
the expected value hypothesis was not consistent with observed patterns
of decision-making.

Bernoulli pointed out that it would not be unreasonable for "a very poor
fellow" faced with the following lottery to sell the lottery ticket to a rich man
for 9000 ducats. Bernoulli claimed that the evaluation of a gamble is not independent of the individual but depends crucially upon the circumstances of
the decision-maker.

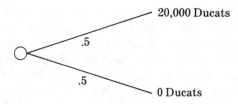

These circumstances were taken to mean the individual's wealth and Bernoulli argued that "there is no doubt that a gain of one thousand ducats is more significant to a pauper than to a rich man though both gain the same amount."

This proposal of declining marginal utility provides the characteristic attribute of risk-averse behaviour. Furthermore, Bernoulli asserted "now it is highly probable that any increase in wealth, no matter how significant, will always result in an increase in utility which is inversely proportionate to the quantity of goods already possessed."

This type of utility is logarithmic. If we denote the utility of an amount x as U(x) and use logarithmic utility we have

$$U(x) = \log (x)$$

$$\text{marginal utility } = \frac{dU(x)}{dx} = U'(x) = \frac{d\log(x)}{dx} = \frac{1}{x}$$

which is what Bernoulli asserted. It is interesting that, to this day, because of its descriptive and analytic properties, logarithmic utility remains the most widely used utility function in theoretical work.

To this point, Bernoulli's comments constitute little more than careful observation or reasoning. But Bernoulli concluded his observation on risk-aversion and insurance with the following ingenious example.

I am forced to admit many novel remarks though these would clearly not be unserviceable. And, though a person who is fairly judicious by natural instinct might have realized and spontaneously applied much of what I have here explained, hardly anyone believed it possible to define these problems with the precision we have employed in our examples. Since all our propositions harmonize perfectly with experience it would be wrong to neglect them as abstractions resting upon precarious hypotheses. This is further confirmed by the following example which inspired these thoughts, and whose history is as follows: My most honorable cousin the celebrated Nicolas Bernoulli, Professor . . . at the University of Bassle, once submitted problems to the highly distinguished mathematician Montmort . . . The last of these problems runs as follows: Peter tosses a coin and continues to do so until it should land heads when it comes to the ground. He agrees to give Paul one ducat if he gets heads on the very first throw, two ducats if he gets it on the second, four if on the third, eight if on the fourth, and so on. So that with each additional throw the number of ducats he must pay is doubled. Suppose we seek to determine the value of Paul's expectation. My aforementioned cousin discussed this problem in a letter to me asking for my opinion. Although the standard calculation shows that the value of Paul's expectation is infinitely great, it has, he said to be admitted that any fairly reasonable man would sell his chance, with great pleasure, for twenty ducats. The accepted method of calculation does, indeed, value Paul's prospects at infinity though no one would be willing to purchase it at a moderately high price.

The fact that this gamble has a infinite expected value is undeniable. The payoff to Paul is 2^n where n is the number of tails tossed before a head turns up. The probability of tossing exactly n successive tails with a fair coin is $(.5)^n$. The expected value of the gamble is thus

$$\sum_{n=1}^{\infty} 2^n (.5)^n = \sum_{n=1}^{\infty} 1$$

this is an infinite sum. If we admit that no one would be willing to pay an infinite amount to participate in this gamble, we are implicitly recognizing declining marginal utility and its consequence, risk aversion.

To illustrate Bernoulli's idea, suppose that Paul owns the rights to the above lottery and has no other assets. If Paul's utility function is logarithmic, then the utility value of the lottery to Paul is

$$EU(x) = \sum_{n=1}^{\infty} \log (2^n)(.5^n)$$

$$EU(x) = \log 2 \sum_{n=1}^{\infty} n(.5)^n$$

note that
$$\sum_{n=1}^{m} n(.5)^n \equiv S = 1(.5)^1 + 2(.5)^2 + \ldots + m(.5)^m$$

and
$$(1/.5) \sum_{n=1}^{m} n(.5)^n = 1 + 2(.5)^1 + \ldots + m(.5)^{m-1}.$$

Thus $\quad [(1/.5)-1]\ S\ =\ S\ =\ 1+\ \sum\limits_{n=1}^{m-1}\ (.5)^n -m\ (.5)^m$

and as $m \to \infty$, $\quad \sum\limits_{n=1}^{m-1}\ (.5)^n \to 1$ and $m(.5)^m \to 0$.

Thus $\quad S = EU(x) \cong 2\log 2$

and the selling price is 4 ducats.

(ii) Markowitz and Portfolio

Markowitz [1952] addressed the issue of selecting securities for investment. Commenting on the net present value hypothesis, Markowitz reasoned as follows: "the hypothesis (or maxim) that the investor does (or should) maximize discounted return must be rejected. If we ignore market imperfections the foregoing rule never implies that there is a diversified portfolio which is preferable to all non diversified portfolios. Diversification is both observable and sensible; a rule of behaviour which does not imply the superiority of diversification must be rejected both as a hypothesis and as a maxim . . .

We . . . consider the rule that the investor does (or should) consider expected return as a desirable thing and variance an undesirable thing."

This led Markowitz to the so called mean-variance criterion which stipulates that the investor will seek to choose a portfolio with the smallest variance for a specified level of expected return. The actual expected return variance pair chosen by the investor will be a function of the investor's utility function. However the set of portfolios from which any investor will choose can be specified in advance. The members of this, efficient, set will be all portfolios which either:

(i) have the smallest amount of variance for a given level of expected return or

(ii) have the highest expected return for a given level of variance.

The relevance of Markowitz's contribution was that he pointed out a market phenomenon, diversification, which suggested risk aversion.

To illustrate the point made by Markowitz, consider the following example. An investor is considering investing in securities. Security 1 promises a return of $10 if State 1 occurs and $2 if state 2 occurs. Security 2 provides a return of $2 if state 1 occurs and $10 if state 2 occurs. Security 2 is thus perfectly negatively correlated with security 1 and each provides a perfect hedge for the other.

Markowitz suggests that, in this case, the investor will always hold security 1 and security 2 simultaneously since, by doing this, portfolio variance can be reduced to zero.

In fact, this is the foundation for the modern theory of financial economics. Only risk which cannot be diversified away by inclusion of the security in a portfolio will earn an incremental return for risk in an efficient capital market.

Unfortunately, the mean-variance criterion and the expected utility hypothesis are not surrogates. The mean-variance criterion is, only in very special cases, equivalent to the expected utility hypothesis. Hanoch and Levy [1969] constructed and discussed the following example:

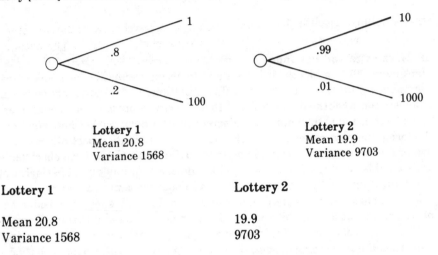

Lottery 1
Mean 20.8
Variance 1568

Lottery 2
Mean 19.9
Variance 9703

	Lottery 1	Lottery 2
Mean	20.8	19.9
Variance	1568	9703

Using the mean-variance criterion, lottery 1 is preferred to lottery 2.

Suppose however the investor exhibits logarithmic utility. That is, the utility number associated with an outcome is the natural logarithm of the outcome. The expected utility associated with lottery 1 is 0.921 and for lottery 2 it is 2.349. Lottery 2 is clearly preferred to lottery 1. This example implies that, in general, the mean-variance criterion violates the axioms of expected utility. It turns out that if: (i) the utility function is quadratic and/or (ii) the distributions of all portfolio returns are all members of the family of stable Paretian distributions (the normal distribution is the only, well-known, member of this family), then the mean-variance criterion is consistent with utility maximization.

5.   Representing Risk Aversion

We have established that to represent a risk-averse utility we need a function which is concave in wealth. Utility, as Bernoulli suggested, is a personal thing. Thus one person's utility function will not necessarily do for another person.

Theoretical work requires utility functions which can be stated in some form. In addition, ease of manipulation requires that the function be continuous.

In order to facilitate the discussion in this article we will assume functional forms such as power, logarithmic, or exponential. But this does *not* imply that utility functions *must* assume such a form. *Any* concave function can represent some form of risk aversion.

In a seminal work, Arrow [1971, Chapter 3] developed the primitive concepts of utility theory. We now briefly review his development.

Let x be wealth and
U(x) be the total utility of wealth x.

The first derivative of the utility function, with respect to wealth, denoted $U'(x)$, is the rate of change of utility with respect to wealth. The second derivative of the utility function with respect to wealth, denoted $U''(x)$, is the rate of change of marginal utility with respect to wealth.

Recall that the utility function serves a ranking task only. There is no cardinality associated with a utility number. Consequently, the only matter of relevance concerning a utility function is the derivative $U'(x)$ and the behaviour of the derivative $U''(x)$.

Arrow demonstrated that, because of this, the following two measures summarize all there is needed to know about a utility function.

$$R_A(x) = -\frac{U''(x)}{U'(x)} \qquad \text{Absolute risk aversion}$$

$$R_R(x) = -\frac{xU''(x)}{U'(x)} \qquad \text{Relative risk aversion}$$

Pratt [1964] has suggested a more direct way of showing that the measure of absolute risk aversion summarizes all that is important about utility.

Integrating $R(x)$ we have $-\log u'(x)$.

Thus $\exp[-\int R(x)] = U'(x)$
and $U(x) = \int \exp[-\int R(x)]$

Thus, a person's absolute risk aversion measure and relative risk aversion measure reveal all there is of importance about a person's utility function. Readers will often find reference to the *risk tolerance measure* which is the reciprocal of the risk aversion measure.

Pratt [1964] developed a practical interpretation of the measure of absolute risk aversion. First, we define the risk premium of a lottery as the difference between the expected value of a lottery and the amount for which the decision-maker would sell the lottery. Pratt showed that the risk premium for a lottery with mean m and with a small variance is approximately one half of the variance of the lottery multiplied by the measure of absolute risk aversion evaluated at x+m where x is the decision-maker's current wealth.

To illustrate the above discussion suppose that the decision-maker faces the following lottery.

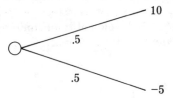

The decision-maker's current wealth is 50 and the decision-maker's utility function is given by log(x) where x is terminal wealth.

If we add the decision-maker's wealth to the incremental payoffs from the lottery we have

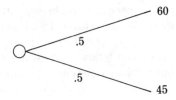

The expected utility of the lottery is

$$(.5) \log(60) + (.5) \log(45) = 3.951$$

Suppose we wish to determine the certainty equivalent. This is the amount such that the decision-maker would be indifferent between facing the lottery and selling the lottery. The amount, S, can be found as

$$\log(50 + S) = 3.951 \text{ or } 50 + S = e^{3.951} \text{ or } S = 1.96$$

Since the expected value of the lottery is 2.5, the risk premium is 2.5 − 1.96 = 0.54.

We have U(x) = log(x).
Thus:

$$U'(x) = \frac{1}{x}$$

$$U''(x) = -\frac{1}{x^2}$$

and $R_A(x) = -\dfrac{u''(x)}{u'(x)} = \dfrac{1}{x}.$

Note that this investor's measure of absolute risk aversion is decreasing in terminal wealth. It is true for most utility functions that risk-attitude is a function of wealth (the exceptions are linear and exponential utility). This is why outcomes from lotteries are always stated in terms of terminal wealth.

The variance of the above lottery is 56.25. The decision-maker's measure of absolute risk aversion evaluated at $x+m$ is

$$\frac{1}{50 + 2.5} = 0.019047$$

Thus Pratt's formula would predict

$$R P = (1/2)(56.25)(0.019047) = 0.54$$

A more direct interpretation of the measure of absolute risk aversion is a reflection of the decision-maker's willingness to accept risk.

To illustrate, suppose we have an investor with wealth w who is considering investing a fraction x of wealth in a risky asset. It can be shown using comparative statics, that the fraction of wealth invested in the risky asset is a decreasing function of the risk aversion measure. Thus it is meaningful to say that the risk aversion measure is a reflection of the decision-maker's attitude toward, and willingness to accept, risk. The higher the measure is, the less willing the decision-maker is to accept risk.

We must be careful in interpreting the above statement since the risk aversion measure is a local measure. To illustrate, suppose that a decision-maker has power utility of the form $U(w) = w^{1/4}$ where w is wealth. The measure of absolute risk aversion is

$$R(w) = \frac{3}{4w} \cdot$$

Note that this measure is defined for each level of wealth w. Thus if we have two decision-makers with absolute risk aversion measures $r_1(w)$ and $r_2(w)$, we can say, in general, that decision-maker 1 is less risk averse than decision maker 2 if

$$r_1(w) < r_2(w) \quad \text{for all w.}$$

That is, for each level of wealth, decision-maker 1's absolute risk-aversion measure is less than decision-maker 2's.

One situation where this occurs is where two decision-makers have utility functions of the same functional form but decision-maker 1 has more wealth.

Savage [1971] has suggested that the following function should be a useful approximation of most utility functions:

$$U(x) = (1-e^{-\lambda x})/\lambda$$

Where λ is a parameter which is individual specific. Suppose a decision-maker exhibits the above utility function with $\lambda = 0.001$.
The utility of the above lottery is 51.12. To find the certainty equivalent, solve

$$\frac{(1-e^{-\lambda(x+S)})}{\lambda} = 51.12 \quad \text{or} \quad S = 2.4719$$

The risk premium is $2.5 - 2.4719 = 0.028$
Using Pratt's formula we require

$$U'(x) = e^{-\lambda x}$$
$$U''(x) = -\lambda e^{-\lambda x}$$
$$-U''(x)/U'(x) = \lambda$$
$$\text{R.P.} = (\tfrac{1}{2})(56.25)(0.001) = 0.028$$

6. HARA Class Utilities

An important class of utility functions which form the basis for virtually all the theoretical work involving utility theory which has been done in Finance and Economics is the so-called HARA class of utility.

These utility functions are called HARA (for hyperbolic absolute risk aversion) because the measure of absolute risk aversion is a hyperbolic function of wealth

$$R(w) = \left(\frac{w}{1-\gamma} + \frac{\eta}{\beta} \right)^{-1}$$

where β, γ, and η are parameters of the utility function.

Notice that the reciprocal of $R(w)$, the risk tolerance measure, is linear in wealth, consequently the HARA class exhausts the family of utility functions whose risk tolerance measure is linear.

The parameters of the utility function are subject to the following restrictions

$$\gamma \neq 1, \quad \beta > 0, \quad R(w) > 0.$$

There are two special cases of HARA utilities: $\gamma = \infty$ and $\gamma = 0$.

(i) $\gamma = \infty$
    As γ goes to infinity, $w/1-\gamma$ goes to zero and $R(w)$ becomes $(\eta/\beta)^{-1}$

$$-\int R(w) \text{ yields} \quad -\beta w/\eta \quad \text{and}$$
$$U(w) = \int \exp \{-\beta w/\eta\} = -(\eta/\beta) \exp \{-\beta w/\eta\}.$$

Thus if a person's attitude towards risk is to be independent of wealth, that person must exhibit exponential utility.

(ii) $\gamma = 0$

$$U(w) = \int (\beta w + \eta)^{-1} = (1/\beta) \log (\beta w + \eta).$$

This is logarithmic utility, which was, apparently, first suggested by Bernoulli and remains very popular in current theoretical work.

If $\gamma \neq 0$

$$U(w) = \int ((\beta w/(1-\gamma)) + \eta)^{\gamma-1} = ((1-\gamma)/\beta\gamma) ((\beta w/(1-\gamma)) + \eta)^{\gamma}.$$

This is the class of power utility functions.

These utility functions: exponential, logarithmic, and power comprise all the utility functions assumed in finance and economics.

With this development in mind, we can return to the previous discussion of interpreting the expression *more risk averse*.

For HARA class utilities we can show, by taking derivatives, that r(w) is

(i)   decreasing in w if $\gamma < 1$, increasing otherwise
(ii)   decreasing in η
(iii)   increasing in β
(iv)   decreasing in γ .

We can see that, while statements about the risk aversion properties of a given decision-maker can be unambiguously related to the utility function parameters, it is not possible, in general, to compare utilities of different forms.

For example, if we have two decision-makers with the following utility functions

$$U_1(w_1) = (w_1)^{1/2}$$
$$U_2(w_2) = 3(w_2)^{1/4}$$

we can say unambiguously that decision-maker one is less risk averse than decision-maker two. If, however, we have two decision-makers with the following utility functions

$$U_1(w) = (w)^{1/2}$$
$$U_2(w) = \log (w + 10{,}000)$$
$$R_1(w) = \frac{1}{2w}$$
$$R_2(w) = \frac{1}{w + 10{,}000}$$

Thus $R_1(w) > R_2(w)$ only if w $<$ 10,000.

In this case, decision-maker one is more risk averse than decision-maker two only if terminal wealth is less than 10,000.

7. Expected Utility Calculations

A decision-maker's choice of an optimal course of action under conditions of uncertainty can be replicated by the following method for decision-makers who subscribe to the axioms of expected utility.

(i)   determine all states affecting outcomes
(ii)   specify all courses of action
(iii) for each state/outcome pair, determine the outcome
(iv)   determine the utility number associated with each outcome
(v)   choose the course of action with the highest expected utility.

To illustrate this process, consider the following example.

An investor faces an investment which pays $10,000 if state 1 occurs and a loss of $4000 if state 2 occurs. The investor assesses a prior probability of 0.4 that state 1 will occur.

The decision-maker has a current wealth of $50,000 and has a utility function such that the utility number associated with terminal wealth is the square root of terminal wealth.

The decision-maker has been offered $1000 for the investment.

The payoff table faced by the investor is (note: payoffs are stated in terms of terminal wealth)

	S_1	S_2			S_1	S_2
keep investment	60,000	46,000		keep investment	244.95	214.48
sell investment	51,000	51,000		sell investment	225.83	225.83

Dollar Outcomes	**Utility Outcomes**

The expected utilities are:

keep investment: $(.4)(244.95)+(.6)(214.48) = 226.67$
sell investment: $(.4)(225.83)+(.6)(225.83) = 225.83$

The optimal course of action is to keep the investment.

Note that the expected values of the two courses of action are:

keep investment: $51,600
sell investment: $51,000.

Thus, in this case, the course of action chosen by the decision-maker assumed here and a risk neutral decision-maker would be the same.

To see how this can change, suppose that the decision-maker in the above problem has a current wealth of $4000. The revised payoff and utility tables are:

	S_1	S_2
keep investment	14,000	0
sell investment	5000	5000

Dollar Outcomes

	S_1	S_2
keep investment	118.32	0
sell investment	70.71	70.71

Utility Outcomes

Expected utilities are:

  keep investment: $(.4)(118.32) + (.6)(0)$ $= 47.33$
  sell investment: $(.4)(70.71) + (.6)(70.71) = 70.71$

Expected values are:

  keep investment: $(.4)(14,000) + (.6)(0)$ $= \$5600$
  sell investment: $(.4)(5000) + (.5)(5000) = \$5000.$

In this case, the optimal course of action for the decision-maker is to sell the investment, whereas a risk-neutral decision-maker would invest. What has happened here, in the alteration of the initial example, is that the decision-maker has become more risk-averse by virtue of decreased wealth and the investment opportunity is no longer attractive.

8. Expected Value of Perfect Information

Since the non-linear utility function can take on any form there is no single computation for the value of perfect information in the case of non-linear utility. Instead the approach used is to:

(i) Determine the maximum outcome when each state occurs. (Since the decision-maker has perfect information the optimal course of action will be chosen.)

(ii) Subtract a number from each outcome such that when utilities and expected utilities are computed the expected utility with perfect information is equal to the expected utility of the optimal course of action based upon prior beliefs. This number is the expected value of perfect information.

Step (ii) is an iterative process which must be repeated until an equilibrating number is found. A useful number to begin this process is the expected value of perfect information for the risk-neutral decision-maker.

To illustrate, reconsider the example in section 6. The expected value of perfect information is found by solving for x in the following equation

$$(.4)(60,000 - x)^{1/2} + (.6)(51,000 - x)^{1/2} = 226.66.$$

Using a trial and error process, we can find x = $3133. Thus the decision-maker would be willing to pay up to $3133 for perfect information.

Recall that the optimal course of action for a risk-neutral decision-maker is to keep the investment. Thus the expected value of perfect information for the risk-neutral decision-maker is given by:

$$EVPI = (.4)(0) + (.6)(5000) = \$3000$$

Thus, in this particular example, perfect information is worth more to the risk-averse decision-maker than it is to the risk-neutral decision-maker. This may *seem* natural since risk-aversion renders a decision-maker more eager to avoid risk and buy information. However this conclusion is erroneous.

Return to the revised example in Section 6 where the current wealth is $4000.

The optimal course of action is to sell the investment. The decrease in wealth, and corresponding increase in risk aversion has caused the decision-maker to choose the safer course of action.

The expected value of the perfect information is found by solving for x in the following equation

$$(.4)(14,000-x)^{1/2} + (.6)(5000-x)^{1/2} = 70.71$$

Solving we find x = $2771. In this case, the expected value of perfect information is worth less to the risk-averse decision-maker than the risk-neutral decision-maker.

Thus the value of information is problematic. We can make no generalizations concerning how risk-aversion will affect information value. This is because of the dual nature of perfect information. While perfect information does eliminate opportunity losses, a new risk is imposed. In the above example, after the information is paid for, the decision-maker expects that 60% of the time the information will merely confirm what the decision-maker's prior information suggested. Thus it is expected that 60% of the time the perfect information will be redundant and useless and the cost of the information will be a loss.

9. Expected Value of Sample Information

The expected value of sample information for a risk-averse decision-maker is found by an iterative trial and error process as in the case of perfect information. The expected value of sample information is a number which, when subtracted from all outcomes, causes the expected utility of decision-making with the sample information to be equal to the expected utility of decision-making without the sample information.

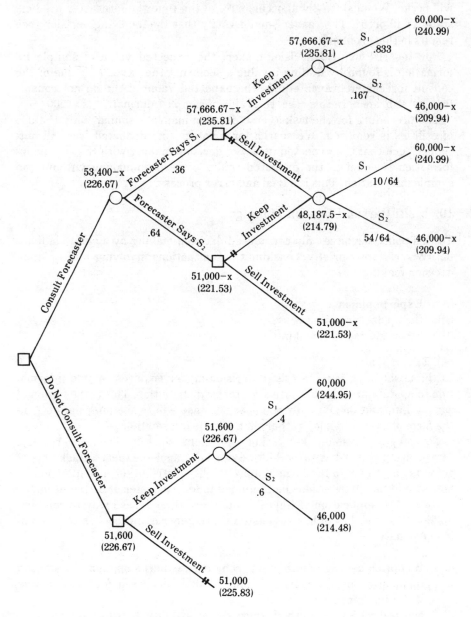

Risk Neutral: EVSI = 53,400 − 51,600 = $1800

Risk-Averse: All utility numbers shown in brackets. Disregard expected values and dollar outcomes. EVSI = $1925 to make expected utilities equal.

To illustrate, let us extend the data in the example introduced in section 6.
Suppose that the investor can consult a market forecaster whose predictions follow the following pattern (likelihood function).
When state 1 will occur, 75% of the time the forecaster predicts state 1 will occur. When state 2 will occur, 90% of the time the forecaster predicts state 2 will occur. The reader should verify that the following decision tree results in this problem.

For the risk-neutral decision-maker, the expected value of sample information is found by finding a value x such that the expected value of the consult forecaster branch equals the expected value of the do not consult forecaster branch. In this case, the value of sample information is $1800.

The procedure for the risk-averse decision-maker is similar, only the use of utilities is required. We search for a value of x , deducted from all outcomes, such that the expected utility of decision-making with the sample information is equal to the expected utility of decision-making without the sample information. This is a trial and error process.

10. Multi-Person Decision-Making

To this point, we have only considered decision-making by a single individual. We will now, briefly, consider three situations involving multi-person decision-making:

(A)   Expert opinion
(B)   Group decision-making
(C)   Strategic decision-making

(A) Expert Opinion

In the usual Bayesian analysis, a decision-maker acquires sample information to up-date prior beliefs into a posterior distribution. This is the notion of sample information. We now consider the case where the information is in the form of expert opinion rather than sample information.

Consider a decision-maker facing a problem which involves uncertainty. The decision-maker has turned for advice to a panel of experts. Each expert submits an opinion in the form of a probability distribution. The question is: how should the distributions be combined to form a posterior distribution?

Unlike the application of Bayes' Rule, there is no agreed way to combine opinion. Winkler [1968] has suggested three general approaches to combining information:

(i)   Weighted average method whereby each expert's opinion is weighted to form a posterior distribution. Winkler proposed four alternative weighting methods.
(ii)   Natural conjugate method where the probability distributions are combined in a manner similar to successive applications of Bayes' Rule.
(iii)   A consensus method whereby the experts interact expressing their individual views with a view to adopting a common belief.

It is beyond the scope of this article to evaluate these suggestions but, by way of illustration, consider the following example:

A decision-maker faces an investment involving uncertainty which depends upon which of two states will occur. Probabilistic beliefs of two states will occur. Probabilistic beliefs are as follows:

	State 1	State 2
Decision-maker	.7	.3
Expert 1	.9	.1
Expert 2	.5	.5

Suppose that the decision-maker wants to determine a posterior distribution by weighting all beliefs equally. (Recall that normalization requires that the sum of the weights must equal one.)

The posterior belief assigned to state one would be

$$\frac{1}{3}(.7) + \frac{1}{3}(.9) + \frac{1}{3}(.5) = .7$$

Suppose, alternatively that the decision-maker wishes to suppress his/her own beliefs and weight the others on the basis of a ranking weight based upon the experts' competence in assessing uncertainty. Suppose expert 1 is ranked first. Thus the ranks are 1 and 2 and the weight assigned to expert 1 is $2/(2+1)$ and the weight assigned to expert 2 is $1/(2+1)$. Thus the posterior belief assigned to state one would be

$$(\tfrac{2}{3})(.9) + (\tfrac{1}{3})(.5) = 0.766$$

(B) Group Decision-Making

In group decision-making, we envision a group of decision-makers who have banded together for the purpose of determining a joint course of action. Examples include an underwriting syndicate and an oil exploration venture by several oil companies.

The most systematic consideration of this problem was undertaken by Wilson [1968]. Wilson considered the problem of finding a way to share the outcomes of a group investment such that the choice of the optimal course of action is unanimous. The analysis consists of finding, when it exists, a group utility function such that maximizing group utility leads to the same joint action as would be selected by the individual members.

Wilson called the group, for which a group utility function exists, a syndicate. Wilson showed that, in general, a group utility function exists, if, and only if, all members either have exponential utilities or agree on the probability assessment of outcomes.

The existence of a group utility is coincident with the existence of a sharing rule which describes how any joint outcome is to be partitioned between individual members. If there is agreement on probability assessments, the sharing rule is linear in the outcome. That is, each member receives a pre-specified (not necessarily equal) share of any outcome. In addition, there may be a (prespecified) set of transfer payments between members which are independent of outcomes. In the case of divergent beliefs, the members' sharing rule is non-linear and reflects, among other things, each member's relative beliefs. We can say, crudely speaking, each member takes more of a share of the outcomes relating to states which he believes are (relative to the other members) more likely to occur.

A more detailed discussion of Wilson's results is beyond the scope of this article but the interested reader is referred to Wilson's work for, what remains today, the most comprehensive analysis of this organization design problem.

11. Stewardship Value of Information

Wilson's syndicate formulation sought an organization design, in the form of a sharing rule, such that a consensus between owners resulted.

Agency theory deals with the relationship between a principal (owner) and agent (manager). Here there is no question of consensus, the issue is motivation. In an agency, a superior/subordinate relationship exists.

Within the context of agency theory, researchers have developed a new concept of information value — namely the control value or stewardship value of information. Gjesdal [1981] has presented an eloquent discussion of this point of view to which you are referred. We will discuss here, only in a superficial way, the control or stewardship value of information.

The stewardship value of information is implicit in legislation regarding public disclosure for firms whose shares are listed on organized exchanges. Basically the idea is that the existence of an independent auditor and public reporting will deter, to some extent, defalcation which might otherwise occur. This implies a value of auditing in the mitigation of instances of fraud.

The focus of agency theory in establishing a stewardship value for information is more subtle than the detection of fraud but relates to the nature of the owner-manager relationship. In brief, the stewardship value for information relates to the increased efficiency in motivating behaviour which results from information.

In agency theory, results are established using embellishments of the following basic scenario. An owner hires a manager to whom decision-making responsibility is delegated. Both the owner and manager are motivated by self-interest. The owner's utility is usually defined as linear in wealth. The manager's utility is usually defined as risk and effort averse. That is, the manager's utility is concave and increasing in wealth and convex and decreasing in effort expended.

The owner's objective is to maximize expected utility. The means to this goal is to develop an incentive contract which motivates the manager to act in a way such that the owner's utility is maximized.

The manager, once presented with an employment contract, maximizes his expected utility.

The environment of the firm is such that there is an external state uncertainty which affects outcomes. In addition, the manager's actions (or effort) increase the probability of more favourable outcomes.

In order to render the situation opaque, and thus non-trivial, the analyses assume that what is observed is the outcome which is jointly determined by the external state and the manager's action, neither of which are directly observable by the owner.

To conceptualize this, think of the firm's profits as uncertain and, approximately normally distributed, reflecting generally uncertain market conditions. Increased effort by the manager results in increasing the mean of the distribution of the firm's profits.

The difficulty is developing an employment contract in this type of environment. Any contract conditioned on effort is unenforceable since effort is not observed. The manager can always claim that poor outcomes are due to adverse states occurring and not because of low effort. Thus any contract based upon effort poses a moral hazard for the manager since it encourages reneging (shirking) on the agreed effort.

In this setting it has been shown that the manager's compensation should be based, in part, on outcomes. This type of contract imposes risk on the manager. Since the manager is risk-averse, he must be compensated for bearing risk.

Given this scenario, the contract value of information is established as follows. If the manager's actions were observable, the manager's compensation could be based upon the action taken and no risk would be imposed on the manager for motivation purposes. This would be desirable since the risk-neutral owner could bear all the risk and would not have to compensate the manager for bearing risk. Thus observing the manager's effort provides access to more efficient contracts and establishes a value for that information.

The agency literature, which elaborates on this basic theme, has been summarized by Jennergren [1980] and Baiman [1982].

Conclusion

The theoretical treatment of risk aversion is highly simplified and relies heavily on mathematical representation. This has lead to considerable resistance to this literature as a useful and insightful guide to practice.

Notwithstanding the mathematical representation and limitations of the existing treatment, there is little sympathy for the point of view which ignores the behavioural and institutional consequences of risk-aversion. For this reason, the effort required to understand both the implications and limitations of this approach are worthwhile. Moreover, since much of the emerging literature in Accounting, Finance, Marketing, and Economics relies on these models, the student is well served by an understanding of their perspectives and limitations.

Group decision-making, which has enjoyed some popularization under various names, has usually been described in mechanical or sociological terms.

In this review, a brief summary has been provided of the statistical approach to developing consensus opinion. It is emphasized that there is no agreed method of affecting this combination. In true group decision-making, characterized by Wilson's Syndicate Theory and the literature on workers' cooperatives, the importance of simultaneous consideration of beliefs, risk attitudes, and work preferences (in the Agency literature) has now been formally recognized. This has had two positive effects: *first*, many of the results confirm methods which, with others, are currently in use and suggest ways of choosing among alternative practices. *Second*, the results and models suggest areas where theory and practice are weak and suggest avenues for further investigation.

Bibliography

Arrow, K.J., *Essays in the Theory of Risk-Bearing*, Markham, 1971.

Baiman, S., "Agency Research in Managerial Accounting: A Survey," *Journal of Accounting Literature*, Volume 1, Spring, 1982, pp. 154-210.

Bernoulli, Daniel, "Exposition of a New Theory on the Measurement of Risk," *Econometrica*, Volume 22, No. 1, January 1954, pp. 22-36.

Friedman, M. and Savage, L.J., "The Utility Analysis of Choices Involving Risk," *The Journal of Political Economy*, Volume 56, No. 4, August 1948, pp. 279-304.

Gjesdal, F., "Accounting for Stewardship," *Journal of Accounting Research*, Volume 19, Number 1, Spring 1981, pp. 208-231.

Hanoch, G., and Levy, H., "The Efficiency of Analysis of Choices Involving Risk," *Review of Economic Studies*, Volume 36, 1969, pp. 335-346.

Jennergren, L.P., "On the Design of Incentives in Business Firms — A Survey of Some Research," *Management Science*, Volume 26, February 1980, pp. 180-201.

Markowitz, Harry, "Portfolio Selection," *Journal of Finance*, Volume 7, No. 1, March 1952, pp. 77-91.

Pratt, J.W., "Risk Aversion in the Small and in the Large," *Econometrica*, Volume 32, No. 1-2, 1964, pp. 122-136.

Savage, L.J., "Elicitation of Personal Probabilities and Expectations," *Journal of the American Statistical Association*, Volume 66, No. 336, December 1971, pp. 783-801.

Swalm, R., "Utility Theory Insights Into Risk Taking," *Harvard Business Review*, Volume 44, Nov.-Dec. 1966, pp. 123-136.

Von Neumann, J. and Morgenstern, O., *Theory of Games and Economic Behavior*, Wiley, New York, 1944.

Wilson, R., "The Theory of Syndicates," *Econometrica*, Volume 36, January 1968, pp. 119-132.

Winkler, R.L., "The Consensus of Subjective Probability Distributions," *Management Science*, Volume 15, Number 2, October 1968, pp. B-61 to B-75.

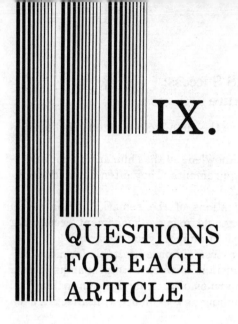

IX.

QUESTIONS
FOR EACH
ARTICLE

Simon Says . . . Decision Making is a 'Satisficing' Experience

1-1. Simon mentions that "Managers . . . really need systems 'more oriented toward data that come into the organization from the environment rather than information generated inside the organization'."
Required: Is management accounting primarily concerned with internally-generated or externally-generated information? Explain, giving the implications for management accountants.

1-2. In awarding Simon the 1978 Nobel laureate in economics, the Swedish Academy of Sciences mentioned that modern business economics and administrative research "are largely based on Simon's ideas."
Required: Summarize Simon's principal ideas.

1-3. If managers "satisfice" rather than "maximize," does this render some management accounting techniques useless or possibly misleading? Which ones? Why?

1-4. Simon mentions the term "aspiration level."
Required: Relate aspiration level to performance evaluation using a management accounting technique.

1-5. ". . . the next generation of information systems . . . will start with the concept of performing a decision making job, planned with the realization that the aim of an information system is to conserve attention, not simply to flood people with data that, in some wild way, might have some potential use for them."
Required: Assuming that Simon is correct, what are some important implications of the above quotation for teachers of management accounting?

Individual Differences and MIS Success:
A Review of Empirical Literature

2-1. According to the author what are the main factors that are believed to influence the success of MIS?

2-2. ". . . it has become generally acknowledged that humans do not understand their own information requirements. They often demand too little or too much information. . . ."

Required: What are the implications of the remarks in the above quotation for persons designing and using management accounting systems? Give a concrete example to support your remarks.

2-3. "Probabilistic analysis appears extremely uncomfortable for most individuals. Humans tend to be reluctant to work with probabilistic data . . . to systematically violate the rules of rational decision making . . . and to exhibit difficulties in weighing new evidence as it affects a decision situation."

Required: What are the implications of the comments in the above quotation for persons designing and using management accounting systems? Explain thoroughly.

2-4. List some topics affecting MIS where there has been little empirical research. Which are important to management accountants? Why?

Framework for Analysis

3-1. Anthony states that mistakes are made when generalizations valid for one subsystem of planning and control systems are applied to another subsystem.

Required: Explain and illustrate Anthony's point.

3-2. List and explain some important characteristics of a management control system.

3-3. Distinguish among the following terms: strategic planning; management control; technical control.

An Executive View of MIS

4-1. Critically evaluate the author's comment: "Taken by itself, an accounting system is an accountant's information system and not a managerial information system."

4-2. Do you agree with the author's comment: "Can the controller recapture the information monopoly he once embraced? . . . I think not." Explain thoroughly.

4-3. Critically evaluate the author's comment: "Accounting, control and audit are essentially an evaluative system — a system for evaluating management's performance and hence necessarily outside of the management function."

Management Misinformation Systems

5-1. According to the author what is the most important information deficiency which managers suffer from? What are the effects of this deficiency, and what does the author recommend to overcome the problem?

5-2. Do Ackoff and Vatter appear to be in substantial agreement on the relationship of the information provider (e.g., accountant or operations researcher) to the manager? Explain, and state whether or not you agree with the stated position of each author.

5-3. What are the five common "errors" made by designers of management information systems? Explain in detail.

Cost Concepts for Control

6-1. Explain the author's reasoning underlying this statement: "We eventually concluded that an attempt to find objective means of differentiating among the various control systems in current use was not feasible. . . ."

6-2. Explain the significance of the following quotation to the conclusions reached in the article: ". . . not everyone is motivated identically by the same stimulus. That this is so is undeniable. Nevertheless, there must be some common patterns of human behavior that apply to large numbers of people."

6-3. In which respects would Anthony's views agree with those expressed by Vatter and Ackoff?

Control and Freedom in a Decentralized Company

7-1. Review several behavioural articles in this book (for example, those of Ridgway and Villers) and comment on the following quotation: ". . . a decade or so of intensive research in human relations shows with equal conclusiveness that our large organizations and our methods of planning and control are, more often than not, antagonistic to good human relations."

7-2. What control concept does the author advocate to help overcome the difficulty mentioned in the quotation in 7-1?

7-3. Discuss the meaning and significance of the following quotation: ". . . control is not by itself a hindrance to individual freedom. Rather, control is in fact a prerequisite to decentralization, and without decentralization there can be no real freedom."

7-4. Examine the facts about the Hart Manufacturing Company and Richards' problem with part 1234. Do you agree with the position taken by the arbitrator, Villers? Explain.

Dysfunctional Consequences of Performance Measurements

8-1. What might Anthony ("Cost Concepts for Control") say about Ridgway's comment that "Quantitative performance measurements — whether single, multiple, or composite — are seen to have undesirable consequences for over-all organizational performance"?

8-2. Distinguish among the terms single, multiple and composite, and explain why each measure might have undesirable side effects.

Divisional Performance Measurement: Beyond an Exclusive Profit Test

9-1. What arguments or issues does the author raise "against the validity of (the) goal congruence concept. . . ."?

9-2. "Modern organization theory would appear to suggest that accountants' encouragement of congruence between divisional and corporate goals is both unnecessary and misdirected."
Required: If the foregoing quotation is accepted as correct, of what use are performance appraisal management accounting techniques such as return on investment and related transfer pricing? (Also discuss other techniques.)

9-3. "If accountants recognize that the performance of divisions can only be judged in relation to the whole corporate 'goal set' then they must be prepared to reject any divisional profit measure as the sole test of performance."
Required: What does the author suggest to overcome the limitations of sole tests of performance.

9-4. Would Ridgway ("Dysfunctional Consequences of Performance Measurements") agree with Parker's suggestions?

Profit Centers, Transfer Prices and Mysticism

10-1. Summarize the author's theme as reflected in his comment: "A good deal of accounting, as currently practised, has a mystical quality."

10-2. According to the author, which management evaluations, as noted in Section I of this book, require the use of transfer prices when goods are switched between divisions of a decentralized company.

Pricing for Profit in the Printing Industry

11-1. What factors are likely to be critical to success, and to failure, in a company in the printing industry? Why?

11-2. Explain the author's comment ". . . pricing must not be reduced to a strict formula but should be dynamic and made with full knowledge of the four basic factors that affect profit: cost, volume, efficiency and price."

11-3. The author distinguishes between pricing when the company is "operating at or near capacity" and when it is not. What are the important distinctions?

11-4. What suggestions does the author make for compensating salespersons? Do you agree?

Anyone for Widgets?

12-1. What are the author's main themes?

12-2. Do you agree with the author's views on the "tightness" of standards? If so, for which decisions noted in Section I of this book? If not, why?

12-3. Would Vatter ("Tailor-making Cost Data for Specific Uses") likely agree with Greer? Why? Why not?

Accounting Logic?

13-1. Do you agree with the accounting-efficiency-expert (AEE)? Explain fully.

13-2. What management accounting techniques should Joe have used to:
A. Decide whether he should have acquired the peanut rack? (Assume that he has not bought it yet.) Why?
B. Decide whether he should keep the peanut rack? (Assume that he bought it a few weeks ago.) Why?

13-3. If you were Joe what would you do after the accounting-efficiency-expert (AEE) left your shop?

13-4. What factors are critical to the success or failure of Joe's business? Why?

The Price of a Flight

14-1. What are the factors that affect "Just how much does it cost to put a plane into the air"?

14-2. Which costs incurred by an airline are likely to be variable? (Variable with what?)

14-3. When an airline calculates the cost of a flight, of what use is the figure (or figures)?

Product Contribution Analysis for Multi-Product Pricing

15-1. Explain the following quotation concerning the role of accounting techniques in pricing decisions: "The product life cycle . . . consists of the following stages: development, introduction, growth, maturity, decline, and phase-out. For pricing decision purposes it is also important to recognize management's objectives during any given stage."

15-2. Explain this quotation: "What is really significant in a pricing decision is neither cost nor price but rather the present value of the contribution that the product makes toward the recovery of period costs and profit over each product's life cycle."

15-3. State the significance to management accountants of the following quotation: "... management's objectives will dictate which ranking is most significant. That is, if the short-run objective is to raise revenue, the revenue ranking will be important. If the management wishes to increase earnings per share, however, the contribution ranking would be more significant. In either case, the reliance on one at the sacrifice of the other would be detrimental to the firm."

Is Your Cost Accounting Up To Date?

16-1. List several "unmistakable signs of a cost accounting system that is in trouble."

16-2. What objectives of a new cost accounting system are mentioned by the authors? Do you agree with them?

16-3. Explain the authors' comments: "The successful cost system will support the economics of your business."

Tailor-making Cost Data for Specific Uses

17-1. "... in our zeal to get the one true and simple answer we frequently overlook the real nature of the problem."
Required: Relate the above quotation to management accounting.

17-2. (a) Do you agree with all parts of the following quotation? "It is not enough to present all of the data, leaving the interpretations to the readers of the reports. The responsibility of the cost accountant is to learn the uses to be made of his cost data . . . and to see that relevant and irrelevant data are handled properly."
(b) Would Ackoff agree with all parts of the quotation in (a)?

17-3. To what extent would Vatter's main theme be appropriate in a financial accounting (external reporting) course?

The Fable of the Accountant and the President

18-1. Which three factors are combining to cause the problem set forth in Act II? What is the problem?

18-2. For which management decisions is the cost data being used?

18-3. The Fable employs the term "contribution margin" in Act III. Do you agree with this usage?

18-4. Explain the trick mentioned in Act III.

18-5. What price should the Board set to sell off excess inventory? State your assumptions clearly.

The Chop Suey Caper

19-1. Speculate on why the author is "not all that fond of chop suey."

19-2. What reply would you give to Hobb's assertion that: "You cost men are supposed to know how to allocate costs."

19-3. Summarize the author's theme about the railroad cost controversy.

For Direct Costing in the Steel Industry

20-1. What factors are likely to be critical to success, and to failure, in a company like the one described by the author (International Harvester, Wisconsin Steel Works)? Why?

20-2. Explain the author's comment: "A discussion of cost variability generally assumes that the costs are totals for some period of time. . . . The time factor is important."

20-3. What use likely would be made of the "direct costing" figures being generated by the company? Might they help in specific management decisions? Which ones? Why?

Formal Decision Making Under Uncertainty: A Structure

21-1. Explain Tables 1 and 2 in the article.

21-2. For which management decisions or evaluations might the various techniques described in the article be used effectively and efficiently? Be specific.

21-3. How might the management accountant obtain subjective probabilities that are needed for some of the computations described by the author? Is too much guesswork involved in deriving subjective probabilities?

Cost Information and Competitive Strategy: Lessons from Japan

22-1. Explain the author's comment "Curiously, research on American firms shows that information is usually aggregated around very broad product definitions or organizational groupings. . . ." (Does the author believe this approach is wise?)

22-2. What impact does the existence of experience or learning curves have on management accounting techniques and management judgments?

22-3. Explain "competitive analysis" and "design to cost" and the implications for management accounting.

22-4. Compare Herbert Simon's views on information systems (see article 1) to the following comment of the author: "Japan has probably the best statistical bureau in the world, collecting mountains of information on every conceivable aspect of the global economy and what these imply for Japan."

Control Systems Supporting Economy, Efficiency and Effectiveness

23-1. Distinguish among the terms economy, efficiency, and effectiveness.

23-2. Relate the terms economy, efficiency, and effectiveness to the management decisions mentioned at the beginning of this book: performance evaluation, pricing, output, and so forth.

23-3. The report mentions that "Management control can be exercised effectively only if" four characteristics exist. Explain why these are important.

23-4. What factors are critical to the success or failure of *governments*? Explain.

The Stressful Effects of Budget Cuts in Organizations

24-1. Explain the author's comment: ". . . the fiscal benefits of cutback management must also be weighed in relation to their downside human risks and the difficulties in implementing cutbacks."

24-2. What are the implications to management and management accounting of the following comment by the author: ". . . employees may have doubts that they can perform well even if they try to when they perceive themselves to be overloaded, under unrealistic deadlines, and/or in chronic conflict with their peers over scarce resources."

24-3. What are some important signs of budget cut stress?

Cash Flow Analysis: More Important than Ever

25-1. Explain the authors' comment: "Although one might expect that a rise in the selling price would generate cash, it generally does not."

25-2. Explain the authors' comment: ". . . a change in either market share or investment intensity can affect cash flow."

25-3. Explain the authors' theme: "Cash flow is predictable and manageable." Do you agree?

Identifying and Resolving Problems in Corporate Liquidity

26-1. According to the authors, what are the prime factors "which could trigger (an executive's) awareness of a liquidity problem? Do these survey results appear to make sense?

26-2. According to the authors, what important measures help "to remedy liquidity problems."

26-3. Discuss the interrelationship for liquidity and profitability management of increasing debt to equity ratios, increasing inflation rates, and rising interest rates. (E.g., If inflation is expected does it make sense to borrow? at what interest rates? with what consequences?)

Strategic Capital Budgeting

27-1. Comment on the following quotation from the article: "Obviously systematic biases in the capital budgeting analyses of the past should not be ignored, but rather they should affect the way in which we evaluate the present proposals." (Do you agree or disagree? Why? Explain.)

27-2. "But the frontier of capital budgeting, uncertainty, has tended to resist efforts to find easily computed feasible solutions to accept or reject decisions."
   Required: Given the nature of uncertainty, how much progress should we logically expect in finding "easily computed feasible solutions"? Explain.

27-3. Refer to the author's example with Division A and Division B. Give several reasons why the capital expenditures for one division could be much, much higher than those for another division.

Structuring Capital Spending Hurdle Rates

28-1. What reasons does the author give to try to explain why "Many companies do not establish capital spending hurdle rates."

28-2. Compare and contrast the author's views with those of Bierman ("Strategic Capital Budgeting").

28-3. What are the benefits and limitations of "multiple hurdle rates"? Consider different types of businesses (e.g., size, industry, geographical locations, etc.).

28-4. Critically evaluate the author's comment, "This means that different business units will use different hurdle rates."

Capital Budgeting Using Terminal Values

29-1. What does the author claim are the advantages of using terminal value capital budgeting? Do you agree with him? Explain.

29-2. How useful is the terminal value technique when "wealth maximization is rejected as a goal"?

29-3. Explain how the terminal value technique helps to highlight reinvestment of the "cash throw-off."

29-4. List the different circumstances where the terminal value technique would have no appreciable advantage over NPV.

Anatomy of an Auto-Plant Rescue

30-1. What factors are likely to be critical to the success, and to the failure, of an auto-plant? Why?

30-2. What management accounting techniques are relevant in deciding whether to close an auto-plant? Why?

30-3. What types of costs would Chrysler not save by closing the plant? Be specific.

30-4. "Instead of creating a budget on the basis of its costs, each plant had to compare its numbers with the costs of buying the same products outside the company."
Required: Evaluate the procedure mentioned in the quotation. When does it make sense to use this procedure? Why?

Recovery Rate and Cash Flow Accounting

31-1. Why is the author suggesting that "Perhaps the time has come to go back to cash flow and see what can be done without mixing it with a host of noncash items."

31-2. What is meant by the "recovery rate"? Would you regard this as a crude or refined technique? (Specify the circumstances you are assuming when making your assessment.)

31-3. Critically evaluate the author's comment: "Complex concepts and systems of information processing . . . are . . . not necessarily of value in the art of management."

How One Financial Officer Uses Inflation-Adjusted Accounting Data

32-1. What are some factors that are probably crucial to the success or failure of the author's employer, American Standard Inc. How might management accounting assist in the decisions that have to be made to pursue success?

32-2. Explain the author's comment: "There are at least three areas in which problems can arise if a corporation uses only historic cost accounting information in measuring performance. . . ."

32-3. What are the main "amendments" to accounting reports that are made by American Standard to convey to management the effects of inflation and changing prices on the company? Do they appear to be sensible "amendments"?

A Cash Flow Model for the Future

33-1. What are the possible benefits of cash flow financial statements for external users (e.g., stockholders; creditors)?

33-2. In which respects does the author agree and disagree with Y. Ijiri? (See also the article "Recovery Rate and Cash Flow Accounting" in this book.) Explain fully. Whom do you support? Why?

33-3. What are the strengths and limitations of the author's cash evaluation techniques when applied at the operating *segment* level? (Be specific and state any important assumptions that you have made.)

An Activity Analysis Approach to Unit Costing with Multiple Interactive Products

34-1. The authors state: "Most traditional cost accounting treatments of product costing deal with extremely simple production process."
Required: What do the authors mean by "extremely simple production processes"?

34-2. What are the benefits of an activity analysis approach to unit costing?

34-3. "Thus a variety of internal and external forces may be operating which makes the computation of a reasonable and defensible average variable cost figure a useful exercise."
Required: What are the "internal and external forces"?

Decision-Making Under Conditions of Uncertainty: Expected Monetary Value and the Value of Information

35-1. For which principal management decision-making situations might the techniques described in this article be useful?

35-2. Explain the concept of "opportunity loss."

35-3. Explain "Bayes' Rule."

Decision-Making Under Conditions of Uncertainty: Risk Aversion, Group Decision-Making, and Agency Theory

36-1. What is meant by "risk aversion." Give an example.

36-2. Which management decisions might be aided by the techniques described in this article? Be specific.

36-3. Explain the concept "expected value of sample information."

36-4. Explain the concept of "agency theory."

Everlasting Love

Everlasting Love

A Collection of Three Complete, Unabridged
Inspirational Romances
in One Volume

The Starfire Quilt
Alice Allen

Journey Toward Home
Carol Cox

The Will and the Way
DeWanna Pace

BARBOUR
PUBLISHING, INC.
Uhrichsville, Ohio

© MCMXCIX by Barbour Publishing, Inc.

ISBN 1-57748-621-8

Published by Barbour Publishing, Inc., P.O. Box 719, Uhrichsville, Ohio 44683
http://www.barbourbooks.com

Member of the
Evangelical Christian
Publishers Association

Printed in the United States of America.

The Starfire Quilt

Alice Allen

ALICE ALLEN's home is in Kansas with her husband Bill. They have a close-knit family of three grown children and four grandchildren. Alice hopes to reach both children and adults with God's truth through her writings, which include curriculum, plays, poems, and more.

one

September 12, 1777

Fair Lady sailed effortlessly over the stone fence and thundered into the meadow. The surrounding woods were just beginning to show glorious fall colors. Pulling up on the reins, Meredeth Elliott headed for the shade of the trees. Heat had already dampened her linen shirt and flecked her horse's neck with perspiration.

"Oh, Matt, why haven't we heard from you? I miss you so much," she said as she gazed ahead.

A snort from Fair Lady was the only warning when, from the cover of the trees, a blaze-faced sorrel came pounding straight for them, its rider hunched low over the horse's head.

"Why, he's trying to run us down!" Meredeth screamed.

As survival reaction overcame shock, Meredeth turned her mount's lead and dug her heels into the horse's sides. Fair Lady responded promptly, but there was so little time as the big sorrel brushed past and then sped off across the field. By the time Meredeth had eased Fair Lady to a stop, the intruder had disappeared from view.

Swiftly dismounting, the petite rider checked her mare for injuries. Fair Lady limped a few steps, then halted and nuzzled Merry's shoulder.

"The brute! Whatever was he thinking of to careen into us like that?"

Gently she touched the mare's flank and leg. "I think it's only a strain, but we'd better walk you back to the stables. Jeremiah will know if there is any serious harm done."

With an angry glance in the direction that the retreating horse had taken, Merry reached for her bonnet. There, on the ground, she noticed a package wrapped in brown paper. Frowning, she slowly picked it up and turned it around in her hands.

"Could that rider have dropped this? But why?" Dejected, Merry started for home.

Jeremiah Grundy saw her coming and loped toward her. "Did she ketch a hoof in a hole, Miss Meredeth?"

"No, she didn't. Jeremiah, have you seen strangers about lately?"

"No'm. Cain't say I have," he responded solemnly as he leaned to inspect the damage.

"A rider on a big sorrel came racing out of the woods near the meadow. He'd have knocked us flat if I hadn't turned Fair Lady. I think he did graze her, but you'd better check her carefully."

"I surely will, Miss Meredeth."

Merry gave her horse a pat of reassurance, then ran for the house and hurried up the back stairs to her room. Instead of changing her clothes, she sat for several minutes and examined the packet. With thin-lipped decisiveness, she tore the paper off and out fell a minuscule parcel of linen squares, each with a set of numbers inked onto it. Beneath was a folded parchment. In spite of shaking hands, she opened and read the letter.

> *Dear Merry,*
>   *I hope you receive this as it will be my last letter to you. Someone's been following me. I have only one sheet of parchment. The squares cut from my shirt are for General Washington, who is in the Philadelphia area. Please get them to him as soon as you can. Find John Clark or Charles Craig. They will know what to do. Don't talk about this to anyone else.*
>   *I love you and Papa.*
>
>   *For freedom!*
>   *Matt*

Meredeth sat stunned, the linen squares clutched in her hands. Tears fell, but they could not wash away the possible meaning of his message.

"Oh, Matt, I can't believe you might be dead. With Papa in Philadelphia that would leave me alone, except for Aunt Mina. She's a dear, but her mind functions on only two subjects: food and the latest fashions. I need your encouragement and steady strength."

Such small snippets of cloth to be so important! That thought slammed Meredeth right back to the monstrous problem at hand. *Now I must get them to the Patriots. How am I going to do that?*

"Oh, dear Lord, guide me," she whispered. "I want to help, yet I have no idea how to do this."

"Merry love, luncheon is all set out for us," Aunt Mina called up the stairs.

"I'll be right there, Aunt Mina, as soon as I put things in order."

Hastily she racked her brain for a secure hidey-hole. The sewing basket on the work table! What better place to conceal small bits of linen? She snipped threads holding the lining in place along one side of the basket to make an opening long enough to insert the cloth pieces.

A quick glance in the mirror confirmed that, as usual, tendrils of her red-gold hair had loosened from their pins. She took time to smooth her hair and add a few pins. Then, tugging her skirts into place, she hurried down the stairs.

"Did you enjoy your ride, my dear?" Aunt Mina glanced briefly at her niece.

Meredeth caught the soft "tsk" of reproach, but after grace was said, the food claimed all of her aunt's attention, and Meredeth hoped she might forget to chide her for coming to the table in riding clothes.

Indeed, Aunt Mina was full of gossip, with which she eagerly enlightened Meredeth throughout the meal. Somehow Merry responded in the right places, though her mind raced ahead, planning. When her aunt's chatter subsided for a moment, Merry plunged in.

"Tomorrow we should make a trip to Philadelphia. I hear there is a new shipment of fabric available at the linen drapers'. We need long cloth for bed gowns, some silk for ribands, and perhaps a bit of lace."

"That sounds delightful, Merry. What time do you want to leave?" Aunt Mina asked.

"I'll order the coach for seven tomorrow morning. That will get us to town before ten. While I'm down at the stables, you can take your nap and I can exercise Papa's stallion."

As soon as Meredeth could excuse herself, she hurried to the stables and, once in the meadow, she let Othello, her father's horse, have his head. Taking the bit eagerly, Othello pranced a few paces, then settled into a steady canter.

"I feel better doing something, even if it doesn't ease the ache in my heart. Should I tell Papa about Matt? But no, Matt said not to mention it to anyone else, except John Clark or Charles Craig."

The sound of hoofbeats close behind pierced her mental detachment and, with every nerve on edge, she slowed Othello to a trot and swung him slightly to the left. She realized that the approaching horse was not the same one that had almost run them down, and she relaxed a bit. This beautiful horse was all of sixteen hands at least, and the man atop the horse was also large, had wide shoulders, and was sitting on his mount as if he had been carved there.

When they were within easy speaking distance, the rider lifted his hat in greeting, revealing dark hair worn a bit long but well groomed. The sun added gold flecks as his head bent in a slight bow.

"My lady, I am ashamed to admit I have been led astray by the beauty of this area. Can you tell me, please, whose land this is?"

"You are in Cresswick Manor Acres, owned by my father, Dr. Lawrence Elliott. What manor are you seeking, sir?"

"Oliver Moreland invited several of his friends to a house party, but as it is difficult for me to remain indoors on such a lovely day, I decided to go for a ride. My horse, Ahmed, was as anxious as I for a run."

"He shows his heritage. He carries that proud head like a prince."

"He is a prince, a foal of Queen Serenay."

Merry's gaze shifted from the horse to the stranger and his fathomless pair of dark blue eyes. *This man is a charmer and he knows it.* That thought brought a warmth to her cheeks.

Chagrined at her obvious response, she turned her face away as she said, "There's a path through this end of the trees that will take you back to Moreland's. I'm sure you will have no trouble finding it."

"I thank you, my lady. William Castleton, at your service. If you are ever lost on my land, or anywhere else for that matter, my specialty is helping damsels in distress." With that, the great horse swiveled at his master's touch and loped away.

"His specialty! Well of all the conceited, arrogant dunderheads!"

At this emotional outburst, Othello sidestepped and it took all of Merry's strength to calm the animal. By the time she raised her eyes to the woods, the stranger was gone.

"And good riddance," she mumbled. "We are in the midst of a war and he attends house parties."

Suddenly she realized how strange it was to have encountered two strangers within hours of each other, and that made her lose all desire to ride any farther that day. Turning, she headed back to the stables.

At table that evening Meredeth did not mention either encounter. There were other decisions to be made, and if any more of that house party lost themselves, they could just talk to the stable lads. She certainly needed no strangers in her life at present. It was complicated enough already. The idea of getting away for a few days pleased her.

☙

When Merry, Aunt Mina, and their maids, Anna and Dela, climbed into the traveling chaise the next morning, wispy ghosts of fog haunted the countryside. Merry stared out, unseeing, as they rumbled along the veiled landscape. Aunt Mina and the maids settled in for a few hours' relaxation. Fortunately they did not require Meredeth's attention.

Should she tell her papa about Matt? Her last memory picture of her parent was that of a weary man, surrounded by pallets of injured; months of serving at the hospital had taken their toll. No. She would stop by the hospital, perhaps bringing him a big meat pie filled with ham and sauer-kraut. She still could not believe that Matt might be dead, and it would be cruel to burden her father with that possibility when he was already inundated with wounded soldiers.

"In case the British come as far as Philadelphia," Aunt Mina said with loud determination, "I think we should move to Cousin Ferdy's. His manor is rather hidden away in the hills. Don't you think we'd be safe there, Meredeth?"

"If Washington holds Philadelphia, we won't have that problem," Merry said, sagging back into her corner.

It had been only a year since independence was declared, and already the British had taken Boston and New York. Most folks expected Philadelphia to be the next target. Could that be the information Matt was sending with those bits of linen? Nervously she clutched her reticule tighter; the small mound that those linen pieces made was not enough to be obvious.

"Halt!" someone shouted.

"May the Lord preserve us. Is it a road bandit?" Aunt Mina gasped, clutching the opal pin fastened to her woolen cloak.

"There's two men. Why one of them is Jemy Prentis," Dela, Aunt Mina's maid, said.

Meredeth and her maid, Anna, turned in their seats to see what caused the delay.

With an angry scowl, Jeremiah Grundy, their coach driver, swung down. Chin to chin with the lanky young man on the road, Grundy spoke in unconcealed contempt. "Just what're you up to, Jemy? There's no need for you to stop honest folk on this road."

"Gotta do it, Jeremiah. It's orders. Honest. The Brits have taken Chadd's Ford and word is they're headin' east."

"East?"

"Yessir, Mr. Grundy, toward Philadelphia."

"How soon do they 'spect they'll git there, Jemy?"

"Don't know. Washington's trying to hold them at the ford. That young Frenchie, Layfay. . .somethin', is helpin' him. No tellin' how long they can hold out."

"We're headin' for Philadelphia," Grundy advised. "Think we can make it?"

"It'd be better than goin' back to Cresswick," Jemy said.

"I'll see what Miz Elliott wants to do. Don't rightly like havin' a coachload of women on the road if the Brits are near." With that, Jeremiah walked back to the carriage, doffed his cap, and informed his passengers of the problem.

Meredeth did not hesitate to respond. "Step up the pace and make a run for it," she ordered. "We'll be safer there than at the manor. Surely General Washington won't let them take Philadelphia."

"You want I should send word back home?" Jeremiah asked.

"Yes, if it's possible. Mrs. Tulley and Barnabas could hide the silver and send the stock back to Cousin Ferdy's. I don't want to lose Fair Lady or Othello."

"Yes'm. I'll tell Jemy. He'll see to it."

After a quick word with the young man, the coachman leaped to his perch and clucked the team into action. In less than an hour, the exhausted horses swirled into the courtyard of Conners Inn, causing a tempest of dust.

"Mistress, do ya mind if'n I go see what the news is here?" Jeremiah asked as he helped the women down.

Smiling, Meredeth sent him on his way then herded her aunt and the maids into the common room, where Elijah Conners was leaning over his counter to greet them warmly.

"Just sign right there, Miz Elliott. I'll send Poll up to fix rooms for ya. Yer pa is in the second room, left. Don't see 'im much, but that's where he keeps his clothes."

"I'll stop by to see him after I find a friend of Matt's," Meredeth said. "Have you seen John Clark or Charles Craig in town this morn?"

Conners thoughtfully tapped a long pipe stem against his chin. "Wal now, lessee. Reckon the major will be up at the Thompson-Neely place and I heard Craig was riding south a ways. If ya want to reach him, ya oughta catch Jim Hanks when he comes for his lunch at City Tavern. In fact, he might be there now. Tell ya what. I'll call back to Zeke an' find out where he's headed. He might take ya there."

Zeke, the inn's ostler, offered them a ride as far as Walnut and Second, where he had a delivery. "Be ready ta leave in 'bout ten to fifteen minutes, Miz Elliott. You and Anna kin wait on the dock."

Clutching cloaks tightly against a gusty north gale, Merry and Anna watched loaders place the last few rows of boxes on Zeke's wagon. Next to them, a brewer's dray was already loaded with kegs and two men were attempting to tie a piece of oiled cloth over the lot. The sound of an angry voice turned Merry's head toward them.

"Thet keg done slipped, it has!" one of the men yelled as he danced about, holding up his wounded foot, while his companion leaned over to examine the injury. Meanwhile, the runaway keg tumbled across the wooden planks of the dock.

"Miss Merry, look out!" Anna screamed, pushing her mistress forward and getting herself out of the way of the rolling keg. But Anna's foot slipped and, with a sharp crack, her head hit a post and then she collapsed in a silent heap.

Merry was struggling to pick herself up when she heard a voice ask, "May I be of assistance? You look very much like a damsel in distress."

That lazy drawl was simply too much. Hands on hips, a blistering set-down on her lips, Merry turned around and found herself looking at the gentleman who was too busy attending parties to fight a war.

"Is he botherin' you, Miz Merry?" Zeke inquired. Pushing Merry back, Zeke stuck his pointed beard right into Castleton's chest, just as if the man were not a good head taller and at least thirty pounds heavier.

At the sight of her would-be rescuer, Merry's anger melted into chuckles and she tried to keep a straight face in the blast of Zeke's indignation.

"Zeke, let me introduce Mr. William Castleton to you. He is not the one who caused the trouble. That black-cloaked loader over there. . ." Her voice dwindled into exasperated silence for, in all the excitement, the dray, its kegs, and the two men had vanished.

Castleton gently eased Zeke back a few steps and then whispered to Meredeth, "When I saw you fall, I feared he had attacked you."

"Wal, they're gone now," Zeke muttered. "Don't do no good to shut the barn door once the cow's vamoosed. Be ya still ridin' with me, Miz Elliott?"

Quickly Merry straightened her cloak, pulled her hood up, and clutched her reticule closely to her side. "Yes, we're ready, aren't we, Anna? Anna?"

"She hit her head on that post when she jumped out of the way," Castleton advised.

In a flurry of skirts and petticoats, Meredeth rushed to kneel beside the still form. "Anna! She's unconscious. Please get me some water."

"You want I should get the doc?" Zeke offered.

"He is so busy. Could we just take her to him at the hospital? Surely there will be a spare pallet somewhere."

"Let's git her in the wagon. We kin be there in fifteen minutes," Zeke promised.

Castleton carried Anna to the wagon, where Merry padded some empty flour sacks. As soon as Zeke and Merry climbed to the seat, the vehicle rumbled away. She was surprised to see Castleton mount his Arabian and trot alongside the wagon.

"You do take your rescue work seriously, don't you?" she quipped as they pulled up in front of the red brick hospital.

"I thought you might need help getting her in," Castleton answered.

His reason was valid. Chagrined, Merry lowered her eyes and spoke softly. "I'm sorry. My sarcasm was uncalled for. You have been a great help. I do appreciate your time and effort on our behalf."

His eyes shone with humor again. "Very prettily said. You are most welcome. Come, let's be friends. You lead the way and I'll carry your maid."

It did not take them long to find Dr. Elliott. At his daughter's greeting, he came toward his visitors, a smile on his face.

"Merry, I didn't know you were coming today. Why, 'tis Anna. What happened?"

"She's unconscious, Papa. Could you take a look at her?"

"Of course. Bring her back to my examining table, please."

When Dr. Elliott discovered the lump over the maid's ear, he looked up at Merry. "How did she hit her head?"

"She slipped and fell into a post near the inn. Will she be all right?"

"Oh, Anna is a strong country girl. I'm sure she will recover. I have never known her to be clumsy before."

"She tried to protect me. We were waiting on the dock while Zeke loaded his wagon. A keg fell from a dray nearby. Anna pushed me out of the way, then she jumped aside, but she lost her footing on the wet dock. Fortunately the keg didn't hit us."

"It's a good thing she saw it in time to avoid it," Dr. Elliott said as he held the lamp closer to check Anna's eyes. The maid moved her head and groaned.

"She'll come around any time now. If there is no problem with her vision or balance, a few days' rest should do the trick. You'd best leave her here with me. I'll keep an eye on her."

Dr. Elliott suddenly realized another figure stood behind Merry. "You have a young man with you. I don't believe we have met."

"Oh. . .yes. He was at the inn and offered his help. Papa, this is William Castleton. Mr. Castleton, my father, Dr. Lawrence Elliott."

Both men nodded tentatively.

"While I was exercising Othello yesterday, I met Mr. Castleton. He is visiting the Morelands. I believe he said it was a house party?"

At the words "house party," Dr. Elliott's eyebrows furrowed in a frown, but his innate good manners urged him to shake the man's hand.

Castleton explained, "The Morelands are cousins of my mother's. I had been visiting relatives in Virginia when I met Trevor Moreland."

"You are not from this part of the country then?"

"No. My home is in England. An uncle in Boston offered me a partnership in his shipping line. For the last few years I have been living there, though responsibilities often call me elsewhere."

Even though Castleton had resided in Boston for several years, both the doctor and his daughter stiffened when he called England his home. As if he felt the icy edges of that wall of distrust between them, the young man bowed and turned away.

"Thank you," Merry called after him.

"I hope to see you again, Miss Elliott, Dr. Elliott. I pray your maid will recover quickly. Good day."

For just a moment, blue eyes met her green ones. Then he was gone and she jerked her attention back to Anna. It would be far too dangerous for all of them to think of friendship with that young man.

When the door closed behind the Englishman, Dr. Elliott drew Meredeth into the small room he used as his own.

"That was a very personable young man, my dear. I think caution will be wise. He is British and the Morelands are trying to ride the fence between Tories and Patriots. Think carefully what you say about Matt when Castleton is around."

"Papa, I am not a child. I can guard my tongue."

"Now don't get your back up. I meant that only as a reminder. You are a young lady now and he is—"

"A very personable young man. Yes, Papa, but I love Matt too well to give him away, especially to a stranger from that country. Most likely I will see little of him. He is too busy being introduced to Tory society."

"I know you would do nothing to harm Matt. Forgive an old man his concern."

"Don't ever stop being concerned for us, Papa. Knowing you are gives us hope and courage."

Kissing him on the cheek, she made her farewells. When she closed the hospital door behind her, the smiling face of the waiting Englishman stopped her midstride.

"Could I escort you to your destination, Miss Elliott?"

"Oh. Oh no, thank you. It is not far from here and the streets are busy with townspeople. I may even see some friends on the way."

The smile disappeared from his face. She reminded herself he was not quite a friend. Still, a small portion of her heart questioned that assumption. With a brief nod, he accepted her dismissal and walked away.

Merry suddenly remembered she must catch Jim Hanks and so she quickened her steps in the direction of City Tavern. When she arrived, she found that the lunchroom was crowded, for this was one place in Philadelphia where travelers could be assured of a good meal. Locals thronged there for its fried chicken and meat pies. Merry had never seen Jim Hanks, but was sure that Molly, one of the serving girls, would know him if he were a regular customer. Molly, carrying a large tray, smiled as she hurried by.

"I jus' cleaned off a small table over there." Molly nodded direction.

Merry sat and removed her cloak. The serving girl soon returned for her order.

"Haven't seen you for a while. I heard yur pa was busy at the hospital. Are you visitin' today?"

"Aunt Mina and I came in to shop. We have been homebodies since Matt and Papa left. How are you doing, Molly?"

"Oh, things are quiet here, with all the young men off fightin'. I hope this war gits over soon or I'll be an old maid afore I have a steady gentleman. Whatcha want?"

"Could you make me two meat pies with ham and sauerkraut? Papa is partial to ham and I know he's not eating as he should."

"It'll be ready quicker'n a cat can lick its whiskers."

"Before you go, Molly, has Jim Hanks been in today?"

"No–o. I don't rightly recall seein' him."

"If he comes while I'm here, will you point him out to me, please?"

"Oh, Miz Elliott, you don't wanta go anywhere with him. He's jus' sorta lazy, good-for-nothin'. There's plenty gents be callin' on you when the war's over."

"I don't want him for that kind of friend, Molly. I just want to talk to him about Matt."

"Oh, that's all right I s'pose. Well I'll git those meat pies."

Merry sat quietly, intrigued by the variety of patrons. A rather rowdy group of young men entered and took possession of one of the larger tables. They had barely made themselves comfortable before another person joined them. It was Castleton! Had they moved the house party here?

"Miz Elliott," Molly said.

Meredeth looked up just as Molly leaned closer to whisper in her ear. "That's Jim Hanks, the one with the red hair."

"Thank you, Molly. Could you ask him to come over here, please? I'd rather talk to him alone."

"Alright, Miz Elliott, if you want me to."

Molly's heels clicked briskly across the floor. Clearing her throat loudly, she leaned over to speak to the red-headed man. Grinning, he looked up at the serving girl then stretched to see around her. For a full minute he stared at the quiet, auburn-haired woman across the room. Merry sat in strained silence, then lowered her eyes. Jim made some remark to his comrades that produced a wave of hilarity.

Pushing back his chair, he rose and ambled over to plant big hands on Merry's table. His brown eyes smiled just ten inches from her reddening face as he said, "I hear you're anxious to talk with me?"

Hardly knowing how to respond, Meredeth reached into her reticule and, with trembling fingers, she pushed the linen squares across the table to him. "My brother, Matt Elliott, sent these to me in a letter. Will you please be sure that either Major John Clark or Captain Charles Craig receives them immediately?"

"Matt? Are you his sister?" Then, at her stiff nod, the man's stance altered abruptly. "Thank you, ma'am. My horse is just outside. I'll see that Craig gets them as soon as I can find him."

The indolent slouch turned and, with three big strides, he returned to his table, issued a sharp command, then walked to the door. The remaining men at the table leaned heads together in earnest conversation, then exited the lunchroom with their voices raised in amiable joking.

The other customers continued to talk and eat as if nothing had happened. When Molly brought the meat pies, Merry paid for them and forced herself to walk from the restaurant at a normal gait, even though she felt like running.

Once outside the tavern, Merry glanced around. There was no sign of Jim Hanks's friends, and she swiftly made her way back to the hospital. When she arrived, her father was busy with a patient. Hesitant to disturb him, she smiled at the helper and pointed to the food. When the woman nodded her understanding, Merry left. Her walk to Conners Inn seemed long. She felt a sudden chill as the sun hid behind dark clouds and the wind increased.

That evening, Philadelphia's population huddled in homes, making plans. At the inn there was a great deal of commotion, and Aunt Mina insisted upon leaving immediately for Elverson. Merry shook her head sadly for the sound of artillery fire could be heard already and she knew they would not make it. The British had surely taken Chadd's Ford and possibly they were as far as Germantown. It would be much safer to remain in Philadelphia.

Kneeling beside the window, Merry wearily closed her eyes and prayed. "Heavenly Father, we are all so afraid. We've heard so many stories about the British troops in Boston. Please keep us all safe. If Matt still lives, bless him and help him. Show us what You would have us do and. . .oh Lord, please be with Papa. Send someone to help him with all the injured and, dear God, help the wounded Patriots, too. Amen."

That night Meredeth tossed fretfully on her bed, going over and over the day's events. Had she done the right thing?

Conners was a close friend of Papa's and a well-known Patriot. She hoped Jim Hanks was all that Conners believed him to be for he certainly was not what she had expected. Then there was Castleton. Why did he run with that group? Was he a spy, an English spy?

By morning, many had packed all the goods they could manage into wagons or carriages, and the road to Morrisville and Trenton was choked with traffic. Bulletins were nailed to trees, informing folks that Benjamin Franklin had sailed for France to enlist aid from friends there.

Merry tried to block out the noise and chill. She pictured them back at Cresswick, with Papa reading the Bible each morn before the fire and Mama telling them stories of great men and women of God. How she wished they had Elijah's army of angels in Philadelphia to defend them now!

All that week the sounds of warfare punctuated every sentence and sent shivers of warning to the entire population. Clark's spy network kept the leaders informed of Howe's every move, and trickles of news leaked down to ordinary citizens. At the inn, Conners proclaimed his favorite topic tonight. Merry wondered if he had more information than most or if he simply talked more convincingly.

"Yes sir, that Washington's a smart man. Those Brits had a right-knowing spy system. Washington and his men were bumfuzzled at first, but then he called John Craig to 'im. Now thet's one canny major. He's done set up a reg'lar comp'ney of spies. Nobody but Craig knows 'em all. He keeps 'em moving round so's nobody kin guess where they'll be two days runnin'. Like a chess player, he moves 'em. You jus' wait. He'll let tha Brits git so fur an' then he'll jump."

The innkeeper clapped his big hands together, causing two-thirds of his customers to jump. Satisfied that he had made his point, he went back to puffin' his pipe. Meredeth grinned at the dead silence in the room. Conners could hold an audience enthralled just with a clap of his hands.

"Wal, jus' hope he jumps soon afore it's too late," one of the customers mumbled as he made for the door.

Silently Merry agreed with him. Certainly Washington was intelligent and Craig was known for his ability, but they were fighting the largest and oldest army in the world. The Brits called the colonists "Rebels." What would happen if the Redcoats did take Philadelphia? It was the nearest thing to a capital that the Patriots had. There were rumors claiming that the citizens of New York and Boston were little more than prisoners. The English took whatever they wanted and none dared say them nay.

By ten o'clock, most of the customers had departed for their homes. Merry climbed the stairs to her room, thinking over all that she had heard. Artillery fire began again; it seemed to be north of the city now. No doubt they were attacking Germantown. After blowing out the candle, Merry leaned on the windowsill and stared out at the blackness. A pink glow lit the northwest. In the city a low, dark fog established itself, like an omen of doom. Buildings were snared in its grip; a stifling miasma of fear filled the air.

She moved like a sleepwalker to her bed and pulled the coverlets over her ears. Just before sleep claimed her, a niggling thought teased her mind: She had not seen Castleton for three days. Before, he had followed her like a pet dog. Where was he? Busy directing Howe to Philadelphia? That night a few tears fell before she finished her prayers for Philadelphia, for the Patriots, and yes, even for Castleton. He might be the enemy, but the Bible urges folks to pray even for their enemies, doesn't it?

Though an eerie light danced on the walls, it was still dark when shouts of alarm woke her. Women and children were crying amid a storm of sounds. Stumbling to the window, she opened it and leaned out. The streets were filled with people, horses, and wagons, all desperately trying to push through the crowd. Someone banged a fist on the door of the inn. Conners's shouted question was answered by a troubled voice.

"The Brits have crossed Swedes Ford! They'll be here by sunrise! Germantown is already in their hands."

Sunrise! That was but a few hours away.

A terrified Aunt Mina charged into the room, her abigail trailing after her like a ghost. "Oh, Meredeth! I just knew we should have gone straight to Elverson. Cousin Ferdy would have taken us in. The British are no better than scoundrels. What will become of us now?"

"We are no more at risk here than at home," Meredeth said. "Papa is here. Perhaps he will let us help with the wounded. If we just stay together, we will be in less danger. Besides, Conners is Papa's friend. He will watch out for us. We shall keep our spirits up, obey their rules, and guard our tongues."

"I do hope you are correct, Meredeth, my dear. These are such trying times, but I suppose we must learn to live through them as you say. I just know I cannot go back to sleep. My mind is in a tizzy. Perhaps if Dela reads to me, my nerves may quiet."

"An excellent idea. Dela," Merry said as she turned to the maid hovering in the doorway, "help Aunt Mina to bed. A warm cup of milk might be just the thing. I will dress and go down to see what the latest news is."

Quickly Merry donned bodice and skirt, then hurried down the stairs. The common room overflowed with townspeople.

Though Conners's voice was strong, he had difficulty speaking over the din. Merry stood back, close to the wall.

A loud clatter brought instant silence as Conners, his face red as his shirt, clambered upon a table and shouted for attention. Except for a low buzz of whispers, the startled group complied.

"Now I want tha lot of ya ta listen. Yer in no danger here. This be a respect'ble inn an' no Brits er gonna make it any different. Jus' go back ta yer beds an' try ta sleep. There's no sense in gittin' all stirred up afore tha puddin's set. We'll break our fast at six like always an' there'll be plenty ta eat. Go on now, back ta yer rooms." He climbed down from his perch mumbling, "An' tha good Lord watch o'er us."

Merry was close enough to hear the last. When Conners came past her on his way to the kitchen, she reached out and touched his arm. "Thank you, Conners. That was well done," she said.

Wearily, Meredeth retreated to their rooms. Aunt Mina and Dela were sound asleep, the book open on the bed between them. With a soft sigh, Merry crawled into her own bed.

In the morning there was no danger of oversleeping for the street below her window was noisy and full of activity. The wagons today were piled with injured British soldiers, headed for the hospital. What would they do with the Patriots who nearly filled the place yesterday? She dressed, then peeked into the other room. Aunt Mina and Dela had not awakened yet.

The common room was already crowded and most of those seated were strangers. Some wore Redcoat uniforms, but all spoke with a British slant to their words. As unobtrusively as possible, Merry made her way around the side, through the hall, and back to the kitchen. There a red-faced Conners muttered to himself as he bustled about. The entire staff, which usually ran his kitchen so effortlessly, was stalking here and there like a flock of angry chickens. There was not a smile to be seen.

Merry almost turned back to her room, but Mrs. Landers, the head cook, saw her. She motioned for Merry to sit at the long table where the kitchen help had their meals. Covering a pot she was tending, the cook sailed around the other workers and leaned over so Merry could hear her in spite of the clamor.

"It's so full out there the rats couldn't find a hole. Though, come to think of it, there's a lot of 'em sitting right there. We got flatcakes left and apple-sauce. Would you like some?"

"That sounds wonderful. Yes, thank you. Are those all British out there?"

"You'd think they owned the place. Mr. Conners had a time saving your rooms for you. If more of them officers come, I don't know if he ken. You might want to keep an eye out for another place to stay, though it beats me where you could go. Those evil men are taking over all the nice homes and either putting folks out or making them move into a back room or two while the Brits claim the best parts. They're almighty high in the instep an' that's a fact."

"Perhaps we will have to return to Cresswick."

"You won't be going anywhere but what they tell you. They got troops all around the city. Won't let none out atal."

"But where can we go then?"

"They already claimed your pa's room. Mr. Conners done took all the doc's things and stored 'em in a cubby. Mebbe you ken take 'em to him in case he has need of 'em. Have you any kin here in the city?"

"There are some friends, but I suspect their homes have been confiscated, too."

"If you cain't find a place, you let me know. Mebbe I ken help you. I'll keep me thinkin' box on it."

Mrs. Landers produced butter, a bowl of applesauce, and utensils. She maneuvered between workers to the fireplace and returned with a platter of flatcakes.

"They're nice and warm yet. Now you jus' eat up while I get the rats some cheese. Whoever heard of cheese on flatcakes! Tis disgusting." With a shake of her gray head, the cook went back to her duties.

Amid all the uproar, Meredeth asked the blessing quietly. Fear floated through that room like fog on water. When she finished, she caught Mrs. Landers's attention.

"May I take the rest up to Aunt Mina and her maid? They should be awake by now."

"Here, let me get a tray for you. Ken you carry it all right or should I send a potboy up with it?"

"I can manage, thank you. That was delicious."

Merry started toward the stairs; she shivered when a rough hand stopped her.

"Here now, missy. Haven't seen the likes of you serving before. Where have you been hiding?"

Standing as tall as her five feet, two inches allowed, Meredeth tilted her chin and forced herself to calmness. "I am not a servant. I am a guest here. Now please have the goodness to let me pass."

"Well now, don't be so high and mighty, missy. A pretty young thing like you shouldn't be wandering around alone. Don't know what kinds of villains you might meet up with. Now I'll just escort you to your room to be sure you get there all safe and sound like, hmmm?"

"I am perfectly capable of making it to my room without help, thank you. Please remove your hand from my arm."

"You don't want to be so hard to get along with. I have authority to guarantee you'll be treated like royalty while we are here."

"The lady already has an escort, Hastings," a voice interrupted. "Sorry. I saw her first. We have become well acquainted this past week."

With one hand on the tray and the other around Merry, Castleton faced down the Redcoat officer. With sputtered anger, Hastings backed off and said nothing more, but his snapping black eyes followed them as they walked to the stairs.

"I must admit you are very good at your specialty, Mr. Castleton. Thank you again," Merry said softly.

"My name is William, but most of my friends call me Will. Surely my adroit rescue of a lovely maiden should prompt her to consider me a friend?"

Soberly, Meredeth searched his face. The congenial smile, the humorous twinkle in his blue eyes, the boyish lock of hair that seemed to have a mind of its own, and the firm but gentle hold on her arm all encouraged her to accept him for what he claimed to be. After all, she did not know for sure that he was a spy. That was only a figment of her imagination. Perhaps he helped the Patriots just as he helped her. She certainly needed a friend right now.

"Very well, we will be friends then. You can call me Meredeth if it pleases you."

"I've heard them call you Merry. I like that much better."

A teasing sparkle lit her eyes as she said, "Let us test your mettle, sir. If you can manage that tray up the stairs to our rooms without spilling anything, you may call me Merry."

The warmth of his answering grin touched her as she led the way up the steps. At the landing, a clatter behind her made Merry turn. She glanced down, following his gaze, and abruptly she lowered her skirts. Better she should fall on the stairs than have Aunt Mina chide her for showing her ankles.

Will looked up with no repentance whatsoever in his smiling features. "Those dainty feet were made for dancing."

With a huff over her shoulder, Merry hurried to the door and held out her hands for the tray. Before she could close the door on him, Will dug into a pocket and handed her a piece of paper.

"If I don't happen to be around when you need me, my helpful service is still at your command. Just send a message to this address. I mean that very seriously," he spoke low but firmly.

"Thank you Mr. . .ah, Will."

When Merry entered the room, Aunt Mina and Dela were dressed, ready to descend to the common room.

"I think you might be much more comfortable eating up here. The dining area is filled with Brits. Mrs. Landers sent up some delicious flatcakes."

"Humph! I suppose we are expected to remain secluded while those atrocious Englishmen are in charge. Well, let's see what the cook has provided. This will doubtless be our lot for some time," Aunt Mina complained.

"Mrs. Landers suggested we seek other quarters for our rooms here will soon be confiscated. Do you know of anyone who might take us in, Aunt Mina?"

Her brow furrowed in concentration, the older woman commenced to deplete the flatcakes swiftly. At last she sat back and gently patted her mouth with a napkin.

"There is an old acquaintance of mine. Her name is Elvira Clairmont. I haven't seen her in years, but she lived in an older place on the north side. I believe it was on Arch Street. She is a widow, just a year older than I, but we grew up together as girls and attended the same schools. As I recall, she lived near Christ Church. That's about Second Street. I doubt the British would confiscate a home there. They prefer the more aristocratic places."

"If you can spare Dela, she and I can try to locate it this morning," Merry said.

Concern evident in her wide eyes, Aunt Mina nodded her agreement. "I will remain here so no one makes off with our belongings while you are gone. Such terrible times these are, when a person can be put out helter-skelter. It's shameful, that's what it is."

Swiftly donning their cloaks, Merry and Dela slipped down the back stairs to the kitchen. Conners sat, eating his own meal. The morning rush was finished and the room was much quieter.

"Mr. Conners, have you seen Jeremiah this morning?" Meredeth inquired.

" 'Tis sorry I am about the fracas this mornin', lass. This oc'apation by tha Brits ain't goin' ta be easy, that's a fact. Good thing Castleton came along when he did. That fella's right up ta snuff. Now, lessee. Jeremiah wuz here but t'wern't no place ta park tha coach. I sent him around ta tha back. Ya might just take a looksee on tha dock."

"Thank you. Oh, and Mr. Conners, Aunt Mina is staying up in our rooms while Dela and I go to speak to a friend."

"Ya best be careful now, Miz Elliott. With the whole place ov'run with Brits, there's no tellin' what could happen."

"We will be on guard. We plan to return by noon or shortly after."

Fortunately their coach was snuggled into a corner not too far away. Jeremiah left the small knot of men with whom he had been talking and hurried toward Merry.

"Can you take us to Christ Church, Jeremiah? We must find some other place to stay."

"I kin take ya there, but then I gotta git this load ta the Brits quick like. They're making use of everything on wheels. Cain't take the chance o' gitting their dander up."

"Of course, Jeremiah. It's not your fault. They've taken over everything. Aunt Mina wasn't sure of the address, anyway. We will stop to ask the Reverend Harrison at Christ Church when we get to the neighborhood."

Everywhere they looked, the city was cloaked in subdued conversation and furtive movements. Wariness weighted the air and soldiers were stopping many vehicles and pedestrians. Merry was glad when they reached the church without incident.

They bid Jeremiah farewell and approached the familiar building. Merry knocked on the heavy wooden door leading to the Reverend Harrison's study. He must have been watching from the window, for the portal opened immediately.

"Miss Elliott, what a pleasant surprise. Do come in. Please be seated, my dear, and tell me what is on your mind."

"Reverend Harrison, I am looking for an older woman by the name of Elvira Clairmont. She is a friend of my Aunt Mina's. Is she a member of your congregation?"

The preacher's eyes twinkled. "I cannot claim the lady as part of my flock, Miss Elliott. However I have heard of her." He lowered his voice to a whisper. "She is a member of another church, but the dear lady has quite a reputation. She is extremely diligent in aiding the poor and is well thought of. She is a widow and lives just down the street on Arch. I am not sure of the address, but look for a two-story, red brick home with bright blue shutters. It is very eye-catching."

Merry smiled at his colorful description and rose to leave. "Thank you, sir. We will pay her a call. We hope to see you Sunday. Surely they must allow us to attend services. Good day."

"We should all pray for good days. Things appear quite dark at present," the reverend remarked.

"You speak truly. Thank you again for your assistance."

The two women had gone only a short way down Arch before both began to chuckle. "I think it is safe to assume that we have found the lady," Merry murmured. "Undoubtedly Mrs. Clairmont is partial to blue."

"I have never seen a home with such bright colors," Dela agreed.

The walkway was bordered on both sides by a variety of plants and the wooden door boasted a large wreath of flowers in various shades of blue cloth and tied with a red bow. Merry's knock brought a tiny, white-haired woman to the door. She wore a blue, floral-print dress of an outdated style; a white lace collar framed a face that seemed to be painted on china. Somehow the dress was at peace with the fragile figure it adorned. She smiled, though breathing a bit hard from her haste to answer the door.

"Good morning, my dears. I don't believe I've had the pleasure of meeting you, but come in. Sit a spell and tell me how I may help you."

She ushered them into a cozy parlor filled with greenery. Waving a hand in the direction of some cane chairs fluffed with pillows, she seated herself and turned to Merry and Dela in eager expectation. Merry could not help responding with a smile as she and Dela sank into the cushions.

"Mrs. Clairmont?" Merry inquired.

"Yes, that is my name and who may you be, dear?"

"I am Meredeth Elliott and this is Dela, my aunt's maid. My aunt, Mina Elliott, remembers you from her early years and wondered if you were still in the vicinity. We are staying at Conners Inn and she would dearly like to visit with you and renew the friendship you shared as girls. We set out to locate you this morning while Aunt Mina waited at the inn."

"Mina Elliott? Well, I never! It has been years since I saw her and we were such close friends. How is she?"

"Except for the passing years, she is much the same girl you knew in school. She would so enjoy meeting you again. Would it be possible for you to come to the inn or could we meet you elsewhere?"

"Why, there's no reason for that. You must come here. My cook would be pleased to show off her skills. It's so seldom we have company anymore. So you are Mina's niece. Well, child, you are a beauty if ever I saw one. It will be a delight to have you visit. My family has moved away and I see them only occasionally. Oh but," she suddenly sobered, "have those terrible invaders come to your inn yet?"

"Yes, they have. We are taking our meals in our rooms for the men at the inn are rather brash in their conduct."

"I'm sure they are. The military men are often so uncouth. Oh child, you must come stay with me. Would it be difficult to move your things? You cannot possibly stay in a public inn under these present circumstances. I will call Nell to spruce up some rooms for you."

"I know Aunt Mina would be pleased to come, but we do not want to put you to a lot of trouble."

"Why, it will be no trouble at all. It will brighten my life to have you. Mina and I could leisurely recall old times. Do say you will come. I have plenty of room and it will be such a joy for me."

The rattle of plates announced the other member of the Clairmont household. Beaming as if she had won the lottery, a well-endowed gnome of a woman entered.

"Here ya be, Miz Clairmont. Since it was close to noon, I just thought I'd make up a batch o' butterfly cakes. You like 'em so well."

With a wink in the direction of the guests, the rotund cook placed a large tray on a nearby table. Towels were whisked away to reveal plates heaped with pastries and tiny cakes. Aunt Mina would think she was in heaven here, Merry thought as she took several pieces. Dela was given her choice of the goodies, as well.

"These are almost too pretty to eat," Meredeth said. "I have never seen such before. You call them butterflies?"

That praise brought an enormous smile to the cook's face. "They are delicious. You have a rare prize in your kitchen, Mrs. Clairmont."

"Oh, forgive me. I forgot to introduce you to Mrs. Nell Schoengert. Actually she is far more than a cook. She is my closest friend. Nell, this is Miss Meredeth Elliott, the niece of a dear friend of mine, and here is Dela, her aunt's maid."

This produced a flurry of bows until the hostess leaned toward the cook and whispered loud enough to be heard at the inn. "We need some tea, dearie. Bring some freshly brewed tea, if you please."

"Oh yessum, Mrs. Clairmont. It's all made right and proper. I'll be just a minute," Mrs. Schoengert said and then away she bustled, humming to herself.

By the time Meredeth and Dela left, it was well into the afternoon. They hurried down Arch and turned on Eighth toward the hospital. Merry had to ask where her papa wanted his things sent and make him aware of their change of residence.

three

Just as Merry and Dela reached Chestnut Street, a dark buggy stopped beside them to let the heavier traffic go by. When the wagons had passed, Merry and Dela started across the street. A sharp command from the driver of the buggy, startled them and, uncertain, they halted. The driver then leaned forward and his whip lashed out to make stinging contact with the rump of the horse pulling the buggy. It snorted savagely and reared, pawing frantically at the air, and another flick of the whip sent the beast lunging toward the two women. Screams and shouts covered the thump of running hooves. Merry and Dela grabbed each other as they leaped to escape. Two figures rushed to them, lifting and rolling with them across the thoroughfare.

Meredeth, gasping for breath, pushed herself up to a sitting position as the buggy rattled off crookedly, the horse still fighting the reins. A small crowd soon surrounded the four people on the ground.

"That horse was crazed!" Meredeth exclaimed.

"No. It was the idiot driver. He lost control."

"Shouldn't a' beat at the critter like that. Bound ta spook the beast."

Strong arms turned Merry to face her rescuer, who asked, "Are you injured?"

"Mr. . .ah, Will. Imagine you turning up just when I required rescuing."

For several long moments they stared at each other while their breathing became more normal. Then with a shaky smile, he stood and held out his hand to help Merry to her feet.

"I didn't get a good look at the driver, did you?" Will asked.

"I couldn't see his face; his hands were raised in front of it. He wore something red around his neck. I have never seen its like before."

"Something red?"

"Yes, it hung down in a V shape, not at all like a proper neckcloth."

"Did it look like a napkin folded in half?" Will asked.

"I suppose so, but who would use red napkins?"

"It sounds like a Belchior neckcloth. In England some wear them to sporting events."

Her eyes widened and a soft gasp escaped her before she covered her mouth. Somewhere else she remembered seeing another person wearing such a neckcloth.

Will started to speak, but bystanders demanded his attention. "I think we'd better get out of the way of traffic," he suggested.

Merry nodded, for the middle of the street was no place to solve mysteries. They then turned to see how Dela had fared. A man was busily brushing dust from her skirts.

"Merry," Will said, "this is my friend, Warren Trent. He is one of the best ship captains in the business. Warren, meet Miss Meredeth Elliott."

"My pleasure, Miss Elliott," Warren Trent said.

"Can we escort you? Where were you bound?" Will asked.

"We planned to stop at the hospital. The innkeeper was unable to prevent British officers from appropriating Papa's room. We wondered where he wanted his things delivered."

"You are welcome to the use of my buggy," Will offered.

"That is kind of you. If you could wait for us to ask his wishes, we would be grateful for your help."

Will glanced toward his friend. "Are you free for a time, Warren?"

"Certainly. I am not due back at the ship for hours."

"Then let's go."

When the young people started down the street, the crowd dispersed rapidly. Within minutes the four friends reached the hospital. While Merry and Dela went in to speak to her papa, the men waited outside. Warren sent Will a knowing grin.

"I was not aware you had female friends here, Will. Is she some local contact?"

Will's face tightened and his eyes narrowed to slits. "She is a lady, my friend, certainly not a mere contact. I met her purely by accident."

"Do you think it wise to start a relationship at this time?" Warren asked.

"We do not have a relationship. She is Matt Elliott's sister, but I am convinced she knows nothing of import. She has a perfectly legitimate reason for being here."

"Touché, Will. Just take care. A lot depends on us in the months ahead."

"I know our responsibilities full well. She will cause no complications."

"I have heard men say that before."

Will's glare brought a chuckle from his companion. He threw up his hands and kept his silence. When the women joined them, there was no sign of conflict, just two gentlemen discussing trivialities.

Warren was dispatched to bring the buggy from their lodgings, and Will walked back to the inn with Meredeth and Dela. Many of the officers recognized Will, greeting him jovially. Conners led them back to a pantry off the kitchen, and he handed the large bag there to Merry.

"Ev'rything from your pa's room is here," Conners said. "Twarn't much."

"I talked to my papa a few minutes ago. He has a room in the hospital where he can sleep and work. Thank you for your help."

"Ah. . .Miz Elliott. . .you didn't by chance find a place to stay yourself, did ja?"

Meredeth smiled at Conners's embarrassment.

"Yes, we did, Conners. We can move tomorrow."

"I thank'e, Miz Elliott. That there Major Hastings is a mean'un, he is. I'll have Zeke take you and yer things to the new place soon's you're ready tomorra."

"The major does seem to have a nasty streak. I'm glad we won't have to deal with him after today."

Conners chewed on his pipe and walked away muttering, "Gittin' to be a hard thing when a man cain't even run his inn without a Brit o'erseein' him."

Will's brows ridged together in a frown as he looked after Conners. Merry bit her lip. Should she warn the innkeeper to watch what he said around Castleton? But, no. She had no proof against him. After all, he had been more than helpful to her.

Mr. Trent pulled the horse to a stop in front of the inn just as Will and Meredeth emerged. After tossing the bag into the buggy, Castleton put his hands on Merry's shoulders and looked deeply into her eyes.

"Please stay in your room tonight. Conners will send food up to you. You didn't say where you are going. I would like to see you again."

"We are to stay with an old friend of Aunt Mina's, Mrs. Clairmont. She lives on Arch Street, between Fourth and Fifth. I don't think she will mind your calling on me there. Just look for the red house with all the blue trim. It stands out."

"Good. If you need help tomorrow, send a note by Conners's potboy. I may be out, but the landlady will see that I get it."

Will scanned the street. Only a handful of men strolled away to the north; there were no others in sight. Drawing Merry closer to the buggy, he raised her hand to his lips. A smile tugged at his mouth when her complexion pinkened.

"I like the way you blush. Not many young ladies are able to do that so beautifully. Instead of a fiery red, you turn a delicate pink, just like one of my mother's favorite roses."

"You are a great tease, sir," Merry admonished him.

"Merry, I am not teasing," Will said as he leaped into the buggy.

Meredeth heard Warren's laughter as they drove off, but she also heard

Will's reply. "Enough, Warren. I was not teasing. If you keep this up, I may have to retire you to captain the *Katie Lou*."

Just what was Will doing? She wished she knew. Swiftly she went into the inn.

≥∙

Promptly at eleven o'clock the next morning, Zeke tapped on their door. "Be ya' ready ta go, Miz Elliott?" he asked.

Meredeth opened the door and directed him to the trunks standing to one side. She, Aunt Mina, and Dela made their good-byes to Conners and climbed into Zeke's wagon. Within the hour they were shown to bedrooms on the second floor of Mrs. Clairmont's home. Aunt Mina was delighted with her room, done in blue muslin and white lace. Their hostess begged Merry's forgiveness when she led her into the next room.

"My husband, bless his soul, was not overfond of blue, so I had a few rooms done in other colors to please him. I hope this green and red room is not offensive to you."

"Not at all," Meredeth answered, biting the inside of her cheek so she would not laugh.

She fingered the beautifully made coverlet. "This is lovely. Did you make this quilt? I don't recall ever seeing this pattern."

"It is the Starfire pattern. The coverlet was a bridal gift from my mother and I have always cherished it. But I cannot understand why she made it in red and green. Perhaps she wanted to please George, my late husband. He did have a preference for those colors. There is also a smaller, matching piece to place over your knees when riding in the carriage. If you are fond of the Starfire pattern, I will look through our trunks in the attic and find the smaller piece for you. With winter coming on, you could use it in the carriage."

"Starfire. That is a perfect name. Thank you again for your warm hospitality. Conners said the British are pressing him for more rooms and that they plan to take over the inn completely."

"Tsk. Just like the lot of ruffians they are. We shall pray Ben Franklin brings us help swiftly."

"It will take time for him to make two trans-Atlantic crossings as well as to talk to his friends. I fear we will be under British rule for some time."

"Then we shall simply have to make them leave by ourselves, won't we, dear?"

A smug smile lit the determined woman's face as she stalked off down the hall. Open-mouthed, Merry stared after her. What did she suppose four women could do to defeat the British army?

Aunt Mina and Elvira, as Mrs. Clairmont preferred to be called, spent every minute reviewing the span of their lives. After a few days, Merry felt utterly useless, and she spoke to them the next morn.

"Anna surely is ready to leave the hospital by now. Papa said just the other day she was doing well. Conditions there are crowded. Do you have need of Jeremiah today, Aunt Mina?"

"No, my dear. There is no place to go since the British set such drastic rules. Redcoats control the market and evening entertainments. No one but their Tory friends dares break the curfew. Take Dela with you."

"We may go as far as the inn. I would like to speak to Conners. With troops all over the city it is difficult to walk even a few blocks without being stopped for questioning."

The older women returned to their reminiscing. Smiling, Merry climbed the stairs to find Dela busily hanging gowns she had just ironed.

"When you are finished, Dela, can you accompany me to bring Anna back to us?"

"Oh yes, Miss Elliott. I can do mending later. It will be good to have Anna with us again."

"Then I will tell Jeremiah to bring the carriage around in ten minutes. Meet me downstairs."

Merry was not chicken-hearted but she was relieved they did not have to walk today. Normally she enjoyed exercise, but troops were everywhere. Couriers cantered past toward headquarters; soldiers stopped many pedestrians to question them. When they approached the hospital, they saw a line of injured Redcoats waiting. Would Papa have time for visitors?

Fortunately, a buggy was pulling away.

"Just sit tight, Miss Merry. We'll swing right in behind them," Jeremiah said.

That maneuver completed, the driver helped his passengers down. With concern, he saw every one of the men standing there turn, like dominoes falling, to watch the women.

"You want I should go ta tha door with ya?" he asked.

"No, thank you, Jeremiah. You stay with the carriage. I've heard the English are looking for horses to replace animals injured or lost in battle. I wouldn't put it past them to take any animal they saw standing unattended."

"Yer prob'ly right but I'll keep an eye out for ya 'til ya git inside."

The men did not leave their places but a few called out ribald comments. One young soldier glared at his comrades, then held the door open for Merry and Dela.

"Mornin' ladies. When you're finished with your business here, I'd surely be pleased to share a cup of tea with you."

His smile was genuine. Meredeth appreciated his kindness, but his red coat reminded her of Matt. Had he been killed by one of these men?

"Thank you for your help, but we have tasks we must do." They hurried in, closing the door quietly behind them. Merry raised an eyebrow at the sight of her papa's office. Books and papers lay in staggering heaps on his desk and furniture had been pushed to the center, leaving space for one pallet on each side. There was barely enough room to walk.

In the area beyond, straw carpeted the floor. Every sort of bedding formed long rows of pallets, separated by narrow walking spaces. The next chamber was the same. Finally they found her father. Anna, holding a small tray of instruments, knelt beside him while he worked on a patient's head wound.

"Ah, there we have it! You'll recover a lot faster, my friend," the doctor said, placing the bloody bullet on the tray. Standing, he wiped his hands down his white coat.

"Now, Anna, if you'll clean that out and stitch it up for me—" His mouth gaped when he noticed Meredeth, standing not five feet from him.

"Papa," she grinned up at him, "can this be the man who required two fresh coats each day when he worked in his office?"

With a laugh, he threw one arm around her, hugging her to his side. "Hush now or I'll put you to work as I did Anna. I suppose you have come to take my assistant away from me?"

His daughter scrutinized his tired eyes and the new lines in his face. In an instant her plan was changed.

"No, Papa. It looks to me as if you are working too hard. Are you getting any rest at all?"

"Oh, I spend a few hours sleeping each night."

"But that is not enough."

She saw sad agreement in his eyes. Pictures of Aunt Mina and Elvira, so happy together, flashed through her mind. There was nothing for a young lady to do at Mrs. Clairmont's.

"Papa, I did come to take Anna back to Arch Street, but if she is able to help you, she must stay here. Could I come help, also? Aunt Mina and her hostess have so much to talk about, they don't even know I'm around."

Dr. Elliott frowned.

"Papa, this is a war. So many men are hurt. You can't do everything yourself. Please let me help. . .for Matt."

His eyes filled with his love for her. He smiled and hugged her again. "You are much like your mother. Very well, we will try it, my dear. But if the men give you the least bit of trouble, you must tell me. We'll see how it goes."

"Good. Anna and I can go back to Mrs. Clairmont's at night and bring you clean clothes each morning. Papa, where do you sleep?"

"I have been sleeping in my office. There is a small dressing room down the hall where Anna sleeps. It would be better if she could sleep elsewhere."

"Agreed. Give me your soiled clothing and I will see that it is clean for tomorrow. I'll send Jeremiah back for Anna at six. Papa, can you eat with us tonight?"

Dr. Elliott slumped. Wearily he looked around at the multitude of injured men. Squaring his shoulders firmly, he replied, "Someone has to be here for them. The other doctors in town have practices of their own. Perhaps you could send me something with Jeremiah?"

At her nod, the twinkle came back in his eyes. Meredeth felt such pride in her heart for him, it brought tears very close to overflowing.

"I love you so much, Papa," she said.

"As I do you, my dear. Now off with you and see if you can find some food for me."

Merry gave him a crooked grin. She and Dela stepped carefully between the long rows of soldiers covering the floor. The line at the door was unchanged. Ducking their heads, the young women hurried to the carriage. Jeremiah leaped down from his perch to help them in.

"Jeremiah, could you stop by Conners Inn please, before we go back to Arch Street?"

"Be glad to, Miz Elliott."

When they arrived at the inn, there was no room to pull aside and wait, so after Jeremiah helped Meredeth and Dela down, he drove around to the back. At the front of the inn, Redcoats lounged about, talking in groups. Meredeth and Dela wove a path through them to the door.

A large hand on Merry's elbow made her twist away, a haughty expression tightening her face. When she saw that it was Will, a huge sigh escaped her. Delight shone in his eyes.

"I believe you are truly glad to see me. May I help you through this crowd?" Will asked.

"Yes, please. I'm afraid my five feet and two inches will not impress any of this group and, yes, it is a relief to see you here. I'd prefer not to encounter Hastings."

Pleased with her answer, Will put a protective arm around her and motioned for Dela to stay close behind.

"Ah, Castleton is taking his little ladybird for a walk. In such close quarters, it does give one opportunity to take liberties, does it not?"

Will stopped short. Pushing Merry between himself and Dela, he turned to glare at Hastings's sneering visage. A large mug of ale was within Will's reach. His eyes intent on Hastings, Will picked up the drink as if to take a swallow, but a swift movement upturned the mug over Hastings's head. Conversation quieted. The Redcoat's guttural reply was easily heard.

"I will see you dead for this!" Hastings exclaimed.

"I will meet you any time," Will said, tossing the metal cup aside with a grimace of distaste.

Enraged, Hastings snarled, his hand dropping to his sword before he realized the impossibility of a sword fight in such a crowd. His jaw hardened and his voice dropped an octave.

"You know full well we were told not to make trouble among the populace, you swine," Hastings muttered.

"That did not occur to you when you maligned this lady. You are all mouth and no muscle. I insist you owe Miss Elliott an apology."

"Englishmen do not apologize to Rebels."

A swift movement slammed Hastings against the wall. The major's mouth gaped at the slim French dagger making a deep dent in his waistcoat. Instantly the crowd hushed, except for one rough voice that said, "Poke 'im with it, matey. Let's see if he does have blue blood as he claims."

"Apologize," Castleton growled.

Perspiration popped from the major's brow. Swiftly his eyes assessed the disgusted looks of his countrymen and the eager expectations apparent in some ragtag seamen standing at the bar. He struggled to clear his throat.

"I. . .I. . .ask your pardon," he said.

Will eased the pressure of the blade. "Get out of here before I forget who we both are."

Those around them immediately moved, making way for Hastings, who, without a backward glance, stumbled from the room.

"Aww right now, let's git back to our vi'tals. There's a flummery for dessert tonight. Got some fresh apples an it's right tasty."

Conners's suggestion brought most of the men back to the tables. Will moved his charges around the group and out to the warmth of the kitchen.

Mrs. Landers hurried to greet them and she pointed to the big table. "Thar now, jus' set you down an' I'll dish up some fried chicken an' dumplins'."

Meredeth was not sure if she wanted to thank Will or scold him for taking such a chance. As if he knew exactly what she was thinking, he leaned over to whisper.

"I knew he wouldn't fight," Will said. "Hastings talks brash, but he's a coward at heart. I carry weapons for protection, but I've never yet had to cut or shoot anyone. Christ managed without sword or gun. My tutor was a clergyman and he told me a true gentleman uses the good sense God gave him first and his fists second, if necessary. Weapons are to be used only when lives are in danger. I think he was a very wise man."

Merry's eyes misted over. "I think so, too," she murmured, "but what am I going to do with you? You always arrive just in time to rescue me, but then I never needed rescuing until I met you."

"Merry, if I could get you and your aunt out of Philadelphia, would you go?" Will asked.

She stared wide-eyed at him for a few minutes before answering, "How could you do that? Who, or what are you, Will?"

He swallowed hard as if he hadn't meant to say that at all. Clearing his throat, he spoke more softly. "Merry, I must leave town for at least a week. If that fiend, Hastings, dares to harm you while I'm gone, I would never forgive myself. Please believe me. I'm part owner of a shipping line operating out of Boston. My home is there, but I have to travel because of business. I work hard, go to church on Sundays, I'm a gentleman and try to behave as one. . .and I like you very much. I don't want Hastings to get his dirty hands on you. Can you understand that?"

She saw truth in what he said, but there was so much he was not saying. In any event she could not leave. Her papa must remain and he needed her. She would be careful to have Dela with her at all times.

"I know there is danger for all of us, but my family is here in Philadelphia. Papa is working so hard I fear for his health. Today he agreed to let me help him. I am going to do that, Will, but I do appreciate your friendship. . . truly."

He closed his eyes and ran nervous fingers through his hair, pushing it back from his forehead.

"I should have known you'd say that. There's got to be a way. . .someone I can trust to protect you. Merry, you have no conception of the devilish things Hastings might do. All right. I do understand what you're saying, but I want you to promise me one thing."

His eyes held hers and she felt his piercing gaze all the way down to her heart. Merry licked her dry lips.

"What do you want me to promise?" she asked.

"Just that you will think carefully about any letter that comes to you that is sealed with this ring. Take a close look at it. . .memorize the pattern. Promise me that, please, Merry?"

He reached a hand to cover hers. She was struck by the force of his concern and his. . .what? What exactly was the message he was trying to convey to her?

"I will try," Merry answered. She could tell he was not satisfied with her response, but it was all she could give at this time.

Mrs. Landers plopped down a platter of chicken and a bowl of dumplings, moist with butter. One look at their sober faces made her frown. Within minutes she was back, bringing warm bread and a small bowl of peas. Hands on hips, she regarded the two young people.

"Thar's e'nugh fightin' goin' on round here without you two starting a battle. Now jus' you fill up on that and talk nice to each other, you hear? I saved this special fer you an' I don't wanta see good food go to waste." With that pronouncement, she stomped away to tend to other chores.

The somber moment broke Merry and Will into smiles, and they did justice to the delicious food before them. From the big hearth, the cook nodded wisely and set up a new batch of dough. When they were done, Will left and Merry went back to Mrs. Clairmont's.

four

The next morning when Merry awoke, a note lay beside her pillow. Startled, she picked it up. The seal of the letter had been imprinted by Will's ring. Quickly, Merry opened and read it.

> *My dear Merry,*
> *There is a soldier, Douglas McClanahan, at the hospital. He is badly injured and will be there for sometime. If for any reason you need my rescuing services, don't write a note. Just tell him. He'll contact me. I beg you to trust me.*
>
> > *Your friend,*
> > *William Castleton*
>
> *Please destroy this note immediately.*

Meredeth sat straight up in bed. Will was gone. Why hadn't he told her he was leaving so soon? Was it such a big secret? Don't write notes, he had said. Destroy this letter. Trust him. *Oh, Will, what are you involved with that must be hidden?*

"William Castleton, don't you dare be a British spy or I. . .I'm afraid I will be left with a totally broken heart. First Matt and now this!"

She threw the letter from her as hard as she could, but a brisk morning breeze wafted it back to the coverlet. After stretching to reclaim the bit of parchment, she jerked the Starfire quilt up over her head. Muted sobs shook the bedclothes until all her despair and frustration drained away. Only the loneliness was left. She drew in a jagged breath and whispered a prayer.

"Dear heavenly Father, thank You for Your promise that You will never leave me nor forsake me. Give me the courage I need to do what I can and trust in You to watch over us. I know You can do all things. Grant me the patience to wait for Your grace to unfold Your Will. Amen."

A gentle rap at the door alerted her to the fact that the sun was well up. Dela came into the room, balancing a tray of food. The smell of honey muffins coaxed Merry from the bed's warmth, and she quickly pulled on her robe and sat cross-legged on the bed. She had plans to help her father today.

"It was getting late, Miss Merry, so Cook said to bring you a tray. Why, Miss Meredeth! Whatever made your eyes so red? Is there aught I can do?"

"Thanks, Dela, but there's nothing anyone can do. It's the way the world is. With war, occupation forces, and Papa so busy he looks sick, I guess it all overwhelmed me a bit. I'll wash my face with cold water. We should leave as soon as possible. Are Papa's clothes clean?"

"Yes, Miss Merry. They're ready. I'll lay your things out for you. Should I tell Jeremiah to bring the coach?"

"Please do. It won't take long to eat. It smells so good and I am hungry. If you will help me dress, we should be able to leave in thirty minutes. Is there a fire in the kitchen hearth, Dela?"

"That there is, Miss Merry. Cook's baking butterflies again."

"Good. You might save a few for me. Aunt Mina likes those so well they may be gone when I come home this eve."

"Yessum."

Merry rolled the note in her hand into a tiny cylinder and then she sped down the back stairs to the kitchen. Good. It was empty. Swiftly she dropped the message into the flames, staying long enough to be sure that only ashes remained.

The cool water in the basin felt good when Merry splashed it on her face and hands. The weather was warm for October, and she thought of her father in the crowded rooms of the hospital and the Patriots surrounded by smoke and heat from the big cannons. Suddenly it occurred to Meredeth that lately there had been no gunfire and that all that the townspeople heard were rumors of British victories. Were they fighting now? Where was Will? She shook that thought away and tugged on her chemise as Dela entered.

"The coachman is bringing the carriage around, Miss Merry. Here, let me help you with those buttons."

Their four hands made swift work of the task, and by the time Aunt Mina called up to inform them that the coach awaited, Merry and Dela were descending the stairs.

The heat that day was the talk of the entire city. Some said it was a belated breath of summer, others dourly whispered it was unnatural, the work of the devil, or perhaps the British. By noon, when the hospital workers stopped to eat, Merry longed for a cool bath. Perspiration ran in trickles down her back, and her hair not only rejected pins but even the riband that she tied about it.

After lunch Merry went to check on a young English soldier, little more than a child, whose fever was aflame. She hurried for more cool water for, British or not, the lad was too young to die. While she bathed his head and neck, her papa came to see the patient.

"I don't like the looks of this. His wound must be festering inside. Do you feel up to helping me or should I ask Anna?"

"Just tell me what I must do," Merry replied.

"Get the tray of instruments Anna keeps ready for me. Bring plenty of cloths and the bottle of laudanum on my desk. It's best he does not regain consciousness while I work."

Merry knelt beside the pallet, as she had seen Anna do. Dr. Elliott pierced the partially healed wound, releasing a pool of noxious ooze.

"Catch it in some cloths, Merry. I want to look at it closely when we are finished. Now pour some of that clear liquid into another cloth and hand it to me."

The boy's body jerked as her papa dipped the cloth into the wound, swathing it clear of all infectious matter.

"Give him a bit of laudanum. You'd better hold his head so he swallows it."

Obediently Merry performed that task, then sat back on her heels as she watched her father close and bandage the shoulder again. Merry felt sure her face must be white as parchment, but she lifted a determined chin and tried to smile for her papa's benefit.

"Thank you, my dear. You are an excellent assistant, much like your mother. Now perhaps you could sit and read letters to some of the men? It will cheer them to hear from loved ones. Sometimes that is as good as any medicine I can give them."

"I don't know what they would do without you, Papa. You treat them as you would any of our men."

"Each is someone's husband or son, Merry, and I hope that Matt would receive the same care if he is ever wounded. I can do no less."

As Merry collected all the letters, she thought soberly of her feelings toward the British. Her papa was right, but it was hard to feel sorrow for them, especially since they might have killed Matt. She flicked through the correspondence.

"Douglas McClanahan," she read. "That's the name Will mentioned. I must see him next."

A craggy featured Scotsman lay staring up at the flies on the ceiling, his hands crossed over his chest, his fingers drumming that part of his anatomy as if he were playing a tune. Her approach brought a big smile to his bearded face.

"Well now, lassie, it's a sight for sore eyes to see you coming to me wi' mail in your hands. Is it a letter you bring then?"

"I do, indeed. Let me kneel here beside you so I don't disturb the others who are sleeping."

"Some sleep because they ha' no letters. 'Tis a hard thing for a mon to lay when he's used to doing a day's work. Do you write to some lad, too?"

Merry's lashes lowered and her tears trembled close to spilling over. How she wished she could write to Matt.

"Och, forgive me, lass. I dinna mean to cause sadness for someone as bonnie as you. Have you lost a loved one then?"

She looked up, cleared her throat, and attempted a smile.

His big roughened hands gathered hers gently between his.

"Mr. McClanahan—"

"I'd be asking you to name me Red Mac, ma'am. That's how my friends call me."

Merry glanced at the brilliant shade of his hair. This time her smile was real.

"Red Mac. That's a fitting name, sir. I am Meredeth Elliott." She leaned closer to whisper. "Will Castleton told me to speak with you if I ever needed his help."

A grin divided the Scotsman's face, ear to ear. "So you are Will's lassie. The boy always did have a good eye for the bonnie ones. Did you want a message delivered?"

"Not at present. I truly came to read your letter to you unless you'd prefer to do it yourself."

"Oh, I'm right able to read, Miss Elliott. It's my legs that give me trouble, but I'd much rather listen to you. Don't think there's aught in there your ears shouldn't hear."

That earned a big smile and, with quick fingers, she broke the seal. A warm feeling flowed through her as she read of a loving family, a cottage with a glowing hearth, and freshly baked bread with molasses. When she at last folded the missive and handed it to him, she caught a hint of moisture in his eyes.

"You must miss them greatly," she said.

"Oh aye, but a soldier learns to hold his dear ones in his heart 'til he can hold them in his arms, you know. 'Tis not likely I will see them for a long while yet."

Merry surprised herself by blurting out, "I pray it will be very soon you are united with them, Red Mac."

What amazed her most was that she meant it with all her heart, and she had to admit that all Englishmen were not bounders. When she rose to leave, he grabbed her hand.

"Be sure if you need help, lass, I'll get word to Will for you. I think the lad's outdone himself this time."

"You, sir, are as big a tease as Will." With that, Merry went on to the next recipient of mail.

Somehow the rest of the day breezed by as if on wings. When Jeremiah came for the women, hovering storm clouds foretold of a noisy bit of weather ahead, but the world looked brighter in her eyes at least.

It was a wild night. Lightning flashed gaudy streaks across the sky while the accompanying thunder rattled windows in the old house. What did men in the battlefields do during a storm? Was Will on one of his ships? There were often disasters along the coast.

"Oh please, God, send Your holy angels to keep him safe."

ঌ

After the storm moved on, the temperatures cooled a bit. As the weeks passed by, each day became much like the one before as healed British soldiers were replaced by newly wounded ones. All the injured Rebels were taken to prison. Merry listened anxiously to the men's conversation, hoping for some news of the war, but they spoke only of their homes and families.

At the Mrs. Clairmont's, Elvira and Aunt Mina continued to chatter like children about the early days. Merry sighed for no one wanted to talk about the war and she longed to hear of the Patriots' progress, of their small army, and the ships at sea. Now and again, though, her papa would go to a meeting and from him she learned several things. Congress had fled to Lancaster; the State House bell, and all other bells in town, had been hidden so the English would not melt them down for cannon balls; and Washington had attacked Howe's main camp in Germantown, but had been repulsed.

One cold night Merry and Dela stayed until ten o'clock to care for the patients, while Dr. Elliott slipped away to a secret town meeting. There the populace was in an uproar for the Brits had invaded the Old Pine Church, chopped up the pews for firewood, and took the minister away for questioning. Howe was angry because the preacher had spoken strongly against the English.

"It was all a few sane citizens could do to prevent open rebellion. We'd have been shot down before we'd gone ten paces from the meeting site. The place was surrounded by Brits when it was time to leave. Fortunately the brewer had an old tunnel he used to unload kegs from the ships and store them in a small cave under his property. We all escaped undetected," Dr. Elliott whispered as Merry donned her cloak to leave.

"Oh, Papa, please be careful," she implored.

"I will, my dear. We can change our meeting place. John Craig is searching for the informant. Let me see if Jeremiah is waiting."

He glanced outside, then nodded to Merry. "You go right to Mrs. Clairmont's now. If anyone stops you, tell them you worked late at the hospital. Most of the men know you help me and they will not cause trouble."

After a last hug, Merry and Dela ran swiftly to the vehicle, and within minutes of reaching Arch Street, they hurried in silence to their rooms. Merry leaned against the closed door; an icy shiver shook her. What sort of men would damage a beloved landmark? A church!

"I wonder what the minister said that put them into such a fury? How I wish I could have heard him."

The water in the basin was cool, but it felt good against her skin heated by the anger building up inside. She pulled on her gown, climbed into the big bed, and went to sleep.

When she awakened, the air was much cooler and it was still dark out. A scrabbling noise outside brought her fully alert. Did Mrs. Clairmont have a cat? Perhaps a wild animal was looking for something to eat. Curious, she tugged on her robe and hurried to open the window, where a fist-sized rock lay on the sill. From the yard below, a sudden movement made Merry turn. Was that the tail of a cloak whipping around the gate? She could not tell for bushes hid the answer. Her gaze again centered on the rock and she realized that someone must have placed it there by climbing up one of the nearby maples thrashing a macabre dance and beating time on the house.

Merry stepped away, her back to the wall, until her hand touched the bed. A tug drew the Starfire quilt closer to her and she wrapped it around her shoulders like an overly large cloak. Bone-chilling shivers shook her slender form and shallow gulps of air only made her colder, but the approaching dawn lent enough vague light to assure her that the room was now empty, except for the simple furnishings.

Aftershock turned her limbs to jelly and she sat on the bed, her head in her hands. Who would do such a thing? The rock! There was parchment tied to it. Merry hurried to the window, knowing that she would simply read the note and all would be explained.

It took a disgusting amount of time to untie the string and free the parchment. Merry then fumbled for taper and flint and, after several strikes, it was lit. Squinting in the meager glow of candlelight, she stumbled over the water-soaked words.

D r M ry,
   T is mus re h ohn Cra im edi ly.

The second page was a jumble of letters and numbers. The outer sheet had protected them fairly well.

"Evidently it is intended for John Craig, but who could have sent it? It's not Matt's handwriting. Oh, it just doesn't make sense," Merry muttered to herself. In her heart she knew it had to be code.

"I'll have to take the morning off at the hospital and get this to Jim Hanks. I wonder if the British have taken over City Tavern, too?"

Dela tapped at the door, then entered with a bowl of applesauce pudding and morning chocolate. Swiftly Merry hid the rock and note among the covers. Only after she was fully dressed did she place the parchment in a pocket of her petticoat.

When Jeremiah helped her into the carriage, she asked, "Could you wait for me this morn? After I see Papa, I must go to City Tavern."

"Of course, Miz Elliott. I ken wait and take you back to the hospital, too."

"That won't be necessary. I don't know how long it will be. I will take Dela with me."

The coachman nodded agreement, but later, when he noted the groups of Redcoats inside, he spoke up. "Miz Meredeth, it jus' ain't proper to leave you like this an' you know it."

"I can't keep you waiting all day for me, Jeremiah. You know full well Aunt Mina and Mrs. Clairmont will need the coach today. It's market day."

The faithful Jeremiah scowled but could not argue with the truth. He reluctantly pulled away.

As they entered, Merry whispered to Dela, "Look for a table in the corner near the kitchen door. Molly will keep an eye out for us. She is a good friend."

The luncheon crowd had not yet arrived. Two waitresses were busily serving the Redcoats. After a lengthy wait, a younger girl came to take the women's order.

"We got no ham today, nor taters, either. Ma says you can have fried chicken or clam chowder. We got plenty biscuits."

"Is Molly here today?" Merry asked with a smile.

"No'um. She done took sick an' went home yeste'day."

Merry's hopes disintegrated. She feared Jim Hanks might not come since the Brits had discovered the source of good food here. She had seen no sign of the tall redhead.

The child misunderstood their silence. Eagerly she added, "I can bring ya' milk with tha' biscuits. Ma jus' took 'em from the oven. She says long as we got chickens, an' the cow don't go dry, we'll have somethin' at least. Can't hardly get beef or ham no more."

"Milk and biscuits sound very good," Merry said, her eyes twinkling at the child's gamin grin as she marched off.

"They've been having trouble getting supplies for the hospital, too. Papa is discouraged about it because he can't get some of the medicines he needs. You'd think it was to their advantage to provide medicines for their own troops," Merry told Dela.

"Here ya' be, ma'am, nice and hot from the hearth fire." The child placed two brimming mugs of milk plus a mound of fragrant biscuits in front of them.

"That smells delicious. What is your name, please?" Merry asked.

"I be Jesse, ma'am."

"Well, Jesse, we thank you for your help. I didn't know there was such a scarcity of food in town."

"The Brits take ev'rything. Don't know what we'll do for next week. Jim Hanks done promised he'd bring us some if he can."

"You know Jim Hanks, Jesse?"

"Yessum. He's my cousin."

Merry's heart did a flip-flop. Could she find a way to reach Jim without entering City Tavern? She felt so vulnerable sitting here.

"Jesse, is there a table in the kitchen where Dela and I can eat? The Redcoats stare at us here."

"Ma said she worried 'bout you. She'd not fuss if you came back there. I can help carry the plates."

Within minutes they were seated at a long table used by the help. Mrs. Wilkins welcomed them; a few minutes of conversation made clear her feelings toward the Englishmen.

"Does Jim Hanks still come in regularly?" Merry ventured.

"He takes his lunch back here. He's a good boy. We'd pro'bly be out of food by now without him."

"Mrs. Wilkins, is there some way I could get a message to him?"

"I'd be glad to give him your message, ma'am," the cook promptly replied.

"Oh, I do thank you, Mrs. Wilkins."

Lifting her skirts, Meredeth removed the folded note from her petticoat pocket and handed it to the cook. With a wink, Mrs. Wilkins shoved it into her bodice and quickly smoothed the material over it.

The door to the kitchen banged open. A red-coated officer stood glaring at them. It was Hastings!

"Just what is going on here?" Hastings demanded. "We ordered some of your biscuits at least a quarter-hour since. I see you serve Rebels before us.

Just remember who the majority of your customers will be from now on, Mrs. Wilkins. Henceforth you will serve us immediately and respectfully or this place will be closed!"

five

Major Hastings stomped out the door, slamming it behind him like a petulant child.

"That's Hastings, Howe's right-hand man. He's got a mean temper, he has. Why don't you two jus' leave by the back door? No sense in you havin' to walk back through there."

With a last thank you, Merry and Dela left and started for the hospital. They had gone only a few feet when an unfamiliar voice stopped them.

"Miss Elliott, is it not?" the voice asked.

Merry jerked around to face a pleasant smile above a red coat. "Y–yes, I am Miss Elliott."

"I saw you at the hospital the other day. I'm going there. Would you object to my walking with you?"

"Why no, certainly not, sir. I would welcome your company. It is not easy for a lady to walk these streets now, even though her abigail is with her."

She managed a smile and motioned for Dela to follow; her mind racing, she tried to behave normally. Had Hastings sent this man to check on her? He appeared to be very congenial, but an apprehensive shiver flickered through her. Merry took a deep breath; she could act a part as well as the next one. Perhaps his presence would prevent them from being accosted by others. He was an officer, after all.

"Permit me to present myself," he said. "I know under other circumstances I should wait for another to introduce us, but the conditions make that unlikely. I am Major Henry Stanfield and you are. . .?"

"Miss Meredeth Elliott. My papa is the doctor at the hospital on Spruce. Because of the extra burden of patients, I am helping him." That should sound friendly enough and quench any doubts he had about her.

"What a diligent young lady you are. You remind me much of my sister. That's why I wanted to speak with you. Truth to tell, all my friends will be jealous, I assure you, to see me walking with such a lovely lady."

Merry ducked her head. *Flattery will not go far with me,* she thought, *especially from an Englishman.*

"I'm from Hambledon in Hampshire, England, a sleepy little town. Philadelphia is larger, but its countryside is similar. Have you always lived here, Miss Elliott?"

"We live west of here. My aunt and I were visiting and shopping when your troops took Philadelphia. Now we must remain."

"Then I am doubly fortunate in meeting you. I realize this is most hasty, but would you object to attending a ball with me this Friday eve? When we see your father, I would be pleased to show him my credentials. There will be other young ladies from town there."

"A ball? In the midst of a war?"

"Perhaps it seems callous, Miss Elliott. Yet we men must have some recreation. Do at least consider my invitation. It is lonely for those of us who have no kin in this area."

Merry looked up at the young man beside her who was as tall as Will. He sounded sincere, but a true Patriot should not attend a ball with a Redcoat officer! "You must see the position into which I would be placed. I understand that you could be lonely, so far from home. Yet I must refuse your offer."

"Please think on it. I would like to know you better. I'm a gentleman of very good background, truly."

He said no more until they reached the red brick hospital. When he accompanied her through the entrance, she glanced up at him.

"At least let me come in and meet your father," he requested. "I have heard much good of him."

"Of course. I will introduce you and then I must attend to my duties."

When they found Dr. Elliott, he was about to set a broken leg and Anna stood ready to help. Dr. Elliott noticed Merry and then began to give brisk orders.

"Anna, hold his left arm. Merry, take his right. Your friend can anchor the right leg, if you will, sir?"

The startled expression on Stanfield's face changed to one of understanding and, with a nod, he stepped forward and grasped the soldier's leg. Merry brimmed with pride as her papa worked carefully to ease the disconnected bone into place. When the wound was clean and bandaged, Dr. Elliott looked up.

The Englishman extended his hand with a smile. "Well done, Doctor. I've heard of your excellent reputation but never dreamed I'd be able to participate in your work. Thank you for allowing me that experience. I'm Major Stanfield, sir. I just had the pleasure of meeting your lovely daughter and escorting her here."

"Then I am in your debt. Do you have a friend in the hospital?"

"Yes I do, but I fear that was not my reason for coming today. I was attempting to coax your daughter to attend a local ball with me. Before you say yea or nay, sir, may I present my credentials to you?"

His daughter's low sound of distress was not lost on Dr. Elliott and he raised a warning eyebrow. Patiently he read the papers given him, then handed them back.

"My lord, I am sure you are all you claim to be. I have no objection to your taking Meredeth to a ball for she has had little enough enjoyment lately. Yet she is of age to decide for herself and I have respect for her judgment."

"But, Papa—"

"Meredeth, I know of the major from others. He is a gentleman and a scholar." The doctor's eyes twinkled as he continued. "He is also a friend of Benjamin Franklin. Is that not true, sir?"

Merry stiffened. For some reason, Papa wanted her to accept this man's invitation. But why, when their countries were at war? She looked up to deep blue eyes and a boyish smile. Oh well, if Will could dance at balls during a war, so could she!

"Major Stanfield, I thank you for asking me to attend this party with you. If you promise to tell me of your knowledge of Benjamin Franklin, I accept."

He could not be all bad. The eager look of delight was surely real. He caught her hand in his and raised it to his lips.

"Thank you, m'lady. I look forward to it. The ball will be held at the Nicholas Curry home. I'll pick you up in my carriage at eight, Friday next. Now, if you will excuse me, I must go." As he exited the hospital, there was a jaunty step to his gait.

Merry turned a calculating gaze to her papa. "Now, Papa, what was that all about?"

"It can do no harm for you to be seen with him, my dear. His escort will insure your safety. He appears an agreeable chap and. . ."

"And what, Papa?"

"You need some frivolous pleasure in your life, and I think you could have no better friend among the British."

"Oh, Papa! Very well, I will go with this paragon."

⁂

In her room that evening, Merry held up one of the gowns she had with her. Yes, it would do for the ball. Humming a melody, she circled the room, imagining herself waltzing at the ball. Somehow Will's face replaced Stanfield's in her mind's eye and the room suddenly felt warm. She put aside the gown and moved to the window. Raising the sash, Merry leaned into the welcome breeze. The trees waved in a waltz of their own.

Just then she noticed a cloaked form scurry from a shrub to the tree! Her first reaction was to close the window and move to one side, but a small, rotund person slipped out to meet the intruder. For mere seconds they made one misshapen shadow, and then the short figure returned to the kitchen. Suddenly, Merry shrank back, for the cloaked stranger was climbing the tree outside her window!

Quickly she ducked behind the curtains in the corner where her clothing hung. He was almost to the windowsill! Then his hand reached out and, with a mighty leap, he dropped from sight.

Merry's shaking fingers flung open the curtains behind which she had hidden. It took no more than a second for her to reach the window. He was gone! Gathering the rags of her courage about her, she lit a candle, picked up the rock, and removed the note.

> *My thanks for the quick delivery last time. This must go the same route. Take care what you say at Nicholas Curry's ball.*

Merry fell back on the bed, her mind awhirl. How could the sender of these notes know she was going to the ball? She only learned of it herself late today. Somehow she must find time to deliver the message. Would she ever know the mysterious stranger's identity?

28.

The next morning when Merry stopped in the kitchen to ask Nell to pack a lunch for them, she watched the cook carefully. It must have been Nell in the garden, for Mrs. Clairmont was far too slim. Later that day the message was duly delivered to Mrs. Wilkins. She and Jesse appeared pleased to be taking part in the subterfuge.

That week there was no word from Jim Hanks, and Merry alternated between excitement and concern. The night of the ball her eyes sparked with anticipation as she twirled before the oval mirror in Aunt Mina's room.

Mrs. Clairmont called up the stairs, "You have a gentleman caller, Meredeth."

Merry caught up her shawl and reticule, then walked sedately down the stairway. The major stood there at the bottom of the steps, awaiting her. From the expression on his face, he was well pleased with what he saw.

"Lovely lady, I shall be the envy of all my colleagues," he said softly as he bowed before her.

Aunt Mina was right behind her. "Mind you now, Meredeth must be home by one of the clock," she informed them.

Stanfield smiled indulgently. "I have given my word, ma'am. Be at ease."

When the major's carriage pulled up before Nicholas Curry's home, a warm welcome awaited them. The ballroom shimmered with gaily swinging skirts and red uniforms twirling about to the music. A great many eyes inspected Stanfield's partner. Meredeth was introduced to several of the major's close friends, then whisked away as a new set formed.

"I believe ladies are allowed to give their escort two dances and the supper dance in your society. Is that correct?" he asked as they followed the pattern of the steps.

"That is true in most cases, but I have no dance card yet," Merry reminded him.

"Then we will acquire one before I relinquish you to the others. You are by far the most beautiful lady in attendance. I refuse to give my partner up except when absolutely necessary. Will you save your waltzes for me?"

Merry teasingly glanced up through her lashes. He was a marvelous dancer and all she could ask for in a partner. His charm seemed genuine and, whatever his motive, she was having a delightful time.

"I will save two for you, Major Stanfield. Thank you for bringing me. I have missed dancing and parties."

He twirled her through the final steps, leaving her breathless. When he bowed over her hand, Merry could feel others crowding around them. Before she could be seated, three young men bowed before her. Two had big smiles and shining eyes. The third was very angry! Merry's mouth flew open and she backed a few steps.

"Sorry, friends. This dance is mine." Castleton clamped one large hand over her small one and pulled her toward the set that was forming.

"Will, whatever is the matter?" she whispered to his back.

Without a word he whirled her into place and took his stance opposite her. His almost-smile was grotesque and his eyes glared as if she had trounced on his foot.

"Will. . . ," she began, and then the music sent the couples dipping and turning and it was impossible to carry on a conversation.

"What are you doing here?" he muttered when they had a few steps together.

"I was invited," she retorted before they moved apart.

"Who?" was all he had time for at the next meeting.

"Stanfield," she sputtered angrily back at him.

Who did he think he was that he might dictate where she went and with whom? She thought they were friends, but she did not need a papa. She had a very good one.

His eyes were softer when he put his arm around her waist for the final promenade under raised hands of the other dancers. He leaned close to whisper.

"Don't you realize this is dangerous for you, Merry?"

"Dangerous? Why? Papa thought it was a good idea."

"But he doesn't know all the facets of it. Don't mention Matt, whatever you do. Promise?"

With a quizzical expression, she examined the worry in his eyes. "I won't, unless someone asks if I have a brother. Then I will only give his name. How do you know Matt?"

There was no time for him to answer for she was deluged with requests for dances. Stanfield shouldered through the press of admirers to hand her a dance card. No sooner had he given it to her than Will's big hand took it away. Only after filling in three dances did he return it to her. Before others claimed the card, she was able to glance at it. Stanfield, true to his word, had marked his name on two waltzes and the supper dance; Will had taken the other two waltzes and a promenade.

In a daze, she managed a smile for the young officer who claimed the next dance. Her mind and heart were both behaving badly. The first was confused, the second was both pleased and worried. She smiled, bowed, and dipped in time to the music, but her thoughts danced to a wilder step. Why was Will so angry at first? How much did he know about Matt? He wasted no time in coming to the dance. Yet he hadn't let her know he was in town. When Will bowed to take her off to the next waltz, she had come to no conclusions.

They said nothing at first, but his hand held hers tightly. She felt his chin brush the top of her head when they twirled, and he clutched her as if he feared she might spin off on one of the turns.

"I am glad you are back in town. Will you be able to stay awhile now?" she ventured.

"I have a ten-day here before my next ship sails. I know you help your father, but when can I see you?"

"We come home at six each evening. I'm sure Mrs. Clairmont would be happy to have you call."

"How about tomorrow and Sunday?"

"It is the same on Saturdays. Sundays we all attend church and rest. I just wish Papa could do the same. He is so tired."

"I'll be at Mrs. Clairmont's at seven tomorrow eve. Is that agreeable?"

"We will be glad to receive you then. Will, why were you so angry when you first saw me tonight?"

He pulled her a bit closer, then relaxed. "I suppose it was the shock of seeing you with a Redcoat. Oh, Merry! I wanted to take you to dances and parties and I have not been able to do that. You are a very special person to me. I want to know you better, much better. Also I worry about Hastings hurting you in some way. He can be a terrible beast when angered."

For a moment they simply stood, staring into each other's eyes and hearts. Then a chuckle nearby awoke them to the fact that the music had stopped and the dance floor was clear. Will's head jerked up to find another Redcoat waiting very patiently for the next dance. Gruffly, Will tried to smile at the man as he handed Merry over to him.

six

Promptly at seven, Will's buggy stopped in front of the Clairmont home; he covered the space from there to the house in giant strides. Nell Schoengert opened the door and directed him to the parlor, where Mrs. Clairmont smiled a welcome.

"Do come in, young man, and be comfortable. We are enjoying evening tea and cakes."

Merry introduced him to their hostess and her aunt. Will bowed to the older women before he allowed his gaze to stray toward Merry. Elvira poured each a cup of tea, while Nell offered plates of butterflies and lemon tarts.

"Have you ever tried these, Will?" Meredeth asked.

She was happily devouring a confection in the shape of a butterfly and held a half cup of tea. Obviously he couldn't carry her away immediately, so he sat down and reached for a butterfly from the plate offered him.

"I don't believe I have ever seen such before. They certainly look good."

One bite made him more than pleased to take another and another, until he was quite as enamored of the cakes as the rest of them. He matched Merry's grin and reached for more cakes. Pure mischief danced in Merry's eyes and soon there was but one cake left. Since all were too polite to claim that one, Will handed over his cup and napkin to Nell and turned to Merry.

"Could I take you for a short ride?" he asked.

"I would enjoy that," she agreed. "Wait just a minute 'til I get my shawl and Anna, my abigail."

Soon they were enjoying the evening breezes while Will told them of his uncle's favorite ship, the *Orient Pearl*, which had returned recently. He urged the horse to a good pace. Near the edge of town, he pulled up at a blacksmith shop. A broad-shouldered man poked his head over the double door to greet them.

"What ho, Will? Did your buggy break a spring?"

"No. I beg your indulgence to let us drive out the Old River Road through your farm. The lady and I have some serious talking to do and we'd prefer not to be interrupted."

"Ha! So that's the way the wind blows, is it? My land is yours to use any time, friend. Just don't scuttle your ship out there, you hear?"

Laughing heartily, Castleton jumped down to open the wide gate. The smith called out over the clang of the hammer. "Leave it open. I'm goin' to supper soon's I finish this."

"Thanks," Will called as he sprang up to his seat and urged the horse into motion.

A soft chill permeated the river area. When Meredeth pulled her shawl about her, Will secured the reins in one hand and tugged her closer.

"It is a bit crowded with three in the buggy, but it will keep you warm," he said with a grin as he set the horse to a faster pace.

When they came to a rocky promontory, Will tethered the horse to a tree, then helped Anna alight. She wandered a short distance away to admire the view. After he helped Merry down, Will did not release her but stood gazing at her for several moments. Tenderly he tilted her elfin chin to the right angle and, with feather-light fingers, brushed a wayward curl back from her brow. Her wide eyes deepened to exotic blue-green. There was a world of wonder in her face. His finger trailed down her cheek. How he longed to bury his face in her hair, now lit to glorious gold in the sunset.

"Merry," his voice was low and urgent. "There are going to be times when I must leave to take care of Uncle Reggie's affairs. It wouldn't be fair to offer for you now. I'm not yet able to provide a home for you, but I want you to know what is in my heart. As soon as I can purchase a home and take care of you, I intend to ask for your hand in marriage. Do you. . .can you feel that way about me?"

She lifted sparkling eyes to meet his. "I have never felt so close to anyone before. It may take time to become sure of my feelings, but I do like you very much."

"Will you promise me one thing, Merry? Will you agree that neither of us will marry another until we learn to know each other better and I can be the kind of husband you deserve?"

She searched deeply into his eyes, shining with entreaty, and felt the gentle grasp of his hands on her arms. What would it be like to have those strong arms holding her close, her head fitted into his shoulder?

"Yes, Will, that I will promise gladly and. . .and I would like to know you better."

With a shout of joy, he swung her around until they were staggering from dizziness. His expression grew soft as he dipped to brush his lips across her cheek and gathered her into his embrace. Somehow they managed to climb into the buggy. It was fortunate that Anna came running for they might have forgotten her in their excitement.

All the way back to Mrs. Clairmont's, starlit silence wrapped them in its magic. Anna went inside while Merry and Will said good night.

Holding Merry's hands in his, Will raised each finger to his lips for a brief salute, then folded her hands around the imprint of his kisses. Merry stepped inside to find Nell watching her, a wide smile on her face.

"That be a right young man, Miss Merry. Just remember to keep him close, but not too close 'til he declares himself as he should."

Merry smiled, content to keep their secret to herself for the present. She climbed the stairs with a little skip in her step and closed the door of her room behind her. She had a lot of thinking to do, and the window seat provided just the space she needed. After awhile she saw great, billowing clouds growing into an autumn storm. She remembered that her family often sat entranced by the changing colors in the night sky. Tonight, though, it was not their faces in her memory, it was Will's.

Lightning crackled and sent fingers of blazing color across the heavens. A boom of thunder startled her from her reverie and she sat bolt upright. Wind whipped the trees into a mad whirl. With an eerie cry, a cat sped across the yard. There, just inside the gate, was a cloaked figure, carrying a rather bulky package. A moment later he left, empty-handed. A gentle knock at her door made Merry's heart race faster than her feet. Mrs. Clairmont stood there, looking for all the world like a drowned rabbit.

"My dear, your young man brought this for you through all this deluge. Can you imagine that?"

After thanking her hostess, Merry retreated once more to the window seat. This was much too big to be a message. Perplexed, she tore the paper eagerly. The wrapping underneath held the most beautiful piece of silk cloth she had ever seen. Her fingers traced the embroidery, radiant in the candle-light. A note lay tucked in the folds.

> *My dear Merry,*
> *This came on the* Orient Pearl. *I will look forward to seeing you wear it. Word came that my uncle is ill. He wants me to come to Boston, but I don't leave until tomorrow afternoon. I have seen you at Christ Church. Look for me tomorrow.*
>
> *Will*

Merry slipped the note beneath her pillow and carefully placed the silk in her trunk before surrendering to sleep. The thunderstorm still filled the night with noise and flashes of light, but her dreams were all of blue skies and sunshine, with Will beside her, of course.

❧

By morning the storm had passed. When Merry entered the church with her aunt, she glanced around quickly but did not see Will. She had almost given him up as they rose to sing the first hymn, but when the chorus rang out, there was a shuffling of feet and Will's rich baritone voice joined her soprano as if they had practiced together. The congregation was seated and Merry's cheeks grew warm as Will's eyes held hers. The Reverend Harrison gave an excellent sermon on faithfulness to the beliefs they held. The last hymn was "O Come, All Ye Faithful," reminding Merry that Christmas was very close.

After greeting the Reverend Harrison, Merry was surprised when her papa joined them. "I arrived late, so I had to sit in the back, but I did want to speak with you and Mina before I leave," he said, smiling at Merry.

"Dr. Elliott! How nice to see you." Mrs. Clairmont hurried to them. "Mina and I were just saying how good it would be to enjoy your company for luncheon today. Can you spare that much of your time? And you are invited, too, Mr. Castleton. I promise you some more butterfly cookies."

Dr. Elliott looked doubtful at first but soon was convinced to accept. Will glanced toward Merry; her little nod and bright smile were all he needed to agree.

"I am honored. I have some time before I sail," he said.

When they arrived home, Nell had everything ready for them and Dr. Elliott said grace.

"That is the same prayer my father says at meals," Will confided as the plates were passed.

Conversation came easily among them, and the women managed, with natural skill, to learn a great deal about Will. Far from embarrassed, he told them of his uncle, the ships of their line, and finally his family back in England. His father raised and trained horses for the nobility's use. His mother had her favorite recipes, just as Mrs. Clairmont did. He had not seen them or his brother and three sisters since he graduated from Oxford.

"Did your father train Ahmed?" Merry asked when the last bite of blueberry pie disappeared.

"He insisted I help train him to make a deeper bond between us. My father was usually so busy I saw little of him, except for church each week. Those two years of training were not only a means of becoming friends with Ahmed, but with my father, as well. They are wonderful memories. My mother writes each week and insists upon an answer, so we are still a close family. How about your folks? Do any of them live nearby?"

"My mother died of a fever when I was twelve. Aunt Mina came to us to assure I had the proper bringing up. There's just Papa, Aunt Mina, Matt, and me."

"Matthew is off fighting with Washington. We don't see much of him," Dr. Elliott swiftly explained, "and I must return to my duties. I pray for good news about your uncle's health when you reach Boston. It was interesting to talk with you, Mr. Castleton."

With Dr. Elliott's departure, Will was reminded of his own journey. "I must go, but thank you all for inviting me today. I enjoyed it immensely."

"Will you be here for Christmas?" Merry asked as they said good-bye.

"I cannot promise that, Merry, but I will certainly be wishing I were here. Take good care of yourself. If you dance at any balls, pretend you're dancing one waltz with me, please."

With Aunt Mina standing by, Will held Merry's hand to his lips for a last kiss, then set off at a fast pace.

ða

The weather changed abruptly after that; winter moved in, cold and wet. Merry and Aunt Mina had no warm clothes with them, so Elvira led them to the attic, filled with chests and boxes. Merry found a blue cloak and hood, warmly lined with soft white fur; there was even a muff to match. A fur cloak trimmed with red braid took Aunt Mina's fancy and the maids were each given sturdy cloaks.

Weeks went by with no word from Will or Jim Hanks. One evening, when Merry returned from the hospital, Nell held out a small packet.

"This gent handed it to me at the back door. Didn't say much, just that it was for you, Miss Merry."

Meredeth simply said, "Thank you," but she thought Nell knew a lot more than she told.

In the privacy of her room, Merry opened the missive. As she read, dread washed over her and her hands shook for the note warned she must be cautious. British authorities were searching for anyone sending information from the city. Some had been questioned already. Merry vowed she would go early tomorrow and deliver the message to Mrs. Wilkins.

During the night it snowed; at least three inches lay on the ground and more fell steadily. Merry got dressed and donned her half-boots in preparation to go see Mrs. Wilkins. While eating a bowl of oatmeal, Merry mentioned telling Jesse of the butterfly cakes and the child's wish to taste one. Nell, who had baked a large batch yesterday, offered to send some of the sweets for Jesse.

With the message tucked into her petticoat pocket, Merry and Anna hurried to the back of City Tavern. Much to their chagrin, that gate was locked and that meant that they must enter the common room, filled with Redcoats! Staunchly ignoring the British soldiers, Merry and Anna marched through the common room and to the kitchen door. But, as soon as they entered, her bag was torn from her hand and she was pushed against the wall. Anna screamed. Startled, Meredeth raised indignant eyes to confront Major Hastings. His florid face was set in stern lines and a sneer twisted his mouth.

"What a pleasant surprise," he said. "I have missed your pretty face around here for some time, Miss Elliott. What brings you out on such a cold day?"

"Major Hastings, keep your hands to yourself. You have no right—," she sputtered.

"Oh, but I do have the right, my dear. You see, I have been ordered to find traitors amongst us."

"Why should that concern me?"

"Spies often appear most innocent. You have been consorting with some of our men. What better way to pry out information, hmm?"

"I did not instigate those friendships. They approached me. That should prove your case is ridiculous."

Anna found courage to say, "That's right—"

Hastings shoved her aside. "All women are born temptresses. They know how to entice a man."

"Like yourself, sir?" Merry demanded. "I have done everything in my power to discourage you, yet you persist in molesting me."

With a livid snarl, he lunged for her, grabbed a fist full of her hair, and forced her head back against the wall. Screams from Mrs. Wilkins, Jesse, and Anna brought instant reaction from the common room. The door was slammed back and several officers rushed in.

"Major Hastings, sir, what—" The young officer swerved to a stop.

Hastings clutched Meredeth to him and covered her mouth with his. Eyes wide in outrage, Merry beat at his face and shoulders, but her struggles only incited his fury. Mrs. Wilkins grabbed Jesse, who was pounding small fists in Hastings's side.

Eyes wide, Anna cried out, "Please, someone help her!" Hastings looked up, his eyes hard. "Do any of you dare challenge me?" he roared.

More men poured into the room. Most of the younger officers stood undecided, but one man pushed his way through the group and stood before Hastings.

"Yes, I think I must, Major. I happen to know this young lady and she is no spy. Now, unless you want me to bring charges against you, release her immediately. In any case, General Howe must hear of your conduct. You go too far." Turning to Mrs. Wilkins and Jesse, Major Henry Stanfield gentled his voice, "Will you tell us what has happened here, please?"

"You can't take the word of a servant over mine. I am—," Hastings sputtered.

"I know your name and rank," Stanfield retorted. "Let the women talk."

Bereft of speech for the moment, Mrs. Wilkins stood silent. Suddenly, chin jutting out like a ship in full sail, Jesse pulled away and stood defiantly.

"Please, sir, Miz Elliott didn't do none of the things he says. He jus' grabbed the bag from her an' pushed her into the wall. Then he kissed her but she tried to stop him."

Terrified, Anna nodded her head in agreement.

"Thank you, child, for your honesty and courage. I will make sure there is no retaliation against any of you. Now, Hastings, will you explain why you attacked this lady?"

"She's a spy, I tell you. Why else would a lady come to the kitchen like this? She carried a bag, no doubt a ruse to slip messages to Rebels. I have orders to detain any I suspect of passing information."

"Is this the bag, Major?" Stanfield asked as he bent to pick it up from the floor.

He held it above the table, letting the contents tumble out. A half-dozen sugared cakes fell for all to see.

"My butterflies! She brought my butterflies, Mama. Aren't they pretty?"

An undercurrent of chuckles erupted from the other men. They sobered immediately at a glance from Stanfield.

"Your accusations are false, Hastings. I must insist you release this young lady at once."

Glaring at the men who had laughed, the red-faced major removed his hand from Meredeth's hair. She backed away, her eyes huge and full of sparks. Anna replaced the cakes in the bag and Merry handed it to the child.

Hastings growled, "Get out of my way!" and stomped out the door, his face twisted in rage.

"I think we can all return to our food now. This display is over, men," Major Stanfield said quietly.

When the room cleared of Redcoats, Stanfield crossed swiftly to Merry, easing her down to a chair. Her eyes were still dilated in shock and tears streamed down her cheeks.

"Do not think all Englishmen are like Hastings. Howe will not put up with conduct like this, even from a distant cousin," he assured them.

Mrs. Wilkins brought a cup of cool water. Jesse knelt beside the chair, patting Merry's arm.

"Miz Merry, please be all right. I 'preciate you bringing me butterflies."

After a wrenching shudder, Merry sat straighter and breathed more evenly.

"Thank you, Major Stanfield, for your intervention. Just his touch makes me feel as if snakes crawled over me."

"An apt description. Now, if you are feeling more the thing, may I take you to your father?"

"That is thoughtful of you but my coachman waits for me outside."

"Then allow me to escort you. I would be sure you are protected before I leave."

"Thank you. If I could just speak with Mrs. Wilkins and Jesse a minute."

"I will make sure Hastings has taken his leave," Stanfield promised as he left.

When the door closed behind him, Mrs. Wilkins whispered, "You'd best not bring any more messages. No tellin' what that devil will do. They're watchin' everywhere."

"Oh, Miss Merry, be careful," Anna murmured.

Meredeth looked to the door, then removed the packet from her petticoat. "They told me this is the last one. It is getting too dangerous. Can you handle this without putting yourself or Jesse in jeopardy?"

The cook's troubled face suddenly beamed. Grabbing some bread dough from the table, she inserted the small note, then folded the dough around it, molding it into a butterfly. She sprinkled some sugar on top and slipped it to the bottom of the bag.

"Ain't nobody goin' to notice that under all the rest. They've already seen what was in that bag. Now, Jesse, you skip out the back door like you're goin' to play. Sit there for a minute and eat one of the cakes. Don't be in a hurry, but soon's you finish, you head right home. No dawdlin', now."

"Yessum," the child replied, winking at Merry. Saucy as a chipmunk, she sat on the porch with the goodies in her lap.

Merry clasped hands with the cook. "Thank you for being a true Patriot and friend. I may not see you for a while, but I will think of you and Jesse often."

Head high, Meredeth tugged Anna behind her and across the common room and stepped outside. Major Stanfield leaned on the carriage, talking to Jeremiah. As the Englishman helped her up, he spoke softly.

"May I call on you this eve?"

"Of course. You are always welcome at Mrs. Clairmont's."

He kissed the tips of her fingers, then stood back to watch them leave. Merry felt secure once again. She had a deep respect for some of the British. Her papa was right, but then he usually was.

seven

Merry did mention to Mrs. Clairmont and Nell that they should take no more messages for her to deliver. Still, she could not erase the fearful memory of Major Hastings. Why did she have this certainty that he watched her wherever she went?

At the hospital the next day, it was a struggle to appear cheerful. When her papa handed her the mail, she gladly left a dreary routine of changing bandages and feeding those who could not help themselves. There was a letter for Red Mac. She smiled as she approached his pallet.

"Well now, lassie, you've come to make my heart happy. I wondered how I could amuse myself the rest of the day."

"Will you read or shall I?" she asked.

"I'd much rather hear your sweet voice, if you please."

Merry began with a smile, but when she reached the last paragraph, her voice faltered.

"I fear 'tis not good news, my friend." When she did not meet his gaze, he leaned closer. "Just tell it out, lass. It's better that way."

Clearing her throat, she continued, "It grieves my heart to tell you this, Son, but I dinna want you to come home not knowing. Mary Duncan was wed to Jamie Fergus this day. She said she would be an old woman afore you came to her. She could'na wait longer."

Red Mac's face whitened and he closed his eyes for a few seconds. When he looked at her, his chin firmed in calm acceptance. He patted Merry's hand with a weary gesture that brought mist to her eyes.

"Och now, don't you be acryin' over a big lump of a Scotsman like me. I've weathered harsher storms than this. I well know there's a chance I may never walk again wi'out sticks to hold me up. That would be a hard thing for a bonny lass to love. 'Tis better this way."

"You would be a fine figure of a man even with crutches, Red McClanahan! If I hadn't already given my heart, I'd be tempted to marry you myself. You're good and kind and you have a gift for making people around you happy. She is the loser in this."

Meredeth's outburst brought a whoop of laughter from the Scotsman.

"If Will was'na me best friend, lass, I'd grab you up and carry you off in a minute. By me granny's pipe, Will is a lucky man. I thank you for caring."

A chorus of clapping hands startled Merry, and she looked up to see most of the patients grinning at her. Across the room, her own papa stood very still, a quizzical look on his face.

"Oh my," was all she found to say. In truth, she had said far too much already. With flaming cheeks, she fled the room.

A few minutes later, she entered her father's office. He did not appear angry, just surprised.

"That was a stirring bit of oration, my dear. I'm afraid I've been so busy I didn't notice my only daughter has given her heart to some fortunate man. I don't even know who he is. Something as important as that should be shared. Sit and tell me, child."

"Papa, I—"

"Never fear. I'm not angry. I'm ashamed I have been too occupied with a war to know my own family. I will do better."

She sat. After twisting her handkerchief so it was wrinkled as a washboard, she raised her eyes. Her papa's caring look sent her flying into his arms.

"Papa, I love you so much. I didn't mean to keep anything from you. We only promised not to marry another until we had a chance to know each other better."

"It surely isn't Stanfield. You met him only recently."

"He is very nice, but no, it is not him. It is Will Castleton."

"The young man who helped bring my things from Conners Inn? Let's see, he shared Sunday dinner with us one day, didn't he?"

"Yes. His uncle invited him to join his shipping business in Boston. He is there now. His uncle is ill and called him back."

"This is the one who goes to Tory parties?"

"Yes, Papa, but he is not at war against us. He is kind and gallant and. . . and I trust him. Mrs. Clairmont and Aunt Mina both like him."

"Then I am sure I will like him, too. Merry, it was hard for me when your mother died. I have immersed myself in my work, but I don't want to lose the closeness we've always had. I will always take time to talk to you."

"I know that, Papa. You are always close to my heart."

"Well, my dear young lady, I fear I must return to work. You will bring your gentleman around when he is in town so I might get to know him better?"

"Of course, Papa."

With that promise between them, Dr. Elliott resumed his rounds while Merry, Anna, and Dela donned their cloaks. Their carriage awaited them.

❧

The promised snow fell all the next day and the day after that. Iridescent reflections of bright sunlight changed Philadelphia into a living Christmas display. As Merry went about her duties, she began to wonder how she could make or purchase gifts for her family. Would Will come for the holidays? She would have to find some linen to make him a shirt. She was positive that the fabric he had given her would make a lovely gown with some left over for a reticule. Aunt Mina would like that. Perhaps there would be enough to make a similar one for Mrs. Clairmont.

"Food!" Aunt Mina groaned. "There will be no Christmas goose this year. We'll probably be fortunate to have stew."

"Meat is becoming very scarce. Why, last week there was not even a fish to be had at the market," Elvira sighed.

They must be content with what they had. Merry was well aware of the scarcities this winter. The minister was right about Mrs. Clairmont. Often a knock at her front door would result in a trip to the cellar or the attic to find help for those less fortunate. One day a much greater call for help came via the grapevine. Washington was asking for cloaks and blankets. Some folks said that his men did not even have shoes but had to tie rags around their feet.

Local residents passed the word from one house to another. They had extra cloaks and blankets, but the problem was collecting them and getting them to Washington. He and his men were but fourteen miles away in Whitemarsh, but with none allowed to leave the city, it seemed hopeless.

"Where are Craig and Clark when we need them?" became a familiar query around town. No one had heard of them recently.

When this word came to Meredeth, she spoke to her papa.

"I may be able to get in touch with Craig or Clark through Jim Hanks."

"How do you know Hanks?"

"Do you remember Jesse and Mrs. Wilkins at City Tavern?"

"That was the cook wasn't it?" Papa asked.

"Yes, they are related to him. She might know where they are."

"I can't like your getting mixed up in this, Merry. Do you think she'd tell me?"

Memories of Hastings convinced her to agree. "I'll write a note introducing you to them." At her papa's nod, she quickly penned a letter to her friends.

It was a long time before the doctor returned. His eyes were troubled as he led her into his office.

"Your friends are gone, my dear. No one seems to know what has become of them. Stanfield was there, but he knew nothing. The officers loudly complain of the food there now."

"Hastings," Merry muttered.

"Is he the one who has been questioning folks lately?"

"Mrs. Wilkins said he'd been watching them. He is a beast."

"Do you think he might have arrested your friends?"

"I can only hope they have hidden where he cannot reach them."

"There's to be a meeting tonight. I'll ask some of the men. Perhaps they will know."

When Jeremiah came for them that eve, he wore a long face but only shook his head when she asked if he were ill. Shrugging, she entered the house, hoping to learn what was wrong. The scene she walked into was certainly not what she expected. At least ten women sat in a makeshift circle, teacups in hand.

"Come in, Meredeth, and join us. I believe we have a plan."

In a daze Merry sat. Mrs. Clairmont appeared to be the instigator of the plot. The women listened eagerly.

"Walsh, the printer, the brewer's son, Horace, and Conners, the innkeeper, have all been collecting blankets, shoes, and clothing for sometime. However, it would be extremely difficult for any of the men to get the load to Whitemarsh. Anything going in that direction will be under suspicion."

There was a general bobbing of heads in response.

"Now Mrs. Graham has a daughter and four grandchildren up in Horesham. They have chicken pox and the Brits already signed a pass for her to go help them. I won't mention names, but a farmer has offered his wagon, which has a false bottom in it. In view of the trade in smuggled goods up Boston way, we won't ask how he happens to have that, either."

A round of chuckles made Merry smile and shake her head. Leave it to Elvira to know about that!

"Mrs. Graham has agreed to take the wagon, but she cannot drive. Would any of you ladies offer to go with her?"

"I can drive," one matron spoke up, "if you get me a pass to show the Brits when we're stopped."

"Excellent!" Mrs. Clairmont beamed. "Will they allow two on your pass, Mrs. Graham?"

"General Howe knew my father back in England. I think I can persuade him to do that."

"Then our plan is complete. Nell, will you please pour each of us another cup of tea. We will drink a toast."

Elvira rose, holding up her cup just as she had seen her husband do on occasion. "May Britain go limping home and let us get on with our lives."

"Hear! Hear!" they all replied stoutly.

When the women filed out to return to their homes, Meredeth knelt beside her hostess. "You are an amazing person. I am so proud to know you."

"Mrs. Pringle suggested I might be getting too old for this. I guess I showed her!"

"Indeed, you did," Merry agreed, hugging the thin shoulders.

ॐ

Two evenings later Merry, Anna, and Dela came through the door, shaking the snow from their cloaks. Their laughter swiftly stilled when they noticed that both elderly women had tears in their eyes.

"What happened?" Merry asked.

"Just minutes ago word came that Mrs. Graham is safely with her family in Horesham, but Carrie Grinnel, who drove the wagon on toward Whitemarsh, was stopped by Redcoats. They were spying out the area."

"What did they do to her?" Merry asked breathlessly.

"They found the secret compartment and questioned her for sometime. She told them some of the women wanted to send warm clothes to their menfolks."

"Was she arrested?"

"They finally released her, but she will never be issued another pass and the wagon was smashed to pieces."

Gloomily they sat around the table to eat, but talk was desultory. Merry soon excused herself and went to her room. One look out the window at gray clouds fading to utter black induced her to pull the curtain across.

"No matter what we do, it seems the British are right there to thwart us. Will we never win our freedom?"

Shivering in the woolen robe that Elvira had loaned her, she sought the warmth of the Starfire quilt. A full moon outside promised frost before morning. Even in sleep she felt chilled, a parade of terrible dreams plaguing her rest.

The next day Merry, Aunt Mina, and the maids walked to church in silence; the sparkle on the snow went unnoticed. Not many of their friends had smiles to share. Merry sang the old, beloved hymns, but nothing broke the ice of sadness in her heart. Papa stopped by after church.

"They say Washington may move his men. Perhaps he has found more secure winter quarters. Whitemarsh is so close to Philadelphia. Howe might take it into his head to make a raid on them."

"Surely there must be a place in the hills where they would have more protection from the cold. Papa, do you truly think we have a chance to win against the might of the British Empire?"

"My dear, there is always a chance when men determine to make a change in their lives. Very small armies have triumphed over great nations. Washington is a skilled leader. I think much of the trouble is getting the men who do the speaking and the men who do the fighting to work together. They have been quibbling for weeks over sending help to the general and his men, but nothing has been done. If a few of the speakers were put in the front lines, it might change some of their ideas."

"I hope they decide soon," Merry murmured. "Sometimes I wonder if it is really worth all the killing and damaging of property and living with the Brits watching every move you make."

Her papa's voice was very soft and gentle. "Would you rather have the English ruling over us again, passing taxes that do not allow local businessmen to make a living, and treating us like so many slaves to provide their wastrel lifestyle?"

With a strong shake of her head, Merry answered, "No, Papa, you're right. I've just been so discouraged lately, I can't think straight."

"Never forget to pray, Merry. God can do so many things that are impossible for us to accomplish. If it is right that we should be free, and I truly believe it is so, God will provide a way."

"Papa, will you pray with me?"

"Gladly, Merry. I do miss our family devotions when Mama was with us," he replied, circling his arm about her.

"Lord God, Creator of all things, we seek Your help. Our world seems intent upon ruling over others. If it is Your Will, help us to be free of the bondage, free to live without violence, a people serving You only. Bring us out of this valley of death and destruction. Show us how You would have us live and worship You in freedom and grace. Give us Your strength, Lord, and have mercy on us. In Christ's name we ask it. Amen.

"Now hold that chin up and let me see you smile," he ordered, his eyes twinkling.

eight

For over two weeks they heard no gunfire, no mention of battles won. Merry, Anna, and Dela took turns helping at the hospital because there were fewer patients. The younger set converged on the library at least once a week, but the foul weather today made that unlikely. Merry sat in the window seat staring at the whirling snow until a wind-whipped cloak at the back gate brought her upright, nose against the pane. It was Jim Hanks!

She hurried down the stairs and into the kitchen, just in time to see Nell hanging a snowy cloak over chairs by the hearth. Jim was already chewing on a dried apple and some bread still warm from the big brick oven. Without a word, Nell pulled up another chair and motioned for Merry to sit.

She was about to burst with questions. When Jim had swallowed the last bite, he was bombarded from both sides.

"Did Washington move yet?"

"How did you know I stayed here with Mrs. Clairmont?" Meredeth blurted out, suddenly realizing she had never given Jim Hanks Elvira's address.

Jim's demeanor was serious, a portent of trouble. He answered neither of their queries and did not meet their eyes as he growled out information. "We knew the Brits kept war prisoners at the Walnut Street prison and on ships. The prison was overflowing with men wounded at Brandywine and Germantown and one prison ship was destroyed when they took Fort Miflin. We heard they moved the survivors to the top floor of the State House. I went there with a repair crew today." He covered his face with his hands, muffling the rest. "I've seen cleaner sewers. God help those poor miserable men!"

"Did you see anyone we know there?" Merry asked softly.

"Most looked like they hadn't been fed in a month. It was hard to recognize anyone."

"Jim, do you know what happened to Mrs. Wilkins and Jesse?" Merry asked.

"They're not in Philadelphia. We got them out awhile back."

"Could you maybe bring us a bit of meat someday, Jim?" Nell wanted to know.

"I'll try. The farmers don't come in lately. The old High Street Market now serves as stables for British officers. You know marshy old Franklin Square has long been a burying place, but it is filling rapidly. Ben

Franklin's *Gazette* and several other papers are doing their best to get a list of the dead Patriots, though few names have been revealed yet. If I'm lucky, maybe I can bring you some meat in a week or two. Can't promise though. It's getting tough to get. Sorry, I gotta go."

He was out the door, jerking on his cloak as he ran, before Nell could hand him a bag of bread. Merry and the cook exchanged worried glances.

"Wouldn't it be grand if he could find us a chicken for Christmas? And maybe some oranges," Nell said, wiping at her eyes with her apron.

"I'd even welcome a crow," Merry groaned as she stumbled upstairs again.

Anna awaited her at the door to her room. "Is there anything I can do for you, Miss Merry? I finished all my chores and I don't feel right just sitting. Could I put your hair up in a new way? Lord Stanfield might call and take you to another ball or something."

"I haven't seen or heard from him, Anna. Well, see what you can do with my hair, just in case."

As if they had conjured up his presence, Major Stanfield came to call that eve. After the usual welcome, plus a plate of butterfly cakes that appeared by Nell's magic, Stanfield gave them some good news.

"I am pleased to report a British ship is due in Baltimore tomorrow. There should be a goodly supply of food in the hold. I shall see that you have some treat for the holidays. I know food has become scarce of late."

"Why, how thoughtful of you, my lord. What a delight that will be for all of us," his hostess responded.

"I cannot stay long for I am shortly to report for duty. Miss Elliott, there is to be another ball this Saturday eve. Dare I hope you will allow me to escort you?"

Merry smiled as she answered, "Yes, my lord, I would be delighted to accompany you. Where is this one to be held?"

"Mr. and Mrs. Carruthers have invited a number of the officers to their home. Are you familiar with that family?"

"The Thomas Carruthers family?" Merry asked. "I went to school with Cecelia, though I have not seen her lately."

"She will announce her marriage to a captain in my command. Forgive me, but I must take my leave. They have kept us busy lately with guard duty."

At his request, Merry accompanied him to the door. He stood, awkward and embarrassed for a moment, before meeting her gaze. He handed her a card.

"Please, don't misunderstand my motives. I cannot help but be aware of the difficulty of finding fabrics here. I know you came with few gowns. If you will visit this dressmaker, she will make a gown for you of whatever material you choose."

Cheeks aflame, Meredeth shook her head. "Thank you for your offer, but I cannot allow you to do this. My other gowns are at home, but it is impossible to get them. I will simply wear what I have."

"Where did you say your estate is?"

"Cresswick Manor is a two-and-a-half- to three-hour ride northwest of Philadelphia."

"Hmmm." He rubbed his chin thoughtfully. "I'm off duty tomorrow. Do you have any plans for the day?"

"No. I am not needed at the hospital lately."

"Very well then. We can make an outing of it. Will you accept my escort?" Stanfield asked.

Merry's eyes danced at the thought. It had been so long since she had ridden. . .then her face fell. "My horse. . .we came in the carriage."

"I can borrow a mount from one of my men. Captain Severn is promised to a card game tomorrow. His horse is a bit frisky, though."

"I am an avid rider, my lord." Merry grinned reassurance. "I will find a more placid horse for your abigail. My valet can do without his steed for one day."

When Stanfield left, Merry excitedly reported the news to the others. Nell packed a basket lunch for them. It proved to be a perfect winter day, cold but bright with sunshine. The trio set out in great spirits, allowing the mounts their heads. The major had no problem exiting the city's boundaries.

As they neared the manor, Meredeth eagerly watched for some sign of life. Had Mrs. Tulley and Barnabas taken the cattle to Cousin Ferdy's? Was the family silver hidden? Not that she expected Stanfield to appropriate them, but he might mention them to others. At least their home still stood intact. Two figures appeared on the veranda.

The riders heard Mrs. Tulley cry out, "It's Miss Merry, the Lord be praised! And Anna, too, I declare."

The housekeeper ran toward them, arms outflung. Swiftly dismounting, Merry ran to embrace her.

"Oh, Miss Merry, is everything well with you and your family?"

"We are all in good health. Mrs. Tulley, Barnabas, let me introduce our escort, Major Henry Stanfield. We have need of more gowns and he was kind enough to bring me here. Barnabas, can you find Papa's boots and a warm cloak for him?"

"Sure will, mistress, soon's I show the major where to stable the horses."

While Stanfield and the old man strode off, Meredeth hugged the house-keeper and urged her inside, where they could talk quietly.

"Mrs. Tulley, we brought a picnic lunch. Can we eat here on the veranda? We don't have much time. I want to choose some gowns for Aunt Mina and me."

"I'll prepare a table for you, Miss Merry. Anna and Abel, the stableboy, can get trunks from the attic. And don't you worry none, mistress, your silver and the cattle are all at your cousin's place, though nobody has come here 'cept two soldiers. They asked for something to eat, but they didn't bother anything."

"They were probably seeking horses. Thank you for sending our stock away. Do you have enough food here, Mrs. Tulley?"

"I put up lots of green beans, peas, and potatoes from the garden and your cousin sent some chickens back with Barnabas. We'll manage for the winter. Is food scarce in Philadelphia?"

"We are staying with an old friend of Aunt Mina's, but the farmers haven't come to the market much lately."

"Well you just go find the clothes you want to take and I'll put together a bit of food for you. Your cousin checks now and then to see if we need anything," Mrs. Tulley assured Merry.

"Thank you. We will all appreciate that. I'll go pack our clothing."

Merry had never before realized how much her home meant to her. She looked at her mama's portrait for a few minutes, then set about gathering what they would need. Abel and Anna brought down trunks and Merry soon had them filled. At the door of her room she paused for a long look, then hurried downstairs. She must get the books Papa wanted.

The picnic proved to be a delight; Major Stanfield was an adept story-teller and coaxed others to contribute. With a last hug for Mrs. Tulley, Meredeth rolled one of her best gowns carefully into a bundle to fit a saddlebag and then they left.

On the way back to the city, Stanfield stopped at a checkpoint and ordered a guard to deliver Merry's trunks to Mrs. Clairmont's the next day. When the trio dismounted in Philadelphia, Merry turned shining eyes to Stanfield.

"Thank you, not just for bringing our clothing here, but for a wonderfully pleasant day."

"It was most enjoyable for me, Miss Meredeth. I was able to see a bit more of your country. I understand why you love it. Someday I hope I can give you a tour of my home and introduce you to my sisters. This war cannot last forever."

She shook her head. "I doubt if I wil ever get to England. I am promised to a young man here, but I have quite changed my mind about you British. I do not condone what your king is doing to our country, but some of you are very congenial."

With a gallant bow, he raised both her hands to his lips. "Until tomorrow eve then."

Merry stood staring at his back as he rode off with the other horses in tandem. He was an exceptionally nice man. A small voice inside whispered, *Will, why haven't you written? I miss you so much.*

Later that evening, Aunt Mina came to Merry's room to say good night and thank Merry for arranging to get more gowns for them. "So Cecelia is to marry one of the British. Well, some of them are quite pleasant. Hopefully she has chosen well."

"It will be good to see her again. We have drifted apart the last few years. I wonder if she has changed."

"You will soon see. Perhaps this war is nearing an end. It is at least much better without the sound of gunfire disturbing our sleep each night."

The next day, in spite of heavy snowfall invading the city, their trunks were promptly fetched. Merry was glad to have her lacy, silver-threaded wool shawl again for it was warm in spite of its fragility. Her ice blue gown was rather lightweight and ballrooms were not always well heated. She hoped Stanfield brought a closed carriage to ride to the ball in for large, white flakes were falling and being driven by a strong east wind.

Thankfully, he had. Trust him to prepare for just such a contingency. When they arrived at Thomas Carruthers's home, the stairway to the ballroom was so crowded they had to wait sometime to reach the receiving line.

A familiar voice welcomed her. "Meredeth Elliott!" Cecelia Carruthers said. "I'm so glad you came. It has been an age since I saw you. We must find time for a cozy chat." She lowered her voice to add, "Right after the supper dance, follow me to my room."

Nodding her understanding, Meredeth moved on into the ballroom with Stanfield. It was draped with holly and ivy, tied up with red velvet ribands. A small orchestra was playing a promenade. As before, Stanfield did not release her dance card until he had signed for two waltzes and the supper dance. He handed Meredeth to her first partner, then set off to find his friends.

Merry was familiar with many of the officers now and found conversation much easier. The swirling movement of the waltz made her a bit lightheaded as Stanfield claimed her for the supper dance. He twirled her into the hallway and stopped beside a window alcove. With gentle hands he cupped her face. "You mentioned being promised to a young man here. In England that often happens when the participants are children. Yet when they become adults, they change their minds. Is it the same here?"

Merry could not have moved if her life depended upon it. This man was kind, intelligent, and strong, but she did not love him. He was a good friend, no more.

She breathed a silent prayer. *Oh Lord, help me to explain in a way that doesn't hurt him.* "You are a dear friend, my lord, but I made this promise just a few months ago. I love him very much, though I will always thank God for sending you into my life."

Meredeth inched away from Major Stanfield's embrace, but he captured her hands and held them loosely between his. "Then we will be good friends, Meredeth. May I continue to see you?"

"I would like to count you friend, my lord."

With a resolute sigh, he offered his arm and led her back to the ballroom where several others joined them for the midnight supper. When the music began once more, Meredeth excused herself and hurried to the room reserved for the women.

Cecelia led her down the hall to a spacious bedroom. "Sit here on the bed. I can't wait to show you my trousseau and the gifts he's given me."

Cecelia brought out one lovely gown after another, a sparkling necklace of garnets with matching earbobs, a gold-embossed jewelry box, and a watercolor of the castle that was to be their home.

"They are truly beautiful! Cecelia, tell me, how did you know he was the right one for you?" Merry inquired.

"Oh, he is pleasant to be with. Father says he is one of the wealthiest men in England and Mother is in alt over it. Just think, I will be the Baroness Delverson!"

"Do you love him?" Merry asked softly.

"Well, we've only known each other for a few months. Mother says love will come. At least I will not be left on the shelf when this war is over. So many of our men are dead. I will have everything a girl dreams of."

"Then I wish you the very best. Perhaps we can continue seeing each other and renew our friendship."

Cecelia tilted her chin up, but her eyes failed to meet Merry's. Nervous hands in her lap made a shambles of her lace kerchief. Troubled, Meredeth reached to touch her, and Cecelia grasped her tightly. A sob caught in Cecelia's throat as she leaned forward, afraid that someone would hear.

nine

"Do not speak of this," Cecelia said. "I must tell someone. Delverson says I must be prepared to leave right after Christmas. He is sure our Rebels will be crushed by then and the British troops will leave only a small contingent here to oversee the colonies. Delverson says they have Washington right where they want him, and once he is captured, the rebellion will fall apart. Merry, I am to return to England with him. I'm so frightened. Delverson is nice, but what shall I do in a strange place, knowing no one?"

"You will know Delverson." Merry feared that was spoken with little sympathy. She tried to give some encouragement, while absently patting the sobbing young woman's shoulder.

Inside, though, her mind churned with memory of recent events. Was Washington in danger? He had escaped capture at Fort Miflin and earlier in Boston. The colonists considered the "wily old fox" invincible. No, she could not accept the possibility of his capture or the Patriots' defeat, though England had far more wealth and men-at-arms. Pulling herself together, she tried to ease her friend's anguish.

"Cecelia, remember the dreams we had at school? You were going to marry a great lord and I planned to marry a doctor or scholar. Your dream is coming true. None of us knows much of our future husband's family, but we accept them and learn to live with them. Delverson sounds like a pleasant young man. Think of this as an adventure into a new world and remember that no matter where you go, God will be there with you."

After a few noisy sniffles and a hiccup, Cecelia raised her eyes to meet Merry's. "You are right. Oh, I'm so glad I talked to you tonight. Delverson is a dear and I think I can learn to love him."

Questions still circled Meredeth's mind. She could not help asking, "How can they be so sure of taking Washington?" in a shaky voice.

Her eyes wide, Cecelia gasped, realizing she had confided more than she should have. Setting her shoulders firmly, she lifted her chin to reply, "Everyone knows he is camped at Whitemarsh. It is a perfect trap. The British can easily surround his troops."

"I heard he was there, but I think he may be more difficult to catch than they believe. He has always had an uncanny intuition. In any event, I wish you joy in your marriage."

Together, they returned to the ballroom, where sets were forming. Both were swiftly whirled away.

Later, at Mrs. Clairmont's door, Stanfield did not linger, the sharp wind flinging snow at them even under the protection of the roof. After he left and when Merry entered the house, she found Aunt Mina propped crookedly in a wicker chair, soft snores coming from her open mouth. Merry smiled fondly as she reached over to waken her aunt. There, in the dim light, two long legs came into view. Merry stepped closer, biting her lip to keep from shouting, for beneath the tousled hair of the second sleeper was the face she so longed to see.

"Will," she whispered in his ear, "when did you get here?"

Abruptly he jerked upright, shaking his head to chase away deep sleep. Bleary eyes met Merry's and they both chuckled, a bit embarrassed at the position in which they found themselves. That woke Aunt Mina, who vaguely told them to be quiet. A bit discomfited herself, she rose, twitched at her skirts, and smoothed her hair.

"I shall retire to my bed, where all good people should be at this time of night," Aunt Mina said, glaring at Will, her finger pointed at his chest. "You may remain five minutes, no more. Merry, I will speak to you in the morning. I am far too tired at present."

Will lurched to his feet, urgently smoothing his clothes. When Aunt Mina's indignant tread was silenced by a closing door, he and Merry stood staring at each other like two fish in adjoining bowls. Finally realizing their allotted time was swiftly passing, he reached for her. Face aglow, she came to his arms.

"How I have longed to do this these last weeks," he murmured in her ear.

She drew back as far as his arm would allow. "Weeks? It's been a month and five days with no word from you."

"Has it now?" he said softly but with a twinkle in his eyes. "Then you must have missed me as I have you."

"Yes, well, I truly thought you would write since you were gone so long."

She dipped her head, but he did not want their eyes to break contact. His finger under her chin restored visual communication. With deliberate slow motion, he claimed her lips.

"You taste sweeter than Nell's butterfly cakes. There were so many things to do when Uncle Reggie died, yet through all the rush and sadness I kept seeing your face. I couldn't wait any longer to hold you in my arms. Fortunately I had no problem leaving Boston. Washington's new counter-intelligence force has more control over that city than the English do, in spite of their reputation."

"I am so pleased to hear that. A friend told me something tonight that left me concerned about Washington's safety."

"I suppose no one can be counted safe these days, but Washington is no fool. His grasp of human nature and success in fielding an army constantly amaze me," Will assured her.

"I did not mean to interrupt. Tell me more of your uncle and the shipping business. I know so little about either."

Merry snuggled a bit closer, enjoying the scent of the pine soap he used and the warmth of his arms. Will's voice grew huskier as he continued, "Uncle Reggie was a hard man in his business dealings, but he had a soft spot in his heart for me. Whenever I showed promise, he let me know he was pleased. Usually he gave orders and expected them to be obeyed. Even when he elevated me to partner, he controlled all decisions."

"You were gone so long, I feared for your safety."

"It was just as long for me. The memory of you kept me sane amid all the business decisions I had to make."

He relaxed back into the chair, pulling her beside him. "In the end, he provided for all the relatives, but the entire business is to be mine if I run his affairs well for two months. I've been working eighteen hours a day to tie up all loose ends. There is one thing more I must do to prove myself. Uncle's favorite ship of the line is due in port."

"Does that mean you must leave again?"

"I am afraid so. Because of the British blockades, Trent is bringing the ship into Baltimore Harbor instead of Boston. I have buyers coming to meet it and another cargo waiting to go out. It is due in three days, so I must leave early this morn. I had no idea how I would get through the guards, but God provided the way. I met Jim Hanks out near Whitemarsh and he brought me in. Your aunt was none too pleased that I asked to wait for you, but I had to see you, Merry."

The small clock on the mantel pointed to half-past-two. "Jim will come for me around three," Will warned.

"When was the last time you ate?" Merry asked.

"I recall a small meat pie about ten yesterday morn."

"If you have a hard ride ahead, you will need food to sustain you. I think Nell will forgive me for invading her kitchen. Come on. There was some hearty stew left from supper. I'll warm it for you. I may be able to find some of her biscuits, too."

Taking his hand, Merry tugged him through the dark hall to the kitchen. Much to their surprise, a candle burned on the table and stew bubbled in the pot over the hearth. Nell appeared with warm biscuits and a bowl of butter.

Two places had been set.

"I jest thought ya might be hungry. They don't always feed ya much at them balls. Well, sit down and I'll fetch some milk from the cellar."

"Thank you, Nell. That was thoughtful of you." Will grinned at her.

"Humph! Don't take no thought to figure two young'uns are gonna be hungry this time of mornin'. I had to do some chores, anyhow. Miss Merry, mind you clean up when you're done now."

"I will. Thank you. You are a dear."

"Ain't never been nobody's dear. If I like ya, don't mind atal doing fer ya and that's that."

Off to bed she marched, leaving them alone. The aroma from the hearth lured them to investigate. Suddenly ravenous, they devoured biscuits and stew with little conversation. When they finally pushed aside the bowls, Will reached for her hands. His thumbs made tiny swirls over their fragile bone structure, though his eyes never left her face.

"Merry, I stopped by the hospital on the way here. Your father and I talked for a while. I inquired if he had any objections to me as a son-in-law." Will grinned broadly before continuing, "He looked down his nose very sternly at me and wanted to know who or what was in control of my life."

Merry's face sobered as she stared wide-eyed at Will. Faintly she asked, "What did you say?"

"I'll admit I thought hard about that before I answered. Finally I said the only thing I could, truthfully. I told him God had been in charge of my life since I was a small child, and after Him, I loved you more than anyone or anything."

Merry's mouth trembled into a smile. Her eyes danced as she urged Will to continue. He caught her to him in a tight embrace.

"He slapped me on the back so hard it almost buckled my knees. They were shaky anyway. Then he told me to go find you and see what you thought about it."

"That's my papa!" Merry's smile burst into laughter.

"How much time will you need for the Reverend Harrison to marry us properly in church, love?" Will asked.

Merry tried hard to keep a straight face as she inquired, "Is that a proposal, Mr. Castleton?"

"Your pardon, my lady. I have not been able to think properly since I left you. If you desire a formal proposal, you shall have it. Will you marry me, Meredeth Elliott?"

The seriousness of the situation was only slightly marred by a smudge of stew on his chin, the shadowy crescents under his eyes, and the thick lock of hair that plopped onto his forehead as he descended to one knee. At the sight of that cherished face looking at her with adoration, Merry whispered, "Yes, Will. Oh, yes."

One finger wiped the smudge away, while her other hand swept the errant hair back from his eyes. Cecelia could have all the castles in England. Merry wanted only to follow this man to Boston and become a part of the rest of his life.

He caught her hand and gifted it with a kiss. Eagerly she leaned forward into his embrace. Will caught her tightly enough, but they were both off balance and tumbled to the floor as a faint knock at the back door brought Nell hurrying in.

"Well, I ain't never seen a man propose that way afore," she said. "Looks like you found the right words, Mr. Castleton. Sorry to bust in like this, but someone's at the door."

Before Will could lift Merry to her feet, Jim Hanks stood, arms akimbo, shaking his head at them. "You Brits sure have some strange ways. Looks like it all worked out, though. I'm happy for you, but we've got to ride. Howe's got men out skirting the city. I brought your horse all packed up and ready to go."

"I'll be right with you," Will promised, pulling Meredeth up with him.

He held her close as he whispered in her ear, "I love you so much. I'll be back as soon as I can. Talk to the reverend and take care of yourself."

Jim had been standing looking longingly at the biscuits. With a sweep of her hand, Nell dumped the lot into a bag and handed it to him. He rewarded her with a hug, then whisked out the door. Will flung his cloak around his shoulders, took one last look to memorize the face of his future wife, and dashed outside. There was no sound for a few minutes except the beat of pounding hooves and the utter silence that followed. A tiny shudder of apprehension shivered along Merry's spine. Nell gave her a comforting embrace before wishing her good night. The next day several of Mrs. Clairmont's friends came to visit. Meredeth sat quietly as they shared bits of news. No mention was made of arrests or confrontations on the roads during the night. By evening, she felt certain that Will and Jim had made it through the British guards. Now it was just a matter of waiting, but that could be a worrisome thing.

Word came of another meeting of the Patriots. Merry and Anna stayed at the hospital that eve. To Merry's surprise, Red Mac already knew of Will's visit and the promise made between them.

"Och, lass, my Scottish heart couldn't be happier. I knew the lad had good sense and a large portion of luck. May the good Lord bless you both."

A loud knocking at the entrance sent her hurrying to open the door, but it slammed open before she reached it. Three Redcoats pushed into the room. One of them grabbed Meredeth's arm in an iron grip.

"Where is he? Where is the doctor?"

ten

Before Merry could answer, another large man pushed through the doorway. It was Jeremiah, and in his arms was a blanket-wrapped figure!

"Miss Merry! Where's your papa? Mrs. Clairmont's been hurt."

Merry was speechless. In shock she looked from one to the other, then said the first thing that came to her mind. "He. . .he went to get some medicine. I don't know when he will be back. What happened to Mrs. Clairmont, Jeremiah?"

Elvira's face was pale. With a wavery voice she explained, "I fell trying to reach a jar on a shelf too high for me." Then with a barely perceptible wink, she added, "Your papa said we should come here. He'll be here as soon as he finds that medicine."

Merry glared indignantly at the man clutching her arm. "Let me go. I must tend to this patient."

The man frowned, but released her. Although he gave his comrades a signal to stand aside, they watched every move that was made.

Jeremiah gently lowered Elvira to the examining table. As if they knew what they were doing, Merry and Anna made her as comfortable as possible, checking first her heart and pulse.

"My ankle hurts something terrible. Do you think I've broken it?" Elvira asked.

Solemnly Meredeth exposed the swollen ankle, carefully moving her fingers over it.

"How long has Dr. Elliott been gone?" one of the Brits asked.

"I. . .I do not have a watch," Merry answered. "It was a short time ago he left."

"There's word out that the townsmen are having a Rebel meeting tonight. Our men are checking everywhere. He'll wind up in prison if he's caught at that meeting," he warned, jerking Merry's arm toward him.

"You will release my daughter immediately! You have no right to mishandle her," a voice demanded.

"Dr. Elliott!" Anna cried out.

Merry closed her eyes and forced herself to take a deep breath. When the

Redcoat dropped her arm, Jeremiah tugged her behind him. Papa stepped closer to confront the soldiers.

"What is it you want?" he asked in a quiet voice.

"We heard you went for medicine but I don't see any. Where were you, Doctor?"

"They told you. I was seeking medication. It is, like most things these days, very hard to come by. I found none. As a doctor helping your own men, it seems to me it would be wise for your people to provide the necessary medicines. I will speak to General Howe about this."

The man's eyes flickered toward his companions. Then, with a grimace, he motioned for them to follow as he strode away, muttering under his breath.

Meredeth ran to her papa. When she opened her mouth, he placed his finger across her lips. Hugging her close, he turned to the others.

"Let me see the patient, please."

When he had inspected the swollen leg, Dr. Elliott declared, "It is not broken, but it will need to be tightly wrapped and you must stay off your feet until the swelling is gone. I'll give you some herbs for the pain. Don't put your weight on it for a few days at least."

When that was done, Mrs. Clairmont was taken home and made comfortable in her favorite chair. She soon fell fast asleep and Jeremiah carried her up to bed. The others were about to retire when there was a soft knock at the back door. Nell reached it first and pulled it open. There was genuine relief all around when they saw Dr. Elliott. He slipped inside and the candles were snuffed out. They all sat around the kitchen table.

"As I neared the meeting place, I saw it was surrounded by Brits, so I hurried back," the doctor told them, "and none too soon. We men must make other arrangements to meet in the future. Thank you all for your help. That was well done. You will not work at the hospital anymore, Merry. I want you to remain here as much as possible."

"Very well, Papa. If Stanfield asks me to go with him, what shall I tell him?"

"You will tell him you are pleased to accept his invitation. I hardly think they will bother you in his company. Friends, we stand in need of God's help. This is getting beyond our control. Please join hands with me.

"Dear Lord God, we come to You with humble pleas. First we ask Your forgiveness for wrongs we have done. We are earthen vessels in Your hands. Fill us with Your Will and Your ways, that we may be reflections of Your grace and mercy. We ask You to please watch over our families and friends. Keep them safe, Lord. If it is Your Will, bring this terrible war to an end so that we may live in peace again. Until then, grant us strength and patience to be Your people in deed as well as in Your Word. In the name of Jesus, we ask Your help. Amen.

"Now I must return as swiftly as I came. Perhaps they will not be so vigilant since they saw me there tonight."

≥∙

The next week, several folks came requesting aid. Supplies, though, were nearly gone. What sort of Christmas could they have? Unless Stanfield brought something, they would be fortunate to have stew. One night there was a knock at Mrs. Clairmont's door. Mrs. Clairmont greeted a Quaker woman, then asked Nell's help in the kitchen.

It was sometime before Mrs. Clairmont returned and, to Merry's surprise, her guest was not with her. Mrs. Clairmont's eyes were downcast and a frown marred her brow. She spent the rest of the evening muttering to herself and jabbing at her needlework haphazardly. Merry and Aunt Mina finally excused themselves and went to their rooms.

Snuggled under the Starfire quilt, Merry blew out the candle and settled herself for sleep. Darkness lay thick and heavy; her thoughts were troubled. Something disturbed her awareness. Had someone called her name?

"Merry," the whisper came a bit more urgently.

At first she looked to the window. The trees made wild, scrabbly noises against the house and a bright moon cast familiar shadows.

"Merry, please."

This time she turned toward the door. Chewing at her underlip, she slid from the warmth of the bed and, bare feet cringing on the cold wooden planks of the floor, she turned the knob. The door swung back and a whirlwind of muslin entered. One small hand closed the door while the other reached toward Merry.

"Do not light a candle, child. It goes against all the rules of hospitality, but I need your help desperately. Do say you will do it."

Merry chided herself mentally for it was only Elvira Clairmont. What had she expected? Hastings? "Come, sit on the bed with me and tell me what you want."

Her guest perched, like a recalcitrant bird, on the edge of the bed. Absently she fingered the quilt's pattern. "I used the small one, you know. You are most welcome to do the same."

"The small one?" Merry questioned.

"Oh, yes. It has hidden pockets just the right size, you see."

"The right size for what?"

Mind awhirl, Merry wondered if the dear woman had hit her head when she fell or had been dreaming and was not fully awakened yet.

"Why the notes, my dear. Like the ones you have been receiving."

Merry froze, mouth open like a doomed flounder.

Mrs. Clairmont continued with a sly smile. "Nell told me all about it. Then she said who brought the packets and I knew right off what they were. I've made a few deliveries myself. It was quite exciting."

Meredeth collapsed in a shaking heap, laughter bubbling over like boiling syrup. Elvira watched for a moment before dissolving into giggles herself.

"Well, if that don't beat all! A fine bunch of conspirators we be," Nell said from the doorway. "If you two don't hush up, the whole world will know afore you git the news to the man himself."

"Did Jim want us to deliver a note?" Merry asked.

"Jim hasn't been here lately. It was Lydia Darragh, the lady who was here tonight. You see, she's got a son in Washington's camp and she hates to see him captured. She lives just across the way from a Tory family where General Howe is quartered. Last night they needed another meeting room, so they took over a floor of the Darragh's home. Can you believe it? They made the Darraghs go to bed and set a guard on their room. Then a large group of them met in the room upstairs."

"What happened?"

"Well, you see, the Darraghs need some work done on their chimneys. There is an open space between the fireplace in their room and the one upstairs where the Redcoats met. Lydia heard everything they said. They plan to raid the camp at Whitemarsh and capture Washington. We can't let that happen."

"What can we do?" Meredeth groaned.

"We must get word to Washington. He'll think of something."

"How can we get out of Philadelphia?"

"Lydia knows a way. She feeds a bunch of Howe's men, so she needs flour. A mill just north of here still has some. Lydia is going to take two flour sacks and go to the mill. They'll let her through for that, you see."

"Is this mill near Whitemarsh?"

Mrs. Clairmont shook her head. "It's about six miles from the mill. While the miller is filling her sacks, Lydia will say she has to visit her young'uns, who are staying with their grandma on her farm. Instead, she'll go to a tavern nearby and get one of Washington's patrols to deliver the message to him."

"Mrs. Darragh will do this by herself?" Merry sputtered.

"Well, she wanted me to go with her, but with my ankle hurting just to walk to the kitchen, I can't do it. Could you go with her, Merry? We'd give you a sack for flour, too."

Meredeth remembered the day Matt's note came and how she had prayed to be able to help the Patriots' cause! This was her chance. If they stopped her, she would have a valid excuse to be on the road. She turned a brave smile to her hostess.

"I will do it. Even if it snows, I have that warm cloak you gave me, plus my spencer and my woolen shawl."

Elvira clasped Merry in a hug. The older woman began to cry. "I always try to help others, but I knew I couldn't walk that far. It made me feel so useless. Thank you, my dear."

"You opened your home to help us and you give aid to so many people. You should never feel useless. God works through you in lots of ways. Let Him use me this time."

Elvira wore a misty-eyed smile as she hobbled to the door. "Meredeth Elliott, you are a lovely, Christian young lady. I am so proud of you and I know the Lord is, too. Lydia plans to leave at first light. I'll ask Nell to wake you. Thank you and may God watch over the two of you."

Merry closed the door and climbed back into her bed. She would need her sleep, but she remembered to thank the Lord.

ℬ

Small, scudding clouds along the horizon were already tinged with a faint wash of gold when Merry and Lydia waited patiently for the guards to examine their passes. The wind blew gently, like an old man puffing on his pipe, and the sun's warmth welcomed them. Their passes returned, they were motioned on their way. In the city, neither said much. Now there were only the birds seeking breakfast and a lone horse watching them from the pasture nearby to overhear.

Mrs. Darragh patted the quilted muff with which she warmed her hands. It was Elvira's Starfire pattern!

"Our passes are here. If anything should happen to me, you must take them and the note and slip away immediately. Go to the first tavern beyond the miller's and give it to the proprietor. Tell him it is for Washington. He will understand."

"Do you think someone patrolling the road would search us?" Merry asked.

"Some men would not put hands on a lady, but there are others who find wicked delight in doing so. We cannot take the chance. If we see Redcoats before they notice us, we shall hide. If they see us, I will delay them while you get away. Do you understand?"

At Meredeth's nod, Lydia continued, "My firstborn boy is in that camp. I will do anything to prevent him or General Washington from being taken by the British. At least one of us must get this message through."

"Of course. I will help in any way I can," Merry assured her.

Smiling, the Quaker mother stepped out at a brisk walk. They did not stop until the sun was well up. A cold drink from a creek beside the road refreshed them. Surprisingly the journey went well that morn. Two British patrols hesitated, but when they saw Lydia's Quaker dress and the empty flour sacks, the captain nodded and rode on. Everyone knew that Quaker "Friends" took no part in war. By the time the women reached the mill at Frankford Creek, both were very tired. The miller agreed to fill their bags as soon as he had enough grain processed.

Mrs. Darragh raised a hand to shade her eyes as she said, "The Widow Kress keeps the Rising Sun Tavern just a little west of us. We're outside the territory usually patrolled by the British. We can walk toward the tavern. It may be we will meet one of Craig's men there."

"Will you recognize them if you see them?" Merry asked as they hurried along the road.

"I know most of them. Hark!" Lydia stiffened as she squinted to see in the distance.

A sturdy beat of hooves approached. It was a lone rider.

"Wait." Lydia caught Merry's hand. "He is not wearing red. Let us stand here and see who it is."

The rider pulled up with a flourish, raising a hand to his cap. A broad grin crossed his face. "Mrs. Darragh. What are you doing so far from home?"

"Charlie Craig! If you aren't a sight for sore eyes! We have a message for General Washington. Can you get it to him swiftly?"

As Mrs. Darragh told him of Howe's scheme to capture their leader, Craig nodded. "Washington heard rumors similar to this from another source. He's got patrols around the area as a precaution, but this confirms it. We'll need to take stronger steps. I have to meet John Clark in five minutes. It may be sometime before I get back to camp. Just over this hill is Tilson's farmhouse. Give the message to Mrs. Tilson. She'll take it to Sergeant Walsh at the tavern. She might give you ladies a hot meat pie if you smile at her. I just had one and they're delicious. Tell her I sent you."

With a wave, he galloped off. Lydia and Merry climbed the hill and soon knocked at Tilson's door. They remembered to smile. When the good woman heard their tale, she urged them to sit and enjoy a meat pie and hot biscuits while she dressed in warmer clothes. They were more than pleased to comply.

"If Sergeant Walsh is not at the tavern, Colonel Boudinot will be. He comes every day for his lunch. I've got a nephew at Whitemarsh. I wouldn't want to see him in a Brit's prison."

In just a few minutes they were all ready to leave. Mrs. Tilson waved them off, then set out for Whitemarsh. When Lydia and Merry reached the mill, their flour was waiting for them. The bags' weight slowed their return, but they reached the sentries on the north side of Philadelphia before true dark. Both women breathed easier after the men let them through. Mrs. Darragh gave Merry a warm hug as they parted.

"With so many of our young lads risking their lives for our freedom, it makes my heart feel warm to know a young lady like you is so brave and patriotic, too. Your papa will be proud of you."

"It made me feel that I was at least contributing to our fight for freedom. Thank you for giving me the opportunity," Merry replied.

There were only a few blocks to go and Merry hurried to get inside before the British began night patrols each half-hour. She was breathless when she tugged the door closed behind her. Nell had stew waiting and some warm biscuits. Of course they all had to hear about her adventure and, by the time she dragged her weary feet up the stairs, Meredeth was half-asleep. She wrapped the Starfire quilt around her and went to sit at the window to say her prayers.

"Heavenly Father, thank You for walking with us today and keeping us safe. I'm so glad I was able to do something to help our Patriots. I hope it helped Will, also. Please watch over him, Lord, and bring him back to me soon. And please help Papa with all his duties. In Jesus' name, Amen."

Nell must have brought up hot bricks for the bed for warmth welcomed Meredeth as she crawled between the coverlets. Drowsily she vowed she would sleep at least a full day.

eleven

Merry did sleep well, and it was late afternoon of the second day when she became aware of the wood seller's heavy wagon and a whole troop of men on horseback going by. At last her dawdling mind focused her attention. Stanfield planned to stop by tonight!

The coverlets were thrown back, and Merry quickly washed, then donned her chemise and underskirt. Anna bustled in with an armload of fresh clothing.

"Which gown were you wanting to wear, Miss Merry?"

"The peach with the velvet trim, please. What hour is it, Anna? I can smell Nell's vegetable soup."

"It is four of the clock, miss. Here, let me do your buttons. I think there's some other guests right now, but they'll surely be gone before your gentleman arrives."

To her dismay, Meredeth walked into a parlor filled with Mrs. Clairmont's friends, anxious to hear of Merry's jaunt with the Quaker woman. At least she could tell it to all of them at once, Merry realized as she joined the circle.

She whispered to Nell, "I don't know how long this will take. Keep watch and let me know if Stanfield arrives before they leave."

Nell winked and disappeared into the foyer. Merry looked at the expectant faces. For a moment, her mind went blank.

"Meredeth, why don't you just begin when you and Lydia left here?" Mrs. Clairmont suggested.

Taking a deep breath, Merry told the entire tale.

"Everything went so smoothly," she concluded. "I must admit I was very thankful the Lord brought us safely back. Has anyone heard rumors of Washington's plans?"

"We were discussing that before you came. No one has any idea what he can do. It's so difficult to move a large group of men without the English noticing," Mrs. Clairmont mused. "Meredeth's idea of thanking the Lord is a very good one. Let's all remember the general and his men in our prayers and give our thanks for watching over our friends on their long walk."

After the women left, the conversation turned again to the problems of finding enough food for growing families. It was too early to expect Stanfield, and the aroma of Nell's soup tugged the Elliotts and Elvira into the kitchen. Elvira said grace, then nodded for Nell to serve them.

After the first bite, Mrs. Clairmont's eyes grew large and round as she beamed at Nell. "Why, wherever did you find meat? None of our friends have been able to purchase any for weeks."

Nell busied herself slicing bread, completely ignoring the question.

Elvira took another bite, chewing tentatively. When that was swallowed, she speared a lump from the broth and held it out to examine it. "Mrs. Schoengert, you will please do me the respect of looking at me and answering my question!"

Nell reluctantly glanced at her employer. With a sniff, she murmured, "Little Jamie Conway found a nest of black snakes in his pa's pasture. He and Sam Williker hit them on the head with sticks 'til they was dead. Then they sold them 'round the neighborhood. Sam says they's real tasty, honest, Mrs. Clairmont. An' I done cleaned 'em extra good afore I cut 'em in the soup."

The fork dropped from Elvira's hand. She sat as if turned to stone, staring in horror at the bite she had almost put in her mouth. "Snake? You have cooked us snakes?"

"Well, ma'am, they jus' don't have nuthin' else at market and a body needs meat. That's a fact."

"You know, my dear," Aunt Mina pleaded, "it truly doesn't taste as horrid as it sounds. Take another bite and see what you think. If she hadn't told me what it was, I'd not have known."

"Humph!" Elvira looked from one to the other. Gingerly picking up her fork, she puckered in distaste, squeezed her eyes shut, and nibbled at the piece. A small frown still crinkled her brow, but she managed to swallow.

Then she reexamined the bowl before her. "Well! It's a crying shame when honest folk are forced to eat reptiles. However, I must admit it tastes better if I close my eyes. I suppose we must eat it, but I can't like it."

Merry and Aunt Mina carefully schooled their faces to indifference and continued the meal. Later, as the women sat stitching on their needlework, Nell brought in a berry bread pudding. Mrs. Clairmont complimented her cook and Nell reclaimed her usual look of pride. By the time Stanfield arrived, the atmosphere was one of satisfaction.

"Why, Major Stanfield! How good of you to call," Mrs. Clairmont welcomed him.

"I regret I can't stay long. I have duty tonight. This Saturday there is to be a musical evening at the Lorings' home. They'll have a theater production and several of the ladies will sing or play for us. Would that interest you, Miss Meredeth?"

"I have always enjoyed plays. Yes, I would like that."

"Then I will come for you at seven. I truly must go now, but I'm pleased you will come." He raised her hand to his lips, then left with a smile.

When Elvira went to her room, Aunt Mina stopped by to chat with Meredeth. At the mention of the snakes, they both laughed heartily. The Elliotts had eaten snake before and found it fairly tasty. When her aunt retired, Merry put on her nightgown and retreated to her place in the window seat. She opened the window just enough to smell the pines at the back of the yard. The cool breeze felt good for a few minutes.

From the direction of Whitemarsh, a lone wood duck's call winged over the silence. Normally she enjoyed the sound, but why did it fill her with apprehension tonight? If only Will would return. She missed him. That must be why she was so gloomy.

ᵗᵃ

The expression on Anna's face answered any questions Merry might have asked. She gave one last twirl of her sea green marquisette, then let the dainty folds drift toward her toes. The maid had fashioned a crown of curls, twisted with a narrow strip of lace, and had left one plump coil to trail down her neck to her shoulder.

Just in time, too, for she could hear Nell welcoming Stanfield. Snatching up her cloak, muff, and reticule, Meredeth started down the stairs.

Stanfield halted in the middle of a sentence, just staring at her. "You are exquisite," he said.

"Thank you, kind sir," Meredeth smiled back at him.

It was a perfect beginning to a wondrous night. They were ushered into the Loring estate to find a ballroom filled to overflowing with young people. At one end of the room hung a huge curtain of maroon velvet. Chairs were placed in a semicircle. Slowly the guests moved toward this area.

A very young man stepped forth from the curtain, his eyes aglow with excitement. He took a deep breath, then loudly said, "The Unsung Oracle of Delphia." Curtains were pulled back to reveal three young maids, bowing low. In the background was a painted scene of Philadelphia. The audience applauded generously as the maids enacted a whirling dance of swaying arms and skirts among bowers filled with blossoms.

Music was provided by a string quartet. No one was sure what the tale was about, but it was all beautifully done. Everyone cheered the three blushing maidens and their stiletto-wielding true loves, assuming that all had ended well for them. There were the usual renditions on harp and harpsichord, plus a trio of songs sung by a shy maid whose voice could not be heard above the chatter of the crowd.

Finally a sweet, clear voice captured the entire group. The room became silent but for the lilt of old folk songs and a slight Scottish accent. The crowd responded with enthusiasm.

Leaning over to Merry, Stanfield murmured, "It seems they saved the best for last."

"Yes, Caroline MacDuff is a wonderful singer. She and I were schoolmates, but her family moved to Boston a few years ago. I haven't seen her since. I wonder if she's living here again."

The butler directed the guests to step into the next room for refreshments, but two words stopped them just a few feet from the cluster of folks around the vivacious singer.

"Meredeth Elliott!" a voice said.

Merry looked up to see Caroline hurrying toward her and saying, "Oh, I so hoped you'd be here and we could talk! Tell me everything that has happened since I saw you last."

When they had embraced, Merry held out a hand to bring Stanfield closer. "This is Major Henry Stanfield, Caroline. Stanfield, meet Caroline MacDuff. You must come visit me, Caroline. I am staying with a friend on Arch Street. Where are you lodged?"

Merry's friend nodded pleasantly to Major Stanfield before continuing, "My mother and I are visiting an aunt who lives on Spruce and Seventh. She's been very ill and Mother has been attending her."

"Why, that is close to the hospital where my papa stays. We've been so near to each other all this time and didn't know it. How wonderful to see you again," Merry exclaimed.

"We enjoyed your singing very much, Miss MacDuff. Do you have an escort?" Stanfield inquired.

"N—no. I came to perform. Mother knows the Lorings and they requested me to sing. Perhaps I shouldn't—"

"If you have no objection, I believe I can find a partner for a foursome and a small table where we can talk," Stanfield said sotto voce.

"That would be just the thing! Thank you, Stanfield. We'll wait here," Merry agreed.

Caroline looked searchingly at Merry. "Tell me quickly before he returns. Are you seeing a British officer?"

Merry's cheeks pinkened. She met her friend's eyes squarely and chose her words with care. "We are friends. He has taken me to a few parties in town. Papa likes Major Stanfield and thought I should attend some of the entertainments with him. I do enjoy his company. He is a friend of Ben Franklin's."

Caroline hesitated. With a duck of her head, she glanced around. No one appeared to be watching. "Merry, are you a Tory or a Whig or. . .?"

Merry's instant response "I'm a Patriot" widened Caroline's smile.

"Good. I'm surprised you don't have a steady beau. I don't, either, though there's one man I'd truly like to see again. You mustn't ever mention his name. He works for the Patriots. They call him Jim Hanks, but that's not his real name. His whole family is involved in helping Washington," she confided."

"Jim Hanks? I met him recently," Merry informed her.

Caroline beamed. "We danced several times at a party up in Boston and he visited with my family. I heard he was somewhere near Philadelphia, but I didn't know where."

"I think he is one of Washington's couriers," Merry said.

Caroline sighed. "Maybe I'll see him again. He's so interesting to talk to and he's done so many exciting things."

"With Major Hastings haunting City Tavern, Jim doesn't come in town much," Merry advised.

Caroline's eyes darkened as she asked, "Hastings? Isn't he that cousin of Howe's who caused so much trouble in Boston?"

"I don't know about that, but few people here like him. If it hadn't been for Major Stanfield, Hastings would have arrested me as a spy. He swore I carried secret messages in a bag I brought to the tavern. Stanfield turned the bag upside down, dumping out the cakes I had promised the cook's daughter. You should have heard the men laugh! Hastings was furious."

"You were fortunate, Merry. Hastings was behind the killing of a good many Patriots up in Boston. He has an evil reputation. We feared to be found on the streets while that fiend was around."

"Even his own men don't like him," Merry said. "Will says he is an evil person."

"Will?" Caroline questioned.

Eyes twinkling, Merry whispered, "I do have a steady beau. He's English, but he's lived in Boston with an uncle for several years. He's been a partner with him in a shipping business. He's in Boston right now."

"Doesn't he mind your seeing Stanfield?"

"Oh, I think he does, but he can't offer for me until he can afford a home for us. He knows Papa wants me to have a little social life. Also, I've explained all this to Stanfield. He is lonesome for his family, so we agreed to be friends. He's been a perfect gentleman."

Before more could be said, Stanfield and another officer, Captain Richardson, joined them. They carried plates of tempting food. The women were escorted to a small table and Captain Richardson was introduced. He promptly decided to remain in their company.

ક

During the days before Christmas, Captain Richardson invited the three young people to share his box at the theater. Except for the men who had drawn guard duty, all the English troops attended, most with local women on their arms. While they waited for the play to begin, Merry and Caroline delighted in seeing all the lovely gowns, jewelry, and flirting fans. Most of the men wore their regimentals, making the colorful frocks of the women look like jewels set in red and gold braid.

Stanfield directed Meredeth's attention to a couple entering the first box. "Have you ever met General Howe?" he asked.

Merry shook her head. Leaning closer, Stanfield informed her, "He just arrived with several ladies, there in the front box. I believe the matron on his arm is his hostess. Her husband is right behind—"

He frowned, muttering under his breath. Meredeth followed his gaze, wondering what had caused his consternation.

"Forgive me, Meredeth, I understood Hastings had been sent back to New York, yet he is sitting there in all his finery."

Perhaps the man felt their scrutiny for his eyes swiveled to meet theirs. Merry knew the second he recognized them. His body stiffened and a fierce scowl invaded his face.

Merry's hand reached for Major Stanfield's arm. "He. . .he wouldn't make a scene here, would he?"

Stanfield lifted his chin and glared down his nose at Hastings. In the face of that blazing frown, Hastings lowered his eyes, but Stanfield and Merry noted the feral smile that crossed the man's face before he turned back to the woman at his side.

An arctic wave of fear washed over Meredeth. She said no more of the incident, but in her heart she felt pinioned by Hastings's hatred.

ક

Snow fell heavily Christmas Eve. Merry watched the flakes tumbling past her window as she wondered what Will was doing. Had he disposed of the ship's cargo and sent it off yet? Could he possibly make it through the British guard again?

Stanfield stopped by to present Mrs. Clairmont with a fat goose and a bag filled with fresh fruit. Elvira dashed to the kitchen to give the food to Nell. While she was gone, the major presented Meredeth and Aunt Mina each with prettily wrapped boxes. All aflutter, Aunt Mina opened hers to find a lovely woolen shawl, which she immediately tried on.

Meredeth's package was smaller but more difficult to open. After removing several layers of paper, she held up a carved wooden box.

"It's beautiful!" she exclaimed happily.

"You must open that, as well," Stanfield said with a pleased smile.

"Oh, how lovely," she sighed as she lifted out a fan of lacelike ivory with clusters of birds painted upon sheer Egyptian linen, "but we don't usually give gifts except for family."

"We do not do so at home. I wanted to give these as a thank-you for the warm hospitality." He nodded to Aunt Mina. "And for your kindness in accompanying me to parties and such, Meredeth. You have taken away much of the loneliness that plagues a man away from his family. Enjoy your goose tomorrow. I will see you again soon."

Snow was still falling on Christmas Day. Dr. Elliott joined the women when they attended church in spite of the weather. At lunch, Nell proudly carried the roasted goose in to the table. When the doctor said grace, he added a thanks to God for friends like Stanfield.

Merry had stitched lace collars for Aunt Mina, Mrs. Clairmont, and Nell. The cook's eyes nearly popped from her head and she was still admiring hers when she excused herself to go to her room that night. Merry had bought a book for her father. Dr. Elliott produced a pair of ebony combs for Aunt Mina and, remarkably, a pair of blue combs for Elvira. Both women were in alt over the choice. For Merry, he had found a beaded reticule. The Christmas spirit was obvious as they all enjoyed singing well-known carols and remembering Christmases past.

Later, as Merry watched the snow drift past her window, she thanked the Lord for her family and asked Him to send angels to watch over Will. It had been such a pleasant night with her family, but how she missed Will's presence. If he were waltzing, would he pretend that she was in his arms?

❧

Shortly after the new year began, they heard that Washington had successfully moved his troops to Valley Forge, where, although they had log huts, many doubted that they could survive the winter. More and more snow fell, making movement difficult even in town. Caroline and Merry managed to visit once or twice a week, and the old friendship became much stronger. Merry thanked God for that gift. It helped her forget the ache in her heart. There was no word from Will or Jim Hanks. Stranger yet, there had been no notice of Matt's death. Because of his spying activities, was he in some unknown grave? Would they ever know his fate?

An unexpected thaw at the end of January brought with it the first serious bout of illness. Most of the city folk sneezed, coughed, or became fevered, and the hospital overflowed with patients. Merry, Anna, and Dela were again recruited to help the weary doctor. Caroline offered her services and was gratefully put to work whenever she could come.

Overwork and lack of sleep finally took its toll on Dr. Elliott. Merry was assisting him with his rounds when her papa staggered, then slid down the wall to the floor. When she touched his forehead, she found it burning with fever. Swiftly she, Anna, and Dela dragged the limp form to a clean pallet and sent for an elderly woman who also assisted at times.

Merry stayed by his side, bathing his face with cool water and giving him herbal tea. What would they do without him? She knew that none of the helpers were able to take over such a responsibility.

A short time later, a matron bustled in with another woman in tow. She approached Meredeth.

"I am Mathilda Atherton. This here's Mrs. Wilcox. We ain't either of us doctors, but I helped my pa with his practice all my life and my friend and I are right handy with herbs and such. If you can use us, we'd be proud to help. We heard you were shorthanded."

"Oh, how kind of you! Do make yourselves at home. I've been helping, but I do not know what to do without my papa's guidance. I am Meredeth Elliott. Anna, Dela, and I will be thankful for your experience. Tell us what must be done and we will help you do it."

"Could you show me where Dr. Elliott's casebook is? Soon's I study that a bit, we can get busy here."

Merry showed the women to her father's office, pointed out the ledger on his desk, and let Miss Atherton take over. Papa became Merry's main concern. She sat beside him, wiping his face and chest with cool cloths, but, so far, his temperature remained high. Weary to the bone, she closed her eyes for a minute. Suddenly she awakened with a start.

"Young lady, you won't do your pa any good atal if you don't get some sleep. Now you just march back to his office and lie down," Miss Atherton scolded. "I'll sure call you if there's any change."

With a rueful smile Merry did as she was told. Soon, she was fast asleep.

twelve

February 1778

It seemed as though Merry had hardly slept when a hand shook her awake again. She squinted to see who knelt by her pallet. "Caroline!" Merry said. "What are you doing here in the middle of the night?"

A closer look at Caroline's strained face brought Meredeth straight up, her hand reaching out to the trembling young woman. "What's wrong?" Merry asked.

"Jim's been badly hurt. I brought him in my aunt's carriage, but I can't carry him in. Could your papa take a look at him? He's bleeding so much."

"Papa is unconscious with a fever. There is a lady here helping. I believe she is a staunch Patriot. I will ask her to see to him. Stop crying now. We'll all help."

Quietly Merry tugged Miss Atherton into her father's office and explained the problem. With a sober nod, Miss Atherton swiftly collected her bag of supplies. Within minutes they huddled around the long, still form slumped in the carriage.

"He has a knife slash in his side that is fairly deep. We must staunch the flow of blood, but his pulse is strong and his heart sounds good. It's the fever we'll have to fight mostly. He's too warm."

Merry stood watch while Miss Atherton cleaned out the wound and bandaged it to stop the bleeding. They had almost finished when they heard the rough voices and marching feet of a patrol.

"You two spread your skirts right here over him, one on each side. Quickly now!" Miss Atherton whispered. "I'll roll my cloak and set it by his head and shoulders like this."

She upended Caroline's large bonnet over Jim's head and adjusted her to a sprawled position. "Now, Miss Caroline, you act like you fainted. Miss Merry, you lean over her like this."

By the time the guard reached the coach, Meredeth and Miss Atherton were crowded around Caroline, waving smelling salts under her nose and patting her cheeks as if they were trying to revive her.

"What is the trouble here?" the man demanded.

"Young man, haven't you ever seen a lady swoon? It happens all the time." Miss Atherton leaned over to whisper in the soldier's ear. "They have such delicate sensibilities, you know. She'll come around shortly."

The man lifted a small lantern to look at the white, strained face. With a gruff "Humphh," he returned to his unit. After a brief conference, they went on their way.

"You couldn't have been more convincing if you had truly fainted," Meredeth chuckled, helping her friend up.

Caroline shook her head as she muttered, "I never felt more like expiring in my life."

It was unlikely that another patrol would accost them there. Still, Miss Atherton hurriedly collected her equipment. "Best I be back about my business," she said. "If any comes by with questions, I'll say you went home to rest, Miss Merry. You go with your friend. Get her young man to a safe place and tend him 'til he recovers. We'll take care of things here."

With that assurance, Merry braced Jim's slack figure in the seat. Caroline, the reins limp in her lap, turned frightened eyes to Merry. "I can't take him to my aunt's. He won't be safe there. Where can we take him?"

"Mrs. Clairmont and Nell! He can stay in the spare room. I think they'd let him, if we can get him there. I'll help care for him," Merry offered.

"Oh, thank the Lord!" Caroline sighed.

She snapped to attention and within minutes they were off at a good pace. They passed a patrol, but the men were busy questioning some pedestrians. The leader gave the carriage only a passing glance.

As they opened the door, Nell peeked out from the kitchen and hurried to help. When she saw who had been hurt, her lips tightened as she muttered about "those Brits." Between the three of them, they dragged Jim's limp body up the steps to a vacant room.

"How did he get hurt, Caroline?" Merry asked when they were alone.

"I have no idea," Caroline replied. "I saw him this afternoon in the library. We talked for a long time and he said he had to return to duty. On my way home, I stopped to get some medicine for my aunt. As I came out of her doctor's office, I heard something heavy fall back in the trees on the adjoining lot. No one answered my call, so I walked closer. He was in a heap on the ground. I ran to my aunt's, told Mother I had to help someone who was hurt, and asked for the carriage. She gave me permission, but it took so long to get him into it and I was terrified someone would see us. Thankfully most folks were inside eating supper."

"You go home now or your family will wonder where you are. We'll take care of him. He'll probably sleep all night," Merry assured her friend. Nell offered to peek in on him through the night, so Merry wearily sought her bed. Worries plagued her, but before she reached the end of the list, sleep erased the problems.

She had just filled her bowl with oatmeal the next morn, when Caroline slipped in, quickly closing out the cold wind.

"How is Jim?" she asked immediately.

"Nell has been watching him through the night. Why don't you have some breakfast with me and then we'll both go up and relieve her?"

"You two go on and eat," Nell said as she bustled in. "I came down to fix some broth for that lanky hunk of man. Soon's you finish, go up and tell him how sick he looks. Then mebbe I can keep him in that bed today. He's too frisky for his own good."

"Did the bleeding stop?" Caroline had to know.

"A mite dried on the bandages is all. He'll do if he stays put for a day or two."

When the two women arrived with the broth, Jim was tossing and muttering under his breath, but one sniff of food and he became docile as a lamb. After dunking biscuits into the broth, he popped them into his mouth with the concentration of a dog on a meaty bone. His face reddened at Caroline's giggles but that did not slow him. After the last biscuit disappeared, he laid back against the pillow, a satisfied smile on his face.

"Now that's the way to begin a day. When do I get breakfast?" he asked.

Nell stuck her head in long enough to reply, "You'll get more soon's you prove you can keep that down. Jackanape comes in here and 'spects to be treated like a king!"

Mrs. Clairmont was disturbed when she heard the news. "We can't keep him in a room. I heard they've been searching homes of suspected spies. We'd better put him in the hidey-hole, if he isn't too big to fit."

"Yessum. I already got it cleaned out," Nell agreed.

Jim was able to walk although he made a point of leaning on Caroline's shoulder. By midday they had him safely hidden in the secret alcove. Nell promised to stay with him, so Merry went to the hospital to see how her papa fared. A welcome sight awaited her. He was sitting against a wall, still pale, but his fever had broken.

"You have found me an admirable staff of helpers, my dear." He lowered his voice to continue, "I hear you had an unexpected patient last night. How is he doing?"

Merry laughed. "He is sitting up eating everything in sight and making jokes. The bleeding has stopped. There's no sign of fever as yet."

"He's a strong young man. We'll hope there is no complication. Is Mrs. Clairmont—"

The front door slammed open with a crash and every head jerked to see a troop of Redcoats stomp in. Faces sharp and intent, they scanned the room.

Dr. Elliott pushed himself up a bit. "Is it necessary to create such a clatter? These men require rest and quiet. How may I help you?"

One of them stepped forward. His voice was hard and angry. "We seek one, Douglas McClanahan, a patient here. Where is he?"

"He is in the next room. Merry, will you direct these men?"

Warily she skirted the band, then led the way. "Mr. McClanahan, you have visitors."

The Scot turned with a smile for her. In seconds it was replaced with a sober look.

"That's him. Just pick up the pallet and get him out of here. They'll question him at headquarters."

Merry was pushed aside roughly. In a flash, the soldiers gathered the corners of the pallet, hefted it up along with the wide-eyed McClanahan, and marched from the room. As they passed by Meredeth, one of them thrust a chin in her direction and muttered, "Yeah. That's her."

When the outer door banged shut, Merry ran to her papa. "What is it? Why would they want to question Red Mac?"

A thoughtful frown puckered his brow as he answered, "I don't know, my dear. Have you had anything to do with him outside of the hospital?"

"Not really. He knows Will and he told me if I ever had a message for Will, he'd see that it was delivered. I never sent one. Will! Could he be in some kind of trouble with the Brits? He went to Baltimore to meet one of his ships."

"I'm afraid we won't have the answer to that until Will returns. Merry, don't come to the hospital anymore. You may be in danger. Until I discover some reason for their attention to you, please do not leave Mrs. Clairmont's home."

When the problem reached Jim's ears, he called Merry to him and questioned her for sometime. Caroline soon joined them. It was her mention of Hastings that made Jim sit up with a worried frown.

"Hastings is arrogant, evil-minded, devious, and half-mad, besides! I don't want either of you ladies near him. So Will and Stanfield have both had confrontations with the man and now someone is after you, Merry. It's Hastings. I'd bet on it. Stanfield is English, but he's a good man. I'm glad he's trying to bring Hastings to justice."

Jim suddenly fastened an intent gaze on Merry. "I'll do all I can, but whatever happens, you keep away from Hastings! And that includes you, as well." Jim's hand caught Caroline's and demanded her attention.

They all agreed to keep out of sight and work together. Merry managed a smile for them, then went to her own room. She sat staring out the window. Jim and Caroline were so happy to be together, though he was injured and might be executed if caught. The memory that Will could be involved in something just as serious hit her like a thrown stone. How she wished she could see him, just to know he was alive and well.

❧

Several weeks passed uneventfully. The hidey-hole was open and ready and it would take only a few seconds for Jim to disappear into it. He roamed the house, but spent most of his time in the kitchen. Nell was hard-pressed to find enough food.

When the women teased him, he retorted, "If you were with Washington and his men, you'd understand what hunger truly is. Did you hear he's moved? What an escapade that was! Washington heard, from several sources, of Howe's attack plan at Whitemarsh. We dug trenches and had our guns ready. Howe slipped out of town late on the night of December fourth, even sent some wagons in another direction to fool any spies who watched. McLane and Washington had a good laugh over that. Howe came marching in on the road Washington said they'd use."

"That was right after Lydia and I delivered the news she'd heard," Merry said.

"Right. The Brit's surprise failed dismally. When they arrived, our men were in ditches with all the guns trained on the Redcoats. The two armies stood there looking at each other for a full day. Howe sent men to reconnoiter, but found no openings."

"Howe is Hastings's relative, isn't he?" Caroline asked.

"He was also the one who led that disastrous charge on Bunker Hill. He knew the deadly aim of the Patriots. Actually we were outnumbered, but we were in more protected positions.

"Next day, about noon, Howe marched his troops back to Philadelphia, 'like a parcel of dumb fools,' one man said. Then it snowed so much, Howe wintered in for the year. That's when Washington moved. Most of his men are used to snow."

"It's so good to hear that kind of story for a change. Have you heard anything about Will?" Merry wondered.

"Don't you worry about Will. He's a canny fellow. Truly he's not part of our army. He just helps at times. The shipping business keeps him busy," Jim told them.

"How does he help you?" was Meredeth's prompt question.

"Oh. . .ah. . .I really shouldn't have mentioned that. Please don't repeat it or I'll be in big trouble."

Merry said no more, but that information made her feel better. At least Will was helping the Patriots, not England.

"Meredeth! Come down, please. You have a visitor."

"I'll be right there, Aunt Mina."

She hurried down to find Major Stanfield, very much ill at ease, in the foyer. His troubled eyes met hers.

"Do come in and be seated, Stanfield. Perhaps Nell can find—"

"Merry, I must talk to you."

Aunt Mina disappeared like a rabbit into its hole. The major took several deep breaths before blurting out the reason for his call, distress flaring in his eyes.

"Meredeth, I don't know quite how to say this. Hastings has been spreading lies about you, claiming you, your aunt, and Mrs. Clairmont are spies for the Rebels. He accuses you of harboring Rebel soldiers in this house."

"Hastings!"

"Yes. The man's gone completely mad. He will do anything to prove those charges."

Stanfield dropped the hat he had been turning round and round in his hands. He leaned toward Merry as he said, "I must know if his charges are based on even the slightest bit of truth before I can help you."

Merry willed her hands to relax in her lap. Like shooting stars, thoughts flashed through her mind. Truly she had spied on no one and Jim was not a soldier.

"How can he think such things when his soldiers patrol so closely we hardly dare step out of our homes, much less the city?"

"Have you ever left Philadelphia?" he asked softly.

"Only that time with you and once with a friend of Mrs. Clairmont's."

"Why—," he began, but she answered before he might ask a question she could not respond to truthfully.

"We needed flour. Mrs. Darragh knew of a mill where some was available. She got a pass and we walked there and back in the same day. The road guards saw us return with the flour. You could check with them."

"Please tell me you did not go to Whitemarsh," he pleaded.

She took a deep breath, long enough to say a swift thank you to God, before meeting his worried gaze squarely.

"We did not go to Whitemarsh. We went to Frankford Mill to get flour. We had lunch at a farmhouse nearby and then returned home."

Stanfield sagged back in relief. "Very good. Merry, I have seen Hastings gun down people with no more than a laugh of scorn. I have always considered myself loyal to England, but if Hastings ever harms you, I think I will kill the beast. Promise me you will stay inside this house until he is sent back to Boston. I will do all I can to hasten that day. I must go. We have duty in half an hour. Be very careful, Merry."

She waved him off, her thoughts twisted and knotted inside.

"Is he gone?" Aunt Mina called softly from the kitchen.

"Yes. Did you want to speak to him?"

"Oh no, my dear. We are thankful he is gone."

At Meredeth's look of confusion, Aunt Mina continued, "I mean. . . Oh, Merry, we feared he came to search the house. We practically folded Jim in half to get him into the hidey-hole quickly. I'm sure he'll be pleased to return to his room again. Is something troubling you, Meredeth?"

"I'll tell you all about it later. Let's get Jim out of the hole."

They were all seated around the kitchen table when Merry shared Stanfield's information with the rest. Sober faces stared at each other. Caroline's voice shook. "What if that terrible man comes here with a warrant?"

"There will be no problem," Jim replied. "I am well enough to leave. It is time I reported back to headquarters."

"But, Jim. . . ," Caroline objected.

"There is a little matter of unfinished business I'm determined to see completed. I'll return before I leave Philadelphia. Chin up, my girl."

With a sigh, she followed him from the room and by midnight he had said his farewells.

A few tears traced a path down Caroline's cheeks as she turned to her friends with a crooked smile and said, "Thank you all. It is so good to have friends you can depend upon. I'd better get back to Mother and Aunt Bertha. They have been a bit petulant at my absence."

❧

It was almost a week before Stanfield returned. Hastings was at least under surveillance. Regretfully, Stanfield informed Merry that his troop had been ordered to outside patrol duty for the next few weeks. Merry's heart sank at the thought of more fighting if the spring thaws came early. He did mention one more item of interest.

"Howe may be leaving us. There is talk that he is to be replaced by General Clinton. I can only hope Howe takes Hastings with him."

In the following weeks, the city's residents heard the boom of big cannon toward the northeast. Could there be more trouble at Trenton or Morristown? There was no word from Jim or Stanfield. Merry thought surely she had worn down at least an inch of her room's floor with her pacing. The view from her window changed to faint green as snow melted and tiny signs of spring appeared. How she wished she could go for a long walk! When her papa stopped by to see them one eve, she fairly leaped into his arms.

"Oh, Papa, it is so good to see you! Are you better now? Is Miss Atherton still helping at the hospital?"

"Miss Atherton and her friend could practically run the place by themselves," he said. "They are gems, both of them. How is my favorite girl?"

"Your only girl had better be your favorite, sir. I am perfectly healthy, but driven to distraction cooped up inside all the time. Could I not take a walk with you at least?"

"I'm afraid not today, my dear. I must return promptly. I came back to get an address of a friend in New York. There is a new sort of sickness taking its toll of the men. My colleague may have knowledge of it. Please bring me my small leather book while I speak to Aunt Mina."

"Of course, Papa," she said, hurrying up the stairs. It took only a few minutes to locate the volume.

An uneasy silence greeted her when she pushed open the kitchen door. A bit embarrassed, she glanced from one blank face to another.

"Is something wrong?"

"Why of course not, Merry," Dr. Elliott smiled. "We were just talking and didn't hear you approach. Thank you for finding my book."

There was something almost tangible in the air. Aunt Mina's hands were fluttery, as if she could not think where to put them. Elvira cleared her throat nervously and sat down, almost missing her chair. Nell spun on her heels and became very busy at the stove.

Dr. Elliott shook his head, smiling at the lot of them. "I suppose it's no use trying to keep it from you. We've all been concerned over Hastings's threats. I've spoken to several friends and they agree we must get you out of Philadelphia as soon as possible. Jim Hanks will help, but he has to work out arrangements first."

"But where would I go?" Merry asked in a startled voice.

"I don't have the answers yet. You keep out of sight as much as possible. Perhaps it is best you do not go with Stanfield. He is doing his utmost to bring Hastings to trial. It might be held against both of you if the top men see you together. I'm sorry, my dear."

As he said his farewells at the door, he tilted her face to look into her eyes. "Perhaps your young man from Boston will be back by then. He might be of help. It is rumored Howe is in disgrace and will be replaced by a man named Clinton. That might solve our problem. Washington's new spy system has evidently been a great success. Between all those good men and the Old Fox's keen mind, I believe we can defeat the British."

thirteen

By the middle of March all Philadelphia turned green in the sunshine and the loons could be heard calling from the marshes again. Nell tapped on Merry's door to tell her that Caroline had come to visit. For a few minutes they chatted of nothing and everything with Aunt Mina and Elvira, then Caroline signaled the need to meet in private. Laughing together, the two women were soon ensconced on the Starfire quilt.

With a serious face, Caroline spoke softly. "I can't stay long but I had to tell you. There's rumors that Howe may leave Philadelphia and some think he will take some of the troops with him."

"But where are they to go? I heard Clinton was to replace Howe."

"Jim thinks Howe will be sent to New York, or possibly Boston."

"But why?" Merry could not help asking.

"There's rumors France might attack England while so many British soldiers are over here. They've been enemies ever so long, you know. The main flank of the Brit's army is based in Boston, but there's a large contingent in New York. If they sent back only half of the men at either place, it would be sufficient to defend England fairly well. Of course, Jim doesn't think highly of Clinton, either."

"Maybe Ben Franklin had something to do with it. He said he would get help from the French."

"I don't know, but Jim is excited about it all. Oh yes, he said to tell you he is sending something special he wants you to take care of for him."

"Something special?"

"I have no idea what he means."

"That's strange. The last message said there would be no more letters because it would put me in danger. Caroline, I'm not supposed to leave the house. Besides, Mrs. Wilkins is no longer at City Tavern. How will I get a message to anyone?" A frown crumpled her brow as another thought came. "Jim is with Washington now, isn't he?"

At Caroline's nod, Merry continued, "Why would he need to send a note to me to deliver to Washington?"

Caroline's mouth opened but no sound came out. She shook her head and whispered, "I don't know. It makes no sense to me, either. I've got to go back, but I'll keep you posted."

Merry sat in the window seat, brushing her hair, her mind a maze with no exit. She shuddered at the stark stillness of the city. As she climbed into bed, the rhythm of hoofbeats kept her from blowing out the candle. It was a single horse, trotting. The hooves slowed to a walk, almost inaudible, coming through the alley behind the house. She heard the rasp of the back gate opening and then a thud.

Without another thought, she slipped out the doorway and raced downstairs. She was just in time to see Nell opening the back door.

"Now whatever made that racket?" the cook mumbled. Leaving the door ajar, she went to her room, no doubt to get her cloak.

Some inner force prompted Merry to grab Elvira's cloak from its hook and tug the hood over her hair. She stepped outside, straining to see in the dim light from the lantern. A trembling spread from her head to her toes. The air was chilly. Goose bumps climbed her spine and froze her heart.

Had Jim made that delivery for her? But then why hadn't he come in? She could see no movement. Was it Jim? Could it be some devious trick of Hastings's. . .a lure to get her outside?

"Dear Lord," she prayed, "send Your angels to watch over me. Help me to know what You would have me do."

A black cloak lurched from the gate. Both fists tight against her mouth, Meredeth swallowed the cry lurking deep in her throat. Tenuous, furtive movements sent her back into the arms of the shadows. But it was no use, for the dark shape came toward her in jerky strides. She should run for the kitchen door, but her feet were imprisoned in the grass. Her heart leaped, almost strangling her with its frantic beat.

It looked as if the cloak reached out. Her own whimper acted as a catalyst of release for her. Stumbling, grabbing at the shrubbery, she pivoted and dashed for the kitchen door, but a dull thump from behind stayed her hand on the knob. Her swift glance revealed a humped cloak on the grass. One white hand lay outstretched as if in supplication. Curiosity overcame her fear and, clutching the post, she eased down the steps.

"Miss Merry, what is it? I went to get my cloak," Nell said.

The warm hand on Merry's shoulder stilled the tremors racing through her body. "I. . .I don't know, Nell. Look! Someone fell out there. What shall we do?"

"Wal now, I'd say the canny thing to do is take a peek and see who it is. Don't seem to be moving. Mebbe someone's hurt. Ain't heard of no ghosts 'round here lately."

Kneeling on either side of the cloak, the two women lifted the hood cautiously. Light from the kitchen revealed a small portion of a white face, nose down, in the grass. Long, dark hair partially slipped from a narrow black band at his neck. Merry lifted a lock of hair from his eyes.

A faint cry escaped her as she sat back on her heels and stammered, "M–Matt! It's impossible but he looks like my brother, Matt. How can this be?"

"Wal from the looks of him, we'd better get him inside or he will be dead. Don't see no blood, but he sure looks pasty. Here, you take that end and I'll take this'n."

When they had him safely in the kitchen and the door locked, Nell set about removing the shabby cloak. Merry's eyes grew large as she brushed her fingers over his face. She bit her lip at the haggard look of him, so pale and worn.

"Oh, just look how thin he is!" Merry said.

"Looks near starved, he does," Nell muttered. "His breathin' is a mite ragged, but his pulse is beatin'."

"Nell," Merry's voice was but a wisp of sound, "I think we'd better put him in the hidey-hole before we do anything else."

The cook nodded her agreement and took the emaciated shoulders from Merry's arms. "You take his legs, real careful now."

They maneuvered him down the narrow stairs and placed him on the cellar floor. Straining together, they moved the big rack of shelves away from the wall. The straw pallet Jim had used still lay there. Gently they lowered the young man. Merry loosened his cloak and opened his shirt, while Nell went up for the lantern and some soft cloths.

The light from the lantern only magnified the extent of his injuries. A deep knife slash had been sewn together with little skill; there were bruises beyond counting; a gash on his head still seeped blood, which had been transferred to his hands and chest.

"It's a wonder he still breathes," Meredeth whispered, wiping tears from her eyes with one hand. "I must go get Papa!"

She leaped to her feet but Nell caught her before she reached the steps. With a gentle shake, she admonished the distraught young woman. "You just think this out afore you run off, child. What if a patrol, or worse, that ornery Hastings should find you out on the streets at night? Let's take a good look, wash him down, and see what he needs first. Then I'll send Jeremiah to get your papa."

"You're right, but we must hurry," Merry admitted, kneeling to help ease off his cloak.

Her eyes blazing with fury, Nell held up Matt's wrists. "Lord, help us. Look at that."

"He's been in prison, hasn't he, chained up like an animal? I wonder how long?"

"I'd say it was way too long, Miss Merry. When did you last hear from him?"

"Just before we came to Philadelphia. That was months ago. How could he have escaped, weak as he is?"

"You didn't see no rider?"

"I heard a horse just before the thud. It sounded different though, almost muted. There was another horse several blocks away, too. It was galloping."

"Mebbe like one was trying to be quiet so's the other wouldn't hear him?"

Merry's eyes met Nell's in sudden understanding. "Someone helped him escape but he was followed! That's why he didn't come in. Do you think Jim. . .?"

"I'd just about bet on it, child. You were right to bring your brother down here first thing. I'm goin' up and turn off the other lantern. We can make do with a candle in the kitchen. There's no windows down here, so no one will see. I'll bring some soap and towels and warm up a bit of broth."

"Thank you, Nell. I truly appreciate your help."

"Nuthin' to thank a body for. Does my old heart good to put one over on them Brits, it does."

Carefully Merry turned the limp form on its side, trying to remove the torn shirt. He groaned but showed no sign of regaining consciousness. His body jerked when she pulled the fabric from his back. He muttered something she could not understand.

At that moment, all the hatred she had felt for the English returned in full measure. She feared to touch the red stripes, but they had to be cleaned. Thankfully the cloths were soft.

"Is it not enough that they seem to defeat us in every conflict? Must they also torture the men they hold prisoner? They're sadistic fiends, the lot of them!"

Except for medication, she knew what her father would do. As she cleansed the wounds, a softer expression crossed her face.

"But not Stanfield. He would not do this. And not Red McClanahan," she murmured. "Surely they would not be party to this sort of thing."

fourteen

April 1778

The next day Jeremiah brought Dr. Elliott, whose knowing hands thoroughly examined Matt's battered body. Papa's mouth was a grim line when he sat back on his heels. "Has he been conscious at all?"

"No, Papa. He spoke awhile back but it was delirium. How badly is he hurt?"

"His heart is strong. The pulse is a bit fast. It's a wonder he didn't die of fever. I brought some ointment. You must rub it in carefully, like this."

Dipping his finger into the jar, he touched the abrasions lightly, but generous portions of the ointment soon covered the wounds. "That's the best thing we have available at the moment."

Merry reached to wipe Matt's brow with a cool cloth. She gasped as a hand caught her arm. Matt's glassy eyes riveted on her face.

Dr. Elliott swiftly knelt beside them. "Matt?"

"Becka. You've got to help me. Take this to one of our men. See that it gets to Jim. You understand?"

"Matt, it's all right. You're safe now. Just lie back and rest," Dr. Elliott urged.

Matt's hand clamped so tightly, Merry winced, and the stark vacancy in his eyes terrified her. Dr. Elliott eased his son back to the pallet. Merry and her papa exchanged glances.

"Who is Becka?" Merry asked.

"Evidently someone important to Matt. Here now, Son, it's all taken care of. Just try to sleep. That will help you heal." The doctor gently patted Matt's shoulder as he sagged into unconsciousness again.

"I'll be back as soon as I can. Keep me informed. And, Merry, whatever happens, do not come yourself. They have been closely watching me ever since McClanahan was taken." Dr. Elliott gathered her into his arms for a brief embrace, then retrieved his bag and trudged up the stairs.

Nell brought some warm broth and, between them, they got a small amount down Matt's throat.

Aunt Mina joined them. "Merry, I had a full night's sleep. Let me sit with Matt while you go up and try to rest."

"I wish I could talk to Caroline. Couldn't I have Jeremiah take me—"

"You are not to leave the house, Meredeth. Those are orders from your papa. Now go get some sleep, my dear. You will need it if we are to bring your brother out of this."

"Yes, Aunt Mina. Thank you."

Curled up on the window seat, Merry sat gazing out at the colors of spring adorning the world. The call of a loon off in the distance brought back memories.

"Will, please come back. I'm so frightened for Matt, for Papa, and all of us. It is like being caught in a terrible storm that never ends. I miss you so."

She reached for her Bible and opened it to her favorite bookmark. Her voice was low as she read the words she so often turned to, Hebrews 13:5 and 6.

" '. . .For he hath said, I will never leave thee, nor forsake thee. . . The Lord is my helper, and I will not fear what man shall do unto me.' "

"Even Hastings," she reminded herself. "I do believe, Lord, but it is frightening. Help us to put our trust in You and continue on our life road bravely."

ॐ

Except for Dr. Elliott's visit, no one came calling, not even Caroline. Strange, Merry mused, leaning her head back against the wall. There had been so many visitors before. She rubbed her weary arms. Matt often thrashed about and it was hard to keep him on the pallet during those shows of strength. He was so worried about this Becka, whoever she was. Merry stretched to relieve cramped muscles, then glanced at her brother. Sweat poured from his brow down his gaunt features. When she lifted the coverlet, she found moisture beading on his chest and shoulders. Was he worse or was his fever breaking? She bent to soothe him with cool cloths.

"Matt, can you hear me?" she asked.

His entire body convulsed, then lay limp.

"Matt!" Fear nearly choked her. Swiftly she checked his heartbeat and pulse.

His eyes flickered several times before two blue-green circles stared back at her in shock. "M–Merry?"

"Yes, oh yes, Matt," her voice trembled. She reached to wipe her tears from his arm. His skin was cool!

"What are you doing here?" he asked shakily.

She giggled like a child. "I am trying to take care of you, that's what I'm doing."

His puzzled regard moved from her to the cramped hidey-hole, the wooden shelves protruding beyond, and finally the stairwell.

"Where. . .? Jim! Did we make it to Mrs. Clairmont's then?"

"Yes, though you gave me a fright, falling so dramatically, face down on the grass. Matt, when I got that package, I thought you were dead. By the way, did you send that wild man on horseback to deliver it? He nearly ran Fair Lady and me down!"

Matt managed a wry grin before he replied in a strained attempt at conversation. "I thought I was as good as dead! They had the tavern surrounded. Somehow Becka must have gotten me up the stairs to her room and hidden me. Bless her heart and her quick mind. I lost consciousness. When I awoke, I was in a wagon, trying hard not to black out again. The rickety wheels hit every rut in the road. Then I vaguely recall being on a ship. . .or maybe I dreamed that."

"Probably a prison ship. The Brits have several."

"No, I don't think so. Those two men cared about me. They couldn't have been the enemy. Next thing I knew I was in Boston and some of Washington's men put me in a small cabin and told me to lie low. Someone was to pick me up, but the Redcoats found me and took me to prison. It was a nightmare. I was there for quite a while."

He rubbed a hand over his face. A slow, tentative smile almost changed him into the Matt she knew so well. "Then one night a rock came flying through the window. Somehow Jim Hanks located me. He told me to be ready, he'd come for me the next night. There was a fire in the trash at the back of the building. While all the guards raced to quench that, Jim climbed through the window, released me, and half-carried me out to his horse. What a wild ride that was! He dumped me off and told me to get inside the house quickly. Then he took off immediately. I don't remember anything after that."

"Jim sent word he was bringing me something," Merry informed him. "I was to take care of it for him. I thought he meant another note for Washington. Oh, bless Jim Hanks for bringing you back to us! We didn't know what had happened to you."

"What do you mean you expected a note for Washington?" His startled expression erased the grin from her face.

"I've been delivering messages now and then," Merry said.

Matt reached for her, but his energy faded and he fell back to the pallet, panting. "Merry, you shouldn't be involved in all this! You're a. . .a. . ."

"I'm a woman, just like a good many others," she replied, her chin tilted up.

He sighed. "Yes, I guess you are, but I don't like to think of you in danger."

"Just who is this Becka you keep talking about?"

His grin returned. "Another Patriot, daft as you. I hope you get to meet her someday. You two will get along just fine."

"Probably we will. Which reminds me, I think you and Will should be good friends, also."

"Will who?"

"Will Castleton. He's the man I'm going to marry."

"Hmmm. That name sounds familiar for some reason. Do I know this future brother-in-law?"

"No. He's from Boston. He and his late uncle own a shipping line. Jim Hanks knows him well. Will's in Boston right now. His uncle died and he had to go back. The last time he was here he talked to Papa, then proposed to me."

"Do you love him, Merry?" Matt asked softly.

"Oh, yes, very much."

"Then I'm happy for you."

Nell appeared on the stairs. Her worried frown alerted Merry and Matt to the world around them. "Dela and I'm goin' to have to close this quick. You two stay there and play mum."

The shelves were pushed in place, closing them off. They heard the scrape of barrels heaved across the cellar floor. Then total silence enveloped brother and sister like a funeral shroud. They stared at each other, grasping hands. For what seemed like hours they waited, hardly daring to breathe, while heavy feet pounded on the stairs and doors slammed. Quiet returned almost secretly, a little at a time.

At last a whisper reached them. "Stay hidden awhile. That was Brits and some of them are still in the yard. They're standing there talking."

It was another eternity before barrels and shelving were pulled back. Mrs. Clairmont's pale visage peered at them. "They've gone at last, thank the good Lord."

Later that night, a subdued group gathered around the table in darkness. Dr. Elliott, Jeremiah, Jim Hanks, and Caroline joined them.

"What are we to do? That man is determined to arrest one of us." Dr. Elliott put all their thoughts into words.

"I probably shouldn't be telling this," Jim spoke up, "but we heard the northern campaign is going in our favor.

"One day Burgoyne was on the march when a whole contingent of men appeared, claiming to be Loyalists. They carried German guns just like the Redcoats and had papers of introduction. Burgoyne was overjoyed to get them. He sent them to guard his rear."

Jim chuckled as he continued, "They came to a wooded area and Brits began falling like birds on a fence. About a dozen men waited in the trees ahead. They knocked out the whole center section of the Redcoats, including two officers. When the Brits turned to see what had happened, they looked right into the rifles of Daniel Morgan's men. They were Loyalist, all right. . .loyal to the Patriots. That's only one confrontation. Our men practice a few Indian tactics, and the Redcoats are losing a lot of men up north."

"Is that why Howe is going to Boston?" Elvira asked.

"He was supposed to go to New York. Clinton and Burgoyne were to join him and hold out there. Well, Howe delayed, Burgoyne was near wiped out, and Clinton is still in winter camp. It's been misunderstandings and bungles throughout their army. Also, the Indians they hired have not been paid as promised and they are rebelling."

"Where do you think Howe will go?" Dr. Elliott queried.

"Washington's had some victories in New Jersey. I think Howe will go to New York. That's why Hastings is so set on getting his hands on Merry before he leaves, Doc."

"Is there any way we could get her out of town for a while, to protect her?"

Jim answered slowly, thoughtfully. "If we could get her past the guards to the river, I know a man who has a canoe. He could take her upriver at night. From there I could get her to one of our safe houses, then to New Jersey."

Dr. Elliott's deep voice broke the silence. "I think I can get her past the guards."

Everyone looked to him in surprise.

"I know of a secret tunnel that will take her to the river. Could your man be waiting there in a boat?"

Jim leaned forward in excitement. "That sounds good to me!"

"Merry, you go pack and bring a change for Matt. We can't let Hastings find him, either."

Merry dashed upstairs. The doctor left to see Anders, the brewer. Jim and Caroline went to get a buggy. Elvira hugged Aunt Mina, then sent Nell to pack some food.

Soon, they had Matt in one of Mr. Clairmont's suits. By the time Merry was dressed and a small carpetbag had been packed with a few extra clothes, Dr. Elliott came bustling in. "A boat will be waiting for them at the exit of Anders's tunnel," he said. "The brewer has his hounds on guard as a precaution."

When Jim and Caroline drove up with the buggy, the entire group gathered to wish the refugees well.

Dr. Elliott took a deep breath and smiled. "Before we leave, let's clasp hands and ask the Lord's blessings on those who leave us and those who remain."

He reached for Merry's hand and Matt's. The circle formed, quiet but for the doctor's soothing words.

"Lord God, we must part from these we love for sometime. Thank You for Your promise to be with us. Keep us close in our hearts and thoughts, though we may be far apart. Watch over us, guide us in the right directions, and in ways pleasing to You. Thank You, Lord, for all the love and mercy You pour out on Your people. In the name of Jesus, Amen."

"Dr. Elliott, can you drive?" Jim asked. "I have to set things up on the other side."

"I'd be happy to. Here, Merry, help me boost Matt up." Once his son was settled, Dr. Elliott climbed in and pulled his daughter up to his other side. "If we should be stopped, I stand the best chance for getting us through as far as Anders's place."

Matt and Merry squeezed themselves into the corners, tugging their hats low. The horses took off at a good clip. They passed a troop of soldiers, but a glance at Dr. Elliott produced only a shrug among them.

Anders was waiting with a lit lantern. Swiftly the family hustled through his office and into the tunnel. The door closed behind them and two dogs sat as sentinels when the camouflage was put in place.

It seemed they descended for miles. The lantern at last promised a level path, and soon they trudged upward. Twice they halted to let Matt rest. He leaned heavily on the doctor's arm and Meredeth's shoulder. Finally, they reached a short flight of steps where two more dogs sniffed at their heels. A quiet command from Dr. Elliott sent the hounds pushing out a small door.

They stopped to listen. Water licked the shore; a minute creak of oars and the shush of a beached boat encouraged them. The doctor leaned out far enough to insure they met friend, not foe. Dr. Elliott gave them a last hug, then helped them into the boat. Their bag was tossed in and a hefty push set them afloat.

"Now I know how the parents of baby Moses felt," Dr. Elliott said to himself.

By the time they reached the bend in the river, they saw only Papa's white face at the tunnel exit. The canoe smoothly caught the current and left the city behind them. A short time later, the boatman turned into the bank on the far side of the river and tied up to a huge oak. He shouldered Matt up the bank to a cluster of brush. There was not so much as the glow of a candle. All they heard was the croak of frogs, the gentle murmur of water, and

Matt's labored breathing. That also quieted.

There they huddled for a long time, not daring to speak. Their minds imagined all the things that could have gone wrong. Where was Jim? Did he get out safely?

Merry did not at first catch the small sounds approaching them, but the boatman stiffened to alertness. His keen eyes searched the fields and the river.

Somebody stumbled, falling into them. The old man grabbed the intruder, jerking the body away from the two huddled at the foot of the oak. A long, lanky figure folded into a compact heap nearby. It was Jim!

"Thanks, Haggis. It was impossible to see clearly in all this brush. Come here to me, darlin'."

"Whew! You near scared me out of my boots," the boatman whispered as he lowered the body he held to Jim's lap.

"Caroline! What are you doing here?" Merry gasped.

"At the moment I am sitting in my future husband's lap. Surprise!"

"You're getting married?" was all Merry could think to say.

Jim grinned. "I'm being transferred north to Boston. Didn't want to leave her here with monsters like Hastings around, so I proposed and she accepted and here we are. You two can be chaperones."

"I left a note for Mama," Caroline added. "She plans to stay with Aunt Bertha. They don't really need me, but I figured this fellow needed a wife to take care of him. Will said you two were to settle in Boston and that way we can be close."

"You know I wish you the best," Merry smiled broadly. "I will enjoy having a friend nearby, too."

Haggis rose and stretched. "It looks clear as fer as I kin see. Best we git agoin' afore someone else comes along."

In mute agreement they all squeezed into the boat. Jim helped Haggis paddle and they set out, keeping close to the bank. The only living things abroad seemed to be night animals. On the distant bank, a group of riders cantered by. . .probably a British patrol. They took no notice of the small craft tucked in the shadows.

"Haggis," Jim spoke softly, "start watching for a narrow bit of land reaching out into the river. There'll be a tree hanging over the water."

A grunt from the old man was the only answer, but all eyes focused on the left bank.

Jim saw it first. He tapped Haggis's arm and pointed ahead. Merry realized she was shivering, no doubt as much from fear as the cool air. They were so close to success.

"Now listen, each of you," Jim said. "No talking. Just follow me."

He led them unerringly through woods and meadows, past a group of horses in one narrow valley.

"The Brits must not have been here," Jim remarked. "They've been confiscating every horse they could find."

In the distance, a small tongue of smoke rose from the chimney of a farmhouse. With practiced cunning, Jim led his friends past the fringes of civilization and into deep woods, where they finally stopped to rest.

"I think I recognize that house. Stay out of sight while I check it out."

He came back with a broad grin on his face. "I should earn a medal. Wait 'til you see what I have." With a dashing bow, he laid out a cloth filled with a round of cheese, a loaf of freshly baked bread, and some dried grapes.

Matt managed a crooked grin, but he was almost too exhausted to eat. With exchanged looks, the others agreed it was time to stop and let him recuperate a bit. Merry closed her eyes. Ummm. Never had warm bread and cheese tasted so good. Within minutes she, Matt, and Caroline were fast asleep. Jim kept guard for several hours before waking them.

"We should get farther from town before we hole up for the day. If we travel at night there's less chance we'll be seen."

The food must have given Matt new strength for he managed to walk by himself for several hours. Low, scudding clouds brought a light rain that persisted, and Jim took advantage of the miserable weather to get his small group into the wooded hills. There they found a cave where it was safe to build a fire, and by nightfall all were dry and warm. Jim returned from a hunt with two rabbits hanging from his belt.

"I think each of us should take a blanket, just in case the rain continues. I'll carry Matt's. We can't take a chance on any of us getting sick. There shouldn't be too many folks out tonight. As long as we keep to the brushy areas or thick woods, there's little chance of running into a Brit patrol. Keep close, now. This is rocky ground," Jim warned.

Matt walked closer to his sister. "Tell me more about this man you love so much," he demanded.

"He is an Englishman who came to the colonies a few years ago to help his uncle run a shipping line. We met when he was riding one day and wandered onto our land. He helps Jim Hanks at times and has been very helpful to us in various ways. I love him, Matt, with all my heart."

Matt grinned. His little sister had become a grown woman when he was not looking. Shaking his head, he put an arm around her shoulders.

"I guess a lot of things have happened to both of us. We need time to catch up. I want to tell you about the love of my life, too."

"I'm looking forward to that. This Becka you mentioned several times sounds like a brave woman," Merry replied with a spark in her eyes.

Jim led them through a dense stand of trees, then halted as they came to a fenced meadow. A hound howled in the distance; it was answered by another much closer. Suddenly a low, menacing growl made Merry and Caroline jump. The animal was some forty feet away, its eyes bright, glaring at them. It stalked closer, a deep rumbling in its throat.

fifteen

"Move slowly back to that tree just behind you, ladies. Grab a low branch and climb fast. I'll hold its attention. Go now!" Jim ordered.

Matt urged the women up into the tree, then tried to pull himself up, calling, "Come on, Jim!"

Jim bolted. Caroline and Merry clung together as the dog attacked the base of the tree, snarling and jumping. Jim tugged Matt higher until they were all out of reach.

"That was close," Merry whispered. "What do we do now?"

"Wait for the beast to get tired and go home," Jim muttered.

Caroline looked at him in astonishment. "How long will that be?"

"How do I know? We'll just have to wait. If it can't reach us, it will look for better game."

The dog circled the tree, trying on all sides to leap high enough. When that failed, it sat on its haunches and glared at them.

"He's not going away, Jim," Caroline mumbled.

"Be patient. We can wait it out. Oh no," Jim groaned, "there's another one coming!"

"What are we going to do now?" Merry asked when the second dog trotted up to nuzzle around the tree.

"Wait a minute. Maybe the second beast will talk the other one into going for better game," Jim insisted.

Caroline humphed. "And maybe we can pretend we are birds and fly."

"You've got to learn to trust me, Caroline, or how are we going to make a marriage work?" Jim retorted.

Silence reigned for a few minutes.

"Ha! I've got it!" Jim informed them. "Leave it to the master spy. I'll save you, my beauties, and you, too, Matt. When I say the word, run as fast as you can."

He stood precariously on the limb, holding to the trunk with one arm. His free hand reached for his belt.

"The rabbits." Merry grinned at Caroline, who clutched the tree desperately. "He's right. They're probably hungry."

Jim removed the first animal and dangled it to get the dogs' attention. Then, with all his might, he flung the rabbit away. Howling in unison, the two hounds raced after the enticing smell.

"Now everyone get ready to go!" Jim ordered, sending the second rabbit in a neat arc even farther away.

"Good shot!" Matt exclaimed as he started down the trunk.

"Ladies, it is time to retreat." Jim looked pleased with himself, jumping to the ground and bowing. "Climb down, Caroline. I'm right beneath you."

Merry turned to look at her friend who stared into space, still clinging to the tree as if her life depended upon it. "Caroline, we've got to go before those dogs come back!" But Merry might as well have been talking to the wind. She tugged at the dazed young woman's arm, but it made no difference.

Jim's voice came softly, beguiling, "We must go, Caroline. Come to me, love. You can do it."

"Jimmmm! What if I fall?"

"Then I'll catch you. I've got muscles you haven't seen yet, young lady. Now get down here where you'll be safe. . .with me."

Without a reply Caroline squeezed her eyes shut and slid off the limb. Fortunately, Jim had his arms out to encourage her.

"Umphhh!" he sputtered as they both went down in a heap.

Merry quickly climbed down, shaking her head at their antics. They were both gasping for breath, but Jim laughed in spite of his battered body.

"May I hope you will always obey me as well, my sweet almost-bride."

Merry darted after Matt, who set a surprising pace. When they reached the river, Jim leaned against a tree to get his breath.

"I don't think the beasts followed us. You three stay here while I reconnoiter the area."

Noiselessly, he disappeared. Now that the emergency was over, Matt fell to the ground, bracing himself against a tree. Merry went to offer him a drink from their water bag. Her brother swallowed once, then closed his eyes, snoring slightly. Merry and Caroline kept watch.

"Our luck's in tonight." Jim's confident voice raised their spirits immensely. "There's an old, abandoned shack about a hundred yards from here. Fur traders used it years ago to overnight when they worked their trap lines. It's not much, but it will keep the wind off. We may have more rain soon."

Matt was hoisted to his feet with effort. "I can make it that far. Let's go before my legs turn to mush again."

Their shelter was not very promising. The roof was in bad shape; hopefully it would not leak. One shutter was missing and they would have to cover that window. Jim looped his blanket in one hand and swept out the debris, evidently left by some small animals seeking refuge. An old piece of canvas served to cover the window.

"Now," he said, "if we each wrap up in a blanket, we should keep reasonably warm."

Jim dug into a bag he had brought from the farm the day before. Grinning, he handed each one an apple. "Try not to think of those hounds eating our supper. Give me the water bag. I'll go fill it."

Eagerly, Meredeth and Caroline accepted the fruit. "At the moment, all I long to do is sleep, but this does taste good," Merry said.

Caroline stared at Jim's retreating figure. "Isn't he wonderful? I simply couldn't let him go without me. I do love him so."

"I pray Will is safe. I wonder if he is on his way back by now."

"Maybe Jim knows where he is. Why don't you ask him in the morning?"

Merry nodded, too tired for further conversation. She took a blanket and wrapped it snugly around Matt, who had fallen asleep with the uneaten apple in his hand. Merry slipped the fruit into his pocket, then reached for her own coverlet. She and Caroline snuggled together for warmth.

A storm roared across the land; startling cracks of thunder and lightning, like evil fingers, grasped at the trees.

Merry sat straight up, breathing hard. Matt lifted his head groggily, his face a twisted mask of pain. "Becka?" he whispered, reaching out.

"Matt, you're here with Jim, Caroline, and me."

"Oh, yes. I remember. I'm worried sick about her, Merry. Jim has heard nothing of her since that night. None of the men have seen her. She could be dead for helping me! If anything happened to her. . .Merry, I love that girl."

"I feel the same way about Will. He should have been back weeks ago. But we can't help them now. We have to trust the Lord to watch over them, Matt."

Tears came then in a flood and Matt gathered her into his arms. "Sis, are you sure Will's working for the Patriots? He is British, after all."

"He came from England, but so did our family, Matt. He is one of us. I truly believe that," Merry insisted.

"He loves you, Merry. He'll be back," Caroline spoke softly from the darkness.

The storm moved on and, in the sudden quiet of the cabin, they all slept again. Dawn brought a heartening promise when Jim strode in the door, his face beaming in triumph. He held up a string of fish that made them all forget their problems for a time. In a sheltered crevice of rock, they built a fire and hung their breakfast on sharpened sticks over it. Nothing had ever tasted quite as good!

When they were done eating and everything was packed, Jim urged them to hurry. "I've seen no British patrols this far east, but we must keep a sharp lookout. The safe house is only a few hours away."

There was plenty of cover. Evergreens grew thickly around them until they reached a summit overlooking a deep valley. There they rested, sharing the last of the water.

"Do you truly think the Brits might retreat?" Caroline asked.

"I wouldn't say retreat, exactly. If Washington has many more victories, the Brits won't be able to hold the land they have taken. I think they will give up Philadelphia and concentrate on holding Boston and New York. The harbors there are the best mooring, safe from storms."

"How about Baltimore?" Merry wondered.

"That would be too far from the rest of their troops," Matt broke in. "Their supply lines would be stretched to the breaking point."

"One thing's sure." Jim frowned as he spoke. "If they move, they could have reconnaissance patrols anywhere from here to Boston. Keep on the alert."

With that warning, Jim urged them to a faster pace. About noon he herded them into a copse of trees and slipped out to scout again. Matt, his energy drained, promptly fell asleep. Merry and Caroline filled the water bags from a nearby stream, then crouched where they had a good view of the surrounding area. Both leaped to their feet when Jim silently came up behind them.

"The conquering hero returns with food for all!" he declared, holding up a good-sized turkey.

"But we heard no shot fired," Caroline exclaimed.

"A gun firing could be heard a long way in these hills. Didn't I tell you? Washington says I can throw a knife better than any in his army. Not that I wish to brag, but. . ." Jim grinned, tying the bird to his pack.

"Oh, of course not." Caroline gave him a big smile.

"How does the Old Fox manage while you are off seeing us to safety?" Matt chuckled.

"He's got Craig and Clark. Those two can run rings around me and never miss a breath. I'm acting confident to hide the feeling someone is following us. Can't explain it. It's only a strange sense of presence. Keep as quiet as possible."

They kept to the woods until a rocky bluff confronted them. Jim signaled them to follow and started up a zigzag animal track. By the time they all reached the top, they were all stumbling on uneven ground. Often, Jim stopped to listen. At last he shinnied up a tree for a better look.

When he leaped to the ground, a satisfied smile filled his face. "We're almost there. Follow me. Matt, if you need a shoulder to lean on, just say so."

A short trek through woods brought them to a small cabin. Its crudely hewn logs sagged in places, but someone had filled the cracks. It looked sturdy enough. Digging a slim metal rod from his pocket, Jim inserted it between the planks of the door; a quick twist of his wrist brought the heavy door swinging outward. His eyes searched the woods carefully as he urged them into the surprisingly clean interior.

A dilapidated table with four ancient chairs took up half the space. One wall offered four bunks complete with blankets. Two more pallets were arranged in one corner near the tiny hearth.

"It shouldn't get too cold tonight. We'd better forego a fire and use blankets. That way no one will notice smoke. Water's in the well just outside the door. I am going to get Nathan. He'll be your guard while I make a thorough search of these woods. Matt, you keep this gun."

"Thanks. The Brits took mine."

"We can keep watch," Caroline offered. "Matt, why don't you lie down for a while. This trek has been hard on you."

The women discovered several knotholes in the shutters, through which they had a fair view of the immediate area.

"Listen to all the birds up here," Merry whispered. "It's almost like being at Cresswick Acres. I wonder. . .will we ever see our homes again?"

"It seems we've been trudging these hills forever. When Jim and I get married, I think I'll talk him into a home in a valley."

They enjoyed the pleasant sounds of the small wildlife, and to pass the time, they called to memory a great deal of their school days. When they were tired of standing, they pulled the chairs close to the window.

It seemed to be hours before they noticed anything other than the local animal life. A sudden silence dominated the space they watched. Both focused eyes and ears as tension tightened.

"Caroline, what's that?"

"I saw it, too. What shall we do?"

"I'd better wake Matt," Merry muttered as she shook his shoulder.

Matt raised himself to one elbow. "Wha—"

"Someone's coming," she spoke in his ear.

In one heave, Matt was on his feet and went to the window. A low, crouching figure sped toward the cabin, using the screen of shrubs to hide. Matt drew the gun Jim left with him and he steadied his hand.

sixteen

"It's Jim. He's back." Matt sagged in relief. Caroline went to open the door.

"Who said there wasn't a rainbow at the end of a storm?" Jim grinned as he dumped cheese, bread, carrots, and apples on the table, then reached to hug Caroline. "And here are some cinnamon rolls and honey cakes. A feast!"

After taking one look at Matt, Jim made a decision. "Matt's wound has opened again. I'd better get him to the hospital tent. It's only about a day's ride north. I brought two mounts for us, my friend. You've been looking green around the gills too long."

"Can't we come with you?" Caroline pleaded.

"That's no place for you, ladies. I'll be back in two days and take you two east to Washington's camp. You'll be a lot safer there. I filled the water bucket as I came in. It's by the door. Caroline, Merry, let me show you something just in case of emergency."

He led them to the table and lifted the worn rag rug. "Watch how I do this now. See this knothole? You lift it this way."

Though uneven ends of wood did not betray a trap door, the planks opened to reveal a ladder. Jim held his lantern to show them a small dugout beneath.

"If anyone else comes, you open this without moving the table. When it's almost closed, pull the rug back to the trap door. This has served us well, even from Indians. It should fool the Brits. You two be as quiet as you can and keep a sharp ear for any noises. I brought Nathan back with me. He's posted right out there where the woods begin. You know I wouldn't leave you with anyone I didn't trust completely."

With a swift hug for Caroline, he hurried Matt out. Merry and Caroline watched through the knotholes until evening shadows devoured the men.

❧

By afternoon the next day, both Meredeth and Caroline were shivering, either from the cold or apprehension. They huddled together at the table, listening to the raging storm outside.

"I think I know every chink in that wall for memory," Merry said, finally breaking the silence. "Tell me more of the plans you and Jim have made."

Caroline happily covered that topic. They dreamed out loud of things they could do together in Boston. Each mentally planned her wedding, while the rain slashed at the cabin and the crashing thunder tore at the fragile threads of their inner anxiety. Both were pacing the floor when they heard the first shots.

Terrified at the realization of their worst fears, Merry and Caroline slipped under the trap door. There was more gunfire. Angry shouts and the pounding of horses' hooves turned their stomachs inside out. Merry tugged the rug back over the trap door, then closed it firmly. She noticed an iron rod hanging to one side. Carefully she threaded it through two straps on the facing board as further precaution. The women clung together for warmth and support. Both jumped when the cabin door slammed back with wooden thunder. Boots stomped front to back; a window smashed, sending a shower of glass to the floor. The footsteps halted.

"They've been here. Look at this food. Why would they leave it?"

"Someone used this pallet. It's rumpled."

"The water bucket's near full. Could anyone live here?"

"Look around you. There's no wood for the hearth. No cooking pots or clothing. Could it be a camping place for hunters?"

"I tell you she was here. A scout saw four of them climb the bluff. He said she was with them."

Meredeth bit her lip to restrain her gasp. She knew well the man who answered. Caroline looked to her in query, but she received only a shake of her friend's head and an admonishing finger over her lips.

Some of the men tramped out, but two remained, arguing loudly. "But they might come back here! Why can't I set a torch to it?"

"Hear me and hear me well! I make the rules for this force! We go after them now! They couldn't have gotten far. I want those women, do you understand? If we don't find them, we can check this place out for more clues. Besides, think what a beautiful sight it will be, burning at night atop this bluff. All the Rebels within miles will see what we do to traitors! When I say we are finished with this shack, then you can put it to the torch. Now mount up! After them!"

At the sounds of hoofbeats retreating, both women closed their eyes and breathed deeply. Their bodies still shivered; cold hands were stiff from holding each other so tightly. They remained motionless until the birds again began their chirping. Only then did relaxation come completely.

"We've got to get out of here, but let's go slowly. That was Hastings. I trust him no farther than I can throw his horse," Merry advised.

She eased the rod loose, then lifted the trap door an inch at a time. There was no sign of Hastings's men. Cautiously, they climbed up into what was left of the cabin. The door hung sideways from one leather hinge. Glass was everywhere. Shutters were torn off and pallets lay in a heap. Still crouching low, they peeked out a window. They could see no one, but they knew there was no safety here for them.

"Nathan, where are you?" Caroline said softly, her face frozen in a white mask.

A glance outside provided the grisly answer. Nathan lay face down; his body, riddled with wounds, was still.

In a panic of fear, Merry and Caroline raced through woods and small clearings with no thought of destination. They had to get away from Hastings and the cabin that was no longer safe. Only when they reached a well-beaten track did the enormity of their plight stop their frantic haste. Dropping to the ground under a stand of thick pines, they assessed the options while they caught their breath.

"We must try to reach Washington," Caroline insisted. "I have only a vague idea of his location, but we can't stay here."

"Do you think we can find the way by ourselves?" Merry asked.

"We have to, Merry. We're on our own now. Jim won't know where to find us."

Merry lowered her gaze, painfully opening fingers nearly frozen in their grip on a small knife she had grabbed up as they made for the underground hole. "I have this," she said.

"One small knife between us and that brute of a man."

"Caroline, when we began this journey, Matt and I turned our lives over to God. He's the only one Who can get us out of this predicament now. Will you pray with me. . .ask for His help?"

"I've gone to church all my life, Merry, but do you honestly think the Almighty Lord is going to take an interest in two lost women? He has much larger problems on His mind."

"Caroline, when Abram went into a strange country because God sent him there, when David was being hunted down by Saul's army, or when Elijah thought he was the only believer left in his world, did God take a vacation or a nap and refuse to help them? God promised He'd be with them and He kept that promise."

"You truly believe He will bother Himself about us, don't you?"

"Yes, Caroline, I do. Will you pray with me?"

"Well, it certainly can't do any harm."

Eyes bright, Merry clasped Caroline's hands. Bowing her head, she spoke with new energy, as if God had already picked her up in His arms.

"Dear Father in heaven, please hear our prayer and come to our rescue.

Hastings is a powerful man and has many others to help him, but You are far more powerful than any man. You can call hosts of angels to help us. Oh, my Lord, we need Your help desperately. Please look down on us with Your love and mercy. Show us the way to go and please watch over Matt and Jim and keep them safe, too, Lord. We ask it in the name of Jesus, Your beloved Son and our beloved Savior. Amen."

Their eyes met and hope blazed there. Carefully they searched the trees around them and the visible length of the road. There was no sound, no movement; it was as if they were the only two people in this part of the world.

They rose and set out with blade-sharp awareness, moving carefully through the trees. Stealth was the only weapon they had other than the thin knife clutched in Meredeth's hand. She nodded encouragement when Caroline stooped to dislodge a sharp-edged rock from the soil. As their confidence grew, they ran, in the easy lope of an Indian, toward the northeast and Washington.

A minute vibration under her feet slammed Merry to a stop and, without a word, she dragged Caroline into the brush beside the track they followed. Horses pounded closer and they were almost past the bushes where the women hid.

The last rider, though, cantered by with easy grace, and Meredeth gasped at the sight of that well-known profile. She stood and called out in a wavery voice, "Stanfield!"

Caroline jerked her friend to the ground, but not before that last Redcoat slowed and turned.

In a scattering of turf, the first three horsemen pulled up with questioning looks, but Stanfield pointed in another direction and shouted to them, "I thought I saw a deer. We could use some venison for supper. Go on. I'll check it out."

Grinning their approval, the others wheeled their mounts and were soon out of sight. Stanfield waited until he was sure they were gone before he maneuvered his horse into the woods.

"Who called me?" he asked the bushes.

"No, Merry, we don't dare!" Caroline whispered.

But that anxious whisper coaxed Stanfield nearer.

Merry stood, dragging a reluctant Caroline with her. "Stanfield. Help us, please."

His startled exclamation was barely voiced before he was out of the saddle. "Meredeth, what are you doing so far from Philadelphia?"

"Hastings was determined to prove me a spy. We had to leave town, but he had us followed. He almost caught us in a cabin back there."

"So that's why he sent our troop on duty up here in the woods! He was trying to get us out of his way," Stanfield muttered.

"We stayed overnight in a cabin," Merry told him. "There was a man guarding us. They killed him. Hastings's men came storming into the cabin and. . .and. . ." Merry's speech broke into sobs.

Stanfield reached for Merry. Caroline's eyes opened wide, though she said not a word.

"And we were but a mile away!" he exclaimed. "Hush, now. It will be all right. I'll see you to Patriot territory. I know an old woman there. She'll keep you safe until you can notify your family. It's not far. I can still make it back to our camp tonight."

"Will that make trouble for you. . .coming back so late?" Meredeth inquired.

"I'll simply tell them my horse cast a shoe and I had to go to a blacksmith. You and Caroline can ride Thunder. I'll walk alongside. Now, up you go."

As they rode, Merry closed her eyes and thanked the Lord for sending Stanfield. It was far too dangerous on their own. Even if they did not fall into Hastings's hands, other soldiers could cross their trail. Stray women were often molested. She was sure Stanfield was trustworthy.

"I'll keep a sharp lookout, but please stay alert yourselves. Tell me if you see anything out of place or moving," he cautioned.

Darkness closed them in its fist. Every small animal came alive, adding its own rustling to the chorus of strange noises. When they found a stream tumbling over a rocky bed, Stanfield halted and helped them down. Wearily they fell to their knees to drink the chilly water. For a few minutes they sat on the mossy bank, until the quickening wind gave the air a frosty bite.

"Be very quiet," he warned. "I'm going to take a look around."

In an instant, he disappeared. Caroline reached for Merry's hand and held it fast. Faintly, a drunken voice stumbled over the words of a lusty tavern song, making Merry wonder if there were more soldiers camped in these woods.

Stanfield returned on the run, scooped Merry up on Thunder, then reached for her friend. "We must circle an encampment," he whispered, moving them off to the left.

Clouds raced from east to west and fog swirled in uncertain circles around them; they could see only a hand's-breadth away. Tensely they put all their senses to work. Recent rains had left the forest floor wet, deadening the sound of hooves. Their breathing seemed loud in their ears. When

Stanfield's horse stumbled, he muttered under his breath and swiftly covered the animal's muzzle with his hands. Then he ran a practiced hand over his mount's foreleg. "It's not a serious injury. Lean close to Thunder. We'll move on slowly," he reported.

There was no change in the sounds from the soldiers and hope fluttered exultantly in Merry's heart. They were going to make it! Ahead of them the woods became sparse. For a fleeting second the moon knifed through the clouds; a silver sliver of light revealed an open meadow and, at the edge of that, a stream danced over jutting rocks.

Meredeth turned to Caroline. "It's beautiful, isn't it?" she whispered.

"Hold!" The major's quiet command hit them like a cold wind.

seventeen

From the meadow, a single rider sped toward Meredeth, Caroline, and Stanfield. There was little cover in which they could hide. He was upon them in seconds.

"Ho, there!" the rider said. "Speak up or you are dead men!"

Stanfield moved a bit forward. "Major Stanfield, Scout and Search Troop. What are you doing in these parts, Hastings?"

"Humph! I go where duty calls. Why are you afoot? Did your mount cast a shoe?"

Merry ducked low over the saddle, bringing Caroline down with her.

Hastings must have caught the movement for he came closer, peering intently at the humped shadow. "By the devil's own luck, you've found some women in this dreary place. How fortunate for you."

"They are but children who are lost. I'm taking them home, just north of here. I know their papa," Stanfield tersely replied.

Hastings's horse sidled close enough to brush Merry's leg and Stanfield jerked his horse away so hard that Thunder bucked at the harsh treatment.

But it was not fast enough and, swift as a rattler, Hastings's hand reached to pull back the hood of Merry's cloak. His breath hissed in triumph. "This is, indeed, a fortunate meeting," he snarled.

Both men drew weapons simultaneously.

"You coward!" Stanfield said with a slap on Thunder's hindquarters. "You would harm your own brother if he got in your way. You will not take these women!" The horse raced away into the trees.

A mocking laugh erupted from Hastings as he dug his spurs in savagely and he charged after Thunder.

Just before Thunder passed Stanfield, Stanfield leaped aside. He leveled his gun and, when Hastings turned to charge again, a bullet cracked Hastings's crazed laughter midway.

With a choke of dismay, Hastings clutched at the reins to retain his seat. His mount slowed as the rider collapsed in his saddle. Seconds later, Hastings tumbled to the ground like a broken puppet. His mount galloped off.

Stanfield saw the riderless horse and set out to check on Hastings, but the dark fog hid him. Swerving in the direction that Thunder had taken,

Stanfield charged after the women when a lone shot echoed behind him. He spun, arching in pain, and fell heavily to the rocky trail.

"Oh, God! Get them away from here to safety," Stanfield pleaded as blackness invaded his sight and mind.

It took Merry some time to slow and quiet Thunder. The first gunshot had shrieked through the air behind them, but fear and anger spurred her back the way they had just come. Deadly stillness iced the night as a second report split her anxiety into a dozen haunting thoughts.

"No!" her scream tore the night apart.

"Don't go back," Caroline whimpered. "We daren't go back."

Thunder leaped across the stream. Merry was sure it was the same place but the happy skip of the water had dimmed. An eye-blinking wind rushed at them as if to push them away. Incoherently, Her mind asked only one thing: *Have I led Stanfield to his death?*

Meredeth tossed the reins to Caroline and slid to the ground. Panting, she strained for signs of either man, but there was no body in sight. She glared at the clouds. Why couldn't the moon shine now? One hand jerked the hair from her eyes as she struggled through the brush. When several circles had been completed to no avail, she braced herself against a tree, her chest heaving. She must think this out. Where had they gone?

"Merry, come back. We'll never find him in this darkness." Caroline's plea went unnoticed.

This was about where she had last seen them, Merry decided. Who shot first? She would bet it was not Stanfield. He must have been wounded. The other shot had come fast upon the first. Hastings's horse was gone. Did that mean he had left or had dismounted or fallen? Stanfield had not followed them, so he had to be somewhere nearby. She hastened again through the trees. He could not have gone far if he was wounded.

A root caught her foot, throwing her to the ground, and she reached out a hand to minimize the fall. There. . .there was another hand! A gun lay beside it! Heart hammering, she explored the arm, the shoulder, the still-warm liquid pooled on a broad back. Blood? Her fingers found the face, the tousled hair.

"Stanfield? No! Dear Lord, don't let him be dead!"

Drawing a deep breath, she forced herself to do what must be done. With shaking fingers, she tore a strip from her petticoat and wadded it over the wound.

Another body fell to the ground beside her. "Is it Stanfield?" Caroline asked.

"Yes," she bit the word out, filled with helpless fury.

"Where is Hastings?" Caroline persisted.

"I don't know."

Caroline moved away, but Meredeth had no thought for anything but stopping the flow of blood. Hurrying to the stream, she soaked another portion of her undergarment and cleaned the wound as best she could. A memory gave her sudden hope as she reached into the pocket of her underskirt.

Thank the Lord. The tin of salve she had brought for Matt's back was still there. She dabbed the salve liberally on Stanfield's back, then wrapped the wound with another strip of cloth.

In the dim light of dawn's promise, there was no evidence of other injuries. His pulse was ragged, but it would do. She brushed a lock of hair from his forehead. Only then did she become aware of sounds behind her.

"Caroline?" she whispered.

"Stanfield, a traitor? I may not make it back to my men, but you'll not leave here alive, either, Rebel!"

Merry jerked around.

Hastings clung to a tree not ten feet away, a useless leg dangling behind him. His coat, hands, and face were smeared with blood. He propped himself against the tree and took deliberate aim, a satisfied sneer cutting across his face.

Merry closed her eyes. A shot broke through the fog. Then a thin shred of a scream echoed from rock to rock as she collapsed in a heap.

The crash of bodies through the brush claimed Meredeth's wavering thoughts. She opened her eyes wide just as arms caught her up, crushing her to a broad, wool-cloaked chest.

"Thank God we were in time!" Will's voice soothed her. "Jim and I heard you scream. Then we saw Caroline stumbling toward the track. My heart almost died inside me when I saw that gun pointed at you. Oh, Merry! I've never prayed so hard in my life."

Suddenly aware of her attempt to change position, Will held her a few inches from him. "Did that miserable excuse for a man hurt you?"

In response to his intense question, she giggled almost hysterically. "No, he. . .I'm. . .please keep holding me. But it's just that I need to breathe and your heavy cloak was not allowing much air to get through. I thought I would never see you again. Hold me tight, Will, so I know I'm not dreaming."

With infinitely gentle hands, Will lifted her face to his and she felt the tremor that shook him. In wonder, she raised her arms to bring him closer and his mouth claimed hers. Vaguely, they were aware of Jim and Caroline behind them, but the near-tragedy made that moment too precious to share with anyone else.

"My dear heart, we must get away from here. There may be other Brits in these woods."

Will kept a strong arm around her but started off toward his mount. Merry's sharp "No!" halted them.

"Stanfield!" Merry said. "We've got to get help for him. He tried to protect us and he's badly hurt. Will, we can't leave him here to die!"

"Stanfield? You mean the British officer who took you to that ball?"

"Yes." Meredeth's eyes filled with tears.

"Merry, do you. . .I mean, is he. . .?"

Will set her on her feet. One big hand plowed a path through his hair as he struggled to gain control of himself. When he looked at her again, his bleak expression sent her flying to him.

"He is a friend, Will, only a friend, but I cannot leave him here to die. I cannot."

Eyes closed tightly, he threw back his head and took a deep breath. His voice was low, strained. "He's a Brit, Merry."

"That Brit was almost killed helping us," Merry said.

With a sigh, Will drew her close, tucking her head into his shoulder. His rueful chuckle relaxed her taut muscles.

"All right, my dear. I have you back safely, thanks to him. I shouldn't quibble, even if he is the enemy."

She reached a hand to his cheek. Her words were barely audible. "I do love you, Will."

He heard and lifted her in his arms to hug her properly. After checking Hastings to be sure he was dead, the four of them found Stanfield unconscious, but the bleeding had stopped. Will mounted his horse and Jim carefully hoisted the Englishman up to Will's arms. The women rode Jim's horse while he walked alongside. Swiftly they left the forest and turned in at a small village nearby.

Right at the edge of the buildings, they stopped at a big red barn where a plump, older woman sat on a three-legged stool, milking a cow. At the sight of her visitors, her mouth formed a large O. She leaped up, smiling as Jim approached.

"Aggie, can the ladies stay here while we take this Brit to a place where his men will find him? He did us a favor."

If the good woman had questions, she did not ask. Nodding happily, she ushered Merry and Caroline into her home. With a wave, Will and Jim rode back into the woods. By the time the women had washed and eaten a bowl of oatmeal, the men were back.

"His troop was out looking for him. We found their camp and left him there. Is that your cinnamon oatmeal I smell, Aggie? Could you spare a bowlful for two hungry Patriots?" Jim flashed her his best smile.

An hour later they left, with Merry and Caroline riding behind the men. Jim called back, "I'll bring you some catfish to feast on, Aggie. You're an angel in disguise."

"Oh, go on with you," she flustered when he threw her a kiss.

By midday they reached the Delaware River, twenty miles above Fort Mercer. There, they ferried over to the New Jersey side and, within another two hours, they rode into Washington's camp.

While Jim and Will reported to the general, one of his men escorted Meredeth and Caroline to Kate Stillwell's home, where an unexpected surprise awaited in the parlor.

"Papa and Aunt Mina! What are you doing here?" Merry asked.

"You can't imagine how worried we've been. Mina and I left Philadelphia shortly after the British did. We feared Hastings had found you. Oh, the good Lord be thanked!"

"We had a few delays. The British left Philadelphia, then?"

"Yes, every one of them, including some of the Tories, pulled out the evening of June eighteenth. Rumor has it that Ben Franklin made an alliance with France and he will return soon. According to Major Clark, the English fear an attack by the French. Many of the British troops are going back home. We don't know if Hastings went with them or not."

Meredeth lowered her eyes, her lip trembling. "Hastings is dead, Papa. When he tried to kill me, Stanfield shot him. Then Hastings shot Stanfield. Just as Hastings pointed his gun at me, Will and Jim came along. They killed him, then took Stanfield back to his camp. I think he will be all right. Stanfield tried to save us Papa. He is a good man."

"I will make inquiries to be sure. I think highly of him, too," Dr. Elliott responded.

"Merry! Look who I found wandering around as if he were lost." Will grinned and stepped aside to reveal the big man behind him.

"Red McClanahan! I can't believe it's truly you. We were so worried when they took you from the hospital. How did you come here?"

"It pleases me to see you, lassie. The British left me fevered in a prison tent when Clinton took his men back to Boston. If Will hadna' come looking for me, I'd be in me grave. He brought me here. You know, 'tis a Rebel, I think, this Scot's becomin'. Mayhap I'll bring me family over."

"It's good to see all of you again. Did Dela and Anna come, too?" Merry asked Aunt Mina.

"Well, of course. I could hardly manage without them, although we could bring very little with us. I'll be happy to get back to our normal life again. Such a hurly-burly time we have had, to be sure."

The call for dinner brought them all together around an extended table. Probably Aunt Mina was the only one who could tell afterward what delicious foods were provided. Everyone else was much too busy enjoying the company.

"Miss Merry, would you like a piece of the cake Ma baked?" a voice asked.

Merry turned a startled face to the little serving wench behind her. "Jesse! You're safely away from the Brits! I feared they had arrested your ma."

"Jim heard Mrs. Stillwell was looking for a cook and he brought us up here. I get to serve sometimes. I'm so glad you got away from that wicked Hastings man."

"He won't hurt anyone now. I'll see your ma a bit later."

Beaming her delight, the child marched back to the kitchen.

When the meal was completed, Will invited Merry out to walk in the garden. Moonlight wrapped it in glowing silver and ebony; a wooden bench beckoned under a latticed rose arbor. When Meredeth was seated, Will knelt beside her.

"I must ask your forgiveness, love," he said.

"Whatever for? For rescuing me?" she asked.

"Of course not that. You see, when I was here before, I mentioned my hopes of marriage and taking you back to Boston with me."

"I shall happily go with you wherever you wish."

"I'm glad, but that's not the problem. Mrs. Stillwell is a dear person, but sometimes she takes things into her own hands and. . ."

Merry's eyes danced as she replied, "What has she done, Will?"

"She's planned our wedding for us. It's to be tomorrow. She has the preacher and all the guests coming."

"Tomorrow?" Meredeth stiffened, a look of horror on her face. "I don't have a gown or any clothes other than these. We haven't had the banns read. How can we be married so quickly?"

Will ducked his head. "You two are much the same size. She wants you to wear her wedding gown and her seamstress is making your traveling clothes and a few other dresses. She said that would do until we reach Boston, where you can have more made."

Merry stared back, glassy eyed. "Tomorrow. What about the banns?"

With a quirky grin he said, "The preacher said it could be overlooked this time in view of the fact that I have to be in Boston in five days to receive my inheritance. Everyone wants us to marry here so they can all attend. Do you mind a terrible lot, my dear?"

She looked lovingly at that worried face. With one hand she lifted the errant lock of hair, fallen to his forehead, as usual.

"Don't fret yourself. I know few people in Boston. It is better that we marry here."

"Then you will? Wonderful! I want to make you mine as soon as possible, and Mrs. Stillwell has worked so hard to make everything work out well. Tomorrow eve. Oh, love, you are all I ever dreamed of in a wife."

He smiled into her moon-starred eyes and ran fingers over her silvered hair before cupping her face and lifting it for his kiss.

"I love you so much, Meredeth Elliott."

"And I love you just as much, Will Castleton."

"I was so frantic with worry over you being subjected to Hastings's wrath. A British patrol gave us trouble at the Maryland docks. It took far too much time to get loaded again."

"Knowing God was with us and thinking of you were the things that gave me strength when Caroline and I had to strike out on our own," Merry murmured into his collar.

Words got in the way. There was a healing hush while they clung tightly to each other. The Stillwell garden quietly folded its trellised enclosure and stole away, leaving only the entwined shadow defined by moonlight.

eighteen

A bit dazed, Merry looked into the mirror the next eve. Her gown was lovely, tiered lace starred with pearls and crystal baguettes. A creamy white veil was poised to lift down over her face. Papa brought her an armful of flowers with one perfect rosebud tied in the center by silk ribands.

"Papa, it is beautiful. Thank you."

"The rose is from Will. He picked it from Stillwell's garden. Merry, we've had word from Matt. He is much better and should be able to visit us soon. He said to wish you happiness."

Vaguely they became aware of music from below. They descended into a flower-laden foyer and then into the parlor. Merry saw nothing but Will's adoring smile and the strong, steady hand he held out to her. The harpsichord ceased its wondrous melody and they turned to the preacher.

Will's big hand shook as he placed the ring, an oval sapphire, edged with pearls, on her finger. The words were spoken at last, making them one. She smiled up at him, her eyes sparkling with happiness. So intent were they on each other, a small ripple of laughter crossed the room.

The preacher said, for the second time, "You may kiss your wife, young man."

A faint pink shaded his face as he gently drew her into his arms and did just that.

They were quickly surrounded by well-wishers, all gaily talking at once. Much later, after small cakes and a bowl of punch satisfied the guests' appetites, Merry and Will slipped away upstairs to a bedroom prepared for them.

"You are so beautiful," he spoke softly, his fingers playing in her hair, then cupping her face for a long kiss.

"Forgive me, but I much prefer your hair down. I love what the candlelight does to it." Before he finished speaking, his nimble fingers had loosened all the combs, letting the waving strands fall in a copper-sparked curtain to her waist.

"That's much better. Before I forget completely, Mrs. Clairmont sent you a gift. She said you could carry on now that she has finally admitted she is an older lady. . .not old she insisted, just older."

Will reached into his trunk and pulled out some folded material. Striding to the hearth, he spread out the Starfire quilt onto a woolen rug. Smiling, Merry helped him smooth out the pattern.

"She couldn't have given me a better gift," she said.

"You are the only gift I want," he murmured, pulling her closer. "You are dearer to me than life itself. I can't wait to show you our new home. Uncle Reggie left us his house and also a small retreat by the ocean. By the way, after we send the British back to their island, Jim has agreed to work for me. He's good with figures and I don't plan to spend all of my time at the shipyards. There is an uninhabited small home a few blocks from ours. It will do them nicely until they can afford better. That way you and Caroline will be close."

"Will we ride to Boston?"

"I've hired a carriage. Jim and Caroline can travel with us. There's a lot of beautiful country on the way. I wish I could take you home on one of our ships, but that is not possible at this time. We'll do that later."

"So many perplexing things have happened. I've longed to ask you, but when you put your arms around me, I can't think."

"Questions, hummm? I hope they are about how gloriously happy I am to hold you close again."

"In truth they are much more mundane. How did you know Matt?"

"I suppose a lady's curiosity must be appeased," Will sighed but refused to relinquish his hold on her. "Clark brought him to me. I heard that a pretty redhead had delivered him in a bloody cloak. She begged Clark to get him to safety. He knew I was moored there in the harbor, waiting for a message. You should have seen him carrying Matt up the gangplank with the fussy old doctor running to keep up with them! Matt wavered in and out of consciousness. After about a week, Clark and his men carried him off in a barrel to get him by the Brits who were coming to check out my cargo."

"Matt wasn't sure if he had been on a ship or if he dreamt it. Do you know how they delivered the notes I sent on to Jim Hanks?" she asked.

"Oh, that was one of Jim's cousins. That whole family is involved in Washington's spy system. The boy was just fourteen, but he wanted to help. He was sorry he almost ran you down that day. He feared the Brits had seen him, so he set the horse at too fast a pace, then had difficulty controlling it. When I heard how they were using you to get messages through, I'm afraid I lost my temper. They promised they would not make you a go-between anymore."

Merry's mouth opened again, "Do you think the war will—"

Chuckling, Will promptly covered her lips with his own. When she gasped for breath, he nibbled at her ears and softly murmured, "Enough, wife, we have more important things to do. God alone knows when this war will end. He brought us together and gifted us with each other's love. We can trust our futures to Him."

Will caught her to him and in one fluid movement lowered them to the quilt. Merry soon stopped thinking altogether and simply relished the wonder of their new life in the marriage covenant. That seemed to please Will immensely.

And God smiled.

Journey Toward Home

Carol Cox

CAROL COX wants to give her readers a message of hope based on the unchanging truth of God's love. Carol is a native of Arizona whose time is devoted to being a pastor's wife, homeschool mom, church pianist, and youth worker.

one

It was unseasonably warm, and a muggy stillness hung over St. Joseph. I sat in the big wicker rocking chair on Aunt Phoebe's front porch and fanned myself. Aunt Phoebe sat facing me, bolt upright in her chair. Her iron-gray hair, pulled into its customary bun, was drawn so tight that I wondered for the thousandth time how she was able even to blink. She pursed her thin lips in disapproval.

"You're a foolish, ungrateful child, Judith. How you can disregard the kindness and generosity I've shown you these past ten years, I cannot imagine. Your mother would never have considered doing such a thing. It is obviously the bad blood you inherited from your father."

I clamped my own lips together to keep silent. We had been over this same ground endlessly in the last two weeks. It would be pointless and perhaps fatal to my plans to open another argument and antagonize my aunt further.

Aunt Phoebe had taken my father and me into her home after my mother died in the influenza epidemic when I was ten. At the time it seemed like the most natural thing in the world, given her autocratic personality and the need to "keep a firm hand" on my father, as she put it.

Papa had been a point of contention between us for years. Gentle, fun loving, and idealistic, his was the complete opposite of Aunt Phoebe's pragmatic nature. Her determination to have us share her large house owed more, I believed, to duty than to affection—an attempt, perhaps, to atone for her lapse in allowing her younger sister to marry him.

"I don't mean to seem ungrateful," I said, choosing my words with infinite care. "But in his letter, Uncle Matthew sounded as though he really needed me to come." I didn't mention how much I longed to go.

"Matthew!" She sniffed in contempt. "Your father's brother, through and through. A complete reprobate if ever I saw one! Whatever possessed him to write after all these years of silence, I will never know."

I didn't know what had prompted his letter either, but I blessed him for sending it. We had never had the opportunity to know one another well. He had left for the gold fields in 1859. I remember seeing him off, holding my father's hand and waving frantically at his wagon, lettered on the side with "Pike's Peak or Bust." He had waved back jauntily, his merry voice booming out, "Come and join me when I get settled, Robert. We'll both make our fortunes!"

After that we received a few sporadic letters, each one from a different gold camp, until finally they stopped coming altogether. Then two weeks ago, another one arrived, a heaven-sent missive addressed to Miss Judith Alder. It read:

> *Dear Niece,*
>
> *Word has reached me that my brother Robert has been dead these three years. I am now the proprietor of a trading post near Taos, New Mexico Territory. I can no longer share my good fortune with your father, but if you choose to join me, I can offer you a home and a share of my future profits. I could sure use your help, as I'm a poor hand at housekeeping and worse at dealing with figures. If you decide to come, anyone in Taos can tell you how to reach me.*
>
>

Your loving uncle,
Matthew

>
> *P. S. I cannot pay for your passage at present, but I am sure that in short order we can build a prosperous business.*

My heart had soared as soon as I finished reading it. Here in my hands lay the possibility of escape from dependence on Aunt Phoebe. After opening her home to us, she had never allowed us to forget the debt we owed. I felt gratitude toward her for all she had done, but I yearned to shake off the status of poor relation.

I thought back to my father. He had rarely mentioned his brother in his later years, the time that stood out in my memory being during his final battle with the consumption that had claimed him.

"They tell me that a drier climate in the early stages might have helped," he said wistfully. "Perhaps I should have followed Matthew west, after all."

In that moment my mind was made up. I would follow my uncle in my father's stead. All that remained was to convince Aunt Phoebe.

I broached the subject as delicately as I could, but my caution didn't soften Aunt Phoebe's reaction one whit. She alternated between stony stares of disapproval and long tirades in which she took me to task for my ingratitude. I was tempted to answer her sharply, but I held my tongue. I had been left without a cent of my own, and if she refused to help me with the cost of my passage, my adventure would be over before it had begun.

"As I've told you," I said, trying not to let desperation show in my voice, "I promise I'll repay the money for my fare west just as soon as I've earned it in Uncle Matthew's trading post."

Her sharp eyes studied me for a long moment before she spoke. "I have made inquiries and have been informed that it is possible to make a comfortable income from such an enterprise. I am certain, though, that wastrel uncle of yours will squander every dime before you ever lay eyes on it."

I swallowed hard.

"However," she continued, "I can see that you are determined to go." Her eyes misted over. "Just like your mother, you are bent on following the Alder will-o'-the-wisp, probably to your ruin. But, foolish or not, I will not stand in your way."

"Oh, Aunt Phoebe!" I cried joyously.

"Just a moment," she snapped, and her eyes were once again hard and bright. "You may delude yourself if you choose, but I will not. You say you will repay the cost of your fare. Very well. I accept your intent, although I do not foresee that you will be able to earn enough in your uncle's care to have more than you need just to keep body and soul together. Nevertheless, I am prepared to finance this venture of yours."

She raised her hand warningly before I could interrupt. "But I refuse to throw away any more money than necessary on a fool's errand. I have looked into the various means of transportation to Taos. The railroad and stagecoach would be the fastest methods, but the fare is over two hundred dollars, far more than I am willing to spend."

I looked at her, puzzled. What on earth did she have in mind?

"I have, however, discovered a way for you to go that should suit us both." She gave me a wintery smile. "As you know, with the advent of the railroad, most of the travel west by wagon has ceased, at least those wagons starting from Independence. It is my understanding that most of those who use that method of travel go as far as possible on the train and outfit themselves at the terminus.

"But I would hardly send a young girl, no matter how headstrong, to choose someone suitable to travel with in that rough environment. Therefore, I have made arrangements for you to leave from here by wagon."

My head spun. A trip by covered wagon, taking weeks instead of days? Surely she wasn't serious! But a look at the grim set of her jaw assured me that she was.

Well, I considered, *why not?* Uncle Matthew had gone that way himself. It would be arduous, I was sure, but what better way of experiencing the country that was to be my new home than to see it at a slow wagon's pace, rather than whizzing by on a train? The more I thought about it, the more enthusiastic I became.

Aunt Phoebe was speaking again. ". . .a family of good character, but without funds to make the journey by train. They will leave St. Joseph on Saturday, four days from now. They have agreed to take you along for a nominal fee and for your help in cooking or any other tasks that should arise. If your desire to go trailing off after your uncle is as great as you say it is, I'm sure you will be willing to employ whatever means necessary to get there."

"I'll do it," I told her, without hesitation. "And I *will* pay you back, every penny."

She might have thought this scheme would discourage me, for my quick acceptance seemed to surprise her; she had little to say after that. The days flew by as I made my preparations, considering what to take, what to leave, packing and repacking as I changed my mind. I decided in the end to take little besides my clothing, toilet articles, and my Bible. I was to have a roof over my head at journey's end, and surely Uncle Matthew would help me secure anything I might need after my arrival.

My trunk was packed and ready early Saturday morning. Aunt Phoebe refused to go with me to the Parkers' home, but did unbend enough to allow Peter, the handyman, to drive me there in the buggy.

At our parting, she surveyed me one last time and said, "When you've seen the folly of your ways, you may come home," and went back into the house.

Peter and I drew up in front of a run-down house on the edge of town. A gaunt woman was supervising the loading of box after box into a covered wagon already laden with tools and furniture. I stepped down, surprised at my nervousness. "Mrs. Parker? I am Judith Alder."

Ignoring my outstretched hand, she said, "Let's see how much extra weight you've brought."

I signaled Peter to carry my trunk to the wagon. "Put it down!" she ordered. "Just as I thought. You've loaded up with so much finery you won't be leaving any room for us and the things we need."

She hauled an empty box, identical in size and shape to the others being loaded, over to my trunk. "You can take just as much as you can put in that, and no more. These crates will just fit inside the wagon, and I'll not have a big, fancy trunk cluttering things up. I've no doubt you'll all but eat us out of house and home on the trip, but there's no need to start out taking up more than your share of room. We might just as well understand each other from the first." And with that, she went back to bullying the men working at the wagon.

I stared at her retreating figure. So this was the woman of good character Aunt Phoebe had chosen! And we would be spending weeks in each other's company. I groaned inwardly, then squared my shoulders. Life with Aunt Phoebe had increased my immunity to intimidation. I could tolerate a few more weeks of the same if it helped me reach my goal.

Frantically, I transferred as much as I could to the rough box. Some of the clothes would have to be left behind. I picked up my Bible and bag containing my personal items. If I had to, I would carry those myself.

"Are you sure you want to do this, Miss Judith?" Peter frowned, concern in his eyes. "If you want to go back, I can have you home in no time."

I shook my head quickly, before my resolve weakened. "Thank you, but no. If you'll just take my trunk back, I'll be grateful." I gave him a smile that was meant to look confident and walked over to the wagon.

Mrs. Parker barely acknowledged my presence beyond nodding her head in my direction and informing her husband that I was "the girl." He looked me over and grunted. Evidently I had been weighed in the balance and found wanting. A boy who looked to be sixteen or seventeen jumped down lightly from the wagon and wiped his brow on his sleeve.

"I think that's it, Ma." He grinned.

Ma? It was hard to believe that this pleasant-looking youth could be the product of the two sullen individuals I had just met.

Seeing me, his grin broadened. "You must be Miss Alder. I'm Lanny Parker. I'm sure glad you're going to go with us. It'll be real good to have company."

The shock of finding a Parker capable of such a lengthy statement rendered me speechless, but I was able to return his smile with enthusiasm. He might be glad of my company, but he had no idea how profoundly grateful I was for his. At least there would be one friendly face along the way.

The boxes were stowed, the mules hitched. Everything appeared to be set for our departure. I looked around, struck by the fact that I was leaving and how little it mattered to me. In my mind, St. Joseph had already ceased to be home.

Mr. Parker mounted to the driver's seat, his wife beside him. I put up my hands to catch hold of the sideboard and pull myself up and over the tailgate.

"What do you think you're doing?" Mrs. Parker's voice rasped. "You and Lanny will walk. We'll spare the mules as much as we can."

Lanny fell in beside me as I walked with my head bowed, trying to hide my mortification. "Don't mind Ma," he said. "She's got a sharp tongue, but a good heart."

Well hidden, I thought. But the friendly overture had its effect, and soon

I was telling him about Uncle Matthew and my hopes for the future.

Mrs. Parker looked back. "Lanny! Come up here and walk by me."

He gave me an apologetic look and trotted off.

I plodded along by myself, staying off to one side to keep out of the dust. *Think about Taos*, I reminded myself. *Just keep that thought before you for the next few weeks. This won't last forever.*

Days later, I questioned that last thought. We had been on the trail for less than a week, but already it had given me a new perspective on eternity. Day followed day with tedious predictability. We awoke before daybreak, ate, and moved on with as little talk as possible. Mrs. Parker, holding steadfastly to her sullenness no matter how pleasant the circumstances, assigned Lanny and me to opposite sides of the wagon each morning, giving us little opportunity for conversation.

I didn't understand her motive for this until I overheard an exchange between her and her husband on our third morning out. I was busy packing the cooking utensils away inside when they stopped just outside, their voices clearly audible through the canvas.

"I never reckoned on making the girl walk all the way to New Mexico." Mr. Parker sounded troubled. "No reason she can't ride a bit. It'll give us a chance to stretch our legs."

"And who would be driving while she rides? Lanny? Can't you see he's got eyes for nothing else? You're a man. You know where that leads.

"We agreed to take her on," she continued, "but she'll keep to herself on the way. And, mind you, keep your own eyes where they belong!"

I pressed my fist against my mouth to stifle a cry of dismay and sat quietly until they moved away. Angry tears mingled with a desire to laugh. Never before had I been cast in the role of a Jezebel! Couldn't she understand that I only wanted human companionship?

Very well, I would walk every step of the way, if necessary. Only a few weeks to endure this, and then I would reach Taos and Uncle Matthew.

two

It was a great relief when we arrived at Council Grove and Mr. Parker announced that we would be staying there for a day or two.

"There's three other wagons waiting here already and more expected," he said that night over supper. "We'll form a train and have just that much more protection the rest of the way."

The prospect of being around friendly, talking human beings was encouraging. The wagons clustered together a little way outside town on the banks of the Neosho River. Cordial-looking women approached as we cooked supper over our fire, but a few sharp words from Mrs. Parker soon sent them on their way, shaking their heads.

I started to speak, but Mrs. Parker's warning look made me hold my tongue. I gazed after them wistfully. It would have been refreshing to have had a good woman-to-woman talk. Maybe things would change once we got under way.

Two more wagons arrived during the next day, and the men from the six groups met together to elect a captain, choosing a self-assured man named Hudson. He had had experience with the trail ahead and made the announcement that we would leave the following morning.

I had hoped for more interaction with the others of the train—perhaps with women who, like myself, walked much of the time. But the Parkers discouraged contact and kept our wagon well to the rear of the train. So we made our way across the plains with the wagon train, yet not really a part of it.

The sheer size of this land was staggering. For mile upon mile, I saw a billowing sea of green everywhere I looked. The stems of the grasses reached to the horses' bellies, and many of the seed heads grew well above my eye level.

At Cow Creek we stepped out of that world and into another, as though we had crossed an invisible boundary line. Listening to Mr. Parker repeating what he had picked up from Mr. Hudson that day, I learned that we had come to the short-grass prairie.

The buffalo and grama grasses grew only inches tall, and instead of the waving softness of the tall grass, the land stretched out in a stark panorama as far as the eye could see.

Moving out of the cover of the tall grasses and into the open made me feel more vulnerable. I was grateful for the protection of the others in our party.

Lanny made things more bearable when he could by talking to me at breakfast and after supper. Once he slipped me a nosegay of wildflowers he had picked, still wet with dew. I smiled at him, grateful for his thoughtfulness, and hid the bouquet before his sharp-eyed mother could spy it.

On the first evening past Dodge, we assembled for a meeting. Mrs. Parker, Lanny, and I sat well away from the rest of the group, but Mr. Hudson's voice carried clearly.

"Folks," he said, "we need to take a vote on the direction we follow next. As some of you know, the trail divides a little way from here. We need to make a choice on which fork we take.

"The easiest way, and the one I recommend, is the Mountain Branch. It's about a hundred miles longer, but we follow right along the Arkansas River like we've been doing, and we're sure of water all along the way."

"What's the other fork like?" asked one of the men.

"The other way is the Cimarron Cutoff. It's sometimes called the *Jornada de Muerte*—the Journey of Death." Prickles ran down the back of my neck as he spoke.

"The first fifty miles are without water at all. You'd have to take all your wagons can carry and pray that it was enough to last you until you reached the Cimarron."

"What then?"

"The Cimarron's a contrary river. Maybe it'll be running, maybe it won't. The decision is up to all of you, but my advice is to take a little longer and be sure of reaching Santa Fe."

The general murmur of assent reassured me even before the vote was taken that the other men saw the wisdom of his advice.

"All in favor of following the Mountain Branch say 'Aye,' " called Mr. Hudson, and a chorus of "Ayes" rang out. "Anyone in favor of the Cutoff?"

"I am," said a lone voice, and I realized with horror that it belonged to Mr. Parker.

A man standing nearby wheeled and stared at him. "Are you crazy, man? I've heard stories about that stretch. We'd all be risking our lives and our families."

"You heard Hudson. It's a hundred miles shorter. I'm in a hurry to get where I'm going."

"So are the rest of us. But we want to get there alive."

"All right, then," said Mr. Hudson. "It looks like it's settled. The majority votes to take the Mountain Branch, and I must say I'm relieved. When we come to the fork tomorrow, we'll follow the right-hand branch."

"Not me." The words fell like a heavy stone into the startled silence.

"He can't be serious," I whispered to Mrs. Parker. "We can't undertake a trip like that alone."

"He knows what he's doing," she replied. "We aim to get this over with as quick as we can."

"But she's right, Ma." Lanny looked as worried as I felt. "We get off by ourselves like that and we're in trouble. If we can't find water, or if we run into outlaws or Indians, we're all alone. There'll be no way to get help."

Mrs. Parker gave him a withering look. "Siding with her against your own parents, are you?"

The men followed Mr. Parker to our wagon, trying to reason with him.

Mr. Hudson grabbed his arm. "Listen to me, Parker. I've been down the trail before. I know the Cutoff. Why, even the jackrabbits carry three days' rations and a canteen of water out there. Think of your women, if nothing else."

"My mind's made up." Mr. Parker's face was set. "The rest of you do as you like. We're taking the Cutoff."

Sleep did not come easily that night. Fragments of conversation tumbled through my mind. *Fifty miles. . .no water. . .Jornada de Muerte. . .Journey of Death.*

By morning, the rest of the train seemed to have accepted the Parkers' decision, although I saw worried glances cast in our direction more than once. Shortly before we started out, Mr. Hudson came over to our wagon and handed Mr. Parker a sheet of paper.

"If you're bound you're going that way," he said, "at least take this with you." Peering over Mr. Parker's shoulder, I could see that he held a crudely drawn map. "I've marked the route the best I could, and I've circled the places where you'll find springs. You'll need 'em, especially if the riverbed's dry."

Mr. Parker thanked him with a grunt and we waited to hear the order to move out for the last time.

My palms were growing sweaty as we reached the point where the trail forked. Five wagons moved on ahead. Ours pulled to a halt and watched as they became smaller and smaller dots on the landscape.

We forded the Arkansas and headed southwest.

We had taken Mr. Hudson's advice and drunk as much as we could hold before leaving the river. The water barrels were filled to overflowing. I breathed a prayer that Mr. Parker knew what he was doing.

The heat was not the only thing against us. Dust, churned up by the wagon wheels and the mules' hooves, billowed into the air in great clouds. When it settled, it blanketed everything—the wagon, the mules, and us. I gave up trying to brush it off my clothes after the first day and concentrated on keeping it out of my eyes and mouth as much as possible. It made me even thirstier just to see it constantly swirling about.

Our pace had slowed as the heat increased, and by the end of the second day, we were all concerned about whether the water supply would hold out. I sipped my evening ration slowly, savoring every drop.

The mules needed an ample supply to pull the heavy wagon. I felt sorry for the hollow-eyed creatures, but it was hard to watch as Mr. Parker and Lanny poured the precious liquid for them to drink. Mrs. Parker evidently felt the same way about me, for I saw her jealously eyeing every drop I swallowed.

Late in the afternoon of the third day, Lanny spotted trees on the horizon. We pressed on, bone weary, and eventually reached the banks of the Cimarron.

It was dry.

"Where cottonwoods grow, there's bound to be water," Mr. Parker said, and began scooping sand from the riverbed. The sand grew darker as he dug, and finally a chalky white liquid began to ooze into the hole. The mules strained to pull the wagon closer to the water.

Lanny moved a little farther up the riverbed and soon had enough in the hole he scooped out to fill a cup for each of us. It was brackish, and back in Missouri would have been scorned as unfit to drink. But it was water nonetheless, and we drank deeply of cup after cup.

In the morning, Mr. Parker consulted the map he had been given. "I figure we're right about here," he said, indicating a spot with his forefinger. "We need to find one of the springs. Looks like the closest one is here." He pointed to a circle on the map.

"How far?" Lanny asked.

"Ten miles. No more."

"Then how far to the next water? And the next?" Mrs. Parker's voice rose shrilly and I looked at her in amazement. It was the first real emotion that she had shown in all our time on the trail.

"We'll make it," said her husband.

"What about her? She'll use up water the three of us need." She seemed on the verge of hysteria.

"We'll make it," he repeated.

We reached the spring sooner than we expected, before noon. *Now*, I thought, *I understand what an oasis is.*

The water bubbled up, clear and fresh, in the middle of a stand of tall, cool grass. Scattered trees afforded shade from the sun. After blissfully drinking my fill at the spring's edge, I sank down in the grass under spreading branches and felt a light breeze play over my face. I loosened my bonnet strings and let the bonnet slide back on my shoulders so the breeze could stir my hair. It felt wonderful.

The Parkers sprawled around the spring while the mules drank and drank. Relief from the heat and thirst made them seem almost companionable.

We sat like that for a while, enjoying the breeze, the shade, and the freshness of the grass. I hoped we would camp here for the night, but after a time, Mr. Parker got to his feet and nodded at Lanny.

"Give me a hand with the water barrels. We've got to fill up and keep moving."

"Now, Pa?" Lanny's plaintive tone echoed my sentiments. "We're just beginning to cool off a little."

"Get a move on, boy. Your mother and I know what we're doing." Lanny groaned, but rose to obey.

I sighed. At least we would have fresh water for the next leg of the journey. I jumped when I realized Mrs. Parker was standing beside me. I hadn't heard her approach.

"Mr. Parker and I have been talking," she said abruptly. "We're all tired and covered with this awful dust. Would you like a chance to wash here before we go on? We can pull the wagon over beyond those trees so you'll have some privacy."

I could hardly believe my ears, but she looked as though she sincerely wanted me to agree.

"Why. . .thank you. I'd like that very much." I was touched by this unexpected concern. Perhaps she was trying to make amends for her earlier attitude.

No matter, I thought, as the hoofbeats of the mules grew fainter and I could no longer hear the creak of the wheels. Whatever the reason, I had the opportunity to get clean, and I intended to make the most of it!

I shook as much dust as I could from the folds of my dress and spread it out on the grass to air a little. I had taken a piece of soap from my bag before the wagon moved away, and I carried it with me as I stepped into the spring.

The cold water closed around my ankles with a delightful shock. It was deeper than I had expected, and I squatted down in the center, enjoying the luxury of washing the caked dust from my arms and shoulders.

I scrubbed and scrubbed until my skin glowed, then undid the pins holding my hair and soaped and rinsed it until it lay clean and shining across my shoulders.

I dried off as best I could, feeling revitalized, but somewhat guilty at the amount of time I had spent in the water. Dressing hurriedly, I hastened to the other side of the grove of trees, hoping the Parkers wouldn't be too angry about my prolonged absence.

I needn't have worried.

When I emerged from the screen made by the trees, the Parkers and the wagon were nowhere to be seen.

three

I stood facing a vast emptiness, my clothes still sticking in places to my damp skin, and searched vainly for the white canvas wagon cover. Always before on this trip, it could be spotted at a distance, the cloth rippling in the breeze like mighty sails.

Nothing.

They must have gone a little farther ahead. Perhaps they had changed their minds and were finding a place to camp nearby, after all. Even as I considered the possibility, my mind rejected it.

What if the Parkers had fallen asleep, and the mules had wandered off? If they had woken up to find the wagon gone, they might even now be trying to catch up to it. We had entered rougher terrain; the landscape might look flat at a distance, but it held an amazing number of rises and depressions. It would be possible, in this broken land, for a whole wagon train to travel along the bottom of a draw and remain all but invisible save to one at a higher elevation. Yes, it was possible they were only hidden from my sight, in one of the distant ravines.

But the head start needed would surely be greater than any distance covered by an aimlessly wandering mule. I fought down a rising sense of panic and began to follow the wagon tracks.

My legs wanted to betray me at every step and break into a headlong run, but I fought the feeling back. Had I begun to run wildly as I wished, the panic would have overtaken both my body and my reason in short order. I forced myself to walk along the track deliberately and to marshal my thoughts.

I had half expected the wagon tracks to wind deviously to some place of concealment, but to my surprise, they continued openly along the trail. The wagon itself, though, was nowhere to be seen. Not even a cloud of dust marred the western sky.

An idea was creeping into my mind and I made every effort to subdue it. The very thought was enough to give me a chill, even in the noonday heat. But it teased and pulled at the edges of consciousness until it had made its way to the center of my thinking and had to be faced head on: I had been deliberately left behind.

The full implications of that did not strike me all at once, which was a mercy. My first feelings were of disbelief and outrage. I was hardly a piece of excess baggage to be cast aside when its burden became too great to bear! I was ready to march into the nearest town, tell the local constable what had happened, and demand that he take action. So great was my wrath that I had actually taken several steps down the trail before I came to myself and realized that the nearest town was a good many miles away.

I stumbled to a halt, knocking one foot against an object I had not previously noticed in my anger. It took a moment to gather my senses and realize what it was.

It was my box of belongings. In a last uncharacteristic act of charity—or was it merely to drop surplus weight?—the Parkers had stopped their wagon to leave the pitifully few items I had brought with me. My Bible lay on top, along with the bag containing my small personal effects.

The enormity of my situation hit me then, and my knees gave way, dropping me down next to my box. I truly had been left, and I faced whatever perils might come upon me quite alone. Incidents along the journey came to mind—comments and complaints about the amount of space my belongings and I took up, the quantity of food and water consumed, and particularly Lanny's supposed infatuation with me. In Mrs. Parker's mind, I *was* merely an excess piece of baggage and a potentially dangerous one at that.

I recalled her kindness to me, her suggestion that I might like to bathe. Once I had been disposed of, it would have taken them little time to put enough distance between us so that there was no possibility of my overtaking them.

The crate puzzled me. Perhaps a twinge of conscience prompted them to set it by the trail, where it presumably would be found. On a less charitable note, it also gave Mrs. Parker more room to arrange her own belongings.

At least I had my Bible. I reached for it with a hand that trembled and opened it on my lap. A light breeze fluttered the pages. The underlined words in Proverbs, chapter three, caught my attention: "Trust in the Lord with all thine heart; and lean not unto thine own understanding. In all thy ways acknowledge him, and he shall direct thy paths."

Papa had always stressed the importance of applying the truths of the Scriptures to daily living. "Do not read God's Word merely for the pride of having read it, Judith. Head knowledge without heart knowledge is an empty thing." If ever I needed my path directed, this must surely qualify as an applicable time.

I stood up and gazed as far as my eyes could see in either direction. With the sun nearly overhead, east and west looked much the same. For a few panic-stricken moments, I couldn't tell the difference in direction, didn't know which way would take me back to St. Joseph and which would lead me, eventually, to Uncle Matthew. Reason reasserted itself, and I reminded myself that if I waited a short time, the new position of the sun would point me westward.

Nothing in my life up to this point had prepared me for any such turn of events. It was difficult to decide on a course of action without any prior experience on which to base such a decision.

As far as I could tell, only two courses were open to me. I could give way to my feelings, fling myself down upon the trail beside my belongings and weep with abandon, or I could choose to travel either east or west and proceed steadily and rationally in the chosen direction.

The first alternative was by far the more tempting, especially as the shock bore down upon me. But I realized that would only exhaust me and leave me prey to any danger that might arise.

Traveling alone, on foot, and helpless was hardly a thing to be desired, but I determined that even if the end should come soon, as seemed all too likely, it would not find me groveling mindlessly.

Not knowing how long this frame of mind would last, I turned to open my crate before my resolve faltered to see which belongings might reasonably be carried along with me.

I pried up the lid and stared in disbelief. Even in their one act of thoughtfulness, the Parkers had managed to leave me high and dry. The clothes in the crate were not mine, but Lanny's.

I sank to my knees beside the crate. How—*why*—could they have done such a thing? Perhaps it was foolish, but somehow not having even the meager consolation of my own belongings seemed the crowning blow.

I remembered then how, after my morning devotions, I had set my Bible down with my bag on the crate closest to me. I groaned. Mrs. Parker and her look-alike boxes! Being in a hurry, they would have connected my Bible with my box and dumped it all together.

Now what? Pillowing my head on my arms on the edge of the crate, I felt my hair brush against my face. I had left it loose to dry. My hands reached mechanically to smooth it into a coil at the base of my neck and I fumbled in my pocket for my hairpins to make myself presentable.

A sudden shock ran through me. Suppose some other traveler happened along. What kind of woman would they take me for? What sort of woman would be put off a wagon in the middle of nowhere? I could think of only one, and the very thought made me blush.

I had envisioned a possible encounter with kindly people, other emigrants perhaps, who would sympathize with my plight, take me aboard their wagon, and see me safely to Taos. But now—the more I thought over my story, the more unlikely it sounded. If it appeared so even to me, how could I hope to convince others that I was indeed an upright, respectable young lady? And failing to convince them, what would be the dangers of being a woman alone in this wilderness?

Snatches of stories I had heard and put out of my mind came back to haunt me—stories of outlaws, coarse frontiersmen, and rampaging Indians. To be sure, the Indians were supposed to have calmed down, and Uncle Matthew had reported no trouble at his trading post, but mightn't there be renegade bands roaming the plains?

I suppressed a shudder and glanced over my shoulder, half expecting to see dark, hostile eyes peering over a rise.

When loose, my hair rippled over my shoulders, a golden cascade gleaming in the sunlight. It was by far my most attractive feature, and I brushed it faithfully one hundred strokes each night. Now my waist-length tresses seemed nothing but a liability.

Wouldn't such long golden hair be prized as a scalp to hang from a savage's lance? Tears of self-pity stung my eyes. It was all so unfair! Abandoned here through no fault of my own, left to the mercy of hoodlums and renegades far from any form of civilization. I scrubbed at my eyes with the back of my hand.

If I were a man, I thought, *I wouldn't be so lost.* Men always seemed to know what to do. Men carried guns to use for protection. A man alone could travel with relative safety. A man. . .

The idea came with startling clarity, fascinating and repulsive at the same time. It was possible, barely, but surely not dignified. On the other hand, how much dignity was attached to becoming an addition to a warrior's scalp collection?

My mind whirled as I reached into Lanny's box, sorting through the clothes there. Two pairs of sturdy pants lay on top, followed by three shirts, a pair of overalls, socks, and a suit of long underwear. I laid the pants, overalls, socks, and shirts out on the ground; I saw no need to get involved with a man's undergarments.

There were certainly possibilities. Lanny was stockier and taller than I, but with some adjustments, it just might work. I selected the overalls and the cleanest shirt and made my way back behind the trees.

Some time later, a boy stepped out carrying a neatly folded parcel of ladies' clothing. The clothes had not proved to be such a bad fit after all. Granted, the heavy overalls bagged about me, and the cuffs were rolled up to keep them from dragging in the dirt, but that seemed to conceal, rather than emphasize, my figure.

Years before, my father had dressed me in a pair of boy's overalls and smuggled me out to a pasture for a clandestine riding lesson. Sitting astride, he said, was the only sensible way to ride a horse, and his daughter was going to experience that at least once in her life. It was one of many things that would have scandalized Aunt Phoebe, and it was understood without a word being said that neither of us would mention it to anyone.

I remember shrieking with delight as the horse cantered around the pasture. I was able to cling to the mare like a burr and felt that nothing she could do would dislodge me. Overalls or dresses, it made little difference to me in those days. How differently I felt now! Camouflaged or not, I felt undressed and indecent. I nearly changed my mind right then and decided to take my chances dressed as a lady.

Finally, I decided upon a compromise—I would use my new identity only as a protective measure. If I met up with ruffians or hostiles, I would keep quiet, letting my disguise speak for me. If, as I hoped, some kindly people were to pass by and offer to take me with them, I would—if I judged them upright people—disclose myself rather than accept their hospitality under false pretenses.

This decided, I squared my shoulders and prepared to make the best of a bad situation. My hair caused me concern. I debated the wisdom of cutting it off short and was rummaging through the lower layers of Lanny's crate for some sharp implement when, to my delight, I unearthed not only a hat, but a sturdy pair of shoes as well.

I coiled my hair high on my head, pinned it in place as well as I could, and with the hat jammed down over my ears, fancied I could go on my way with little fear of discovery. The shoes were rather large, but strips torn from one of Lanny's shirts and stuffed into the toes made it possible for me to walk without stepping out of them.

I fashioned a sling out of the remainder of the torn shirt, folded my small bag and Bible inside, and fastened it inside the baggy overalls. Then taking a deep breath, I resolutely turned my face toward the west.

four

By sundown of that day, my brave resolve had shattered into a million hopeless pieces. Never before had I felt such utter despair. I had no idea how far I had come or how far I had yet to go. The long drink I had taken at the spring before leaving hadn't quenched my thirst for long on the dusty trail. And the oversized shoes had rubbed my feet to a raw, painful mess.

How far did Mr. Parker say we had to go until we reached the next spring? Ten miles? But I had no idea how near the trail it might be. I tried not to think what it would mean if I had already passed it.

Doggedly, I planted one foot more or less firmly in front of the other. Even in my exhausted state, I held fast to the knowledge that the only way to be rescued was to keep moving. The setting sun dazzled my eyes, and I stumbled over a stone.

The fall took every last bit of reserve I had. I pushed myself up on my elbows and tried to gather my knees under me. But my strength was spent, and I pitched forward into sweet oblivion.

The next thought that entered my consciousness was that some large dogs had found me and were sniffing my inert form. I waved an arm feebly, trying to shoo them away, and my hand encountered an enormous wet muzzle. Calculating the size of the beast from the dimensions of its nose, it must have been monstrous.

The realization jolted me into a sitting position. The sky had darkened, and I could just make out huge shapes milling about me, making snuffling sounds.

I rose cautiously. Fright drove all power of speech from me, and I began backing away from the creatures, but they followed me, sniffing ominously.

Hunger, thirst, fatigue, and the sheer terror of being alone to face this peril nearly drove away my reason altogether.

"Never give way to panic." How many times had I heard my father say that? "Panic will keep you from thinking clearly, and clear thinking is the best weapon you have in a dangerous situation."

I tried to think as I shuffled backward, wincing as the rough boots rubbed my blistered feet. I had no gun, no knife, not even a stout stick to use as a weapon; I couldn't keep the beasts at bay much longer. I was dimly aware of the blood pulsing in my throat, throbbing in my temples. The throbbing increased to an audible pounding, vibrating through the sand at my feet.

It was several moments before I recognized the sound as the galloping of horses' hooves and a potential rescue. No sooner did that recognition strike me than I had wheeled and was staggering toward the sound with all the strength I had left. Darkness was closing in, and I stumbled over the shadowy ground. The thought that I might come this close to rescue and miss it was too great to be borne.

My throat was so parched from thirst that I was unable to scream. I swallowed painfully two or three times and managed a hoarse cry. Hoofbeats clattered nearer, and a black shape drew up almost on top of me.

"Lookee here!" cried a gravelly voice. I sensed, rather than saw, a figure dismount and step close to me. However, I could not pinpoint the location accurately due to the overpowering aroma of tobacco and perspiration.

"Over here, boys!" my rescuer shouted, his breath nearly bowling me over. He fumbled for a moment, then struck a match and held it toward my face. The sudden light hurt my eyes, and I threw a hand up to cover them, stepping backward as I did so.

"Aw, now, if it ain't a kid. Don't be scared, son. You'll be all right. What happened? You wander off from your folks?"

I was saved from answering by a clatter of hoofbeats as two more riders drew up.

"Found 'em, did you, Jake?" asked one.

"Them, and something extra. Look here."

"Where?" spoke yet another disembodied voice.

"Right under your ugly nose," said my protector. "It's a kid. A poor, lost kid."

The moon rose as if on cue, brightening the scene enough to reveal three rough, unshaven men, all staring at me.

"Now don't be scared, sonny," said the one called Jake. "We're not going to hurt you. You just tell us where your folks are, and we'll see you get back first thing in the morning."

I opened my lips to speak, but could only manage a croak.

"Jake, where's your sense?" said one of the mounted men. "Can't you see the kid's dyin' of thirst?"

Jake hurriedly untied a canteen from his saddle, mumbling under his breath. The water tasted as sweet to me as it must have to the children of Israel at Elim. I sipped slowly, letting it trickle down my parched throat, and felt its restoring coolness spread throughout my body.

I used the few moments' respite to compose my thoughts. My original plan, to disclose my identity as soon as I was rescued, did not seem wise at this point.

True, the three men did seem inclined toward kindliness, but they believed me to be a young boy with family nearby. What they might feel about a young woman whose only family was hundreds of miles away might be another matter entirely.

Evidently my disguise was working in the moonlight. But I had no way of knowing how well it would conceal my identity when day came. In the meantime, I decided, I would adopt a cautious policy. I would not deliberately mislead these men by my answers, but neither would I volunteer information unnecessarily, at least not until I was more sure of the type of men they were.

I swallowed again. My voice came out in a raspy whisper. "My parents are dead. I was traveling with another family to go live with my Uncle Matthew, but they left me back down the trail."

"*Left* you?" Even by the light of the moon, amazement was plainly written on Jake's countenance. "You mean they just hauled off and left you in the middle of nowhere?"

It was a difficult question. In my new role, I could hardly say that Mrs. Parker had considered me a threat to her son's virtue.

"I guess I ate more than they liked." That much was surely true. I was saved from closer questioning by a snort from one of the other men.

"Leave the kid alone, Jake. Can't you see he's tuckered out? We'll talk to the boss in the morning and figure out what to do with him. Come on, you take him up behind you. Shorty and I can push these strays back to camp."

Jake spat—tobacco juice, I believed—and mounted before turning to me again. "Come on, kid, climb up here. Those two should just about be able to handle half a dozen steers by themselves."

For the first time since hearing the hoofbeats, I remembered the threatening creatures. Now I saw them standing not many yards distant, long, curving horns clearly outlined in the moonlight.

"Steers," I croaked. "Why, I thought they were some kind of huge dogs." Whatever else I might have said was drowned out by wild roars of laughter, which threatened to unseat all three men. Shorty fairly howled, leaning forward almost double and pounding one fist against his leg.

I could feel an embarrassed flush rise from my neck and wash over my face and was doubly grateful for the darkness. Mutely, I accepted the hand Jake extended between guffaws and scrambled up behind him with as much dignity as I could muster.

As the horse carried us away at a trot, the whoops continued but grew fainter. Jake's shoulders convulsed from time to time, although he at least tried to subdue his mirth.

The day's events had taken their toll, and I found myself struggling to stay awake and upright. Eventually, I managed to balance myself so that I could fall into a light doze without danger of slipping off the horse. I had not asked where we were going or how long the trip would be; I was simply too tired to care. Tomorrow could take care of itself.

At some point we stopped and there were other voices. Hands lifted me from the horse and carried me to a blanket roll beneath a wagon. The last thing I remembered was pulling my hat down securely with both hands.

Morning was heralded by the rattle of tin plates, the creaking of saddle leather, and a general flurry about the camp. These things penetrated my consciousness despite my exhaustion, but I wasn't brought fully awake until a pair of feet flying past the wagon kicked a shower of dirt into my face.

I raised my head and looked about wildly, trying to remember where I was. No one had taken notice of me yet, so I lay peering into the hazy light of false dawn, trying to take stock of my surroundings.

As my field of vision was limited, the closest things I could make out were occasional pairs of boots striding by the wagon. Farther out, other objects were beginning to take shape in the brightening sky. A large group of horses was off to one side; some were being saddled, others rubbed down. Farther along to my right was a vast herd of the cattle that had frightened me so the night before. Evidently the men who had found me were part of one of the cattle drives I had heard about.

A sudden chill crept over me. Did women come along on these drives? I was fairly sure they did not. In that case, I must be the only female among all these rough-looking men, and with no idea how long they would travel until journey's end.

Cautiously, I rolled to my left side, remembering to make sure my hat was pulled firmly in place. I tucked a few stray hairs back up under the crown and peered out. A group of men sat cross-legged in a circle not ten yards away. Most were wolfing down the contents of the tin plates on their laps, while a few slurped their coffee.

Coffee! The aroma made my stomach double up in a hard knot. I had been so tired the night before that even hunger had not kept me awake. But now I was ravenous.

How should I make my presence known? I recognized none of the men whose faces I could see, and I shrank from revealing myself before strangers. Furthermore, my male garb had proven effective last night, but just how much could I rely on it in the light of day?

I was saved from further speculation by Jake, whose head suddenly appeared beneath the wagon's floorboards.

"Well, so you've come around, have you?" The kindness in his eyes belied his attempt to make his voice sound gruff. I nodded, trying to shrink back into the shadows.

"I never saw anyone before who could sleep through Cookie's 'Come and get it.' And right under the chuck wagon, too."

"Jake!" called a stentorian voice. "Is that boy still asleep?"

"No, boss," returned Jake over his shoulder. "He's awake and rarin' to go."

"See that he eats before we pull out. He's probably half-starved." As if in agreement, my stomach gave a loud rumble.

"Look, boy," said Jake, his attention focused on me again, "you roll right out the far side of this wagon. There's some water there, and soap. And after you've scrubbed off some of the trail dust, you come over and get something to eat."

I moved to follow his instructions, but found I had to grasp the wagon wheel to pull myself upright. I could feel the sores on my feet breaking open again.

A basin of water stood on a small shelf jutting out from the side of the wagon. A bar of soap lay beside it, and a grimy towel hung from a nail.

The soap and water felt heavenly, and I wished that I could use them more extensively. My face stung as I dried it on the rough towel. I noticed a small mirror propped up on the shelf, and looked in it to prepare myself for the inspection ahead. I gasped in surprise. If Aunt Phoebe had walked past me on the streets of St. Joseph, she would have gathered her skirts about her and gone by without a second glance.

No wonder the towel had made my face sting. Lanny's hat, while good for disguise, had a much narrower brim than my sunbonnet. My face, with no protection, had been sunburned beyond recognition, and my nose had already started to peel. With the battered hat jammed down on my head, I hardly recognized myself.

The freckles I had treated so diligently with lemon and buttermilk were putting in a fresh appearance, and I wrinkled my nose ruefully. That was a mistake. My face felt as though it would split. I could feel heat radiating from it even in the crisp morning air.

Well, I thought, *sore it might be, but surely not fatal.* And I looked more like a boy than I ever dreamed possible. If I watched myself closely and guarded my tongue, I believed I would be safe for the time being without resorting to overt deception.

Still feeling almost undressed in my rough shirt and baggy overalls, I squared my shoulders, then settled into a slouch, which I told myself looked more boylike, and hobbled around the wagon.

Most of the men had finished eating and were already busy breaking camp, although the first fingers of sunlight were just reaching over the horizon. Three men still sat around the remains of the campfire sipping coffee. One of them was Jake, who motioned me to sit next to him.

He placed a tin plate heaped with beans and biscuits on my lap. "Here you go. Now just set here and eat your fill. We won't worry you till you've had a chance to fill your belly."

I was so hungry that the familiarity didn't even make me blush. At Aunt Phoebe's, we would have been helping ourselves from chafing dishes arranged on the sideboard. The scrambled eggs would have been fluffy delights, the sausages perfectly brown, the toast a delicate gold. There would have been a selection of jams and marmalade in cut glass bowls, and low-pitched conversation would be heard above the soft clinks of silver touching bone china.

Here, a tin plate had been thrust at me, its cargo of beans a towering brown mass. Biscuits dotted the top and their undersides were already getting soggy. But food had never tasted so good.

The beans swam in some sort of broth and I used pieces of biscuit to sop up the last of the juices. The biscuits were surprisingly light. I glanced at the dour-faced man putting things to rights around the chuck wagon. If he was, as I assumed, the cook, then it wasn't necessarily true that it took a merry heart to make a good meal. The conglomeration on my plate hardly had visual appeal, but it was delicious.

After I had bolted the meal, my hunger was assuaged sufficiently for me to give some attention to my companions. I eyed the two across the fire from under the brim of my hat.

One was drinking coffee, holding the tin cup in both hands to take full advantage of its warmth. His profile looked vaguely familiar, and I thought he might have been one of Jake's companions of the night before. His youthful movements as he rose to stir the embers of the fire contradicted the age suggested by his weather-beaten face and hands. His eyes, too, were those of a young man and held a glint that promised a sense of mischief.

I turned my attention to the man standing directly across from me. My eyes traveled up a substantial length of denim-clad leg, took in strong, lean hands holding the inevitable cup of coffee, and came to rest on a face seemingly carved of granite. A firm chin jutted out, the mouth set in a determined line above it.

Suddenly, he glanced my way and his blue eyes looked into mine with an intensity that seemed to bore straight through me. I dropped my eyes and hoped my confusion didn't show. My conscience was pricking me painfully.

I picked up my coffee cup. The steam rose to warm my face as I took my first sip. I gasped and was seized by a fit of coughing. Tears stung my eyes as I tried to catch my breath. I had almost succeeded when Jake began pounding on my back solicitously.

"Are you all right, kid?" he asked, his grizzled face close to mine. I managed to nod and secured my hat, which threatened to fly off under his ministrations.

"Fine," I choked out. Either the coffee or Jake's pounding had made me slightly giddy, and I blinked, trying to clear my vision. "Just fine."

"Coffee's no good to a cowboy 'less it's strong enough to float a horseshoe," drawled the weather-beaten man, rising to his feet.

"You hush, Shorty," snapped Jake. "This young un's had enough trouble without you making fun."

Shorty drew himself up to his inconsiderable height and stalked off with as much dignity as a bowlegged man could muster.

Jake turned his attention back to me. "Now that you've gotten filled up and woke up, you and the boss here need to talk a bit before we head out." He jerked his head in the direction of the man across the fire. "I'll go see to my horse."

I steeled myself to meet that intense gaze again and rose to my feet to reduce somewhat his advantage in height. Even across the fire, I could see that my head wouldn't quite reach the top of his shoulder.

They were broad shoulders. His height was not the gangly awkwardness of some of the young men I had known at home, all arms and legs and lack of grace. He was well-proportioned, and his movements as he set down his cup and turned to study me were smooth and agile. I wished I knew what manner of man lay beneath the exterior.

"What's your name, boy?" he asked.

"Ju—" I caught myself, floundered wildly, and managed to stammer, "Judah." Foolishly, I had been unprepared for the question and came up with the first compromise that entered my head.

"Judah. All right. Don't be frightened, son. We only mean to help." He took a long step over the dying coals to stand at my side and threw a muscular arm around my shoulders.

I caught my breath. There was only kindness in the gesture, but the proximity was unnerving.

"Jake told me how he found you. I know it's tough, being without your folks. Mine have been gone a good many years now, since I was fifteen." His grip on my shoulders tightened as the expression on his face softened.

"But we'll see you through till the end of the drive, and then see about finding a way to get you to your—uncle's, was it?" I nodded. He gave a final squeeze and released me, much to my relief.

"How–how long will the drive last?"

"Not long. We're three days at most from the ranch."

Three days alone with all these men! Resolutely I choked down my alarm. This was all the help that was available and I was powerless to change my situation. I would have to make the best of it.

"Let's get moving. It's time to head out." He seemed to be in a hurry, and I tried to match his pace as he strode toward the horses. He noticed my stiff gait and frowned.

"Your feet are raw from all that walking, aren't they? Well, come along, you'd better ride in the wagon."

I limped along behind him to the chuck wagon, where the cook had made ready for departure with amazing speed.

"Cookie, this is Judah," he announced. "He'll be riding with you today." The heavyset man gave me a sour look and began clearing a space near the wagon's tail. Evidently I wasn't going to sit next to him on the seat.

But that meant less chance of being questioned, I thought, brightening, and it would give me time to reflect on what my next move should be.

The space cleared, Cookie climbed up to the seat and my benefactor turned to go. "Don't worry, Judah. Cookie's bark is worse than his bite. At least," he said with a sudden twinkle, "I think it is. He hasn't bitten me yet."

I repressed a smile as I scrambled to my perch and raised my eyes to meet his. "Thank you, Mr.—"

"Jeff will do. Short for Jefferson." With that he was gone. Moments later a roar of "Move 'em out!" echoed through the camp, and we were off.

five

From my cramped seat I could see the cowboys in position alongside the herd. There was beauty and precision in the way they kept the cattle grouped together, slowing the ones in front who would forge ahead and prodding those who tried to lag behind. From time to time, one of the men would have to veer away from the group in order to head off a stray, and the cooperation between horse and rider was a marvel to watch.

Engrossed in the strange ballet, my spirit soared and I rejoiced in being a child of the God of creation. My throbbing feet soon claimed my attention, however, and I gingerly eased the boots off. Both feet were terribly swollen, as well as being raw and covered with blisters. I winced as the throbbing increased and wished I had a pail of cold water to bathe them in.

Lacking that, I wriggled around sideways so my feet could rest on sacks of flour and my back was propped against the wagon's side.

When I was reasonably comfortable, I leaned back and felt the weight of my Bible pressing against me. I looked around cautiously. Cookie sat hunched over the reins, as unconcerned as if he had nothing more than beans and flour riding behind him. No one was riding near the rear of the wagon, so I reached inside my overalls and drew out my Bible.

I sighed. At least one thing remained constant in my madly changing world. Hardly a day had gone by in recent years that I hadn't begun with time spent reading God's Word. I turned the well-thumbed pages to Paul's epistle to the Ephesians, where I had marked my place—was it only the day before?—and settled back to read.

Chapter four. Paul talks about the unity of believers, their edification, and speaking the truth in love. I was squirming uncomfortably by the time I reached verse 25: "Wherefore putting away lying, speak every man truth with his neighbor. . ." There was a distinct twinge in the area of my conscience.

I flipped the page, and a verse fairly flew out to meet me: "Stand therefore, having your loins girt about with truth. . ."

The Bible lay open on my lap, but my eyes tried to focus on the sacks of flour, the sideboards of the wagon, anything but the printed page.

Shame swept over me. Deception and falsehood—hardly the path I had committed myself to follow! It had seemed such an innocent thing at first, and the initial goal of protecting myself from marauders had not been a bad one. But now I was becoming more and more enmeshed in the lie I had begun.

The Lord had seen fit to bring me to a point of rescue; could I not then trust Him to provide protection from that point on? Granted, last night's exhaustion had muddled my thinking, but I bitterly regretted not having told Mr. Jefferson the truth this morning.

I resolved I would do so as soon as I saw him. After all, he was the one to whom I had lied directly. This resolution made, I asked forgiveness from the Lord and drifted into an uneasy sleep.

A particularly hard jolt of the wagon woke me. From the sun's position and the heat, I judged it to be about noon. The back of the wagon was stifling. I longed to get out and walk in the fresh air, but my feet were so swollen that I couldn't begin to put the boots back on.

I leaned back and consoled myself with the thought that we would soon stop for the noon meal and I could take that opportunity to confess to Mr. Jefferson.

The wagon lurched along and my stomach began to complain. "Biscuits and some jerky in the box next to you," said Cookie, without turning his head.

I reached into the box and helped myself. The biscuits, I knew, would be good, but I looked skeptically at the strips of dried meat. I tried nibbling at the end of one. That proved fruitless, and I soon found that the only way to take a bite was to grip a chunk firmly between my back teeth and tear it off.

Chewing it was another matter entirely. It took considerable time for it to soften enough to chew at all. It made for slow eating, but surprisingly it was all the more satisfying for that.

The last of my meal gone, I realized I was thirsty and summoned up my nerve to speak to the dour cook.

"Excuse me, will there be coffee when we stop for lunch?"

"Stop?" He snorted. "You just had your lunch. There's water in that canteen in front of you."

There was, although it was tepid and stale. But it did quench my thirst. I began to develop an appreciation for the men who sat on horseback without a break. Some of them were digging into bags behind their saddles and pulling out what looked to be more biscuits and jerky.

I was anxious to have my talk with Mr. Jefferson. Once more I addressed the cook's forbidding back. "When *will* we be stopping?"

He snorted again. It seemed to be his most expressive means of communication. "We will be stopping," he said mockingly, "about an hour before sundown. Boy, if you're in such an all-fired hurry, why don't you hop out and run over to some of them bushes over there?"

I blushed hotly as I realized his meaning. That would be the last time I addressed the man, I vowed. He was exactly the coarse type of person I had been hiding from in the first place.

Hiding. That reminded me of my postponed interview with Mr. Jefferson. Now I would have to wait until sundown! Much as I dreaded it, I wanted the peace of having it over and done with.

The pile of sacks wasn't as comfortable now as it had been earlier. I rearranged them as best I could and found some empty sacks to place under me, where the floorboards were growing harder by the minute. With that accomplished, I stretched out as far as I could in my cramped quarters and resigned myself to riding out the intervening hours.

The prairie grasses rustled softly in the light breeze. Cattle bawled from time to time, their voices interspersed with yips from the cowboys. The wind shifted, and the breeze played lightly inside the wagon, cooling my hot face. My hair was still coiled on top of my head under my hat. Its weight was oppressive, but I didn't dare take the hat off. . .not yet.

We rolled across the vast prairie, a herd of cattle, a dozen rugged men, and me. Despite our large numbers, we were no more than a speck in that wide and empty land. I dozed off and on during the afternoon, lazily tracking the sun's path as it headed down toward the horizon.

Late in the afternoon, one of the men rode up alongside the wagon and spoke to Cookie. "Got a place spotted?"

Cookie nodded. "Bunch of trees up there. Should be water. I'll go on ahead and set up if it looks good." The team picked up speed and we moved away from the herd.

Apparently there was ample water, for Cookie brought the team to a halt. I was pleased to see that keeping my feet elevated during the day had reduced the swelling, and they were nearly back to their normal size. I tried to slip my socks back on, wincing as they touched the raw places.

Cookie pulled down the tailgate, glanced at my efforts with an impassive face, then reached into a box and tossed me a roll of soft cloth strips. "Bandages," he said.

My feet were still tender when I stepped out of the wagon, although the soft bandages did help a lot. My concern for my feet, however, was dwarfed by the pains that shot through every other part of my body. After a full day of cramped inactivity, my muscles felt as though they had frozen stiff.

Cookie was busy building his fire, but he watched as I staggered around stiff-legged, trying to straighten up. A raspy sound came from his direction, like the wheeze from an organ that has long gone unplayed.

He wheezed again. Why, the man was laughing! My pleasure in discovering that he was capable of such a thing was dampened by the fact that I was the object of his merriment, but it was an encouraging discovery, all the same.

"Boy," he said when he had regained some control, "why don't you go on over and wash yourself?" I was touched by his concern until he added, "You surely look like you could use it." And began wheezing again.

I found a towel in the wagon and went off, reflecting on the strange humor of cowboys.

I returned feeling much refreshed. I had even been able to unwind my hair and brush through it, and the few minutes' respite from its weight on my head had been wonderful.

"Is there anything I can do to help?" I asked Cookie. It was hardly fair to expect to be waited on when these men had so kindly taken me under their wing.

He looked at me appraisingly. "Why don't you scout around for more wood? We'll need enough to keep it going all night long to keep the coffee hot for the night crew."

I stared. For Cookie, this was being positively chatty. I wondered what had brought about the change as I began to gather firewood.

The exercise helped loosen my stiff muscles, and as long as I walked gingerly, I got along rather well. I was proud of the pile I had collected by the time the men had brought the herd up and gathered for supper.

They sprawled around the fire in a variety of attitudes, but none of them displayed the bone-weariness I would have expected after a full day in the saddle. Cookie unbent still further and let me help him dish up the supper. The plates were filled with succulent steaks and the ever-present beans. Coffee that looked strong enough to float any number of horseshoes added its fragrant aroma to the evening air.

I scanned the faces in the group. Mr. Jefferson was not among them. I told myself not to worry. He would surely be in soon.

Taking my own plate, I sat at the edge of the firelight. Some of the men had finished eating and were settling down to talk.

"Good thing Andy got that buffalo yesterday," said one.

"Mm," agreed another around a mouthful of food. "Best steaks we've had the whole trip."

I glanced at the bite on my fork. So this was buffalo and not beef. I took a tentative nibble and found it delicious. There was a lot I had to learn in this new land.

"Anybody seen Jeff?" asked Cookie. "He'd better show up while there's food left."

"He and Jake went to doctor a cow," answered Shorty. "She got a leg tangled pretty bad in some cactus."

So now I would have to wait even longer. I watched idly as Shorty rose and left the circle. He picked up a bedroll and looped his rope around it, then strolled over to a nearby tree. Standing beneath it, he gave the bedroll, rope and all, a toss into the air.

My interest quickened. What new practice of the west was this? The roll fell at his feet, and he threw it again, harder this time. The rope caught around one of the branches about ten feet up and hung in a fork, the bedroll swinging from one side, the end of the rope dangling from the other. I waited to see how he would get the tangle loose, but he walked back to his place in the circle and sat down as if satisfied.

One of the other cowboys shook his head sadly. "Shorty, one of these days, someone's going to dangle a loop over a limb that's meant for you."

Shorty grinned. "No chance, Neil. I'm as pure as the driven snow."

Neil grunted. None of this exchange made sense to me, but so far, very little had.

"Here you go, boys." It was Cookie, bearing a tray of steaming pies. "Enjoy the apples. They're the last you'll get on this ride."

I helped him cut huge wedges of the pies and serve them to the men. Shorty looked up as I gave his piece to him. "Well, boy," he said, "what do you think about those three thousand head of big dogs we're herding?"

The chuckles around me revealed that my comment had been repeated and apparently enjoyed. I ducked my head in embarrassment and kept on serving.

"His name's Judah," Cookie growled. I turned to look at him in appreciation and he glared back at me, but this unexpected championship made me feel more protected than I had since Jake had left me that morning.

Shorty, however, wasn't one to give up easily. "Judah, is it?" he asked politely. "Well, that's fine. Judah, are you feeling better today?"

I nodded, sitting down to eat my pie. His face betrayed nothing, but I was confused by his sudden interest, embarrassed at being singled out, and altogether suspicious of his motives.

"That boy don't talk much, does he?" he muttered. I glanced up to see him eyeing me speculatively.

"Shorty?" It was Neil. "Do you think we'll have any trouble with skunks like we did back in Texas?"

"Well, now, it all depends," Shorty drawled. I breathed a sigh of relief.

His attention had been diverted from me; he didn't so much as flicker an eyelash in my direction.

"It all depends," he repeated. "I surely hope not. I recollect what happened to poor Lem Harris. You all know that story, of course."

"Can't say I've heard it," said a man sitting a few feet from me. "Why don't you tell us all about it?"

"It's a sad and terrible story," Shorty began. "About five years ago, I was on a drive near the Brazos. There were only ten of us, including the cook and the wrangler.

"We'd had trouble all along the way, what with Indians, dry waterholes, and wolves waiting to pick off the stragglers if we gave them half a chance. But the worst problem we had to put up with was the hydrophoby skunks."

I shuddered. Here was another new peril. I listened intently to prepare myself in the event I came across one.

"You've all dealt with hydrophoby skunks, haven't you?" Several of the men nodded solemnly. "For such timid critters, they turn mighty mean when the disease takes them. Cunning, too. They're just itching to bite someone, but they know they don't stand a chance when you're up on horseback."

"What do they do?" asked the man near me.

"Why, they wait around a cow camp, like this one here, and hide in the grass until everyone's asleep. Then they come creeping out and check the bedrolls, one by one. And the amazing thing is how they always check the head end."

"Can't you just cover your head and fool 'em?" asked my neighbor.

Shorty shook his head. "I told you, they get mighty cunning. They have some kind of instinct for finding the head. Maybe it's the sound of breathing. But they'll creep up and pull the blankets right back from your face."

I looked around cautiously, trying to search out the shadows. None of the men seemed particularly concerned, though, and no one took the slightest notice of me.

"Anyway," Shorty resumed his tale, "we'd noticed signs of them hydrophoby skunks for some time, and of course, I'd warned all the new men about them. Told them that the only way to keep from getting bit if one comes up to you is to lie perfectly still. You know, they have bad eyesight, and they wait for a body to move so they can take proper aim."

"Tell 'em what happened to Lem," prompted Neil.

Shorty sighed mournfully. "That Lem never was one for listening. One night, we were all layin' in our blankets, when I heard a rustling in the grass. I knew it was some kind of varmint, but it wasn't until it began tugging my blankets away from my face that I saw for sure it was a hydrophoby skunk."

"What did you do?" This from my neighbor.

"Do? Why, I just laid there as still as death, and when he couldn't take a proper aim at me, he moved off to check the others.

"Once he was gone, I kind of eased up on one elbow, and I saw him sizing up old Lem. Lem hadn't taken my warning to heart, and no sooner did the pulling and the tugging wake him than he started up with a yell.

"That was all the skunk was waiting for. As soon as Lem moved, the skunk spotted his target and jumped him."

"How bad was it?" asked one of the men.

"Bit the end of his nose clean off. Lem was up dancing around, whooping and swearing, and in all the excitement the hydrophoby skunk moseyed off and we never saw him again. Lem never did look quite right after that. Them hydrophoby skunks are mean—poison mean."

In the silence that followed, I realized I was holding one hand protectively over the lower half of my face.

The cowboys got up, stretched, and one by one started laying out their bedrolls. Shorty stopped next to me and laid a hand on my shoulder. "I already spread your blankets out for you, boy," he said kindly. "You'd best get some sleep."

The fire had burned down and the night air was chilly. I would roll up in my blankets, I decided, and wait for the return of Jake and Mr. Jefferson.

Shorty had thoughtfully spread my blankets next to the chuck wagon, and I welcomed its now-familiar shelter. I tossed and twisted, trying to fit my body to the unrelenting contours of the ground.

Overhead, the sky was an indigo blue, with the lighter clouds scudding across it. The moon had nearly completed its circuit and was casting a cheerful glow across our campground. The beauty of God's creation held me spellbound, and it seemed impossible for any but the most friendly creatures to exist in the peaceful setting.

Footsteps sounded on the far side of the fire, and I raised my head to see Jake walk into the circle of light. He looked exhausted. He stood for a moment as if puzzled, then frowned and began pacing around outside the circle of sleepers. "All right, where is it?" he yelled. The cowboys lay undisturbed, apparently sound asleep.

Jake turned away, mumbling, and enlarged his circle. He stopped short under a tree and stared up into its branches. "Hey, Shorty!" he roared. "Can't a body come back all tuckered out after a long day's work without finding someone's gone and strung his bedroll up in a tree?"

The bodies around the fire were suspiciously quiet, but I heard a muffled snort of laughter. Until that moment I had forgotten Shorty's strange behavior. The sight of Jake clambering up the tree to untangle his bedroll might have been funny if I hadn't been so tired myself lately and had a fair idea of how he felt.

A movement behind me claimed my attention. On the opposite side of the chuck wagon I could see two pairs of boots and hear the murmur of voices.

One I recognized as Cookie's. "About time you got in. You look about played out. Here, I saved you a plate. It's cold now."

I strained to hear more. This must be Mr. Jefferson.

"Thanks, Cookie. I am tired." It was undoubtedly his voice. My moment was at hand.

"Cow going to be all right?"

"I think so, as long as infection doesn't set in. We'll do the best we can."

I drew a long breath and offered a prayer for strength. I was in the very act of slipping from beneath the covers when Mr. Jefferson's next words arrested my movement.

"How's Judah? Did he give you any trouble today?"

I froze, straining to hear Cookie's reply. "You know, that boy's really something. I figured he'd be up beside me, wanting to drive and jabbering in my ear all day. But he sat in the back where I put him and hardly said a word."

"Is he rested up from yesterday? He's had a pretty rough time of it, being deserted like that."

"I'll tell you, Jeff, that boy's got spunk. His feet were worn as raw as anything I've ever seen, but he never once complained. I gave him some bandages, and darned if he didn't come offer to help me! Gathered that pile of wood all by himself.

"That boy's game, Jeff. I'll stand by him."

"He must be something special to get you to open up," Mr. Jefferson said, chuckling. "That's more than I've heard you say on the whole drive."

Cookie resorted to his characteristic snort and withdrew into silence. I could see the other pair of boots walk away into the night.

It's said that eavesdroppers seldom hear good of themselves. I wondered how many eavesdroppers heard themselves described in such glowing terms, especially when they knew the praise was undeserved.

I could no more have interrupted that conversation than I could have held the chuck wagon up with one hand. My misery increased—not only had I failed to confess my duplicity, but by my silence I had allowed the two men to form a wholly undeserved opinion of me.

The fire was merely a bed of glowing coals by now. I could not make out

Mr. Jefferson's form in the darkness, nor could I call out to him for fear of rousing the camp. My confrontation had been postponed again, at least until breakfast. I rolled up in my blankets, thoroughly disgusted with myself, and went to sleep.

I don't know what startled me out of my sleep, but all at once my eyelids flew open and I knew something was wrong. A tug on my blankets told me I was not alone; someone was gently pulling the blankets away from my face.

A confusion of thoughts whirled through my mind in what must have been only a split second. One of the men, perhaps. Should I cry out? But surely none of our number would come meaning me any harm, not with a dozen strong, armed men sleeping only yards away. It must be Mr. Jefferson, or Cookie, or Jake, come to bring me some message. But then why not shake my shoulder? Why this insistent tugging to uncover my face?

Something in my sleep-numbed brain fought for recognition, something that lay just beyond my grasp.

Of course! I almost moaned aloud in despair. Shorty's story of the marauding skunks! What had he said to do? Lie perfectly still. That was it. Don't give the poor-sighted brute a chance to take aim.

The blanket inched away from my cheek, my nose, my chin. *Remember Lem Harris,* I warned myself. *Lie still, and it will go away, and you can raise the alarm to warn the others.*

The pulling stopped, although I still felt a vibrating tension on one corner of my blanket, as though the beast were trying to focus on my face, to take aim at my nose. It was almost more than I could bear to lie motionless under its steady, if nearsighted, gaze. The black night hid it well, but I could feel its presence as it waited for a chance to spring.

There was a sudden rustle, and to my terror, a furry body leapt full into my face. I screamed, fighting wildly against both my attacker and the tangle of blankets that held me.

I screamed again and kicked my way free. I caught hold of a fistful of fur and tore it away from my face. There was a roaring in my ears, and I steadied myself. This was no time to faint.

Movement stirred among the bedrolls, and someone threw wood on the fire, sending up a shower of sparks followed by a strong flame that lit up the camp area.

Through my panic, I became dimly aware that the roaring in my ears was the sound of the men's laughter—laughter that died away as they stared at me, open-mouthed.

I dropped my eyes before their gaze and became aware of three things. One was the piece of rabbit skin I still clutched in one hand. Another was the rope tied to one corner of my blanket and trailing away toward where the men lay. The third was my hat, lying on the ground.

To pick it up and replace it would have been pointless. My hair had fallen loose during my frantic struggle and now hung down to my waist.

I looked back at the men. They still gaped at me. Only Shorty, absorbed in his hilarity, had failed to notice what had happened. He rocked back and forth, the end of a rope trailing from his hand, whooping and slapping his leg.

"Hear that?" he cried. "Did you hear that? I told you I'd get that boy to talk! I told you—" He broke off, eyes bulging as he finally focused on me.

It was Jake who broke the silence. "My word!" he roared. "He's a girl!"

No one else made a sound. I waited hopefully for the earth to open and swallow me up.

Across the fire, a figure stepped into the circle of light and I found myself looking straight into Mr. Jefferson's eyes.

six

The next day found me rocking along in my seat in the rear of the chuck wagon. My feet were over much of their soreness by now, but my pride was grievously tender.

The much-delayed talk with Mr. Jefferson had finally taken place the night before. We had walked to the edge of the firelight while the cowboys rearranged themselves in their blankets. Not one of them had uttered a word following Jake's outburst. Even Shorty had remained silent.

We stopped just before the darkness enveloped us. I was grateful for the effort made to have a private conversation and devoutly hoped that we were indeed out of earshot. I was sure that anything that might be overheard would spread through the group like wildfire. From what I had seen thus far, when it came to passing along scraps of information, Aunt Phoebe's sewing circle had nothing on these cowboys.

Mr. Jefferson turned to face me. He said nothing, but his eyes demanded an explanation.

"I meant to talk to you earlier," I faltered. He raised his eyebrows. I took a deep breath and plunged into my story.

"My name is Judith Alder. That's the only thing I lied to you about. I really was traveling west to help my uncle Matthew at his trading post. The family I was traveling with drove off and left me yesterday morning, just as I said."

"Why?"

"We were running low on food and water. They'd be more sure of getting to Santa Fe if they only had three mouths to feed. And Mrs. Parker. . ." I hadn't planned to elaborate on that portion of the story, but I had made up my mind to make a clean breast of things, and I would, despite my embarrassment.

"Mrs. Parker, the woman I came with, felt I was an. . .an unsettling influence on her husband and son."

"I can imagine," he said drily. "You've certainly succeeded in unsettling this camp tonight. And did your Mrs. Parker outfit you before she left?"

"Not intentionally. They set out a crate they thought was mine, but their son's clothes were in it. I felt I would be safer traveling alone if I were, ah, incognito."

"I see. But after Jake found you and brought you in. . .?"

"Please try to understand," I pleaded. "I was so terribly tired and afraid and confused. I had no idea what sort of men you were, and there weren't any other women around.

"After I'd lied to you about my name, I knew I had to tell you the truth and make it right, but I didn't see you anymore today. And after I got in bed, I heard you come in, but then I heard what you and Cookie were saying about me, and I just couldn't bring myself to do it then.

"And then," I gulped, my emotions getting the upper hand, "when you went away, I decided I'd tell you at breakfast, but Shorty played that horrible trick about the hydrophobia skunk, and. . .and. . ." For the first time since being left, I gave way to tears, and they came in abundance.

I covered my face with my hands to muffle the sobs that shook me. Never had I felt so alone and so ashamed. Not only had I purposely deceived the kind people who had taken me in, but I had failed miserably at following the example of Christ.

Mr. Jefferson shuffled his feet. Apparently he was as uncomfortable as most men around feminine tears. Wiping my eyes with the backs of my hands I choked back the sobs and waited for whatever censure was to come.

"You're tired, Ju—Miss Alder. You'd best go get what sleep you can. If we push ourselves, we may be able to make the ranch by sundown tomorrow, and you can have a decent bed." His lips tightened. "And a change of clothes."

"Thank you," I said meekly. He stretched out an arm as if to throw it around my shoulders as he had that morning, but drew it back abruptly.

"Go get some rest," he said.

After the evening's turn of events, I expected to lie awake for hours. Instead, I slept dreamlessly, noticing nothing until Cookie's "Come and get it!" roused the camp. I elected to stay close to the wagon to eat the plate of biscuits and beans Cookie silently handed me rather than join the men around the fire.

Now it was nearing noonday, and I helped myself to biscuits and jerky. Cookie made no effort at conversation, but then, no one had spoken a word to me all day. I felt a twinge of self-pity.

You've only yourself to blame, I scolded myself. I wondered, though, if I would be ostracized like this once we reached the ranch. If the story was passed along to the owners. . . If! How could I doubt its being told, and with suitable embellishments, at that.

But they would have to talk with me at least long enough to let me know how I was to reach Uncle Matthew. I sighed. Being passed from hand to hand was growing tiresome.

Late in the afternoon, one of the men rode up next to Cookie. "Jeff said to tell you we're making better time than we thought. He's scouted on ahead and he says we ought to be at the ranch in an hour or so."

"Good," Cookie said. "It'll give me a chance to unload in the daylight."

Yes, unload, I thought wearily. *Unload the food, unload the equipment, and unload me.* I pulled out my bag and found my comb, then set to work on the snarls in my hair. If we were getting back into civilized country, I had better make myself presentable. Well, as presentable as possible. I fervently hoped that the rancher's wife wasn't another Aunt Phoebe.

At least I could make a reasonably fresh start there, and I would be free of the cowboys' scrutiny, Shorty's practical jokes, and the look in Mr. Jefferson's eyes in which I was sure I had read disappointment and reproach. Once I was safely inside the ranch house, I need not see any of them again.

I found a small handkerchief tucked away in my bag, soaked it with water from a canteen, and used it to scrub my face and hands. The trail dust, I knew, would settle and cling again almost as soon as I had washed it off, but it boosted my morale to make the effort.

There was little that could be done about my clothes. I slapped dust from the overalls with my hat as I had seen the men do. Thank goodness I wouldn't have to wear it again! I smoothed my hair as best I could into a coil at the back of my neck, thinking how good it would feel to have it clean once more.

The wagon rocked more slowly now. I tried to peer out the front, but could see nothing beyond Cookie's broad back. He seemed to be maintaining his cold-shoulder treatment to the end. I had tried to apologize earlier, but he had gone about his business as though I were not even there.

Cookie drew the team to a stop and jumped off the seat, not bothering to glance back at me. I was sorry to leave him on such a cool note.

Jake's face appeared at the back of the wagon. "Miss Judith, we're at the Double B now. Come on out and I'll take you to meet the Bradleys."

He helped me down with such courtly manners that I almost laughed in spite of my nervousness. "Jake," I said, "I want to thank you for rescuing me. And I'm sorry—very sorry—that I deceived you as I did. Please forgive me."

To my surprise, he turned as red as a beet. "Don't you worry about that, Miss Judith. I've been talking to Jeff and he explained it all to me. You kind of bowled us all over last night, but I think you're one spunky little lady."

My spirits soared. "Thank you, Jake. You don't know what it means to have one friend left among you."

"*One* friend?" His eyes widened, then narrowed. "Miss Judith—" He broke off at the approach of a tall, smiling man.

"Jake! It's good to see you here. Jeff tells me you have something to show me."

My embarrassment returned full flood. Some*thing*, indeed! Jake reached out eagerly to pump the man's hand. "Yep, we rounded up more than our share of strays this trip. Miss Judith, may I present Mr. Charles Bradley, owner of the Double B Ranch. Charles, this here is Miss Judith Alder, late of St. Joseph, and on her way to live with her uncle over in Taos."

Mr. Bradley took my extended hand and immediately endeared himself to me by ignoring my strange garb entirely.

"Miss Alder, I am pleased to make your acquaintance. I hope you will do us the honor of being our guest for some time." He turned at the sound of approaching footsteps and smiled. Two women were walking toward us. The younger woman, slight and fair-haired, leaned on the arm of the older one, whose sharp, disapproving glance took in the group and focused on me.

"Allow me to present my wife, Abby," said Mr. Bradley. "Abby, Miss Alder." His wife was as gracious as her husband, smiling and completely overlooking my unconventional arrival. She released her hold on the older woman's arm and took a step toward her husband, who smiled and put a supporting arm around her waist.

"I'm glad to meet you, Miss Alder." Her voice was soft and her speech bore evidence of a southern origin.

The older woman stood as stiff and straight as if she had swallowed a poker. Her eyes had not left my face since she had first seen me, and they glittered now with animosity.

The Bradleys seemed to recall her presence. "My apologies," Mr. Bradley said, smiling. "Miss Alder, this is Mrs. Styles."

Her sharp eyes looked me up and down. I tentatively offered a hand, which she ignored. "And your family, Miss Alder? Are they stopping here also?"

Somehow I felt instinctively that the Bradleys wouldn't blink at my strange situation, but I hated to explain in front of Mrs. Styles. "I am not traveling with my family. I was on my way west when the people I was with deserted me. These trail drivers were kind enough to bring me here until I can make arrangements to finish my journey."

"And how long have you been in their company. . .alone?"

I made an effort to speak evenly. "I have been with them for two nights and two days, and all of them have behaved as perfect gentlemen." I put as much dignity into this speech as I could, considering that I was hardly dressed as the perfect lady.

Mrs. Styles sniffed and looked me up and down. "I shall be on my way, Abby. I will return to see you and Charles at a later date." She gave me a final scathing look and walked to a buggy standing in front of the house.

The four of us—the Bradleys, Jake and I—let out a collective sigh of relief and looked at one another guiltily.

"Please, Miss Alder—may I call you Judith?" said Mrs. Bradley. "And you're to call us Charles and Abby. Things aren't nearly as formal here as they are back east. Don't be too upset by Lucia Styles. It's just that she has exceptionally high standards and so few of us manage to live up to them." Her pale cheek dimpled as she smiled mischievously.

"Won't you come in and sit with me? I believe I need to rest a bit." She certainly looked it. The hand resting on her husband's arm was trembling.

"I'm sorry, dear," he said in a stricken voice. "I'll take you in at once." And with that he swept her up in his arms. He turned to me. "She only came out to greet the drivers. She isn't supposed to be up for long periods. Please do come in. You must be exhausted."

I took my first look at the ranch house as I followed them inside. It was huge, a long, low, rambling affair of stone. Off to the west, the sun was setting in a glorious array of pink and gold, its last brilliant rays picking out the soft hues in the stone walls. Different styles of building seemed to be represented, as though several additions had been made to the original structure, but all in all the effect was one of strength and permanence.

The house stood on a level area at the top of a low hill, commanding the view for miles in all directions. In the distance, cattle dotted the slopes.

Inside, the house was furnished elegantly and with taste, making one feel at home immediately without any hint of pretentiousness. Charles laid Abby gently on a couch, arranging cushions at her back to let her rest comfortably.

I sank gratefully into a deep chair he pointed out to me. It was my first taste of comfort in many days, and I felt as if I could sit there forever.

A plump woman in a gingham dress brought in a tea service, and Charles poured out steaming cups for the three of us.

"Now, Judith," he said, "you say your party deserted you along the trail?"

I retold my story for what seemed the thousandth time while we sat sipping our tea. I went back to Aunt Phoebe's choice of the Parkers to take me along and omitted nothing along the way, including my decision to wear Lanny's clothes. Abby's dimple deepened at that, but she said nothing.

"And so they brought me here, and it appears they have decided I'm to stay with you until I can contact Uncle Matthew to make further arrangements. But I don't want to impose."

Abby laughed softly. "Judith, if you only knew how I welcome your company! Of course you must stay with us. Charles, please show her to a room and have Vera bring her plenty of hot water. I still have some dresses that haven't been taken in. She can try them on." She added to me, "I think you're much the same size I was before I lost weight."

I followed Charles down a long corridor to my room. He stopped at an open doorway. "Please make yourself at home, Judith. I'll see Vera about the water and Abby's dresses."

The room carried the same stamp of elegant simplicity that I had noted before, nothing lavish, but everything comfortable and lovely. The bed drew my attention first, and I settled myself gingerly on a corner. It was a wonderfully soft mattress, especially tempting after so many days of bedrolls on the ground. I didn't dare lie upon it now, or I was sure I wouldn't move until morning.

A small overstuffed chair sat in one corner next to the stone fireplace, and there were a wardrobe and dresser on the other side of the room. The bed, chair, and floor had been covered with bright rugs, which I guessed were Indian in design and added a warm glow of color to the room.

There was a knock on the door, and the plump woman came into the room, carrying an armful of clothing. She was followed by two young boys, one bearing a bathtub and the other buckets of steaming water. The boys set down their cargo and left, but the woman lingered behind.

"Charles said to bring you dresses, but I figured you'd need more'n that, so I brought along some necessaries, too." She grinned and produced an array of undergarments from beneath the pile of dresses.

"That's very thoughtful." I smiled back at her. It was easy to relax in the face of her good humor.

She hefted the buckets as though they weighed nothing and poured them into the bath. "Soap's over there." She nodded toward a small table next to the dresser that also held a basin and pitcher.

"After you get all clean, I'll come if you want me to and help you try on the dresses. If they need some taking up or letting out, I can do that, too. But they should be pretty close. Abby used to be just about your size."

"Is she. . ." I trailed off, not knowing exactly how to ask about my frail hostess.

Vera understood. "No one's sure what's ailing her. She just started wasting away about six months ago. Nobody knows why, but Charles is worried sick about her."

"But surely a doctor could help."

"Honey, we don't have a doctor handy. There've been a couple passing through, though, and neither one of them could find a thing wrong." Her eyes misted over. It was plain to see that she was as worried about Abby as anyone.

"But what you need right now," she said briskly, "is a long soak, some supper, and bed. I'll quit talking, and you get on with it."

Left to myself, I peeled off Lanny's shirt and overalls and the rest of the clothes I had worn, now filthy. Bless Vera for having thought of the "necessaries!"

The hot water felt heavenly. I soaked and scrubbed and rinsed, then scrubbed some more. I lathered up my hair and washed it until it squeaked and my scalp tingled. When the water began to cool, I got out and wrapped myself in one of the huge, fluffy towels Vera had brought. I used another to get as much water as I could out of my hair.

I sorted through the clothes on the bed. They were all well made, with the attention to detail that transforms an ordinary garment into one of distinction.

I had just finished putting on clean undergarments when Vera tapped on the door and came in.

"My land, there was a pretty girl under all that grime," she said with a chuckle.

Together we held up the dresses and Vera helped me into one that took my fancy. It was a pale blue, simply made, which brought out the blue in my eyes that my father had always called cornflower. Vera provided a supply of hairpins and we dressed my still damp hair into a simple style low on my neck.

"I need to see about supper," said Vera. "You come back to the parlor with me so you don't get lost your first night here."

Back in the parlor, I realized that despite the hearty helpings of beans, biscuits, and more beans that I had eaten the last two days, I was famished for a home-cooked meal served at a table.

No one else was in the room, so I wandered around, admiring several of the different objects. My skirts rustled and swayed as I moved, and it was a welcome feeling after having been encased in boy's clothes.

I sighed. Being clean again, wearing a dress, and once more looking like myself would have been enough, even without the Bradleys' kind hospitality. Their warm welcome, this lovely home, and the tempting smells that were finding their way from the kitchen made the Parkers' perfidy and my masquerade fade away like a bad dream.

And I would not have to face the shunning of the cowboys any longer. I had known them only a short time, but I still did not like the thought of losing their respect.

I turned to see Charles Bradley standing in the open doorway, a pleased smile on his face. "You look refreshed, Judith. And that dress suits you admirably. Supper is ready now, but if you don't mind waiting a few moments more, my brother will join us."

I smiled back at him. "Thank you. I'm sure I can last a few more minutes. Is Abby feeling better?"

A shadow crossed his face. "She is having her supper on a tray in her room. I shouldn't have let her stay up and get so tired. But she was so excited about the rest of the cattle arriving safely that I thought it might do her good." He smiled again. "For all of her frailty now, Abby loved being involved in the ranch and the life that goes with it."

"I can see how she would. You have a beautiful home and a perfect setting for it. I want to thank you for your hospitality, especially to an unexpected guest. I do hope I won't need to impose on you for more than a short time."

"Please feel free to stay as long as you like. Both Abby and I are delighted to have you. So now, you see, you're an invited guest and don't need to consider your stay an imposition."

"I'll try not to. But is there some way of sending a message to my uncle? He'll be expecting me soon and I need to let him know where I am and ask him to arrange for some kind of transportation for me."

"Of course. I know you must be concerned for him and anxious to finish your journey. If you'll write out your message tonight, I'll send it with one of my men to the stage station tomorrow morning. And now," he said, turning, "I believe I hear my brother coming."

Footsteps sounded in the corridor, and a tall man stepped into the room. I gasped and felt the warm blood rush to my cheeks.

"I believe you're already acquainted with my brother, Jefferson," Charles said.

seven

His brother! Our eyes met and held while I struggled to keep from gaping and to make some sense of this new development.

Charles looked confused. "I'm sorry. I thought you two had met. Miss Alder, my brother, Jefferson Bradley."

"No, you're right, Charles. We have met," said his brother, the corners of his mouth twitching. "But it appears neither one of us made our identity quite clear."

Charles's brow furrowed again and Jeff laughed. "Don't worry, I'll explain later. Right now, I'm sure Miss Alder must be as hungry as I am. Let's go in to dinner."

The aroma that had drifted to me from the kitchen had awakened a delicious anticipation of the supper to come. But after meeting Mr. Je— Bradley, I corrected myself—I could not have told what we ate.

The brothers were clearly delighted to be together again, but made every effort to include me in their conversation. I appreciated their attempt to smooth over the awkwardness we all felt and soon became caught up in their discussion of the ranch.

"Something puzzles me," I ventured. "I always thought cattle were driven *from* the ranch *to* the market. But you brought thousands of them here."

Charles answered my question. "You're right, Judith. This is a little out of the ordinary. You have to understand that we grew up ranching in Texas and built up quite a herd. But times aren't easy in Texas these days. Abby and I moved up here a little over a year ago and brought half our herd with us. Jeff kept the rest in Texas in case the experiment failed.

"But this New Mexico Territory is open and fresh and ready for new blood. The cattle thrive here. And best of all, the railroad will extend this far west in just a few years, and we'll be able to drive cattle to a railhead in just a few days, instead of taking them all the way up the trail to Abilene."

"So now you've brought all your livestock up here?"

"That's what we've done. We're sure now that the land will support the cattle, and Jeff and the hands we had left drove the rest of them here. Your arrival along with them was a pleasant surprise, eh, Jeff?"

"She was certainly a surprise," Jeff replied drily.

I chose not to rise to the bait.

After dinner, Charles excused himself to check on the new stock. Jeff walked with me as far as the parlor.

"It's a little different, seeing you like this," he said, smiling.

I ducked my head in confusion. "I'm really sorry about the mix-up. I never meant to—"

"I didn't mean that as a criticism," he said. "It's a nice difference."

"Thank you."

"You said you overhead me talking to Cookie last night?"

I nodded. "I couldn't help it. I don't eavesdrop as a rule."

"I just want you to know that. . .all the things Cookie said about you. . .I still think they're true." He cleared his throat. "Good night." And then he was gone.

I floated down the corridor to my room. Trying to think sensibly, I told myself that a total stranger had said I had spunk, that I was game. It should hardly have produced such a heady sensation. I climbed into bed feeling ridiculously happy.

Next morning, after eating the breakfast Vera brought to my room on a tray, I dressed in another of Abby's dresses, a flowered print this time, and sat down to compose a note to Uncle Matthew, explaining my plight. With that done, I managed to find my way to the front of the house.

Charles was at one end of the broad porch, talking to his brother, while Abby lay in a hammock at the other. I felt my cheeks grow warm at the sight of Jeff and hurried to a chair next to Abby, hoping the others had not noticed.

She smiled. "That dress looks charming on you. I'm so glad you are able to wear it."

"It was good of you to lend your dresses to me. I'll return them once I've reached my uncle and can make more."

"No, don't worry about that. I'd like for you to have them. I have plenty for myself now, and I'm not likely to need that size again." A swift shadow crossed her face, to be replaced by her gentle smile.

"Don't look so distressed, Judith. Vera said she had told you about my illness. I would like to grow well again, of course, but I know the Lord as my Savior, and I'm sure of a home in heaven if I don't recover." Her gaze rested on her husband lovingly. "It's Charles that concerns me most. Charles and the children."

"Children?" I don't know why that should have surprised me, but I had seen no evidence of them, and it only seemed to compound the tragedy.

"We have two," she said, laughing, "although they get into so much mischief that sometimes it seems like more.

"Charles is so busy running the ranch that he can't spend as much time with them as he'd like, and Vera has all she can handle managing the house. Since I've been ill, I'm afraid they've run rather wild." The shadow crept into her eyes again. "It's for them that I mind most."

I tried to think of something to say. Surely there were words of comfort, but they eluded me. Her faith touched me deeply, and I was grateful that she knew the Lord.

Would I be able to face death as calmly as she, even though it meant leaving a beloved family? I wondered.

She seemed to sense my distress, for she smiled again and tactfully changed the subject. "Tell me," she said, her eyes twinkling, "how did the men react when they found out you were a young lady instead of a boy?"

I groaned. "It certainly wasn't what I had expected. I was prepared for all kinds of recriminations, but when it came down to it, I don't believe one of them actually said a word. Except Jeff, of course. Even Jake kept away from me after that until we arrived here.

"They must have been even more embarrassed than I was, but I still felt bad that they were all so angry they wouldn't even speak to me."

"Angry?" Abby raised an eyebrow. "Judith, is this your first trip west?" I nodded. "Well, brace yourself, my dear. I think you're in for a surprise."

Before I could ask what she meant, Charles and Jeff had come up behind us. Charles smoothed his wife's hair tenderly. "Did you write your message to your uncle?" he asked me. I took the note from my pocket and handed it to him. "One of the men is leaving for town soon. I'll send it along with him," he promised.

Abby looked up at Jeff and smiled. "Welcome home," she said. "I didn't get a chance to greet you last night. I hope you were comfortable."

Jeff grinned back at her. "After all those nights on the trail, anything would have been an improvement. But my bed felt wonderful, Abby. The place already feels like home."

"Did Charles tell you the news?"

"Nothing but news since I got here. Was there any particular thing you had in mind?"

Abby made a face at him, and I gathered that the lighthearted banter between these three was of long standing. I wondered if this was too tiring for Abby, but her color seemed improved and her manner more relaxed.

"Why *the* news, of course. Just in time for your arrival, we have acquired a minister at Three Forks."

Jeff whistled and a grin broke out on his face. I felt my heart quicken and told myself it was due to the news and his infectious grin. I would surely be here at least throughout the weekend. How wonderful it would be to attend a worship service again before traveling on!

"How did you manage that?" Jeff asked.

"Really, he just fell into our laps," answered Charles. "He had to give up his church in the east because of ill health and traveled out here under his doctor's orders. If the climate suits him, he may stay permanently."

"Wouldn't that be fine!" Jeff's eyes glowed with a happiness that—I checked myself. I was becoming all too interested in the moods of a stranger, even one who had rescued me. I would be gone in a few days to a new life filled with new people. The thought should not have left me feeling so bleak.

I forced my attention back to the conversation. ". . .only had time to shake his hand and say hello," Charles was saying. "But this western air should make a new man out of him, if he'll stay long enough to give it a chance."

He broke off and frowned, sniffing. There *was* a peculiar smell, sweet and cloying, even though we were outside. We were all looking for its source when Shorty and Neil stepped around the corner of the house, bringing an even stronger cloud of the scent with them. They stopped before us and shuffled their feet.

"What on earth!" sputtered Charles. "Did you two tangle with a skunk this morning? Back away so the rest of us can breathe, won't you?"

Shorty looked hurt. "Aw, Boss, you ain't making fun of my cologne, are you?"

"Cologne?" Charles stepped down off the porch and circled the pair slowly. "Hair combed," he said in awe. "Clean shaven, and, I declare, I believe those shirts have been washed sometime within the last six months. What's gotten into you boys?" Behind me, I heard Abby giggle.

"Why, Boss," said Shorty, with an attempt at wounded dignity, "we just came in off the trail and wanted to make ourselves presentable. Right, Neil?"

Neil, his eyes fastened on the toe of his boot, mumbled assent.

"And being naturally kindhearted, we thought we'd come and see how Miss Judith was doing this morning. We wanted to see if there was anything we could do for her. Right, Neil?"

Neil gulped and nodded.

"I see," Charles said kindly. "I appreciate that, boys, and I'm sure Miss Alder does, too. As a matter of fact," he continued, "there is something you could do, but it's a job for just one of you."

Shorty stepped forward. "I'm your man," he announced.

"Good for you," Charles said. "Take this message to the stage station at Three Forks. It's on the trail, about fifteen miles southwest of here. You can't miss it."

Shorty stared, crestfallen, as Charles handed him the note and gave him a hearty clap on the shoulder. He looked mournfully at the paper, then shook his head and started toward the corral.

Charles turned his attention to Neil. "Well, what's keeping you from your chores?"

Neil turned brick red and stared intently at his boot. "Begging your pardon, Boss, but I twisted my ankle something awful this morning, and I thought maybe I ought to sit down and give it a chance to heal." He raised his eyes hopefully. "Like maybe on the porch?"

Charles rolled his eyes skyward. Neil heaved a sigh and walked away with a pronounced limp I was sure had not been evident earlier. Jeff and Charles watched him go, then walked off toward the corral, chuckling.

I had sat wide-eyed through this performance, unable to utter a word, but now I turned to Abby. "Was that really for my benefit?"

She nodded, still trying to control her laughter. Evidently, her illness had not dampened her sense of humor. "Oh, Judith!" she burst out, "I knew your coming here would do me good, but what havoc you've wrought on these poor cowboys!"

I sighed. If nothing else, my presence here seemed to be highly entertaining to everyone else. No, I shouldn't feel sorry for myself. If I could do anything at all to lighten Abby's spirits, I would do so.

We talked on in the warm sunshine. A light breeze stirred from time to time. Abby told me of her girlhood in Virginia as the youngest daughter of a wealthy plantation owner and of her family's dismay when she married and left with Charles, who had been visiting relatives nearby.

"They told me I would regret marrying 'beneath me,' " she said. "But I've never regretted one instant with Charles. Judith, I hope that when the time is right, you will find someone who will make you as happy as I have been." Her eyes sparkled with mischief. "You realize, of course, that you have only to say the word to have the pick of any of the cowboys on the ranch."

I pretended to consider the matter. "Shorty, perhaps? No, I don't think I'd care to go through life wondering if a skunk was going to creep up on me in my sleep." We both laughed.

When Abby felt she could walk a bit, she showed me around the house. The arrangement was much less complicated than I had thought. The house was made up of four wings forming a hollow square, in the center of which was a spacious courtyard.

Nearly all the rooms in the house opened onto the courtyard, except for a few, including mine, which were located in a sort of annex that projected beyond one corner of the square. The annex itself was connected to the court-yard by means of a covered walkway that separated the north and west wings.

A tall cottonwood tree grew in the center of the courtyard, with a bench encircling it. Bright flowers bloomed near a well, and two sets of hitching rails flanked a large gate set in the east wall.

"How lovely," I breathed. "It's like having your own little world."

"It is peaceful here," Abby agreed. "It started out as a trading post, and they had to build it almost like a fortress for protection. The fur trade started to die out, so it was sold several years ago to an Englishman. He had a sub-stantial amount of money, but, as a younger son, no hope of inheriting prop-erty in England. So he bought this place and transformed it from a trading post into a showplace.

"He added onto the original building. I rather imagine he planned to build more on bit by bit and create his own 'ancestral home.' By the time he had fin-ished the annex, he'd grown lonely and bored and went back to England where he could spend his money in a more populous area."

"And then you moved here?"

She nodded. "When we first saw it, it seemed like home. Charles and Jeff were determined to leave Texas so we could have a better life, and it seemed this place was here just waiting for us."

We were interrupted by Vera's call to lunch. Today, I joined Abby for the meal, which she ate in her room. She seemed to have enjoyed the conver-sation and walk, but she tired so quickly, she explained, that it was easier for all concerned if she could eat and go immediately to bed for a midday rest.

The next few days fell into a pattern. I would spend the morning visiting with Abby, then eat lunch with her and help her to bed. I usually took a brief rest at that time myself, then the rest of afternoon was mine to use as I wished, exploring the immediate area or relaxing on the bench in the court-yard with a good book.

The fellowship with Abby was sweet, and I was grateful that the Lord had given me this oasis of calm in the midst of the upheaval in my life. I wished, though, that Uncle Matthew would hasten his reply. Despite the Bradleys' glad acceptance of my company, I had no wish to be a burden.

It was during my third afternoon on my own that I became acquainted with the Bradley children. I had ventured out the gate and had walked for some distance, reveling in the view and the pure air. Surely, I felt, in such vast surroundings, a person ought to expand in character to match it.

I had made my way back to the house and was passing through the wide gate when something hard was pressed into my back.

My knees went weak. Abby's words came back to me: fortress, protection. This was still wild country. How could I have forgotten?

A voice behind me piped, "Hands up, and don't try anything."

Piped? Either I had been accosted by a soprano ruffian, or. . .I took a chance and turned my head. I had to drop my eyes to come in contact with those of my assailant, who was holding a stick rifle in the small of my back and trying to maintain a stern expression.

Another small figure moved from behind the gate and stood beside the first. Both wore rough clothing, a miniature replica of the cowboys' garb. Both wore hats several sizes too large pulled down over their eyes and held wooden rifles. And both glowered at me.

The smaller one spoke first. "See, Lizzie, you spoiled it! If you hadn't gone and talked, it would've been fine. She turned just as white as a sheet."

I knelt down in front of them and raised their hat brims so I could look into their faces. "What on earth were you two doing?"

Again, it was the smaller one who broke the silence. "We were bein' outlaws. And if Lizzie here hadn't of opened her mouth, I bet we could have gotten all your money. You were really scared, weren't you?"

"As a matter of fact," I admitted, "I was. How did two youngsters like you learn to be outlaws?"

"Aw, we hang around the bunkhouse a lot," said my young informant. "They tell real good stories, and they don't mind us bein' there, as long as we keep quiet. They even let Lizzie stay around, and she's a girl." He lowered his voice conspiratorially. "Even if she don't dress like one."

At this, Lizzie found her voice. "I don't have to dress any different if I don't want to!" she shouted. "Shorty said I look fine just like I am. He said it didn't matter if I didn't want to wear girl clothes. He said. . .he said there was a lot of it going around," she ended defiantly.

It was time to change the subject. "All right. I know you're Lizzie. My name is Judith." I looked over at the other aspiring outlaw. "Now, what's your name?"

"That's Willie," Lizzie answered. "He's my little brother. Our last name is Bradley. What's yours?"

"Alder," I said, trying to come to terms with the fact that these little hoodlums belonged to Charles and Abby.

I wondered if Abby was aware of just how wild they had become. I had been under the impression that they were cared for during the day in a part of the house where their noise wouldn't disturb her rest. Apparently they ran loose, unattended. Hanging around the bunkhouse, indeed! I could imagine the kind of stories they were likely to overhear.

This, I realized, *could be a way to repay Charles and Abby in part for their kindness in letting me stay.* If I could do nothing else, I could at least look after the well-being of their children while I was here.

"Why don't you both come with me," I said, rising. "We'll see about cleaning your hands and faces, and then we'll try to find something for you to eat while you tell me about those outlaws you seem to like so well."

To my surprise, they each took one of my hands and walked along docilely to my room, where I poured water into the basin and scrubbed their hands and faces until they fairly shone.

"Underneath all that dust, you were hiding some very good-looking children," I said, surveying my work with satisfaction. Willie was a miniature of his father, with a naturally cheerful expression not even his assumed scowl could hide. Lizzie had her mother's fair hair, but along with that went the determined Bradley chin I had noticed on her uncle.

They both stood and stared at me. I thought of how their lives must have changed over the past few months, with their mother suddenly unable to care for them and their father busy building up a new ranch. Everyone was so occupied with their own duties that the children were, for the most part, forgotten.

The poor things were trying to adjust to the upheaval without any consistent guidance. They had been passive enough about doing as I had bidden, but it was little wonder that they were reluctant to open up to a stranger.

"How about something to eat?" I asked.

Vera had been in the habit of bringing a late-night snack of cookies and milk to my room, and I had some leftover cookies wrapped in a handkerchief in a dresser drawer. When they saw what I was offering, their faces lit up, and in no time the three of us were munching away at our impromptu tea party.

My heart went out to them. How long had it been since they had had a bit of fun, I wondered. I discounted story hour in the bunkhouse. From my acquaintance with the cowboys, I felt certain that it was not the sort of entertainment the children needed.

Lizzie, having finished her cookies, eyed me steadily. "That's my mama's dress," she announced. I nodded, wondering if she felt I had no right to be wearing it and whether I should explain. "It still smells a little like my mama," she said, and to my surprise, snuggled up next to me. I put my arm around her and blinked to keep back the tears.

"Wouldn't you like to go with me to your room, Lizzie, and pick out a dress for you to wear?" I was totally unprepared for her reaction.

"No!" she shouted. "I won't! If I wear a dress, everyone says I'm just like my mama. And I don't want to get sick like she is. I don't!" With that, she burst into sobs and buried her face in my lap. I stroked her fair hair and let her cry. She had to have some way to turn loose of the pain she had been carrying.

Willie looked on with a stoic expression until I tentatively held out a hand to him. Then he, too, snuggled into the circle of my arm and the three of us huddled together in a tight little knot while Lizzie's sobs racked her small body and even Willie sniffled occasionally.

Poor little things! I held them even closer to me. Lizzie couldn't be more than nine years old, and Willie looked to be six or seven. I tried to picture the family as they must have been, with Abby caring for her children and Charles romping with them, before this wasting illness took its toll. Abby was right; she was not the only one to suffer.

I promised myself to bring up the subject gently with her at the first opportunity. She had told me that the children ate their meals in the kitchen and that she seldom saw them until they were brought to her room at night, freshly scrubbed and ready for bed. I was sure she believed they were being properly tended to, for I could not believe for a moment that she would rest easy if she had any idea how much time they spent on their own.

The shadows were growing long by the time the emotional storm had subsided. I washed the children's hands and faces again and sent them along to the kitchen for their supper. I was touched by their reluctance to leave me and promised them we would spend more time together during my stay.

The next day was Saturday, and Abby took a turn for the worse. Charles turned full responsibility for the ranch over to Jeff and spent the day hovering over her. Vera, solemn-faced, rushed to and from her room with supplies and tonics I gathered had been left by the doctors she had mentioned.

I felt utterly useless. I tried to find the children, but was informed they had been taken for a ride in order to spare them the tension of the day. So I found myself empty-handed and restless.

I decided to take a walk. Maybe the exercise would work off some of my own tension. How long had I been here? Was it only four days? And yet these people had become so dear to me that I hated the thought of being separated from them.

I sank down under a spreading cedar tree and prayed, first for Abby's recovery, then for my own situation. Would there ever again be a place where I truly belonged and had a right to stay?

The smells of summer were all around me, the scent of the scrub brush and the dusty ground where I sat. The land rolled away from me, the grasses waving in the gentle wind. Off in the distance I could see groups of cattle, and here and there a rider appeared against the skyline. It was a calm, pastoral scene, belying the worry in the house and the tumult within me.

I stayed under my cedar until most of the afternoon had passed, alternately praying and wondering what the future held in store. When the sun was well down in the sky, I stood, dusted myself off, and turned back toward the house.

Jeff's figure loomed in the open gateway as I approached, and I hurried toward him, fear mounting within me. "Abby," I faltered. "Is she. . .?"

"She's resting," he said, and I sighed with relief. His mouth curved in one of his slow smiles. "I didn't mean to frighten you. I wondered where you were, and nobody had seen you for some time, so I thought I'd make sure you were all right."

"I wanted to stay out of the way, and I was worried about Abby, so I went for a walk," I said, lowering my eyes to hide my pleasure at his concern.

"It's been rough on you, hasn't it? Have you had any word from your uncle?"

I shook my head and raised my eyes to search his. "Shouldn't I have heard something by now? It seems that a stagecoach would have had time to get there and back."

"That would be cutting it pretty close. And if there were any problems at all, it could delay your message, or his, or both."

"What kind of problems?"

"This is still new country. A lot of things can happen. But I wouldn't be too concerned just yet. Give it a few more days."

He walked with me to the door of my room. "I'll have supper sent to you. What with all the worry over Abby, our routine is a bit off today."

"Of course. Isn't there something I can do? Maybe sit with her tonight?"

He shook his head. "Charles will insist on doing that himself. They're devoted to each other, as I'm sure you've noticed. I just hope this doesn't last too long. He's about done in, what with trying to handle the ranch alone and worrying about her on top of it. I wish you had known her before she got sick."

He seemed lost in thought for a moment, then pulled himself together. "Well, I'll see you tomorrow," he said. He turned as if to leave, then hesitated. "Judith? I know Charles and Abby won't be up to going into town for church in the morning. But if you'd like to go, I'd be happy to drive you."

"All right," I said. "I'd love to go." I entered my room before he could see the foolish grin that spread across my face. It wasn't until I was almost asleep that I realized he had called me by my Christian name for the first time.

eight

By the next morning, it was clear that Abby was going to rally, and I readied myself for my first church service in weeks. Was it really possible that only a week before I had been rolling along in a wagon with only the Parkers for company?

I hummed a happy little tune as I tried to decide which dress to wear. Truly, there was a great deal to be thankful for on this Lord's Day.

I chose a sprigged muslin with ruffles at the wrists and throat. Vera had thoughtfully provided a number of hairpins, so I was able to dress my hair more elaborately than usual.

I looked in the mirror for a final appraisal and saw a sparkle in my eyes and a pink flush on my cheeks, due, I assured myself, to the excitement of going to a church service. How wonderful it would be to worship in company with other believers and hear the Bible taught by this learned man from the east!

Muffins and coffee were waiting in the kitchen. Everyone was too tired from the strain of the day before to care much about a formal meal.

A glance out the window showed a team and wagon approaching the house, so I gathered up my Bible and a light shawl and hurried outdoors. Jeff sprang down to help me up to the wagon seat and handed me my shawl.

"We'll be all set as soon as our other passengers are ready," he said, smiling up at me. Good heavens! Up to then I had completely forgotten the need for a chaperon. I smiled to cover my confusion and said a silent prayer of thanks that he was gentleman enough to have thought of it as a matter of course. After my experiences on the trail, I knew I would be perfectly safe with him or any of the cowboys, but we were heading for civilization of sorts, where tongues would wag if given half a chance.

I turned at the sound of footsteps and drew a quick breath in astonished delight. Lizzie and Willie stood beside the wagon, scrubbed and dressed in their Sunday best.

Willie looked gentlemanly, if uncomfortable, with his stiff collar and slicked-down hair. And Lizzie was the very picture of an angel with her hair neatly combed and in, wonder of wonders, a dainty ruffled dress. Jeff lifted them into the back of the wagon, where they scooted up behind the seat and looked at me shyly.

"One more and we'll be off," said Jeff. I looked at him in surprise. Neither Abby nor Charles would be in any condition to stir today. Perhaps Vera was coming. A broad smile broke out on Jeff's face and I followed his gaze to see Jake emerge from the bunkhouse and walk our way.

His hair was plastered as close to his head as Willie's, and he wore what must have been his best pair of work clothes. I hoped he hadn't felt it necessary to borrow Shorty's cologne.

His expression, his walk, his every move showed resignation rather than pleasure at the prospect of going to church. I couldn't quite suppress a smile at his hangdog look.

"Hurry up, cowpuncher," called Jeff. "We're ready to roll!"

"So help me, Jeff, I don't see why you needed someone to come along to play nursemaid," Jake muttered, his eyes gloomily fastened on the ground. "Seems to me you ought to be able to handle a couple of half-pints by yourself."

"Why, Jake," Jeff said, all innocence, "I asked for one of you boys to volunteer to come along this morning. Do you mean you aren't here by choice? I really do need you. You see, I have three on my hands, instead of two."

"Three?" Jake looked up at his employer for the first time, then glanced around. His eyes lit on me and his jaw dropped ludicrously. "Excuse me, ma'am," he sputtered. "I surely didn't know any young lady was going or I wouldn't have talked so."

"Good morning, Jake," I said demurely. "I've missed your company."

He peered up at me, squinting, then his eyes grew round in surprise. "Will ya look at that!" he exclaimed. "If it ain't Miss Judith!"

If I had needed any gratification for my feminine vanity, I couldn't have asked for more than Jake's reaction. He climbed silently into the back of the wagon and sat, shaking his head from time to time.

It wasn't until we had driven a mile or so that he began to chuckle softly. The chuckles increased until he was leaning against the side of the wagon, his head thrown back and tears streaming down his cheeks.

"All right," said Jeff. "Better tell us what it is before you hurt something."

Jake pulled a bandanna from his back pocket and mopped at his face. "It's . . .it's seein' Miss Judith up there lookin' like that," he said, gasping for breath. "Won't Shorty be sore when he finds out who I'm goin' to church with?"

"I don't understand," I said. "Why should Shorty be angry?"

"He's the one that slipped me the short straw when we were deciding who was going to 'volunteer!' " And he went off again into gales of laughter.

Jeff looked at me as if wondering how I would react to learning I was the loser's lot. When our eyes met, we both laughed heartily. The children, too, joined in the general merriment, and the slight tension that had been present dissolved.

The drive into town took about three hours in the wagon, and we whiled away a good bit of the time singing hymns. Jeff had a pleasant baritone and started us off on song after song in seemingly endless procession.

I was pleased to find I knew most of the hymns he sang and could join in with him. What Jake's voice lacked in quality, he made up for in enthusiasm on the songs he knew, and on some he didn't. The children, I noted with approval, knew a good many of the hymns. I made a mental note to teach them one or two more before I left.

The settlement was small, not much more than a store, a warehouse, two saloons, and a dozen houses along a wide, dusty street.

Jeff drew the team to a halt in front of the store and checked his watch. "Thirty minutes to spare," he announced with satisfaction. "That gives us a chance to look the place over."

Jake stared wistfully at the nearest saloon. "I don't suppose. . ." he began.

"Not today," Jeff answered. "Today you are coming to church. Take Lizzie and Willie in and find us *all* a place to sit, will you?"

He grinned as he lifted me down from the seat. "This is hardly the way Jake planned to spend his Sunday. He's a good man—one of the best—but he relies too much on his own merit. Hearing a real man of God may be just what he needs to realize that no one can be 'good enough' on his own.

"Tell me," he went on, tucking my hand under his arm, "what kind of miracle have you worked on Lizzie and Willie? They've always had a mischievous streak, but as soon as they heard you were coming to church with me, they were wild to come along. They look positively angelic this morning. Vera tells me it's the first time Lizzie's worn a dress in months."

As I related my meeting with the children, his face sobered as he realized the depth of their feelings about their mother's illness. "Poor kids! I guess we've all been so busy that they've been 'out of sight, out of mind.' " He gave my hand a gentle squeeze. "It looks like your coming has been good for all of us."

I floated into the store where the service was to be held and had to make an effort to respond sensibly to the people I met. I shook hands with people whose names I barely heard and could not remember, until a familiar face loomed before me, and I recognized Mrs. Styles.

"Mr. Bradley," she said archly, "I am pleased to see you here this morning. Is Abby better? I drove out yesterday to visit her, but was turned away most abruptly by one of your hands."

Jeff nodded politely and said, "She seems to be better today, thank you," and was about to walk on to our seats when she stopped him.

"Come now, aren't you going to introduce me to your charming companion? We don't see many fresh young faces around here, you know."

"But I thought you had already met her. This is Miss Judith Alder, Mrs. Styles. She's a guest at the ranch." The smile froze on her face and she peered at me more closely.

"Oh," she said. "Oh!" She withdrew the hand she had extended toward me, turned stiffly and marched to a seat on the front row of chairs.

The encounter brought my feet back to earth with an effective thud. We spotted Jake. He had found seats for all of us on the last row, which suited me fine. I sat between the children, leaving the two men to flank us.

Jake leaned across Lizzie and whispered hopefully, "The place is fillin' up, don't you think? Maybe I ought to slip on out and give other folks a chance to sit down."

Jeff responded with a look that made him sit back in his chair, shoulders slumped. It would have been funny if I hadn't felt so mortified. Mrs. Styles had obviously formed a most unflattering opinion of me. I would have to be careful to behave in an exemplary manner around her.

A hush fell as a middle-aged man stood and led the congregation in singing hymns. I tried to recapture the joy of worship I had anticipated, but the mood wouldn't come.

You're being ridiculous, I scolded myself. *Letting yourself get caught up in romantic notions when you're only going to be here a short while! If you're not careful, Judith Alder, you'll appear to be just what Lucia Styles thinks you are.*

That was enough to settle my thoughts in preparation for the sermon. Wasn't this why we had come—to hear a man of God bring a message from the Word?

I deliberately focused my attention on the man who now stood at the front of the worshippers. He was younger than I had expected, probably around Charles Bradley's age, and the black frock coat he wore accented the pallor of his skin. He had come west, I remembered, for his health.

"Welcome, my friends," he intoned. "As many of you good people know, I am the Reverend Thomas Carver from Philadelphia, Pennsylvania. I have come to this savage land seeking a climate conducive to recovery from a wasting illness and have agreed to preach in your quaint settlement this Sunday. If we find each other satisfactory, I will consider lengthening my stay to help you profit from the knowledge I have acquired."

I felt a stab of disappointment, though I could not pinpoint the cause. His preaching style was different from what I was accustomed to, that was all.

He was quite slender, as might be expected of one who had recently been ill. His face was long and narrow, the features almost delicate. His hair was a very light blond, and his eyebrows and lashes must have been as well, for from my seat I could not distinguish them. He was, I judged, in his early thirties—still a young man, but old enough to have had experience in the pulpit.

I heard the rustle of pages and realized that he had announced the Scripture text for his sermon and I had not been paying attention. I peered over Willie's head at Jeff's Bible, trying to see what page he had turned to. Isaiah 61. I hastily turned there myself.

"The Spirit of the Lord God is upon me; because the Lord hath anointed me to preach good tidings unto the meek; he hath sent me to bind up the broken-hearted, to proclaim liberty to the captives, and the opening of the prison to them that are bound; To proclaim the acceptable year of the Lord. . ."

The words lingered in my mind as Reverend Carver stood for a moment, surveying the congregation. He sighed as if disappointed in what he saw, then took a deep breath and began.

"Brethren," he said, "I see unhappy faces here among you. I see faces lined with bitterness and despair. Why? Why are you discouraged? Why do you feel you have failed in some way? Because, my friends, you have succumbed to the philosophy of many that there is no inherent goodness in man."

There was a stirring among those present, whether of interest or antagonism I could not tell. I was having a difficult enough time trying to concentrate on what he was saying rather than on the rise and fall of my emotions.

Really, I chided myself sternly, *whatever is troubling you can wait until after the service. An opportunity for spiritual feeding may not come often in these parts.*

"Certainly there are those who do not treat others as they should, those who are bad neighbors, those who fall into crime. But why are they this way? I tell you, it is not due to any evil within themselves, but to the lack of love given them from parents, friends, society itself!

"Friends, no one ever bothered to look for the good that was in them, to bring it out and nurture it. And how could they love others if they did not love themselves first and foremost? Therein lies the key to the evils in this world. Many have failed to look for the good."

Even my wandering attention was held by this. The sermon went on interminably in the same vein, seeking to point out man's innate goodness.

I wondered if anyone else was bothered by the lack of concern with sin and man's unrighteousness. A quick glance to my left showed Jeff's mouth set in a thin line. I relaxed a little. So it wasn't only my own perception.

It was an effort to stay awake until the end of the service, too much effort for Lizzie and Willie, who slumped against me and slept.

After the final prayer, people rose and milled around, talking quietly. Reverend Carver positioned himself at the door to greet the worshippers as they left. As I tried to wake the children, I couldn't help but notice that while the preacher's comments were enthusiastic, the responses he got were lukewarm at best.

By the time we were ready to leave, there were only a couple of men left in the store putting away the chairs. I took a drowsy Lizzie by the hand and started for the door, wishing there were another exit.

Reverend Carver smiled at Lizzie, who glared at him. He then turned to me. "Ah, Miss Alder, is it not?" he asked with a wonderful display of white teeth. I managed a nod. "Mrs. Styles has told me a great deal about you."

I hope you told her to look for the good, I thought rebelliously.

He went on without bothering to lower his voice. "I believe you were stranded alone on the trail and arrived here under the, ah, protection of a group of trail drivers. Is that correct?"

I looked around frantically, not wanting my experience to be overheard and misinterpreted by the whole town. "As I told Mrs. Styles," I said in a low voice, "they were kindness itself and absolute gentlemen."

Behind me, Jake and Jeff had given up trying to rouse Willie, and Jake was carrying him out. "These are two of the men who helped me," I told the minister, turning gratefully to Jeff, who was by this time at my elbow. "This is Mr. Bradley. I believe you have met his brother."

"Of course, of course. Good morning, Mr. Bradley. I hope you enjoyed the service." I didn't hear Jeff's reply, as I had propelled Lizzie toward the wagon at the first opportunity and now stood leaning against it.

The morning had started out with such promise; now even the brightness of the noonday seemed to have dimmed. Mrs. Styles alone had been bad enough, but knowing that she had spread her version of my arrival made me want to crawl under the blanket on the wagon bed and remain there until we were out of town.

The pastor's inflection had left no doubt in my mind as to the picture that had been painted of me. I thought of the people I had met before the service. My head had been too much in the clouds at the time to take note of their reaction, but now I wondered. Had there been a hidden meaning behind the smiles and friendly words? Suddenly, I couldn't wait to get away.

I hoisted Lizzie to the wagon bed, gave her orders to sit quietly, and scrambled to the seat. If only the men would hurry! I imagined curtains being drawn back furtively to take a look at the questionable newcomer.

To my intense relief, Jake and Jeff came striding toward the wagon at that moment and arranged a comfortable place in the back for Willie, who was snoring gently.

Jeff was just settling onto the seat beside me when a man ran out of the store, waving at us.

"Miss Alder?" he said. "I'm Fred Kilmer. I run the general store. I have a letter here for you, but I didn't realize who you were until Reverend Carver pointed you out."

My cheeks burned as I envisioned the scene, but I reached for the letter with hope rising in my heart. "Thank you," I said as we pulled away.

Joyfully I tore at the envelope. I need not stay here to suffer further humiliation. Soon I would be heading west once more to begin my new life. I read:

> *Dear Judith,*
>
> *Sorry to hear of your delay, but it may be for the best. There was a fire at the trading post. Burned the place clear to the ground. I don't have the money to rebuild and restock, so I'm off to find greener pastures. Glad to hear you have found a place where they're good to you. Stay put until I send for you. Don't know how soon it will be.*
>
> *Your loving uncle,*
> *Matthew*

I stared at the paper. *Stay put?* Tears stung my eyes and blurred the landscape. How could I stay? I could not presume indefinitely on the Bradleys' hospitality. I had no money to pay for my board, either there or in town. And the thought of remaining, to be an object of community scorn, filled me with dread.

The only course that seemed open to me was one I dreaded as much as Mrs. Styles's wagging tongue. I could wire Aunt Phoebe, throw myself on her mercy, and beg for forgiveness and passage back home.

I knew that would end any further hopes of going west to be with Uncle Matthew. My rebellion in doing so once would never be forgotten.

We were over halfway back to the ranch when Jeff spoke. "Have you had bad news?" he asked softly. I handed him the brief letter, which he scanned and handed back.

"I'm sorry," he said. "You've had a hard time of it lately." I nodded, too miserable to speak.

He turned his head toward the back of the wagon. I followed his gaze. Lizzie had curled up next to her brother, and Jake leaned against the wagon's side, head back and eyes closed.

"Do you want to talk about it?"

I struggled to force words past the obstruction in my throat. "I guess the only thing for me to do is to go back to Missouri, to my aunt."

"And try again when your uncle has relocated?"

I shook my head and managed a small laugh. "No. I'm afraid this will be my first and last trip west. Once I go back, my aunt will see to it that I never leave St. Joseph again."

He stared straight ahead. "Will that really be so bad? It isn't civilized out here yet, at least not in the way you're used to."

"But I like what I've seen. There's a wildness here, a bigness that's almost frightening, but I want—wanted—to be a part of it."

"Then why go back?"

"It's the only thing I can do. I have no choice." A warm breeze rustled the grasses and played with loose strands of my hair, but the beauty of the day was lost on me as I stared at the rolling hills through tear-filmed eyes.

When we reached the ranch, Jeff took the children to see their mother and I closeted myself in my room. I lay facedown on the bed, trying to adjust to the idea of returning to a way of life I thought I had left forever.

My brain was numb, unable to deal with the blow I had received. Could I go back again to being the poor relation, tolerated only because of a blood tie? My whole being rebelled at the thought, but what else was there?

The return of the prodigal. That's how Aunt Phoebe would see it. But there would be no joyous welcome, no fatted calf. It would be back to life as usual, dancing attendance on Aunt Phoebe and being the object of disdain among the ladies of her circle. They would have plenty to fuel their imaginations as they tried to figure out what I had really been up to during my absence.

The tidy streets of my aunt's neighborhood would be the same, yards neatly trimmed, picket fences faithfully whitewashed. It was the scene from my growing-up years, constant and unchanging since the day we came to live with Aunt Phoebe.

I closed my eyes wearily. In my mind's eye I could see the vast land outside the courtyard walls. It, too, had remained the same, and for much longer than St. Joseph. But here, there was openness and freedom. The very landscape had a life of its own as it responded to the wind, rain, and sun.

One could spend a lifetime here getting acquainted with the country, always discovering something new.

A figure appeared on my imaginary landscape, a figure who turned and looked at me with smiling blue eyes, called out a glad welcome, and waited with open arms for me to come. I shook myself back to reality and noticed how far the sun had moved across the sky. I must have been dozing.

I poured water into the basin and scrubbed at my face. I wanted to stay. But how? Resolve began to stiffen my drooping spine. I didn't know how, not yet. But for once in my life, I would fight for something I wanted.

Pacing the floor of my room, I began to make my plans. Surely I could find a job in town and a place to stay. Since I'd planned to help Uncle Matthew in his trading post, perhaps I could get a job helping Mr. Kilmer at the general store.

The more I mulled over the possibilities, the more enthusiastic I became. Even the thought of Mrs. Styles and her venomous gossip could not dampen my mood. I knew I had done nothing wrong, and it was high time I started holding my head up.

For the first time in days, I felt sure of where my path led. Yes, I would stay, I determined. There would be no slinking off, no whimpering in defeat. This was where my heart lay. This was where I belonged.

I patted my hair into place and headed for the parlor, bursting with the need to tell someone of my plans. I nearly collided with Charles in the doorway. He looked tired, and I remembered how much sleep he must have lost caring for Abby. Perhaps because of that, he was quick in coming to the point.

"Jefferson tells me you're leaving us," he said without preamble.

"Yes, but—"

"Don't do it," he interrupted. He seemed to realize how brusque this sounded and made a visible effort to collect himself. "I mean, don't do it, *please.*"

Still bubbling with my newly devised strategy, I didn't see at first what he was getting at. "Charles, I appreciate so much the hospitality you've shown me, but I can't abuse it. That's why I've decided—"

"Have you talked her out of it yet?" This time the interruption came from Jeff, who strode into the center of the room and stood clenching and unclenching his fists.

I stared from one brother to the other, trying to understand. Jeff seemed to sense my bewilderment.

"Charles, do you mean you haven't asked her yet?"

"You haven't given me much opportunity," Charles said mildly.

"Ask me what?" I nearly shouted. "Will someone please tell me what's going on?"

Jeff looked at me, then at his brother, turned on his heel and was gone. I stared openmouthed at Charles.

He smiled and shook his head. "Please forgive us both, Judith. We've both been under a great strain.

"I talked with my children a little while ago. Talked *and* listened for the first time in longer than I care to admit. I had no idea they'd been allowed to go unsupervised all this time.

"That leaves me in a dilemma. My time will be fully taken up for some time. Abby is in no condition to do anything but rest, and I have no people here whose work will allow them to take on the added responsibility for the children.

"Would you consider staying here to care for them, at least for a while? Until we send some cattle to market, all my transactions will be on credit, so I can't offer you more than room and board for the time being. But the children seem to like you a great deal, and you'd be doing us all a great favor— myself, Abby, and Jefferson."

"Jeff?"

"My brother is not ordinarily a highly-strung person," he said with a smile. "But you saw him just now. And I've never seen him in as excitable a state as when he told me you were leaving and ordered me to find a way to keep you here."

I looked at him in surprise and he grinned back. "If Abby and I hadn't already decided to ask you to stay, I would have had to create a reason, just to pacify him.

"So what do you think, Judith? Could you put up with us all a little longer? Would you like some time to consider the matter?"

"No! I mean, yes. I mean. . .I'd be very happy to stay on. Thank you." I managed to contain myself until I got back to the privacy of my room, where I spun about with wild abandon. Jeff had demanded that Charles ask me to stay!

I could hardly contain my joy. He wanted me here!

nine

It was with a light heart that I was able to pen a letter to Aunt Phoebe, telling her of my safe arrival in New Mexico Territory, the unfortunate fire at Uncle Matthew's, and my temporary position at the Bradley's. I was sorely tempted to give her my opinion of her carefully chosen chaperones, but I could so easily picture her deriving a perverse sense of satisfaction from my plight that I focused only on the positive aspects of the situation.

I placed the letter with others that would go out as soon as someone made a trip to town. Knowing Aunt Phoebe, I expected no reply but felt better having discharged that obligation.

The speed with which news traveled among the widely scattered inhabitants of the territory never ceased to amaze me. No sooner had I announced my intention to remain than a trickle of would-be suitors began showing up on the Bradley doorstep.

In the weeks that followed, the trickle became a steady stream. I was puzzled at first, then amused, and finally driven to seek Abby's counsel.

"What have I done to make myself fair game?" I cried in frustration. "Abby, I promise you I have never given any of them an indication that their attentions would be welcome. But just yesterday a total stranger rode in out of nowhere and asked me to *marry* him! When I turned him down, he just shrugged and rode off again. What am I to do?"

Abby pushed herself higher on her pillows and managed a weak chuckle. Her strength seemed to diminish a fraction with each passing day, but her good humor and interest in events at the ranch never wavered. The crisp fall air had brought a tinge of color to her cheeks, and she looked at me now with a hint of the old sparkle dancing in her eyes.

"Why, Judith, what you've done is very serious," she said, attempting to sound stern. "You've become a permanent resident. An attractive, single, *female* resident. It's started every one of those lonely cowboys thinking how good it would be to come home to a wife and a place of his own.

"In a way," she said, laughing softly, "you really can't blame them. I guess they feel there's no harm in trying."

She became suddenly grave. "None of them have tried to force their attentions beyond decent limits, have they?"

"No," I admitted. "I have to give them credit for that. Nearly all of them have given up after the first 'no.' And the rest have gotten it through their heads after two or three tries. . .all except Shorty."

"Shorty! I should have guessed."

"I can't go anywhere or do anything without that man popping up. Just yesterday, the children and I were out walking. I would have sworn there wasn't anyone but the three of us around, but all of a sudden, there he was, all big soulful eyes and deep sighs, come to 'walk with us a ways.' Is this going to go on until I've exhausted every single man in the territory?"

"Well, there is one thing you could do."

"What?" I asked eagerly.

"You could take one of them up on his offer."

"Oh, Abby! I thought you were serious."

"I am. You're not planning to stay single all your life, are you?"

"Of course not. It's just that. . .well, the right person hasn't asked me yet."

"I was afraid of that. I don't know why Jeff's dragging his feet so." She laughed at my expression. "Don't worry. You don't make it terribly obvious, if that's what you're afraid of. Sometimes we women are just quicker to read the signs, that's all. Don't forget that I fell in love with a Bradley man myself."

"Maybe it's more one-sided than I thought. Maybe there's someone else?" She averted her eyes, and my heart sank. "Abby, please! You've got to tell me. There is someone, isn't there?"

"No, dear," she said, meeting my eyes again. "At least, not now. It happened a long time ago, and I hadn't thought of it for some time."

"Please. Tell me anyway."

"I hate to. No," she added hastily, "not for the reason you think. A member of my family was involved, and I suppose I feel responsible.

"It was while we lived in Texas," she continued. "A distant cousin of mine came to visit. I hadn't seen Lorelei since we were children, and she had grown into the most beautiful woman I have ever seen. She had skin like fine porcelain, with dark curls and deep blue eyes, and a way about her that could make you feel you were the only other person on earth.

"Jeff was much younger then and was absolutely captivated by her. It was a whirlwind courtship, and I'd never seen Jeff in such a fever. He had plans to expand the ranch, add stock, build a house. He seemed to be everywhere at once. . ." Her voice trailed off.

"What happened?"

Abby sighed. "She left. Just up and left one day. Charles told me later that she'd laughed at Jeff, told him it was foolish to think she would consent to live in a barren wasteland where she couldn't have the social life she was accustomed to.

"Jeff was devastated. It was his first love, and he'd believed it would last forever, that Lorelei felt as deeply as he did. We were terribly worried about him, but time seemed to heal the wounds, and he has never referred to her again. But now. . ."

"Now?" I prompted.

"I wonder if he's afraid of being hurt again. This country is terribly different from what you've been used to, and he knows you have family in Missouri you can return to if you choose."

"Oh, no," I moaned. "If he only realized! I sometimes think that if I had to choose between an Indian raid and Aunt Phoebe, I'd take a chance on the Indians. But even if things had been better back there, it's not home to me anymore. I can't explain it, but I feel that I belong here, that I was made for this place. It's never seemed barren or desolate to me."

"Does Jeff know that?"

"I've barely been able to speak to him the last few weeks. He's spent so much time out on roundup, and when he is at home I seldom see him, except at supper. That's hardly the place to start that kind of conversation, with Charles and the children there, too. It's almost as though—" Sudden panic gripped me. "Abby, you don't think he's changed his mind, do you? That he's avoiding me?"

Abby laughed softly. "I don't think you need to worry about him changing his mind. As to avoiding you, he may need time to come to grips with himself and realize you won't change your mind and leave. Can you be very patient, if need be?"

"I can wait as long as it takes, as long as I know he cares for me!" The heavy weight that had oppressed me lifted, and I felt light, free, and capable of all patience. "Now if I can just convince Shorty that I'm not refusing everyone else to leave the way clear for him!"

We both laughed, and I went off to collect the children for their lessons with a lighter heart than I'd had for many a day.

Both Lizzie and Willie had bright, inquiring minds, and with the help of books I chose from Charles's library, I was trying to channel their curiosity in a more acceptable direction. Although I had no training as a teacher, I was pleased with the progress they were making.

We were sitting on the porch, reading aloud from *Ivanhoe,* when Reverend Carver drove up in a rented buggy. I stood and went to greet him, assuming he had come to call on Abby. It was rather late for that, I thought peevishly, as he had not been to the ranch before in all the time he had been in the territory.

Reverend Carver had been the topic of many a puzzled conversation among us. He had indeed stayed on, "to bring light into our dark corner of the world," as he put it, but his idea of being a shepherd seemed to stop at preaching a lukewarm sermon once a week on the goodness of man and the ills of society.

He turned a deaf ear to complaints that he ignored the sick and ailing of his flock. Attendance at the Sunday services had dropped to a pitifully low level.

Jake and the other cowboys had had their fill early in the minister's tenure. Once, during a time of sharing testimonies, Shorty had stood up and announced that he wished to speak.

"Preacher," he had drawled, "it seems you do a powerful lot of talking about bein' good and kind to one another, and that's all well and good. But me and the boys have been comin' to hear you for three weeks now, and you haven't said anything different from one time to the next. I've never even heard you mention the Good Book.

"Beggin' the pardon of everyone here, but if this is all there is to your brand of religion, I guess the boys and me can save ourselves the trip and talk to each other about how good we all are."

And with that, he, Neil, and two other men stalked out, leaving the congregation and Reverend Carver in stunned silence. Even the Bradleys and I had not attended a service in several weeks. I had spent much time reading my Bible, finding in it the guiding truths Reverend Carver's sermons had lacked. And now, after all these months, he had come to call.

I said a quick "good day" to him and turned to lead him through the house to see Abby. I was anxious to get back to Lizzie and Willie and their reading lesson. To my surprise, he laid his hand on my arm and whispered, "Please, may I speak with you alone?"

Annoyed at the delay, I showed him to a seat in the parlor, hoping Charles, Vera, anyone would come along to take over. His face shone with beads of perspiration, and his hands shook. I wondered if he were becoming ill himself. I was about to offer him a drink of water when he spoke.

"Miss Alder." He cleared his throat nervously. "Judith. I. . .I hardly know how to begin."

It was all I could do to keep from tapping my foot impatiently. This was usually a busy area of the house. Why didn't someone come?

"I find great gratification in my work here," he went on. "But some days the time does lie heavy on my hands, and I begin to think."

I thought to myself that if he would spend more time visiting the sick and tending to other pastoral duties, he would have less of it on his hands.

"A man gets lonely, Judith," he said, and I realized with a sick feeling where this conversation was leading. "He begins to realize his need for a companion, someone to share the lonely times, the bleak moments, as well as the joys of success."

"You hardly paint a happy picture of married life," I said tartly. To my relief, I heard footsteps approaching from the hallway. Rescue was at hand!

"Your smile, your sweet disposition, all lead me to believe you would make an ideal companion."

Hurry, I willed whoever was beyond the door. My heart leaped as it opened and Jeff stood framed in the doorway. He opened his mouth to speak, but at that moment, Reverend Carver flung himself on his knees before me and cried, "Judith, I am asking you to be my wife."

The three of us remained frozen for what seemed an eternity. It was Jeff who finally broke the silence.

"Excuse me," he said. "I seem to be interrupting." He turned on his heel and was gone.

"Jeff, wait!" I cried, utterly ignoring the Reverend Carver, who still knelt on the floor. I ran to the doorway, but Jeff's long strides had already carried him out of sight. I turned in exasperation to find my suitor standing immediately behind me, hands clasped in pleading.

"Judith, please. What is your answer?"

"My answer is no!" It came out sharper than I had intended, but I was too vexed to care.

"I see." He drew himself up with far more dignity than he had shown up to now. "I have tried to bestow upon you the greatest honor a man can give to a woman. You have refused me most abruptly. May I hope that, after you have had time to give the idea due consideration, you may change your mind?"

"Please," I said, fighting to keep my temper in check. "I appreciate your kind proposal, but you must accept my answer as final."

"Very well," he said stiffly. "Then I will not trouble you again." He stopped at the door and turned. "Judith, this was intended as much for your good as for mine. Considering the. . .unorthodox manner of your arrival here, do you think you can ever truly be accepted by the people? Come away with me, and we'll start a new life together."

My temper was slipping its restraints. "You're quite mistaken about my acceptance here. The Bradleys have opened their home freely and have entrusted their children's care to me. Surely they wouldn't do that for anyone whose morals might be suspect.

"Any other notions about my respectability come from the fevered imagination of Lucia Styles. I am not concerned about her malicious gossip, and

I beg you not to be, either."

His lips tightened and he closed the door behind him with more force than was strictly necessary. I breathed a sigh of relief and ran to look for Jeff. Not finding him in the house, I hurried outdoors toward the corral, where I found Jake leaning against the rail.

"You wouldn't be lookin' for Jeff now, would you?" he asked, a twinkle in his eye.

"Have you seen him, Jake? Where is he?"

"He came stormin' out of the house a few minutes ago, threw a saddle and some gear on his horse, and said he was going to check the stock up on the north range. Said he'd be back in about a week."

"A week!"

"Uh-huh. Kept mutterin' something about women while he was gettin' ready. Any idea what he meant?" he asked, with an air of innocence a child could have seen through.

I was beyond answering. I turned and scanned the horizon. He must have ridden like the wind; the gently rolling hills held no sign of him.

A week to live through before I could see him and explain. A week for him to imagine all sorts of mistaken situations. I forced one foot in front of the other and made my way back to the front porch to finish the interrupted lesson.

"Did the minister come to see Mama?" Lizzie asked.

"Why was he so mad when he left?" Willie wondered. "He jumped in his rig and took off like he was gonna run that horse to death."

"He did seem upset, didn't he?" I murmured. "Let's see, what page were we on?"

"I'll bet he didn't come to see Mama at all," Lizzie said. "He wasn't here long enough for a real visit. And besides, Mama doesn't make people mad like that."

"Here we are," I announced brightly. "Page thirty-eight. Lizzie, I believe it was your turn to read."

"You're right," Willie said, as though I weren't there. "Mama doesn't make anybody mad." He eyed me speculatively. "But *she* does."

"I. . .I what?"

"Make people mad," Willie answered solemnly. "I heard Jake say he never saw any woman in his life that got people stirred up more."

"Willie!" scolded his sister. "You're not supposed to say things like that."

"But it's true, Lizzie! You know it's true. Like when you told Shorty he ought to ask her to marry him—"

"Willie, don't," Lizzie warned.

"—and he did, and she said she wouldn't."

"Willie!" Lizzie shrilled.

"Remember how mad he was before you told him he ought to keep trying and not give up?"

"*Willieee!*" Lizzie screeched, leaping upon her brother and trying to cover his mouth with her hands.

By this time, I had recovered sufficiently to pry them apart, and the three of us stood looking at one another.

"Lizzie," I panted, "you didn't really tell Shorty to. . .to. . ."

"Sure she did," Willie bragged. This time Lizzie silenced him with a look.

"But why?"

"Well," she said reluctantly, "Vera said you looked sad one day, and she thought it was because you were pining for someone. So I thought if you got married, you'd be able to quit pining and be happy."

"I see. Uh, Lizzie, you didn't say this kind of thing to anyone besides Shorty, did you?"

"Well. . ."

"Oh, she told lots of people," put in the helpful Willie. "Lots and lots. *Lots* and *lots* and. . ." Catching sight of both our faces, he trailed off. "We just didn't want you to pine," he mumbled.

"Children," I said, "our lesson is over for today. Go to the kitchen and see what Vera can find for you." They scampered off in relief, and I sagged limply against the porch rail.

ten

Much to my surprise, the week flew by in spite of Jeff's absence. I had fully expected to "pine," as Lizzie put it, worrying about his frame of mind. Instead, the week was so full of activity that I had little time to dwell on my problem.

Charles had given a steer to an old settler and his wife in the next valley. The man had broken his leg on a hunting trip and had been laid up for weeks, unable to work or hunt. Pride had kept the couple from asking for help, and by the time one of the Double B cowboys noticed their plight, they were subsisting mostly on apples from their orchard.

In gratitude, they had sent over a wagon load of apples, and Vera and I fell heir to the task of putting them up.

We peeled and cored and sliced all week long. Some went in the canning kettle to be added to the glistening rows of jars already lining the pantry shelves. Others, Vera baked into pies.

The smell of their baking brought more than one cowboy to the kitchen, where Vera had them sweep the floor, carry out ashes, or bring in wood for the stove before she served them a generous helping.

"Baking takes extra time," she said, grinning, "but this way we have a lot of chores taken off our hands."

I laughed and agreed that it wasn't a bad trade.

Most of the apples were cored and sliced, and the slices strung to hang over the woodstove to dry. These would keep almost indefinitely and could be taken along by the men when they rode out on the range or be used by Vera for baking as the winter progressed.

Lessons were suspended for the time being; Lizzie and Willie sat on low stools in the kitchen and strung the slices as we cut them. I was touched to see how seriously they took the task, carefully spacing the rounds so they didn't touch and the air could move freely around them.

Willie was impressive, going through his bowl of slices nearly twice as quickly as his sister. I noticed, though, that we didn't hang his strings over the stove any more often. I was about to comment on this when he let out a horrible groan.

I looked to see what was wrong. He had turned a light shade of green and was doubled over, clutching his stomach.

"Willie!" I cried, kneeling beside him. "What's wrong?"

"Oooh, it hurts. It hurts!" was all he could say before he went off into a series of pathetic moans.

Vera felt his forehead. "He's cold and clammy," she told me. "No fever. Help me get him to bed."

Between us, we carried him to his room. By the time Vera was turning down the covers on his bed, beads of perspiration were standing out on his forehead.

We laid him between the sheets, still moaning, and I found I was trembling almost as much as Willie.

"What is it, Vera? Do you know?" Memories of a child back in Missouri whose appendix had ruptured rushed into my mind, and the memory of the tragic consequences chilled me.

"I have an idea," she said. "You go on back and tend to Lizzie. She looked almost as scared as you do."

I marveled at her calm as I ran back to the kitchen where Lizzie sat, white faced. I sat in the big rocker and held out my arms, and she came readily. We took comfort in each other's presence as we rocked silently, waiting. I was debating whether or not to disturb Abby with the news when Vera appeared in the doorway.

"Is it serious? Should we call his parents?"

"How's my brother?" Our words tumbled over one another as we scrambled out of the rocker.

Vera settled herself comfortably in her chair and mopped her forehead before she spoke. "Willie's just fine," she said.

"But his stomach. . .I'm sure he was really in pain. . ."

"Oh, he was in pain, right enough," she agreed as she picked up her paring knife and another bowl of apples.

"Vera!" I cried in exasperation. I was astonished to hear her chuckle.

"Now, didn't you notice how fast Willie strung those apples?"

"Yes, but what—"

"And didn't you think it was peculiar that with all that speed, he had only finished as many strings as Lizzie?"

"Yes, I wondered about it. But what does that have to do with it?"

"That little scamp was eating a slice for every one he strung." She grinned. "He must have popped one in his mouth whenever he figured we weren't looking."

I looked at the strings festooned over the stove. Half of them were Willie's, and to eat that many apples at once. . . "Good heavens! Why, that would. . ."

"Uh-huh. Young Master Willie had a good old-fashioned bellyache."

I laughed in relief. "But you're sure he's going to be all right?"

"Let's just say that nature has taken its course," she said drily. "He'll feel a mite puny the rest of the day, but by morning he'll be looking for new mischief to get into."

"Thank goodness." We settled back into our routine. Lizzie seemed rather subdued, which could have been expected after the scare we had just had. But I had noticed that many of her quiet spells were followed by some type of prank, and I wondered uneasily what we might be in for next.

Vera broke into my reverie. "Have you decided how you'll decorate your box?" she asked.

"What box?"

Her hands flew to her face. "Mercy! Don't tell me I clean forgot to tell you?"

"Tell me what?" I asked, bewildered.

"About the box supper social this week." She sighed. "I must be getting old. I didn't say a word about it, did I?"

"I guess not. I'm still not sure what we're talking about."

"There's to be a get-together in town next Saturday night to raise money for a school. People will be coming in from all over this part of the territory."

"Oh. That sounds nice."

"Honey, haven't you ever *been* to one?"

"No," I admitted. "Are we going to this one?"

"You'd better smile, we're going! All of us except Charles and Abby and the children. And you'll be a little more excited once you hear what it's all about."

"All right." I laughed. "Satisfy my curiosity. You've certainly stirred it up."

Vera took her time removing the core from the apple she was working on. "Well," she began, "all the single ladies cook up the best supper they can and pack it in a box. Then they decorate their boxes real fancy and take them along to the supper.

"When it's time to eat, the men bid on the boxes. The highest bid gets the box, the supper, *and* the company of the lady that fixed it."

"You mean they auction them? But how do they know whose box they're bidding for?"

"It's all supposed to be a secret," she said. "And some of the fellows don't care so much about whose it is as they care about getting a good home-cooked supper and some female companionship while they're eating.

"But the ones who really want to sit with a certain young lady usually have some way of finding out ahead of time." She eyed me slyly. "Might be worth your while."

I shot her a sharp glance. "What is that supposed to mean?"

"Nothing," she replied airily. "Just that when a man and a woman are having trouble getting off on the right foot, a long conversation over a good meal sure can't hurt."

I bit off a tart reply and peeled apples with fervor, hoping Vera would think the flush I could feel on my face was due to the heat of the stove. She wouldn't be fooled for a minute, though. She seemed to have a sixth sense when it came to human relationships.

Well, why not take her advice? The way to a man's heart might not really be through his stomach, but it might help to pave the way.

The more I thought about it, the more my spirits rose. Jeff's initial reaction to the scene he had witnessed with Reverend Carver was understandable, but he'd had nearly a week to think about it. Granted, he hadn't heard my refusal, but surely he realized I wouldn't accept.

If he returned on time, he should be home tomorrow. I built up the scene in my mind. I would go to meet him and simply explain what had happened. He would have regained his good humor during his week away, and we would laugh together over the incident.

With the ice thus broken, the box supper two days later would give us the perfect opportunity to iron things out. Maybe reach some kind of understanding. Maybe even. . . I took a firm hold on my soaring imagination before I became positively giddy. There would be a lot of planning to do over the next few days—what dress to wear, what food to prepare—but it would all be worth it in the end. Vera was right, I was sure. It would all work out.

That evening I sat on the porch, watching a harvest moon rise above the hills. Its brightness washed the countryside with a silver glow. It was a pity, I thought, that its beauty would be waning by the night of the social. I consoled myself by thinking of Jeff lying in his bedroll under the stars, staring at the same moon. Was he thinking of me at this moment?

Next morning, I took special pains with my appearance before hurrying to help Vera finish the last batch of apples. Both the children worked with us again, Willie having recovered according to Vera's prediction. I noticed that today he conscientiously strung every slice. It would be quite some time, I suspected, before he was tempted to gorge on apples again.

With the last of the strings hung over the stove, I put the children through their lessons at a rapid pace, and sent them, protesting, to straighten their rooms. I gathered up some mending and stationed myself on the porch, where I could watch the horizon. Today was the day.

The sun was nearly at its peak when a shout from one of the stablehands drew my attention to a rider coming from the north. I leaned against the porch rail to watch, turning over in my mind exactly what I would say. It was silly to have let silence come between us when a few words of explanation could have smoothed the way.

The rider drew closer, and as he neared the bunkhouse, I could see that it was Jeff. Just the sight of him astride his mount made me catch my breath with love and pride. He reined in his horse and swung down from the saddle.

I drew a deep breath and started toward the stable to greet him. Jeff had his hat off now and was mopping his brow. The boy who had come to take his horse looked past me and gestured toward the road. I glanced over my shoulder and saw a buggy coming. It looked like the Styles's.

I nearly laughed out loud. Let Lucia Styles come, disapproving glares and all. This was my moment, my turning point. All the busybodies in the world couldn't take it from me.

Following the gesture, Jeff, too, had seen the buggy, but now his eyes were fixed on me. I stopped under a cottonwood and waited for him, trying to remain calm. He smiled, and there was only warmth and tenderness in his glance. It was just as I had imagined; soon we would be laughing over the incident together.

I stretched out my hands to him. "I'm glad you're back. There's something I want to explain." My hands remained suspended in the air as he stood stock-still in front of me, his eyes riveted on a point somewhere over my shoulder.

Turning to locate the distraction, I found that the buggy had drawn up behind us. It was indeed the Styles's buggy, but alighting from it was the most beautiful creature I had ever seen. Finely chiseled features, raven hair, and a porcelain complexion combined to give an impression of exquisite loveliness and fragility.

She smiled radiantly. "Jefferson, dear. It's been so long."

I wheeled around to face Jeff. He gaped at the newcomer as though seeing a ghost and choked out one word: "Lorelei!"

eleven

I stared at the array of frills spread across my bed. Scraps of fabric and colored paper, bits of lace, ribbons, and buttons of assorted sizes, all donated by Vera to decorate my box. I moved different items around in various combinations, without finding one that suited me. But then, nothing seemed to please me lately.

The entire household had felt the strain of the last two days. Lorelei, it seemed, had heard of Abby's illness through the family grapevine and had taken it upon herself to come out to "care for dear cousin Abby through these last trying days."

My own feeling was that the days hadn't been nearly so trying before Lorelei arrived, but I took care to hold my tongue. She was, after all, a member of the family.

She had taken up residence in the room next to Abby's to be available whenever she was needed. I couldn't help noticing that Abby's periods of rest came more frequently and lasted longer, and I wondered whether her condition was worsening or if this was her only means of gaining some moments of privacy.

Whatever the case, it gave Lorelei ample time to explore the ranch, in Jeff's company, more often than not. During the children's lessons on the porch, we often saw them strolling arm in arm.

Lizzie and Willie didn't seem to be any happier about her coming than I was. She had made overtures to them both on the day of her arrival but soon retreated under their sullen glares. I chided them for their lack of courtesy, but the rebuke was halfhearted on my part, and they seemed to sense it.

My own conversations with her had been as brief as I could politely manage. I could see that she was curious about me. She approached me shortly before supper on her first evening at the ranch.

"I can't tell you what a relief it is to see that the children are being cared for properly," she said with a bright smile. "That was worrying my poor mother to death. And here they are with a regular. . .governess, would you call yourself? What an asset you must be! Did Charles advertise back east?"

Knowing full well by then that she had met Lucia Styles upon her arrival in Three Forks and had prevailed upon her to drive her to the ranch, I confined my answer to a simple no. She would have already heard the Styles's version of my arrival, and I had no intention of trying to defend myself.

"Jefferson has told me what a help you are with the little dears." She lowered her voice to a confidential tone. "Jefferson and I are old, old friends, you know."

I clenched my teeth and displayed them in what I hoped would be convincing as a smile. Vera came to call us for supper at that moment.

"Well, dear," Lorelei said, "I'll see you after supper, and we'll have a cozy little chat." She looked surprised as I followed her to the dining room. "Oh, do you eat here with the family? Why, how very. . .democratic!" And with a flash of dazzling white teeth, she swirled away to her seat.

Despite the addition of a guest, dinner that night was not a festive event. The children stared steadfastly at their plates. Charles, usually the perfect host, made several attempts at conversation, then trailed off, at a loss for words. Jeff was apparently still in shock from her unexpected arrival and alternated between staring at Lorelei and pushing food aimlessly about on his plate. My appetite, too, had vanished.

Only Lorelei seemed unaware of the lack of conviviality. She chattered on and on about her journey by train and stagecoach, about the relatives in Virginia, and how wonderful it was to be with dear Charles and Abby and Jefferson.

By the time dessert was ready to be served, I pleaded a headache and went to my room.

Things continued in much the same fashion over the next two days, with Charles struggling to be courteous, Jeff in a daze, and Lorelei either attending Abby or attaching herself to Jeff.

"Like a. . .a leech," I complained bitterly to Vera on the morning of the box supper. Deprived of Abby's counsel, I had turned to Vera with my doubts and frustrations. Knowing that she was well aware of my feelings for Jeff, it had been a relief to unburden myself to her.

"Just when I thought it was all working out, she comes along and everything falls apart."

"Well, for heaven's sake, girl," Vera snapped. "If something's worth having, it's worth fighting for, isn't it? She's with Abby most of the time, isn't she? Get out there when you've got a chance and talk to the man."

"It's not that easy. He's away from the house so much of the day, and when he is around, Lorelei's free and needs him as an escort." I slumped miserably against the kitchen counter. "And what would I say now, anyway? 'Make up your mind, Jeff, and choose between us?' I couldn't do that."

Vera sniffed. "I didn't say it was going to be easy. Nothing worth having ever is. All I know is, if I cared about someone as much as you care about Jeff Bradley, you can bet I'd be willing to put up a fight!"

I had to smile at the thought of Lorelei and me dueling over Jeff in the courtyard. But Vera's talk had its effect. I didn't have to resort to punching and jabbing, but neither did I have to crawl away like a whipped pup, handing Lorelei the victory by default. There were more ways to win a fight than with a clenched fist.

Under Vera's guidance, I soon had an apple pie in the oven, with biscuits to follow. Crispy fried chicken, potatoes, and gravy would complete the meal, which Vera assured me was Jeff's favorite.

Lorelei came to the kitchen in the afternoon while Vera was finishing her own box supper, to fix, as she put it, "some fancy sandwiches for that quaint little social." We watched in astonishment as she cut bread into elaborate shapes and filled the sandwiches with bits of ham.

I had been on the ranch long enough to know what a hard day's work did for a man's appetite. Any one of the cowboys could easily have devoured the entirety of Lorelei's meal without batting an eye and then looked around for the main course. I felt a stab of sympathy for her and hoped that whoever bought her supper would be gentleman enough not to complain too loudly.

Watching Lorelei's lovely form while she worked at the counter, I was assailed by a flood of doubt. I had looked upon her as an interloper, but what if Jeff honestly did prefer her to me? He had loved her once; had he really gotten over it, as Abby thought?

Now the time had come to decorate my box, and I was busy wrestling with my feelings. "All right," I said aloud. "Suppose the worst happens. Do you love him enough to want him to be happy? Enough to be glad to let him go to Lorelei if that's what he truly wants?"

I did, I realized with a mixture of pain and relief. I had done nothing to be ashamed of in loving him. I would do nothing now to embarrass him or hurt him in any way. It was his choice; he would have to make up his own mind.

I picked up a length of red ribbon. A milliner had once shown me how to fashion a rose out of ribbon. Did I still remember how? A fold, a few twists, and while the end result wasn't of professional quality, it was at least recognizable. Jeff and Charles had mentioned once how much they missed the roses that grew at their Texas ranch. I would give him a garden of roses.

I twisted ribbon after ribbon, forming roses of varied sizes and hues, enough to nearly cover the top of my box. I wrapped the box in soft green cloth as the base of my "garden," then carefully fastened the roses to it. Lizzie and Willie burst through the door when I was nearly finished.

"Oh, it's beautiful!" Lizzie cried, and I basked in the warmth of her praise.

"Green, with flowers," muttered Willie to himself, as if committing it to memory.

"We were hoping you had it finished," Lizzie said.

"Yeah," said Willie, " 'cause someone's been asking us what it looked—ow!" He broke off as a well-aimed kick caught him on the shin.

"Well, now you've seen it. But you know," I added virtuously, "that no one is supposed to know who made which box."

"We know," Lizzie agreed cheerfully. "And we wouldn't tell. . .not just anybody, anyway!"

I hugged myself in delight as they left, giggling. "Not just anybody," indeed! I hadn't imagined his feelings for me, after all. Of course Lorelei's coming had stunned him; that was only natural. And it was just as natural that he could not avoid her. After all, she was a guest at the ranch, and Jeff would have to be gracious out of courtesy.

But tonight—tonight when the bidding was going on for the supposedly anonymous suppers—it could hardly be considered neglect of Lorelei to fail to bid on hers. I fastened the last few ribbon roses to the box with tender care. It did look lovely, if I said so myself.

I realized with a shock that I had spent so much time preparing the box that I had left barely enough time to get myself ready.

The dress I had chosen was pale blue with a tight bodice and puffy sleeves. It had seemed too lovely to wear before, even to church, and I wondered about the wisdom of subjecting it to the long wagon ride into town. But I was determined to shine, this night at least.

The dress fit as though it had been made for me, and for the hundredth time I blessed Abby for her generosity. She must have looked stunning in this dress, I reflected, and turned to study myself in the mirror. Excitement and the mounting anticipation had brought a pink flush to my cheeks and an expectant sparkle to my eyes. I smoothed a stray wisp of hair into place and grinned at the girl in the glass.

Vera had found a dark blue cloak for me to use as a wrap, and I was glad of its warmth when I stepped out to the waiting wagon. The rays of the late afternoon sun didn't do a thing to combat the crisp chill. Autumn was definitely in the air.

Vera was waiting just outside the kitchen door. "Here, give me your box before anybody sees it," she said. She set it carefully inside a covered basket next to two other boxes of similar size. One was wrapped in calico, the other in a cloth of delicate blue which had a wide ruffle of lace around the edge and a large velvet bow on the top. It wasn't difficult to decide which box was whose.

"You did a nice job." She smiled approvingly. "The roses were a nice touch." She gave me a sly wink as she closed the basket. I laughed happily, letting the mood of the evening take over.

Shorty and Neil had placed a box at the end of the wagon for us to use as a step and stood ready to assist us as we climbed in. Shorty was wearing his cologne again. The aroma wafted over us as he helped me step to the wagon bed, and I hoped it would not cling to my hair or clothes.

Vera shook off their hands and stepped up herself, carefully balancing the basket as she did so. Neil reached out to take it from her, but she slapped his hand away.

"Keep those hands to yourself," she snapped. "You're just dying to lift that lid and see how those boxes are done up. But you're just going to have to wait your turn like everyone else!"

Shorty hooted at Neil's discomfiture until Vera wheeled toward him and said, "And you, you'll do us all a favor if you'll stay downwind."

I sat on one of the blankets that had been laid over fluffy piles of straw, carefully smoothing my skirts to avoid as many wrinkles as possible. Vera sat opposite, guarding her basket jealously.

A strangling noise from Shorty made us turn. He and Neil were gaping at a vision of loveliness framed in the doorway. Lorelei had a knack for making an entrance a grand event. She had only to stand, as she did now, looking helpless and appealing, and every man in the vicinity would fall all over himself to go to her aid.

Shorty and Neil sprang forward, each trying to be the first to reach her. They collided, bounced apart, and stumbled to her side together.

"Looks like a tie," Vera muttered.

Lorelei appeared to regard it as such, for she favored each contender with one of her brilliant smiles and allowed each of them to tuck one of her dainty hands in the crook of his arm. They led her to the wagon in state, the picture of well-trained footmen, and helped her tenderly into the wagon as though she might break.

"I never saw anything like it," Vera said to me in a low voice. "All she has to do is stand there." We watched, fascinated, as she seated herself upon the straw as though it were a throne. She smiled graciously at her courtiers, dismissing them, and turned to us.

Evidently, Lorelei was not immune to the excitement of the evening, for she seemed as inclined to giggle and chatter as a schoolgirl.

"Isn't this quaint?" she gushed. "It'll be such fun to tell everybody back home about it. Imagine. . .taking a chance on spending the evening with a total stranger!" She shivered in delicious anticipation.

"Appears to me that it's the men who are taking the risk," Vera said drily. "They're buying two pigs in a poke—the company and the meal."

"Why, what an unflattering comparison, Vera dear!" Lorelei laughed gaily.

Vera opened her mouth as if to make a retort, and I was relieved when Jake's sudden arrival interrupted them. "Your driver at your service, ladies," he announced grandly. "And there's no one who'll be driving any lovelier ladies to the supper."

"I'm inclined to agree," said Jeff, stepping out of the doorway.

"Jefferson!" Lorelei exclaimed. "Don't you look fine!" He stood tall and straight in his black frock coat and striped pants.

"Thank you," he said, stepping easily into the wagon and settling himself between us. "May I return the compliment?" While Lorelei fluttered happily, he turned to me and said softly, "You look lovely tonight, Judith." His smile was like a caress. I found myself suddenly unable to speak, but smiled back at him with my heart in my eyes.

Jake stepped nimbly to the seat, shook out the reins with a flourish, and we were off. Neil and Shorty had mounted their horses and rode beside the wagon. The evening's excitement was infectious, and good-natured banter flew back and forth between the wagon and the riders. Even Neil shook off some of his shyness and ventured an occasional comment.

Lorelei dominated the conversation, batting her eyes first at one cowboy, then another, archly accusing all the men of trying to find out which basket belonged to which girl.

Shorty's and Neil's mounts proved unexpectedly susceptible to injury, Neil's bruising its foot on a stone and Shorty's acquiring a limp perceptible only to Shorty himself.

Both tied their horses to the tailgate and climbed into the now crowded wagon. As the only available space was along Vera's side, it placed both of them opposite Lorelei, which seemed to satisfy them admirably.

Vera grumbled and held on to the basket. Jake remarked loudly that there was plenty of room next to him on the seat, but no one seemed to pay any attention.

With Lorelei holding court and the cowboys eagerly competing for her attention, the rest of us were left to amuse ourselves. This suited me well enough; it was pleasant just to sit close to Jeff without having to say anything.

The sun had slipped behind the mountains and there was a chill in the air. I drew my cloak around me and shivered.

"Cold?" Jeff reached around me to tuck a blanket about my shoulders.

At that moment, one of the rear wheels hit a hole, and the wagon lurched violently. I was thrown back against Jeff, whose arm tightened protectively around me. It took a moment to recover my balance sufficiently to right myself. Recovering my composure took longer. Fortunately, everyone else had been similarly thrown about, and no one seemed to notice.

"I'm sorry," I whispered, dismayed to find my breath coming in little gasps.

"I'm not," he said quietly. His smile had faded, and he looked at me intently in the twilight.

We said nothing more during the ride into town, but that moment hung between us like a promise.

twelve

Lights spilled out of the windows of the warehouse and painted yellow squares on the darkened street. Jake let us out at the door and went to find a place to leave the wagon.

We moved through a swirling throng of gaily laughing people, only a few of whom I recognized. I followed Vera as we threaded our way to a long table already covered with decorated boxes. I looked them over quickly, but none resembled my "rose garden." My breath whooshed out in a sigh of relief. There shouldn't be any doubt as to which was mine.

Vera handed her basket to one of the women presiding over the table, and we retired to a corner, out of the crush.

"I had no idea there were this many people to be found around here," I said, panting slightly.

Vera produced a handkerchief from her sleeve and dabbed at her forehead. "They've come for miles in all directions. Anything like this happens so seldom that it brings them right out of the woodwork. Those who aren't in on the auction brought potluck suppers and will donate money, anyway. And the thought of having a school and a good teacher for their youngsters—the bidding ought to go high tonight."

I looked at the children scampering around the room and felt a momentary pang of regret for Lizzie and Willie. How they would have loved playing with them! But, no, they needed a quiet evening alone with their parents even more. There had been little enough time for them as a family lately.

A tall, lean man stood up on a platform behind the long table and tried vainly to get the crowd's attention. He called, he whistled, he clapped his hands, but even though I was watching him, I couldn't hear him over the din.

Finally, a husky, square-shouldered fellow motioned him off the platform, mounted it himself, and let out a screeching war whoop. The effect was almost miraculous. All eyes turned toward the man, who bowed, stepped down with a grin, and pushed the tall man back up again. "They're all yours, Sam," he announced.

"All right, folks," said the one called Sam. "It's about time we got started. Ladies, please have a seat on the benches over there along the wall. Gentlemen, you line up here on this side so you can all see what you'll be bidding on. I'm your auctioneer for the evening, and I hope you men all brought good appetites and full wallets so we can raise plenty of money for the new school!"

A cheer rose and died away as we all moved to find our places. I had begun to feel guilty about leaving Lorelei to her own devices, but as we made our way toward the benches lining the far wall, I saw her talking animatedly to a group of young men. Even here, she was the undisputed belle of the ball.

Her admirers escorted her to one of the benches and left, reluctantly, I thought. I sat between her and Vera and scanned the group of men opposite. Jeff leaned comfortably against the wall. His eyes met mine and a smile lit his face.

"Isn't this exciting?" Lorelei whispered delightedly. I nodded, in complete agreement with her for once.

"Ladies and gentlemen," intoned the auctioneer, "the auction will now begin!" He held up a box covered with yellow paper cutouts of the moon and stars. "What am I bid for this box, which promises to contain a heavenly feast?"

A ripple of nervous laughter swept the room, but no one seemed inclined to open the bidding.

"Come, come," the auctioneer chided. "No need to be shy, folks. Let's start the bidding at twenty-five cents. Who'll be first?"

A hand went up across the room. "That's more like it! Now do I hear thirty cents? Thirty cents for the new schoolhouse?"

"I'll bid thirty."

"Thirty-five."

The bidding began to grow more spirited, and a final bid of fifty-five cents brought the auctioneer's gavel crashing down on the table.

"Sold!" he cried. "To Eb Winters for fifty-five cents. Step right up, Eb. Claim your dinner and your partner."

Eb Winters, a tall gangly youth who looked to be barely out of his teens moved forward, grinning sheepishly. He handed over his money amid good-natured catcalls, took his box, and turned to look hopefully for his dinner partner.

A pleasant-faced woman of about fifty stepped out of the crowd and went to join him. Eb made an obvious effort to control his disappointment and escorted his companion to a table with dignity.

I began to wonder just how enjoyable the evening would be for most of the participants. My concern must have shown on my face, for Vera patted me on the knee and said, "Don't worry, honey. She's one of the best cooks around.

By the time he eats his fill, and she gets finished mothering him, he'll feel like he got more than his money's worth."

Sure enough, Eb was tucking into his supper as though he hadn't eaten for a month. His partner watched with pleasure, smiling maternally and urging him to take even more. Looking at it from Vera's point of view, it made sense. In fact, judging from the crowd's reaction, a good deal of the fun was in the unlikely matches that occurred.

More of the tables were filling up as the boxes went to their various buyers. I became interested in watching the reactions of the girls and women around me as the tension mounted as to whose box would be offered next.

The auctioneer held aloft a box wrapped only in brown paper, with birds drawn on it. It was easy enough to see that it belonged to a young girl sitting back near the wall by the wave of crimson that spread over her face. The bidding started slowly, to the girl's obvious embarrassment.

A flurry of activity on the other side of the room caught my eye. A boy of about the same age as the girl was sidling along the wall, stopping first at one man, then the next. Some of the men slipped something from their pockets into the boy's hand, while others shook their heads. The boy reached the end of the line and hurriedly examined his collection.

"Forty cents," said the auctioneer. "Are there no more bids? Going once. . . going twice. . ."

"I bid seventy-eight cents!" cried the boy. The auctioneer swept his gavel down, and the girl, still blushing, walked away with her hero.

There were now no more than half a dozen suppers on the auction table, Vera's, Lorelei's, and mine among them. The men left waiting to bid began to take special notice of the boxes being presented.

Once Jeff offered a bid on one of the suppers, and my heart stopped. Again it was Vera who reassured me. "See the 'RT' down in the corner? Everybody knows that's Rose Taylor's box and that she's sweet on Bill Carson," she said. "Bill doesn't want anyone else to have her, but he's one of the biggest skinflints you ever saw. Jeff just wanted to make him pay what the supper's worth, that's all."

As usual, Vera was right. After giving Jeff a baleful look, a glowering man with shaggy black hair made the final bid and led Rose away.

Vera's box was the next to go. She was calmer than I was as we watched the bidding mount. I wanted to cry out with pleasure when the gavel rang out on the final bid of a dollar. She squeezed my hand and gave me an encouraging wink. "It won't be long now," she whispered as she left.

And it wasn't. In no time at all, only two boxes remained—my garden of roses, and Lorelei's lace-trimmed confection. I was glad now that most of the room was engaged in eating; the strain of waiting was bad enough without being the center of the whole group's attention.

Lorelei wore the look of a contented, cream-fed cat. She was actually enjoying the suspense, I realized. The whole thing couldn't be over soon enough for me.

The auctioneer paused dramatically and made a show of deciding which box to pick up next. His hand moved from one to the other and back again before finally settling on mine.

He held the box under his nose and inhaled deeply. "Aaah," he sighed. "Gentlemen, I won't tell you what is in here, but I guarantee that if it tastes as delectable as it smells, it contains a meal fit for a king!" I felt pleased despite my nervousness, but I wished he would get on with it. I was interested in only one particular bidder.

My eyes sought out Jeff. He was lounging casually against the wall, a slight smile on his face. I was glad that he, at least, could relax, but did wish he would show a little more enthusiasm.

"Men," cried the auctioneer, "if you're hungry, you'd better wake up and bid. This is almost your last chance. Let's hear an opening bid."

"Twenty-five cents."

"Thirty."

"I'll go thirty-five."

Something was hurting my arm. It was Lorelei, gripping it tightly with both hands. "Who do you think it will be?" She looked unaccountably anxious.

"The highest bidder, I suppose," I replied, trying to keep my voice steady. I laced my fingers tightly together and willed my hands to lay calmly in my lap, hoping no one would notice the white knuckles that betrayed my nervousness.

Now that the moment had come, I was assailed by sudden fears. What if something went wrong? But how could it, barring fire, flood, or imminent collapse of the roof? My lungs ached for air, and I realized I had been holding my breath.

"Forty-five cents," called out a cowboy.

"Sixty!" I recognized the voice as Shorty's. I started, then smiled shakily as I remembered Jeff's ploy with Bill Carson. Jeff would want to make a nice contribution to the school fund; evidently he was using Shorty to drive the price up.

"Seventy-five." I breathed a sigh of relief. Jeff was joining the bidding at last.

"Eighty-five," sang out the cowboy, getting into the spirit of things.

"One dollar," called Jeff, grinning.

Shorty looked irritated. He was playing his part well. He felt in one pocket, frowned, and explored the depths of the other. His face cleared. "I bid two dollars," he announced. We had everyone's attention now. A jump of a dollar in the bidding was unheard of.

"Two fifty," Jeff said.

The cowboy sat down resignedly. Silence fell, and the auctioneer raised his gavel. "Two fifty," he announced. "I have two fifty. Will anybody make it three?" He paused hopefully, scanning the men's faces. "Going once. . . going twice. . ."

"Three dollars!" shouted Shorty, his face as red as mine felt.

"Three dollars," echoed the auctioneer. Silence again.

"Going once. . ."

"Hurry, Jeff," I breathed.

"Going twice. . ."

"Please. Just get it over." I fidgeted, exasperated. This charade had gone on more than long enough to suit me.

"Sold!" The gavel rang out on the table. "Folks, let's hear it for Shorty Nelson, the highest bidder so far tonight!" Enthusiastic applause rocked the room. Lorelei gave my arm another squeeze.

Shorty swaggered to the table and counted out his money with a flourish. I sat in stunned disbelief. Could Jeff possibly have run out of money? He stood watching, grinning broadly. He didn't look at all like a man disappointed.

I rose woodenly and somehow got to Shorty's side. I didn't dare risk another look at Jeff.

How Shorty managed to get himself, the three-dollar supper, and me to a small table in a corner of the room, I never knew. The whole evening seemed like a bad dream. I had to make a determined effort in order to be aware of anything at all.

It struck me then that Shorty was fumbling with the wrapping on the box and I roused myself to help him. It was hardly fair to him to be penalized for making such a gallant gesture. Three dollars, I knew, was the equivalent of several days' wages to the cowboys—hardly a sum to be dismissed lightly.

My fingers moved mechanically, trying to disturb the ribbon roses as little as possible. The room began to come back in focus again, and I realized that Lorelei's box, the last of the evening, was being bid on.

Evidently the remaining group of hungry men was being spurred to new heights both by Shorty's high bid and by the realization that Lorelei and the last box must go together. Pockets were being turned out, money hastily counted, and enthusiasm was at a fever pitch.

"A dollar seventy-five." Apparently the bidding had been going on for some time before I had come out of my stupor.

"Two fifty." Jeff spoke clearly.

"Two seventy-five." I looked at Jeff, tall and remote across the room. He had stopped at two fifty before. Would he do it again?

"Two eighty." To my relief, the voice was not Jeff's. The momentum of the bidding was slowing down.

The auctioneer scanned the men as if to draw out any more prospective buyers.

"How about two ninety?" he called. "Do I hear two ninety?"

"Three dollars and fifty cents." Every head swiveled to see from whom the bid had come, but I didn't need to look. I knew that voice well enough.

I watched Jeff pay for his supper after the auctioneer's gavel had descended for the last time. Lorelei stood and swept toward him, grace and elegance in every line of her bearing. I could picture her moving the same way down a curving staircase at a lavish ball. She would always be queen of whatever group she chose to rule.

They did make a handsome couple. It wasn't hard to see how any man could lose his heart to Lorelei. I just wished it hadn't been the one man to whom my heart would always belong.

Pull yourself together, I reminded myself. *If you love him, love him enough to let go. Remember?*

"Anything wrong, Miss Judith? You're not feeling sick or anything?" Shorty still beamed triumphantly, but a touch of concern crept into his voice.

I forced a smile, although my face felt as though it would shatter. "I'm sorry, Shorty. I guess I was just woolgathering."

A smile of relief brightened his face still more, and I felt ashamed of myself. I hastened to take two plates from the box and fill one of them with pieces of fried chicken, fluffy mashed potatoes, biscuits, and gravy. I wouldn't have thought Shorty's face could have gotten any brighter, but now he fairly glowed.

I took smaller portions for myself and bowed my head to say grace. Shorty looked at me quizzically for a moment after my amen, then began tucking into the food. He concentrated solely on eating for several minutes, and when he finally stopped to catch his breath, his face wore an expression of pure satisfaction.

"No lady's cooked a supper just for me since my ma died when I was fifteen."

"I'm glad you like it." And to my surprise, I found that I meant it. To keep the conversation going I added, "That was quite a bid you made."

He grinned, then his face darkened. "I thought for a moment ol' Jeff was going to bid me clear out of the running, but he stopped just in time."

That was an area I didn't care to explore. "Tell me about your mother," I ventured.

I had found the right tactic for keeping the talk away from dangerous subjects. Shorty told story after story about growing up as the son of a sharecropper in Arkansas. His father had died when he was ten, and he and his mother had barely managed to keep going by taking in laundry and doing odd jobs. When she passed away five years later, he decided to head west.

I felt an unexpected softening toward Shorty. I could understand his feelings on the loss of his parents, and the west had seemed to me, too, the door to a brighter future. The realization that we had so much in common brought me up short, and I looked at him with new eyes. When he wasn't devising practical jokes or begging me to marry him, Shorty could actually be pleasant company.

When he saw the apple pie, he set to with relish, polishing off all but the narrow slice I had cut for myself. Remembering Willie's experience, I hoped Shorty wouldn't fall prey to the same malady.

He leaned back in his chair and sighed blissfully. I returned the empty dishes to the box and wondered what came next. I steeled myself and glanced covertly at the table where Jeff sat with Lorelei. They were smiling and chatting merrily, and Jeff was devouring her little sandwiches with every bit as much enjoyment as Shorty had shown with my meal.

People around us were beginning to stir, clearing away the remains of their suppers and shoving chairs and benches back up against the tables. Evidently the evening was over. I dreaded the long drive home.

I swept the last of the crumbs off the table and brushed them into the box. Shorty looked up at me and said, "You know, I really didn't think it would be like this, me actually getting to eat with you and all. I guess I've been pretty hard to be around. Can we kind of. . .start over, do you think?"

I sighed. "Shorty, I just don't know. Right now, I need some time. But. . . I would like for us to be friends, if that's all right."

"Well," he said, pushing away from the table and helping me with my cloak, "it's better than nothing." He grinned and held out his arm.

The crowd had thinned out by the time we made our way to the door. Outside, Jake had drawn the wagon up. Shorty boosted me easily to the wagon bed and said, "Thanks for tonight."

"Thank you for buying my supper," I managed. "And thank you for being my friend." He nodded and gave me a cheerful wink, then went to mount his horse, which had apparently recovered from its limp.

A wave of weariness and misery engulfed me, and I was grateful to be able to settle myself in a front corner before the others got aboard. I pulled the hood of my cloak up so that it shaded my face.

The rest of the party came out on a wave of Lorelei's prattle. I was too tired and heartsick to rouse myself to greet them, even when Vera laid a solicitous hand on my shoulder.

Neil joined Shorty on horseback, which left only the four of us and Jake in the wagon.

Once, Lorelei directed a remark to me, but before I could make the effort to reply, Vera intervened.

"She's asleep," she snapped, in the manner of a hen defending her only chick. "Just keep your voices down and leave her be."

All I remember of the endless ride home was that we seemed to float on a stream of Lorelei's constant chatter. Even when I didn't catch her words, her tone indicated that she was immensely pleased with herself.

After what seemed an eternity, we pulled up before the ranch house. Charles had left lamps burning low for us and I was glad as I stumbled to my room that I hadn't had to carry a candle.

I threw the cloak and the lovely blue dress over the back of my chair, flung myself across the bed, and slept.

thirteen

The following days went by in a blur. My senses were numbed by my emotional upheaval, and I was content for the time being to go along in that unfeeling state. I knew that at some point in the near future I would have to face the prospect of my future and make plans. But for now a sort of protective cocoon enveloped me, and I welcomed it.

Avoiding the other adults on the ranch became an obsession. The children made a good excuse, and I took them on long walks on the pretext of getting in as much exercise as possible before the snow fell.

Lorelei unknowingly aided me by monopolizing as much of Jeff's time as possible. "I guess I'm just not cut out for full-time nursing," she declared. "If I spend too much more time in that stuffy little room, I'll be laid as low as Abby. You don't mind giving me a little break now and then to get fresh air, do you?"

Actually, I didn't. Vera agreed to keep Lizzie and Willie under her watchful eye while I was with Abby, so I was able to spend nearly all my time either alone with the children or in the sickroom. Abby slept for a good part of each day, which left me free to brood. I found myself with more time to do this as Lorelei discovered an increasing need for fresh air.

"That woman is acting like she owns the place," reported Vera, setting my lunch tray down in Abby's room with a muffled thump. "She actually had the gall to ask me if she could rearrange some of the furniture in the parlor!"

I knew her words were intended to rouse me to action, but I had tried Vera's philosophy of "stand up and fight" and had been defeated soundly. Right now, all I wanted was to lick my wounds in peace.

Charles came to Abby's door every evening and said he would relieve me for supper, but I always insisted he go instead. I was grateful for the excuse not to have to face Jeff or watch Lorelei's possessiveness. It was cowardly, I knew, but it was hard to care about that or anything else from within my protective cocoon.

But little by little, small things began to work their way through unsuspected chinks in my carefully constructed armor, fanning to life sparks of feeling I thought would never surface again.

Lizzie and Willie dogged my steps every time I set foot outside their mother's room. They had been models of good behavior ever since the night of the box supper social, and it was evidence of my numbed state of mind that that alone didn't send me flying into a panic.

During one of our long walks, we stopped to rest in the shelter of an enormous cedar. The children arranged themselves on either side of me, each holding one of my hands. We sat like that, listening to the wind stirring the branches, until I felt their small bodies slump against me. I eased them down so that their heads could rest in my lap.

Lizzie stirred and reached for my hand again. Taking it, she pressed it against her cheek. A lump formed in my throat. Willie slept contentedly, a soft snore escaping his lips from time to time. Lizzie, however, whimpered repeatedly and squirmed in her sleep, squeezing my hand as though for reassurance.

The lump in my throat grew until it reached the bursting point, and by the time both children's eyelids flickered open, slow tears were coursing down my cheeks. Uncharacteristically, they didn't say a word all the way back to the house.

I left them with Vera and fled to the sanctuary of Abby's room, thrusting an astonished Lorelei out into the hallway. I sat straight in the bedside chair, lips pressed together, hands clasped in my lap, feet arranged just so, as if by holding my body in rigid alignment I could calm the tumult that raged within.

"Abby," I whispered to the sleeping form through lips all too inclined to tremble, "I wish you could hear me. I thought things would be so different by now. I'm so confused. Jeff and Lorelei are together all the time now, and ever since the social, he's seemed like a total stranger.

"Right up until that night, I was sure there was something wonderful between us, but I guess I was wrong. Maybe he never really did get over Lorelei, after all. I turned it over to the Lord because I. . .I love Jeff and I want him to be happy. I thought that would solve everything—but then, why am I so miserable?"

I put my face in my hands and wept, trying to stifle the sound so that Abby wouldn't be disturbed. If only she were well again! I needed her counsel and friendship now more than ever.

A gentle touch on my knee made me bring my head upright with a start. To my surprise, I found myself staring into Abby's calm gray eyes.

"What is it?" she asked gently.

"Oh, Abby!" I cried. "I didn't mean to wake you."

"Why are you crying, dear? Can I help?"

"It's. . .it's not important," I answered, trying to keep my voice level. Much as I longed to share everything with her, the burden of my problems was the last thing she needed to bear.

"But, Mama, dear, you seemed worried over something."

I stared uncomprehendingly as the impact of her words sank into my consciousness.

"Mama?" I repeated blankly.

"Is it about Charles? I know you think I'm making the wrong choice in marrying him, but I love him, Mama, truly I do. And I know he'll make a kind and wonderful husband."

The gray eyes held mine steadily, but there was no doubt that the face she saw was from another place and time.

I drew the covers up over her gently, patted her hand, and murmured sounds that were meant to be comforting. I withdrew from the room, closed the door softly, and bolted down the hall in search of Charles, Jeff, Vera, anyone who could dispel this nightmare. My own troubles were, for the moment, firmly thrust aside.

Worried days and wakeful nights followed each other in a seemingly endless procession. Abby went from delirium to lucidity and back again while we all performed what tasks we could for her comfort and chafed at our helplessness to do anything of significance.

Vera, Lorelei, and I took turns watching at her bedside during the day, while Charles took the night watches himself. Consequently, Jeff shouldered full responsibility for the ranch. He was away from the house all day, except for supper, the one time we all gathered for a meal.

I alternated between helping Vera in the kitchen and minding the children when I was not on duty in the sickroom.

"What do you think?" Vera asked me as we peeled potatoes one morning. We tried to keep enough food available during the day so that any of us could eat whenever we had a free moment.

"About Abby?" I asked.

She nodded, her brow furrowed with worry. "I thought she looked like she'd gained a little this morning, didn't you?" She looked at me hopefully.

"I honestly don't know what to think," I replied cautiously. "Sometimes she seems as if she's almost back to normal. Then she starts talking like she's a girl in Virginia again."

"I know." Vera sighed. "I'm so afraid for Charles and those little ones." She paused in her work to wipe the back of her hand across one cheek.

"Isn't there anything we can do? There must be something! It's unbearable to sit by and watch her waste away like this."

Vera shook her head wearily. "There's not a thing more that any of us can do. . .except pray."

"I've been praying for her almost constantly. We all have."

"Then I guess we'll just have to leave it in His hands, won't we?"

I nodded. A feeling that a turning point must soon be reached pervaded the house, and the resulting tension spread over us like a pall.

Everyone felt the strain, but I ached especially for the children, who were denied even the satisfaction of performing little duties for their mother. Charles had ordered that they be allowed in the sickroom only when Abby was asleep. I knew they missed her company, but had to agree that they needed to be protected from the shock of realizing that their own mother didn't always recognize them.

The nightly gathering at the supper table was primarily for their benefit, to preserve a sense of normalcy, but it served to give the rest of us an anchor as well. I had resumed eating with the family, finding that the sense of unity gave us all added strength.

It was at the dinner table one evening that Jeff had a piece of astonishing news. "I had a long visit with the Reverend Carver today," he said, helping himself to slices of roast beef.

I winced and fastened my eyes on my plate. I hadn't seen the pastor since the day of his proposal, nor did I care to.

"And what did the good reverend have to say?" asked Charles, with a sarcasm I knew would not have been present if not for his anxiety.

Jeff took a moment to swallow his food. "I think I've discovered the reason his sermons have seemed so far off the mark. The man doesn't know the Christ he preaches."

I stared at Jeff in spite of myself.

"Do you mean he's here under false pretenses?" asked Charles. "He isn't even a Christian?"

"I should have said he *didn't* know Christ," Jeff replied. "He met the Lord this afternoon."

"I don't understand," put in Lorelei. "How could he be a minister and not be a Christian?"

Jeff looked at her thoughtfully before replying. "I had business in town this morning," he said, "and as I was about to head back home, I bumped into him on the street. He asked me about Abby, and I told him she wasn't doing well at all."

"As he'd know if he ever bothered to call out here." Charles snorted in disgust.

"Yes, we touched on that topic," Jeff said with a crooked grin. "I told him that it was hard to see her this way, that if it weren't for knowing the Lord, it would be more than any of us could stand.

"And do you know what he did?" He shook his head, remembering. "He coughed and spluttered and said, 'Yes, I'm sure Mrs. Bradley has led an exemplary life. And if her days should be drawing to a close, her works will precede her and open the way to paradise.' "

"He actually said *that?*" I gasped. Jeff didn't even glance in my direction.

"He did. So I sat him down in front of the store and asked him just exactly what he did believe."

"I'll bet it has something to do with 'the inherent goodness of man,' " Charles quipped.

"That, and a lot besides," Jeff said. "It seems his grandfather and two uncles are ministers at churches back east. When it came time for him to decide on his life's work, he just figured he'd follow in the family tradition."

"And what's wrong with that?" Lorelei challenged. "It's a noble and respectable calling."

"Yes," Jeff answered slowly, "if it's the Lord who's doing the calling. But Carver never saw it that way. He just looked on it as a job like any other.

"Apparently he got in with some progressive-thinking church that thought his brand of religion was fine. Then when his health failed, he decided he'd spread the light of all his knowledge to the poor, backward souls in the west while he recuperated. He never could understand why he got such a cool reception here."

"Until today?" Charles prompted.

"That's right. We took a long walk through the Bible he was carrying, and he found out that man has no inherent goodness and that our works don't mean a thing if they're not based on faith in Jesus Christ as Savior and Lord."

"You mean he was converted right then and there?"

"Right where we sat. Once he got past the idea that he was able to make himself good enough for heaven, he asked me, 'Then how can I be saved?' Just like the Philippian jailer," he chuckled.

"It was wonderful to see. He bowed his head and repented and asked the Lord to save him. He's a new man in Christ!"

"That is wonderful," Charles agreed. "Will he stay on and preach, then?"

"No." Jeff shook his head. "He said he thought he'd spend some time in study to see what he really is supposed to be saying. I think that in time the Lord will have a fine spokesman in him."

"What does 'repent' mean?" Lizzie asked. I jumped a little. The children had sat so quietly through supper that I had almost forgotten their presence.

"What does it mean?" she repeated, wide-eyed.

"Well, honey," said Charles, "it's kind of like when a man realizes he's been going down the wrong trail and he needs to turn around and go back the right way. It's when you decide to turn back from going your own way and go God's way instead. Understand?" She nodded, and Charles rose from his seat and gave her a warm hug.

We all prepared to go our separate ways—Charles to sit with Abby, Jeff to a final check of the ranch for the night, me to see the children to bed, and Lorelei to her beauty sleep. I dipped a corner of Willie's napkin in his water tumbler and was using it to scrub his face when I heard a cry behind me. Lizzie had laid her head down on the white tablecloth and was sobbing wildly.

Charles and Lorelei had already gone. Jeff looked at me with as much astonishment as I felt.

"What is it, Lizzie?" I asked, giving Willie's cheek a final rub.

Her sobs turned to wails and I hurried to quiet her.

"I. . .I. . .I repent!" she choked out.

"Of what, honey?" I stroked her hair.

"I lied to Uncle Jeff, and I knew it was wrong, and I want to repent!"

"Lied to me?" Jeff knelt beside her, eyes full of concern. "What about?"

Lizzie sat up, her face swollen and tear streaked. I handed her one of the napkins and she blew her nose thoroughly. Her breath was coming in quick little gasps as she turned to her uncle.

"It was the day of the box supper social," she gulped. "Remember when you asked Willie and me to find out what Judith's box looked like so you could bid on it?"

Jeff nodded. I stirred uneasily, thinking that this was a line of thought neither of us would wish to pursue.

"I remember," he said. His voice betrayed nothing.

"And remember I told you she said that her box and her dress would match?"

I drew a quick breath, remembering my blue dress and Lorelei's blue box. He nodded solemnly.

"Well—," she faltered, "I lied. I knew her box was the green one with the pretty flowers."

Jeff glanced up at me. Our eyes met and held, but neither of us spoke.

He looked Lizzie squarely in the eye. "Then why? Why tell me something that wasn't true?"

Her shoulders shook as the sobs took hold of her again. "I thought it would be funny," she said. "A good joke. But it wasn't funny at all. I never thought about you getting that old Lorelei's box by mistake, and now she says she's going to marry you, and Mama's so sick, and, oh, Uncle Jeff, everything's going wrong!"

She threw her arms around his neck and he held her close. "It's all right," he said, rocking her in his arms. "Everybody does wrong sometimes. But now you've told me about it, and I forgive you. So it's over. You don't need to worry about it anymore."

Instead of being soothed by this, Lizzie's agitation increased and she clung to him all the more tightly. "But I want to be clean," she wailed. "I want to be all new, like Reverend Carver."

A joyful smile broke out on Jeff's face. "Well, Lizzie," he said, "that's a real easy thing to arrange. Let's go find your father." And he carried her out of the room in search of Charles.

I let out a pent-up sigh of relief. It looked as though two new children would enter the Kingdom of God that day. I turned to the wide-eyed Willie and herded him off to bed.

I lay awake for a long time, thinking over Lizzie's confession. How different things would be right now if she had not unwittingly fabricated a story that would play right into Lorelei's hands!

Or would they? I wondered.

On the one hand, Jeff had not denied Lizzie's statement that he had intended to buy my box at the social. I had not, then, been mistaken about the warmth of his manner toward me on the way to town that night.

But, I reflected, there had been opportunity since then to explain the mix-up if he had wanted to. Had the mistake turned out to be a favorable one for him, rekindling his feelings for Lorelei? If what Lizzie had quoted Lorelei as saying was true, it would certainly seem that the social had acted as the catalyst that brought them back together.

I tossed and turned, pummeling my pillow into a myriad of shapes as I examined the pieces of this puzzle and tried to fit them into a meaningful pattern. Finally admitting defeat, I breathed, "Lord, it's all Yours. I can't begin to understand what's happened," and promptly fell asleep.

fourteen

I awoke well before daybreak, feeling fully rested and ready for action. No matter how hard I tried, I could not go back to sleep, nor could I convince myself to burrow under the covers against the chill morning air.

I dressed quickly and crept down the hall to the kitchen. Even Vera wasn't up and about yet. I pulled one of her shawls from a peg near the door and stepped outside.

If I hadn't been fully awake, it would have taken only that first moment of contact with the frosty air to make me so. Even the warm shawl couldn't stop the icy fingers from raising gooseflesh along my arms.

I paced up and down the porch and filled my lungs with the invigorating air. A light frost crunched beneath my feet, and I reveled in having this moment to myself.

The indigo hue of the sky was fading to gray. One by one, the stars were lost to sight. It was impossible, I felt, to witness all this beauty without being aware of the One who made it. I brought my concerns to Him one by one: Abby's failing health; Lizzie and her new life in Christ; Jeff, Lorelei, and their engagement; and direction for my own future. In this time alone with God, even that uncertainty paled in significance.

Back inside, I had biscuits mixed and in the oven by the time Vera walked in. "Well, aren't you bright-eyed this morning!" she said, blinking in surprise.

I smiled at her. "I couldn't sleep. I've been getting some things straightened out between me and the Lord."

"Good for you." She squeezed my shoulders. "I've been worried about you."

"I'm sorry. I guess I've been feeling so sorry for myself that I didn't think how my attitude might affect anyone else. It won't happen again. We all have enough to worry about without my adding to it."

"Well, it's over now." She eyed me critically. "You're feeling a lot better, aren't you?"

"I feel fine," I said, laughing. "Ready for anything." And it was a good thing, because Vera kept me flying from one task to another until well after lunchtime.

We were standing on the porch, taking a few moments to catch our breath, when Neil rode up.

"I had to go into town yesterday. They were holding a bunch of mail. It was late when I got back, so I held on to it till today." He tossed a bundle of envelopes to Vera and loped away.

Vera glanced through the envelopes quickly, then went back to examine each one more thoroughly. She pulled one, grimier than the rest, from the pile. "Miss Judith Alder," she read, holding it gingerly by one corner. "Looks like the dogs delivered this one." She handed it to me, and I accepted it with quickening breath.

A glance at the handwriting verified that it was from Uncle Matthew. No one else I knew used quite the same slapdash scrawl.

I stared at the missive. There was something awe inspiring about receiving word from him only a few hours after praying for guidance.

The confusing whirl of thoughts from the night before renewed their dance through my mind. Jeff had been ready to buy my box. So, buying Lorelei's instead hadn't really been his intention. He had to dance attendance on her that evening, but certainly no one had forced him to do so since. All he had to do was say the word, and I would be willing to stay forever. Abby had said he was through with Lorelei. But Lorelei said. . .

Impatiently, I wedged my finger under the flap and ripped the envelope open. All I was doing was indulging in idle speculation. I had prayed for direction; was I willing to accept it?

"Would you look at this!" Vera exclaimed. "Charles! *Charles!* "

"What is it?" I asked, almost glad of the interruption.

"What is it?" Charles echoed, striding onto the porch, followed by Jeff.

"Look at the return address." Vera waved the envelope under his nose. "Isn't that the name of one of the doctors who came through last spring?"

Charles had to grab it from her to hold it still enough to read the name. "I think so," he agreed. "Jeff, come take a look at this."

As the two men moved farther down the length of the porch, I pulled my own letter from its envelope and read:

> *Dear Niece,*
> *There have been a few problems with creditors since the trading post burned down. I have decided I'd be healthier in a different climate. By the time you get this, I'll be headed for greener pastures. Your aunt always said I was a shiftless no-account, and I guess maybe she was right. You'll be better off staying where you are or going back to Missouri.*
>
> > *Your affectionate uncle,*
> > *Matthew*

I stared at the paper, willing it to say more. Was this the divine guidance I had sought? All it did was close one door and leave me as much in the dark as before. Stay or go back east—those were my choices. My heart was here. But was there a reason to stay? The reason I hoped for?

"Praise the Lord." I looked up at the sound of Charles's voice. He and Jeff stood grinning at each other. "Praise the Lord!" he repeated, and the brothers slapped each other on the back.

"Well, are you going to share it with Judith and me," Vera snapped, "or are we going to have to take that letter from you and read it ourselves?"

Charles looked from one of us to the other as though he didn't know where to begin. Jeff clapped him on the shoulder and laughed. "You'd better tell them before they come after you."

His brother grinned and shook his head as if to clear it. "You're right, Vera. This is from Dr. Anderson. He was out in this area last spring," he explained to me, "and examined Abby while he was here. He was just as puzzled as anyone and had no idea as to what was causing her illness.

"However, he writes that on returning to Boston, he has learned that promising work is being done with patients who have symptoms similar to Abby's. He believes that if we take her back east, there is every hope that she'll recover."

This time I was able to add my heartfelt praise to the others'. To think that after all, Charles and the children might not lose Abby! Truly, this was a day of answered prayer.

"When will you start?" Vera demanded.

"Just as soon as possible," said Charles. "This week, if we can. Even though her mind wanders, it seems to me that she's rallied physically the past few days. I want to do it soon, before she loses any more ground. There's no point in starting for Boston if she can't stand the trip."

"What about the children?"

"I think they should come with us. Abby's mother would be glad to take care of them, I'm sure. Jeff will have to run the place alone, and he'll be busy enough without having to watch out for them."

Jeff chuckled. "You sound as though you've been planning this for weeks instead of five minutes."

Charles smiled. "The Lord must have been laying the groundwork for this in my mind all along. The ideas just seem to be falling into place." He stopped abruptly. "Except for one thing." He looked at me intently.

"Judith, I know it's presumptuous of me to ask this of you, and I wouldn't except for Abby's sake. I know how much it means to you to be able to join your uncle. But we'll need someone to care for the children on the trip back.

Could you possibly consider postponing your plans long enough to help us?"

Uncle Matthew's letter seemed to burn in my hand. Little did they know how my options had narrowed. I thought rapidly. If Abby and Charles were going to leave, I could hardly remain here. Unless. . .I looked at Jeff, hoping he would step forward and give me a reason to stay.

He didn't make a move.

This was, then, evidently the guidance I had looked for, though hardly in the form I had hoped. I looked at Charles, squared my shoulders and said, "Of course I'll go."

The days of preparation flew by as the details for the trip were worked out. Vera and I starched, ironed, and packed clothes for the five of us who would be traveling, took turns tending to Abby, and tried to maintain some semblance of control over Lizzie and Willie, who were wild with excitement at the prospect of the journey.

Charles ran himself ragged trying to get all the travel plans in order before Abby's slight increase in strength waned. We would go by wagon to Raton, where we would rest overnight before taking the eastbound stagecoach to Dodge and the train to Boston.

He had wired Abby's mother, who had replied that, rather than having the children stay with her, she would take rooms in Boston. That way she could be near her daughter, and the children wouldn't have to be separated from their parents.

And Jeff—Jeff worked as though driven, trying to live up to the responsibility placed upon him, consulting with Charles to be sure they were in agreement over what should be done during the coming winter. If our time together had been scarce before, it was all but nonexistent now. We didn't exchange more than a few words during the days of preparation.

I told myself it was just as well. There was nothing left to say.

I, too, pushed myself to the limit through the long days of activity, trying to stay busy enough to ignore the growing sense of loneliness. Not since the Parkers had slipped away, leaving me on the prairie, had I felt so utterly alone. The fact that I was in the midst of people only made the emptiness more difficult to bear.

I knew well that once we arrived in Boston, with Abby's mother at hand to care for the children, my usefulness would be at an end. They would all expect me to make my way back and join Uncle Matthew.

Charles had generously insisted on paying my way back to New Mexico, and I hadn't been able to bring myself to tell him, or anyone, that I was even more adrift now than when I had first climbed out of the chuck wagon at their doorstep.

I knew the Bradleys well enough by now to realize that if they had any inkling of my true situation, they would feel obligated to help me. I could no longer presume on such generosity when I could in no way repay them.

"Fight for what you want," Vera had advised. I had fought, in the only ways I knew how, and had come out the loser. I was completely at loose ends, totally dependent upon the Lord to show me the next step to take.

In due time, I supposed, I would get over Uncle Matthew's betrayal and would be able to look back on my months in New Mexico as a lovely interlude, a memory to be treasured through the remainder of my life. I wondered dully if time would also heal the aching void I felt when I thought of leaving Jeff forever.

One day, in the midst of all the preparations, Vera and I were folding clothes and arranging them in a trunk with Lorelei's indifferent help. After Vera had to refold a third dress that Lorelei had carelessly wadded, she told her to sit on the bed and watch.

Lorelei moved instead to the mirror and occupied herself with twisting already perfect ringlets into shape around her lovely face.

I was smoothing the folds of the sky blue dress I had worn to the box supper social when Charles looked in through the open door.

"Everything going all right?" We assured him that it was. His eyes lingered on the dress in my hands and grew wistful. "I'm glad you're taking that dress, Judith. Abby would want you to consider all the clothes she gave you as yours to keep."

"I'm not taking this for myself," I told him. "This is for Abby to wear when she's well." His eyes misted over, and he turned abruptly and left.

"Do you know," said Lorelei, still primping, "I believe I'll travel back with you all. All this nursing has just about worn me out, and I think I need a change."

I stared at her, dumbfounded. "But what about the wedding?"

"Oh, that," she murmured vaguely and swept out of the room.

"Well, forevermore!" Vera exclaimed. "What on earth's gotten into her?"

I had no answer for her. The question in my mind was how Jeff would feel, being turned down twice by the same woman.

Somehow we all managed to complete our assigned tasks, and the day of departure came. I hurried outside at dawn to have a few minutes to myself. My eyes swept across the landscape, taking in the shrubs and trees close at hand as they emerged from the dark folds of night and moving on to the vast reaches of prairie that swept out to the horizon.

I felt a part of this land. It was home to me in a way that the once-familiar streets of St. Joseph never had been. It drew me now, and I stepped back almost involuntarily, as if to break the spell.

"Good-bye," I whispered, knowing that a part of me would always remain here.

Saying good-bye to Vera was nearly impossible. Poor Vera! She had taken care of Charles, Abby, and the children for so long that it was almost as if part of her was being physically torn out to see them go. If she had her way, she would have gone all the way to Boston to be sure her charges were properly cared for. But Charles had convinced her that she needed to stay and keep house for Jeff.

I waited until she had finished tucking Abby in and making sure that she had done everything possible for her comfort. She stood back from the buggy, biting her lower lip and blinking rapidly.

Finally the last piece of luggage had been loaded, and we were ready to go. Charles had hired a buggy for Abby to ride in to Raton, and he was to ride with her, with Jeff driving them. Lorelei, somewhat miffed at being left out of the more comfortable arrangements, was seated next to the driver of the wagon carrying our luggage. Lizzie and Willie were waiting for me in a second wagon.

I turned to Vera, trying for her sake to keep the parting on a steady note. "Good-bye," I said. "You'll never know how much your friendship has meant to me. I'll never forget you." I heard my voice climbing higher, nearly breaking, and it proved Vera's undoing.

Her face working, she drew me into her arms and we clung to each other, letting the tears flow. Then we stood facing each other, mopping our cheeks with sodden handkerchiefs, and Vera tried to speak, but the words would not come. No matter. I knew how she felt and knew that her friendship and respect were things to be valued highly.

I sat between Lizzie and Willie and we waved until the house and Vera were out of sight. "Thus ends the pioneer life of Judith Alder," I murmured.

The nip in the air made the horses lively and anxious to be moving, but even so the ride into Raton lasted the whole day. Charles hurried into the hotel to secure rooms for all of us, and I helped him settle Abby for the night after he had carried her upstairs. The long drive had not fatigued her as much as we had feared, and I prayed her stamina would hold throughout the trip.

We gathered in the dining room adjacent to the hotel lobby. The food was well prepared and plentiful, and it was a relief not to have to cook and help clean up after the meal.

Tired as we were, no one spoke much except Lorelei, who managed to find something to criticize about her room, the food, and the service. When

Lizzie and Willie all but fell asleep at their places, I used the excuse to take them upstairs and put them to bed in the room we shared. Lorelei's constant faultfinding was more than I could bear just then.

fifteen

Once again I rose before the sun. Dressing quietly in the dark, I managed to slip out without waking the children. The stage did not leave until mid-morning, and I wanted to come to terms with myself on my last morning in New Mexico Territory before I had to face the others.

I dared not go too far away in case someone should need me, but I walked softly along the boardwalk until I was several buildings away from the hotel and stood facing the east, awaiting the sunrise.

So much had happened; so many changes had taken place. I was not the same person I had been when I left Missouri.

I could just make out the building across the street. The telegraph office. I wondered if I should wire Aunt Phoebe when it opened to let her know I would be returning soon.

Everything within me rebelled at the thought. Even though I was no longer the same person, I was limited in what I could do on my own. I wondered idly what positions might be available in Boston for a Christian young lady of moderate education and no experience.

"Good morning."

I gasped and whirled, a hand at my throat. So engrossed had I been in my thoughts that I hadn't heard him approach.

"G–good morning," I faltered, fighting for composure.

Jeff looked down at me through the graying light. "I didn't mean to frighten you," he said gently.

Caught off guard like that, I couldn't think of a thing to say. The lines around his eyes were more deeply etched than before, and his face looked thinner. I thought angrily of how much damage Lorelei had done and with what little feeling.

I longed to trace the contours of his face with my fingertips. Instead, I laced my fingers tightly together so they would not betray me of their own accord and turned away slightly, feigning interest in the telegraph office across the street.

"Planning to send a wire?"

I shook my head yes, then no, then shrugged. "I don't know. I thought I might let my aunt know that I'd be coming back soon." The prospect seemed no less dismal when voiced aloud. I placed my hands around a post and held on for support.

"I guess you'll be glad to get back to your family and civilization again."

Splinters from the post bit into my fingers as I gripped it to keep from crying out that what I wanted was to stay with him, wherever he might be.

He didn't seem to notice my lack of response. "Seems like the people you care about the most always leave," he said, almost to himself.

"Maybe they don't always want to." It was out before I could stop myself.

"You mean Lorelei?"

"I wasn't talking about—" I wheeled to face him. "What do you mean?"

"I mean," he said slowly, "that Lorelei wasn't any too happy when I sent her away."

I must have been even more tired than I thought. Nothing was making sense this morning. "You *sent* Lorelei away?"

He nodded. "I told her we had found out long ago that we weren't meant for each other. No use raking up dead coals. She didn't take it well. I think she's been used to being the one who's called it quits."

I thought back over the last few days. "Then that's why she's acted so strangely lately." A thought was trying to penetrate my fog-enshrouded brain, but I couldn't quite grasp it.

Jeff seemed to be having the same difficulty. "If you weren't talking about Lorelei. . .what *did* you mean?" I started to turn away again, but he placed one hand on each shoulder and looked squarely into my eyes. "What did you mean?" he repeated.

"I just meant that. . .that people who leave don't always go because they want to." My voice shook. I wasn't saying it well at all.

He wet his lips and spoke carefully, as if searching for the right words. "Do you mean, Judith, that *you* don't want to go?" I nodded mutely. "Then why—?"

"What choice do I have? Uncle Matthew wrote that he couldn't take me, and I couldn't very well stay on at the ranch with Charles and Abby gone. And I thought that, well, you and Lorelei. . .I mean, I didn't think there was a reason for me to stay."

The next thing I knew, his arms were around me, holding me close. One hand pressed my head tight against his chest. His breath stirred my hair as he whispered, "To think I was almost fool enough to let you get away!"

I drew back a little, still remaining within the circle of his arms. The lines in his face had disappeared and he looked boyishly exuberant. I found that my arms were wrapped around him and were clinging as though I would never let him go.

His work-hardened hand caressed my cheek. "It's been tearing me apart to think of you leaving, but I know how hard life can be out here. I didn't want to take you away from the comforts you'd known, when I had so little to offer."

"Little!" Tears stung my eyes. "Everything I'd ever want is right here." I searched his face. "You're sure?" I asked, and his response was more than enough to convince me.

The dawn broke then, bathing us in a golden haze. Joy welled up inside me and bubbled over into a spring of delight. Let Uncle Matthew and others like him search for hidden riches. It was enough for me to have the treasure of Jeff's love.

"We'll have to make some plans," he said softly.

"Plans?" I repeated dreamily. Then awareness jolted me back to reality. "Why, I suppose—Jeff! What about Abby? What about the children? What about—?"

He stopped the flow of words effectively with a kiss that left me breathless. "What did you have in mind?" I asked meekly.

"I suggest," he said, tucking my hand into the crook of his arm as we walked back toward the hotel, "that I send word to the ranch that I won't be back for awhile. Jake and Shorty can hold the fort for a couple of weeks.

"Then I can ride along with you on the train as far as, oh, say Missouri. If you like, we can go ahead and wire your aunt from here and ask if she'd like to attend the wedding.

"And then," he said, cupping my cheek in his hand, "we'll travel back to the ranch—back to our home—on our honeymoon."

I sighed in blissful contentment. Once again, though, duty reared its stern head. "But what about the children?"

One corner of his mouth turned up in a crooked grin. "We'll let Charles put Lorelei in charge of them. It will be a good experience for her."

I turned back to face the sunrise. The golden glow was giving way to a rosy hue. It was a new dawn, a new day.

A new beginning.

The Will and the Way

DeWanna Pace

DEWANNA PACE is a multi-published, award-winning author of historical novels. She is also very active in Romance Writers of America of the Texas Panhandle where she makes her home.

one

February, 1868
Lodgepole Creek, Wyoming

"Are ye the man who was with Clancy when he died?" Key Calhoun's eyes narrowed and adjusted from the blinding white snow to the darker confines of the command tent. The wind had steadily increased since dawn and now billowed the canvas walls. Key shivered as she awaited the man's reply.

"Depends on who's asking."

The buckskinned man sitting on the opposite side of the makeshift table rose, his gaze slowly examining her. His hands inched toward the two Colts holstered against his hips. Like his rugged face, the weapons looked as if they had survived several battles.

It would take more than muscle and gruff to frighten her away from what she'd come several territories to accomplish. She knew what her brother had hoped to achieve, and Key would rather be six feet in the grave than let anything or anybody keep her from completing that goal for him.

She lifted her palms wide and slow, revealing she meant no harm to the blond-bearded man. "I just wanted to meet the man who couldn't find the courage to put my brother out of his agony."

"Your *brother*?" Davage Jansen's hands remained poised near the pistols. "Which one are you?" His gray eyes searched for some resemblance. "Shamus, Peter. . ." he rattled off the other three brothers' names.

Key's face turned red, making her more aware of how unladylike she looked in the layers of clothing she wore. The steady clang of iron being strung together along the track outside only added to the painful tempo that beat at her temples. She had donned the nut-brown linsey shirt and trousers beneath the woolen parka as part of the new life she intended for herself. What had God said?—*to walk among them?* She supposed that meant dressing as they did, as well.

It seemed foolish to be annoyed because the crew chief endured a bad sense of humor or poor eyesight. The men outside had certainly suffered no such trouble defining her gender through the layers of garments.

Key brushed the parka backward, revealing a long ebony braid that unfurled and hung to her waist. "I'm Key."

A flicker in his steely gaze betrayed his surprise and attraction, planting a seed of challenge within Key. As Jansen masked his astonishment behind pursed lips and a tightening jaw, mischief sprouted in her thoughts like newborn heather on a highland glen. Seeing if she could unnerve him appealed to her sense of adventure. She started to flirt but then realized he'd never take her seriously if she attempted to use her feminine wiles to coerce him into agreeing.

Key extended her hand. "I represent all the Calhouns in asking why ye allowed Clancy to linger in his misery. It was unchristian of ye."

Jansen's large hand gripped hers. "As a *Christian*, Miss Calhoun, I have no right to take God's will into my own hands. I wish I could have stopped your brother's suffering sooner, but I did not have the right to take a life."

The coldness of his touch permeated her glove and hinted that he had been working for hours at the maps and diagrams strewn across the table. Yet his bronzed skin exposed him as a leader who did not remain behind a desk.

"Then ye wear those Colts for adornment?"

"For keeping the railbed clear of snakes and other annoyances." He waved her to a camp chair. "Please sit, Miss Calhoun. I'm sure you didn't travel half the continent just to challenge me. If you had, you'd be wearing a gun."

Before she could answer, he acknowledged the large auburn-haired man who had escorted her into the tent and now waited at attention near the entrance. "Duffy, have some coffee brought in."

Key sat and turned toward the Irishman. "Thanks for your help, Mr. McDonough."

Duffy's beefy palms circled the hat he'd doffed, crushing the rim. "No trouble at all, Lass." He stood there, staring, waiting, gawking as though he'd never seen a female before.

"If it's no trouble, man," Jansen repeated, "then get moving and bring the lady some refreshment."

"That I'll be doing." Duffy's handlebar mustache puffed out as he exhaled a bit of embarrassment for having lingered. "But, sir, the men." He motioned toward the flap at the entrance. "They're thicker'n buffs out there. What do I tell 'em?"

"Tell them not to listen so hard, or they'll lean too far into the stakes and send this tent down on the lady's head. The Union Pacific's got enough problems without sending her home injured."

"No need to concern yerself, Mr. Jansen." Her gaze met his directly. There were other ways to challenge. "I won't be returning east."

Jansen dismissed the Irishman and leaned back casually, triangling his fingers and thumbs just below his chin. "Where out west do you intend to go, Miss Calhoun? I'm afraid, at the moment rails' end is a bit far from any of the stage lines. Of course, I could see you as far as Council Bluff, then you could decide from there."

"I plan to remain here. . .until a few things are finished." Key squared her shoulders in anticipation of his disapproval.

"I seem to remember Clancy telling me you would inherit should anything happen to him." His tone took on an edge of concern. "But I'm afraid I don't handle that part of the U.P.'s business. You'll need to speak with Thomas Durant at headquarters."

"Is that what ye think?" Irritation forced Key to her feet. She felt like David squaring off with Goliath. "Do ye think Clancy meant no more to me than thirty pieces of silver? The Calhouns have never asked for charity, and I refuse to be the first."

He reached out to calm her, but she shrugged away. "I didn't mean to imply you wanted a handout."

Family pride made her bristle. "Then mind yer words. I've a Scot for a mother and an Irishman for my da. You'll soon see I've Clancy's temper, as well, but perhaps ye've been too long in this tent to see my likeness to him." Her eyes narrowed in warning. "It's my Christian duty to tell ye of my lashing tongue, but apologizing for it a second time is one obedience God is still trying to soak into my stubborn head."

"You're definitely Clancy's sister. Blue eyes and all." Amusement etched the crew chief's face, softening his angular features.

She simply could not remain irritated at a man with such a gentle smile. "I didn't come to bleed the railroad," she assured Jansen. "Just the opposite. I felt it was my duty as sister to meet the man Clancy had trusted with his life."

She shuddered at the thought of her beloved brother being burned alive as the engine slid off the track and the firebox exploded. "When the letter came about his death, I felt I owed it to him to come and see for myself this dream he had."

The rigidness of Jansen's shoulders remained. "Clancy was a good friend and one of the most dedicated men I've ever had the privilege of working with. The best thing you can do for him is to get on with your life."

The chief's tone sounded final, as if the conversation had ended, but Key was only beginning. "I plan to finish his work."

A sandy brow raised quizzically over Davage's intense gaze. "Work?"

"I know about the trouble with the Lodgepole Creek trestle. I'm told you were blasting a path through solid rock until the deep snow set in. I can see that the wind gusts are keeping the banks adrift, so I've a plan to help clear the tracks."

The slightest smile curved the man's mouth, partially hidden beneath his mustache. "And I'm supposed to believe *you* know how to solve these problems, *Miss* Calhoun?"

"Is that so beyond belief?" She'd been the only girl in a clan of six brothers. Considering the Lord had a sense of humor and forgotten to give her a liking for normal feminine abilities, she'd taken to mastering almost anything that would keep her from domestic chores.

"You do remember *'Pride goeth before destruction, and a haughty spirit before a fall,'* don't you?" Jansen challenged.

"Proverbs. The sixteenth chapter, I believe." Her chin lifted. "And I'm not at all boasting. Clancy surely must have told ye he studied engineering with Ted Judah before the war?"

Astonishment filled Davage's eyes at the mention of Judah's name.

"Ye can bet Mr. Judah didn't snarl a nose at a mind that needed stirring. . . man's nor woman's," Key informed him. Everyone involved with any railroad company knew of the man who had virtually founded the move to connect West with East. Ted's unbiased belief in allowing each man or woman his or her own talent had been the gossip of social gatherings in every part of the country she'd traveled. "And remember what it says in the Bible about making use of one's gifts."

"You studied with Judah?" A grudging respect layered Jansen's tone.

"Is there an echo in the tent, or is it the clanging outside that makes ye hard of hearing?" she asked.

"I have a temper, too, Miss Calhoun." His jaw squared.

"Good, then we'll get along well enough. I like a man who states his boundaries. It makes it easier to know how far one might push." Key appraised him, finding him not at all unappealing. Davage Jansen would never win a most-handsome contest—he was a bit too brawny, slightly rough-faced. But seldom did a man brook her, and she found it appealing that he thought himself up to the challenge.

"Even if what you say is true about studying with Judah, you couldn't possibly have enough field experience to solve our problems," he countered.

Key jammed her hands into her pockets, her patience wearing thin. "Clancy gave me all the details in his letters. I have almost a daily account of yer troubles, Mr. Jansen. Field experience is unnecessary when trusting one's instincts will do."

"Using women's intuition—eh?" He grinned. "I admit that's one commodity we are in short supply of."

"Call it what you want. I prefer thinking of it as trusting God's will." Her tone grew as icy as the wind that slipped under the tent walls. "Perhaps relying on a touch of feminine intuition would offer you a—"

"Bunch of blarney, if you'll pardon me for saying so, Miss Calhoun." The crew chief's white teeth formed a half-crescent in his bronzed face, but his words were biting.

"A few solutions are what I had in mind."

"Around here we work in facts, figures, and accuracy." His brow arched as if he were scolding a rebellious child. "Not wishful thinking nor fanciful daydreams. Cold, hard reality."

Key stood, leaned over and placed her hands on the table, meeting him at eye level. "Ye can wire Omaha and Thomas Durant himself, for all I care."

She'd warned him of her temper, but he hadn't listened. What would the man say if she told him he actually had no choice in the matter?

"Durant?" Denial carved a deep furrow in Jansen's forehead, adding a rosy hue to his bronzed face. "You couldn't possibly be the—," he growled as she nodded, "snow expert he sent from Omaha?"

Satisfaction saturated her. "That I am."

"He's derailed for sure this time! A woman, for Chri—"

"Don't say that." Key wagged her finger at him. "I won't have anyone using the Lord's name in vain around me. Especially, if ye intend to rely on my services."

"Oh, you won't, will you?" The crew chief began to pace. "Lady, don't you realize I have hundreds of women-starved men out there? I'll be surprised if there's one among them who'll give a tinker's. . .uh. . .a second thought that you're Clancy's sister and can't abide the indelicacies muttered, shouted, and swapped by the crew."

He smacked one fist into the open palm of his other hand. "Don't you realize the weather is twenty below if it's a degree? And there's not a hotel for a hundred miles." He pointed to her hair. "The Indians won't be able to resist taking that braid for a coup. And that's not the worst of it. . ."

His blatant look of appraisal stirred strange feelings within Key, making her all too aware that the concho belt she wore accentuated her narrow hips and flat stomach. Pulling the parka closer around her, she stared back. Her teeth clenched as she exhaled a slow, deliberate breath. "Clancy and I both believed I could do the job. You have access to Durant. Ask him yourself."

"I still have the last say around here, Omaha or no Omaha."

He leaned over the tabletop, challenging her in a manner more infuriating than any of his words. She refused to waver, though she knew if the crew chief resisted her presence at rails' end, Durant might reconsider his decision to let her work. "I had hoped ye would let me prove myself by my work, but if ye refuse me the opportunity, then I must insist."

Key hadn't wanted to play her hand, but he'd forced her to do so. Jansen would never let her work with a U.P. crew, if she didn't. She folded her arms in front of her, a habit that warned anyone who knew her that her mind was set and her will immovable.

"Insist?" Jansen straightened. Storm clouds thundered in the gray depths of his eyes.

"Fume and fizzle all you want," she warned. "I own *Credit Mobilier* stock. Enough Union Pacific stock to give me the right to do *as* I please, *when* I please, and *whether* you're pleased or not."

"Lady!" The word rasped through the tent like a saber sliding from its sheath. His mouth halted only inches from her face. "You can own the whole railroad as far as I'm concerned. If Durant really sent you, I may *have* to hire you as an engineer. But if you think for one moment I'm going to put the lives of my survey crew in danger by bowing to your every whim and temper tantrum, you'd better save yourself and me a headache. *I* am chief engineer, and it's *my* duty to see this railroad is built as carefully and as efficiently as possible.

"I've got enough problems trying to keep Fear No Man and his renegade Crazy Dogs in line, much less having to worry about a rebellious petticoat, as well. Stocks or no stocks, no broomtail from back East is going to tell me how to build my railroad. Do I make myself understood?"

It wasn't easy looking into his silver-glinted gaze, but if it was a fight the man wanted, it was a fight he'd get! Key gripped the edge of her chair and again spoke each word precisely so there would be no mistake that *she* was understood. "Despite what ye believe, I did not come here to threaten yer authority, Mr. Jansen. But I cannot let my brother's dreams fall by the way. I mean to complete them and see that his stocks keep their value."

"A woman's pride shall bring her low, but honor shall uphold the humble in spirit," he quoted another verse, changing only the gender.

"Why is it when a man can't handle a strong woman, he tries to switch around the Lord's words to suit his purpose? Am I too much woman for a mortal man to handle, Davage Jansen? *Ye* especially?

"It was Clancy's wish to see the rails meet," she continued, not allowing him time to answer. "Being part of such a fine undertaking gave my brother a sense of purpose and, yes, *pride*." Key stared past him, seeing images of herself and Clancy discussing the kind of life he wanted but would never enjoy now. "Clancy told me to finish all I set my mind upon, but it's his dream I mean to finish. *His* life must count for something."

The fringes of his buckskinned shirt swayed as Jansen stood and motioned toward the entrance. "Would you mind stepping out a moment, Miss Calhoun?"

When Key walked in front of him through the flap and out into the Wyoming morning, a hungry male growl went up from the awaiting crowd. Respect for their boss kept the railroaders at a proper distance, but in many of the men's faces Key saw curiosity mixed with the lust he had warned her about. Suddenly, she knew how Daniel must have felt in the lion's den.

"Are you certain I can't talk you out of this?"

Jansen stepped aside and gave her full view of the ice-covered roadbed. The muddy slush, lack of windbreak, and miserable cold would have daunted a saint's determination.

But the invincibility of faith that inspired her brother's dream and the spirit that urged her mother's clan to follow Bonnie Prince Charlie over the highlands, stirred Key's blood even now. "I am here to work. . .and to *stay* until the job is finished."

"Gentleman," Jansen waved the men in closer, "this is Key Calhoun, Clancy's own sister and. . .Durant's new snow expert."

Someone chuckled. Others jeered. Mumbles rippled through the crowd.

Finally, an irritated voice jabbed, "Sounds like something that desk dandy would do."

"At least she's better to look at than that last fella," came a reply.

Laughter echoed through the gathering. Key steeled herself against their scorn, not letting them see her momentary lack of faith in her ability to control her temper. She would prove her worthiness to them all. She was willing. Now it was up to God to point the way.

The crew chief raised his hat high into the air to silence the men. "Never let it be said we kept a sister from honoring her brother's dream."

Her fists balled against her hips as her gaze met each man's one by one. "Never let it be said a sister of Clancy Calhoun's needs anybody's approval."

"I was just wondering, Miss Calhoun. . .?" Jansen asked as he motioned her toward the city of tents that ran along each side of the roadbed.

"Yes?"

"Does that include God's approval?"

"*My* God doesn't want us to sit around. He says faith without works is as useless as an unsowed seed."

"You have your own time schedule, don't you, Miss Calhoun?"

"For everything there is a season, Mr. Jansen. A time to be born, a time to die, a time to work, and a time for *change*."

"You can lead a horse to water, but you can't make him drink, Miss Calhoun."

"Then perhaps it's time to turn the horse out to pasture, Mr. Jansen. . .for a season. The Lord willing, of course."

two

Wind moved among the tents, swaying the ropes and sputtering the fires that held the cold at bay. Snow shifted and darted against the enclosures. Key pulled the parka close to ward off the chill. The canvas-and-rope shelters looked like a thousand white spiders gathering in one place.

She shook off the feeling of foreboding and reminded herself that there was no challenge too big for God, and therefore none too large for Key Calhoun either. "I can survive with the best of you, make no mistake, Mr. Jansen," she announced with conviction.

"Seems your mind is set, then." Jansen glared into the distance. "If Duffy ever shows up with that coffee, I'll help you set up your tent."

Other offers followed as several of the men jockeyed for a right to help the woman in their midst.

"I thank ye kindly, but I'm as capable as any." Key wanted to dispel the notion she would be a burden to the crew. "I'll set up my own. I'll work equally with the others or not at all."

Six doting brothers intent upon protecting their only sister had clipped her adventurous wings on more than one occasion. It was long past time to soar, and this frigid wilderness seemed just the place to test her feathers. . .and ruffle Jansen's.

A grin spread across Jansen's lips as he directed her to the camp supply. "I don't suppose you'd change your mind and make it not at all, would you?"

"Is that how ye came to be crew chief then. . .supposing?"

"I deserved that. The answer is no. I assume nothing, especially when it comes to. . ."

Women, she completed his statement to herself, but he grinned and gave her a nod.

". . .snow experts. Now, do you know how to put one of those together?"

"Can one tent be that much different from another?" What she lacked in knowledge, she would supplement in willingness. Key studied the canvas housing, refusing to admit her misgivings. No need to tell him she was clumsy with her hands. Certainly, this seemed a fitting start on the road to new experiences. "Are those tents standard issue?"

"The new Sibleys." Humor lit his gray eyes as he turned to the workers following them up the grade. "You men can introduce yourselves properly when Cookie whistles for supper. We've got rails to lay and dark'll be setting in soon."

"A congenial bunch," Key complimented as the crew obeyed. "It's good they respect ye."

"As I respect them. Fear is for fools and failed heroes."

Key gazed up at him. Though spoken softly, the crew chief's words echoed from his heart. What fear of his own lay hidden beneath his words? she wondered. Was he fool or failed hero? An impulse to satisfy her curiosity almost urged her to break the promise she made to herself when she'd left Pennsylvania—but getting involved meant gathering roots, and she had vowed not to do that. She would ride the wind of whimsy and leave worry to those with less faith.

"Speaking of heroes, did the good Mr. McDonough have to grow the coffee beans himself?"

"Patience is not one of your better qualities, is it, Miss Calhoun? I'll have to remember that when we're chugging up a snow-packed trestle."

"The Good Book says 'Be not slothful, but followers of them who through faith and patience inherit the promises.' I intend to inherit every promise I'm offered, Mister Jansen," Key informed him. "So, you're right—I'm not the patient sort."

"*Davage,*" the crew chief insisted. "If we're going to work together, then we can save some of your precious time by being less formal."

"Davage, then," she accepted his terms. "And I shall be Key to every man of ye."

He halted in front of a large three-poled tent and held open the flap at the entrance. "This is the supply tent. You'll find the coffee and everything else you need to set up quarters. Supper will be in about three hours. Two short bursts of the whistle means come a'running. Railroaders are a hungry lot, and I can't promise you the men will wait until you've been served." His gaze surveyed her from head to foot. "Then again, they might."

When she stepped inside, he started to close the flap behind her. "Ye're leaving?"

He shrugged. "I've a railroad to run, Miss. . .Key, and unless you want me to help set up your tent, then I've got a dozen other tasks that need my attention."

"By all means, be about yer busi—," the flap slapped shut as he left, "—ness. And good day to ye too."

The smell of brewing coffee lured her from the abrupt dismissal. Boxes of supplies and tools had been stacked to the canvassed ceiling. A makeshift table standing in one corner of the tented room held a ledger, pen, and inkwell. A curtain of goatskin formed a wall on each side, dividing the dwelling into three sections. The wonderful aroma of coffee wafted from the area to her right.

She raised her voice to announce herself. "Mr. McDonough?"

There was no answer. Could he hear her behind the thick goatskin hide? Pulling back the flap that formed a door between sections, she peeked through. Heat brushed her cheeks and neck. "Mmmm. That smells delicious. I haven't enjoyed a good cup of coffee since—you're not McDonough."

The man turned from the potbellied stove whose stack disappeared through a hole in the top of the tent. A smile lifted the edges of his chestnut mustache and Van Dyke beard. "Hamilton Sax is the name. I'm sure I can be of more help than Duffy. You must be Clancy's sister. Key, isn't it?"

The medium-sized man extended his hand. She hesitated for only a second before allowing the stove's warmth to draw her inside the section. Key meant only to shake his hand, but he lifted hers and brushed a kiss against her knuckles.

"You knew my brother?" She edged away as soon as protocol allowed, then wiped her gloves on her dungarees. His black eyes were hypnotizing, like a snake with a field mouse.

He grabbed a tin cup from a stack of wooden crates and poured it full of coffee. After he refilled another cup resting on a table next to the stove, he offered the fresh tin to Key. "I knew Clancy. Not as much as I would have preferred, but well enough." He waved to one of the two chairs the table provided. "Want to sit? Pennsylvania's a long ride from here."

Key thanked him and sat. Heat filtered through the tin to her kid gloves, thawing her fingertips. Steam rose from the brim as she slowly sipped and the fiery liquid slid down her throat, warming her aching body. The journey had indeed been long, filled with chilly passenger cars and stagecoaches.

Though she was accustomed to dealing with winter weather, the treeless plains had inflicted a biting wind that pierced her to the bone. Yet Key was not about to let anyone know that she felt ill at the moment. Wouldn't they laugh at her if they knew the snow expert had taken cold?

Another sip fueled her purpose, and she stood.

Hamilton Sax did the same. "You're not leaving? We've just met. McDonough's running an errand for me. He'll be back in a moment. I told him I'd make the coffee."

"I must not tarry, Mr. Sax. Perhaps another time. I just needed a sip or two to stop my teeth from chattering. It's a pleasure to meet any friend of my brother's."

"Then let me help you get supplies or at least mark them up for you." He held the goatskin open while she walked past him into the larger chamber.

"Mark them?"

The man shed his hat and placed it on the table next to the ledger. Reaching into his pocket, he pulled out a pair of pince-nez glasses and threaded them over each ear then took the pen from the inkwell and wrote: *Key Calhoun. Harrisburg, Pennsylvania. Female. Born: March, 1848.* "Let's see, that makes you almost twenty. Unmarried." He added with a flourish, "Stockholder."

"Are ye the camp gossip?" she asked, incensed by his knowledge. Clancy would not have told so much. This man had other sources.

Hamilton dipped into the inkwell again. "I'm assistant crew chief. I make it a habit to keep track of all the employees. It makes Jansen happy and keeps trouble at a distance."

"Must be boring. . .knowing all," her tone mocked.

"At times. But it can be equally amusing."

Key didn't quite know how to gauge Hamilton Sax. He both intrigued and inspired caution within her. Though her impulse was always to satisfy her curiosity, she decided to give caution an equal chance. "What are ye marking up and why?"

He tapped the ledger with the feathered pen. "We record everything you purchase. The Union Pacific allots each worker ten dollars for initial set up, then the remaining money owed will come out of your pay."

"Ten dollars! That's barely enough to buy a tent and cot!"

"Food, tools, and two changes of chambray and trousers are also provided." Hamilton shrugged. "Anything else is considered a luxury."

"What of soap, shoes, blankets. . .books?" A list of necessities raced through her mind.

"Considered items of choice, not essentials."

"What if I'd come to ye a poor lass? How would I acquire my necessities?"

"If you were poor, Miss Calhoun, you wouldn't have gotten the job."

The man knew too much. Though his tone was nothing but courteous, Key sensed an underlying edge of mockery. Hamilton Sax had something planned, and Key suspected the results would be at her expense. "Tally the register, then. And be certain of your figures. I want to see them when you're finished." She ignored the look darkening his eyes to onyx. Let his kettle boil a bit.

Making a quick inventory of needed provisions, she waited until his heavy scrawl ended and he replaced the pen in its well. At that moment McDonough entered, introduced himself, and relieved Key of having to check the figures.

"Will ye see that all my supplies are properly accounted?" She smiled at the redhead. "I wouldn't want to cheat the U.P."

Her gaze locked with Sax's in silent challenge, certain she'd made an enemy of the boss. She could feel it to her toes. But he would find her an eager David to his Goliath, if he started casting stones.

" 'Tis a fine day when the U.P. hires such as yourself," McDonough complimented as he checked over the books. "All is in order, Lass."

"Thank ye, Mr. McDonough," she returned. "Yours is the best welcome I've received. I'll be off now to set up my quarters. Does Mr. Jansen fancy a certain location for me to set up?"

Hamilton answered before Duffy could elaborate. "If you want privacy, then I'd set it a good ten yards from any of the others. But don't get too far. Fear No Man and Crazy Dogs are on the warpath—you're too prime a target for him to overlook. You'll want to be close enough for the camp to protect you."

"Crazy Dogs?" Images of wild coyotes and wolves darted through her imagination.

"Renegade Sioux. Indians." Respect mingled with caution in Duffy's tone. "They consider the railroad a threat because we cut across their land."

"I've heard stories of wild savages and their attacks on settlers," she acknowledged. "I wonder if they are any more savage than our own people."

Hamilton lifted his slouch hat from the table and nestled it on his head. "You might not be so forgiving once you stare down the shaft of an arrow."

"True, Mr. Sax," she admitted, "but I'm not one to form an opinion without experience. I think it unjust to wager war against a whole nation because of one warrior's misguided hand. Perhaps we should offer them a Christian's hand instead. Now, if you'll excuse me, I've a tent to raise."

"It's been a pleasure, Miss Calhoun. I'm sure we'll have further opportunity to talk later." Hamilton's smile reached his eyes and turned hard, glittering. With a nod, he exited the supply tent.

"Is he always so certain of himself?"

Duffy gathered the list of requested supplies. "Sax is proficient, Lass, and that keeps Davage content with the man."

Though she could have sworn Duffy didn't particularly care for the crew chief's second-in-command, the Irishman seemed reluctant to criticize him. Well, what did she expect? She was the new employee. She supposed old loyalties died hard. Perhaps one day, she could earn Duffy's and Davage's allegiance as well.

Key blew out a long, cool breath, a sharp pain knifing through her throat.

"Would ye add some camphor to that list, Mr. McDonough?"

"Duffy, Lass. I'm just a lineman. Feeling a bit ill, are you now?" Immediate concern furrowed his broad brow.

A wave of loneliness enveloped her. She missed her brothers immensely, and Duffy's concern brought back memories of their caring ways. "Just a scratchy throat," she reassured the big man. "Nothing to trouble yerself about."

"I noticed you did not come with a chaperon, Miss Calhoun. My mother's third cousin is a Calhoun. That makes it me solemn obligation to look out for you while you're in our midst. A right and proper chaperon I'll be. That is, if you care to do me the honor, Lass."

The man half bowed. Key found it endearing. "It will be my honor, Mr. McDonough—Duffy. As long as it doesn't interfere with either your or my work on the line."

His eyes brightened. "I'm not one to interfere, Lass, unless you call upon me to do so. Now, together we can get that tent up quicker'n you can say Kathleen Killarney kissed a Klacken Clansman."

"I appreciate the offer, Duffy, but being my chaperon doesn't include doing my work. I've a mind to set it up myself."

"All right, Lass, but I won't let you tote these alone." He gathered the tent and cot in his arms. "If you were lad or lass, I'd lend a hand."

Key liked this gentle giant more with each passing moment. She was amazed to see one of the Lord's own take human form on occasion, and the thought crossed her mind that perhaps he had sent her a very special guardian angel this time. "You're a good man, Duffy McDonough, and I thank you for your kindness." She gathered a few of the smaller items. "I saw a fine place to set up quarters near a stand of willow and birch. They ought to provide plenty of firewood."

"I've no mind to tell you your business, but I wouldn't get that far afield."

"Because of the Indians?"

Duffy shook his head. " 'Tis the least of your worries, Lass. 'Tis too near Outlaw Row. Evil—most of that lot be, and the evil will tempt you, mark me words."

Like her parents, Key enjoyed a bit of blarney and thought perhaps the Irishman was teasing her. But when he drew a cross from head to shoulders, she realized the seriousness of his warning. "Outlaw Row?"

"Better to show ye, Lass."

Huge muscles bulged beneath his blue chambray shirt, and she admired the strength she saw carved in the sinews of his broad neck. She wouldn't want to engage Duffy in a battle of fists. The Irishman was a good two hundred and fifty pounds—all of it work-hardened muscle.

When he exited the supply tent, she followed, aware of her own small load compared to his. "Ye make a good wind block, Duffy."

He laughed, but kept on walking. "Aye, Lass. Davage threatened to use me for such, but the rails need me special touch. Who else would make the hammer sing so well?"

"So ye're a pile driver?" She attempted to keep up with his powerful strides.

"*The* pile driver. The best in the whole U.P." His voice held no arrogance, simply a calm self-assurance. "Head this way."

Key followed closely behind, Duffy's body blocking sight of their destination. Carefully, she tried to match the Irishman's exact steps to prevent herself from sinking into snow up to her calves. As she concentrated on the steady plod of feet, she didn't notice that he'd come to an abrupt halt. With a jolt, her body plowed into the iron-honed back. Like a tumbleweed encountering a stone wall, she bounced backward and landed in the snow.

"He's not having you put your tent up here!" Duffy roared with disapproval as he reached out a hand to help her up. "I'll not have it!"

"Where's here?" Key found herself at the end of a row of tents. From the center pole of each tent flew a red banner. Dizziness overtook her, reminding Key she was ill and should prepare her tent and seek warmth as quickly as possible. "Outlaw Row, I take it?"

Duffy deposited her supplies in a rectangle where snow had been shoveled away, avoiding her look of inquiry. He twisted his coarse red beard. "Do not fly the banner and you'll be safe enough, I'll warrant."

"Safe from what?"

Duffy looked pained, then finally exhaled a long white-clouded breath. "You'll discover soon enough. He means to put you with the laundresses."

Key threw her hands wide in exasperation. "Then, Heaven be praised, man. I thought myself the only female in the whole of it. You sound as if they have the pox or something."

"Some of them do"—his cheeks reddened—"but not the sort you need fear getting, Lass, unless you behave in the same unseemly way they do."

Realization crept through Key. Insult ignited her own cheeks and blazed through her. How dare Davage Jansen leave Duffy to handle the telling? If he had the gumption to put her in such a place, then he should have had the grit to tell her himself instead of inflicting such embarrassment on an innocent soul like Duffy.

"Ye tell that. . .that. . ." She refused to resort to expletives. "Survey chief of yers that Key Calhoun will stay with this railroad until the last spike is hammered. I'll put my tent up anywhere his *saintly* self decrees." Her eyes narrowed. "Thinks he can run the likes of Key Calhoun off with a bit of trickery, does he now?"

Her voice lowered to a deadly calm, "I'll *give* away my stocks before I let him prevent me from completing Clancy's goal. You tell your crew chief to mark *that* down in his precious ledger! This is a fine place for a tent."

"Davage said if you should need any help, you're supposed to call on him or me." Duffy attempted to cool her temper.

"No offense to ye, Duffy, but I'd rather play with brimstone than ask for help now."

"Then I'll leave you to your business, Lass."

The big man escaped before she could say more. "Well, this is what ye wanted, Key Calhoun," she told herself as the wind rose in velocity, matching the anger sweeping through her thoughts. "Now, best prove ye meant it."

By the time Key placed each pole an equal distance apart, her mind had set itself upon a course of action no crew chief could daunt. She stretched the canvas, attempting to stake a corner. Though the poles wavered in the strong wind, her will did not. One stake held, then another. The third proved difficult, but finally settled. Just as she hammered the last into the earth, a great gust of wind howled through the ropes, shook the poles to their plantings and ripped the stakes from their moors.

The tent shuddered, and then like the walls of Jericho, it came crashing down. Key scrambled out of the way, dashing for the opening in the front. The center pole careened and flung forward, striking her midcalf. She hit the ground. Moments passed and she couldn't catch her breath. With one great inhalation, she sucked in the frosty Wyoming eve and felt its fierce coldness grip her lungs. Trembling, she rose to her knees, then finally stood.

A movement captured her attention, and she squinted through her snow-dusted lashes to stare at the birch trees. Jansen! Walking with a blond-haired woman. Who was she? Key wondered. One of the laundresses?

The Bible said there was a time and season for everything, but certainly no time to waste on speculation. . .or envy. With all the dignity Key could muster, she began reconstructing the tent.

Again.

And again.

And again.

"Please, God, hold it steady!" Key prayed aloud as the brawny Irishmen strained to keep the span of mortared logs from toppling down the mountain. Davage commanded a group just below her. His men placed boulders beneath the logs to anchor them in their precarious foundations. With one slip of a single boot or one tug too soon, the entire load would rumble down upon their heads. On each side of the grading, the mountain looked as if it had sprouted a mile of wooden wings or was on the verge of birthing two gigantic rafts.

Key's team secured ropes around the trees that lined the crest. Logs and ropes swayed momentarily in the prevailing wind, then settled into place, angled at the same slant as the railway. A great shout from the workers echoed across the countryside. Despite the misery of her drippy nose and wind-blasted cheeks, elation filled Key. She'd spent three cold days and three freezing nights on the construction, and her mind had grown weary of the endless questions Davage asked. Along with his constant examination of her abilities, snow, ice, and wind had tested her worth. But she would walk barefoot from here to the Continental Divide before she let anyone, especially the crew chief, know how miserable she felt, how tired, how utterly cold.

She would give him no reason to send her back, her abilities in doubt. Better she were half frozen out here in this railroad Yukon than face the ridicule back home.

Key watched Engine No. 106 move to the bottom of the grade. Great puffs of resinous black pinewood smoke billowed from the bell stack as the engineer prepared to climb the slope. Her pulse quickened. Her heart increased its beat. *This was how Clancy died!*

His brawny strength had been needed to keep the firebox filled on the long climb. But the ice pack beneath the wooden trestle cracked and jarred the track. The engine plummeted down the ravine, sending hot steam and fire into the cab. Davage was thrown clear, but Clancy had not been so fortunate.

Now Davage filled the firebox while Hamilton Sax commandeered the engine upgrade. Key wanted to close her eyes to the possibility of disaster, but faith willed them open to focus on the train as it moved in slow motion up the mountainside. Her prayers grew louder as the engine's cowcatcher reached the point where Clancy's engine had slid off.

The trestle's iron work gleamed pristine against the rugged backdrop, making her all too aware of the deep ravine below. "H–how be the wind?" Hoarse and shrill from the extreme frost, her voice cracked. One of the workmen bellowed her question down the mountain.

"Slower than a shadow!" Hamilton hollered back, a smile slicing his mustache and beard. "Snow's drifting away, so the track is less slick. The grade seems shielded from the wind."

"Then on with ye," Key encouraged, eager to see their success and prove her capabilities. Again, the worker passed her message to Hamilton and Davage.

They tipped their hats in respect for her accomplishment, then fed the engine. When it slowly chugged up the grade, a mighty yowl of eagerness resounded from the workers. The line that had been stalled for three weeks would crest the summit today!

Heat flashed across Key's cheeks as she stared down at the scattered men along the snow-laden countryside. Sick and elated all in the same instant, her breath took on the engine's slow chugging rhythm. Suddenly, a deeper roar rumbled in her ears as the men's jubilation jumbled together into one loud ovation.

Through fevered eyes, she listened and watched in horror as the ovation became a cacophony of screams. The snow was moving, not in small drifts as before, but with the strength of shifting, quaking earth! Huge chunks of powdery ice broke away from cliffs, rushing a tidal wave of snow down the mountain. Key's feet slipped. Her fingers clutched.

With every bit of strength she possessed, she grabbed the rope secured to the nearest tree. *"Hold!"* she screamed, knowing that God's will and the windbreaks were her only hope. The vibration jarred the trees. Key twisted, first this way, then that, as if she were a string of taffy being pulled.

The thundering white doom made shouting for help useless. Cold rushed down the mountain and boomeranged up from the canyon floor as the snow hit the ravine and billowed in great frosty puffs toward the crest. The stinging blast gripped her lungs and body, making her gasp. Her arms quivered, yet she desperately hung on.

The roar ended. The avalanche stilled.

No. 106 whistled sharp and clear. Every available man grabbed poles and jabbed them deeply into the snow to open airways for those buried beneath. "Drill ye terriers, drill!" A wave of relief washed through Key when she recognized the familiar call that had everyone scrambling to their rescue stations.

Key dared a glance at the summit. The sight of the engine cresting the peak filled her with a moment of strength that denied the fear, the concern for the others, the sheer exhaustion that consumed her. Clancy's crest was conquered; his death was not meaningless.

No, she was mistaken. There Clancy was, climbing the mountain toward her. . .his face happy and smiling. He would save her. He wasn't dead, at all. Davage had lied to her. Played a cruel prank.

"I'm coming, Clancy." She released the rope and gave in to the fever that distorted her senses. Suddenly, she was sliding, sliding, sliding down into her brother's welcoming arms.

≈

Davage's arms ached from carrying Key's limp form, but he ignored the discomfort. Doing so distanced him from the blustery cold that numbed his cheeks and stiffened his fingers. He jostled Clancy's sister closer so that her chin fit snugly to his chest and kept her face away from the chill. Despite her heavy linsey and leggings and his own buffalo robe wrapped around her, the woman shivered. He had to get her back to camp, and soon, or she would die from exposure.

The deep foundations she insisted upon, and he had disputed earlier, had saved the trestle from the force of the slide. The engine could be backed downgrade. That would be the quickest way to get her to camp. As he trod through the snow bank toward the awaiting engine, survivors looked for buried railmates.

The U.P. had suffered many disasters in its five year push across the continent. Though he was sure this would not be the last nor the worst, Davage's heart still felt heavy from the loss of life as he stared at the woman cradled in his arms. Thank God she still lived, for now.

The Crow and Arapaho traveled the warpath lately, unhappy with the Iron Horse cutting into their land. The Brulé and Teton Sioux retaliated for crimes blamed on them, claiming they were committed by the Crow. Fear No Man had broken from Sitting Bull's and Big Nose's pledge of peace, raiding at will. An avalanche and Key Calhoun were the least of Davage's distractions.

But difficulties were inevitable if he intended to succeed in his mission to build this railroad. Davage had called upon his faith when the trestle seemed to best him, and the Lord decided to test Davage's on-again, off-again beliefs by using one of his "mysterious ways."

Though her ideas were maverick and her temper salty, Davage had to admit Key's plan worked. Key could be a real asset to accomplishing his goals. It wasn't fitting to corral a spirit daring enough to challenge a task this size.

Second-guessing God—and Key Calhoun—might be the most foolish choices he'd ever made. Yet, logic told him having a woman this lovely on the roster was anything short of lunatic.

"How is she?" Hamilton Sax jumped down from the engine to help Davage.

"Alive for now. But she won't be if we don't hurry." Davage declined the younger man's offer to carry Key, despite the fact that carrying her tested his own stamina and made walking difficult in the ice.

A wisp of blue-black hair slipped from her hooded parka. Davage found the long tendrils intriguing. Indeed, everything about Clancy's sister amazed him since she'd arrived in camp. Though stubborn as a lop-eared mule, she was as smart as any engineer he'd had the good fortune to work with, including General Dodge himself.

The wind quieted now, only occasionally making a lunge at the engine. Once inside the locomotive, Davage gently deposited Key on the floor and readjusted the buffalo robe. The pale tightness of her lips worried him. To keep his mind off the intense cold and Key's condition, Davage busied himself with loading the firebox.

"No more," Hamilton reached out and stilled Davage's efforts. "We can chuff back down. Save your stamina."

Since Hamilton had arrived, the man had been a constant help. Despite the difference in ages, Hamilton was as good an organizer as Davage. . .but still there was something about the man Davage didn't trust. Some of the ruffians took an immediate liking to Hamilton, which Davage suspected stemmed from his ability to quench the worker's thirst with more than coffee. A fact higher officials insisted kept the crew appeased during the long months away from home, but Davage disapproved of.

Davage bent over his unconscious charge and pretended to readjust her hood. He told himself he was just looking after her, first, because she was a woman, and second, because she was Clancy's sister, to whom he owed an allegiance. Truth was, he didn't like the way Hamilton stared at Key, desire darkening his green gaze.

Davage gently shoved a wayward strand of hair inside her hood, only to make several more fall in its place. The silken curls were cold and thick. She rolled over at that moment, and her lips nestled against his fingers as he tucked in the last strand.

The veins in his hands contracted with an unexpected tingle. *Such a delicately curved mouth.* Cold and bluish-red now, but only this morning spouting words full of spit and vinegar. He ran one finger along her cheek, admiring the softness of her porcelainlike skin.

"Kiss her," Hamilton urged. "She'll never know."

Long-dormant chivalry made Davage angrier at himself than his coworker. After all, he'd wanted to kiss her. Hamilton was only voicing what he'd been thinking. Did *wanting* to kiss her make him just as guilty as actually taking such a liberty? He glared at the man. "*I* would know."

The sound of Hamilton's laughter only added to Davage's silent pledge to resist the temptation Clancy's sister presented and to keep his mind on the work ahead. He wasn't sure which pain presented him the greater danger— the direction his heart was heading or the trek of the railroad west.

❧

Thin pale light greeted Key as she woke to the Wyoming morning that seeped slowly into the canvas tent. She blinked twice and sighed, a heavy sigh that made her wonder how long and deeply she'd slept. She threw back the covers and sat upright. As she wrapped her arms around herself to hug away the bone-chilling cold, surprise, then a thousand questions raced to mind. The blue chambray shirt and trousers she wore were not the clothes she'd put on this morning. A glance around the room reassured her she was at least in her own quarters.

The smell of brewing coffee wafted on the morning breeze, awakening a craving within her. Moving to get ready for the day, Key discovered that every muscle ached, and bruises stained her skin. Quickly, she exchanged the chambray and oversized britches with her brown linsey shirt and trousers that hung on the pegged coatrack in the corner. A momentary reluctance slowed her efforts as she settled into the cooler material. She instantly missed the warmth she'd left in the chambray.

Following her nose, she found her way outside the tent. A cot stood close to the entrance. *Why would anyone leave a bed outside in the cold?* she wondered. Key added the question to those more pressing. Heading for the curling smoke of the cook fire, she knew someone always stood around it no matter what time of day. Meals had to be taken in shifts because of the large number of workers.

Davage warmed his hands near the fire.

"Good morning to ye," she hailed.

He glanced up, nodded, and poured a cup of coffee. "Nice to see you up and about." He handed her the cup. "Feeling rested now?"

"I think so." She reached up to smooth her tangled hair. "At least my eyes are awake. I'm not sure about the rest of me." Key pushed back her shoulders and stretched her neck in a semicircle.

"You didn't like the shirt Peg put on you? It's warmer than what you're wearing."

"Peg?" Key looked up into gray eyes and found they were full of concern.

"One of the laundresses. You were wet when we brought you down the mountain. I had her change your. . .er. . .I thought it best for you to get warm and dry as soon as possible so you wouldn't catch your death. For a while there, we thought we might have been too late."

Key noticed the dark circles under his eyes, his disheveled hair, wrinkled shirt. The cot outside her tent now made sense. "Ye stood watch over me?"

"Peg saw to your needs, Miss Calhoun. I merely made certain I was there if Peg required help." He yawned. "She'll be glad to know you're better. I sent her off to sleep a while, but I'm headed back that way."

"Seems I owe the both of you special thanks. How can I repay you?"

"You owe me nothing, but Peg earns a hard living. Though she would never ask you, you might offer her something delicate and frilly." Davage blew the steam off his coffee. "She loves beautiful things."

Key's gaze focused on his cup. The leanness and grace of his fingers surprised her. *Were they soft or calloused from hard work?* A strong urge to brush her lips against them was followed by an even stranger sense of loss. Was she so weak that she couldn't even control her own thoughts?

"May I sit for a moment?" Key asked, feeling faint. She remembered the slide well now and knew the fate that would have befallen her had Davage not rescued her.

She started to sit in one of the camp chairs, but Davage set his cup down and gently grabbed her by the elbow. "I thought ye were Clancy, ye know," she whispered, unsure why she felt the need to explain.

"Key, you need more rest," he insisted. "Let me help you back to your tent."

She agreed, too unsteady to argue with him. As they lumbered back to her quarters, Davage told her all that had gone on in the three days since the avalanche.

"I should have anticipated something like this," Key admitted. "Had every detail covered, I did. I wouldn't blame you if you ask for my dismissal."

"You couldn't have predicted that earthshaker anymore than I or anyone else could have."

His readiness not to cast blame increased her respect for him. "Does that mean you plan on letting me stay?"

Davage stopped and studied her. "Somehow that word and you don't go together." He grinned, then answered her silent query, "*Let.* I can't imagine you *letting* anyone make any decision that concerns you, Miss Calhoun."

She returned his stare evenly and laughed. "I do get things done."

"You're good at handling snow," he admitted. "But what about people?"

Key hesitated, uncertain where his question was headed. Had he guessed she was a loner? She liked caution, respected it. . .lived by it. A wariness came into his eyes, intriguing Key. Davage Jansen was a cautious man too. "Some people. I don't take much brook from those who show no sense."

"What if I told you I find you exceptionally beautiful? Would you think me senseless?"

"No, I'd say ye've very good eyesight and fine taste. An intelligent man if ever I met one."

A chuckle started low and deep. The rich baritone of his laughter made him appear years younger. What would he look like come spring thaw when he shaved off that thistle of a beard? If she stayed on, Key promised herself she would see him clean-shaven before they reached the downslope of the Continental Divide.

Morning sun filled his eyes with a light that reflected a merrier soul than his duty had allowed her to view previously. Getting to know the gentler aspects of this man might be an added benefit of working the U.P.

He took a gulp of air to calm his laughter. "Are you always this frank?"

"Yes, and you?"

"Not all the time. Hedging has its uses."

"Lies do nothing but hurt."

Davage's features sobered. "Who lied to you, Key, to make you so drawn to truth?"

"Sometimes the lies we tell ourselves are more harmful than any someone else might offer us," she answered, her voice tinged with a truth she knew far too well.

four

In the few days he'd known her, Davage discovered a woman who knew her job well and didn't make spur-of-the-moment judgments. He had followed her all morning and was impressed by her careful study of the land. She looked for a better observation point to create a pass through the Laramie Mountains.

Other engineers assigned to survey the area found the slopes too short and high for the long slanting ridge needed to descend from the relatively flat summit. Seamed and cracked cliffs overlooking the gorge appeared impassable. Craggy buttresses jutted out and blocked a substantial portion of the descent.

"I see you've come to a conclusion." Davage moved closer to view the dark lines Key now inked on the map.

She pointed to the yawning precipice. "I want to try something new, and I'm not sure you'll like it." She took off the slouch hat that shaded her face from the sun, then wiped her brow with the long sleeve of her linsey.

"There isn't much we haven't tried." Davage admired the heavy mass of hair twisted and pinned beneath her hat. He had ordered her to wear her waist-length hair up in the masculine style, hoping a scouting party wouldn't notice a woman in their ranks. Uncomfortable with his growing attraction to her beauty, he added, "This idea can't be any more mulebrained than the rest of yours."

She offered a halfhearted smile to the party of engineers. They all had extended more than their share of effort, time, and knowledge the last two days to overcome this snag in the U.P.'s progress.

Her gaze momentarily locked with Davage's, almost as if she were considering his opinion even before he gave it. The thought pleased him. Yet when a glint of mirth crinkled the corner of her lips, he realized she had done so only to gain his undivided attention, and he had fallen for her tactic!

"I think we ought to shimmy down the cliff and see if we're overlooking something important," she suggested. "Up here, we can't get a clear view no matter which angle we take. From down there looking up, we might see a better way to descend."

"Are *you* willing to do the shimmying?" asked a sullen-faced, chinless engineer. His continual scowl had worn creases in his forehead and soft loose face.

"No one does my work for me." Key motioned the crew forward to the edge. "Now, look here at the way the slope slants smooth from this point to about midway of the buttress. Then see where it picks up about a mile farther down? I think if I could get below, I could see whether it's an unbroken grade or if it matches that cutaway on the other side."

Davage studied the ledge and the path farther down the mountain Key hoped would form a continuance. The angle looked good, but it was unlikely the wind had eroded this side of the gorge in exactly the same manner as the other. Wind tended to carve indiscriminately. Still, it was worth investigating, but he would never allow her to do such a dangerous job herself.

"You've tested the ledge?" General Dodge asked. The leader of the Union Pacific had recently arrived in camp. He would let headquarters know of the impossibility of the task should they fail.

She nodded. "I tied a rope around a couple of good-sized rocks and let them fall. A few yards down they hit. It couldn't have been anywhere near bottom. I knew I'd found a ledge when I brought the rocks back up. My rope was only extended four, maybe five feet."

General Dodge held out his hand, and she offered her own to complete the handshake. "I knew you must be remarkable, Miss Calhoun, when I brought back the railroad car you ordered from Council Bluff. Anyone who had the gumption to bring that out here in the middle of the wilderness must have nerves of iron. I'm pleased to know your tactics are just as bold. Let's try that ledge. Davage, grab the rope."

Davage hesitated just long enough to draw Key's curiosity. He sucked in a deep breath as if to steel himself against a hidden enemy.

Finally he seized the rope, tied it to one of the cedars that fringed the yellow gorge, then secured it with a knot. Before she had a chance to ask him if he was afraid of heights, Davage tied the other end around his buckskinned waist.

"What are you doing?" She grabbed the rawhide. "I said I'd take the risks."

"Not while under my command, you won't." His eyes narrowed as he gave one last glance toward the huge stone wall that bulged over the gorge. He'd listen to no argument this time.

"God be with you then. I don't want to mourn a man I barely know."

Despite her sarcasm, he could hear the concern in her voice. The way her hands gripped the rope harder to help his descent proved she was the type to mourn him if she'd known him at all.

Davage backed slowly down the cliff, his eyes carefully gauging the stone wall and its deathtraps. *Hold,* he ordered silently, fighting off the racing of his heart to calm his breathing. He broadened the length of the rope as he inched his way down, his shoulders and back muscles tightening and flexing with each jerk. One misplaced foot might unearth loosened rock and send a weakened section sliding down from its primeval perch. He maneuvered clear of a dwarf pine that hung lopsided from its unfortunate birth along the high gale-swept ridge.

"A little more," he hollered, drawing close to her estimated five feet. Yes, there it was. Just below the buttress. A smooth running ledge! They'd know if Key was right before nightfall.

Spang! A puff of sand and rock showered from above and dusted his hair. *Sping! Spang! Spang!* Bullets ricocheted off the stone everywhere around him. Someone was shooting at him!

"Indians!" several men yelled from above.

The pressure on the rope eased. Key must have let go! Now only the cedar held him as he dangled over the gorge. Terror gripped him, blinding him with visions from the past.

The rope slowly worked itself up from his waist. Would it settle beneath his arms and rise to hang him? Davage began to pray, knowing now the fear that must have been his younger brother's on that day Davage had almost hanged him accidentally.

Dodging the hail of bullets, Davage tried to inch the rope down to allow him room to get his weapon, but the threat kept coming. *Spang! Sping, spang!* He felt a jerk. His gaze shot upward. Another bullet creased his fragile link to the ledge, and his lifeline snapped.

❧

Key tied the rope around the base of the nearest tree and scrambled for the horses as renegade arrows and bullets found their marks. She prayed the attackers couldn't see the rope snaking through the grass and over the edge. Could Davage hold on until she or the others returned for him?

The only thing she could do now was slap heels to her sorrel. The detachment of troops from Fort Halleck that had escorted the U.P.'s forays into this portion of the Wyoming wilderness seemed nowhere at hand. Had the renegades sidetracked them or led them on a wild chase, then doubled back?

No time to worry about what had happened to the troopers if she intended to save herself and rescue Davage. The general and his men would stay together, but her best chance might come from going it alone. She scaled the ridge, the renegades in a straightaway pursuit. The bulk of the raiders followed General Dodge and his company, as she'd hoped. But to her dismay, a band of three challenged her bid for freedom. Key rode for her life over the rock-strewn ground. Tufts of sage and greasewood tore at her trousers as the animal galloped over the exposed heights.

The attackers steadily gained, their expert horsemanship far superior to her own. Nearing the peak, she realized there would be no turning back now. The horse was already lathered with sweat and foam, his breath labored. Whichever direction she chose, the Indians' swift mustangs would overtake her government-issued animal in a matter of minutes.

Somewhere in the bounding fear, she reminded herself that only God could decide the hour of her death and that he surely had more of a purpose for her than this. What if her survey was correct? What if there truly was a ridge that slanted from the peak to the gorge's floor? What if he meant for her to survive this tribulation?

"I'm willing to do this on my own, Lord. But if You've a mind, I'd appreciate You riding with me on this one and showing me a way." Key urged her mount into an all-out gallop, riding hard for the mountaintop and beyond. "Preserve me, Looord!"

Bracing herself as she sailed through the air, Key's plea was almost instantly and miraculously jarred from her throat. After only a distance of four or five feet, the horse's hooves hit blessed earth, nearly uprooting every tooth in her head with their vibrating impact.

She waited for the animal to regain its footing. The sorrel shied a few steps then gentled under her calm, yet authoritative commands. A glance at the top made her blink in wonder. "T–that's one leap of faith we just took, horse. I don't know about you, but nobody will ever convince me there aren't such things as miracles anymore. I just lived one."

Key urged the animal down the ledge she'd only hoped was there, but now prized as greatly as she did God's mighty hand in her life. There was no time for congratulations. If she dared the peak, so might the renegades.

"Let's find Davage," she told the horse, feeling a new strength of purpose settle within her. Ever since Davage had accused her of challenging God's will with her own, she'd wondered if he spoke the truth. But it seemed the Almighty approved of her daring. . .so far!

She rode down the incline, mentally stockpiling facts—the level of the grade, the width of the ledge—all details she would need to report back to General Dodge. Solitary snuffs of shod hooves against sand and rock assured her she was not being followed. No unshod hoofprints dusted the trail before her, confirming that the renegades did not know this way up Sherman Hill. As she descended, landmarks on the other side of the gorge suddenly became familiar. This must be close to where Davage dangled over the edge.

Whizz! An arrow zipped by and buried itself in the bank to her left. *Spang! Spang! Whizz!*

Bullets and arrows rained over from above. The buttress loomed ahead, and she saw with grim satisfaction that it rose vertically over the incline. No wonder they hadn't been able to see the slope.

The overhang was the answer to her safety. Bullets couldn't reach her beneath it. A glance told her Davage no longer hung over the cliff. Had he somehow managed to climb back over the top, or. . .had he fallen to the bottom of the gorge? Guilt and dread coursed through Key as she realized he might have died doing the job she should have done.

Oh, ye of little faith, the words crashed into her mind, forcing Key to steel herself against the doubt threatening to consume her. She galloped toward the buttress, dodging the hail of bullets. Davage lay motionless on the ledge's rim. Jerking hard on the reins, she narrowly missed sending his unconscious form hurtling over the precipice.

"Davage, are you all right?" Key dismounted cautiously and dropped the reins, knowing the government-issued animal understood this as a command not to move.

Bending over Davage, she felt for broken bones. Finding none, she managed to get him on his back and away from the edge. His forehead bled profusely, but when she wiped away the blood with her sleeve, she found only a deep scratch.

Bullets puffed up spirals of dirt on either side of the stone wall, but for now they were safe. Key prayed for yet another miracle—time to get Davage mounted before the renegades discovered her leap and attempted it themselves.

She placed her arms beneath him and locked them in front of his chest in an effort to get Davage to his feet. He moaned. Key laid him gently back down on the ground. A glance at his ashen face rushed a wave of protectiveness through her. She respected him. Even liked him. Not only as a boss but as a man. Key found herself questioning what it would be like to be courted by such a man, but that thought quickly buried itself to be dug up and examined in less dangerous times.

"I'm going to help you up, Davage." She wrapped her arms around him as she'd done before. "Whatever ye do, don't move fast. Just lean into me and take steps when I tell you to."

The smell of sweat, dust, and fear filled her nostrils and nearly made her choke as she dragged him closer to the sorrel. "Now what?" she worried aloud as she stared up at the saddle and wondered how she was going to get him into it. "Lord, if I ever needed Your mighty hand, now's the time to lend it."

Like a trumpet from heaven, a bugle sounded from the valley below. A thin column of blue riders broke through the cottonwood and willows lining the bottom of the gorge. Volleys of gunshots and whizzing arrows greeted the troops as they split, one column of men riding around the mountain's base, the other heading up the incline toward her and Davage.

Key dared to loosen her hold on him, flailing one arm in a desperate attempt to gain their attention. "Up here. . .on the ledge. Please help us!"

She pushed and gave Davage the upward momentum he needed, then grabbed the reins. "Can ye hold on long enough for me to—?"

"Saddle up!" he ordered through clenched teeth.

Pebbles and sand skittered down the slope behind them announcing otherwise soundless horses. The renegades had jumped the peak! Davage offered her a hand up, and she locked arms with him. Key straddled the horse behind him, her hands encompassing his waist and her cheek resting against his rock-hard back.

"Be careful," she warned. "They're above us, too."

"Guess there's no place but down." He spurred the sorrel into a gallop toward the approaching troopers.

"First time we've agreed on anything," Key whispered against his back, wondering if there would ever be a second time.

five

The renegades fought to the last warrior but were quickly defeated by the overwhelming force of troopers. General Dodge and the remaining surveyors managed to escape and had aided in Key's and Davage's rescue.

"Unusual way to make a point, Miss Calhoun." General Dodge reined to a halt near her. He dusted his hat on his leg. "Seems you've found the grade we need for the pass."

Key loosened her hold around Davage's middle. His heavy exhale of breath hinted she'd been holding on too desperately. "Davage found it first." She silently reminded herself he had also managed to get them down the slope despite his injury. He reined the horse a half-quarter turn to look back up the grade and to the overhang above it, then wiped the back of his hand across his bloody brow. "I would have bled to death if Key hadn't found me."

"Nothing ye wouldn't have done for me." Key knew she spoke the truth but was pleased he had the integrity to acknowledge her efforts. For one brief moment, she felt as if something bound her to him—something far more intense than sharing a horse or surviving the attack.

General Dodge looked from Key to his crew chief. "Well, there's one good thing come out of all this ruckus. . ."

"What's that?" Davage asked as his hand pressed against Key's, silently requesting that she strengthen her grip around his waist once again.

"That blow to your head must have knocked some sense into you because, Son, you're finally treating Miss Calhoun like the beautiful woman that she is."

A loud guffaw erupted from General Dodge behind them as Davage nudged their mount toward camp and away from the U.P. leader's sharp insight.

❧

The camp was astir with more than news about the attack. A letter sent from New York awaited their return. Certain members of the railroad's board of directors were dissatisfied with the construction record. Durant expected the U.P. crew to build more than four hundred miles this year, and that meant added surveys for precautionary measures.

"More head work?" Davage complained as he lay on the sick bed and awaited General Dodge's ministrations to his head wound. "And I don't mean my own."

The U.P. leader had sent away the camp doctor, insisting that he'd see to Davage's injury himself. Davage appreciated the man's concern and knew the general considered him more son than employee. "We've already got five engineers per survey now."

"Just lie still. This is going to sting," the officer warned.

Scalding liquid sent searing pain through Davage's head. "What in high—?"

"There's a lady present." The general nodded toward the sheet that shielded Davage's sick bed from the remainder of the tent. "And it's whiskey, boy. It'll cleanse the wound. Now lie still, as I told you, and that's an order."

Davage did as he was told and peered hard at the sheet, barely making out the form of the woman sitting in a chair. "What's she doing here?" he mouthed almost inaudibly.

"The same thing ye did for me when I was sick," Key answered. "Now behave and do what the good general tells ye to."

From the amused look on his superior's face, General Dodge was enjoying the situation immensely. Davage went on, "We've already got the greater force of our crew working on the masonry foundations at Dale Creek." Talking railroad business would keep his mind off the general's patchwork. "Half our tie-cutters are floundering in three feet of snow, trying to float timber down the Laramie."

"Sounds like your crew is strung from here to Utah," Key commented.

General Dodge pulled back the flesh in order to probe further into the wound.

"You trying to peel me for a spud?" Davage yelled. "Quit dawdling, would you, man? More head work, my eye!"

Anger swelled through Davage, and when the general explored the wound with a fire-sanitized knife, a moan escaped Davage.

"Is he all right?" Key's worry echoed from the other side of the curtain.

"It's full of sand and something else here I can't quite. . . hold still, boy. . . stay calm," General Dodge muttered.

"Our Father Who are in heaven, hallowed be Thy—"

Davage found comfort in Key's soft voice and concentrated on the meaning of her prayer rather than the painful throb drumming at his temples and dulling his senses.

Finally, General Dodge quit probing. "You're lucky the bullet only creased you." His voice raised to include their visitor. "Ma'am, if I'm ever injured, I hope you'll consider sitting at my sickbed. Seems you have a direct line to heaven."

"I hope I never have to grant you the same, General, but if I have a direct line it's only because I learned a long time ago that if I didn't ask, I wouldn't receive. Part of that comes from being the only girl holding her own in a family full of brothers. The other part, well. . .I like to think it's due to faith, pure and simple. Now if you'll excuse me, I'll go get the hardhead something to eat."

General Dodge dipped a white cloth in a clear liquid and placed it over Davage's forehead. "She's a fine woman and has a sharp mind, I must say. You're a lucky man."

"Oww! That'll kill me for sure, Dodge!" Davage bellowed. "What is it? And if you call this lucky. . ."

"Sterilizer. I'm reading a book that says keeping wounds clean will stop the chance of infection. Tried it myself, and it works." He deliberately scrubbed the wound hard. "And the good fortune that's come your way is more than a spared brain. I can see what's going on between you two."

"What?" Davage played the innocent. Yet he suspected Key's presence with the U.P. would effect him more personally than the crew.

"Miss Calhoun's car is a good deal warmer, and from the looks of it, more comfortable." General Dodge tossed the now blood-soaked cloth into the barrel. "That's where you'll stay until you're better."

Davage jerked up to a sitting position, immediately regretting his action. Dizziness assaulted him. He had to lean back far enough to rest on his elbows for strength. "Did she put you up to—"

"Anything the U.P. needs to further its progress is subject to confiscation. You know that." The general wrapped clean bandages around the injured forehead. "And no, she hasn't a clue. . .yet."

One of General Dodge's graying brows shot upward. "I think you're running scared for the first time since I've known you. And Lord knows, I'm having one jolly, fine laugh about it." Good to his word, a healthy chuckle escaped him.

"When I get up from here, Dodge, I'm going to lasso you by your bootheels and drag you clear to the Tetons."

"You do that, Son. But in the meantime, you enjoy that fancy Pullman, and I'll enjoy watching Key Calhoun lasso you in."

❧

"Mighty decorative dwelling you have here." Davage admired the pink Arabian lace gracing the fourteen single-sashed windows along the railroad car's west wall. "Did George Pullman make it for you himself?"

"It's one of his trial models."

A rosewood chest, high-backed chair, mirror, and washstand lined the east wall, while a coal stove provided the warmth that kept out the late January chill. A chair, upholstered in the best grade of plush, offered a place to read, and the carpet was surely Aubusson or better. Cherry woodwork shined with a polished silkworm pattern. The center dot in the cushions' birdseye, diamond-shaped figures seemed to stare back at him as if they were a thousand eyes already accusing Davage of a sin he had not yet committed.

The car's definite feminine interior glowed with a rosy hue embellished by the light of an oil lamp. Pullman knew what it took to make a lady comfortable and a gentleman ill at ease.

The car suddenly jerked forward then back, making Key stumble. "We're moving! What's going on?"

She regained her footing, then raced to the windows, parting the lace curtains. Key gasped as she swung around. Her lips drew into a grim line. "The renegades. They're back!"

"Stay put," Davage ordered, heading for the door that led out to the Pullman's front platform. He grabbed the chair. "Prop this up against the knob and don't remove it unless either I or the general comes to get you."

Though his tone brooked no argument, Key blocked the exit with her back. "You're not climbing up there and take a chance of falling. I'm going with you."

Was the worry darkening her eyes to a deep blue concern for his safety or a reaction to the pair of moccasins they both saw slip up and out of view over the farthermost window? Together they stood a better chance getting to the others. He *was* too dizzy to safeguard her well being. "Alright, but stay behind me. And close." Davage opened the door and pointed to the roof's scalloped edges, waiting for sight of the attacker before attempting the next move. A thick, gray mist shrouded the mountains. Morning had not yet broken over their summits.

The train lurched, throwing Davage forward. He landed against the hard muscular body of a renegade squatting over the coupling between cars.

"He's pulling the linchpin to disconnect us!" Key shouted.

A shot rang out, the noise deafening. Someone was firing from the direction of the tool car. The warrior crumpled into a heap below the fittings, disappearing between the rush of iron wheels.

Davage rolled and landed on his feet only to crash into the door of the car ahead of him. To the relief of both, the shooter was one of his own men.

"Blow those lights!" Davage didn't wait for the startled lineman to obey. Instead, with tremendous effort, Davage swung himself to the top of the car, then offered Key a hand up.

"Is this any time to tell you I haven't done this before?"

He suspected the teasing in her tone was meant to cloak her fear, but safety lay further down the cars. And the only sure way to get past trouble was to walk the roof. "Good a time as any. But once is all it takes to change that. Ready?"

In the same instant she gripped his hand and allowed him to boost her up, the oil lanterns shattered with a last flare. Davage shifted his gaze toward the engine light and, in that exact moment, was awarded with the sight of a silhouetted party of riders. Realizing he, and now Key, must be visible to them, Davage signaled her to crouch low.

Hand in hand, they rushed forward.

"Sort of like w-walking on water," Key tried to appease the mounting tension.

"Comes close." Davage squeezed her hand and willed her to be brave. "It takes the same kind of faith. . .or desperation. Now get ready to leap to the tender car."

"Leap?"

"Yes, jump. On the count of three. One. Two. Threeee!"

They sailed through the space dividing car from car, landing in a pile of coal. Pain coursed through Davage's head, forcing him to blink back the wave of dizziness. Blood seeped through the bandage.

"Remind me never to do that again." Key brushed her hands on her trousers.

Davage held a finger to his lips and pointed. Voices carried on the wind, and it was difficult to discern which direction they came from.

"How much do you think she's worth?" a voice growled.

"Fool! Why don't you just shout out the whole plan? They'll blockade that Pullman so heavy, we'll have to blow the *señorita* out. Wonder if Running Elk's got that fancy car cut loose yet?"

These aren't ringleaders, Davage decided quickly. These *pistoleros* had obviously been told to wait until the linchpin had been pulled.

Stealthily, Davage made his way over the coal until he could see down into the next car—the engine cab. A white man and warrior stood facing Hamilton Sax and General Dodge. The two U.P. bosses had been backed into one window seat, their respect for the menacing guns begrudging and subdued.

Davage warned Key to remain hidden then grabbed a handful of coal dust, swung inside the car and threw it into the attacker's face before dizziness overtook him once more. The sound of guns clearing leather echoed around him.

For a moment, he wondered if he'd failed.

But as clear as Gabriel's shout on Judgment Day, General Dodge's voice rang loud and clear. "You! Keep your hands away from that pistol or I'll finish you off here and now!"

Hamilton confiscated the men's weapons. "They won't be causing any more trouble."

"Will she run faster?" Davage finally regained his equilibrium and stood. "Is the track all right?"

"No blockade that I can see." Hamilton forced the prisoners over to one corner. "These two swung up here just as we started topping the grade."

"Get this thing fanning then," Davage commanded.

Hamilton leaned against the lever hard, instigating a rumbling shudder. Shots rang out in the night, shattering glass to the floor.

"Crest her full!" Davage yelled. The engine slowly nosed over the grade, gathering speed steadily. He resisted the urge to check on Key, praying she had taken cover. The only way to get her out of harm's way was to speed the train back to camp amid a greater number of allies. Key was smart. She'd lie low and not try anything foolish. . .wouldn't she?

Hamilton wiped the perspiration from his brow with his shirt sleeve. The shots diminished, growing faint in the distance. "What do you think they're after?"

Davage nodded at the prisoners. "Unless they want to be taken to the nearest sheriff and strung up for their crimes, I think one of them can give us all the answers we need."

"The woman!" the white man said with apprehension. The other man shot him a look of pure contempt. "Fear No Man wants your Christian. He says there was a good woman with the crew, but we found only men. . .and the laundresses."

"Why is he looking for the Christian among us?" Davage demanded.

The man sneered. "He said you would search for her. You wouldn't be able to boss the gangs, so the work would stop."

Hamilton nudged the talkative prisoner with his boot. "It looks like you put yourselves to a lot of needless trouble. He would've *given* her to you if you'd only asked."

Davage didn't appreciate Hamilton's jest—it had just confirmed Key's presence among the crew.

six

General Dodge looked up from the maps and plans before him with a faint smile. His dark, stern face mirrored his many years as a major-general who expected to be obeyed. "I'm sorry, Miss Calhoun, but those are my orders."

"But I don't need a guard." Key respected the officer as the chief of the U.P., but this time his decision was unfair.

"I'm not sure you understand the many difficulties, the many perils of our undertaking," he said. "With the outside world waiting and the nation doubting we can complete a transcontinental railroad, I can't let a precaution go unheeded nor a possible delay in our progress go unchallenged. I must insist that you have a guard, madame, if you intend to work for me."

His face became grim, hard. "Fear No Man does not make idle threats. The only way we can be certain you're not abducted is for you to be constantly under Davage's watchful eye."

"Constantly?"

"Twenty-four hours."

Her mukluk boot tapped a staccato beat against the camp chair. "Does he know it yet?"

"Do I know what?" Davage stepped through the command tent entrance. "You sent for me?"

He looked remarkably refreshed and comfortable in his fur-lined mackintosh. Living round the clock in his presence would present any number of troubles Key was not prepared to take on.

"I was just informing Miss Calhoun that I've assigned the two of you to work closely together for the next several weeks. I've been requested to return to Omaha, and I want you to ensure our mile-a-day track quota. Jack and Dan Casement can see to business here at rails' end."

"Twenty-four-hour guard were your exact words, General," Key reminded.

Davage slammed a fist down on the makeshift table, sending several papers flying and sloshing the general's coffee. "This has gone too far."

The U.P. leader stood slowly, gathering the papers. "If Fear No Man intends to lure you away by kidnapping her, then I mean to have her constantly within your sight. You will obey these orders—the both of you—or find employment elsewhere."

"Guess *I'm* gonna be guarding *you*." Key finally conceded. And if the renegades took him but left her behind, she might have time to sound an alarm. "They're smart, if you ask me," she said. "The men *do* work faster when you're with them and not surveying ahead with me."

General Dodge cleared his throat. "Well, I see you two have come to terms with it. I'll let you work out your own arrangements."

"Most of the time we'll be surveying ahead and won't have to worry about *arrangements*." Davage backed away from Key as if he already intruded on her privacy. "We'll take our bedrolls and saddles and sleep near the campfire with all the others. But when we're back at base, I'll bunk in the tool car and keep watch. You know I don't sleep much. Hamilton or Duffy can take my place the few hours I do."

20.

That night Key stood at the window of the Pullman, restless, staring out into the deepening shadows of night.

Suddenly, Davage exited the tool car linked to the Pullman, his hands gripping a rope and adeptly forming a lasso. Though she couldn't hear what he said, she could tell he must be talking to someone as he twirled the rope in a wide loop. She wondered if he and the person he called to would mind company. Perhaps a brisk walk would be just the activity that might tire her enough to make her sleepy. Key peered first one way, then the other but couldn't see to whom he spoke.

Curiosity got the best of her. She dressed warmly and went outside. "Davage, what are you doing up this late?" she asked as she attempted to catch up with him. "Don't you know we have two days work to do tomorrow?"

". . .accident. . .s–so sorry," he turned and stared at her, his eyes wide, unseeing. "I didn't mean. . ." He gripped the rope as if he wanted to rip it to pieces. "God forgive me. Tobiah. . .Toby. . .speak to me. . .please, Tobiah. . .*speak!*"

Realization swept through Key like a chilling wind—he was sleepwalking. Talking in his sleep, Davage's words were being spoken to no one. Key glanced around once again to make certain. No one stood in the immediate vicinity. Her attention riveted on him. She'd heard it was unwise to startle someone awake from sleepwalking. What should she do? She couldn't just let him wander the night; he might hurt himself.

His face was etched with an emotion she recognized too well. She had seen its like in her own family's expressions too often during and after the war. Who was this Tobiah person Davage grieved for? And why did Davage seek forgiveness from him? Compassion filled her and she gently touched the crew chief's hand, hoping he would let her lead him back to the tool car.

He dropped the lasso as if it were a snake that had bitten him. "N–never.

Never again. I. . .won't touch. . .I promise, Tobiah. I promise."

Davage looked at her with such need, Key felt compelled to make him think *she* was Tobiah. "That's good, Davage. I accept your promise. You don't have to touch. . ." she stared at the rope, ". . .the rope, is it?" When his eyes widened as if in horror, she reassured him, "You don't have to touch that rope ever again. No one will make you. Ever." Perhaps she could use this mistaken identity to lure him back to the safety of the tool car. "You won't have to. . .if you'll come with me and let me take you home."

Like a small child, Davage allowed her to thread her fingers into his and lead him back to the car. When she knocked gently on the door, a low grumble met her inquiry.

"It be morning already? Why isn't the coffee brewing to wake a man for his day?"

"Mr. McDonough? It's me, Key Calhoun. I–I'm sorry to trouble ye, but Mr. Jansen, well he's—"

"Say no more, Lass. He's taken to wandering again, I warrant. Give me a minute and I'll be out to help you."

Key stared at Davage, unsure what he might do. He kept muttering indecipherable words. Only the occasional reference to Tobiah crept through, warning her that he was still gripped in the misery of his dream. *Please hurry,* she willed Duffy to hasten his efforts.

The door swung open and Duffy's massiveness filled the entrance, silhouetted by the lamp he'd lit. " 'Tis good that you found him, Lass. I normally keep watch over him, but my pillow was too comfortable tonight. I didn't hear him go out this time."

"It's all right, Duffy. We're all tired," Key reassured the Irishman. "Then this is not the first time he's done this?"

Duffy stepped aside and let her lead Davage past him.

"No," he whispered. "He's done this every night I've known him. The lad is troubled, but he doesn't talk about it."

"What can we do?" Key asked, urging Davage toward one of the cots the two men used to bunk down for the night.

Duffy let out a deep yawn. "Excuse me, Lass. 'Tis been a while since I've had a full night's sleep. I usually sit with him until he settles down. He goes out once, mumbles some words and throws a loop or two. Always the same thing. Never changes. A troubled heart, he has. Wish he would talk about it, but he won't. Just bends his back to his work so's he doesn't have to think about whatever 'tis that's bothering him."

"Perhaps it's a memory too deep to share," Key defended the man she knew so little of other than he was Clancy's friend. Perhaps one day, Davage would trust her enough to tell her. But for now, she would simply safeguard him through *this* night.

"Duffy, I'm restless tonight, and I couldn't sleep right now if I wanted. You look exhausted. How about if I sit with him for a while and let you rest?"

"Thank you, but I think I'll go make some coffee and bring you back a cup. It doesn't take him long to settle down once you've convinced him to take to his bed again. See there, he's already quit the mumbling." Duffy pulled over a chair so she could sit next to Davage's cot.

"I'll be back soon as the coffee boils."

Key thanked him, then directed her attention to Davage. Though he no longer mumbled, the crew chief's body was trembling. The night was warmer than most had been, yet she pulled the blankets over his shoulders and tucked them around him to help warm him. It was only then that Key realized he was silently weeping.

Whatever the tragedy that gripped Davage, Key knew of only one source to relieve such torment. "That's all right, Davage. Everything will be all right now. Just put your trouble in the Lord's hands and let Him have His way. Peace will come if you'll just turn it over to God. He promised it would be so. And while He's working His miracles, you and I will watch over each other," Key whispered. "Just like we promised General Dodge."

≥∙

They adhered to the general's orders even after his abrupt return to Omaha. Thomas Durant had requested his presence for a meeting of the board. Companionship developed between them despite Key and Davage's obvious discomfort in sharing such close quarters. Key participated in the daily duties, particularly enjoying the times Davage inspected the construction lines and went among the men, always with a ready *hello*. She was pleased to learn he knew each one by name. But she never mentioned to Davage the nights she followed him, led him back to safety, only to share his tears and pray for him to be comforted.

Now that February days were warming, the surveyors worked ten miles ahead of the rail crew. Key followed Davage down the loose, unspiked ties to where they ended and along the graded roadbed that stretched even farther ahead. She took swift inventory of the possible problems for the next day's work. Gazing over the mountains with a dreamlike contemplation, her mind worked ahead, searching the beautiful, strong, changeless scenery for some hidden secret it might offer. Unlike Davage, who often spoke of the sacrifice it might expect.

The man was an enigma to her. He obviously loved what he did, giving his heart to the project at hand. Davage never gave less, working as the men said, from can to can't. Yet, he did so as if waiting for fate to blow an ill wind his direction. What had happened in his life that made him so distrustful of good things? So willing to work, lest he slow down long enough to live?

Every day was a constant din of hammering, laying rail or raising trestles over the many creeks and streams that flowed on the eastern slope of the Rockies. The grading gang was fast approaching the area just south of Fort Laramie. Already the tent owners and other fold-up businesses were leaving the fort behind to establish the new town of Laramie alongside the intended railbed.

Today, Key walked behind Davage in the shallow muddy water that streamed from the hills. They tramped up and down the ravine which lay far below the trestle being built over the creek.

The rising wind stung as Davage stepped swiftly, his glance keen and roving as he studied the lay of the ground.

"Wasn't this dry when you surveyed it?" Key scrutinized the stream flowing beneath the partially built coffer dam. The other dam near it had collapsed. Tons of cut and uncut stone, piles of muddy lumber, platforms and rafts lay strewn about.

"Yes, it was dry, but I figured on an early melt off. Somebody didn't follow orders." He rubbed his chin in thought. "Where's Hamilton?"

"He made a quick trip back to the line gangs. Said he needed to send some men up on the hills to cut and trim trees for piles and beams."

"Hope he thought about horses to snake down the timbers."

"He did, and I told Duffy to haul the pile driver down to the river and start up the steam."

"Mighty fine, Key."

She warmed to the approval in his tone. Like the linemen, Key discovered she worked harder for those moments when he voiced his appreciation. She tried to convince herself it was for her own self-satisfaction. Yet she was all too aware of her growing interest in Davage Jansen.

Several times, she'd found herself noticing how the sunlight burnished his sandy-colored locks with red streaks, how his eyes looked as distant as the Colorado horizon to the southwest while he estimated the grade. How steely they became when she interrupted his concentration. She noted too that his left foot cocked to one side when he was in deep thought. Key especially liked the way his lips curved and withdrew momentarily from their thin line when he was pleased. She knew she was letting her heart pull her from her goal of fulfilling Clancy's role. Perhaps that was why she had invited

Hamilton Sax to dinner tonight. It might be just the thing to get Davage off her mind.

"There's bound to be a little trouble when Hamilton gets back." Davage's smile suddenly sobered.

"W–what? Oh. . ." For a moment, Key suspected he had somehow read her thoughts. "Because of the orders not being followed, you mean?"

His brow creased. "Remember when we drew plans for breakwaters to be built upstream? You said that the snow-melt would cause high water and that we needed to direct the fast current *between* the piers and not against them. Someone's tampered with your plans."

She assumed Davage and Hamilton's relationship was more friendship than boss and hired hand. "And you think Sax did it?"

"No. But he can help me find out who did. In the meantime, you and I will go over my instructions while we wait for his return. I'll tell the men to rest until we're finished. We might as well send wagons back for supplies so we can make good use of the delay." His gaze softened. "Do you want anything brought up from camp?"

Key wiped a smudge of dirt from her cheek and brushed back a wayward wisp of ebony that had fallen from the slouch hat she wore. "There wouldn't be a spare bathtub, would there?"

Davage bent and playfully splashed a handful of water at her. It felt cool against Key's skin, but his playfulness surprised her. She suddenly remembered she'd opened the top buttons of her blouse earlier to relieve the effects of the blazing sun. Her fingers rushed instinctively to refasten the breech. The warmth of Davage's gaze prickled the back of her hand like heated tingles from the sun. Key glanced up at him, staring as he did at her.

After a moment, the silence grew awkward. Not knowing quite what to do with herself, she relied on what she'd always called upon in times of nervousness—her spunk. She dipped her own hand into the current and splashed the water back at him.

A challenge ensued, splashing first with hands then with legs. He chased her downstream, and she squealed in mock fright as she sloshed through the shallow stream and red clay. Her hat flew off. Key tried to catch it, but her legs quickly tired after all the trampling from the day's work.

"You want the whole Sioux nation down on our heads?" Davage half-complained, half-laughed as he grabbed her from behind.

"So keep me quiet," her heart took voice and challenged. Key realized what her words suggested and refused to find fault with the truth of her feelings.

Davage pulled her back into the wet, hard planes of his chest, turned her around, then kissed her. Key surrendered to the feelings that had been stirring since she'd met him, the adventure beckoning from her very soul.

He finally pushed away, his breath ragged, his eyes smoke-gray and hooded. A tremor of cold raced through her even before Davage's words left her chilled with their denial. "I can't, Key. I won't."

She watched contrasting feelings war through him. He ran a hand through his hair, then grumbled when he noticed his palms were full of red mud from the streambed. Davage glanced at Key, looking self-conscious and uncertain what to do about the uneasiness that spanned the short distance between them or the mud that now glistened in his hair.

She bent and cupped water in her hands. Approaching him slowly, she poured the water over his muddied temple. To her surprise, he allowed her to touch him. She repeated the procedure several more times until the mud was gone.

"I don't have time to play, Key."

His breath whispered against her cheek, sending a shiver of attraction to the tips of her toes. Her heart felt like a fish flipping in the afternoon sun. She searched his eyes for an explanation of his abrupt withdrawal. "This is about Tobiah, isn't it?"

His hands clutched her shoulders. "How do you know about my brother?"

When Key squirmed, his grasp slackened. Davage rubbed his hands up and down the lengths of her arms from shoulder to elbow to erase any pain he may have caused.

"I've been sleepwalking again, haven't I?"

"Aye."

"Talking in my sleep?"

"Nothing I could understand. Just that name. But you've repeated it many times."

"It's happened more than one night then?"

Key told him of his many walks but did not confide the part about his tears or her taking turns with Duffy, staying until dawn. Let him think her occasional exhaustion stemmed from their strenuous work schedule.

Apology softened his gaze. "I didn't mean to keep anyone awake."

"You didn't. You have so much on your mind, it's probably difficult to turn off the thoughts." Perhaps now was the right time to satisfy her curiosity. "I don't suppose you'd want to talk about Tobiah?"

Davage looked toward the horizon, then started toward the bank. "No, I wouldn't."

"Then, I don't suppose you'd want to kiss me like that again, would you?" Key joked, trying to ease the sudden tension.

He halted, his gaze sweeping over her. Attraction sizzled between them like new wood to a hungry flame.

"All in good time," his tone was low and husky.

seven

She had tried to concentrate on her work, but Key's mind wandered to the kiss she and Davage had shared. Calculations became frustrating numbers. She finally realized she was not doing herself, or the Union Pacific, any good. If Davage could put away the equipment, she would have enough time to bathe and prepare herself for the dinner invitation she'd extended to Hamilton.

Taking a last look into the survey glass mounted on the tripod, Key unhinged the three wooden legs and folded them. After gathering her notebook and pen, she followed the roadbed to Davage, who was heavy in discussion with several stonecutters. Key waited for the conversation to end, staring appreciatively at his tall, lean physique.

The day's heat had forced many of the workers out of their shirts. Davage was no exception. Though his duties consisted of mental as well as physical activities, he always lent an extra hand where needed whether it was hammering ties, lifting stone, or laying rail. His face and neck were a golden bronze, tanned by the reflection of the earlier snows. The man certainly presented a handsome image.

When the conversation lulled, Key took the opportunity to interject, "Excuse me, Davage." She motioned him to move away from the group so they might talk privately. "I was wondering if ye would mind putting the equipment away tonight? I'd like to head on back to the Pullman now."

He untied his bandanna, then wiped his brow and the back of his neck. Key forced herself to focus on a point beyond him to keep from wondering how it might feel to be held in his arms again. Somehow she found her voice and was surprised that it sounded steady, with no sign of her overwhelming attraction to him. "That is, if it's no trouble to ye."

"Sounds like you've made plans."

"I invited Hamilton to dinner. But I haven't had a chance to entertain since I went to work for you, so I wanted to make him a home-cooked meal."

"You cook?" His mouth twisted into a teasing grin.

Key didn't take offense. "Quite well. I rather enjoy it too."

"Lucky man. Cookie isn't known for his variety."

She laughed. "No, he's not, but don't let him hear that. He'll be sourer han that dough he calls biscuits." Key held out the tripod. "If you'll put his away for me, I'll save you some of my stew. It'll have choice cuts of beef, sweetbreads, and a few secret ingredients that are very appetizing."

He took the equipment. "I'll look forward to it. Go ahead. I'll finish up." She started to walk away, but he quickly added, "Oh, and when you're done with your bath. . ."

"Yes?" She turned around to see why his voice still sounded amused.

". . .don't forget to rinse the tub out extra good. Last time you didn't do t so well, and I happened to be the man to use it after you. I woke up smelling like lilacs or lavender or whatever flower's in that soap you use. Took me four hours of honest sweat for that stuff to wear off. I even threatened to wallop the next man who teased me."

She could imagine the pleasure the men took in taunting him. Key smiled and walked away again. "I'll be more careful."

"Key?"

Sighing, she halted. *Why is he deliberately stalling me?* "Yes?"

"What kind of soap *is* it?"

"Lavender."

"Smells good," his gaze held hers for a moment, "on you."

"Thanks." It was the first compliment he'd given her that didn't have to do with maps, grades, or courage.

"Hamilton's a decent sort," Davage informed her, "but you've kind of fit n here like one of the fellows. So he's not used to thinking of you in a lady-sort of way. I know you've got your doubts about him, but I haven't ever seen him treat a woman with anything but kindness and manners. If he decides to overdo his stay in any way, or. . .uh. . .gets out of line. . .just give me a shout. I'll be over in the tool car, if you need me."

Davage looked past her toward the winding road. "Sometimes this stretch of lonesomeness gets to a man, and he doesn't act like his usual self."

Something haunted his tone, but Key knew whatever troubled him was now locked behind his iron will. "Thanks, I'll remember that." She glanced at the afternoon sun already spreading its fire across the snowcapped peaks and knew if she dallied any longer she'd be late with the meal. "Now I really must be going, or I'll not get everything done."

Key hurried down the roadbed and stopped to pick up the necessary supplies for the meal before riding the five miles back to the Pullman. By the time she'd reined to a halt at the horse corral, she was ready for a hot bath. With the men spending most of their free time gambling in the tent cities, she figured no one would be willing to earn extra money by drawing water for her. Fortunately, one such soul needed the extra money to send home to his wife and children. Arriving at the Pullman, she discovered all was in order.

Soon the sides of her speckled kettle glowed with a reddish tint, cooking the wild onions, alder mint, potatoes and tenderized beef she'd marinated yesterday.

Key hurried to the huge mahogany wardrobe that took up one corner of the Pullman. Inside hung the black velvet dress that brought out the dark blue highlights of her hair, especially in candlelight and made her eyes more vivid in contrast. "So pretty," she murmured aloud and looked forward to the feel of it against her skin.

She dug through the gunnysack of supplies and found the new cake of soap. Key smiled as she thought of Davage's compliment and wondered what he would say now that she'd purchased another. Testing the water's temperature, Key then stripped off her remaining work clothes and settled into the tub with a long, satisfied sigh.

She leaned back against the tub's rim and rested for a few moments. Hot steam rose off the water, flushing her face, soothing her tired back and easing her thoughts into welcome oblivion.

Reluctantly, she scrubbed her hair and skin then stepped out onto the marble floor to dry. Out of one chest drawer, she chose black stockings and a matching chemise. The silk felt deliciously cool. Stockings and pantaloons came next. She refused to wear hooped crinoline beneath the sheath-styled dress; they would ruin the effect and were much too hot and cumbersome.

Key glanced at the clock. She had taken longer than planned. There was no opportunity to do more than brush her waist-length hair and let it dry. Not that she minded. Key loved the feel of her long curls as they cascaded down her back and brushed her waist. Keeping her hair pinned up beneath the slouch hat made her face look wide. Down, the thick mass framed the curves of her high cheekbones and complimented the fragile grace of her features. The blue-black length contrasted sharply with the creamy white of her shoulders and made her feel feminine in its full, shining glory.

From her jewelry box, she pulled two diamond earrings and a matching necklace, then put them on. Placing the lace tablecloth on the table, Key set the dinnerware and linen napkins in their spots. Two long, tapered candles formed a centerpiece surrounded by fresh, winter roses. Lighting the candles, she surveyed the table and decided all was indeed in order.

The intense smell of lavender overpowered the other aromas. Frustration wrinkled her brow. How was she supposed to dump the bathtub water and get rid of the prominent smell? Hamilton would be arriving any moment. She certainly wouldn't get it all bucketed out in time. Perhaps his sense of smell would not be as sensitive as Davage's.

A knock on the door offered no time to worry over the matter. Nervousness settled in her stomach as she anticipated the evening ahead. Key had never deliberately set a trap, yet she could sense something just beneath the surface with Hamilton, as if he were playing some kind of master game everyone else was unaware of. She had to get to the bottom of it—her curiosity wouldn't let her rest. She felt like David must have when he faced Goliath. Alder stew seemed a sorry weapon, but she reminded herself that David's aim remained true because he believed in what God had sent him to do. So she must believe that she was only doing what was best for the Union Pacific.

Opening the door, Key greeted Hamilton Sax's startled expression with a smile she hoped would disarm him.

He found his voice after a moment. "You look lovely this evening, Miss Calhoun."

His Adam's apple warbled up and down in his high-necked collar. Hamilton had donned a three-piece suit of green silk and brocade and his voice cracked like a schoolboy addressing the first girl who'd shown interest in him.

"Thank you, Hamilton. Won't you come in?"

"You know how to travel well." He forced his emerald gaze away to survey the room he'd just stepped into. "Looks like you have everything you could possibly need."

"Not everything." Key waved him to one of the chairs at the table. "I know you must be starving. Let's eat. We can talk over our meal."

He doffed his broad-brimmed hat. She offered to hang it on the wooden rack by the door. "Your coat as well. It'll take a while for the stove to cool down."

Hamilton gave her the jacket and sat in the chair she indicated and waited for her to scoop two bowls of the hot stew.

"I didn't think I'd ever be invited here. Thank you."

She appreciated his honesty. "You're welcome. But I find that puzzling. I thought we were becoming good friends." It pleased her that he was just as nervous as her. She'd watched Hamilton with the men and discovered him to be a man of purpose. He laughed quickly at the men's jokes and never quarreled, preferring to remain everyone's friend. As a Christian, that trait should not have troubled her. . .but it did. She sensed something beneath his friendliness.

Yet his knowledge of the U.P.'s plans was often as great as Davage's. This man meant trouble. She needed evidence either way—to prove his innocence or incriminate him. Key whispered a prayer that she was no[t] guilty of judging the man unfairly.

"I'm glad you consider me a friend, Miss Calhoun—Key." Hamilton'[s] tone was an obvious attempt to warm her, but she warded off a chill as sh[e] felt his gaze follow her every move. *A quickening of the spirit?* A warnin[g] flag raised the fine hairs along the surface of her skin. *Don't trust this man*, her senses said. She turned and concentrated on buttering two slices o[f] sweet bread.

"I was certain Davage had made a claim on you, and that you hadn'[t] objected to the idea."

She ventured a peek over her shoulder, careful not to disclose the irritatio[n] rising from his suggestive tone. "Our closeness is purely by order of Genera[l] Dodge."

"Perhaps in your judgment, but not so with Davage." He ran a forefinge[r] repeatedly over his mustache and beard.

She deliberately turned away again, not wanting him to read any stra[y] emotion. "Oh?"

"I've never seen him like this. He's grouchy when he gets up, then agai[n] about an hour before we roll up for the night. One of the men can look a[t] you, say something about how you look, and Davage will threaten to ben[d] a rail over the man's head and send him packing. I'd say Davage is follow[-] ing more than the General's orders where it concerns you."

A blush worked its way up Key's shoulders and neck. Better to guide th[e] subject to safer grounds. "I'm sure it's simply protectiveness because I'm [a] woman. Now, what about you? Tell me how you came to be with the Unio[n] Pacific. Your accent isn't Southern. My guess is it's Western. Far Western. Sa[n] Francisco, maybe?"

She placed the bowls of stew on the table. His look of unguarded surpris[e] rewarded Key as she retreated long enough to add the sweet bread and th[e] coffee to the table.

"You have a keen ear." He rose while she seated herself. "It all looks del[i]- cious. Shall I pour?"

"After we've said grace, please." She bowed her head and asked him [to] lead them in prayer.

He completed the task in short order. Hamilton poured the coffee, raise[d] his cup, then offered a toast. "To the most beautiful lady ever to work th[e] railroad."

She gently clinked her cup against his. "And may I add, to the most inter[-] esting man I've met." Key noticed how her compliment smoothed the line[s] of his face into a smile of appreciation.

Her conscience balked at the words until she reassured herself she wasn't lying. He had aroused her interest more than any other man on the Union Pacific—her interest and her suspicions. She knew men loved to be asked questions about themselves, to receive compliments, but Hamilton would not abide a liar. If he truly had ulterior motives for the U.P., he would be clever enough not to take her flirtation seriously.

"Here, here. But not as interesting as you may believe."

Key tried to read innuendo into his tone but found none. As the meal progressed, she learned that he'd come from a good home and a well-respected family. He admitted being from San Francisco. "Did ye know Ted Judah?" she asked, hoping to catch him unaware.

Hamilton spilled the coffee he sipped.

She rose and dampened a towel, offering it to him. "I'm sorry. I didn't mean to startle ye."

"You didn't. I guess I drank too much at one time." He stood to wipe the stain but kept missing the soiled spot.

"Here, let me help." She took the cloth and gently wiped the offending liquid from his collar. The effort brought her dangerously close to his face. His eyes darkened to forest green.

"I thought it was the flower arrangement," his voice seemed unusually low, "but it's you who smells so lovely."

A knock on the door startled her. Key moved away from Hamilton as the door opened. The scowl on Davage's face warned he wasn't happy with what he saw.

"Looks like you two are enjoying the evening."

Hamilton grinned. "I'm afraid I've had a spill. Key was merely cleaning me up."

Davage studied Key and the obvious the care she had taken to make herself beautiful for Hamilton. His features hardened with every step into the car. He walked past her, toting his saddle and saddlebag toward one of the reading chairs.

Key couldn't believe his audacity. She excused herself from her invited guest and marched over to the crew chief.

"Just what do you think you're doing?"

Davage turned and brushed the dirt from his buckskins. Dust particles flew in the air, making her jump back in order to protect the black velvet. He let the saddle slide in a dirty heap on the carpet. "I'm supposed to keep an eye on you, aren't I?"

Before he could turn around, she tore into him with her forefinger, thumping him on the chest to punctuate her anger. "Don't think for one minute that you're going to hold to those orders while I'm entertaining. If I get into trouble tonight, Hamilton will get me out."

She offered her guest a look of confidence. Let him think she didn't get along near as well with Davage as he first believed. Perhaps then Hamilton would open up enough to trust her with his secrets. Her nose wrinkled at Davage. "Not to mention the fact that you smell worse than ten polecats and look like a porcupine who's met up with a sandstorm. You are not going to sit on my furniture looking and smelling like this, Davage Jansen—orders or no orders."

Davage's eyes lit with something more than anger. "Just what do you think you can do about it, Miss Calhoun?"

The cost of a bathscreen might be worth convincing Hamilton that she and Davage tolerated one another only for the general's sake! Pushing his chest hard, she sent him falling backward into the screen. The water she'd accidentally splattered on the floor during her own bath made him slip. Backward Davage teetered, heading directly for the lavender water.

Worried that she'd gone too far and fearing he might get hurt, Key tried to break his fall. But the momentum was too great. Davage landed with a tidal splash that drenched not only himself but her from head to foot. He sprawled in momentary shock. She stood there and tried not to laugh. Their gazes locked.

"Are you two all right?" Hamilton sped to lend a hand.

"I'm fine." Key brushed him away. She may be laying a trap for him, but she didn't have to let him touch her. Her lips quirked despite her struggle to keep them straight. "How about you, Davage? You okay?"

"Never been *wetter*." Davage raised his arms letting the water splash again.

Key squealed as she dodged out of the way.

Hamilton looked from one to the other and straightened his string tie. "The dinner was lovely, Miss Calhoun. Perhaps we can continue our conversation another day."

She did not want the evening to be a total waste. Remembering his jacket and hat, Key retrieved them and walked Hamilton to the door. "Another time, then."

He tipped his hat and rushed out onto the platform that formed a porch for the Pullman. "I'll look forward to that. . .when there's less company."

As Key closed the door, Davage's voice boomed from the bathtub, "I don't want him ever invited here again when you're alone."

Key settled her back against the door, considering Davage's demand. Of course, she must obey his wishes. After all, he was the crew chief. But why not use this to her advantage. . .and to his?

She marched over to her bureau and withdrew a razor strop and comb. Taking them to him, she countered with a demand of her own. "I'll agree, but on one condition. . .that I get to see how you look without a beard."

eight

Davage rubbed his chin, then rose awkwardly. "I'm going to be laughed at from here to Salt Lake."

Key jumped back, trying to avoid the puddle forming beneath his soggy buckskin. "Here, take this."

She offered him the razor strop. He accepted it and the towel she grabbed from a nearby hook. His hand lingered with her own. His pulse throbbed in his palm, revealing that Davage's heart raced as quickly as her own. "You're getting more water on the floor," she reminded softly.

"Guess I'd better change." His voice descended an octave lower.

"I'll heat up the stew while you're gone." She withdrew her hand from his, finding more than a little regret in how empty it now felt. Her gaze met his for the briefest moment. "The stew won't take long to reheat."

Key hurried to the stove to busy herself and keep her mind off the sensations spiraling within her.

"Would you like to ride into Fort Laramie with me tomorrow?" He moved toward the door. "I've got some business to take care of and thought you might enjoy spending the day with a friend of mine. You'll like Uva, and she'd enjoy attending church."

A day at the fort sounded wonderful, if only to give her a break from the monotony. Tomorrow was Sunday, and General Dodge did not allow work on the Sabbath. It would be wonderful to meet another woman brave enough to head west.

"Are you certain your friend won't think I'm imposing? I'm sure she has better things to do than take me to church."

"She'll skin my hide and make moccasins of it if she finds out I brought a woman within miles of the fort and didn't bring her to visit. Uva doesn't have much female company since she runs the bachelors' quarters at the post."

Bachelors' quarters? "I'll let you know when you get back from changing." Key concentrated on the task at hand. Not knowing quite what to do with herself, she poured a cup of coffee, sat down at the table, and sipped it slowly.

From the respect she'd heard in Davage's voice, Key guessed Uva was a fine lady. Yet she'd seen time and again how this rugged territory claimed many a woman's wit, charm, and virtue. Still, Key's curiosity over the bachelors' quarters conjured a dozen images.

Sooner than she expected, the stew bubbled and Davage had returned.

"That smells mighty good." He sat in Hamilton's former place.

"So do you." Key meant to chide him, but when she sat the bowl of stew in front of him, her words faded into an intake of breath. Her heart thumped wildly against her ribcage. She noticed every nuance of his rugged handsomeness once hidden beneath the blond whiskers. Davage looked much younger now, his face divided into two shades—the bronze tan from nose to forehead and the slightly pinker shade revealed beneath the new shave.

The black trousers and white double-breasted cotton shirt he wore fit like second skin. His shirt sleeves were rolled up in a comfortable fashion above the muscular swell of his forearms. Sandy-colored hair dried and curled in thick tufts along his collar, enhancing the rugged handsomeness of his face. She sat, feeling a bit off-balance by the wave of attraction that enveloped her.

"Will you say grace or shall I?"

"Why don't you?" Key bowed her head in respect.

Davage offered no memorized prayer as she expected but instead gave a heartfelt offering of thanks.

"Heavenly Father, bless this food to the nourishment of our bodies. Thank You, Lord, for watching over the families of each of the men while they're so far away from home and loved ones. Continue to walk beside the U.P., Sir, in its endeavor to bring this nation together by rail. For Your many blessings, we thank You and praise Your holy name. May we spread Your word and purpose with as much muster as we do the rails, Lord."

Key thought that even God in His heaven must thrill at the echoes of manly prayers resounding off the Rockies.

"Amen." Davage unthreaded his hands then began to eat.

Key ate sparingly, already full from the portion shared with Hamilton. The candles she'd lit for Hamilton now dripped wax onto the winter roses. She leaned over to snuff them out.

"Please don't." Davage placed a hand over hers. "I like to look at you in the candlelight."

Key rested her back against the chair and considered his compliment. To say it didn't please her would have been a lie, but *why* it pleased her was a truth that she needed to explore further. She studied him quietly as he ate. "I think you'd better tell me what's on your mind. First, you agree to shave off your beard, then you invite me to visit your friend. Now, you tell me you like how I look. What are you up to, Davage Jansen?"

He sipped his coffee, staring at her over the cup's rim. "I had to get your attention, and it seemed the only way. As for the beard, I always shave it come spring. It was time."

"So now that you have my undivided attention, why do you want it?" She liked the way he held the cup in his hands and how his lashes brushed the top of his cheeks as his eyes closed when he drank. The white of his shirt contrasted sharply with the bronze tint to his neck and forearms. He, too, looked attractive in candlelight.

"I've found out some things that may or may not warrant your suspicions about Hamilton. I'd rather you weren't alone with him until I'm sure."

"What sort of things?" She was sorry she might be right about Hamilton, yet grateful that Davage had truly listened to her concerns about the man's trustworthiness. The hard lines of Davage's face took on a luminescence that made her want to reach out and glide her fingers across the rugged firmness. Instead she hid them.

"Someone is buying up U.P. stock. A shipping company in San Francisco seems to be rather handy with funds when we run into delays. That left me wondering who else would be hurt by the completion of a railroad but the shipping companies that use the Cape to transport goods to the East Coast. A shipping company that suddenly has unlimited funds, exchanges those funds for stocks in order to help the railroad out when we get in a pinch. I smell a big fish, and some of its bait is riding the rails with us."

"Hamilton is from San Francisco," Key informed, though she suspected Davage would know that about his second-in-charge.

"I've never had a reason to mistrust Hamilton. . .until now."

"Why don't you just fire him?"

"No, then all I catch is a minnow. If I give him enough net, he'll snare himself and the whole fleet of swindlers. If I wait a while, maybe I'll find out my suspicions are all wrong and he's not even involved."

"Ye like him, don't ye?" Key appreciated his loyalty to his friend, though she suspected it misplaced.

"He was there after Clancy's death. I might have grieved myself to death if he didn't remind me every day that there was nothing I could have done to save Clancy. Your brother was a good friend to me."

She reached out in compassion and closed her fingers over Davage's hand as he toyed subconsciously with his spoon. Davage stiffened but didn't pull away. Key wondered how long it had been since Davage had allowed anyone to touch him so simply. "Did I thank ye for helping Clancy?" she asked softly.

His fingers flexed beneath hers. "I believe you did."

The touch set her soul to humming. "You didn't answer my second question." She needed to know whether he'd purposefully steered the conversation so that he wouldn't have to answer all she asked. "Why do you want me to go to the fort?"

His fingers gently edged away from hers. He lifted his spoon to scoop more stew, but the utensil stopped halfway to his lips. "Uva is all I've said she is. She's fun to be with, but she also listens well. She'll know if there's anything unusual going on in this part of the country that I should know about. She has a way of finding out everybody's business from here to the Tetons."

He finished the bite, then continued. "If I waltz in there and spend time alone with her, everyone will suspect I'm trying to get information. That might alert Hamilton. But if I bring another lady to visit, he and everyone else will expect you two to gossip about everything under the sun."

"I don't know whether to thank you for the compliment or be angry at the insult. Are you sure this will be necessary?"

"Whether he's there or not, we'll still need to be cautious. He may have agents working for him, and that's what I want to find out. I already suspect Coogan and a few others. I just want to be sure before I take action."

"What kind of clothes should I wear? I've been around the crew so long, I've fallen into some less-than-ladylike habits your friend may frown upon."

"Be yourself. Uva will like you just as you are. I do."

Key looked into his eyes and found something warm and inviting, like the soft gray-black shadows of midnight. She searched for some way to laugh off his sudden seriousness. "Is that why you avoid kissing me again?"

Disapproval darted across his features. He rose and grabbed the oil lamp from the reading table. "Pour some more coffee and let's talk."

As she refilled his cup, he sat on the davenport. She started to move toward the reading chair on the other side of the room, but he motioned her to sit beside him.

"What we're going to talk about needs to be discussed like we're old friends, not cordial strangers," he insisted. "Turn around here and tell me why you think you have to impress everyone you meet."

The danger Davage presented took on a more worrisome aspect. "I don't know what you mean," she evaded.

"Now you're lying. And if there's one thing I do know about you, Key, is that you don't lie."

"I don't try to impress people. I just don't want them to see my ignorance about things."

"Do you mind if I prop my knee up?" He looked at the distance that separated them on the davenport. "That spill I took was worse than ten days on a flatbed. I ache all over."

She didn't feel at ease with him making himself so comfortable, but she wouldn't tell him so. Instead, Key said, "Go ahead and stretch out if you like." When he seemed settled, she asked, "Did you see the look on Hamilton's face? He was out of here so fast he forgot to take his shadow! Don't you think he was wondering what I had planned for him?"

Their laughter mingled and a pleasant silence layered the Pullman.

"You're not ignorant, Key. Maybe you're confusing ignorance with something else."

Suddenly, he seemed very close and smelled very masculine despite the lavender. She wished immediately that she hadn't seen how deeply gray his eyes had become.

"I thought you were a brazen petticoat when you first came to work for us," Davage admitted. "Now that I know you better, I think you're playing some elaborate game with me. If that's so, Key, it's time the game ended. I'm beginning to care about you."

Key was drawn to his genuine interest in her and found herself weakening in her resolve not to succumb to his kindness. She could tell him the truth, but would he understand? Would any man understand what it was to be ridiculed because she lusted for life, enjoyed sharing wholly and completely all she had to give? How long had she wanted to share her heart's trouble with someone, yet couldn't? *Why Davage? Why now?*

He locked his fingers behind him and rested his head in his palms. Shifting again, he crossed one ankle over the other and settled in comfortably as if he intended to stay there for a while. "I'm all for talking to sagebrush and prairie chickens when I've got the lonesomes, but sometimes a person needs a voice to answer back. I've got all night and a willing ear. Tell me about you."

Where should she begin. . .or should she at all? Yet, he looked stubborn enough not to move off the davenport until she did so. *That would certainly cause a scandal among the crew!* She and Davage had become friends, good friends as far as she was concerned. She owed him a portion of her past. "You're acting so strange tonight, I'm beginning to wonder if there's anything between those willing ears."

"Blame it on the lavender and shaved beard." He shot her a heart-stopping grin.

"This started long before the lavender." Seeing that he deliberately ignored her delay tactics, Key took one of her waist-length curls and twisted it around her finger. She did not enjoy talking about the past and wished it was as easily manipulated as the strand of hair.

"Da was like most Irishmen who came from the old country," she began. "He took any job he could to make a living and support my mother and us children. The mill seemed a godsend; we were allowed to live in an apartment the company had built for the foreman. Da worked fourteen-hour days, six days a week, all for a boss he never saw. As long as he kept up the cord quota, his payroll came regularly. But when the quota was down, his salary mysteriously became delayed. So all of his time was spent working at the mill. My brothers worked there too, until the war came along and killed them."

She explained briefly about their deaths at Gettysburg, the telling cold and tearless. "All but Clancy, that is."

"Clancy never told me." Davage turned, crooked his elbow and rested his head on one palm. "And your mother?"

"An invalid. Much of the time she didn't know me. She had great memory losses for most of my life. The boys' deaths came as the final blow. She was never quite the same again."

He reached out and took the waist-length curl from Key's hand and began to twist it around his own finger. Then he realized what he'd done and let go. His fingers clenched into a fist.

"She's dead?" he asked roughly, almost as if he were angry with Key.

Once again he hid behind whatever barricade his past had erected to protect him from his feelings. Yet that single touch of compassion threatened to release the dam of tears that had welled in Key's eyes as she told of those hurtful years. "Aye," Key replied, the word barely a sigh but carrying with it the burden of grief.

"And your father?"

Key told briefly the story of her father's death at the hands of robbers, merely stating that she'd managed to escape.

"Have you ever been in love?" His eyes penetrated. "You still carry the Calhoun name. I'm assuming you've never married."

"I've been in love before, but the war claimed him too." Key told of John William and of her betrothed's preference to save a general rather than their hope for marriage.

"You wouldn't have loved him if he hadn't been that kind of man," Davage tried to soften her pain.

"I want to be the most important consideration to the man I love. Above everything. That's what I would give him of myself."

"Even before God. . .his *religion*?"

"My God would not require me to make that choice."

"Even before your country?"

"I have no country. This Union took everything and everyone I ever loved."

"Hard words from a Northerner."

"I'm not North or South. I'm Key Calhoun. I'm what matters to me. I have to be."

Davage sat up and crossed his legs Indian-style, rubbing his thighs where they had fallen against the tub. "Key, no man or woman stands alone forever. I'm a Southerner. I know it will take all of us working together to set this country back on its track. The country is kind of like the railroad. Doesn't it take every division of us from surveyor to back spiker to complete the job? Why do you think your brothers fought? Was it for their own safety or for the safety of your entire family?"

"They fought because they received better wages as soldiers than they did in the mill. It didn't matter that they were fighting a rich man's war of ideas and principles. They were poor Union boys just trying to make a better living. I doubt even they considered the issue of slavery other than they knew that our way of life offered them little more than slavery at best."

"And Clancy?"

"He worked the railroad so he could buy easily into its stocks."

"He loved the Union Pacific, Key. It was more than money. He was one of those rare men who saw the future of it, the good it would do the country, maybe even the opportunity it would give those classes of people who couldn't do well in the East."

"But it didn't do him any good, did it?" Anger sharpened her tone. "He died, like all my family. Working for someone else. Killing themselves for nothing." Her shoulders straightened. "Not me. No one's going to stop me from making my fortune and living my life the way I want. How I want."

"Sounds like someone has tried to tell you how."

"They have." She said no more. Harrisburg was no one's business but her own.

"Then why run? Why hide?"

Her back stiffened as resentment coursed through Key. "I'm not running. What do ye think I'm hiding from?"

"Yourself." He cupped her chin with his hand and gently urged her toward him. "You might say this isn't my business, but you're my friend. That makes you my business."

He rubbed one thumb against the bottom swell of her lips. "I care about you, Key. I see you hurting inside. You say all you want to do is to live some wild adventure, test your talents. But I see you testing your will against God's. I'm by no means a man of the cloth, and Lord knows, I've got my own troubles to set right with Him. But I do know this much—the only way you'll ever pass the test is to quit fighting the Teacher."

A feeling swept through Key, more powerful than anything she'd ever felt before. No one had ever looked beyond her outward facade and sought to strengthen her spirit. She memorized his face, full of genuine kindness and concern. Perhaps tomorrow, he would not be so companionable and she quite so ready to believe what she felt for Davage was nothing but friendship. But for tonight, she would let him ease her past miseries and begin a new future.

"I've only one thing to ask ye now." She willed the tension from her body and dared to let him see her vulnerability. "Will ye hold me again? Like ye did before? Not as a woman, Davage, but as yer friend. As one human being who needs to know someone else cares?"

When Davage wrapped his arms around her, Key gave herself to his embrace. His fingers stroked the long tresses that cascaded down her back. She could feel a stiff resistance that kept him distant, if not in body, then at least in mind. After several minutes, he started to move away.

"Please don't go," she whispered. "Just hold me a few moments more. Until I go to sleep."

He nestled against her back. She snuggled against him.

"Davage?"

"Yes?"

"Do ye sing?"

"Why?"

"I thought I heard ye singing with Duffy the other day. If it was, you have a talent other than railroading you need to pursue." She remembered his prayer at the table and knew the rich baritone blending with Duffy's could have only been Davage's.

"Tobiah and I learned to sing when we were in chur—when we were very young. It's difficult for him now."

She heard the loneliness in his voice and sensed he was recalling one sweeter than his own. Key turned over, clutched the white linen of his shirt and clung to him. But as her sympathetic heart reached, the misery that had been her past welled and flooded in her eyes, breaking the dam of tears held back far too long.

"I'm s–sorry." She could not control the sob that wrenched through her.

"Don't be. Cry it all out, Key. Cry until there are no more tears. God knows. . .I have."

Much later, when all the past hurt had been shed, Key fought sleep long enough to whisper, "Davage?"

"Yes."

"Don't ever stop being my friend."

When he brushed a light kiss against her upraised forehead, she thought for a moment that he had moaned. Her eyelids began to droop. His fist wrapped around the long curls that brushed her waist and lifted them to his cheek. Davage rubbed the thick ringlet against his skin then laid the curl back in its place. Gently, almost reverently, his finger began at the top of her forehead and traced a warm path down to the tip of her nose.

"The choice is no longer mine," he whispered.

A low, lulling hum of a lullaby filled the Pullman. Key's eyes blinked away the beloved image and her breath eased into the steady rhythm of sleep, leaving behind a smile to applaud his performance as he exited the Pullman.

nine

Ominous clouds loomed over the lofty brick walls of distant Fort Laramie, built in an oblong formation with bastions of adobe at two corners. The great gateway was floored with planks, while peddler stands, soldiers, and prospectors lined the entrance.

Key rode alongside Davage, wondering why so many gathered there. Reining her horse toward the flow of pilgrims heading into the fort, she soon found the answer. The overhead ramparts made a pleasant, shaded seat for the weary souls traveling to and from the great square. But the brisk breeze sent chill bumps up her arms and made her wish she'd worn heavier attire.

She ignored the cold and studied the individual apartments. They looked like ordinary blockhouses opening onto the inner courtyard. Despite the Sabbath, several whiskey mills and bawdy houses filled the business district with noise. This was certainly not the more genteel quarter of town, it seemed.

Davage had warned these dens would be packed to capacity due to the closure of traffic along the Bozeman Trail leading into the Black Hills. Prospecting in the Yellowstone had become a hair-raising experience since renegade Arapaho, Sioux, Crow, and even Cheyenne were on the warpath.

Standing alone at the north end of the fort, far detached from these rows of side-by-side commerce, rose a large two-story gallery with a sign identifying the quarters as "Old Bedlam."

"That's the place." Davage nudged his horse into a trot.

Key followed him to the freshly painted gallery. As he dismounted, she swung her leg over the sidesaddle. But she came to a jerking halt when the hem of her riding skirt hung on the horn. Davage glanced up and noticed her problem but was gentleman enough to turn away. But not before she saw him bite back a smile.

Still, he had the right to snicker. He'd told her not to exchange the Mexican saddle she'd used since hiring on, but she insisted upon riding sidesaddle, wanting to make a good impression on Uva. At least he didn't gloat. Davage moved toward her to help, but immediately halted. Someone else approached.

"Excuse me, ma'am. May I be of assistance?" a distinguished voice asked.

She tried to determine who among the colorful group of prospectors and bullwhackers surrounding her had spoken. A fancy-dressed man whose hands looked softer and smoother than her own offered to help. The crowd of well-wishers parted as the owner of the intriguing voice moved closer.

One of Key's feet dangled in the stirrup as she tried to work the hem from the horn. The soldier, obviously an officer from the shiny bars sewn on his blue-uniformed shoulders, stepped around to the other side and unhooked her snagged hem. Key settled both feet on the ground, then secured the reins around the hitching post. Offering a hand of gratitude to the handsome man, she thanked him.

"My pleasure, Ma'am."

Instead of shaking her hand as she expected, the soldier bowed and lightly brushed his lips across her gloved hand just below the knuckles.

With a flare, the soldier removed his hat and swept it under his left elbow, revealing a healthy thatch of sand-colored hair. "Sergeant Major Cord of the Third Calvary Regiment, at your service, Ma'am. Cleveland Cord."

"*Miss* Key Calhoun of the Union Pacific Railroad." Key loosened the rawhide knot securing her hat. She let it slide to the middle of her back and toyed with the string.

She brushed away wisps of blue-black curls escaping from the ribbon at the base of her neck.

"A *lady* with the railroad?" one of the rough-looking drifters taunted. He spit a stream of tobacco juice from his bewhiskered mouth. "Them 'Rapaho shot up so many of you railsplitters, you have to call in your womenfolk to string iron?"

Key could almost see color in the acrid puff of his cold breath.

Davage moved to her side and offered an arm to escort her into the building. "You ready? I ought to get you out of this cold."

"If you'll excuse me, Sergeant Major, I must be on my way," she apologized. "Thank you for your kindness."

"May I have the pleasure of calling on you later?" Cleveland Cord persisted. "Perhaps for dinner?"

"Well, I really don't know. . ." She looked at Davage and found only disapproval there. "I've come to visit Uva."

"Mrs. Blanks is hosting a sociable this evening. I'll see you then, Miss Calhoun. Be sure to save a place on your dance card for me. . .in fact, several places. Good day." The sergeant major tipped his hat in salute, then left.

"You make friends easy."

"Let's hope I do with Uva." Her gaze swept the remaining crowd and she smiled. "Good day, Gentlemen."

Key wasn't sure what she expected from a boardinghouse in the West, but certainly not the fine furnishings and harmonious simplicity of decor that she met upon entering. Black walnut walls surrounded floors of an elegant blend of manitou marble and thick carpets. Heavy cowhide furniture that could comfort large man-carved guests filled the massive room, but draperies and doilies sewn in patterns of sunflowers and rosettes gave the room a feminine spriteness.

"Of all people!" a musical voice resounded from above. "Come here and let me look at you!"

Key's attention went from the elaborate furnishings to the owner of the dainty voice—a stunning redhead who swept down the stairway leading to a second floor filled with doorways. The woman opened her green-satined arms wide, revealing a voluptuous figure that filled her shirtwaist to near bursting. But the sparkle in the woman's vivid violet eyes most interested Key as Davage took a bounding leap up the staircase to greet the woman.

He lifted the woman in his arms, each equally thrilled to see one another. Davage whispered something in her ear and she giggled as he carried her down the steps like a cradled baby.

"Put me down, you big Texan," the redhead squealed, waiting until he deposited her on the marble floor. Standing beside him now, she didn't quite reach his shoulders. Barely five feet tall, if that much!

"Who's this beauty you have here?" The woman turned her wondrous eyes upon Key.

"Uva Blanks," Davage motioned toward Key, "meet Miss Key Calhoun."

Uva held out her gloved hand. "Proud to meet you, Miss Calhoun. Hope your stay here is enjoyable."

Key thanked her. "Your place is beautiful." *And so are you,* Key noted, *despite your reported forty-some-odd years.* When Davage had told her about his friend, she'd anticipated a matronly woman with graying hair and grandmotherly ways.

"For now it is." Uva walked behind the long mahogany counter running the length of the wall a few feet from the stairs. She turned the register around for Davage to sign. He stepped aside and let Key sign for herself.

"But just wait until tonight," Uva continued. "You folks came just in time for my sociable, and this one's always the most fun. This place will be full of dirt-tromping, slick-haired, spiffed-up fellows wanting to raise the roof off with their toe-tapping jigs. I'll have to wipe Wyoming clay off the ceiling for weeks afterward."

"A dance?" Key hoped she wouldn't offend the woman, but she'd never learned to dance well. Ma and Da disagreed over whether or not such frolicking was appropriate. Ma won the argument, as she always did. But Key suspected Da stubbornly clung to his opinion because he was as inept as his only daughter at keeping the right foot forward. Ma took solace in having six sons willing to sashay her around the floor.

"Why is this sociable more fun than most?" Key steered the conversation to safer ground. "Is this a holiday I've forgotten?"

"Ought to be. Who knows, maybe one day someone'll make it a custom. You see, the ladies get to ask the gents, not the usual turnabout." Uva chuckled.

Davage didn't laugh. His gaze penetrated Key. "Some of them won't be happy watching their ladies in the arms of other men."

Uva stared first at Davage, then at Key, one brow arching. "It's whose wagon she rides home in after the last dance that counts. Besides, there aren't enough women to go around. It's every woman's Christian duty to dance at least once with every man before the evening's through. We consider it paying her respects."

"Excuse me, Uvvie. I gotta get our warbags so Key can freshen up." He rushed outside as if a fire burned at his heels.

"Well, that's a first." Uva stared at him, her mouth agape.

But Key was too disturbed by something else her hostess had said to worry over Davage's odd behavior. "You did say *Ladies,* didn't you?" she asked hesitantly.

Uva blinked off whatever had filled her thoughts and nodded at Key. "Those other gals who frequent the tents don't come to my place." She patted Key's hand. "And don't you worry, a decent woman in this territory is a real prize and does a man honor by agreeing to sashay with him. Any cayuse tries to get out of hand, well. . ." Uva pointed toward a double-barreled shotgun racked on the wall. "Old Vindicator and I distribute judgment as we see fit."

"You'd actually shoot someone?" Though she'd challenged Davage about not shooting her brother to end his misery, the thought of truly killing someone to settle a difference seemed unthinkable to Key.

Uva glanced to see if anyone was within listening distance. "Of course not," she whispered, "but I figure people tend to respect your territory more if you lay down a few rules to show 'em your boundaries."

Moses and the Ten Commandments sprang to Key's mind. She could imagine Uva in his place, a prophet of goodness, conquering the wilderness of the Black Hills. "So this sociable is a part of a greater plan," Key decided, not realizing she'd muttered it aloud.

"Exactly." Uva's face brightened. "You *do* understand. I can see you and I are going to get along well."

"I certainly hope so." Key didn't tell the woman she couldn't dance. "Can I help during the festivities tonight?

Uva smiled, her eyes softening to deep violet. "I believe you'll be too busy talking with the men about your experiences with the railroad."

"So you do understand." Key warmed to the lady's kindness, echoing Uva's previous statement about their blossoming friendship, "I can see you're right. We are going to get along well."

"You'd like to freshen up, I'm sure," Uva offered. "Let me show you to a room while Davage is putting away your things." She led the way to the upstairs landing and opened the door to the farthermost room in the north corner. "It'll be noisy tonight. I'll apologize for the inconvenience now."

"I don't think we're planning on staying the entire evening." Key decided she needed to explain so Uva wouldn't be offended. "We only have one day to visit before we must be back to work. I'm sure Davage will want to leave early, especially if the weather doesn't hold."

When Uva led Key into an immaculate room, she caught Key's roving gaze. "It's not much for a woman, but the men who bunk here don't spend much time in their rooms. With God's hills to hunt and rivers to fish in, would *you* stay inside?"

Key laughed. "I don't expect I would. And this is more than adequate. Thank you, Mrs. Blanks."

"Call me Uva. Everyone does."

When Uva hesitated to leave, Key felt a moment of awkwardness. She mulled what to say and wondered what was taking Davage so long. "Will I get to meet your husband tonight?" she asked, only now realizing Davage had not spoken of Mr. Blanks.

"Darlin', I do hope so. He's been gone so long, maybe a sociable *would* bring him back." Wistfulness made Uva's face look momentarily older, more fragile.

"Oh, I'm sorry. I didn't know." With Uva's husband gone, had she and Davage become more than friends? Ashamed of herself for considering such a thing, Key blushed when Uva smiled and shook her head.

"No need to fret, Miss Calhoun. Others have doubts about mine and Davvy's friendship. But I let them speculate. Keeps unwanteds away from me. He may look like a big, old, cuddly bear, but Davage can be a handful when he wants to be. He and Grenville—"

"General Dodge?"

"Yes. He and General Dodge helped me search for Shorty when he didn't come back from the Black Hills. I thought I'd needed a man to keep me going that first year, but Davage taught me all I needed was myself and a couple of faithful friends."

She sighed. "My pride and my heart were more than crushed, I can tell you, because I couldn't think of any better man than Davage to nurse my wounds with."

Uva smiled at Key. "But thank the Lord for common sense and Davage Jansen. Because of him, we've been fortunate enough to remain friends all these years. That's even rarer than lovers. It's easy for a man to love you out here where women are scarce, but to just plain *like* you. That's the real challenge. From the way he looks at you, I'd say he likes you extremely well."

"We're just good friends." Key felt uncomfortable discussing him with someone she hardly knew and who obviously cared very deeply for him.

"Be careful. He's tied to a past that won't be easy to fight." Uva gazed out the window. "Maybe I like to tell myself that so I don't have to feel so badly about not being able to win his heart. Then again, maybe I've always known Shorty would return someday and that's why Davage and I are only meant to be friends."

Her eyes now focused on Key. "I tell you one thing, though. Davage never looked at me the way he does at you. But that's not for me to ponder, is it?"

She waved Key toward the bed. "I'm sure you're wondering why I'm stalling. Please sit and rest yourself. We need to hurry or Davage will run out of things to do. He can only take so long to gather baggage. And like you say, it is getting nippy out there." Key sat on the feather-tick mattress while Uva took the chair.

"Davage said I was to tell you the latest happenings at the fort."

"When did he do that?" Suddenly the exact moment registered in Key's mind—when he'd lifted Uva into his arms and whispered something in her ear. She'd giggled as if he'd told her a joke or something saucy. *No one suspected a thing!* "Go on. I remember now."

Mischief lit Uva's eyes. "I'm sorry. At the time, I didn't know if you were friend or foe. It was the only way for him to let me know quickly." Uva leaned closer and, in a hushed tone, said, "Rest a little. Then we'll attend church. I'm not sure that will yield us as much information as tonight's sociable will, however. When you get battering rams together under one roof, they tend to butt heads and brag."

Walking to the door, she barely cracked it open and peeked out into the hallway, then closed it softly. "Talk is a freighting company has Fear No Man on its payroll. I've been keeping my eye on a fellow who's supposed to be working for the company. But he's not real smart. He hangs around town too much, and that makes me wonder when he has time to freight. I think he must be spying for someone and keeping close to the fort. Sooner or later, all business dealings, good or murderous, wind up here. I've sent a wire to an agent friend of mine in Washington to find out what he can about the freighting company, but he's having no luck."

"Ask him if there is a shipping company by the same name out on the West Coast," Key suggested. "Possibly in the San Francisco area."

"You sound like you already know about this."

"Not completely. But we've had some delays with the tracks, one of those being Fear No Man. It makes sense that if he's on the shipping company's payroll, then he's being paid to stop the work. Do you have the name of the freighting company?"

"J & S Cargo Company."

"J & S?"

"Judah and Saxon, prominent families in the Bay City."

Key dropped her reticule and the heavy clink of coins punctuated the thick tightening in her chest. *Ted* Judah, her and Clancy's mentor? Ted and *Hamilton* Sax. Hamilton *Saxon?* Could it be?

ten

The sociable was full-blown—merry, excited and lively. Two hundred people enjoyed Old Bedlam's crowded parlor. Furniture had been moved to the far edges of the wall, some taken upstairs and placed against the landing. The carpets had been removed and now dozens of feet stamped over the marble flooring to the tune of "Turkey In the Straw." Uva wouldn't have to wipe the dust from the ceiling as she feared. A thin layer of snow blanketed the fort's courtyard, providing a welcome cleanliness of boot soles.

Most of the men bore the rough brand of soldier, prospector, or rail-splitter. Unfamiliar with social graces, their feet seemed in defiance of the tune being played. Dressed in their prairie finest, the women reminded Key of the childhood tales of sprite wood nymphs, graceful and glowing from the abundance of male attention.

Though other men were clean-shaven, the cut of Davage's rugged physique in the buckskins made him a favorite choice among the women. Key watched him for several reels, noting that the women who chose him looked spellbound when he escorted them back to the sidelines.

He did have a certain charm about him that few men possessed. A charm and a challenge. Perhaps it was the secure feeling Key had when she was with him, knowing that he wanted no bride and she no husband at this point in her life. Still, she'd chosen her clothes for the gathering carefully. He'd teased her incessantly about Sergeant Major Cord. Now it was her opportunity to torment him.

Key decided it was time to quit watching from the landing and actually join the party. She'd stalled all she could without being rude. Perhaps her good fortune would hold and someone would involve her in a conversation that would keep her from the dance floor. However, the thought of sashaying around held one promise. . .to keep warm. Already the nails on the boards were white with frost, and her fingers felt numb and stiff despite her gloves.

It would be a shame to have spent so much money on a fine dress, then not be able to wear it because of the chilly temperature. Heat from the stoves and the swelling crowd awaited her, offering Key the hope that downstairs might be warmer than her rented room.

She descended the stairs, smiling at the admiring looks from the men who waited below. Her long, blue-black hair was piled on her head in an elabo-rate, formal style, allowing a chill to sweep across the back of her neck. She'd bathed in the lavender soap and corseted and laced herself until she could scarcely breathe. The royal blue, watered-silk gown had been chosen to match the night-sapphire of her eyes. Though Uva offered rice powder to dust her fine complexion, Key elected to forego any enhancement and merely pinched her cheeks to add a slight rosy hue.

"There you are, my dear." Uva introduced her to a circle of men who began to gather near them.

Key smiled, allowing Uva to parade her around, showing off the "new" woman in the territory—a woman whose daily work routine had carved the fine contours of her figure into a radiance of health.

Spit-polished and clean-shaven men deluged her with questions, blatant courting, and astonished respect for the job she held with the Union Pacific. Key found herself the talk of the party. . .but not as she had been in Harrisburg. Here, in this wondrous place called Laramie, she did not have to worry about her past. No one wanted to know. Her personal history was an almost forbidden subject. . .not only for herself, but for anyone else as well.

Everyone accepted her for what she was now. How she could grow to love the kind of territory that harvested this sort of people and this kind of acceptance! Key listened as the conversations fluttered from her to the weather and assorted small-talk. One lady declared to Key that she'd spent all day yesterday and this morning ironing the friz from her hair and wor-ried that she still looked as if she'd met up with a twister. Another lady was certain that her stays would pop the first time she alamanded left. Despite the discomfiture, men and women alike seemed ready to forget their shy-ness, thinness, obesity, small stature, stuttering and other frailties, simply to enjoy the comradery.

"Did you come here to eavesdrop or to dance?" a voice asked from behind her.

Key turned and stared into Davage's eyes as they focused on her in frank approval. She felt as if he were measuring her in some way. Was he compar-ing her with the other women he'd known? "Actually, I came down to stay warm."

"That's a worrisome thought." He stepped back to admire her once again. "You should have told me you were going to dress formal. I'd have worn something better myself."

"You look well enough, but I've noticed several of the men have cuts and bruises. What happened?"

"A fight. No—I didn't join them. I haven't got the time nor the inclination for saloons." He nodded toward a group of strangers whose attention seemed riveted on his and Key's every word. In a hushed tone, Davage added, "You have a room full of admirers, it seems."

"You haven't exactly been Sam-sit-in-the-shade yourself."

"Glad you noticed."

He smiled—a wicked grin that made her look away quickly. The memory of his lips kissing her own was strong. She focused across the room on the table laden with beverages and food. "I always try to find a friend in a crowd of people."

He thumped a fist against his chest, pretending an arrow had pierced him. "You inflict much pain, O one with face of sacred lily and forked tongue of serpent."

She tried not to be amused, but Key was in too good a humor.

Suddenly, he bowed much as Cleveland Cord had done earlier in the day. "If you would do me the honor, dear *friend,* may I have the pleasure of this dance."

Her smile froze, her voice lowering to a whisper. "I d–don't know how."

"Then I'll teach you."

Before she could protest further, he drew her into his embrace and waltzed her out into the swirling crowd. They managed to make it several yards across the dance floor before he halted.

"What are you doing?" Davage asked.

"Counting. What does it look like I'm doing?"

"The waltz is more of a slide this way, up, down. Then slide that way, up, down. Yes, that's right. Slide this way, up, down. Now that way. . .you're doing fine. Ouchhh!"

"Oops. . .forgive me." Key concentrated on watching Davage's feet. But she kept getting distracted by the mass of heated faces, clinging arms, and twirling flounces whirling around her in a kaleidoscope of joy and laughter.

The roar of the fiddler's bow and the wail of the harmonica made talking near impossible. Not that she could talk and dance at the same time, anyway. Too much sliding and up-downing going on. Still, Key wanted to know whether their visit to the fort had been worthwhile and wondered what Davage had learned this afternoon. When she leaned closer to his ear to ask a question, he jerked his face to one side and glanced at her inquiringly.

"I'm not going to bite you," she said.

His mouth moved, but she didn't hear him. Finally, he managed a "What?" over the noise.

"I said. . .I'm not going to bite you," Key yelled over the din. The music stopped, reverberating her shout through the abrupt silence. Heat deeper than the color of Uva's gown scalded Key's cheeks as all eyes focused on her outburst.

Davage chuckled.

"The music was loud," Key began to explain to those around them. "He couldn't hear what I was saying, so I leaned closer." Mortified, she realized she was just digging herself in deeper.

"That's all right, ma'am," the fiddler announced. "I 'spect he's been bit by a sight less pretty than you."

The crowd laughed, and Davage had the decency to flush a distinctive shade of pink. She joined him.

"All's forgiven," the fiddler declared and picked up his bow. "Ladies, grab your partners!"

The reel was a favorite and many of the men were left without someone to dance with. Key noticed as several pulled out red bandannas to wrap over their right arms. "What are they doing?" she asked as Davage and the other men lined up in rows opposite the women.

"Not enough of you ladies to go around. So before the sociable, we drew straws. Anyone who got a short straw has to be a heifer and dance like a gal. The heifers wear the bandannas." The men paired off and extended the rows.

"Did you draw short?" If she was going to stumble around, then she preferred it be with Davage only.

"Salute your partners now!" the fiddler called.

Davage bowed as she watched what the others did, then curtsied. With a wink, he said, "Uva's missing a considerably long broomstraw."

Key laughed as she tried to keep up with the others. She backed away, then moved forward only to lock the wrong arm with Davage. He spun her around the correct way, then gently pushed her toward her next partner, Cleveland Cord! She looked back at Davage and realized that all pairs had exchanged partners. Key started to turn away and head back toward the refreshment table, but a hand shot out and stopped her.

The sandy-haired soldier linked fingers with her and drew her into a human bridge for the other couples to sashay through. This she could handle.

"I'm disappointed, Miss Calhoun," he said, his tone genuinely discouraged.

"Oh?" She glanced down the line to locate Davage. *Please hurry back,* she willed him.

"The party has been going full swing for two hours, and you haven't asked me to dance once," he gently complained. "You do remember, it's *lady's* choice?"

Though marble, Key felt the quiver of the floor through her slippers as those who did not dance clapped their hands and stamped their feet to the lively tune.

The bridge unlinked. Everyone turned their backsides to their partners. Key did the same, wondering what came next. His hands grabbed hers, bring their bodies back to back. He tried to sashay several steps, but her feet tangled in her skirts. Key let go and faced him. "I can't do that part," she apologized.

"No problem. We'll just let the others go by us. But you will dance with me later won't you, Miss Calhoun? This hardly constitutes a full dance."

"I'll try my best to, Sergeant Major," she evaded, glad for the excuse Uva had unknowingly given her earlier. "But I may only have time to dance with each man once tonight."

"Then may the night linger long." He gave her hand a quick kiss before being swept away to his next partner.

Several exhausting minutes later, Davage returned to Key and the last round of the reel ended with thunderous applause. "I'm thirstier than a three-year drought," he announced, his handsome features suddenly wincing in pain. "Want some punch? I think I'll sit this one out."

"Are you all right?" Key noticed his breath had become not only ragged but labored. Did he suffer from more than sleepwalking? "You've hurt yerself, haven't you? You should have said something. You certainly shouldn't be dancing."

"I'm fine. Just tired all the time." Davage waved away her concern. "The post doc said a good night's sleep away from that clanging iron ought to do me good. Now, I suggest we get some punch before everyone else takes the same notion."

Perhaps giving him time to get her the refreshment wouldn't obligate him to dance with anyone. "I'd love some."

While Davage set off toward the punch table, Key searched the crowd for Uva. Instead, she spotted Cleveland Cord. He seemed in earnest conversation with a burly-looking man whose orange-red hair drew immediate attention. Standing beside him was the man she knew as Ox Naagen. Cord's cohorts had not been at the dance long. Flakes of snow still dusted their hats and coats.

The strains of the next song began. An impulse that something of interest transpired with the three men urged Key forward. Perhaps she could learn useful information before Davage returned. She walked up to the sergeant major and grit her teeth against the torture she was about to inflict upon herself. "May I have the pleasure, Cleveland?"

The soldier turned, a look of dark anger storming his eyes. Quickly masking the irritation, his expression settled into one more amiable. "Of course, Miss Calhoun. I'd be delighted. Excuse me, gentlemen."

Something about the red-haired man disturbed Key. The way his jaw tightened and flexed when Cleveland said her name. Did she know him? Key arched a brow of inquiry at her partner. "Aren't ye going to introduce me?"

Cleveland seemed in a sudden hurry. "Gentlemen, Miss Key Calhoun of the Union Pacific railroad. Miss Calhoun, this is Cane Hager of the J & S Cargo Company, and you may already know Ox Naagen, a rail layer on your crew."

So, this was the freighter Uva had described to Davage. She found it difficult to keep suspicion from her tone. "I believe I've had the pleasure of meeting Ox." She tried to ease the conversation by teasing, "It's a tongue-lashing we'll get from the general when we get back, isn't it?"

Before Ox could answer, Cleveland offered his arm and urged her toward the throng of dancers. "I can't share her fine company further, gents. I've waited all evening for this opportunity, and we've used up enough of the song already."

His cohorts doffed their hats, then left as promptly as they'd come. From the way they had to fight with the door and the force of the blowing snow as they departed, Key worried about the worsening weather. The temperature was dropping, yet no one else seemed alarmed. Perhaps she worried needlessly.

When Cleveland led her into the two-step, Key realized that what she had thought was the wail of the harmonica was also the rising moan of the wind. "Trouble?" she asked as she followed his lead. Fortunately, he was little better at dancing than she. He didn't seem to notice her coltish steps.

"No, why do you ask?"

She found herself comparing Davage's and Cleveland's footwork and decided the sergeant major came up short-soled.

"Ox and Mr. Hager left as soon as they came. Since they didn't stay for the sociable, I assumed they had a message to give you."

"I asked them to leave because they'd been drinking. We were discussing their departure when you arrived with your pleasant invitation."

That would certainly explain his look of anger. Perhaps she'd misjudged the man. *Judge not, that ye be not judged,* Key reminded herself. But at what point was suspicion healthy? Caution warned her not to discuss the two men with him any further. "There's Davage. And look, he brought punch. I'm afraid I'll have to make this the last dance for a while. I did send him after refreshment, and it would only be ri—"

Another woman, large and insistent-looking, tapped her on the shoulder and asked if she might intrude. Key smiled at Cleveland who, to his credit, bowed and told the woman of his esteemed pleasure at being chosen. "Perhaps later," Key muttered, relieved to be free of him and the dance floor.

"I'll be waiting," he insisted, then took up the rolling gait of the corpulent woman.

Seeing the expression on Davage's face, Key wondered what had caused him to lose his good humor. She shouldered her way through the crowd to reach him. Accepting the glass of refreshment he offered, Key asked, "Was it that difficult to get punch?"

"You didn't need to send me away." He saluted her with his own glass. "If you wanted to dance with Cord, you should have just said so."

eleven

He was jealous! Deep within two feelings flared—anger at his audacity and pleasure to know he might care more than friendship. "I told you I was cold," Key reminded. "I wanted to stay warm while you were gone. As crowded as the refreshment table looks, I thought you might meet up with Shorty and I'd never see you again."

Davage motioned toward the landing. "Let's drink our punch up there. Uva told you about Shorty?"

Most visitors remained downstairs, all trying to keep warm. One of the davenports was completely empty allowing Key and Davage an opportunity to sit and watch the party below.

"A little," Key said. "About how he'd found gold in the Black Hills and built this place for her. How he didn't come back and you helped her come to terms with it all."

"She hasn't really. Uva still gets up every morning and makes coffee the way he likes it, expecting him to walk into the kitchen hollering for his breakfast." Davage stared affectionately at his long-time friend as she served refills to her visitors. "It's been over five years now. He came up missing about the time the U.P. first surveyed this area and were having trouble with the Crow. Will you look at that?" He pointed to a man snarling his nose up at the bite of sandwich he'd taken then spit the distasteful mouthful in a vase of winter primroses. "I'd do the same, partner," Davage said in sympathy. "I'm a steak man myself."

Key liked the way Davage's eyes gleamed with humor. He always seemed to see humor in the little things in life. He didn't try to impress anyone with what he could be, he seemed comfortable in having people accept him for what he was. Perhaps he wasn't as refined as Cleveland Cord, but Davage had one of the finest souls she'd ever met. She had learned from him that using one's talents was one thing, but the greater talent was letting one's work speak for itself.

Cleveland Cord! "Oh goodness, I forgot to tell you something important!" Key lowered her voice so another couple resting a few feet away from them would not overhear her. She told Davage about the sergeant major's discussion with Ox and Cane Hager. "You don't suppose he's lying, do you?"

Davage stood. "I don't know, but it sheds a new light on the sabotage we've been dealing with if he, and particularly the military, are involved. I'd better hightail it over to headquarters and dig up what background material I can about your sergeant major."

"*My* sergeant major?" Key linked her arm through his and headed downstairs. Halfway she paused, her shoulders trembling and her teeth chattering. "It's terribly cold. I think I'll ask Uva if she has an extra coat I can borrow."

Key walked him to the door, waited to bid him to hurry back, then was astonished when he couldn't get the door open. "What is it?" she asked, a sense of dread filling her as she noted the ice forming around the door hinges.

"I'm not certain. Let me try the back door first. No need to panic anyone . . .yet."

Had the snow fallen so hard that it formed drifts against the door? Were they snowed in? The trek to the back door was slow-moving due to the sheer volume of the crowd. Once there, their luck took a turn for the worse.

"What are we going to do?" she asked.

"We need to make an announcement before anyone gets the idea to try it on their own. If need be, Uva's got plenty of food to keep us fed for a couple of days, I imagine. Just pray this storm isn't one of those two-weekers."

"Two weeks!" Key had known winters back home that kept them in for days, but weeks? The food would never last that long, nor the pile of wood to keep the dampers filled for the sociable. "Will some try to return to their own quarters?"

"I don't know." Davage rubbed a finger over his eyebrow as he considered all the possibilities open to them. "If it's as bad as I think it is, they could get lost two feet off the porch and freeze to death. All I can do is leave it up to each man to make his own choice. The women stay."

Key clung to his arm as he rushed back through the crowd to reach the fiddler's stand that rose above the dance floor. She waited to one side, folding her hands protectively beneath her breasts in order to stop the trembling provoked more by fear now than cold.

The music ended abruptly. "Pardon me, folks. Sorry to interrupt your evening, but Mother Nature has decided to give a final blow before she lets spring set in." A look of concern washed over the crowd as he continued. "Seems we have a storm on our hands, ladies and gents. We ought to be deciding whether we're going to dance it out or try to make an effort to get back to our homes and children."

As if to accentuate his words, the wind howled. Murmurs rippled through the gathering. Several gentlemen fetched their wives then headed for the door.

"Don't mean to tell you your business, but I vote we leave the ladies here at Uva's." Male approval swept the room. "Uva, do you have a rope? A long piece. Hopefully one that will reach from Old Bedlam to the mercantile?"

"I've got one. If that isn't long enough, I could use my linens."

"No, keep anything that can be used for warmth in the event this lasts longer than we expect."

Tension layered the room. Everyone's mind focused on the one fear no one was willing to speak—*blizzard.*

"What are you going to do?" Key asked as Uva returned with the rope.

Davage accepted the rawhide, looped it around his chest and tied it securely. "Plan to see if I can reach another building. If I can, then we men can weather the storm there and leave the food and beds to you women."

Uncertainty filled Key. He meant to spare the women in case the storm lasted so long it forced starvation. "But what about your ribs? The rope will hurt them worse. Don't go, Davage. We can all make it here. Have a little faith."

Her concern that he wasn't listening to her gave way to dread. What if he didn't come back? He was compelled to play hero just as John William had. But heroes died and left brokenhearted. . .friends? She refused to deal with another death. "You w–won't come back," she whispered.

"Where's that faith you spoke of?" Davage teased. "Besides, if I can survive this rope, I'll survive anything."

"What?" Was he making jokes. . .now of all times?

"Long story I'll tell you when I get back."

Key kissed him, ignoring several feminine gasps that erupted from the onlookers. When she moved away from him, she tugged the knot that held the rope tightly against his chest.

"Don't you die out there, Davage Jansen. I don't make friends that easily, despite what you think."

She wrapped the closest edge of rope in her gloved hands. "I'll be the first one to welcome you back. Uva get a coat for Davage, please. Some of you men, open that door if it takes the whole lot of you. Ladies, grab an end of the rope and hang on tightly."

Davage accepted the buffalo skin coat one of the men offered him and put it on. As he did so, four burly freighters managed to jar open the door. Several resounding kicks from the tremendous boots opened a pathway over the drift. Davage waved a jolly goodbye and winked encouragingly at Key. "Last man to the water trough buys me an antelope steak. Horns peeled," he joked. The crowd laughed, eagerly latching onto his buffoonery to boost their lagging spirits.

Davage literally jumped up and onto the drift, his only way to get above the snow holding them prisoner. As she strained to listen, Key willed the wind to stop. The screeching wail muffled any moan he might have made as Davage rolled. She gripped the rope tightly, entreating God to help her hold the lifeline.

Davage disappeared from sight. The rope levelled off at the top of the snow. . .warning that the drifts were already chest-high.

❧

Davage waded through the river of white, the weight of the buffalo robe cumbersome and the pressure on his ribs a constant pain. Occasionally the wind lifted the snow in whirling eddies, giving him moments of vision. But after he'd trekked past the protection of Old Bedlam's framework, the open space between the bachelor quarters and the other buildings he knew stood down the way became a white blast of hell. The fury of the wind as it wailed in madness through the unbuffeted zone flung swirls of driven snow and ice into his face and body.

The blasts hit him from both sides, catching him off-balance. He fell backward, and the rope went slack. Air barreled from his lungs, leaving him empty and shaken. He inhaled. Cold rushed through his nose and throat, stinging his innards and reminding Davage that he was indeed injured. Had the fall jerked the rope loose?

Davage scrambled to regain his footing, clawing his way through the snow. *Lord,* he called upon his Maker, *steady me.* His boots slipped, sending him backward yet again. He couldn't take many such falls or he'd lose consciousness from lack of air. The cold and stinging wind sealed his eyelashes together with ice. *A little help is better than none at all,* he challenged, his anger at the Lord for only partially helping Tobiah recover from the near-hanging still an open sore festering his pride. *I'm not calling on You for my sake, but for Key and all the others. I gotta get back to them or they'll try this again. They'll die out here, Lord.*

Soon he could no longer move by sight alone but was forced to use instinct and memory instead. *Why do You never hear me?*

He knew he needed to get back on his feet and retrace his steps. *Use the rope to guide you back,* an inner knowing wailed with the wind. No one would get anywhere in this blinding storm. In no time at all, it would be an all-out blizzard.

It would take a miracle for him to find Old Bedlam again. And miracles were not something Davage relied on. When he'd played cowboy and cal with his brother, and the rope accidentally tightened around Tobiah's neck, Davage had prayed heaven down to save his brother's life. Though Tobiah survived, he'd never regained his ability to speak. The tragedy convinced Davage that, for him, miracles were offered only in half-measures.

But if something miraculous didn't happen now, he'd be lost in the storm. Someone might foolishly risk his life—or *her* life—to save him. Davage couldn't take the chance on Key daring to search for him in this fury. And she would. . .she believed her will stronger than God's.

He couldn't let that happen. For the first time since Tobiah's tragedy, Davage trusted someone else's faith other than his own. He bowed his head and prayed, not for his life, but that he could overcome his halfhearted faith.

Get on your feet, a voice mingling with the wind ordered. *Grab the rope.* Davage focused all his effort on standing. Suddenly, the rope pulled taut, jerking him backward.

➷

Key felt the rope jerk, tugged on it, then realized there was more slack than last time. Had Davage found the mercantile? Had he loosened the rope? She could think of no other reason for its laxness unless he was in trouble and down. A vivid image of him lying in the snow, face turning blue from the cold filled her mind.

"Something's wrong," she yelled to the leaning line of tuggers behind her. "Some of you larger men, get up here and help me. Davage is in trouble."

Massive hands and shoulders took the forefront. Inch by slow inch the rope grew longer at the gallery door. An avalanche of snow plummeted into the entrance as a furry bulk was tugged into view.

"Davage, are you all right?" Key cried, her voice a shrill screech.

She rubbed his hands to warm them, flicked snow from his face, then brushed the ice from his lashes. Finally his eyes opened, revealing an ornery, conscious Texan.

"I would have been, woman, if you hadn't tried to drag three years of Sundays out of me," he complained.

In exasperation, she brushed away the remainder of snow from the buffalo robe. "You *worried* three years out of me."

A round of tentative laughter filled the room as Davage stood. Key could see he was not at all as unshaken about the ordeal as he would like them to believe. The laughter quickly settled into subdued concern as his grim expression warned what they all feared.

"Certain death awaits anyone who tries to leave."

His words struck the crowd silent as if he'd hit them with a spiker's maul. "Then let's pray for a miracle," Key announced, joining one hand to

Davage's and offering her other to the next man in line behind her. Soon, everyone had locked hands. "Davage, will you lead us in prayer?" she asked.

He hesitated. But the conviction of belief lighting her eyes was so earnest he felt his heart grow lighter and years of anger at the Lord shed itself from Davage's heart. Surprising himself, he bowed his head and thanked God for the miracle he'd already experienced—the miracle of Key Calhoun in his life—then he asked for a second one—that Uva's guests be spared.

twelve

Being the kind of folk who made the best of their trials and tribulations, the people of Fort Laramie dug in and enjoyed themselves. . .for a time. Three days the winter storm raged, taking its toll on the manners and temperaments of the cooped-in crowd.

Uva allotted sleeping shifts on the available beds upstairs. Once every seventeen hours, Key rested her weary feet and back along with three other women. In the remaining hours, the ladies milled about, helped cook, ate, or danced. The wood supply depleted quickly, so now huddling in groups or dancing seemed to be the only way to keep warm.

Like cut flowers, several of the women wilted under the marathon effort. Some of the men fared no better. Stubble sprouted on the once clean-shaven faces, bringing with it prickly dispositions once hidden beneath earlier slick manners. Perspiring bodies, along with the lack of an indoor privy considerably discouraged future marriage prospects.

Gamblers, prospectors, and soldiers alike wished for the wide-open ranges of the Rockies. Ladies complained of the men's arguesome natures, stating they were relatively certain that grizzly bears had better dispositions. But Uva always managed to bring a cautionary peace to the courting room without having to resort to using Ol' Vindicator.

Around midnight of the third evening, someone tapped Key on the shoulder as she stared off into the blinding white nothingness that glared back at her from the window.

"Uva said it's your shift's turn to sleep."

"Thanks, Mary—" Key couldn't remember now if the woman's name was Mary Beth, Mary Ann, or Marybell. Whatever her name was, she looked none the worse for the wear. Mary was one of several women who rose to the occasion and helped serve food, clean dishes, and gentle tempers when others got irritated. Strange, how challenge brought out the strength in some and pinpointed frazzled petulance in others.

Davage unfolded his arms and moved away from the wall next to the window. "Don't have to start cooking till four. How about you?"

"I can sleep in until five. That is, if Mrs. Walburton doesn't start thrashing around again. I wonder how her husband gets any rest at all." When did Davage sleep? Key wondered. He'd been up and busy when she woke and still helping when she went to bed. Exhaustion shadowed his dark eyes. His field expertise in making very little stretch extremely far proved an added advantage in the kitchen. When he didn't sleep, Uva usually had him cooking. But he'd managed to stay on his feet.

Too exhausted for more conversation, they held each other's hand and moved upstairs toward their respective assigned beds. Sleeping bodies stretched out on the davenports and carpeted floors on the landing.

"Get some rest, Davage." She squeezed his hand when he halted at the door of her assigned room. "I'm certainly going to try. Do you think this weather will hold much longer?" Hope echoed in her voice even as she peeked in at the three bodies sharing her mattress. The large woman made the bed sag. Wiggler Walburton, *Winona* to those who didn't bunk with her, had rolled into the middle, legs askew. The other women at their feet seemed oblivious to it all. Davage yawned, stretching his back and shoulders as Key blocked his view of her roommates.

"Keep that special faith you have, Key." He sighed. "It's the only thing that keeps me believing it won't." Davage glanced at the multitude of sleepers in the hallway. "What I wouldn't give for one night's sleep in the tool car. It's hard trying not to step on someone, but half the time I'm too sleepy to tell where I'm going."

Realization dawned on Key. That's why he looked so much more exhausted than everyone else. He wasn't sleeping. He was afraid he might sleepwalk and hurt someone!

A wave of tenderness washed over her. The man needed looking after. Without a doubt, he wouldn't allow himself to sleep until their troubles ended. There seemed only one way to help him. "Davage," she motioned to one of the davenports. "Sit down over there and rest yourself."

"There's not enough room for two. You take it."

She insisted and urged him forward. "We'll compromise. You take the davenport. I'll sit at your feet."

"Like Ruth and Boaz?"

"Your knowledge of the Holy Word surprises me sometimes," she complimented.

He smiled, despite his exhaustion. "I wasn't born a heathen." Davage sat and rested his back against the cushioned rosewood, exhaling a weary sigh. "I wish I could close my eyes for just a moment."

"Then do, Davage," Key encouraged, taking a seat at his feet and tucking her skirts around her. "Don't worry, I'll be here the whole time."

"You get some rest too."

"The only way I can is if you will."

His will deferred to hers. Minutes ticked by as she watched the exhaustion leave his face and his body ease into slumber. Though she wanted nothing more than to close her own eyes, she willed them to keep careful watch.

Less than half an hour passed before he began to mumble. His muscles twitched as if he were under attack.

"No, let me go. I didn't—I'm sorry. So sorrrry."

Key tentatively reached out to touch him but his brow furrowed and his hands balled into fists.

"Davage, wake up. You're having a nightmare. Dav—"

He bolted upright, his eyes glazed. . .unseeing.

Please, Lord, help me wake him, Key prayed, realizing that he might hurt someone or himself if she couldn't pull him from the depths of his dreams. A memory flashed across her mind's eye. Of course! Clancy had used just that method to make her pay attention when she was daydreaming. It ought to work now.

Key pinched Davage's forearm. His eyes blinked open. "Davage, are you awake?"

No answer. She pinched him again. His gaze locked with her own.

"Time to get up?" he asked, reaching out to return the pinch.

Key dodged him, scrambling to her feet. "Now, Davage, you were dreaming. . .I mean. . .having a nightmare."

"Yes, I was," he chuckled. "And a sharp-clawed devil was pinching a hunk out of me. My mother always told me bad dreams can be *chased* away."

❧

Key leap-frogged several sleepers to bolt down the stairs. Davage followed, mindless of the awakening household. "What the daylights has gotten into you two?" Uva scurried from the kitchen.

"Out of my way!" Key yelled and squealed like a greased piglet at a Fourth of July hog-catching contest. She dodged several dancers. "Stampede! Watch out! Coming through."

Laughter and grumbles echoed from all corners as she darted through the human pathway. Davage must have suspected her destination now for he slowed his run to an imperial stroll. Too late, Key realized her mistake. The kitchen had been his domain for three days. He knew its every cranny.

Uva moved away from the doorway, letting Key pass. Unfortunately, she did nothing to stop Davage from following.

The redhead brushed flour from her hands as if she were wiping herself clean of any favoritism. "You need Vindicator?" Uva asked as Davage slowly approached the corner of defense Key had taken up.

Davage shook his head. "No, but maybe a *pinch* of this or that will do."

Key couldn't contain her laughter. "N—now, Davage, I was only trying t k–keep you awake. . .keep you from. . . g–getting too sleepy and stumblin over somebody."

Her gaze swept to the crock of flour Uva had been working with on th counter.

"You wouldn't?" He spied the direction her thoughts had taken. Davag stepped backward. "Would you?"

"Self-preservation is a strong instinct." Key seized the moment and handful of flour, dusting his face and hair with the white powder.

Uva gasped.

"Equal rights you wanted," Davage wiped the powder from his eyes an spit white puffs into the cold air. "So, Miss Credit Mobilier Stocks, equa rights you'll get!"

Uva gaped in horror as Davage returned the rapid fire. "Stop that thi minute!" she finally found her voice. "Have you both gone mad? I'll neve get this mess cleaned up. In fact, *I* won't clean a solitary inch of this ridicu lous display of. . .of. . ." She slid her way to the door, sputtering her outrag With a jerk, she imperiously flung it open and pointed toward the snow, he expression thunderous. "If you're going to act like mulebrains, then b Teton, get out there and stay with them! Quit wasting my food stuff!"

"Uva, you've got the door open!" Key's laughter turned to astonishmen

"The wind's stopped." Davage stuck his hand out above the drift. "Look like the blizzard's over. There's sun out there somewhere."

A gratified grin stretched across Uva's face as her arms folded in front c her. "Good thing there is. There's also a shed with a shovel. You, Mr. Janser can dig us a path through to the mercantile, while you, Miss Calhoun, ca melt some of that snow and clean up my kitchen."

Key shared a conspiratorial glance with Davage. "After we do us first."

She grabbed his flour-dusted hands then flung herself face-first into th drift, taking him with her.

≥≥

The blizzard was long forgotten as spring rushed by. Summer rapidl approached as the Union Pacific crew laid tracks to Bridger's Pass. Muc of the crew's time was spent skirmishing with Fear No Man and rebuildin the roadbed torn up by the buffalo. Policing the men who traveled to Bento on Sundays to drink and gamble became a full-time job. The newest Hel on-Wheels was living up to its name. Still, the U.P. managed to reac Bridger's Pass by the end of May.

It had been a long, difficult struggle but one Davage and his team accomplished in record time. A telegram from Washington now rested in Davage's hand as he sat at the table in the Pullman. A frown wrinkled his brow. Key watched his mouth thin to an unyielding straight line. "What does it say?" She handed him a cup of coffee and took a seat opposite him. "Looks like bad news."

Davage rose and paced. "Over and over again. All they want to do is build this railroad over and over again." He looked like he might smash something. "Thousands of dollars in iron, men's sweat and blood out there, and the directors say our survey must be reevaluated. Twenty miles of track in question torn up and rebuilt. It's just another delay tactic. The track is as solid and smooth-riding as any they'll find."

Key picked up the telegram lying near his coffee and read the message. Not a single track of mile could be laid until both General Dodge and Davage appeared in Washington to meet with the directors.

"This isn't for the sake of the railroad." Key had a feeling who—several who's—had instigated this delay. "This is for the gold. Someone's looking to get a considerable sum if the rails have to be redone. The question is. . . who will profit from both the delay and the reconstruction? Who's financing the supplies?"

Davage gave her his full attention.

"My guess, it's the J & S Cargo Company," Key declared. "And who will profit from you and Dodge being gone? You've headed off trouble for Jack Casement and the graders. You've kept Hamilton from causing any real snags in the line. I'd say he's getting worried because you and General Dodge are moving this railroad faster than he planned. Hamilton's found a prime opportunity to get you out of the way."

She handed him the telegram. "Find the congressman who's shouting the loudest about rebuilding the track. See if his pockets have recently received new lining. Personally, I'd be little surprised to find out he's got some kind of connection to Hamilton or the J & S."

Davage quit pacing. "You're right. The bad thing about this is that the men will be idle and spend more time in Benton. By the time Washington decides, half of them will be gambled out of money and spirit. . .or worse. I doubt any of them will continue attending your Sunday sermons with Hamilton here to keep them traipsing off to Benton instead. Whoever thought of this knew exactly what damage it would do to us."

"We'll have to be smarter." Key rose and pulled a trunk from under the davenport. She opened the latch then began to fill the case with clothing from the armoire.

"You're not going."

Key continued to pack. "Of course I am. As you said, I won't be very effective here. I'd be of better service to the U.P. in Washington."

She retrieved her Bible from the table near the reading chair and wrapped it with one of her garments to protect it during travel. Saving the black velvet dress for last, she carefully wrapped it in paper. "I can get anything else I need when we reach Washington."

"You're not—"

Key waved off his protest. "Don't say it—I'm just following General Dodge's order—remember? We stay together. If the men do as you suspect, then this train will be a sitting target for Fear No Man. I don't intend to be taken prisoner, nor am I thrilled about going into Benton either."

Glancing around the Pullman, Key felt satisfied she hadn't forgotten anything important. "I know several congressmen. Perhaps I can use the influence of my stock to get their unbiased opinions and also find respected engineers who are not on either the U.P.'s, the Central Pacific's, or the J & S payrolls. I just might be able to sway them to make the trip and check the track themselves."

As if estimating her ability to accomplish the deed, Davage eyed her. He finally nodded, a smile easing the concern carved into his earlier expression. "That's a wonderful idea, Key. It would save time we don't have and give less opportunity for Hamilton to mess things up. But just a warning. . . the folks in Washington and I have never talked the same language. I hope you do."

ॐ

Key played the officials like an old political wizard. She listened to their discussions as if she were enraptured. . .as indeed she was in many aspects. Every phase of the work, from the Credit Mobilier to the advancing Central Pacific from the West, seemed topic for conversation. The railroad's core lived, breathed, and thrived in the frock-coated, silk-dressed community that mediated the nation's political arena.

When the conversation lagged or took a turn that did not hold her interest, Key slyly darted glances in Davage's direction. Like many of the women in the crowded ballroom, she noticed the difference between Davage and the Eastern associates of the U.P. He seemed uncomfortable in the stiff collar of his new white shirt, obviously not suited to a man honed from rugged years in the saddle. Though the gray frock coat and silk vest fit him well, he fidgeted in them as if they were made of horsehair. His gait was uneven, and she realized that Davage no longer wore the Colt strapped to his hip. Looking out of balance without its weight, Davage edged around the group like a corralled stallion searching for a weak spot in the fence.

The meadow of spirited "mares" in the room were falling all over themselves to get his attention. The same petite blond who had danced with Davage twice now approached him again. Her blue taffeta dress swayed purposefully at the hips, initiating Key's own need to move.

Key shot Davage a warning look. *Time to save you from yourself.* She excused herself from the Congressmen with whom she'd been talking and made her way across the ballroom floor. Arriving at Davage's side, she noticed the blond flicking her fan and blushing profusely. What had he said to the woman?

"I believe you promised me this dance." Key linked her arm through Davage's. Giving his sleeve a slight squeeze, she let him know she wouldn't be put off.

"If you'll excuse me, Mrs. Cord." Though his tone was pure apology, his expression bordered on relief. "Seems I have a promise to keep."

Green daggers of envy glared back at Key.

"I'll try not to keep him too long." Davage pulled her into his arms. One of his hands wrapped around her waist, the other encompassed her palm protectively, possessively. The healthy beat of his heart sent a warm rush of memories racing through her. "And to think I once wanted to be just like her."

His cheek brushed Key's temple as he held her close. "And what has made the difference?"

You, her heart spoke silently. But she listed the other distractions of late, "Seeing the men work so hard to create something that will help everybody. Using their talents for the good of all." She leaned back to stare at him. "I believe that must surely be the greatest kind of love. I'm beginning to understand why Clancy wanted to see the U.P. through till we lay the golden spike. It wasn't to assure his own fortune, but to show that there's something bigger than our individual dreams—God's will. By joining forces and combining all our talents, there's nothing we can't accomplish together."

Davage stopped dancing and urged her toward the doors leading into the garden. "We need to talk. . .about another combination."

As she stepped outside into the flower garden, a slight breeze brought a shiver to her shoulders. The fragrance of roses and honeysuckle offered a welcome relief from the crowded ballroom.

"Why haven't you married?" He faced Key so abruptly her palms came to rest upon his chest. "There has to be more reason than fulfilling Clancy's dream."

Uncomfortable with the sudden probing of her past, Key attempted to move away. He held her there, silently demanding an answer. Something witty sprang to the tip of her tongue, but she realized it would only delay the inevitable. She knew he would wait until he heard the truth. So be it. He might as well know now before he learned it from someone who wouldn't tell him her side of the story.

"The men who came calling after my fiance's death believed that I had inherited John's gold mine in. . .well, should I say. . .a less than proper way." She looked him squarely in the eye, steeling herself against the ridicule that might fill his beloved gaze with disdain. "My father used to say I have a Sunday-morning heart with a Saturday-night figure. Da was right. No one— not even my good friends—believed that all I'd ever been to John was best friend, confidante, and intended bride. They branded me incapable of talents other than the one their wicked minds wanted to believe. I decided that if I was going to be talked about, then I wanted the whole country talking about me and for the right reason."

"Aren't you feeling a little sorry for yourself, Key?"

She blinked. She had expected disdain, ridicule. . .but an accusal of self-pity? Indignation consumed her. "No, I believe in speaking the truth as I see it. There's a lot I'd like to change about myself."

"Is that why you read those books on etiquette when we stop for lunch? And what about balancing them on the top of your head and practicing the way you walk when you think we aren't noticing. Don't you even like *that* about yourself?"

His voice took on a softer edge. The compassion crumbled her wall of indignation, leaving behind a need for his understanding. "You saw those ladies in there," she said. "I said I didn't want to be like her. And I meant it. Still, her daintiness and well-educated manners make her immediately accepted, even sought after."

Davage ran a thumb up Key's arm and rubbed slow lazy circles on her shoulder. "You earned the respect of every gentleman in the room tonight. You know it. You *felt* it. You got the type of respect you want because you're helping to build something bigger than your own dream."

Urged on by their many days together and the many dangers they'd overcome, the inevitable could not be denied. She sensed the path his words would take even before he spoke them.

"About that combination I want to discuss."

"Davage. . ." His name was but a whispered longing on her lips and a tightening in her heart. Suddenly, Key knew now what she'd only suspected since Fort Laramie. She had fallen deeply and hopelessly in love with him. Key moved closer.

He kissed her softly. Her arms slipped around his neck. Key answered his kiss with all the tender acceptance of her heart's revelation, rejoicing in the homecoming she found there. His mouth was sweet and warm, a treasured taste of heaven that made her tremble in its wake. He pulled away, his dark eyes thrilling her with their intensity.

"I beg your pardon, Mr. Jansen. . ." a man spoke behind them.

"*Miss* Calhoun." A feminine voice stressed Key's unmarried status before the man could finish.

They turned to find Mrs. Cord and one of the men who had paid the socialite notice all evening. The suitor half bowed while Mrs. Cord smiled fetchingly at Davage then focused her attention on Key. The woman's nose wrinkled slightly, and her lips puckered just long enough to fail in greeting Key as amiably as Davage.

"Good evening." Davage coupled his arm with Key's in open defiance of the socialite's rebuff. "A wonderful night to enjoy the gardens, wouldn't you say?"

Mrs. Cord's chin lifted, her gaze examining Davage as if he were the newest fashion hanging in a dress shop window. "Depends on the skill of the gardener," challenge frosted her tone. "Come, Mathias, I need a breath of fresher air."

When the couple's path took them into the shadowed distance, Davage sighed heavily. "Oh dear, my name is ruined. I'll never be able to show my face in Washington again." He attempted to be shamefully serious but couldn't contain his laughter. "Now I'm afraid you'll have to marry me, my dear Key."

"If I thought for one moment that you were serious, I just might take you up on it." Realizing that she'd spoken before thinking, she noted the humor still dancing in his eyes. Common sense said to ignore the hope racing through her bloodstream. Common sense said to play along. But love urged her to challenge him. "Then what would you do?"

"Is a man allowed to swoon?"

Though she laughed, hurt and disappointment seeped into the deepest recess of her heart. He was only teasing. Unwilling to let him know that she *had* been serious, she put on her best protective expression and raised her right arm as if carrying a sword to lead them into battle. "Shall I go talk to the gentleman and explain what we were doing?"

"You'd do that for me?"

"I can't have you scandalized, now can I?"

One eye narrowed at her. "I'm not sure if I'd be scandalized now or *after* you talk to him."

Key laughed. "Point well taken. I hadn't thought of it, but why not?" Suddenly her smile faded. "You don't suppose you would be scandalized, do you? The lady looked like she might—"

Davage urged her toward the main house. "No, I don't. And neither will you. Mrs. Cord is not going to gossip, I can assure you."

"She won't?"

"That, Miss Daring Do, is Mrs. *Cleveland* Cord, wife of your favorite Laramie Sergeant Major Cord. I'm fairly certain when she discovers how well acquainted we've become with her husband, she'll not want us to mention that she too decided to enjoy a moonlit garden. And Key—"

"Yes?"

"I wasn't jesting."

thirteen

The time Key and Davage shared in Washington passed all too quickly. The intrigue concerning the relaying of the track kept their days frustrated by the delay. Key grew tired of the parties and galas, visits in the Senate and the House of Congress, meetings with important voices in the community. *Boredom.* The glittering, expensive, social-climbing hodgepodge left her longing for the ring and clash of iron and Irish voices instead of the soft strains of Chopin and the harsh discord of Washington gossip.

Still, she spent her days drumming up support for the U.P.'s completion. With driving purpose she sought every citizen and Senate committee member who would listen, use their influence, or donate something to the cause. Selling the gold mine John William had given her was the hardest and easiest choice she ever made, exchanging it for more Credit Mobilier stocks. Then she sold all of them to an investor bent on depriving Thomas Durant of further control of the Union Pacific.

Key wired the subsequent funds into an account in Salt Lake City to be used in purchasing the badly needed supplies from Brigham Young. General Dodge would have sole and undenied access to every penny. Yet she told no one of her gift. . .not even Davage. If she was to be God's instrument, then so be it. She needed no other appreciation than to do what her heart compelled her to do.

Thomas Durant, whom they were certain instigated their troubles, had left Washington to go to Laramie with President Johnson's Peace Commission and confer with tribal chieftains. Davage and General Dodge finally called together a meeting of the Appropriations Committee. The meeting lasted more than two hours, and the hoarseness of the general's voice betrayed his irritation.

"All we ask, Gentlemen," he spoke curtly, "is for you to send back a group of unbiased engineers and let them suggest or rule out the changes that might be required on the line. Let us be done with the delays and allow us to return to rail's end. We must get on with the job you're paying us to do, or we'll enter the Wasatch Mountains in Utah during the thick of winter."

"But the work has already been started on the changes we'll make concerning your survey," Colonel Silas Seymour informed as he looked slyly over the rim of his cup. His bearded chin was pointed much in the same style of Hamilton Sax's, and Key wondered if the comparison inspired the impression of evil.

"Alterations are being completed as of this moment on the portion of the line between Laramie and Rock Creek," Seymour added.

"What sort of alterations?"

After learning the survey was now snakelike instead of straight, Davage's temper flared visibly. Key watched the elder statesman's complexion take on a lighter shade.

"The straighter line would have involved a good deal of expensive, time-consuming rock excavation," Seymour argued, his cohort Senator Payne nodding his double chin like a buoyant bottle in an ocean of skin.

Key cleared her throat, drawing the attention of all the men. "It also enabled the U.P. directors to collect six hundred and forty thousand dollars more in U.S. subsidy bonds on that portion of the route than would have been possible otherwise, didn't it, Gentlemen?"

The members of the commission gulped simultaneously. Davage stared at her, his face becoming a mask of stone. *Did he fear she had just lost support of the crowd of influential men by making everyone aware that they weren't fooling anyone?*

General Dodge stood, his face red with obvious anger. "We're taking leave of Washington come sunrise, Gentlemen, and I'll be settling this matter with Durant in Laramie. I suggest you decide who is building this railroad— Thomas Durant or the United States government."

Key approached Davage when all the men had left. "We need to talk," Key said.

"I think you've said quite enough for one day, Miss Calhoun. Now, if you'll excuse me. . .I have a railroad to finish. With or without your help."

❧

As the track carried them far away from Washington, Davage continued to ignore Key. The comfort of friendship had fled with the miles. Though he afforded her all manner of politeness, he treated her as if she were a stranger.

Key hid her hurt and confusion by focusing her attention on General Dodge and Colonel Seymour and the ritual both carried out every twenty miles or so. Each made a trip back to the car behind them, returning several minutes later. She wanted to remember her manners and not be a snoop, but the monotony of the rail's *clackety-clack* only added to her inner discord. She desperately needed a diversion from her thoughts.

Following the two men, she was surprised at her discovery in the next car. A glass filled with liquid stood in the middle of the floor. The men seemed intent upon watching it. She waited for either to speak, but neither did. Finally, she could contain her curiosity no longer. "I don't understand what's going on."

General Dodge faced Key. "I'm trying to prove a point here."

"And he's done quite well, so far." Colonel Seymour rubbed his bearded chin. "I think Thomas will be amazed to hear how well."

General Dodge shook his head. "Doesn't matter if Durant is surprised or not. Only that you witness this and tell the truth of it to those back in Washington."

Key stared hard at the glass as if everyone could see something she couldn't. "What are we witnessing?"

Dodge pointed to the liquid. "I poured that when we left Omaha. We've checked it every twenty miles. Not a drop has spilled. I'd say that's proof enough our survey and grades are the best engineered. Paper and politics can deny it all they want, but there rides the validity that our work is sound."

Key clapped her hands softly. "Bravo, General."

"Durant will be speechless," Colonel Seymour predicted grimly.

છે

Once they arrived in Fort Laramie, surprisingly without Indian attack, General Dodge confronted Thomas Durant on Laramie's hot, dusty main street.

After hearing Seymour's report, Durant conceded. He knew the general had the backing of presidential shoe-in Ulysses S. Grant, Republican candidate. "No more changes," Thomas yielded. "I just needed proof the track was sound."

When the vice president of the U.P. and his circle of henchmen strode away, Key offered General Dodge praise. "You handled that well, General."

He shrugged. "Had to be done."

"If only we could get rid of all of our bad influences so easily," Davage grumbled walking away from Key and the general.

Key's eyes blurred with tears, sensing *she* had somehow become one of the influences Davage wanted to be rid of.

"What's got into that young man?" the general asked, offering an arm to escort Key to Old Bedlam. "He's been stewing since we left Washington. With Seymour and the others on our side, our troubles are just about over."

Loyalty to the man she loved kept her from telling their friend the truth. "Oh, you know Davage. . .he's singleminded about being the first to reach Promontory. He's just frustrated over the delay Washington cost us."

General Dodge patted her arm. "Well, he needs to learn there are far greater costs if he continues to act like that."

❧

When they returned to rails' end, problems kept Davage busy and away from Key much of the time. Though the order for them to remain in close quarters had not been retracted, it seemed to Key that Davage and the general had forgotten it all together. Davage lingered at his chores, assuming she was long asleep before he rested for the night and on duty before she rose every morning.

But his sleepwalking had become a nightly ritual again, each walk ending with him calling out his brother's name and shedding tears. Key prayed earnestly that the demon of dreams he fought would no longer possess him.

If Davage had any knowledge of his nightly walks or her efforts to soothe him, he never showed it during the light of day. The relentless pressure he placed on himself to move faster and make up for lost time allowed no time for them to talk things out or spend time together.

Their most irksome problem was the continued delays that kept Davage from working his crew at a steady pace—survey stakes came up missing; wagons full of rails arrived late; logs jammed upriver; payrolls were waylaid and Fear No Man began to sabotage the tracks frequently.

Then Davage was given the unpleasant task of telling Brigham Young that the U.P. surveys deemed the most practical route west would take them around the north end of Salt Lake, not through their settlement as believed. Young recalled his work force and swung his support to the fast approaching Central Pacific from the west until he learned that their surveys also deemed Promontory Point the proper junction for the meeting of the rails.

And to top it off, Thomas Durant did not keep his word. From September to December, he used the authority of his own Credit Mobilier stocks to take most of the graders off the line and send them into the Utah woods after tie and bridge timbers. Though Davage needed them to continue the grading into Weber Canyon before frost covered the ground, Durant continued his power play, leaving the Union Pacific to deal with the fiercest winter of the past decade.

It seemed heaven itself had turned against the U.P. and Davage planned to have nothing else to do with Key.

fourteen

She ought to just let him roam. It would serve him right the way he'd treated her lately. But try as she might, Key couldn't let Davage wander the night unguarded.

He'd been working himself senseless, dragging in so exhausted he rarely ate more than a few bites of food before washing up and heading to the tool car to turn in for the night. Like clockwork, less than an hour after he'd entered the car, Davage began his nightly ritual of throwing lassos over the nearest bush. Tonight, he'd wandered away from the circle of campfire light and into the deepening shadows of midnight before she'd been able to reach him.

"See, Tobiah, I can do it right," he mumbled. "*Every time*. Again. . ." He threw another lasso and captured the bush a second time. ". . .and again. . . and again."

Key gently touched him, waiting to see if he pulled away as he did on occasion. Davage stared at her vacantly. "Come rest, Davvy," she whispered, motioning toward the fireglow in the distance. "You can show him again tomorrow when there's more light. Tobiah's tired right now. He'll watch again tomorrow."

"He's not talking." Concern deepened his tone. "Toby's not talking and I. . . I. . .never meant to h–hurt him."

"He's knows that Davage," she assured him, knowing without seeing that he cried now. . .as he cried every night when he spoke those same words. "Tobiah understands. Now come rest and everything will be fine in the morning."

Davage blinked once. . .twice. "All right," he sighed and began to walk ahead of her now. Davage's shoulders slumped as if he carried the weight of the world upon them.

Key halted and stared up into the star-filled sky. She knew she shouldn't linger in the dark alone, but right now her heart ached for Davage. She wanted to pray for him out here. . .away from camp. . .where she could enjoy the cloak of shadows. *Lord, I hope somewhere in the world today Your word became truth to someone who'd never heard it before. And Lord, I thank You for the privilege of sharing it with Davage, though he isn't as likable as he's been in the past. But that's not for me to judge, You say, so I won't. I'll get right to the point and not waste any more of Your blessed time. Take this guilt from him, Father. Show Davage that he needs to forgive himself for what he did to his brother. It isn't Tobiah that blames him. Show him that sometime. things just happen and it's just plain no one's fault.*

Suddenly, bedlam broke loose. All around a hail of bullets shattered the night. Arrow's whizzed overhead, arcing rainbows of fire into the railcars' roofs.

"Attaaack!" her scream of warning was cut short as something flew overhead and whipped her neck backward, gagging her mouth. She spun around to see her abductor, but a heavy tarp enveloped Key, shrouding her in blackness. Rope encircled her shoulders, her waist and feet until standing was impossible.

Still, she tried to kick and scream, straining to connect her feet with anything human.

"Get her in the wagon," a gruff male voice ordered. "And don't stop until you reach where you were told to go."

Though she continued to struggle, Key was no match for their manhandling. Soon, they slid her into the back of a wagon. As the conveyance rattled into action, the jostle of wheels jarred her teeth with every bounce. Key offered up a volley of prayers that her abductors would be pitched out into a chasm of cacti.

As the night wore on, the tarp became suffocating. Key willed herself to think about cool waters and mountain winds. Onward they drove the team over what seemed like every stone and rut in the entire territory. Finally her abductors stopped, one of them barking an order.

"Take care of the horses, I'll give the woman some air."

"You take care of the horses. I'd rather take care of the woman," suggestion insinuated itself in the other man's tone.

"Not a hair on her head is to be harmed. I told you that," challenged the first man. "Davage will pay, and pay dearly for her, but he won't tolerate her being hurt."

Though vaguely comforting, Key knew better than to take this kind of man's word as fact. Still, she refused to show her fear. She would fight with every ounce of her will. *Fill me with Your might, Lord,* she prayed as the canvas was pulled back. Her lashes blinked against the sudden light. Night had given way to day. . . At least now she would be able to see who her abductor was.

Hager! His carrot-colored hair was unmistakable. This was no Indian raid. It was only meant to look like one. How much of the troubles that had been blamed on Fear No Man were, in truth, acts of the U.P.'s competitors'

Her eyes narrowed as she struggled against her bindings.

"Saucy slip of petticoat, ain't you, lady?" Hager jeered. "I know just the thing to cool you down."

He moved away from the wagon. Key twisted her wrists back and forth, hoping to weaken the taut rope that secured them. Her skin chafed and burned from hours of trying to free herself. *Okay, Lord,* she offered up a reminder. *You can step in anytime now. Be my guest.*

Nothing happened. *Lord, You said to ask and we would receive. I'm asking. . .please lend a hand, will You?*

"Water them down," Hager told the other men. "I'll be right back."

He sounded as if he was moving toward her. Key struggled in earnest now. *Hey, are You listening, Lord? I'm having a little trouble here. My mouth is gagged, but my heart's calling loud and clear. Can You hear me? I'm willing for You to step in anytime now.*

The face of her abductor wrinkled into a mocking grin as he reached the wagon and lifted the hat he now held in his hand.

Only the Lord shall know the hour of thy delivery. The words echoed through Key's mind like a shout from the top of a canyon. Realization blazed through her. *Lord, I promise I won't question Your timing ever again. . .if You'll just save me from these heathens. From now on Your schedule will be good enough for me. You don't have to hit me over this hard head for me to learn my less—*

With a laugh, Hager dumped the hatful of water over Key. Her body jerked. Her eyes blinked in frenzy. She tried to see everything at once, preparing for the next revelation. The gag became damp, but she refused to show a speck of gratitude for the relief it offered from the heat. Her eyes narrowed as Key called down the rage of angels upon his head.

He glanced at his cohort, then back at Key. "Lucky for you, Wildcat, that I'm in charge. Better pray to that heaven of yours that me and this wagon make it all the way to Rawlins. No telling what might happen to you if I don't."

It took every ounce of will not to show her fear. Rawlins? The roaringest, raunchiest tent city ever to be built along the line—a present day Sodom and Gomorrah! Why was he taking her there?

As if he could read her thoughts, the rogue taunted, "It's the last place Davage Jansen will ever think to look for you."

Night came and with it the amber lights of Rawlins. A dim impression of stale whiskey and rank souls wafted with the breeze that permeated the approach to town. Yellow, glaring torches, bright lamps, and pale lights behind tented walls accentuated the blackness of night. Sounds of brawling followed by gunfire mingled with the furious mirth of hollow-sounding female voices. Perspiration broke out on Key's forehead and made her bound wrists itch.

The wagon stopped. Hager barked orders. One man dragged her over the wagonbed. Key winced as splinters pierced through the folds of her trousers.

Her new prison became a series of tented corridors, a maze of canvas. Finally, Hager entered a room where he set her on her feet. Key stumbled, her legs wobbling as they attempted to regain their strength.

"I'll leave the leg ties for you to do." He unbound her wrists and gag "That ought to keep you from escaping before I get back. And I wouldn't advise trying in this place. There may be a worser hell out there."

Key watched the tent door shut and heard something heavy being slid into place. *Trapped!* She looked around for a knife—anything sharp—to cut herself out of this canvas prison. *Nothing!*

For the first time since the attack, she allowed herself to speculate. Had Davage survived the fracas? Would she ever see him again? His image haunted her. . .the way his eyes turned smokey gray when he admired her, his will of iron that drove him to complete all he set out to do.

She'd get out of this, if it was the last thing she did. *You with me, Lord? I know it's mighty hard to hear in a place such as this, but I'm counting on You. I'm not so tough as I try to appear. . .but You know that.* She wiped away the moisture stinging her eyes. *I don't have to tell You that.*

Someone entered the room adjoining Key's and fumbled with the object that barred her escape. The glaring light of a lantern silhouetted Hager and the bundle he carried as he entered her tent. A beefy hand thrust the bundle out to her. Key refused to take it. He tossed the bundle onto the cot. "Put those on and don't be slow about it."

Key lifted her chin defiantly and glared at him. He'd never see tears from Key Calhoun. "I'll be no man's doxy."

"Good thing I ain't got the mind to prove you wrong. But you're safe for now, Little Lady. Like I told Boots, Jansen won't pay as much if the goods are damaged."

When Hager left her alone, Key searched the room for any other means of escape. Sections of canvas formed the walls and ceilings. Key pushed against the tent and discovered that it swayed and creaked.

She untied the bundle to see if it held anything that might prove useful to help her escape. All she found was a bright red taffeta dress with black chenille around the bodice and hem. Chenille straps as thin as a piece of sinew offered the only covering for the shoulders and arms.

"I won't wear this!" To be held hostage to lure Davage was terror enough but wearing a dress such as this only invited disaster.

Just as she flung the dress from her touch, Hager returned. The dress hit him in the face. His expression hardened.

"Prickly little piece of cactus, aren't you?" Hager grabbed her arm roughly, making her head jerk up. "That's more like it. Do what you're told and things might just be a little easier around here for you."

Trust God's perfect timing, she held onto the promise as if it were a lifeline to pull her from the man's immoral mire. *He'll save me in time. He said just ask. Well, I'm asking, Lord. Step in anytime You feel the urge. . .*

Hager laughed. "Don't go anywhere, Prissy. I'll be right back."

❧

Heavy steps and male voices entered the room that led to this one. It sounded as if they were setting something up. In a mad rush, she hurried to test the barricade that had imprisoned her. To her surprise, the obstruction had been removed.

"Push open the door and come on in, Prissy," Hager ordered.

She stepped into the room and discovered it now contained a table with four chairs and another table with liquor and glasses. Three men, who looked like miners or laborers of sorts, stared at her.

"Yeah, Hager. She's a real looker, that one," one man teased. "Guess that must be the newest Parish fashion."

Key glared at her abductor, then each man in turn, challenging them but grateful Hager had not forced her to change clothes.

"I thought I told you to put that dress on—"

"Maybe she's cold," remarked the short, stocky man whose gaze examined Key from head to foot. His coffee-colored eyes bore into her as if he were ranking her in some way. "What's your name, lady?"

"Key Calhoun of the Union Pacific," she answered. "And I'm being held here without my consent."

To her dismay, none of the men seemed to care. Her bravado shook to its foundations. Perhaps she'd tried to bluff one too many times. Key swallowed back a lump of fear lodging in her throat.

"Even in that getup she looks fresher than some of those wilting violets the Rusty Bucket offers lately." Approval filled the man's tone.

Hager dismissed Key's act of defiance and waved to the table where poker chips awaited them, "Forget the woman and let's get this game underway."

Key stared at her abductor to see what was expected of her. Hager merely motioned to the table where the liquor had been set up. "Pour us drinks and look a little prettier."

Not hardly! She seized a bottle and glasses, then plunked them down on the poker table. "If you're going to liquor yourselves up, then pour your own. I'll be no party to it."

"She's a feisty filly; I'll give you that," one of the men said, grabbing the bottle and pouring the drinks.

"One of those bellringers, they say," Hager informed as he dealt the cards. "Full of sass and Armageddon. Probably doesn't know a shot glass from a tea cup."

The game commenced, several of the men bragging to the others about their card-playing expertise. The man with coffee-colored eyes seemed different than the others. His sole concern seemed focused on the amount of gold bet on each hand. Though she'd learned his opponents' names, Coffee didn't offer his into the conversation. He hadn't even asked for a drink.

Occasionally, a different man appeared from the canvas corridor that led to the room, spoke to Hager in whispers, then left. Was he a guard posted outside?

Coffee won continuously. The winning aggravated Hager. Her jailer lost a considerable amount as the night wore on and the drinks flowed. Coffee was the only man winning now, and Hager's face had swollen into a blue-veined bulb.

"Guess I'd better call it quits, Gentlemen." Coffee tossed in his cards. "Need to turn in and get a few hours of shuteye. I'm heading back to Laramie tomorrow."

"Ye wouldn't happen to know Uva Blanks, would ye, Cof—Mister?" Key asked. The dark look on Hager's face and the swift hand to his holster warned she'd said too much.

Coffee rubbed his chin. "Name sounds mighty familiar, ma'am. Why?"

"I thought if ye happen to see her," she watched Hager's hand slip over the butt of his revolver, "ye might tell her Key said hello. I wish she and my other friends could be here with me."

Coffee's eyes narrowed. He studied her through layers of cigar smoke. "Who might I say is giving this well-wishing? Key, was it?"

"Calhoun, Sir. Key Calhoun. And I'm *much* obliged."

"I'll pass that on for you, ma'am."

Hager was a poor loser. He stood. "You coming back through soon, Pilgrim?"

"Maybe."

"Why just maybe? You won. Maybe you're on a streak."

The coffee-colored gaze shifted to Key. "I like better stakes than gold. You have anything more valuable?"

Hager grinned like a cat who'd trapped a particularly troublesome mouse. "I just might have. . .depends on how much gold we're talking about."

"Enough. But it'll take me a while to get it."

Greed glinted in Hager's eyes. "Not too long or I might just give some-one else the game."

"I'll be back soon enough." Coffee tipped his hat at Key.

Key's stomach knotted with dread. Why was Coffee looking at her like that? They weren't going to gamble for *her,* were they? For a moment, one brief moment, she thought Coffee the kind of man who might save her. Now it seemed she would be delivered from tormentors into the hands of another rake.

When the man took his winnings and left, Hager's face contorted into tri-umph. "Looks like you're my lucky charm. I'll set up more lanterns when he returns. If he gets a *real* look at you, he'll be willing to lose enough gold to buy out the Union Pacific. Fool doesn't know you ain't for sale."

"But he beat ye," Key reminded, wanting to puncture his pride. . .if only with words. "*All* of ye. He's not the losing kind."

With a sneer, Hager eyed the other men. "That's what we wanted him to believe, wasn't it, boys?"

A new fear gripped Key as she realized the lengths this vile man would go to. She ran from the room to the safety of her prison. At least here she would be alone, away from the lawbreakers and their corrupt game. She threw herself onto the cot and cupped her palms around her ears, closing off Hager's shout.

"He'll be back, Lady. You can bet on it!"

❧

Another day passed, the night creeping by terrifyingly slow. Hager invited yet another group of men into his private gambling den.

During this second night of gambling, he gloated about how the J & S Cargo company intended to foil the Union Pacific. He confirmed that Cleveland Cord and Fear No Man were involved as General Dodge and Davage suspected. When she asked about Cornelia Cord, Hager bragged that Cleveland had married the Washington socialite for her money and standing in the community. She was formerly Cornelia Saxon, once married to the half owner of the Judah and Saxon Cargo Company, who happened to die quite unexpectedly two years ago.

That must mean Hamilton Sax was related to Cornelia! Relief engulfed Key. Ted Judah's good name would go unblemished. The Saxons were responsible for this travesty; her mentor was blameless. Still, Ted's widow, Anna, would not weather the news well that someone was trying to destroy the Transcontinental when it had been Ted's dream to unite East and West by means of the railroad.

A great peace filled Key when she realized she did care that Ted's and Clancy's goals were accomplished. A track of iron *would* unite the land as politicians and principles never could. Sympathy welled in her heart for Cornelia Cord as Key realized the intricacy of Sergeant Major Cord's and Hager's scheme. Though Cornelia had been unkind in Washington, she didn't deserve such deception. God willing, Key would escape this tented prison and finish the job she'd been hired to do. "Miss Priss, get in here."

Hager's demand shook Key from her thoughts, but she vowed to find a way to escape. . .this very night. *Just stick by my side, Lord. I need You more than ever now.*

When she entered the smoke-layered room, a friendly voice greeted her. "Hello, Miss Calhoun. You're looking much better than when I saw you last."

Key squinted. Coffee Eyes had returned! *If he rode all the way to Laramie and back, his horse must have wings!*

Two men dressed in the work clothes of the Union Pacific made up the remainder of the foursome. Try as she might, she didn't recognize either and could only pray that they gave their loyalty to Davage rather than Hamilton Sax. She caught her breath, knowing now why Hager seemed so exuberant tonight. Coffee had obviously returned with enough gold to make good his intentions.

The game commenced. Key noticed Coffee played carelessly, as if his mind was preoccupied with something else. At least Coffee had said he might know Uva. He must have a shred of decency if he claimed that privilege.

"Come on, Mister," she encouraged. "You played better than that the first time."

Hager eyed her. "Looks like you've caught the lady's fancy tonight. Too bad you can't say the same about Lady Luck." He glanced at the fan of cards resting in Coffee's hands. "How many you want?"

"None." Coffee slowly drew his cards together. "I'll stand."

fifteen

A commotion outside interrupted the game. A bullet whizzed through the tent near Hager's face. "Better watch where you're shooting out there!" he roared, jumping up to run down the corridor. "Priss, watch my poke. Gents, follow me."

If there had ever been any question whether the other two players were Hager's henchmen, he had just answered it. Coffee stood and moved toward Key. She began to back away from him, looking for something to defend herself with.

He held a finger up to his lips, his eyes slanting in the direction Hager had taken. Then he whispered, "Davage is with me. He'll be here when the time is right."

Davage? His name echoed through Key like a warm wind to chill the cold edge of fear that had taken root since the kidnapping. "Now. I want him here *now!*"

"I don't know how long we have, so listen carefully. Davage thought Hager might have you and knew he'd want to be close to his cronies, so he told Uva if Hager showed up in Laramie to send him word. She sent me here looking for you. When word got around that a white woman was in Rawlins, I figured it must be you."

"Who are you?" she demanded. Was this some sort of trick to get her to trust him?

"Shorty. Uva's husband."

"Her *husband?* Where have you been? She's been looking for you every—"

"No time to discuss that now. I'll tell you later. We're planning to get you out tonight. Keep close watch for his signal, then be ready to move. Don't think. Don't hesitate. Just run."

"What signal?" she asked, mentally blessing Uva for her friendship. The woman had waited years to find her husband only to send him off to help save Key's life. "Where is he?"

"In prayer," Shorty glanced toward the door, then waved her away as the sound of the men returning prevented him from saying more. He reseated himself. The two U.P. men returned only seconds before Hager reappeared.

"What's the fuss?" Shorty feigned curiosity.

"Drunks. Shootin' the town up for the fun of it." Hager sneered. "Don't reckon they'll be target practicing around this end of the tents for a while."

After boasting for several minutes, the game began again. But this time the tide turned. Shorty won with driving purpose. The bets took on a frenzied zeal. A crowd gathered to watch as news of the money being bet spread around Rawlins.

Key tried twice to slip through the gathering, but Hager kept careful watch on her and foiled each attempt.

As time sped by, Key hoped for that single moment when Hager would be so engrossed with the game he wouldn't notice her whereabouts. She glanced at the corridor packed with men and noted a padre entering the throng. Something about him looked familiar despite his low-riding hood. The man looked up, stared directly into her eyes and grinned, then melted into the horde. *Davage!*

"You're done, Hager," Shorty spoke softly.

Everyone held a collective breath.

Like a man doomed for the poor house, Hager's gaze glued to the glistening heap of gold.

Shorty leaned over to rake in his winnings, then paused offering Hager another chance. "You want to bet the lady?"

Hager glanced at Key, as if inspecting his last opportunity. "She ain't for sale."

"I'll double the pot. Winner take all."

Hager's jaw convulsed. "Done."

The crowd moved in like buzzards circling a stricken animal in its death throes. Key saw a movement toward the room with the cot. *Davage?*

Hager cut the cards to see who would shuffle. Shorty won. He began to blend the pasteboards together in a fast-handed shuffle. Sweat broke out along Hager's hairline, his face reddening to a shade as carroty-colored as his hair. A white line tightened his mouth as he asked for two cards and received them. When he glanced at the new additions, his face eased somewhat. Key moved toward the room with the cot.

"Where you going?" he asked.

"Just to my room. I'll be right back."

"I'll take three," Shorty announced, drawing Hager's attention from Key. His coffee-colored eyes shone with victory as he dropped his cards face up on the table. "I believe that beats anything you've got."

Hager stared at the unbeatable hand. Key hurried to her room, sensing the clash about to take place.

"You're a cheater!" Hager shoved the gold so fiercely that he upset the table, its contents jangling to the floor.

"And you're a kidnapper!" Davage rushed forward, his hood falling back to reveal his true identity.

Hager went for his gun. Davage grabbed a lantern and flung it against one wall. The canvas burst into flames.

"Fire!" someone screamed. Men frantically fought for the scattered gold before seeking safety outside.

Davage unsheathed a huge knife from his boot, then slashed his way through the canvas barring Key's escape. "This way," he commanded, gripping her hand. Shorty followed.

"Now where?" Key asked as they entered yet another corridor of canvas.

"We cut until we find the alley between houseboards," Davage informed, slicing into the next canvas, then the next.

"These cities are all made the same. There's got to be fresh air out there somewhere."

With three more cuts, they found themselves in a passage that led out into a square surrounded by low, dark structures.

A light appeared, moving slowly from an obscure corner of the square. Davage motioned Key to follow him. "Shorty, cover her from behind."

The trio stayed in the shadows as they made their way across the square. Dim lamps shown through tents, allowing shadowed glimpses of their pursuers. When they turned the corner, a bullet thudded next to Key's shoulder. Lead struck Shorty behind her. Key flinched at his strangled cry.

"Run!" Davage yelled.

"We've got to take our chances in there," Shorty insisted through gritted teeth.

Running into the saloon, they discovered troopers and Union Pacific men crowding the tables. Men they knew by name and face. Men who would fight on their side if necessary.

"Better get me a place to lie down," Shorty huffed, grasping a bloody splotch on his shoulder. "If I die now after being gone all this time, Uva will dig me up and kill me once more for spite."

"Up there." Key motioned toward the second landing. "I'll help Shorty to a room. Come back as soon as ye can."

Finding a room proved easier than expected. Most of the patrons were apparently downstairs at the gaming tables. She helped Shorty to a bed, then latched the door. Fortunately, the washstand had a pitcher of clean water and a fresh cloth waiting for whoever would rent the room tonight.

Key prepared to cleanse his wound, but before she walked back to the bed, a knock sounded on the door.

"Key," Davage whispered. "Are you in there?"

She opened the door and threw herself into his arms. All the fear, dread, and now relief of the past few days were too overwhelming to hide her emotions. "Oh, Davage, you're here. Don't ever let me go. Please, just hold me."

He didn't release her for a moment. "Are you hurt?"

Thank You, Lord, she offered to her Maker, *for letting me be able to say no.* "I'm fine." She let go of him and stared at her beloved. "Are you?"

His gaze fastened on her lips as his hands gently closed over her shoulders, drawing her back into his embrace. "I'll always be fine with you in my arms," he whispered against her lips, then kissed her.

sixteen

A throat cleared behind them. "I'm glad you two are perfectly healthy," Shorty complained. "But I'm over here bleeding to death. Reckon you could stop kissing long enough to find me a doctor?"

"Certainly," Davage grinned, "but only if you'll satisfy Key's curiosity about where you've been all these years."

"Got caught up in prospecting some of that Yukon gold, ma'am. There was a cave-in and, for a long time, I didn't know who I was. When I finally came to my senses, I not only remembered my identity but that my best prospect might still be waiting for me back home in Laramie. I'm a mighty willful sort, at times. I'm sure glad the Lord, and Uva, stuck around long enough for me to see if I've got the will, He's got the way. Sure was a hard way to learn to let Him lead."

Key offered him a smile, then stared deeply into Davage's eyes. "Oh, He sends an occasional reminder now and then. . .if we're not too stubborn to listen."

えも

They not only found Shorty a doctor, but waited until the man recovered enough to see him home to Laramie. The reunion between Shorty and Uva spurred Davage into a decision he'd tried to ignore since Washington.

When she challenged the Congressmen about their stocks becoming more valuable because of the track relaying, suspicion had ridden the rails with Davage. But try as he might, his heart refused to believe that she was guilty of duplicity. Whatever changing of money and stocks that went on between Key and the senator that last day in Washington had to be for the good of the U.P. and not to cause its downfall. She'd earned his trust and with it. . .love.

Life wasn't meant to be spent alone. Davage couldn't alter the tragedy that caused his brother to lose his ability to talk no more than he could deprive himself of loving Key because he might harm her.

Concentrating on work and squelching any association that didn't pertain to the U.P. had been to safeguard his heart from further pain. But steeling himself against his emotions only hardened his heart into an instrument of lackluster existence. For years, he'd persistently buried his dreams and the hope for his own family, guilt-ridden that Tobiah must suffer the same because of his bungling. But Key resurrected those hopes. Made him dream again. Made him believe again.

Lord knew, she'd shown him that he wasn't living life, just existing. But to love her would be taking the greatest chance of all. He smiled as he watched her wave to the men in the worktrain. She looked at home again in her Union Pacific uniform.

"Ready to leave?" She caught him staring at her.

"Go ahead and board. I've got to send a telegram. I'll be right with you."

"To General Dodge?" Her brow wrinkled in thought. "Isn't he with the directors?"

"Yes, he is. The telegram's to my brother. I want him with us at Promontory."

Key smiled. "I'm sure he'd want to see the rails meet, knowing what it means to you. I can't think of anything more exciting."

You will, love, Davage assured her silently. *It just may prove to be the most exciting day of either of our lives.* But he just smiled back and waved her aboard.

Later when Davage boarded, he realized Key had chosen to ride in front of the long string of box and flat cars loaded with stone, iron, and ties. She wanted to be the first to top the rise outside Garter City.

Davage made his way to the engine, remembering how easily she'd learned to walk the top with him on that fateful first raid on her Pullman. The woman was an escapade waiting to happen. But as he preached to Key time and again, God did have His own perfect timing. It was their duty to trust and believe in Him. Perhaps it had taken preaching this to someone else for Davage to hear it and understand it himself. He'd blamed God for not healing Toby's malady. But the real blame lay with Davage. He'd put a time limit on God's miracle. Perhaps if he believed hard enough in what he'd tried to make Key understand, then there was still hope for Toby to talk again one day. But now he realized it was his lack of faith that drove him. He need to trust God to handle the situation with a wisdom Davage couldn't comprehend, in God's timing.

All along the track from Garter City to the top of the long slow rise, there were implications that Indians had torn up the road bed and attempted to derail the engines.

Moving westward now was slow work. Davage expected the regular train from the east to overtake them, but no smoke for the engine stacks rose in their wake. Could there have been an attack to hold it back? Fear for Tobiah renewed itself. He would be coming from the east in a few days. Could the rail be depended upon?

Your time, Lord, not ours, Davage offered up a prayer to the heavens.

Strengthen my faith. Help me to believe.

Toward evening of the second day, the work train reached the curves of glistening salt flats prized highly by the local Indian tribes. Passing through the two dangerous curves unscathed and heading into the straight stretch of track that would lead them to the highest slope of Weber Canyon forced a sigh of relief amongst the crew.

"The sunset is so pretty." Awe filled Key's tone as she motioned to the sun melting into the large patches of snow cresting the mountaintops. Scrub oak and dwarf maple already painted the slopes a brilliant red and bronze while sego lilies opened their white triangle of flowers. Their yellow, brown, and purple centers bowed toward the dying sunlight. "It's almost as if this is a place for all seasons and the cradle for God's rainbow." She looked straight at Davage. "I've heard lots of stories about where it's supposed to end, but I'll always remember this as its birthing place."

"It is a place of beginnings, Key." Davage took her hand in his. "But beginnings must first begin with belief. I'll trust if you will." He spoke of more than her whimsy about rainbows and sensed that she knew it too.

As the work train lumbered along the crest of the pass, Davage observed a temporary station that had been erected in the shape of several boxcars. Telegraph wires and trooper tents assured all that the station was in use. Someone at the station waved at them with a flag. Davage gave the engineer the sign to stop, though they would have stopped anyway.

As the train rolled to a halt, the flag waver ran alongside. "Who's in charge of this train?" he demanded.

"He is." Duffy McDonough signalled with his thumb toward Davage.

"What's the problem?" Davage leaned out to hear better.

"There's a wire from Garter City." The man's face paled. "You've got orders to stop General Dodge's train. There are Sioux in ambush down in the flats and General Dodge is bringing the directors out from Garter City."

Key gaped. "But that can't be! We just came through there and we passed safely."

"They were after bigger prey. I've tried to get Cardwell at the other end, but the wire's cut!"

"And you say you know for certain Dodge's trains are moving this way?" Davage demanded.

The telegrapher's head bobbed. "He has soldiers with him, but not enough to fight off an ambush in the flats."

"What can we do?" Key looked from Davage to the flagman.

"There's no way the general can make it through," Duffy warned. The roadbed was too high and narrow.

"Then we've got to stop the general before he reaches the pass," Key insisted.

Davage nodded. "At least they can fight. They've stood off attacks before. They might even be able to hold off long enough until the next train comes along."

"We can't stop them," one of the men argued, breaking his way through the crowd of linemen. "The engine is behind the loaded cars. We can't switch. Sax and the Sioux will have them all scalped and rendered before we can even get there."

Lifting the naysayer by the scruff of the neck, Duffy nodded toward Davage. "You take care of the general's train, lad. I'll see to it this bag of coal ash is here when ye get back. Then, we'll let him tell us all he knows about Mr. Sax and them Sooz."

Key wheeled and strode toward the gravel car at the end of the line. Davage followed as she climbed on the car.

"What do you think you're doing?" he demanded.

She pointed toward the linchpin. "Would ye uncouple this for me?"

Davage shook his head, but hopped onto the car with her. "I won't but I'll have Duffy do it."

Duffy handed over his prisoner to a couple of trusted men, then moved to do his boss's bidding. "By Brian Boru, ye might just do it. It's downgrade more'n ten miles, but ye might slip through the pass. Without the smoke stack, they won't see or hear you till it's too late. If you'll lie low, they'll think you're just a runaway car broke loose."

"That's not far from the truth," Davage acknowledged. "Toss me up a couple of ropes and some cartridges."

"The brake won't hold," the prisoner taunted as he struggled against his confinements. "You'll run into the very train you want to save, fools!"

Davage stared at Key. "It could mean death, love."

"We have to take that chance. There are many lives at stake."

Davage reached out and gently caressed her cheek. "He didn't mean for us to take chances."

"He intends for us to save someone's life with any means possible, doesn't He?"

A grin stretched wide across Davage's face. Her unconquerable spirit would either lead him into one long adventurous lifetime or hurl them straight into heaven. Either way, he'd be with Key and that was all that mattered.

Loving was believing they could face impossible odds and win.

Believing was trusting God's will.

"Toss us the Henrys and plenty of ammunition," he ordered. "Then shove us off. Time's wasting."

The gang started the car and cheered as its *clackety-clack* gained momentum.

"Luck to you!" Duffy shouted over the din.

Davage and Key loaded the Henrys. A glance backward showed the station was now out of sight. Fixing his gaze on the curve of the track ahead where it disappeared between snow banks, no one but a railroader could distinguish the imperceptible grade. The car crept along.

"Will it stop?" Key worried aloud.

Davage shook his head. "If it does, we'll just start it up again. The heavier it is, the longer it'll run on this kind of grade."

"I wish there was something we could do about the rattle of the wheels. I'm not so sure they won't hear us coming." The curve straightened into a stretch of straight track and the speed increased.

"We'd best be digging in now while we can, Love." Davage scooped a hole in the gravel. "Might give us more protection from the bullets. And let's tie one of those ropes around the two of us so that we won't be separated from each other for any reason."

He gripped the rope so tightly his hands trembled.

"What is it, Davage? What's wrong?" Concern filled Key's features.

God's schedule, not mine. The reminder echoed through Davage's thoughts. "Nothing. I've just never had much use for ropes." He tossed her one end of the rawhide.

She wrapped the rope around her waist several times, then knotted it. "No need to worry about bringing any harm down on my head," she teased. "*You're* the one who gets in trouble when we're near ropes."

They laughed. As the wind began to blow and whip Key's hair into her eyes, the laughing stopped and she noticed the considerable increase of the car's speed. "Get that rope tied around you, too."

"Davage?"

"Yes?"

"Why were you so angry with me when we left Washington?"

"This isn't exactly the time for that sort of discussion."

"We might not have a better time."

He nudged her chin up. "They'll be time. And there's nothing to discuss. It was me I was angry at. . .not you."

"Then do me a favor."

"What's that, Love?"

She flashed him a smile. "Keep me on your good side."

As they approached the first curve, Davage applied the wheelbrake. I
didn't work well but held despite their first misgivings. "The brake i
gonna be useless if we pick up much more speed," he warned, all humo
gone.

seventeen

Fear rushed through Key as she saw the next curve and knew, without doubt, they would be going too fast to take it safely. The months of working the U.P. flashed before her. Davage's image filled the horizon. His dedication to work and fairness with the men. His reminders that God decided their fates, and that she should stop and listen to *His* will.

Davage gripped the handbrake. The car ran wild now, making a raucous clatter. Before she could worry further, the car lurched and the right wheels left the track. The left wheels squealed and ground hard against the iron railing.

"Lean right!" Davage shouted. The car lurched. Took flight. Banged against the railing. Righted itself and rounded the curve.

"We made it!" Triumph resounded from Key as she watched Davage ease his death grip on the wheelbrake. Not an Indian could be seen. Only patches of snow and salt. Then with a second glance, the hair on the back of her neck and arms raised. There! Amid the maple and scrub oak. Renegades, armed and painted!

The third curve loomed ahead. Beyond that the long stretch of track leading to Garter City. The car entered the cut with a screeching roar. Above the wheel's *clackety-clack,* rifle reports and shrill yells echoed around them. Whizzing arrows spurred Key into grabbing one of the Henrys and sighting down a target. But her heart could not do what her mind said she must. The car traveled too fast. The target whizzed by in a blur.

"Uhhhah!"

Key turned to see Davage grazed by an arrow. "Davage!"

"It's nothing. Stay put." He searched the rail behind them to make sure the Sioux no longer threatened.

Far into the horizon, black smoke from a locomotive rose to dirty the air. "Train's coming!" Key shouted.

Davage applied pressure on the brake, attempting to slow the car, but the brake wouldn't hold. The handle snapped in his hands! "The stress of the curves broke it," he declared. "We can't count on that to stop us."

"But they're too far away to see us. They'll be too close to stop in time." Key's eyes rounded in fear as the train chugged into plain sight now.

Davage lifted a heavy tie and lay it in front of them. "Shove this off with our feet!"

"W–what?"

"Push it, then jump!"

"But. . ."

"Key, trust me!"

She paused.

"It's in God's hands. It's his time for us, or it isn't." Davage stared at her, his eyes softening. *"Trust!"*

Key took a deep breath and held out her hand. "I–I'm ready." *I won't say good-bye. We'll make it.*

Davage gripped her hand and gently squeezed it. "The time we have spent together has been a pleasure, Miss Calhoun."

"The pleasure was all mine, Mr. Jansen."

"Kick with all your might."

"Like a mule." She gave the tie a mighty shove.

๛

Key's lashes fluttered open to the sight of the polished silkworm pattern of the Pullman's cherry woodwork. A glance at the coal stove and chair next to it showed a bedraggled and unshaven Davage, fast asleep. Momentarily confused, she wondered what she was doing here in her Pullman.

She sat up and pain spiraled from every joint in her body. The wild ride down the mountain. Catapulting through the air! "Davage," she whispered, limping over to see about him. "Are you all right?"

He woke and groaned. But when his eyes fully focused, he smiled and gathered her into his embrace. "You're well now. It's been days. I thought you'd. . .well, I see you're perfectly fine now."

Key wanted to linger in his arms forever, but she must know if the train survived. "General Dodge? Is he safe?"

"He and all the other directors. Hamilton's in jail."

"But how. . .I don't remember anything but flying through the air." She closed her eyes, trying to envision what had transpired, but her memory failed her.

Davage brushed the silken curl that had fallen against her cheek. "We landed in the snow. You landed on top of me. The rope helped us stay together."

"It saved our lives," she whispered.

Davage's gaze turned smokey gray. "Would you save *my* life, Key?"

"How?" she challenged, yet willing him to say the words spoken in earnest rather than jest.

"Marry me. Be my wife. Teach me to believe again."

Davage kissed her forehead, her eyes, her cheek. He took her chin in his and and tilted her face up, kissing her slowly and tenderly. It was a kiss illed with faith, hope and, above all else, trust that they belonged together.

Her arms encircled his neck, and she answered him in kind, certain that narriage to Davage would be the greatest adventure she'd ever embrace.

"When?" she whispered against his lips.

"It'll be worth waiting for, I promise. Just remember. Timing is everything."

ða

he ringing sound of success filled the air as May 10, 1869, brought special ains from west and east. Governor Stanford from California, president of ie Central Pacific, arrived and met with the directors of the Union Pacific. Jtah citizens showed up in full force. Dignitaries, officials, government epresentatives, and news reporters from both coasts crowded in to partici- ate in the historical occasion. Most notable to Key was the mingling of rish and Chinese workers. It had taken them all to complete the railroad, nd now the railroad would unite the States as General Dodge and President Grant had hoped. . .as Ted Judah first imagined.

Key linked her arm through Davage's and listened to the murmur of oices in the crowd, watching as the two engines—the Central Pacific's Jupiter" and the Union Pacific's "Number 119"—puffed and billowed team. She felt Clancy's presence here amidst the sound and fury of the inal rail-laying and was glad that she had kept her promise to him.

The military band of the 21st Infantry struck up a drumroll as the iron nen from both crews lifted the final lengths of rail. Governor Leland tanford's six-foot frame looked imposing as he waited for the final tie to e laid. This was no ordinary tie for it was a gift from California, Nevada, daho, Arizona, and Montana. Made of California laurel, the tie was orna- nented with silver and polished to a soft lustrous sheen. Holes had been rilled rather than hammered in it so the last spike, made of solid gold, vould not be damaged.

"The nuggets that were originally at the top of these two spikes," Governor tanford said, "have been formed into seven rings. Inscribed inside each is ie statement, 'Morning Wedding 1869,' to represent the joining of the rail- oads. The rings have been given to President Grant, Secretary of State eward, myself and. . ."

The speech went on endlessly. Key wanted it all over so her life as Mrs. Davage Jansen could begin. The wedding wouldn't take place until General Dodge finished the ceremony.

At twenty-seven minutes after noon, Davage asked the crowd to take off heir hats. He had asked to be allowed to lead the men in prayer. Key ouldn't have been prouder of her husband-to-be than she was in that

solitary moment. He'd finally shone his true colors. He would no long
deny his love and respect for God. No matter what other accomplishme
she managed to achieve in her life, helping to guide Davage back to t
Lord would always be her proudest moment.

Governor Stanford and Thomas Durant hoisted their sledgehamme
above their shoulders and heaved. As the mauls came crashing down
hammer two golden spikes into place at the same time, the locomotive
whistles blasted the news across the countryside, then moved their co
catchers forward until they touched.

"It's time!" Davage announced as the great roar of approval faded wi
the whistle blasts. He grabbed Key's hand and ran toward the Pullman th
had been hitched to the cars that would follow Engine 119.

"But General Dodge. Where is he?" Key laughed at Davage's exube
ance and scanned the crowd.

"Probably already there." Davage urged her into a run. When they arriv
at the Pullman, he swept Key up into his arms and carried her over t
threshold.

Inside, disappointment enveloped her. "You don't think they've all fo
gotten, do you?"

"Not hardly, Lass," Duffy's voice grumbled from behind the bathscree

"Shh, you big oaf," someone berated.

"You weren't supposed to give it away, McDonough," another scolded

Laughing at the big man's blunder, Key smiled and wrinkled her nos
"I smell lavender. Lots of it."

Twitters behind the bathscreen forced her eyes to meet Davage's. "Y
didn't."

"I'm afraid I did."

He carried her past the sleeper and around the bathscreen. Davage stopp
abruptly at the sight of his younger brother and a petite woman standing ne
to him. "Tobiah, you made it!" he exclaimed.

"I w–wouldn't h–have m–missed it," Tobiah stammered, then hurried
made signals with his hands. The woman beside him smiled and offere
word of encouragement.

"He says, he wouldn't have missed his big brother's wedding no mat
where it took place."

"Toby can talk?" Davage whispered reverently, tears of utter joy welli
in his eyes and spilling over his cheeks.

Tobiah's interpreter's face stained a becoming shade of rose as the you
man's fingers moved rapidly. "Yes, and he says your bride-to-be is almo
as beautiful as his."

"Bride-to-be?" Davage looked from brother to interpreter. "You're going to get married?"

Key had to blink back her own happiness, her joy for both brothers overwhelming. Miracles did happen. . .when one was willing to wait for them. *Thank You, Lord,* she offered to her Maker. *Your blessings know no bounds.*

Brother congratulated brother. Several throats cleared. General Dodge, Duffy, Uva, and Shorty stood in a circle around the filled bathtub. The preacher waited, a Bible resting next to his heart.

" 'Tis mighty sweet-smelling in here," Duffy grumbled. "Best be to getting married 'fore I start sprouting petals."

Davage grinned. "Just one more thing left to do."

"You wouldn't." Key noted the challenge lighting Davage's eyes. He deposited her into the water, then stepped in himself, buckskins and all.

"I did," he admitted, then faced the preacher. "And, Sir, I certainly do. . . for better and—I'm sure my adventuresome bride-to-be will bring it down on our heads—for worse. From now until God decides He's had enough."

He lifted Key's hand to his lips and kissed the ring that would forever bind them. "I can't offer you great wealth, but I promise to make our lives as daring as I can stand them and still keep my faith."

"And *I* promise to find out what some of my gentler talents are," Key pledged. "I'm willing to give you a rest now and then from my wilder ones and to let God lead the way."

And so Key Calhoun became the bride of Davage Jansen. Though six of the rings formed from the golden spike had been offered to officials, President Grant allowed Davage to have the seventh. It now rested on Key's finger with a slight alteration in the inscription the others contained. Hers read, *Mountain Wedding, May 10, 1969.*

A simple band. . .all the gold she'd ever need, knowing that the true adventure would be in learning the secrets of Davage's heart that were now hers alone to discover.